The Lives and Times of The Forty Martyrs of England and Wales 1535-1680

Second Edition, Revised and Enlarged

Malcolm Pullan

The Lives and Times of the Forty Martyrs of
England and Wales 1535-1680

Second Edition, Revised and Enlarged

Copyright © Malcolm Pullan 2013

All Rights Reserved

The right of Malcolm Pullan to be identified as the author
of this work has been asserted by him in accordance with the
Copyright, Designs and Patents Act 1988.

No part of this book may be reproduced,
stored in a retrieval system, or transmitted,
in any form or by any means, electronic, mechanical,
photocopying, recording or otherwise, without the prior
permission of the copyright owner.

*Dedicated to the memory of ALL the Catholic martyrs
of England and Wales, those known and those unknown,
and Anna Dimascio (1950-1995) by whose hand
the ikon of the Forty Martyrs was written:
a rare talent snuffed out all too soon.*

So let us now give praise to godly men,
our ancestors of generations past,
men whom the Lord honoured with great glory,
in whom his greatness has been seen ...
All these were famous in their own times,
honoured by the people of their day.
Some left a reputation,
and people still praise them today.
There are others who are not remembered,
as if they had never lived,
they died and were forgotten ...
But we will praise these godly men,
whose righteous deeds have never been forgotten.
Their reputations will be passed on to their descendants,
and this will be their inheritance.
Their descendants continue to keep the covenant,
and always will, because of what their ancestors did...
their fame will never fade.
Their bodies were laid to rest,
but their reputations will live forever.
Nations will tell about these men,
and God's people will praise them.

Sirach/Ecclesiastus: Chapter 44

1. John Rigby
2. Philip Howard
3. Richard Gwyn
4. Philip Evans
5. John Lloyd
6. John Roberts
7. Alban Roe
8. Ambrose Barlow
9. Margaret Clitherow
10. Anne Line
11. Margaret Ward
12. John Houghton
13. Richard Reynolds
14. Robert Lawrence
15. Augustine Webster
16. David Lewis
17. John Jones
18. Robert Southwell
19. Nicholas Owen
20. Henry Walpole
21. John Wall
22. John Stone
23. Cuthbert Mayne
24. John Kemble
25. Edmund Gennings
26. Swithun Wells
27. Edmund Arrowsmith
28. John Southworth
29. Henry Morse
30. John Boste
31. John Almond
32. John Plessington
33. Luke Kirby
34. Thomas Garnet
35. Ralph Sherwin
36. Edmund Campion
37. Alexander Briant
38. Eustace White
39. Polydore Plasden
40. John Paine

Ikon of the Forty Martyrs of England and Wales

By faith, the martyrs gave their lives, bearing witness to the truth of the Gospel that had transformed them and made them capable of attaining to the greatest gift of love: the forgiveness of their persecutors.

Pope Benedict XVI, Apostolic Letter 'Porta Fidei' ('door of faith')
17 October 2011

Contents

Canonization Homily of Pope Paul VI ix

Preface xii

Introduction xviii

CHAPTER ONE: The Henrician Martyrs and the Aftermath 1

CHAPTER TWO: Edward VI and Mary Tudor 75

CHAPTER THREE: The Elizabethan Persecution, 1559-1603 91

CHAPTER FOUR: The Elizabethan Martyrs, 1577-1601 178

CHAPTER FIVE: The Jacobean Martyrs, 1603-1625 388

CHAPTER SIX: Charles I and the Civil War Martyrs, 1625-1649 452

CHAPTER SEVEN: Puritan Parliament and the Commonwealth 514

CHAPTER EIGHT: Charles II and the 'Popish Plot,' 1660-1685 546

EPILOGUE 614

Appendix 1: The Ikon of the Forty Martyrs of England and Wales 627

Appendix 2: Prayer to the Forty Martyrs of England and Wales 628

Appendix 3:
  Beatification and Canonization   628

Appendix 4: The Seal of Confession   629

Appendix 5: Extra Ecclesiam nulla salus   631

List of Sources   633

Index of Persons   647

Canonization Homily of Pope Paul VI

I saw under the altar the souls of those who had been killed because they had proclaimed God's word and had been faithful in their witnessing.
Revelation: 6:9

'To all those who are filled with admiration in reading the records of these Forty Martyrs it is perfectly clear that they are worthy to stand alongside the greatest martyrs of the past; and this is not merely because of their fearless faith and constancy, but by reason of their humility, simplicity and serenity, and above all the spiritual joy and that wondrously radiant love with which they accepted their condemnation and death.

Faced with the choice of remaining steadfast in their faith and of dying for it, or of saving their lives by denying their faith, without a moment's hesitation and with a truly supernatural strength they stood for God and joyfully confronted martyrdom.

May the blood of these martyrs be able to heal the great wound inflicted upon God's Church by reason of the separation of the Anglican Church from the Catholic Church. Is it not one - these martyrs say to us - the Church founded by Christ? Is not this their witness? Their devotion to their nation gives us the assurance that on the day when - God willing - the unity of the faith and of Christian life is restored, no offence will be inflicted on the honour and sovereignty of a great country such as England. There will be no seeking to lessen the ... worthy patrimony of piety and usage proper to the Anglican Church when the Roman Catholic Church - this humble 'Servant of the Servants of God' - is able to embrace her ever-beloved sister in the one authentic communion of the family of Christ ... Perhaps we shall have to go on, waiting and watching in prayer, in order to deserve that blessed day. But already we are strengthened by the heavenly friendship of the Forty Martyrs of England and Wales.'

Homily of Pope Paul VI at the Canonization of the

Forty Martyrs of England and Wales 25 October 1970

Preface

It hath been a laudable custom in all ages, from the beginning of Christ His Church, to publish and truly set forth the singular virtues of such her children as either in their lives by rare godliness did shine above the rest, or by their patient deaths most stoutly overcame all barbarous cruelty, and both by their lives and deaths glorified God, encouraged to like victories their faithful brethren, and with invincible fortitude confounded the persecuting tyrants.

So begins *A True Report of the Life and Martyrdom of Mrs Margaret Clitherow* written in 1586 by one of the most celebrated sixteenth century Yorkshire mission secular priests, Father John Mush; and being so bold as to try and emulate that *'laudable custom'*, I have written this volume.

Why a book specifically about the lives and times of the Forty Martyrs of England and Wales, and why a book now? After all, the martyrs lived hundreds of years ago, so who is interested in them? What relevance do they have today when, in the interests of 'political correctness', it is *de rigueur* for religious differences to be played down? The fact is that I have discovered many people, when told about them, **are** curious to know more about these sixteenth and seventeenth century martyrs. I have been asked several times if I could recommend 'a book' that could be acquired and I have had to reply that I was unaware of the existence of any comprehensive volume on the subject. To which has come back the rhetorical riposte, 'Then why don't you write one?'

I have a personal interest in recusant history. My ancestral family, the Pulleyns of Yorkshire, whose coat of arms was the scallop shell of St James of Compostela, their crest the pelican in her piety, suffered greatly for their Catholic Faith in penal times. In the amazingly detailed list of Yorkshire Catholics compiled for James I in 1604 the Pulleyns of Scotton, Killinghall and Fewston along with their recusant servants, as well as the families connected to them by marriage, are all named. The resolutely recusant Pulleyns of Killinghall and Scotton Hall, Farnham, and their close relatives at Fewston, were people of influence and standing enjoying considerable wealth and property. This was all gradually eaten away in fines and confiscations until by the close of James I's reign their properties were gone and they were financially ruined because of their refusal to 'conform'. Scotton Hall, a substantial mansion, survived in different ownership but was so altered in the early 19th century that scarcely any features of antiquity remained.

The Pulleyns gave seminary priests to the Church, among them the brothers Joshua and William, sons of James Pulleyn of Killinghall. Joshua, born 1543, qualified as a doctor but arrived at Douai 8 July 1577 and studied alongside several future martyrs. Listed as Josue Pullan, he was ordained priest at Cambrai 29 March 1578, together with St Alexander Briant. He returned to England in the same year; the first of many Yorkshire-born Douai priests to serve in his native county. He worked in the area of his birth around Ripon. In 1592 Father Pulleyn's name appears, alongside that of John Mush, in a government list of wanted seminary priests in Yorkshire. He is mentioned in the correspondence between Henry Hastings, Earl of Huntingdon and William Cecil, Lord Burghley in January 1593. He figures in the examination on 30 March 1594 of a cutler named Simon Knowles by the vicious Justice Richard Young. Knowles admitted to acting as a guide for the priest to Brussels. On 20 May 1594 he arrived at Rome and three days later was admitted to the Society of Jesus. Joshua is also mentioned in the autobiography of Father John Gerard SJ, under the name of Pollen. He was staying with Father Gerard, and Gerard's companion, John Lillie, at St Anne Line's house in London in July 1599 when the house was raided. Joshua and Gerard slipped into a hiding place while John Lillie assumed 'grave airs'. This led the searchers into believing that *he* was the priest, and they arrested him and took him to the Tower. Father Gerard and Joshua moved to another house. At one point in the Douai diary Joshua is described as 'impoverished'. How he came to be impoverished we can glean from the Calendar of State Papers (vol. 1603-10) where on 10 September 1603, the Council of the North informs Lord Dorset that Dr Martin Windsor, physician to the Queen, begs the forfeited goods of certain recusants, including those of Joshua Pulleyn. Joshua died 3 June 1607.

His brother William was educated at University College, Oxford. He graduated BA in 1563 and MA in 1566. He was appointed captain of Tynemouth Castle, Northumberland. He arrived at Rheims 7 January 1583 and was ordained deacon in the same ceremony as his kinsman, Blessed Francis Ingleby, who will feature later in the life of St Margaret Clitherow. William was ordained priest at Laon 18 May 1583 and served as a chaplain in Flanders where he died. The Pulleyns were allied by interlocking family ties not only to the Inglebys of Ripley Castle, but also to many of the most prominent, hereditary Catholic landed gentry families of Yorkshire: e.g. Darcy, Conyers, Fairfax, Gascoigne. Together they formed one of the largest, most vigorous - and wealthiest - communities of recusants in England, as well as producing an astonishing number of vocations to the priesthood and religious life. The Pulleyns were also related by marriage to Guy

Fawkes, he of Gunpowder Plot notoriety. Guy's mother re-married a Pulleyn of Scotton and the boy and his sisters were partly raised in their step-father's house - but we don't often mention that! Guy married Maria Pulleyn of Scotton at St Oswald's parish church at nearby Farnham in 1590 and they had a son, Thomas, born the following year.

A later generation of Pullans also produced a priest. Michael Pullan, son of Robert Pullan of Holme, near Hampsthwaite, was born 1653. As he was baptised at St Thomas of Canterbury, Hampsthwaite, his family must have been conforming Anglicans. However Michael returned to the Faith of his ancestors while a teenager and was received into the Benedictine order at St Gregory's Monastery, Douai 8 February 1672. He later returned to England and worked on the mission in Durham as Provincial of York 1693-97, holding the titular title of Prior of Coventry. He served as prior of Douai 1701-05 and again 1710-13, where he had the honour to have been one of the successors of St John Roberts in that office. He died at Douai 3 February 1723.

I also have a more circumstantial link to two Yorkshire martyrs: Peter Snow and Ralph Grimston q.v. Father Snow and his lay companion were martyred at York in 1598 on my birth date: 15 June. Their skulls were preserved, eventually finding a home with the Carmelites at Hazlewood Castle, near Tadcaster. When Hazlewood was sold the skulls were transferred to St Anne's Cathedral, Leeds, and subjected to examination by a forensic scientist. He not only confirmed that they were the relics of the two martyrs, but also carried out amazing reconstructions of their heads and faces. When Leeds Cathedral was re-ordered in 2006, following the ancient tradition regarding the relics of saints and martyrs, the two skulls were placed beneath the altar. At the age of eighteen I was received into full communion with the Catholic Church at St Anne's Cathedral on the patronal feast day, 26 July 1961, so I am delighted that the cathedral possesses the relics of these martyrs.

Furthermore, I have an emotional 'pull' to the history I describe in that many members of my family lie buried in the graveyard beside the impressive ruins of the Augustinian Bolton Priory of St Mary and St Cuthbert (suppressed 1539) in their beautiful setting on the banks of the River Wharfe, on the Bolton Abbey Estate, near Skipton.

I have spent over thirty years studying the lives of the martyrs, trying to make them better known and loved, to keep their memory alive and encouraging devotion to them. It would be callously ungrateful if today's Catholics allow those brave souls to be forgotten and unhonoured who by their steadfastness have left us a laudable example of courage and constancy. Unlike our Catholic forebears, to whom stories of the martyrs were familiar, new generations have grown up knowing little or nothing about the horrendous persecution under which these heroes and heroines of the Old Faith suffered in our land. This book has been written with such in mind and if it introduces the martyrs for the first time to even one new person I shall be content.

There have been many pamphlets and booklets and a few biographies of individuals among the Forty; for example the *Life of Robert Southwell* by Father Christopher Devlin SJ; *Henry Morse* by Father Philip Caraman SJ, and Evelyn Waugh's *Edmund Campion*. But I have always felt the lack of a comprehensive, single volume that gives biographies of all Forty set within their historical context. Most of the publications on the martyrs appeared many years ago, pre-dating the 1970 canonization. Many were written in a high-flown style that is not appealing to a modern readership. In any event most of them are long out of print.

The sources for the lives and deaths of the martyrs are well established. Every writer on the subject inevitably draws on these same sources and subsequently upon each other. My work is no exception. There is no new, hitherto unpublished material and I make no claim to originality or great erudition. By its very nature this is a compilation and I pay heartfelt tribute to all who have gone before me whose works I have culled. I gratefully acknowledge that without their efforts this book would not have been possible. I have utilised just about every previous author on the subject. It is fair to say that I have gleaned something, whether consciously or sub-consciously, from every one of them over many years of reading and in the process of writing this book. As the saying goes, no one is infallible, yet in the course of my research I have been surprised by the number of errors of fact and the self-contradictions that I have detected in the works of highly respected authors on the subject.

This is not a history book *per se*, but historical background has been included in order to elucidate the conditions under which the martyrs lived. This is not a book for academics and scholars: it is intended for a general readership. Thus it would be not only quite impractical, but also extremely tedious and distracting for the non-academic reader, if I was to specifically cite every reference either in the text or as notes. Appended is an extensive list which effectively credits my sources, none of whom must be held responsible for any mistakes in the text. If there are factual errors I accept full responsibility and plead, 'Mea culpa!' The opinions expressed and the interpretation of events and characters, however perverse, are entirely my own.

The first edition of my book was completed in 2005 and published in

2008. Since then I have had time in which to reflect upon it. My original manuscript was longer and far more detailed than the version I submitted for publication. With hindsight I soon regretted that I had not retained my fuller original text, especially with regard to details about the many beatified martyrs who feature in its pages. In relegating these martyrs in most cases to brief notes, I felt I had committed the same 'grave injustice' with which, in my Introduction, I had charged those responsible for promoting the martyrs' canonization. This revised and enlarged edition seeks to rectify that fault by reverting, more or less, to my original version with some updated additions. Consequently it also fills out much more of the historical and political background in the context of which the martyrs lived and died, in the hope that readers might better comprehend the pervasive extent of the prolonged, mindless, insensate violence and wickedness that is chronicled in these pages.

A handful of typographical errors and name spellings have been corrected as well as clarifying a few factual points. The List of Sources has been considerably expanded to more faithfully encompass all the source material and the Index of Persons has been completely re-written as it was very inadequate.

I would like to acknowledge my indebtedness to the Public Record Office (now The National Archives at Kew), The British Library and Guildhall Library, City of London, for providing the historical material I needed to consult.

I hope that this new edition of my book will prove a more fitting tribute to the heroes and heroines of the Catholic Faith in our land. Unlike the Protestants executed under Queen Mary very few of them have any permanent public memorial, although, happily, there are Catholic schools and churches dedicated to some of the blessed martyrs as well as saints in the group of Forty Martyrs.

Malcolm Pullan

23 June 2013
405th anniversary of the martyrdom of St Thomas Garnet

Introduction

The word martyr comes from the Greek meaning 'one who witnesses to the truth'. Today the appellation is frequently misused or, even worse, sacrilegiously misappropriated by terrorist suicide bombers. It is common to hear all manner of people described in the media as 'martyrs' to various causes. They may well have suffered for their consciences' sake but they are not martyrs in the recognised Christian sense. As St Augustine of Hippo (354-430) wrote, 'It is not the pain but the cause that makes the martyr'; and Blessed John Henry, Cardinal Newman (1801-90) wrote, 'No one is a martyr for a conclusion; no one is a martyr for an opinion. It is faith that makes martyrs.'

The Forty Martyrs of England and Wales gave the ultimate witness to the truth of the Catholic Faith. They laid down their lives with an astounding fortitude that is almost impossible for us to comprehend when we read of the privations and sufferings they had to endure. Humanly speaking, how did they do it? A similar question was posed by 20th century Russian writer and prisoner, Alexander Solzhenitsyn, in *The Gulag Archipelago*. 'How can you stand your ground when you are weak and sensitive to pain, when people you love are still alive?' Solzhenitsyn gave an answer that would have resonated with our martyrs: 'my spirit and my conscience remain precious ... to me,' and concluded that 'Only the man who has renounced everything' can win the victory. For love of their Lord Jesus Christ and His Church the Forty Martyrs did indeed renounce everything and they exemplified Christ's injunction in the Sermon on the Mount to 'love your enemies and pray for those who persecute you.' Like that great British Christian heroine of World War I, Nurse Edith Cavell, they could say of those who sought to kill them, 'I must have no hatred or bitterness towards anyone.' The martyrs did not want to die: they shared that shrinking from death that comes naturally to every man. The martyrs did not seek death but rather accepted it when it came, and, while fearful of the horror that awaited them, they were prepared to willingly endure it for the cause of Christ and His truth. The Forty came from many different backgrounds in terms of education, social status, age and temperament. They comprise thirteen secular priests, three Benedictines, three Carthusians, one Bridgettine, two Franciscans, one Augustinian, ten Jesuits and seven laymen and women.

England and Wales has been slothful in promoting the causes of its saints and martyrs compared with the Church in Asia and Latin America or with our Continental cousins. Spain, for example, has successfully promoted the beatification and canonization of many

Introduction

hundreds of its Civil War Martyrs. When Thomas More and John Fisher were canonized in 1935, after the most intense lobbying by Catholics in England and Wales, it had been 534 years since a native Englishman had been raised to the altars. (For the record that was St John of Bridlington; all too little known today.) 1 From the start, those put to death for the Faith were regarded as martyrs by their co-religionists. Pope Gregory XIII Buoncompagni (1572-85) acknowledged this by allowing relics of the English and Welsh martyrs to be used in altars and their pictures to be venerated. This took the form of a group of frescoes painted by Nicholas Circiniani on the walls of the church of St Thomas of Canterbury at the English College in Rome, depicting the martyrs between 1535 and 1583. The cost of the paintings was met by George Gilbert, a wealthy Englishman forced into exile for his faith. The Pope also authorised public *Te Deums* to be sung when news of martyrs was received.

Because the victims were so widely venerated, the first moves to promote the canonization of the English and Welsh martyrs were instituted by Pope Urban VIII Barberini (1623-44) as early as 1642 at the request of the exiled English Benedictines. Because of the ongoing persecution, together with the Civil War, the investigation process was severely hampered by the difficulty of collecting convincing evidence to prove martyrdom, a process wilfully hindered by the obstruction of the government in this country. The most important and valuable work of Dr Richard Smith, Bishop of Chalcedon (1587-1655), was his meticulous catalogue of the English and Welsh martyrs which he submitted to Rome in 1628.

Another individual to whom an incalculable debt is owed was Father Christopher Grene SJ. He was born in Ireland of English parents in 1629. Ordained in Rome in 1653, he came to England in 1658, where he joined the Society of Jesus. By 1664 he was back in Italy and became the English penitentiary (priest appointed to administer penance) at the Holy House, Loreto, and then at St.Peter's, Rome. He died in retirement at the English College, Rome, in 1697. A great lover of the English martyrs, he probably did more than any other person to preserve the records of the sufferings of Catholics during the time of persecution, including detailed lists of those who died in various prisons around the country. He collected, transcribed and catalogued reams of letters and other documents relating to the martyrs; information that is only available to us now because of his prodigious labours, as many of the originals have long been lost. Another valuable source of information is the *Sufferings of Catholics* compiled by Father John Knaresborough. Born in Yorkshire in 1672 he was ordained at

Introduction

Douai in 1699. He served on the mission in and around York from 1704 until his death in 1722 and was buried in the city at St Michael-le-Belfry.

In the eighteenth century, the work of Bishop Smith was updated, amplified and published by a saint who's Cause we English have been neglectful of promoting: the Venerable Bishop Richard Challoner, Vicar Apostolic of the London District (1691-1781). 2 Challoner's *Memoirs of Missionary Priests* became the basis of the records of the martyrs whose cause was not revived until 1855, when following the restoration of the Catholic hierarchy the indefatigable Father John Morris SJ took it up in earnest.

The Synod of Westminster, held in 1859, unsuccessfully petitioned the Holy See in the hope of obtaining a papal decree officially approving the cult of the martyrs. It was not until 1874 that a formal process was opened for 361 martyrs. The process proved difficult and time-consuming, not least because of the sheer number of martyrs involved. Tribute must be paid to the priests of the London Oratory for their commitment and devotion in collecting evidence in a form acceptable to Rome. Pope Leo XIII Pecci (1878-1903) introduced the Cause of 254 martyrs, and fifty-four were beatified 'equipollently' on 29 December 1886, followed by nine others on 13 May 1895. These sixty-three corresponded with those honoured by Pope Gregory XIII, their veneration being judged to constitute an immemorial cult. In 1923 Cardinal Francis Bourne OP, Archbishop of Westminster (1903-1935), resumed the process, and on 15 December 1929 Pope Pius XI Ratti (1922-39) beatified a further 136 martyrs, although 241 had been submitted, entitling them to the epithet 'Venerable'. With the exception of the special case of More and Fisher, canonized in 1935, it was another thirty-five years before any other martyrs were canonized.

The English and Welsh hierarchy decided once more to resume the martyrs' cause, but with just a small group. The names of the Forty Martyrs were submitted in December 1960 to the Holy See, which accepted the group as forming one Cause. Before that date reports of many favours and cures attributed to the intercession of the Blessed Martyrs of England and Wales had been brought to the attention of the hierarchy and the authorities in Rome. Once the group of forty names were known there was an official and intense nationwide campaign of prayer. As a result data on over twenty 'miracles' was presented to Cardinal William Godfrey, Archbishop of Westminster (1956-1963), who passed on the information to the Sacred Congregation in Rome. These claims were examined by medical experts of international repute and two particularly noteworthy cases were submitted to the Holy See.

Introduction

One of these, the cure of a malignant tumour in a young mother, was judged by the medical team to be perfect, constant and inexplicable by any natural means. Pope Paul VI Montini (1963-78) confirmed the miraculous nature of the cure through the intercession of the Forty Martyrs. The Pope signified that he was prepared to go ahead with their canonization on the basis of this one miracle, bearing in mind that in the case of Fisher and More a dispensation had been given to proceed without a miracle. No miracle is required for the beatification of a martyr so why the Church considers it necessary to demand miracles as 'proof' before canonizing martyrs remains a mystery to me. (See Appendix 3) Surely the very fact of their martyrdom for Christ is sufficiently eloquent testimony of heroic virtue practised even unto death: a miracle in itself. Expressing this view I am in good company; no less than the great Father of the Church, St John Chrysostom (347-407) who thought too much importance was attached to miracles. 'What constitutes Christian life, good deeds or a show of miracles? Good deeds, of course', and he goes on to say that given the choice of performing a miracle or dying for Christ 'would you not choose martyrdom? For martyrdom is a deed, but a miracle is only a sign.' He pointed out that our Lord's invitation to the blessed ones to enter into His Father's kingdom was not addressed to those who worked miracles, but to those who ministered to Him in the persons of the hungry, the sick and the sorrowful. Amidst great rejoicing, the canonization ceremony took place in St Peter's Basilica on 25 October 1970, with Pope Paul trying valiantly to cope with the pronunciation of the forty English and Welsh names as he read them out in chronological order. 25 October was fixed in the liturgical calendar as the feast day of the Forty, but the hierarchy has now removed their separate commemoration, which has been subsumed into a feast of all the English Martyrs, kept on 4 May. (Unlike the Church in Wales which not only commemorates the six canonized Welsh martyrs and their companions on 25 October but also observes their individual feast days on the dates of their deaths.)

The canonization of the Forty Martyrs must be set in the wider context of the multitude of martyrs and confessors who gave their lives for the Catholic Faith. The Forty are to be seen as representatives of those Catholics who suffered for their faith in various parts of England and Wales between 1534 and 1729. Some may be surprised that I include this late date when the 'accepted' date is usually taken as 1681, but the fact is that there were priests who continued to be imprisoned in the reign of William III (1689-1702) and under the Hanoverians. For example there was the case of the Yorkshireman, Matthew Atkinson, a

Introduction

Franciscan known as Father Paul of St Francis. He had joined the Franciscans at Douai in December 1673 aged only seventeen years. He had been sent to the English mission in 1687 until on the evidence of a false convert, eager to obtain the £100 reward, he had been arrested in 1699 and condemned to perpetual imprisonment. He served 30 years in Hurst Castle on the Solent dying there on 15 October 1729.

Why the decision was taken by the hierarchy to promote the Cause of only forty of the beatified martyrs, and exactly what motivated the choice of that particular forty in preference to others is not at all obvious. The explanation cannot be that the remainder were regarded as 'second class' martyrs. And it was certainly not the case that there was more information in the form of the requisite documentary proof available about the forty selected than any other martyrs. Reasons advanced for the choice of those included in the Forty were the extent of devotion to each of them and how representative they were as regards place of origin and status. But I have to admit I never found this very convincing, given the equally strong and continuous devotion to many other martyrs such as Robert Ludlam, Nicholas Garlick, George Haydock and above all Nicholas Postgate. I suspect an underlying element not only of timidity on the part of those in Britain promoting the martyrs' Cause but also of 'political correctness' in the selection, long before that expression became current. Providing proof to Rome was certainly a daunting task, so was there fear of the potential costs and time factor? Or was there overanxiety about upsetting ecumenical relations, particularly with the Anglican Church? Whatever the reservations of the Protestant Establishment, it should not have affected the judgement of the Church as to the sanctity of the Forty Martyrs. It was charitably courteous to wish to avoid distressing our Anglican friends by reminding them of the uncomfortable fact that their Church had been established by persecution, but the lengths to which the Catholic Church went to avoid that possibility seemed to me excessive. The Cause was hampered by the monitoring of newspaper and magazine articles and general media reactions to assess its 'opportuneness'. Even the Roman Postulator General, Father Paolo Molinari SJ, devoted an inordinate amount of time in self-justification after, as he put it, 'voices had been raised in England' that the Cause might be 'inopportune for ecumenical reasons.' Holding apologetic press conferences and seeking reassurances from the British Council of Churches - which gave its patronising-sounding 'approval' in 1969 - all looks rather 'over the top' and immature with hindsight. It served only to demonstrate how insecure and unsure of themselves Catholics still were about their place in British society.

Introduction

I do not want to seem sententious and have no wish to be hypercritical of the dedicated efforts of those admirable promoters involved at the time. But, accepting the sincere motivation of those responsible, it can be cogently argued that the very process of selection has resulted, albeit unintentionally, in a grave injustice being done to hundreds of other martyrs, equally deserving of veneration and the honour of being 'raised to the altars'. This applies above all to the inexplicable omission of those who were the actual *companions* in martyrdom of those numbered among the Forty. Even 'secular' authors such as Professor John Phillips Kenyon, in his masterly and definitive study, *The Popish Plot* (1972), are baffled by the apparent inconsistency of the Catholic Church in its canonization policy with regard to the English martyrs. To quote Kenyon, 'This distinction cannot be explained by reference to historical sources', and he cites the specific case of Nicholas Postgate to illustrate his point. Writing in 1999 about the selection of martyrs for canonization, Archbishop Edward Nowak, Secretary of the Vatican Congregation for the Causes of Saints from 1990 to 2007, said 'Ideologies ... serve as a context of martyrdom, but in the foreground the person stands out with his conduct and it is important that the people among whom the person lived should affirm and recognise his fame as a martyr ... It is not so much ideologies that concern us, as the sense of faith of the People of God, who judge the person's behaviour.' If that criterion had been observed, i.e. the judgement of their contemporaries, then most of the English and Welsh martyrs, including Henry Garnet, would have long since been canonized. It is certainly disappointing and frustrating that more of our martyrs have not been canonized, especially those priests who were totally innocent victims of the 'Popish Plot'. It is a major offence against justice, or indeed simple logic, that only six of these martyrs were selected for canonization and the equally worthy remainder omitted. It upsets me when, in comparison with these brave, martyred priests, I think of some of the Church's contentiously dubious beatifications and canonizations in recent decades. I will refrain from naming examples!

Sufficient evidence having been amassed, a further group of eighty-four English and Welsh martyrs, plus the Scotsman George Douglas, who was executed at York, was beatified on 22 November 1987 by Pope John Paul II Wojtyla (1979-2005). There remain another thirty Venerable martyrs whose beatification cause was deferred in 1929; these too were regarded by their contemporaries, and ever afterwards, as genuine martyrs; but obtaining corroborative evidence now seems highly unlikely. The Church is, quite rightly, wary of treating as martyrs any whose deaths may have had 'political' connotations. Yet

Introduction

there are among the beatified martyrs some whose actions which led to their deaths may be construed as 'political', e.g. John Felton 1570, Thomas Plumtree 1570, Thomas Percy 1572 and Edward Coleman 1678. In justification it should be pointed out that they all rejected offers of pardon and their lives if they agreed to conform to the Established Church, therefore it is correct that ultimately they died for their religion. Nevertheless their cases further highlight the Church's inconsistency. Percy and Plumtree were prominent in the Northern Rising of 1569, yet were judged to merit beatification. Therefore, it is pertinent to ask why have those religious who were executed after the 1536/37 'Pilgrimage of Grace' been treated so differently. After all, they too paid with their lives for opposing the religious tyranny of the monarch.

There remains a supplementary list of 242 men and women. Many of these Venerable and *praetermissi* ('passed over') martyrs were products of the seminaries, undertook the same dangerous work and suffered the same penalties, but their lives were spent in such obscurity that little is known about them. A great many others, religious and laymen and women, died in prison, confessors for the Faith. The problem is trying to prove that they died as a direct result of their imprisonment. At this distance in time it is difficult to see how such evidence will ever be forthcoming. But by the same token how can one differentiate between them and the case of St Philip Howard? It is to be fervently hoped that one day at least all the beatified martyrs of England and Wales who, like the canonized martyrs, suffered because they refused to bow down in the house of Rimmon, * will be formally enrolled by the Church among the saints.

Finally a word about nomenclature. Until relatively recent times only priests who were religious (i.e. belonging to a religious order) were called 'Father'; secular priests were always called 'Mr', and that is how it would have been throughout the entire period covered by this book. However, for modern readership unfamiliar with these niceties it might prove confusing, therefore for the sake of clarity I have opted for the anachronism of referring to all priests as 'Father'.

---

* Rimmon, a deity and idol worshipped in Syria. See the Old Testament story of Naaman, 2 Kings 5:18. In modern parlance conforming to a reprehensible act in order to save one's life.

Introduction

Notes to the Introduction

1 St John of Bridlington was born at Thwing, near Bridlington, East Yorkshire and studied at Oxford before becoming an Augustinian Canon at Bridlington. He held a number of offices in the monastery before being elected prior in 1362. A model monastic, he perfectly combined his fervent prayer life with the practicalities of his office. He was a wise, outstanding and greatly loved and revered leader of his community. He was an exemplar of the wry comment made by Pope Clement VIII 200 years later: 'Show me anyone who has lived in perfect observance of the rule, and I will canonize him without any other miracle.' John died in 1379 and many miracles took place at his tomb. King Henry V attributed his success at the Battle of Agincourt to the intercession of John and his Yorkshire namesake, St John of Beverley, Bishop of York (d.721). John of Bridlington was canonized in 1401. There is a wonderful medieval stained-glass window commemorating his life in the church at Morley, Derbyshire.

2 Bishop Richard Challoner was born at Lewes, Sussex, in 1691, the son of a Presbyterian wine barrel maker. When he was thirteen Richard was baptised a Catholic by a famous spiritual writer, Father John Goter. This took place at Warkworth Castle, Northamptonshire, where his widowed mother was housekeeper to the Catholic Holman family. Lady Anastasia Holman was a daughter of the martyred Blessed William Howard, Viscount Stafford. Richard was ordained at Douai in 1716 and spent the next fourteen years at the College as a professor and Vice-President. In 1730 he returned to England and ten years later was appointed a bishop and coadjutor to the Vicar Apostolic of the London District, Benjamin Petre, whom he succeeded in 1758. He was Vicar Apostolic until his death in January 1781. His extensive activities are the more remarkable because most of his life was spent in hiding, often hurriedly changing his lodgings to escape the informers, anxious to earn the reward for his capture. Challoner's *Memoirs of Missionary Priests* consists of biographies of around 300 Catholics who suffered for their faith. It is an invaluable source of information as he made use of material that is no longer extant. Among his many publications he compiled one of the most popular and enduring prayer books for private devotions amongst English Catholics: the *Garden of the Soul*. In 1749-50 he also published his revision of the Douai-Rheims Bible. Since 1946 his remains have rested in Westminster Cathedral. The Cause for the beatification of this wise and holy bishop was introduced many years ago but now sadly seems to have been abandoned.

Chapter One

The Henrician Martyrs

No man is justified in doing evil on the ground of expediency.

Theodore Roosevelt, 1858-1919

The martyrs' story begins in the reign of that abominable Tudor autocrat, the megalomaniac King Henry VIII (1509-47). Like his father before him, Henry ostentatiously paraded his devotion to the Church and the Papacy. His enthusiastic profession of ultra-orthodox Catholicism in 1521 had earned him the title 'Defender of the Faith' from Pope Leo X Medici (1513-21) for his best-selling book in defence of the Seven Sacraments against Martin Luther. Henry was so obsequious in expressing his devotion to the Holy See that when Sir Thomas More counselled him to be more circumspect pointing out that the pope, 'is a prince as you are and in league with other princes ... I think it best therefore that his authority may be more slenderly touched.' The King expostulated, 'Nay, that shall it not. We are so much bounden unto the See of Rome that we cannot do too much honour to it.' Henry said that Luther 'cannot deny that all the faithful honour and acknowledge the sacred Roman See as our Mother and Supreme Judge - all the churches in the Christian world have been obedient to the See of Rome. He considers not, I say, what cruel punishment he deserves, that will not obey the Chief Priest and Supreme Judge upon earth.' However when it came to the crunch and the teaching of the Church clashed with Henry's personal desires his egoism carried the day. Thomas More astutely summed up Henry's character. When congratulated that he so greatly enjoyed the King's favour, under no illusions, More replied, 'If he thought my head could gain for him a castle in France he would not hesitate to have it off.' And More's comment on Cardinal Wolsey was just as apposite when applied to Henry: 'Never was he satiate of hearing his own praise.' Charles de Marillac, French Ambassador in England 1538-42, wrote of Henry, 'Not only a King to be obeyed on earth, but a veritable idol to be worshipped.'

Pared down to its simplest elements, the story ran as follows. Henry was besotted with his pushy paramour, Anne Boleyn. In order to marry her Henry was determined to divorce his lawful wife, Catherine of Aragon (1485-1536), to whom he had been married for twenty years.

The Henrician Martyrs

She had borne him three sons and two daughters, but only Princess Mary had survived. The self-righteous Henry was so egocentric that it never seems to have occurred to him that the Church would do any other than eventually give him what he desired just because he, the King, desired it. His case for marrying Anne was not helped by the fact that her elder sister, Mary, had already been Henry's mistress. In Canon Law this constituted a serious impediment, especially as it was widely believed - and now accepted as true - that the father of her children, Catherine and Henry, later 1st Baron Hunsdon, was, in fact, the King and not her complaisant husband, Sir William Carey, Gentleman of the Privy Chamber. Contemporaries noted that Catherine in particular bore a striking resemblance to Henry and Elizabeth I. Carey profited hugely from his wife's infidelity with gifts of manors and estates. It is hardly surprising that the King may have been too embarrassed to officially acknowledge the children considering that he had embarked upon his quest for a divorce from Queen Catherine in order to marry their aunt.

The King's chief minister, Cardinal Thomas Wolsey, on his knees, pleaded with Henry not to discard the Queen, but failed to dissuade him. This earned the Cardinal the malevolent enmity of Anne Boleyn. Queen Catherine was much loved and undoubtedly enjoyed the support not only of a great many of the nobility and clergy, but also of the majority of the English people. Assailed on all sides, and believing it impossible to obtain a fair hearing in England, in a remarkable *coup de théâtre* at Blackfriars monastery, Catherine referred her case to Rome. In spite of all the bullying pressure exerted on him by Henry, Pope Clement VII Medici (1523-34) for various reasons - by no means all of them edifying or spiritual - vacillated about granting Henry's wish to have his marriage nullified. If Clement had had the courage to refuse an annulment immediately and not let the matter drag on, engendering greater resentment from Henry with each passing year, it is possible that the situation could have been salvaged and England saved from schism. Yet there has to be some sneaking sympathy for Clement. Following the Sack of Rome in 1527, Clement was held in the Castel Sant'Angelo, the prisoner of the Emperor Charles V and as the Emperor was uncle to Queen Catherine Clement dared not offend him by giving in to Henry. Nonetheless the King's agents pursued the Pope relentlessly to Orvieto when he escaped from Rome and treated him with great discourtesy when they found him living in a miserable, poverty-stricken state in the bishop's ruined palace.

Amongst Catherine's supporters were Bishop John Fisher of Rochester and Sir Thomas More. William Warham, the devout and learned humanist Archbishop of Canterbury had at first been lukewarm

The Henrician Martyrs

in Catherine's cause but when he realised the direction in which ecclesiastical matters were going he woke up to the gravity of the situation and opposed the divorce in Parliament and all Acts derogatory to the Pope's authority. Warham died in August 1532, aged eighty-two. Henry was beside himself with rage and frustration at the delay in getting a papal decision. If the Pope could not, or would not, give him what he wanted then he would repudiate the Pope and find someone else who would accede to his wishes. And if the consequence of having his own way meant divorcing not only his wife but also divorcing the entire nation from communion with the Holy See, then so be it.

On 1 October 1532 Archdeacon Thomas Cranmer (1489-1556), [1] a former chaplain to the Boleyn family, who secured his astonishing promotion, was appointed Archbishop of Canterbury. In spite of being warned of Cranmer's unsuitability for the primacy, Pope Clement, anxious to mollify Henry, gave his approval of the appointment to the See of Canterbury. Cranmer, of course, hypocritically went along with his charade of loyalty to Rome just long enough to secure his installation as archbishop. A man of Protestant sympathies, while in Germany Cranmer had defied the Church's discipline by secretly marrying a German Lutheran. Incredible though it may seem, he kept his marriage such a closely guarded secret it is doubtful if Henry ever knew about it. The novelist, Anthony Trollope, succinctly summed up Cranmer as 'a time-serving priest, willing to go to any lengths to keep his place.'

The King's compliant archbishop conveniently annulled his master's marriage to Catherine in 1533, notwithstanding that Anne and Henry had already gone through a secret, bigamous marriage ceremony at Whitehall Palace four months earlier on 25 January, conducted by one of the royal chaplains, Rowland Lee. He would later get his reward with a bishopric and become one of the King's minions for the suppression of the monasteries. Cranmer validated Henry's marriage to Anne in order to ensure that the child she was carrying would be legitimate. On 1 June, the obviously pregnant, deeply unpopular Anne was crowned queen by Cranmer. On 11 July Pope Clement ineffectually retaliated to the news from London by excommunicating Henry and Cranmer, and declaring the purported annulment of the King's marriage to Catherine and his marriage to Anne Boleyn null and void.

In March 1534 the Act of Succession (25 Henr.VIII, c.22) declared Princess Mary, the King's daughter by Catherine, a bastard, and made it an offence punishable by death to deny the validity of the King's new marriage. The first victims of the Act were Elizabeth Barton, the visionary 'Holy Maid of Kent', and some of her supporters. 2 After seven years of vacillation, on 23 March 1534 Pope Clement finally declared the King's first marriage to be valid and his marriage to Anne unlawful. In the end the papal judgment was morally right, but had political circumstances been different it is difficult to resist the conclusion that Clement would have felt it pragmatically expedient to sacrifice Queen Catherine in the wider political interest. However the papal procrastination only served to seriously damage even further the diminished respect in which the papacy was held in England.

Henry, the first English king to adopt the title 'majesty', had initially declared himself Supreme Head of the Church in England in 1531. (In 2005 Richard Chartres, Anglican Bishop of London, speaking of the 'crucial significance of this issue', declared, 'As a matter of historical fact, the title Supreme Head is a direct contradiction of Scripture.') When the Convocation of Clergy of Canterbury and York met Henry completely humiliated the bishops by forcing them to pay £100,000 to obtain his pardon for having recognised Cardinal Wolsey as papal legate in England. The majority of the Convocation then tamely accepted the King's new title with the addition of the proviso, 'so far as the law of God allows' - a meaningless quibble as it turned out. Bishop John Fisher of Rochester was the only dissenting voice. How many of the bishops repented, like the staunchly anti-Lutheran, John Stokesley of London? He was a friend of Thomas More and collaborated closely with him in combating and rooting out heresy. On his deathbed in 1539, he declared that he wished he had stood with 'my brother Fisher.' Stokesley, who had baptised the infant Princess Elizabeth, thought at the time that the King's break with Rome was a tactical manoeuvre to secure his divorce. His episcopal colleagues may well have believed, or wanted to believe, the same. Stokesley was accounted a learned man, but he was clearly not a brave one. The bishops were not to know that the ruthless Thomas Cromwell, Henry's chief minister, was determined that the break would be permanent. Thomas More once sagely told Cromwell, 'If you follow my poor advice you shall in your counsel to his grace, ever tell him what he ought to do, but never what he is able to do ... For if a lion knew his own strength, it would be hard for any man to rule him.' Cromwell chose to ignore that wise advice, encouraging the King to ever greater exploits of egocentric excess, with dire consequences for all who opposed him.

Henry's move to make himself head of the Church may be viewed in the context of the general trend of the times: the consolidation of monarchical absolutism; an omnipotence stemming from the idea of the 'divine right' of kings to rule. No one expressed this doctrine more forcibly than Martin Luther himself. Protestant princes who supported the new religious movement actually strengthened their rule because without any independent arbiter in Rome or any risk of reprisal, they were free to demand not only what their subjects must do but also what they must believe. It is unlikely that Luther was familiar with Niccoló Machiavelli's *The Prince*, which advocated that monarchs should rule by fear, using brute force and deceit whenever necessary to maintain state power, morality having nothing to do with the matter. Luther would have certainly approved of and shared his Italian contemporary's philosophy. Luther wrote, 'A donkey driver has to be always beating his donkey, or the beast will not obey him. This is how the ruler should treat the people. Princes must drive, beat, throttle, hang, burn, behead and torture them, so as to make themselves dreaded and keep the people in awe of them.' Henry VIII may have disagreed with Luther over religious doctrine but he would have seen eye-to-eye with him over this championing of royal absolutism. By declaring himself Supreme Head of the Church in a sense Henry was only extending his autocratic authority over the ecclesiastical as well as the secular sphere. In effect it turned the Church into just another department of state under royal control. (It was a continuation of this policy under his daughter Elizabeth I that brought the Church of England into being.)

In 1532 the Church had surrendered its independence and canon law to the King. In 1533 the Act in Restraint of Appeals put an end to all matrimonial and testamentary appeals to Rome. On 18 November 1534 Parliament subserviently ratified the de facto situation by passing the Act of Supremacy (26 Henr.VIII, c.1) in which, without any qualification, the King was declared to be 'the only supreme head on earth of the Church in England' with full powers, including spiritual, over clergy and laity. As Thomas Howard, 3rd Duke of Norfolk, succinctly put it, 'The king was now emperor and pope in his own dominions.' In a sense the Act only legalised what, in reality, had already been achieved. Papal jurisdiction had been formally severed, thereby putting England and Wales into schism from Rome. The break with Rome was deeply resented by the nation at large. As the distinguished historian, James Gairdner (1828-1905), assistant Keeper of the Public Records, wrote, 'On no other subject during the whole reign have we such overt and repeated expressions of dissatisfaction with the king and his proceedings.'

Henry VIII seems to have been the first monarch to realise the significance of public opinion. In 2005 Richard Chartres, Anglican Bishop of London, described Henry as 'a monster of egotism with a gift for propaganda.' This was exploited by Thomas Cromwell who made every effort to mould the populace to accept the religious changes. In the sixteenth century the pulpit was the chief vehicle for influencing public opinion. Thomas Cromwell issued detailed instructions about the anti-papal diatribes bishops and clergy were required to deliver in their sermons. They were commanded to preach the royal supremacy in all churches every Sunday and feast day of the year. It speaks volumes that it was thought necessary to pump such unrelenting propaganda into priests and people to secure their acquiescence. Only priests who received royal licences were permitted to preach, thus effectively silencing any of them who might voice their opposition from the pulpit. In order to forestall widespread public discontent, when the suppression of the religious houses began unbelievable filth and coarse invective was poured out blackening the reputations of members of the religious orders. The propaganda effort was not confined to preaching alone. Plays and interludes were enacted, often in the churches, purportedly representing the immorality of the clergy, lampooning the pope and cardinals and making a mockery of certain forms of worship. As John Henry Blunt wrote in *The Reformation of the Church of England*, 1878, 'The horrible coarseness of such representations; the immorality and blasphemy of parodizing the Holy Eucharist in the very house of God itself seem not to have struck the writers.'

No one was allowed to express any opinion contrary to official policy and a system of espionage came into being to report on any lapses. What happened to those brave enough to speak out publicly is illustrated by the case of James Mallet who, among other benefices, was treasurer of Lincoln Cathedral. He dared to attribute the root of all the troubles and changes to the 'sin' of the King's divorce from Catherine. He paid for this temerity with his life being hanged, drawn and quartered. Succeeding injunctions made it abundantly clear that the clergy were relegated to being mouthpieces of royal propaganda. The bishops were held responsible for the compliance of the clergy with the injunctions and the bishops were answerable to the sheriffs for their own conformity. It is surely beyond the bounds of coincidence that after 1536 the numbers of men offering themselves for ordination declined sharply in every diocese. (Philip Hughes, *The Reformation in England*, 1963). Perversely, the shortage of priests that resulted worked to Henry's advantage as ambitious curates, who might have had to wait many years for preferment, now found benefices available. This no doubt helped cement their acceptance of the King's new religious regime. When the suppression of the religious houses was implemented it removed one of the chief sources of patronage to benefices. It has been estimated that laymen acquired the right of nomination to around one-third of all benefices. Henceforth the Church's control over priestly appointments was drastically curtailed, whereas that of the King and other lay patrons greatly increased.

With the exception of John Fisher, the bishops, who should have been the chief shepherds of their flock, lamentably failed in their responsibility. Why? Whilst there were those among the hierarchy who certainly fell short of the ideal, there were also conscientious pastors who probably thought that matters would soon revert to 'normal' and they could buy time. Others, no doubt, were anxious to protect their careers by propitiating the King. Some, like Edmund Bonner of London, later claimed that it was 'fear that compelled us to bide with the time'. In any event they allowed themselves to be bullied and cowed by Henry into submission.

Much that was wrong in parts of the Church was epitomised by the career of Thomas Wolsey, by whom many of the bishops had been appointed. Those he elevated were expected to materially show their gratitude. They were men who could be counted on to be loyal to him in order to secure his continued patronage and maintain him in power rather than for their outstanding spiritual attributes. From humble beginnings, Wolsey rose by intelligence, talent, industry and driving ambition to become Lord Chancellor and Cardinal. But alongside these qualities he loved power, wealth and ostentation. His *folie de grandeur* demanded a style of living rivalling that of the King for its lavishness and splendour. An absentee pluralist, in 1514 he was made Archbishop of York, and during the same period he held the bishoprics of Durham and Winchester. When Wolsey failed to deliver the annulment of the King's marriage, he bore the brunt of Henry's anger and his enemies, the Boleyn's and the Howard's, pounced ensuring that he plummeted from power. (Jean du Bellay, the French Ambassador, discerned with prophetic foresight, even at that early stage, that once they had ruined the Cardinal these covetous lords would next seek to take the wealth of the Church.) Facing charges of treason Wolsey died in 1530, remorsefully wishing that he had served his God as diligently as he had served his King. Against this background, it is little wonder then that the bishops, in a weakened Church without a strong leader, had neither the faith nor courage to offer strong resistance to the King.

The new Treason Act of 1534 (26 Henry VIII c.13), the culmination of all the anti-papal measures, was a formidable piece of legislation that trampled on any remaining semblance of civil liberty and gave the King absolute power. Henceforth it was high treason to deny in any way the King's supremacy; the Act making it an offence punishable by death to deny the King his title. The Act introduced a new principle into English law: treason could now be committed simply by words or opinion, and even Parliament's caveat by inserting 'maliciously' into the Act did nothing to lighten its oppressive impact. It was this Act that led to the martyrdoms of Henry's reign. The martyrs wished to continue as loyal subjects of the Crown but conscientiously refused to accept the King's spiritual supremacy, knowing that doing so rendered them guilty under the regime's new definition of treason. E. E. Reynolds in his, *The Roman Catholic Church in England and Wales*, 1973, summarised it thus. The martyrs 'were not put to death for denying any doctrine of the Christian faith; they were not heretics; they did not plot against the state, but their fate was to be beheaded or hanged, drawn and quartered for a newly invented kind of treason that involved the repudiation of papal authority'.

The first martyrs under the Act of Supremacy came from an unlikely quarter: the quiet cloisters of the Carthusian Order, eighteen of whose members were to suffer for their opposition. The chief source for our information about them comes from the contemporary account, *Historia aliquot nostri saeculi martyrum*, by Dom Maurice Chauncy, which exists in several versions. Chauncy, the eldest son of John Chauncy, was born at Sawbridgeworth, Hertfordshire, in 1509 and studied law at Gray's Inn before joining the London Charterhouse at around the time of John Houghton's election as prior. A monk of the Charterhouse during the last few years of its existence, Chauncy was intimately acquainted with the martyrs and the life of the monastery. Although inclined to hagiographical hyperbole, as an eyewitness of many of the events he describes his trustworthiness is unimpeachable.

John Houghton, Robert Lawrence and Augustine Webster

That little spark of celestial fire called conscience.

George Washington, 1732-99

What was to develop into the Carthusian Order was established in 1084 by St Bruno at Chartreuse near Grenoble; hence the Anglicisation to Charterhouse. By the reign of Henry VIII there were nine Charterhouses in England. The first English houses were both in Somerset: Witham, founded in 1178 by Henry II, in reparation for the

The Henrician Martyrs

murder of St Thomas Becket, followed by Hinton in 1227. Next came the Charterhouse of the Blessed Trinity at Beauvale in Nottinghamshire, which was founded in 1343 by Sir Nicholas de Cantilupe. The Charterhouse of the Salutation of the most blessed Mother of God had been established at Smithfield in 1370. Sir Walter de Manny, one of the knights of Edward III, had bought land in 1351 which he donated to the City of London as a cemetery for victims of the Black Death. A small chapel was erected and twenty years later Manny invited Carthusians from Hinton to set up a monastery on the site. Edward III's own master mason was given charge of the building operations and by 1371 enough had been accomplished for the foundation charter to be issued. The monastery must have been planned for a long time because Michael Northburgh, Bishop of London (1354-61), richly endowed the foundation with money left in his will for the purpose. Eventually the monastery occupied about thirty acres, which included not only the monastic buildings but also an orchard and vegetable garden. It had an advanced piped water supply, drawn from a spring a mile or so away at Islington, fed into the monastery by underground lead pipes. The monastery was more than a century in construction. The remnant that exists today dates from the early Tudor period. It is just possible that the initials 'I.H.' that can be discerned in dark brick on a wall of the court are those of John Houghton. The church, as prescribed by the rules of the Order, was plain and austere. The cells, as in all Charterhouses, consisted of a two-storey house which stood in its own garden. Each had a workroom, oratory, bedroom and living room. In one of the most austere of all religious orders, the white-robed monks keep silence and live alone, usually eating alone except on Sundays and feast days, when they congregate in the refectory. They live on a vegetarian diet: Carthusians eat fish but never eat meat. They talk to each other on Sundays after refectory, when it is the custom to go for a walk outside the monastery.

Between 1499 and 1503, while still a law student, Thomas More frequently stayed at the monastery, joining in the offices and testing his vocation. Contemporaries said that if you wanted to hear the liturgy beautifully celebrated, the Charterhouse was the place to go. No religious house had a finer reputation. The monks were deeply respected for their strict observance of the rule and the number of applicants of quality wishing to join the community was so great that there was a waiting list.

In the period covered by this narrative there were three priors at the Charterhouse. Firstly there was William Tynbygh 1500-29, an Irishman by birth. Sixty years a Carthusian, he was a man of conspicuous

The Henrician Martyrs

holiness, to whom must be attributed the high standards that distinguished his community; secondly came John Batmanson 1529-31; and thirdly John Houghton.

Houghton was born in Essex in 1486 or '87. He studied Civil and Canon Law at Cambridge University and can most probably be identified with the student of that name who took his degree in Civil Law in 1506. Having returned to his parents' home in Essex, he found that they expected him to make a good marriage. But John had other ideas: he wanted to be a priest. We are told that he left home in secret to train for the priesthood. When he reached the canonical age he was ordained and went back home, remaining with his parents for about four years, serving as a parish priest before entering the London Charterhouse in 1515. In 1522 he became Sacrist and in 1527 was dismayed when appointed Procurator. The reason for his distress was that this office required him to travel outside the monastery on matters of business which interrupted his observance of solitude and silence.

In 1531 John was elected Prior of Beauvale, Nottinghamshire. Later that same year he returned to London, having been unanimously elected prior of the London Charterhouse. There were thirty priest choir monks and eighteen lay brothers, most of them relatively young men. During his tenure of office the reputation of the house increased to an even higher level, under the guidance of a man who governed by example and whose combined qualities of holiness and leadership skills were an inspiration to his monks. Chauncy tells us John was 'of short stature, of dignified appearance; his actions modest, and gracious and gentle in speech, humble of heart, admired and sought after by all, and by his community most beloved and esteemed.' Chauncy was of the opinion that even had Houghton not died a martyr he would have been worthy of sainthood. In 1532, the General Chapter of the Order appointed John as Provincial Visitor for England. This meant that he was required to make inspections every two years and report on the condition of all the Carthusian houses in the country.

Robert Lawrence, a monk of the London Charterhouse, succeeded John Houghton as Prior of Beauvale. Little is known of his early life. It has been suggested that he came from Dorset, and he may be the Robert Lawrence who took a degree in Civil Law at Cambridge in 1508. It is also possible that he may have served for a time as a chaplain to Thomas Howard, 2nd Duke of Norfolk.

Augustine Webster was born c.1480. He was a monk of the Charterhouse of Jesus of Bethlehem at Sheen, near Richmond, Surrey; the largest of the English Charterhouses, it had been founded by Henry V (1413-22). Augustine too had studied at Cambridge, and is most

The Henrician Martyrs

likely the student of that name who is recorded as having taken the degrees of Bachelor and Master of Arts. In 1531 he became Prior of the Charterhouse of the Visitation of Our Lady, in the Isle of Axholme, Lincolnshire, which had been founded around 1397 by Thomas Mowbray, Earl of Nottingham and Earl Marshal of England.

Henry VIII was determined that the validity of his marriage to Anne Boleyn should be recognised and thereby secure the succession to the throne of their children, so the Carthusians, along with everyone else, were required to swear to the Act of Succession. On 4 May 1534, royal commissioners Rowland Lee and Thomas Bedyll visited the London Charterhouse requiring the monks to take an oath to that effect. Prior Houghton tried to evade the question saying that his position did not require him to pass judgement on such high matters as royal marriages. He told them that monks did not meddle in the King's affairs, but also gave the opinion that he did not see how a marriage ratified by the Church and of such long duration as the King's to Catherine could be invalid. Along with Father Humphrey Middlemore, the Procurator, John was imprisoned in the Tower. They remained there a month and were visited by Bishop Stokesley of London and Archbishop Lee of York who persuaded them that the issue of the succession was not one for which to sacrifice their lives for conscience's sake. They were released after agreeing to take the Oath conditionally, i.e. so far as it was lawful; but the rest of the community were reluctant to swear even on those terms. Amidst their joy at their Prior's return, the monks were deeply disturbed that a similar oath would soon be required of them. John told them, 'Our hour has not yet come, dear Fathers. This very night that Father Procurator and I were set free from prison, I dreamt that I was not to escape so soon, but that I should be brought back, and that very prison would receive me again within a year ... So though I set no store by dreams, I think that something else will be proposed to us before long; but meanwhile let us live without offending God, as far as we possibly can.'

The royal commissioners, Archdeacon Thomas Bedyll and Rowland Lee - since January 1534 Bishop of Coventry and Lichfield - again visited the Charterhouse on 29 May 1534, but achieved only partial success, some of the monks taking the oath conditionally. Only when Bishop Lee brought the lord mayor and one of the sheriffs of London with an armed band of men on 6 June did they manage to secure the reluctant acceptance of all the community to the oath. 'We all swore as we were required,' writes Chauncy, 'making one condition, that we submitted only so far as it was lawful for us to do so. Thus, like Jonah, we were delivered from the belly of this monster ... But it is better to trust in the Lord than in princes, in whom is no salvation. God had prepared a worm that smote our gourd and made it perish.'

In August 1534 Archdeacon Bedyll wrote to Thomas Cromwell about the attitude of the monks at the Charterhouse and the Bridgettines at Syon Abbey.

> I am right sorry to see the foolishness and obstinacy of diverse religious men so addicted to the bishop of Rome and his usurped power, that they contemn all counsel and likewise jeopardy their bodies and souls and the suppression of their houses as careless men and willing to die. If it were not for the opinion which men had, and some yet have, in their apparent holiness, which is and was, for the most part covert hypocrisy, it made no great matter what became of them so that their souls were saved. And as for my part, I would that all such obstinate persons of them, who be willing to die for the advancement of the bishop of Rome's authority, were dead indeed by God's hand; that no man should run wrongfully into obloquy for their just punishment ... I have taken some pains to reduce them from their errors and will take more if I be commanded ... I mean this not only by divers of the Charterhouses and chiefly at London, but also by others, as by divers of the friars at Syon who are minded to offer themselves in sacrifice to the great idol of Rome; and in so minding they be cursed of God ...

The Act of Supremacy came into force, (26 Henry VIII, c.1.) in autumn 1534 and Henry's new title of 'Supreme Head' was incorporated in the King's style by decree of the Council on 15 January 1535. When the Treason Act quickly followed Houghton was under no illusion that he and his community would face further trials. Chauncy tells us that John tried to prepare his community for the worst.

In April 1535 the royal commissioners were due to descend upon the Charterhouse to obtain the sworn acceptance of the monks to the Act of Supremacy, or risk being charged with high treason should they refuse. John asked for three days of special preparation to be held. The first day was devoted to prayers and Prior Houghton's homily was a meditation on Psalm 59: 'Save me from my enemies, my God; protect me from those who attack me ...' He concluded by saying, 'It is better for us to bear some brief punishment for our faults than to be preserved for eternal torments'. Then rising from his place John went to the eldest of his brothers and kneeling before him, begged his forgiveness for any offence he might have committed against him. He repeated this action before every member of the community in turn. The second day was given over to confession and reconciliation with each other. Chauncy writes that,

The Henrician Martyrs

When we were all in great consternation he said to us, "Very sorry am I, and my heart is heavy, especially for you, my younger friends, of whom I see so many around me. Here you are living in your innocence. The yoke will not be laid upon your necks, nor the rod of persecution. But if you are taken hence, and mingle among the Gentiles, you may learn the works of them and, having begun in the spirit, you may be consumed in the flesh ... what shall I say, and what shall I do, if I cannot save those whom God has trusted to my charge." Then all who were present burst into tears and cried with one voice, "Let us die together in our integrity" ...The prior answered sadly - " Would indeed that it might be so; that so dying we might live, as living we die. But they will not do us so great a kindness, nor to themselves so great an injury. Many of you are of noble blood; and what I think they will do is this: me and the elder brethren they will kill; and they will dismiss you that are young into a world which is not for you. If, therefore, it depend on me alone - if my oath will suffice for the house - I will throw myself for your sakes on the mercy of God. I will make myself anathema; and to preserve you from these dangers I will consent to the king's will. If, however, they have determined otherwise - if they choose to have the consent of us all - the will of God be done. If one death will not avail, we will all die". So then, bidding us prepare for the worst, that the Lord when he knocked might find us ready, he desired us to choose each our confessor, and to confess our sins to another, giving us power to grant each other absolution.

The third day was devoted to a votive Mass of the Holy Spirit. It was a most moving experience for all the community. Chauncy writes that the Spirit made His presence felt by them all. 'Some perceived it with their bodily senses; all felt it as it thrilled their hearts. And then followed a sweet, soft sound of music, at which our venerable father was so moved, God being thus abundantly manifested among us, that he sank down in tears and for a long time could not continue the service - we all remaining stupefied, hearing the melody and feeling the marvellous effects of it upon our spirits.' While this triduum was taking place, apparently quite by coincidence, Priors Lawrence and Webster came to London to consult with John Houghton and their brethren.

In an attempt to forestall the arrival of the Commissioners, the three priors sought an interview with Thomas Cromwell, [3] Henry VIII's chief Secretary of State, and since 1535 Ecclesiastical Vicar General. The detested Cromwell was a *parvenu par excellence* and the supervisory role that he exercised over the Church was unprecedented for a layman. His protégé, and second in command, was the double-dealing and treacherous Richard Rich, [4] whom historian Hugh Trevor-Roper dismissed as a man 'of whom nobody has ever spoken a good word.' Cromwell was responsible for the visitation and eventual suppression of the monasteries, euphemistically referred to as the 'dissolution'. The

The Henrician Martyrs

Protestant historian, Dr S R Maitland, sometime secretary to the Archbishop of Canterbury, wrote of Cromwell in his *Essays on the Reformation in England,* 1849, 'He was the great patron of ribaldry, and the protector of the ribalds, of the low jester, the filthy balladmonger, the ale-house singers and the hypocritical mockers ... in short, of all the blasphemous mocking and scoffing which disgraced the protestant party at the time of the reformation. It was the result of design and policy earnestly and elaborately pursued by the man possessing for all such purposes the highest place and power in the land.' This was the character of the man the three monks' naïvely hoped to persuade to give them exemption, or at least to agree a form of the Oath that would be acceptable to their communities. Cromwell treated them discourteously and refused to listen. He committed all three of them to the Tower and on 20 April they were brought before Cromwell, Rich, Bedyll and others. They remained steadfast in their refusal to take the Oath and consistent in the reasons they adduced for doing so. Father Houghton wrote a note of all the questions that had been proposed to them, and their answers. The priors declared themselves willing to take the Oath if, once again, they could add, 'as far as the law of God allows'. But Cromwell would permit no conditions, and insisted that the Oath be taken without reservation.

Richard Reynolds

Integer vitae scelerisque purus
A man of upright life and free from guilt

Horace, *Odes* I, 22 (65-8BC)

Joining the Carthusians in their stand was Richard Reynolds, a monk of the Bridgettine Order from Syon Abbey, Middlesex. Probably born at Pinhoe, Devon about 1490, he had joined the Bridgettine's after an exceptionally distinguished career at Cambridge. (The Reynolds family were still living at Pinhoe a generation later. William Reynolds, son of Richard Reynolds, was born there in 1543. Having been Rector of Lavenham, Suffolk in the Established Church, he converted and was ordained priest 1580. What was his relationship to the martyr?) Richard took his BA in 1506 and his MA in 1509, becoming a fellow of Corpus Christi College, where he attained the degree of Bachelor of Divinity in 1513, the same year in which he was appointed University Preacher.

The Bridgettine Order of St Saviour had been founded in 1346 by St

The Henrician Martyrs

Bridget (Birgitta) of Sweden (1303-73) and developed by her daughter St Catherine (Katrin) of Sweden (1331-81). The monastery of St Saviour and St Bridget, known as Syon Abbey, was the only Bridgettine house in England. Situated by the River Thames near Isleworth, it had been endowed by Henry V in 1415. It was a double monastery, consisting of separate enclosures for men and women with an abbess in overall charge of all temporal affairs. Each community had separate choirs in a common monastery church. An enclosed order, the Bridgettines were noted for their austerity as well as for their strictness in accepting new members. The nuns had to be eighteen years old and the brothers twenty-five. Charles Wriothesley, the contemporary chronicler, called Syon 'the most virtuous house of religion in the land'.

It was well known to Queen Catherine and her daughter Mary, who often paid visits when staying at the nearby Richmond Palace. Syon was also in the vanguard of what we would call evangelisation, taking full advantage of the opportunities offered by the invention of printing. The many spiritual volumes that they produced were intended not only for religious but also for the growing lay reading public. These included an English translation of Thomas à Kempis's *Imitation of Christ* by Richard Whytford, 5 another Cambridge man who joined the abbey about the same time as Reynolds and was probably the best known member of the Bridgettine community at Syon.

The Bridgettine way of life, study and prayer, was eminently suitable for one of Reynolds's temperament. When he was professed at Syon in 1513, he presented his great collection of books to its library. A friend of Sir Thomas More, he was a famous spiritual counsellor and preacher; one of the most respected, wise and learned priests of his time, he was familiar with Latin, Greek and Hebrew. Many people consulted him, particularly when the question of the King's divorce arose. These included Bishop John Fisher, who was Queen Catherine's chief supporter. But apart from his learning, Richard was also renowned for the holiness of his life. Chauncy was not the only contemporary to describe Richard as a man of angelic countenance and angelic life.

Elizabeth Barton, the 'Holy Maid of Kent', paid several visits to Syon and conferred with members of the community, including Richard Reynolds, telling them of her views about the royal supremacy. It was inevitable that Syon would attract the attention of the government, and the 'King's great matter' would soon penetrate its hallowed precincts. In January 1534 royal officials led by John Stokesley, Bishop of London, had visited the monastery in an effort to secure the signatures of the community acknowledging the validity of the King's second marriage. A draft was signed but the wording was too ambiguous to satisfy the King. A second, more explicit draft was submitted, which the brothers refused to sign, urging the nuns to follow suit. In May Cromwell sent Rowland Lee and Thomas Bedyll to get the community to take the Oath of Succession, but were unsuccessful. Queen Anne Boleyn made a personal visit to Syon in September 1534, presumably to see if that might persuade the community. Evidently it did not. By November 1534 the government had made the Oath of Succession obligatory, quickly to be followed by the Act of Supremacy.

Cromwell had to crush the opposition coming from the Carthusians and the Bridgettines, who enjoyed such high reputations. Cromwell clearly thought that if he could induce a man of such intellectual brilliance and holiness as Richard Reynolds to take the Oath of Supremacy it would persuade others to follow. It cannot be without significance that Richard was the only one of the Syon community who was apprehended at this time. His arrest came in the spring of 1535 and he was sent to the Tower a few days after the Carthusian priors. On 25 April Cromwell and the royal commissioners came to see all four prisoners in the Tower, demanding that they should renounce the authority of the Pope and acknowledge that the King was supreme head of the Church in England. The answers they gave to the interrogations they underwent can still be read in the Public Record Office.

John Houghton says he cannot take the King, our Sovereign Lord to be supreme head of the Church of England afore the apostles of Christ's Church.

Robert Lawrence says that there is one Catholic Church of which the Bishop of Rome is the head; therefore he cannot believe that the King is supreme head of the Church.

Augustine Webster says that he cannot take the King to be supreme head of the Church, but him that is by the doctors of the Church taken as head of the Church, that is the Bishop of Rome, as Ambrose, Jerome and Augustine affirm and is made at the Council of Basle.

Richard Reynolds declares that though he would spend his blood for the king, still that the pope is head of the Church.

Speaking for all the prisoners, Richard fearlessly replied that they could only accept the proposition 'so far as the law of Christ allows'. Thus the four made a courageous and principled stand for orthodox teaching, maintaining the integrity of the Catholic Faith. With the scandals of the Borgias and Medicis still relatively fresh in their minds for many people the 16th century had been a period of criticism of the papacy. The nature of the papacy had been under discussion for some time. Was it a human institution or did it have a divine origin in the commission of Christ to St Peter, continued in his successors, the

The Henrician Martyrs

Bishops of Rome? Following this encounter with Reynolds and the three priors, Cromwell and the King agreed that the priests should be charged with high treason and sent for trial, knowing that the outcome of any trial would be a foregone conclusion. On 28 April 1535 the three Priors and Reynolds were taken for trial at Westminster Hall. Earlier, prejudiced 'historians', such as Bishop Gilbert Burnet (1643-1715) in his *History of the Reformation*, tried, for propaganda purposes, to make out that the Carthusians had died for disobedience to the King. Clearly Burnet had never read the original indictment, which is still extant in the Public Record Office, leaving no shadow of doubt as to the reason they were convicted for 'Treacherously machinating and desiring to deprive the King of his title as Supreme Head of the Church and at the Tower of London on 26th April', openly declaring, 'The King our Sovereign Lord is not Supreme Head on earth of the Church of England'. The Carthusians were joined by an elderly secular priest, John Haile, Vicar of Isleworth. 6

A special commission was appointed to hear the case. Its members included Sir Thomas Audley, the Lord Chancellor; Thomas Howard, 3rd Duke of Norfolk; Henry Courtenay, Marquess of Exeter; Henry Clifford, Earl of Cumberland; Thomas Boleyn, 1st Earl of Wiltshire, who was Anne Boleyn's father; and George, Viscount Rochford, who was her brother, together with Thomas Cromwell, Sir Anthony Fitzherbert and other lawyers. All the accused pleaded 'not guilty' and a jury was sworn. Evidence was presented to show that Richard had encouraged others to oppose the divorce and the royal supremacy.

The prisoners were sent back to the Tower while the jury deliberated at length late into the evening. When Cromwell sent to ask why they had not yet reached a verdict, they responded that they could not find such holy men guilty, especially as they did not find it proved that they had - as was required by the Act - 'maliciously' denied the supremacy. Cromwell was furious and personally threatened the jurors with imprisonment and death. Only after this overnight intimidation did they bring in the required guilty verdict. Reynolds, Haile and the three Priors were summoned back to Westminster the following day and urged to recant before sentence was passed. Richard seems to have acted as spokesman for all the accused.

In response to questions from the Lord Chancellor, he started by saying that it had been his intention to follow the example of Our Lord and keep silent before his accusers, but now felt that his conscience required him to speak out. He appealed to the rest of European Christendom and to the continuous history of the Church in England, which had owed allegiance to Rome for a thousand years. Richard

The Henrician Martyrs

declared: 'I say that our belief is of greater weight and has far more abundant testimony in its behalf than yours. For instead of the few whom you bring forward out of the parliament of this kingdom I have the whole of Christendom in my favour. I can even say I have all this kingdom in my favour, although the smaller part holds with you, for I am sure the larger part is at heart of my opinion, although outwardly, partly from fear and partly from hope, they profess to be of yours in the hope of retaining royal favour. As to dead witnesses, I have on my side all the General Councils, all historians, the holy doctors of the Church for the last fifteen hundred years, especially saints Jerome, Ambrose, Augustine and Gregory'.

When warned only to answer to the charge that he had maliciously and against the King's authority tried to persuade many from submitting to the King's Majesty, he replied, 'If I were here arraigned before God's own tribunal, it would be made clear that never to a living man have I declared an opinion of my own maliciously against the King or anyone'. He said he had only spoken of the matter to clear his conscience or when asked about it in confession. 'I was indeed grieved to learn that his Majesty had fallen into so grave an error, but I said so to no one, except as I have declared. And had I not then declared what I believe I would say it openly now, seeing that I am bound by God and my conscience and in doing so neither my Sovereign nor anyone else may rightly take offence'. At this point he was ordered to be silent. 'Since you will not let me say more, judge me according to your law'.

After the inevitable sentence had been pronounced, Richard asked if they could have two or three days in order to prepare for death. He was told this request was not in the judges' power to grant but rested with the King. The request was met, but the condemned were not left in a great deal of peace because Archbishop Cranmer and Cromwell did all in their power to get them to change their minds, sending various representatives to argue with them but without any success. One of these was Dr Thomas Starkey, a chaplain to the King, who later wrote of Richard, 'For sorry I was for many causes, that a man of such fame, and he was here noted both for virtue and learning, should die in such a blind and superstitious opinion. But nothing could avail, but that he would, in that opinion, as a disobedient person to the king's laws, suffer his death with the others of the same mind.' The influential Protestant historian, Dr Samuel Gardiner, in his *Student's' History of England* (1892), wrote of these martyrs, 'They had sown no seeds of rebellion, and they died because a tyrannical king insisted on ruling over consciences as well as bodily acts'.

On 4 May 1535 all five priests, wearing their religious habits in

The Henrician Martyrs

order to make a greater impression upon the people, were dragged on hurdles through the streets of London from the Tower to Tyburn. Sir Thomas More was then a prisoner in the Tower awaiting trial. It so happened that on the day of the priests' execution his daughter Margaret Roper had been given permission to visit him. Through the narrow windows of his cell, father and daughter were able to see what was taking place.

'Lo, dost thou not see Meg', said More, 'that these blessed fathers be now as cheerfully going to their deaths as bridegrooms to their marriage? Wherefore thereby mayest thou see, my own good daughter, what a great difference there is between such as have in effect spent all their days in a strait, hard, penitential and painful life, religiously; and such as have, as thy poor father hath done, consumed all their time in pleasure and ease. For God, considering their long-continued life in most sore and grievous penance, will no longer suffer them to remain here in this vale of misery and iniquity, but speedily hence taketh them to the fruition of His everlasting Deity. Whereas thy silly father, Meg ... hath passed forth the whole course of his miserable life most sinfully, God, thinking him not worthy so soon to come to that eternal felicity, leaveth him here to be plagued with misery.'

Tyburn, to the west of London, had been the place for executions since the late twelfth century. The grisly ritual required the condemned to be tied onto hurdles, primitive frames that jolted along uncomfortably pulled by horses. The gallows consisted of a wooden upright against which a ladder was rested. The rope was placed around the neck and the condemned had to climb the ladder which, at the moment deemed appropriate, was pushed away leaving the victim dangling.

A great crowd of spectators had gathered for the priests' execution. Eustace Chapuys, the Imperial Ambassador, who described the event in a letter the following day, informs us that most of the members of the Court were present, including leading nobility such as the dukes of Norfolk and Richmond and the earl of Wiltshire and his son. Even on the scaffold each one of the priests was offered a pardon if he would take the Oath. Despite knowing the terrible consequences, each one refused. They faced the most barbarous of deaths. They were hung by a rope around the neck, causing slow strangulation, but not long enough for them to die. While alive they were to be cut down, their genitals cut off, their insides ripped open with a knife, their heart and inner organs torn out and burned, and finally their bodies were to be cut into four sections and beheaded. As if that was not enough, there was the stomach-churning stench as the severed quarters were parboiled to help

The Henrician Martyrs

preserve them for public display.

John Houghton was the first to die. He embraced the executioner and forgave him for what he was about to do. He spoke up: 'I call Almighty God to witness, and I beseech all here present to attest for me on the dreadful day of judgement, that being about to die in public, I declare that I have refused to comply with the will of His Majesty the King, not from obstinacy, malice or a rebellious spirit, but solely for fear of offending the supreme Majesty of God. Our holy mother the Church has decreed and enjoined otherwise than the King and Parliament have decreed. I am therefore bound in conscience, and am ready and willing to suffer every kind of torture rather than deny a doctrine of the Church. Pray for me and have pity on me my brethren, of whom I have been the unworthy prior. Then kneeling down he recited verses from Psalm 31. *In thee O Lord have I hoped; let me never be confounded: deliver me in thy justice ... into thy hands I commend my spirit.*

After he had been hanging for a while the rope was cut. John's habit was torn off, revealing his hair shirt, and as the horrific butchery began while he was fully conscious, he cried out, 'Jesus, have mercy on me in this hour!' As the executioner groped for his heart John was heard to say, 'Good Jesu, what will you do with my heart?' The executioner then added diabolical insult to injury by rubbing the heart in John's face.

His companions, who had to watch this ghastly spectacle taking place, showed no sign of human weakness, but rather called upon the crowd to live good lives and to serve the King faithfully in everything that was not contrary to the law of God and His Church. Reynolds, being the last to die, stood encouraging his brothers calling on them to think of the heavenly banquet they would all soon be sharing together after 'their sharp breakfast, taken patiently for their Master's sake'. Eye-witnesses commented that Richard did not appear in the least upset or fearful but submitted courageously to his torments.

The dismembered parts of the martyrs' bodies were displayed around the City of London as a warning to others and Prior Houghton's left arm was hung up over the Charterhouse gate to help overawe those remaining into submission.

On 4 May, the very same day as the Priors' execution, Archdeacon Thomas Bedyll, the royal commissioner arrived at the monastery. He and Rowland Lee had achieved some measure of success in persuading the Carthusians at Sheen. Like their London brethren the monks showed great reluctance to take the Oath of Supremacy. The Prior, Henry Man, had been Prior of Witham, before taking up the same office at Sheen. He was sent to the Tower for a short period and when he returned to Sheen seemed more amenable to doing the King's bidding. As one of the monks reported the house was divided 'many of them were ready to conform ... others I think will rather die from a little scrupulosity of conscience and would not give way for sorrow and despair of salvation.' The community was preached at unrelentingly until most of them gave way. Sheen was finally surrendered by Prior Man early in 1539. Eighteen of the monks and novices who had subscribed to the oath received small pensions. Man received his rewards: a pension of £133.6s and was afterwards made dean of Chester and then Bishop of Sodor and Man.

Cromwell installed resident agents at the London Charterhouse to report on the remaining monks. All their books were confiscated and they were forced to endure violent anti-papal harangues in an effort to break their resolve. We learn from Chauncy that the monks were deprived of food and drink and were constantly harassed so that they could not perform the daily monastic offices, being detained by diatribes from the commissioners. On 6 May, Ascension Day, Bedyll wrote to Cromwell. As it reveals so much about the mind-set of the man, it is worth quoting from the letter at length.

Please it you to understand that on Tuesday, forthwith upon my departure from you, I repaired to the Charterhouse and had with me divers books and annotations, both of my own and others, against the primacy of the Bishop of Rome, and also of St.Peter ... After long communication, more than one hour and a half, with the Vicar and Procurator of the house, I left those books and annotations with them, that they should see the Holy Scriptures and Doctors thereupon concerning the said matters, and thereupon reform themselves accordingly. And yesterday they sent me the said books and annotations again home to my house by a servant of theirs, without any word or writing. Wherefore I sent to the Procurator to come and speak with me, seeing I kept my bed by reason of sickness, and could not come to him. And at his coming I demanded of him whether he and the Vicar and other of the seniors had seen or heard the said annotations, or perused the titles of the books, making most for the said matters. And he answered that the Vicar and he and Newdigate had spent the time upon them till nine or ten of the clock at night, and that they saw nothing in them whereby they were moved to alter their opinion. I then declared to him the danger of his opinion, which was like to be the destruction of them and their house for ever; and as far as I could perceive by my communication with the Vicar and Procurator on Tuesday, and with the Procurator yesterday, they obstinately determined to suffer all extremities rather than to alter their opinion, regarding no more the death of their Father in word or countenance than he were living and conversant among them. I also demanded of the Procurator whether the residue of his brethren were of like opinion, and he answered he was not sure, but he thought they were all of one mind ... Finally, I suppose it to be the will of God, that as their Religion had a simple beginning, so in this realm it shall have a strange end, procured by themselves, and by none others. And albeit they pretend holiness in their behalf, surely the ground of their said opinion is hypocrisy, vainglory, confederacy, obstinacy, to the intent that they may be seen to the world, or specially to such as have confidence in them, more faithful and more constant than any other.

Tactics such as these went on for about three weeks and when they had no effect Father Humphrey Middlemore, [7] whom Houghton had appointed Vicar and was now in charge of the monastery, and Father William Exmew, [8] the Procurator, along with Father Sebastian Newdigate, [9] were arrested. They were first sent to Cromwell at his house in Stepney where each of them declared, 'I cannot nor will consent to be obedient to the king's highness as a true, lawful and obedient subject to take and repute him to be supreme head on earth of the church of England under Christ.' They were then committed to the Tower where Henry VIII secretly visited Sebastian to try and persuade him to submit. They were treated with inhuman cruelty, being tied upright to posts with iron collars and chains around their necks and legs. Unable to move they were left in this state for two weeks enduring the stench of their own excrement. They were tried by a special commission presided over by the Lord Chancellor, Thomas Audley, [10] and defended themselves with arguments from Scripture and Tradition in favour of the papal primacy as to why the King could not be the head of the Church. Having been refused permission to receive Holy Communion, on Saturday, 19 June 1535 they were hanged, drawn and quartered in their religious habits at Tyburn. This was quickly followed on 22 June by the execution of John Fisher, [11] Cardinal Bishop of Rochester on Tower Hill. Sir Thomas More had used all his legal skills to avoid committing himself in respect of the royal supremacy. He knew that his best defence was in maintaining his silence on the subject. But it was galling to Henry that this internationally recognised and respected figure would not support him and he was not prepared to tolerate even mute dissent. In his play *A Man for All Seasons* Robert Bolt has Thomas Cromwell percipiently say, 'His silence is deafening all Europe.' On 6 July Sir Thomas More [12] met the same fate as Fisher.

Cromwell continued to bring every pressure to bear to wear down the resolve of the monks now deprived of leadership. In 1536 he appointed the subservient William Trafford, a member of the Sheen community and a former Procurator at Beauvale, as Prior of the London Charterhouse. Trafford had initially been as constant as his brothers in

The Henrician Martyrs

London, declaring to Sir John Markham, who had been sent to Beauvale to assess its worth, that he 'firmly believed the pope of Rome is supreme head of the Church Catholic', for which boldness he was placed in custody. In order to try and save their house in January 1537 Prior Thomas Woodcock and the monks of Beauvale paid a heavy fine of £166.13s.4d; around £70,000 at today's worth. (Beauvale, with all its possessions in Nottinghamshire, Derbyshire and Lincolnshire, was suppressed in July 1539.) At some subsequent point Trafford had surrendered his conscience to the King. Reading Chauncy it is clear that the monks did not regard Trafford as their true Prior, as he had been imposed upon them. Twenty choir monks and eighteen brothers remained: of the 'refuseniks' two of the most obdurate priests, John Rochester [13] and James Walworth, were sent to the Charterhouse at Hull. This monastery had been founded in 1378 but had been one of the houses already suppressed. A small group of monks had begged to be allowed to return and did so, only to find the place stripped bare. There John and James were left as virtual prisoners until March 1537 when they were placed in custody at St Mary's Monastery, York. Thomas Howard, 3rd Duke of Norfolk, then in residence in the city, was reminded about them. He described John Rochester as a malign spirit who still believed in the primacy of the Pope and who might influence the opinions of others in that direction. On 15 May 1537, refusing to submit, the two monks were hanged in chains at York by order of the Duke; they were left hanging on the walls of the city for several days until they were dead.

Prior Trafford was merely a cipher. Bedyll speaks of him as doing 'howsoever he be ordered'. The Charterhouse was run by Royal Commissioners, termed Governors. Their instructions were:

1. That they should be continually present there every meal and lodge there every night.

2. That they take the keys from the Procurator and other officers, and to govern the house, receive all rents, make all payments and be accountable to the King thereof.

3. That they should call the monks, one at a time, and examine them about their opinions, promising them that if he conformed himself to the King's laws he would have a dispensation to leave the Order and receive a stipend for a year or two.

4. To put all the monks to the cloister for a season, and that no one speak to them but by the leave of the Governors.

5. To take from them all manner of books wherein any errors be contained.

6. To cause them to forsake all their ceremonies that be nought.

7. If they find any of them so obstinate that they will not be reformed, then to commit them to prison.

8. That three or four times every week, a sermon to be made that all were compelled to attend, except those too sick to leave their cells.

9. That the lay-brothers, being more obstinate and unreasonable than the monks, should be punished or expelled.

The Charterhouse became a prison with the monks kept short of food and warm clothing during the winter months and their health began to badly suffer. Chauncy describes how members of the Privy Council would come and harangue them in the chapter house, and detain them deliberately to prevent them singing Vespers and Matins in choir. One Sunday Cromwell ordered four of the monks to be removed from High Mass and taken to St Paul's where, in the custody of the sheriff's, they had to sit and listen to an anti-papal sermon.

Under the strain of this unrelenting pressure their resolve was broken. On 18 May 1537, led by Prior Trafford and Edmund Stern, the Vicar, half of the monks, in the hope of saving the Charterhouse, capitulated by accepting the royal supremacy in the presence of Archdeacon Bedyll of Cornwall and Richard Gwent, Archdeacon of London. Although Chauncy's signature does not appear amongst the names of those who signed the Oath, he nonetheless admitted to having taken it, albeit against his conscience. His cowardice on this occasion seems to have haunted him and he repented it for the rest of his life describing himself as 'the spotted and diseased sheep of the flock.'

Ten members of the community, [14] three priests, a deacon and six brothers, refused to submit and on 29 May were sent to Newgate, where they were chained to posts upright and left without food. Even by the standards of the time Newgate, which had been a prison site since the 12th century, was, in the 16th century, in an appallingly ruinous state. Margaret Clement neé Giggs, [15] the foster daughter of Thomas More, bribed the jailer to let her visit the prisoners disguised as a milkmaid. She smuggled food in and fed them and tried to clean them of their filth, but when queries were raised as to why the prisoners were not already dead the jailer was too afraid to let her into the prison again. Nine of them were deliberately starved to death. After their deaths Archdeacon Bedyll callously wrote to Cromwell:

The Henrician Martyrs

It shall please your lordship to understand that the monks of the Charterhouse here in London, which were committed to Newgate for their traitorous behaviour long time continued against the King's Grace, be almost despatched by the hand of God ... I am not sorry, but would that all such as love not the King's Highness and his worldly honour were in like case.

He then goes on to list by name those who had already died and the two who, although very sick, were still alive.

The sole survivor, Blessed William Horne, was kept in the Tower for three years and finally hanged, drawn and quartered at Tyburn on 4 August 1540. Executed with him were Lawrence Cook, Carmelite Prior of Doncaster, Thomas Epson, a Benedictine and William Bird, Vicar of Bradford-on-Avon, attainted for speaking out against the suppression of the abbeys and the royal supremacy. (Bird acted as chaplain to Walter, Lord Hungerford who was also attainted for employing him, knowing his views. Hungerford was beheaded on 28 July, along with Thomas Cromwell.) Executed with these clergy were two laymen, Robert Bird and Giles Heron, the former ward and then son-in-law of Thomas More. Heron, son and heir of Sir John Heron, Treasurer of the Chamber to Henry VII and VIII was hanged for high treason, although the official records offer no clear explanation as to what precisely he was alleged to have done to deserve such a fate. [16]

In the meantime, in exchange for a paltry pension of £20, on 10 June 1537 Prior William Trafford had surrendered the remnant of the Charterhouse to the King under the most abject terms, dictated to him by Bedyll. The twelve surviving monks and six lay-brothers were finally forcibly expelled on 15 November 1539, each of them receiving a pension of £5. The last name on the list of brothers is that of Maurice Chauncy who recalled with horror how men sacrilegiously played dice on the altar of the church. Archdeacon Bedyll asked that the Charterhouse might be put to some 'better use'. On 12 June 1542 Henry gave the property for use as a store for his hunting tents. In 1555 the buildings were granted to Sir Edward North, who turned them into a stately home for himself. He demolished the cloister and converted the chapel into a dining hall. In 1565 the property was sold to the Duke of Norfolk for £2,500. In turn his son, Thomas Howard, Earl of Suffolk, sold it in 1611 for £13,000 to Thomas Sutton, the founder of what was eventually to become the famous Charterhouse public school. Among its future pupils was John Wesley, the founder of Methodism.

In May 2005, on the 470th anniversary of the martyrdom of John Houghton and his companions, an ecumenical service took place in which Catholic Bishop George Stack and Anglican Bishop Richard

The Henrician Martyrs

Chartres of London in a spirit of reconciliation and reparation jointly dedicated a Commemorative Stone to the martyrs in the former great cloister of the Charterhouse. The inscription reads: May the cause of healing inspire all who study and teach here today. Chartres, describing Henry VIII as a man of 'messianic pretensions' similar to Hitler or Stalin, declared, 'We salute the courage and discernment of those who said 'no'. We are honouring martyrs who deserve to be remembered with thanksgiving by the whole Church.'

John Stone

Nothing in his life became him like the leaving of it.

Macbeth, William Shakespeare, 1564-1616

He was an Augustinian Friar and a doctor of theology about whose early life we know nothing. The Austin Friars had a number of houses in England. John Stone belonged to the Augustinian Priory at Canterbury, which had been established by Archbishop Walter Reynolds in 1318. John had already come to the notice of the authorities when he publicly denounced from the pulpit the attempts of the King to divorce Queen Catherine. On 14 December 1538 the King's agent, Richard Ingworth, schismatic Suffragan Bishop of Dover arrived to suppress the priory. Ingworth, the former Dominican prior of Kings Langley, had been consecrated bishop on 9 December 1537 and shortly afterwards received a commission 'to vex and visit' the various orders of friars, most of whose houses he found 'the poorest houses ever.' At the suppression of the Dominicans in Newcastle Ingworth had sold the goods in the house and the church vestments for less than £5. The only items worth anything were the chalices, which were sent to the royal treasury, and the lead and tiles off the roof. As for the friars the bishop 'gave them a few hours grace to quit their convent' and turned them out in the depth of winter without any provision. Ingworth found the Austin Friars in great poverty and debt. He demanded that all the friars acknowledge the King as head of the Church and sign a document surrendering the priory. John boldly refused to sign the Oath of Supremacy and upbraided Ingworth for doing the King's dirty work. On no account would he acknowledge the King as supreme head of the Church. As he endeavoured to persuade his fellow friars to also refuse he was immediately detained. Ingworth sent a report of his visit to

The Henrician Martyrs

Cromwell.

Being in the Austin Friars there the 14th day of December one friar there very rudely and traitorously used himself before all the company as by a bill enclosed you shall perceive part. To write half of his words and order there it were too long to write. I perceiving his demeanour straight away sequestered him so that none spoke with him. I sent for the mayor [of Canterbury] ... I examined him before the mayor ... and at all times he still held and willed to die for it, that the King may not be the head of the Church in England, but it must be a spiritual father appointed by God.

John was taken to London to be examined by Cromwell. He spent the next year in prison. On 27 October 1539 the Mayor of Canterbury was given a commission for John to be tried under the Treason Act, and for this purpose he was sent back to Canterbury; most likely imprisoned in the castle. John prayed and fasted for three days and while praying in his cell he heard a heavenly voice, although he saw no one. The voice addressed him by name, telling him to be of good heart and encouraged him to remain constant unto death. He drew great spiritual courage and strength from the experience.

Exactly when his trial took place at Canterbury Guildhall is now unknown but it was just before Christmas. The importance attached to the trial may be gauged from the fact that the prosecution was in the hands of Sir Christopher Hales, former Attorney-General and currently Master of the Rolls, who also prosecuted at the trials of John Fisher, Thomas More and Anne Boleyn. No doubt the whole affair was a formality and John was convicted of treason. He was removed to Westgate Tower in readiness for his execution, which was to be very public as a warning to others. He was hanged, drawn and quartered on a hill by the city walls known as Dane John, from where he would have been able to see his old, now empty, friary: the date was most probably 27 December 1539. Early authorities claim that on the scaffold John declared, 'I close my apostolate in my blood. In my death I shall find life, for I die for a holy cause, the defence of the Church of God'.

His head and quarters were displayed at the gates of the city. The bill for his execution has survived in the account books of the City of Canterbury, which lists wood for the scaffold and other items purchased for the purpose. The total cost came to sixteen shillings and one penny, including 3s 8d to the executioner, 1s to the two men who parboiled John's quarters and 1s to the two men who carried his quarters and set them up on the gates.

Despite his relative obscurity, John's martyrdom must have been well known to his contemporaries, and his memory was revered. When Pope Gregory XIII, a great patron of the new English College at Rome, authorised the wall paintings of sixty-three English martyrs at the college in 1583, he thereby also recognised and sanctioned veneration of them. Forty-four years after his death John Stone was among those depicted in the frescoes. It was John's name that headed the list of English martyrs first submitted to Rome for beatification.

The Aftermath

Time unveils all truth.

> S.Hubert Burke, *Historical Portraits of the Tudor Dynasty and the Reformation Period,* 1880

Henry VIII's lust and paranoia, leading to the schism from Rome, was the direct precursor of what is now called the English Protestant Reformation; a process that took a minority many decades to accomplish. The hypothesis on which writers like A G Dickens based his influential *The English Reformation* (i.e. that the state of the Church was so defective that the people were alienated and ripe for Protestantism) has now been largely discredited by more modern historical scholarship. Certainly everything in the pre-Reformation garden was not rosy, not least the state of the papacy, which had fallen to a number of worldly, weak and utterly unworthy men such as Sixtus IV della Rovere (1471-84) who, by promoting relatives and evil-living men to high office, sowed the seeds of the scandals that were to engulf Rome for the next seventy years. The wicked, licentious Alexander VI Borgia (1492-1503) has become a byword for ignominy; while his successor Julius II della Rovere (1503-1513), was almost his equal for corruption and nepotism as well as being a warmonger, more concerned with temporal power than the spiritual welfare of the Church. Loyalty to Rome must have been severely stretched in these years for those who found it difficult to distinguish between the office and the holder.

The selling of indulgences was a sacrilegious outrage. Indeed, the whole issue of indulgences was fraught with asinine superstition. For the repetitious performance of certain prescribed rituals and prayers, like some Eastern mystic mantra, the participant expected to receive spiritual benefits. One such exercise stipulated that it could obtain precisely 52,712 years off time spent in Purgatory! No wonder the reformers derided such arrant nonsense. Too many cases of simony and nepotism existed; pluralism of benefices, which often meant absenteeism by the priest from a parish, was a cause for concern, although in England not universally detrimental because many of the curates were excellent and diligent. By no means was all pluralism motivated by avarice. It has to be borne in mind that many priests were so poverty-stricken that they became pluralists out of necessity to make ends meet, so as to enable them to carry out their responsibilities. The suppression of the religious houses only added to their problem. Abbots and priors had been able to augment clergy incomes with stipends and help in kind, such as providing meals or fuel. Local clergy suddenly found that the laymen who got their hands on Church livings wanted some profit from them, not subsidising impoverished incumbents.

The nature of men and women being what it is, laxity and complacency had crept into some monastic institutions, which included members who certainly fell short of the high ideals they should have professed. This stricture also applied to the secular clergy and there was much that needed to be reformed and renewed. This was a message reiterated by Dr John Colet, the learned Dean of St Paul's, who maintained a lodging at Sheen Charterhouse where he died in 1519, and men such as Sir Thomas More or the scholar and physician - and late in life priest - Thomas Linacre and his pupil, Desiderius Erasmus. In addition to magnificent prelates like Cardinal Wolsey, unfortunately it was not difficult to find examples of similarly unworthy churchmen, more noted for their pride and worldliness than for their spirituality. There were complacent, high-ranking clergy who, wrapped up in enjoying the perquisites of their office, were blind to the imminent danger that threatened. These were not the men to take the action required. In this context Christ's parable in Matthew's Gospel comes to mind. 'A man sowed good seed in his field. One night, when everyone was asleep an enemy came and sowed weeds among the wheat.'

To give credit where it is due, as well as seeking to control every aspect of the Church, Wolsey did try and defend the Church. Half-hearted attempts at reform had been tried by Wolsey under the authority of Pope Leo X, but how could such a degenerate churchman be taken seriously as a reformer when he condemned others for indulging in the same corrupt practices? With the Church under threat from Lutheran ideas, Wolsey, too occupied with matters of state during the fourteen years he held power, failed to take the necessary steps for counteracting Protestant heresy. Thomas More severely criticised Wolsey for his lack of resistance and wholly inadequate response to the danger.

While it is true that some Church leaders behaved more like careerist bureaucrats, among the bishops were good men who demonstrated genuine concern for their clergy and the pastoral welfare of their parishioners. The late-medieval Church, contrary to what has often been portrayed, was not a universally corrupt organisation. Generations of schoolchildren have been fed with biased information

The Henrician Martyrs

masquerading as history, produced by those who, more eager to spread Protestant propaganda rather than the facts, succumbed to exaggerating negligence or immorality amongst the clergy, suggesting it pointed to a Church in decline. That such cases existed certainly cannot be denied - they always have and always will! - but they were relatively rare. In spite of cases of anticlericalism, the weight of evidence points to the respect in which the parishioners generally held their priests and curates and there was no shortage of vocations. The Church over which Henry VIII sought complete domination, far from being a decaying institution, was very much alive and robust. Professor J J Scarisbrick in his *The Reformation and the English People* (1984) stresses the vitality and popularity of religious guilds and confraternities for lay people into the late 1540's. As Professor Christopher Haigh wrote in *The English Reformation Revised* (1987) 'The fact that there *was* a Reformation does not mean that it was wanted: it does not imply that there was a deep-seated popular demand for religious change.' And he comments, vis-à-vis the 'received' version of events, 'The long-term causes of the Reformation - the corruption of the Church and the hostility of the laity - appear to have been historical illusions.' The level of opposition to Henry's take-over of the Church was far more widespread than was once commonly acknowledged. The denial of papal primacy of itself did not precipitate significant open dissent, but anger was expressed in varied ways. Those who were prepared to resist to the death were a small band. Yet modern historians, such as Geoffrey R Elton, have amassed evidence from across the country that there were many arguing privately about the papacy and other religious issues. As this evidence comes from sources that betrayed confidential conversations, one may assume that the level of discontent expressed was even more extensive. The contemporary commentators from Queen Mary's reign may be nearer the mark when they claimed that most had acquiesced to her father's religious changes out of fear. But not all the parish clergy were cowed into submission. At least three priests, John Allen, John Collins and George Croft, and a layman, Hugh Holland, were executed in 1538 for 'adhering to the Pope' and refusing to accept the royal supremacy. It was the wholesale attack on the religious houses that touched a raw nerve among the people. It was one thing to deny the authority of a remote figure in Rome, but quite a different matter to rip the heart out of a local community, many of whom depended upon a monastery for their livelihood or welfare. Even at that stage many people may have acquiesced in the expectation that the confiscated wealth of the monasteries would be used for beneficial charitable purposes, such as schools and hospitals. As will be shown, sadly, none

The Henrician Martyrs

of it was.

The dissolution of religious houses was no new phenomenon. With permission from Pope Clement VII, Wolsey had at least thirty religious houses dissolved, including St Frideswide's Priory, Oxford, for being either too small or allegedly because the religious fell short of their vocations. He used the proceeds to found educational establishments, mostly notably the Oxford college now known as Christ Church. In this he was not alone: other bishops acted in a similar manner, including John Fisher, who dissolved nunneries in order to maintain St John's College, Cambridge. But the depredations under Thomas Cromwell were of a totally different order to previous closures. This onslaught was aimed at nothing less than the wholesale, root and branch destruction of religious life, engendering wanton iconoclasm and gratuitous vandalism on an unprecedented scale.

In 1535 Cromwell designated lay commissioners to make a systematic visitation of the religious houses, to report on their spiritual and moral condition and, most importantly, to assess their monetary worth. The value of the church plate and vestments, the goods and chattels of the community and even the amount of lead on the roof and its meltdown value were all calculated for their likely worth to the King.

The whole process was a pretext to give some semblance of justice for what was planned because, as is clear from contemporary documentation, the closures had all been pre-determined by Cromwell. Regardless of the content of the commissioners' reports, the monasteries were doomed. Take the case of the Cluniac priory at Lenton, Nottinghamshire. Cromwell had written in a memorandum to himself, 'The suppression of Lenton and the execution of the prior', months before any action was taken. Prior Nicholas Heath was arrested in February 1538 with William Gylham and seven other monks and four of their labourers. They were indicted for treason at Nottingham and sentenced to be hanged, drawn and quartered. The remaining monks were expelled without any pensions, together with the five poor men whom they charitably maintained. The revenues of the house and the sale of the monastic goods passed to the King.

Visitations of religious houses, usually by the diocesan bishop, had been taking place for centuries and the records show that admonitions, corrections and, where warranted, punishments were imposed on offending individuals for their misdemeanours. However, such fault-finding was of a completely different order from the commissioner's chief role, which was essentially to denigrate the reputations of the monks and nuns. It is significant that the stories of corruption their reports contain are virtually the only source for such information at this period. If the moral state of some religious houses was as alleged by the commissioners, why is there no other reliable contemporary evidence to corroborate their claims? An immense number of letters from the bishops have survived as well as government correspondence. There is nothing to be found that may be construed as deploring the moral lives of the religious. All the contemporary chroniclers of the period are equally silent on the subject: hardly likely if the moral turpitude of the monasteries was supposedly so notorious. Charles Wriothesley, Windsor Herald of Arms, was a supporter of the 'reformers' and closely connected with Chancellor Thomas Audley. In his *Chronicle* he not only makes no mention of the alleged widespread wrongdoing but writes of the monasteries, 'It was pity the great lamentation that the poor people made for them, for there was a great hospitality kept amongst them, and, as it was reported, ten thousand persons had lost their living by the putting down of them, which was a great pity.' Archbishop Cranmer himself admitted that he could find nothing against the moral character of the monks of Christ Church, Canterbury. Even Bishop Hugh Latimer, in the early stages, was in favour of preserving a few of the monasteries. Richard Ingworth, suffragan Bishop of Dover, who was engaged in the suppressions, especially of the mendicant friars, made no accusations of immorality against them. In his initial report to Cromwell he stated that 'in every place there is much poverty' among them. Ingworth wrote to Cromwell, 'I beg your lordship, to be a good lord to the poor friars.' Cromwell was not happy and chided Ingworth, the former Dominican Prior Provincial, with still having a 'friar's heart'. The thought that he had upset Cromwell clearly worried Ingworth and he wrote an anxious letter back saying that he quaked for fear of offending and to please Cromwell he would make some charges against the friar's houses he had visited.

Thus the truthfulness of the commissioners' reports rests entirely upon the credibility and trustworthiness or otherwise of the commissioners. Chief of these were the equally detested Dr Richard Layton and Dr Thomas Legh, Dr John London, and John ap Rice. Layton came from humble origins in Cumberland but, thanks to the patronage of Cromwell, obtained many ecclesiastical preferments, including the rectorships of Stepney and Harrow-on-the-Hill, and rose to be Dean of York. Judging from his reports to Cromwell he seems to have had a most unhealthily salacious appetite. The zealous Dr London, a former Warden of New College, Oxford had no scruples whatsoever and perpetrated monstrous acts of vandalism and desecration against many of the friaries. At Aylesbury, Bedford, Stamford, Coventry and

Warwick he boasted about smashing all the stained glass windows and defacing the churches so that 'they could not be used again.' At Reading he destroyed everything in the church, which he had converted into a new town hall. The charges against the monasteries largely depend upon the reports of men like him, yet no inquiry was ever undertaken to ascertain the truth of their claims, often based upon the malicious second-hand gossip of ill-disposed malcontents. As sycophantic minions of Cromwell, their veracity is, at least, open to doubt. Layton became the subservient tool of Cromwell and the King and was prepared to say anything required of him. On a 1535 visitation to Glastonbury Abbey Layton praised the great religious house. This brought the wrath of Cromwell down on his head. Cromwell told him that he had not been sent there for the purpose of expressing his approval. Layton sent a grovelling apology 'most humbly beseeching' his master's pardon and promised not to make the same mistake again. To quote John Henry Blunt again in his *The Reformation of the Church of England,* writing about these men, 'It is not impossible that even such bad men *may* have told the truth in this matter: but the character of witnesses must always form an important element in estimating the value of their testimony, and the character of such obscene, profligate and perjured witnesses as Layton and London could not well be worse. These men were not just Lots vexed with the filthy conversation of the wicked, but filthy dreamers who defiled the flesh, despised ecclesiastical dominion, and spake evil of dignities in the very spirit of the evil one.' To quote James Gairdner again, 'We have no reason, indeed, to think highly of Cromwell's visitors', yet it is upon the testimony of these vile myrmidons of Cromwell, totally unsupported by independent evidence, that the monks were condemned.

    To back up the work of the commissioners, preachers were sent out to stir up public opinion against the monks accusing them, among other things, of sorcery and idleness. Cromwell of course painted the blackest picture possible and was carefully selective in highlighting only those aspects of his agents' reports that recounted the immorality and misdeeds of some monks and nuns. Where such lapses were found they were few and far between, usually involving one or two individuals who were failing to live up to their monastic calling. A case in point is that of the sub-prior of Holy Trinity Augustinian Priory, Repton, Derbyshire who, with three of the brothers, was identified as indulging in homosexual practices. Naturally such cases were blown-up out of all proportion in an attempt to destroy the reputation of the whole community by implication. Such independent contemporary evidence as exists paints a rather different picture than the repetitive recital of faults recorded by the commissioners. It gives an impression of vigour in many religious communities who were able to attract new recruits; an unlikely occurrence if the houses were in the dire straits the commissioners would have us believe. Setting aside the obvious fabrications, even if much in the commissioners reports are held to be accurate, the offences catalogued still represent only a tiny percentage of the number of religious. The most that could be alleged against one Lancashire monastery was that the monks were well-supplied with mattresses, pillows and blankets; that they had 'a desk to write on' and glazed windows. In spite of these 'luxuries' the spiritual condition of the house was said to be in good order and it could not be charged with any scandal. In 1539 the only criticism to be made of the monks of Durham was that they had tablecloths and individual drinking bowls and ate lots of eggs each week. Now all this 'luxury' may not have been entirely in keeping with a spirit of unrelieved austerity, but it hardly constituted a monstrous crime, just an all-too-human desire for a bit of comfort.

The greatest modern specialist on the subject, Dom David Knowles, (*The Religious Orders in England,* 1959) is in no doubt that the aim of the commission was to dig out as much dirt as possible and extract 'damaging confessions' to serve as propaganda for suppressions. The fact that the commissioners took advantage and personally profited by acquiring land and property from the monasteries hardly betokens unbiased impartiality on their part. As Edmund Burke wrote in his *Reflections on the French Revolution,* 1790, 'It is not with much credulity that I listen to any when they speak ill of those they are going to plunder. I rather suspect that vices are feigned or exaggerated when profit is looked for in punishment. An enemy is a bad witness - a robber is a worse.' Suspicion is increased when reading the instructions given to the commissioners charged with the suppressions: they were required to ensure that the monks did not cheat the King of any of his potential wealth from the suppressed houses. The real motive for the suppressions - financial gain - is reinforced by the offers made by the commissioners to some houses to keep them open in exchange for a substantial cash payment. There were abbots and priors who tried to buy the survival of their communities by raising loans or by selling property or their livestock. It availed them nothing, but it does reveal that Cromwell's contention that the monasteries had to go because they were too corrupt and irreligious to be allowed to continue, was a sham. Cases of drunkenness, sexual impropriety and financial misdemeanours, sadly, undoubtedly existed, but the stories of widespread dissipation, concupiscence and corruption being rife in

The Henrician Martyrs

religious communities - in short that they were dens of iniquity - were largely false. Most monastic houses were simply busy getting on with the daily routine of prayer, education, employment and charitable work. As James Edwin Thorold Rogers (1823-90), former Anglican cleric turned Liberal MP and historian wrote, 'The monks were the men of letters ... the historians, the jurists, the philosophers, the physicians, the students of nature, the founders of schools, authors of chronicles, teachers of agriculture, indulgent landlords, and advocates of genuine dealing towards the peasantry.'

When the first measure for suppressing the religious houses, the Act for the Dissolution of the Lesser Monasteries, came before Parliament it appears that none of the 'evidence' gathered by Cromwell was presented. In the preamble to the first Act the compliant members of Parliament hedged their bets by stating that they accepted as true the accusations against the smaller monasteries purely because the King had declared them to be true. Yet in the same preamble it reads that those religious displaced from 'the little and small abbeys' should be re-housed 'in the great and honourable monasteries of the realm' where religion was well observed and God well served: perhaps a truer reflection of their real opinions.

Following the passing of the Act in 1536 commissioners were again sent out. As the closure of the religious houses to be visited had already been decided, the purpose of the new visitation was to produce inventories and carefully calculate the value of the properties and their possessions. Judging by their extant reports the new commissioners selected for the task were clearly a more honest - and braver - bunch than their predecessors. There is a striking difference in their reports from those of self-aggrandising Layton and Legh and their cronies. Out of eighty houses visited across eleven counties only four attracted severe criticism. For the rest the commissioners had mostly only commendations: a few random examples will suffice.

Although it was never a wealthy house, nonetheless the Cistercians of Netley Abbey, near Southampton, Hampshire were praised for their hospitality to strangers and travellers. Across the water, at 12th century Quarr Abbey on the Isle of Wight, the Cistercian monks were said to offer 'great refuge and comfort to all the inhabitants of the island and to strangers travelling the seas.' (The godmother of Henry VIII, Princess Cecily of York, daughter of Edward IV, was buried at Quarr.) At Ulverscroft, in Charnwood Forest, Leicestershire the Augustinian Priory, founded 1130, contained 'good virtuous religious, of good qualities as writers, embroiderers and painters and living'. The Prior was described as 'a wise and discreet man'. The Cistercian Priory at

The Henrician Martyrs

Catesby, Northamptonshire had existed since 1175. When the local commissioners visited Catesby in May 1536 they were struck with the admirable condition of the house, which was found to be 'in perfect order, the prioress a wise, discreet and very religious woman with nine nuns ... as religious and devout and with as good obedience as we have in time past seen or belike shall see.' They pleaded for 'the King's Highness to have remorse' and out of charity spare the Priory. The pleas fell on deaf royal ears. When Henry read the report his comment was that the commissioners must have been bribed! For Polesworth Abbey, founded by King Egbert and his daughter, St Edith, in 827 on the Warwickshire/Staffordshire border, the commissioners begged for a stay of execution on the house 'for, as we think, you shall not speak in the preferment of a better nunnery nor of better women.' The monks of the Charterhouse at Hull 'were well-favoured and commended by the honest men of Hull for their good living and great hospitality.' But despite Cromwell's pressure for haste in closing down the houses many earned a temporary reprieve for a simple, practical reason that he had perhaps not foreseen. The displaced religious were given the options of finding places in 'the great and honourable monasteries of the realm' or returning to lay status. The overwhelming majority chose to continue their vocations which meant that it was impossible to find accommodation in the larger houses for so many religious, hence they had to be left where they were for the time being. Those who did find places in larger houses, sometimes at great distances, among strangers, must have found the experience traumatic, being uprooted from communities that had been their homes for most of their lives. Other houses, despite their poverty, managed to raise enough money to bribe Cromwell and his minions, thereby purchasing a temporary stay of execution. Nonetheless, by the end of 1536, 244 religious houses, whose notional annual revenue amounted to less than £200, had been closed, their possessions confiscated, their lands seized and their lay employees and dependants thrown out of work. In Wales, the Augustinian priory at Carmarthen managed to survive until 17 February 1537. The commissioners reported that its yearly value was under £200. The house of twelve canons 'was well built and in a good state of repair.' The priory, they said, 'is an open lodging for all. Hospitality is daily kept for rich and poor, which is a great relief to the country, being poor and bare. Weekly alms are given to eighty poor people, which, if the house were suppressed, they would be in want. These charges are met by good husbandry.' Clearly neither Cromwell nor the King cared a fig about the fate of either the canons or the poor who depended upon them.

The Henrician Martyrs

The plain fact is that the prime motivation for the religious changes from the King and those in power was avarice and venality. It was not only to crush a major source of opposition to his royal supremacy that the King sought to abolish the religious houses, but principally to swell his coffers. Thus the English Reformation was built upon wholesale sacrilege, pillage and greed. In 1536 there were over 800 religious houses containing about 8,000 monks and nuns of various orders; by 1540 there were none. The lot of the expelled nuns must have been particularly hard to bear, compelled to exchange a life of seclusion for an uncertain future providing for themselves in the world. The last of the houses to go was the Augustinian Abbey of the Holy Cross at Waltham, near London, founded in 1060 by Harold II, the last Saxon king of England. The organist at Waltham Abbey at the time of the suppression was the great composer Thomas Tallis.

At this distance in time it is difficult to appreciate the deeply personal element consequent upon all this upheaval and destruction, but perhaps one small example will help put a human face on what it involved. Waverley Abbey, near Farnham, Surrey, was the first Cistercian abbey in England, founded in 1128. In 1536 it housed an abbot and thirteen monks and its annual income was £174. Eric Parker in his 1935 book, *Highways and Byways in Surrey*, writing of Waverley, says, 'Its brethren were simple, kindly men with few wants and little money, who yet were generous hosts and the most skilled farmers of their day'. The last abbot, William Ayling, desperately tried to stave off Waverley's suppression. On 9 June 1536 he wrote a touchingly pathetic letter to Thomas Cromwell:

Pleaseth your mastership, I received your letters of the 17th day of the present month and have endeavoured myself to accomplish the contents of them, and have sent your mastership the true extent, value and account of our said monastery. Beseeching your good mastership, for the love of Christ's passion, to help me in the preservation of this poor monastery, that we your beadsmen may remain in the service of God with the meanest living that any poor man may live with in this world. So to continue in the service of Almighty Jesus, and to pray for the estate of our prince and your mastership. In no vain hope I write this to your mastership, forasmuch you put me in such boldness full gently, when I was in suit to you last year at Winchester, saying, 'Repair to me for such business as you shall have from time to time'. Therefore, instantly praying you, and more poor brethren with weeping. Yes! - desire you to help them; in this world no creatures in more trouble, and so we remain dependent upon the comfort that shall come to us from you - serving God daily at Waverley.

The Abbot's pleading was, of course, in vain. Cromwell's response

The Henrician Martyrs

was that they had to immediately leave their monastery. We do not know what happened to the poor who were sheltering in the guesthouse or to the sick and dying in the monks' care. However, we do know what happened to the monastic buildings: they were largely dismantled and the stone used to build nearby Loseley Hall.

Queen Catherine died at Kimbolton Castle in January 1536. Henry and Queen Anne could hardly contain themselves for delight when the news reached them. But by then Henry had grown tired of Anne and her intractable ways and was casting his lustful eyes elsewhere. Anne's fate was finally sealed when she suffered the miscarriage of a son on the last day of January. Henry decided that God had shown his displeasure at his second marriage by denying him a male heir and he was now considering taking a third wife. Thomas Cromwell engineered the means of getting rid of Anne by providing the King with trumped-up charges against her of adultery with five gentlemen of the Court, as well as incest with her own brother, Viscount Rochford. The courtiers and Rochford were speedily executed. Having heard Anne's confession in the Tower on 16 May the next day Archbishop Cranmer obligingly declared her marriage to the King null and void, just as he had done in the case of Queen Catherine. He then pronounced that the Princess Elizabeth was a bastard. Anne was beheaded in the Tower on 19 May 1536 and buried there in an unmarked grave. So Henry, seemingly without a flicker of remorse, quickly disposed of the woman for whom he had been prepared to take his kingdom into schism. Just eleven days later he was already celebrating his marriage to Jane Seymour.

The religious innovations were not without a great deal of opposition, and soon there took place what was the largest civil rebellion in English history, known as the 'Pilgrimage of Grace'.

In Lincolnshire, the Midlands, Yorkshire, Lancashire, Durham, Cumberland, and Westmorland unrest was fomenting. The first rebellion began at, Louth, Lincolnshire, on 1 October 1536. The locals were angry at the closure of Louth Park Abbey and the actions of the royal commissioners in selling off the abbey church ornaments and vestments. The unrest quickly spread to nearby towns. Supported by the local gentry, up to 40,000 people occupied Lincoln and took over the cathedral, demanding that the religious changes should be halted. The protest was short-lived. When threatened with military action from the forces of Henry's brother-in-law, Charles Brandon, Duke of Suffolk, most of the people dispersed. However, within days Henry had to contend with a far more serious insurrection. Nominally led by Robert Aske, thousands occupied York and the expelled monks and nuns were invited to return to their houses. In the territory held by the rebels,

The Henrician Martyrs

sixteen of the fifty-five suppressed northern religious houses were restored. The 'Pilgrims' manifesto declared that the faith was 'abominably confounded' by 'certain heretics in our time' who 'blaspheme the honour of our Lord God, working most cruelly by spoiling and suppression of holy places, as abbeys, churches, and minsters of the same.' The rebel clergy who met at Pontefract Priory during the rising affirmed that the Pope was head of the Church. The rebels ordered that all men over sixteen should be ready 'to aid us in maintaining of the said faith of Christ and his Church ... for the love you bear to God, his faith, and Church militant.'

Aske, the son of Sir Robert Aske of Aughton, near Selby, was a devout and charismatic figure, a well-connected Yorkshire gentleman and a barrister of Gray's Inn. His mother was a daughter of John, Lord Clifford. By the end of October the 'Pilgrimage of Grace', supported by the local nobility and clergy and with perhaps as many as 40,000 adherents on the march southwards, had grown into a full-scale revolt and posed a real threat to Henry. Aske forbade any use of force, so while maintaining their loyalty to the King the 'pilgrims' drew up a set of demands. These included halting any further religious changes, stopping the suppression of the monasteries and healing the breach with Rome, dismissing the King's heretical counsellors and holding a parliament in the north to address their religious and economic grievances. A report from one of Cromwell's agents in Yorkshire stated that 'The greater part of Yorkshire is up ... and the whole country favours their opinions.' Only Scarborough and Skipton castles held out for the King.

When Thomas Howard, Duke of Norfolk, met the 'pilgrims' at Doncaster he admitted that he could not be entirely sure of the loyalty of his own troops who, he declared, thought the 'pilgrims' had a 'good and godly' cause. Outnumbered three to one, Norfolk sent desperate letters to Henry who, thoroughly alarmed, authorised the Duke to offer a free general pardon and assurances that a parliament would be held at York. Trusting implicitly in Henry's promises, Aske persuaded the insurgent leaders and their followers to disperse. In spite of Norfolk's assurances to the 'pilgrims' that the reinstated religious could remain in their houses - a promise he declared to the King he did not feel honour bound to fulfil - Henry sent instructions to the Earl of Derby to arrest the reinstated abbot and twenty-one monks of Sawley Abbey, who were living off the charity of their supporters, 'and without any manner of delay, in their monks apparel, cause them to be hanged up as most errant traitors and movers of insurrection.' When Henry learned that Derby had still not carried out his orders he wrote again, angrily

The Henrician Martyrs

commanding him to proceed immediately to Sawley to hang the monks.

Needless to say Henry had no intention of seriously negotiating with the rebels and none of his promises were kept. In January 1537 a new rebellion began although Aske did all he could to prevent it. Martial law was proclaimed with legal trials being suspended. The rebellion was finally crushed with incredible savagery. Henry wrote to the Duke of Norfolk ordering 'such dreadful executions to be done upon a good number of the inhabitants of every town, village and hamlet, that have offended in this rebellion, as well by the hanging of them up in trees, as by the quartering of them and the setting of their heads and quarters in every town, great and small and such other places as they may be fearful spectacle to all others hereafter that would practice any like matter: which we require you to do without pity or respect ... that these traitors should perish in their wilful, traitorous follies ... as the dread thereof should be a warning to others'. In many places priests were forbidden to give Christian burial to those executed and their families had to resort to burying them secretly in ditches or fields.

Along with the Cistercians of Whalley Abbey, the Augustinian canons of Cartmel Priory, together with sixteen of their husbandmen employees, were tried for treason at Lancaster. Most of them were executed. Norfolk proceeded to Carlisle from where he complained that he had so many prisoners he had nowhere to keep them. He carried out savage executions hanging seventy-four of the insurgents from the city walls where they remained until they rotted. Some of their wives and mothers had cut down the bodies to bury them. When Henry was told he demanded that the women be punished. Henry's anger was now so great that he wanted 'retribution against the monasteries that went far beyond the destruction of their property and the acquisition of their wealth'. (Geoffrey Moorhouse, *The Pilgrimage of Grace*, 2002.) He urged Norfolk to proceed to a whole list of religious houses in Yorkshire and Northumberland, some of whom had no direct involvement whatever with the uprising. All were suppressed for the benefit of the royal purse and the inhabitants expelled. They included Augustinian Hexham and Lanercost, Cistercian Newminster and Premonstratensian St Agatha's at Easby, Richmond. Henry's instructions were that 'without pity or circumstance' the monks should be hanged 'without further delay or ceremony'. Norfolk personally supervised the suppression of Bridlington Priory and Jervaulx Abbey. He declared his presence to be necessary because the houses were 'greatly beloved by the people' whom he presumably thought might try and prevent their destruction. The people of Bridlington begged - to no avail - that the priory church, and especially the shrine of St John,

The Henrician Martyrs

which stood behind the magnificent high altar reredos, should not be defaced. According to Sir Arthur Darcy, who was present, the church at Jervaulx was 'one of the fairest I have ever seen'. Notwithstanding, it was soon desecrated and demolished and the monks expelled. The Duke took his pick of some of the choicest items of monastic property, plate, vestments and cattle, before transporting what remained to London for the King. After his orgy of slaughter the self-satisfied Duke commented that 'though the number be nothing as great as their deserts did require to have suffered, yet I think the like number has not been heard of put to execution at one time.' He reported to his master, 'I see nothing here but fear.' He persistently petitioned the King and Cromwell for more monastic properties. He wanted Lewes priory but Cromwell had reserved that for himself. As a consolation prize the Duke was given the priory's valuable possessions in Norfolk at Castle Rising and Castleacre, plus over 120 manors in the county.

At the King's request Robert Aske journeyed south to meet him and while there wrote a detailed account for Henry of the 'Pilgrimage'. 'In all parts of the realm,' he insisted, 'men's hearts much grudged with the suppression of the abbeys, and the first-fruits, by reason the same would be the destruction of the whole religion in England. And their especial great grudge is against the lord Cromwell, being the destroyer of the commonwealth ... for there is no earthly man so evil believed as the said lord Cromwell is with the commoners.' Aske went on to enumerate all the good works done by the religious houses for the benefit of the people, for example, that they maintained sea walls and dykes and built bridges and highways. In spite of a pardon promised to him personally by the King, in July 1537 Aske was sent back to York and hung in chains for high treason. His case is not comparable to the deaths of Thomas More, John Fisher and the Carthusians. Yet we may surely hold in honour his memory and that of the men of the North 'Who rose in dark and evil days to right their native land' (*The Memory of the Dead*, John Ingram Kells, 1843) because, like the Biblical Maccabees, they felt that it was better to die than to live to see the desolation and desecration of all they held most sacred. Along with Aske died all the other pilgrimage leaders, including Lord Thomas Darcy of Templehurst, Lord John Hussey, Sir Stephen Bigod, Sir Thomas Percy, Sir Stephen Hammerton, Robert Constable and Sir John Bulmer, whose common-law wife Margaret was sent to Smithfield and burnt at the stake. But vengeance was also visited upon hundreds of ordinary folk, including women and children. Among the religious victims were Bishop Matthew Mackerell, a suffragan to the bishop of Lincoln and Abbot of Premonstratensian Barlings, near Lincoln.

The Henrician Martyrs

Mackerell was a high-profile prelate: he had preached at the spectacular funeral of the 2nd Duke of Norfolk in 1524. The church at Barlings, which was 300 feet in length, was desecrated, the lead from its roof being melted down. Others who suffered were William Wood, Prior of Bridlington; William Thirsk OCist., dispossessed Prior of Fountains Abbey; Adam Sedbar OCist., Abbot of Jervaulx and monk George Asleby; John Paslew OCist., Abbot of Whalley, Lancashire, and monks William Haydock and John Eastgate; John Pickering OSB, Prior of York; James Cockerel, Prior of Guisborough; Richard Harrison OCist., Abbot of Kirkstead, Lincolnshire, with three of his monks: Richard Wade, William Swale and Henry Jenkinson; six monks of Bardney Abbey, John Tenant, William Cole, John Francis, William Cowper, Richard Layton and Hugh Londale; William Trafford OCist., Abbot of Sawley and monk Richard Eastgate. Other priests and monks executed in 1537 included William Burraby, Thomas Redforth, William Coe, Robert Leach and Richard Masters.

Influenced, no doubt, by the happenings in the North in April 1537 serious discontent broke out in Cheshire which was swiftly put down. In Norfolk meetings were held at Walsingham to protest at the suppression of the religious houses. Henry ordered immediate action and thirty or forty men were arrested and put on trial at Norwich in May and condemned to death. Among them were John Grigby, rector of Langham; Nicholas Mileham and Richard Vowell, Augustinian canons of Walsingham; two Carmelite friars from Burnham Norton, William Gibson and John Peacock, and John Punte, rector of Waterlow. Mileham was executed at Walsingham on 30 May and Peacock at Lynn on 1 June. Of the remainder two were pardoned and the laymen were executed at various locations in Norfolk.

Although not directly implicated in the 'Pilgrimage' the opportunity was seized to suppress Woburn Abbey, Bedfordshire. Robert Hobbes OCist., who had been abbot for many years, comes across as a most attractive character. His anguish of conscience, evident in his responses to Cromwell, resonates across the centuries. Hobbes and many of his monks had taken the Oath of Supremacy but, deeply troubled in conscience they soon bitterly regretted doing so. Imprisoned in the Tower in May 1538, Hobbes and some of his monks confessed that they had spoken against the royal supremacy. Hobbes had openly criticised the closure of religious houses, comparing the King to Nebuchadnezzar. Hobbes's plea for mercy for his house fell on deaf ears. He was hanged, drawn and quartered outside the gates of his abbey with two of his monks, Ralph Barnes, the sub prior and Laurence Blonham, both of whom maintained the papal primacy, and John

The Henrician Martyrs

Henmarsh, vicar of Puddington. By attainder the abbey and its lands passed into the possession of the King. Henry made it abundantly clear that he would brook no opposition, and woe betide anyone who attempted it. The fate of those who had opposed Henry's religious changes and tried to save the monasteries had its desired effect in striking terror into the hearts of any others who might contemplate similar resistance.

The Observant Franciscan Friary, adjoining the royal palace at Greenwich, was a religious house of renown. Henry VIII, who was born at Greenwich, was baptised in the friary church and he and Catherine of Aragon had been married there in 1509. Henry's two daughters, Mary and Elizabeth, were also baptised at the friary. In 1513 Henry had written from Greenwich to Pope Leo X that he 'could not sufficiently commend' the Observant Friars 'strict adherence to poverty, their sincerity, charity and devotion.' No Order, he said, was more assiduous or active in 'keeping Christ's fold.' The ascetic friars, among whose number were several brilliant scholars, remained stalwart in their support for Queen Catherine who had always been their friend and admirer. The Franciscan Provincial was William Peto, a friar known for his holiness and learning. He was appointed confessor to Princess Mary. The friars came into direct conflict with Henry over the question of his divorce from Catherine. On Easter Sunday 1534, preaching before the King, Peto bravely denounced the divorce and was subsequently arrested and imprisoned until the end of the year when he went into exile at Antwerp. Other friars were caught preaching against the divorce, and in 1533 secret correspondence between them and Queen Catherine - now styled Princess Dowager - was intercepted by Cromwell.

Because of the friary's close connection with the royal family it must have been particularly galling to the King that the friars opposed him. Hoping to bend them to his will, on 15 June 1534 Henry sent the royal commissioners, Rowland Lee and Thomas Bedyll, to visit the friary to induce its inhabitants to acknowledge the royal supremacy. They interviewed each friar separately and to a man they refused. In his rage Henry ordered the closure of Observant houses in England and the friars were expelled. On 17 June two cartloads of friars were driven through London to the Tower. In all, two hundred friars were thrown into prison. From the severity of their treatment at least fifty Observant friars died in prison. Thirty-two of them, chained together two-by-two, are known to have died very quickly in various prisons as a result of want and sickness in the inhuman conditions. Many of the remainder died in the summer of 1537, at the same time as the Carthusians were

The Henrician Martyrs

being starved to death, and it may well be the case that similar treatment was meted out to the Franciscans. Charles Wriothesley, who wrote the famous *Chronicle* of the Tudor sovereigns, was an admirer of the Observants and he used his influence with Cromwell to enable those who survived to leave for Scotland, Ireland or the Continent. (Not that they would have been very safe in Ireland. On 30 July 1537 Venerable John Travers, Chancellor of St Patrick's Cathedral, Dublin, had been executed. As special punishment for writing against the royal supremacy his hand was first symbolically cut off and burned.) Other friars who had made their submission to secure their freedom, nonetheless continued to uphold and preach the papacy. Henry used the 'Pilgrimage of Grace' as an excuse to renew his attack on them. He declared that the Observant Friars were 'disciples of the bishop of Rome and sowers of sedition.' He ordered that they should be arrested and committed as prisoners to other Conventual houses of friars, 'without liberty to speak to any man till we decide our pleasure concerning them.' Father Thomas Bourchier, himself a Franciscan, wrote a Latin account of the suffering of his brethren: *History of the Martyrs of the Friars Minor of the Observance,* 1583. Three of the friars [17] whose names are known died in Newgate in 1537. In May 1538 the Observant Franciscan priest of Greenwich, John Forest, [18] was executed at Smithfield. The most famous victim of the renewed persecution, he was hung by the armpits from a chain over a fire and literally roasted to death; an ordeal that lasted two hours. And while all this was taking place schismatic Bishop Hugh Latimer of Worcester presided and preached - at great length! John Stow (1525-1605) records in his *Annales* that when Latimer, denouncing the papacy, asked the friar in what state he would die Forest, 'with a loud voice answered and said that if an angel should come down from Heaven and teach him any other doctrine than he had received and believed from his youth he would not now believe him.' When Forest was dead his body, together with the gibbet from which he was hung, was thrown into the fire.

In July 1538, Anthony Browne, another of the Greenwich friars who, on being expelled, had become a hermit in Norfolk, was brought before the justices at Norwich at the instigation of the Duke of Norfolk. Browne denied Henry's supremacy declaring that no temporal prince could occupy that role. He pleaded guilty and was condemned to death, but his execution was delayed for ten days in the hope of persuading him to recant. When he remained steadfast Norfolk proposed sending him to be tortured in the Tower. The judges also suggested that the Bishop of Norwich should be present at his execution to preach a sermon for the occasion, on similar lines to Bishop Latimer's. Norfolk

The Henrician Martyrs

had coveted the Franciscan friary at Norwich and achieved his aim in September 1538 when the friars - whom he referred to as 'very poor wretches' - were expelled. He demolished the buildings, selling off what he could to make a quick profit. He also acquired St Leonard's Benedictine priory in the city which his son, the Earl of Surrey, rebuilt as a lavish Renaissance house.

After the failure of the 'Pilgrimage of Grace', the efforts to stamp out all dissent relentlessly continued. With this object in mind, Henry re-established the Council of the North at York with sweeping powers. The pace of the destruction of images and relics gathered momentum along with the suppression of the religious houses. Throughout 1539 and 1540 Cromwell pursued his vendetta against the monasteries by suppressing the greater houses for the financial benefit of the Crown. Cromwell promised to make Henry the richest king that ever reigned in England. He found Syon Abbey a tough nut to crack, as it refused to play along with the absurd pretence that the surrender of the monasteries was voluntary. In 1538 a writ of *praemunire* was issued against Bishop Stokesley of London and Agnes Jordan, who had been abbess of Syon since 1521. Stokesley was accused of having officiated at the monastic profession of members of the community, citing the Bishop of Rome as his authority, thus rendering himself and all those involved liable to the penalties prescribed. Stokesley, when taken into custody, begged Cromwell to intercede on his behalf with the King, who granted him a pardon. All this was just a means to an end. Cromwell was not interested in Stokesley but in getting his hands on Syon by whatever devious ploy he could engineer. When the abbey was suppressed in 1539, for agreeing to leave quietly Abbess Agnes was given a pension of £200. She and several of her nuns moved to Denham, Buckinghamshire, where she had family connections. When she died in 1545 in her will she left bequests to her nuns and her confessor, a former monk of Syon. In the chancel floor of Denham church can be found a brass showing Agnes Jordan in her abbesses robes. The inscription reads,
Of your charity pray for the soul of Dame Agnes Jordan sometime abbess of the monastery of Syon which departed this life the 29th day of January in the year of our Lord God 1545 on whose soul Jesu have mercy.

At the suppression many of the Syon community went to Flanders. The abbey church was left standing. Part of it was turned into a munitions factory. In 1541 Queen Catherine Howard was held in custody at Syon while Henry decided the fate of his fifth wife. When Henry died in 1547 his body rested overnight in Syon Abbey church en

The Henrician Martyrs

route to his interment at Windsor. Later that year the abbey church was demolished and the stones were recycled by the Duke of Somerset to build his renaissance mansion. It was at Syon that Lady Jane Grey was offered the crown following the death of Edward VI. Under Queen Mary, in 1557 the Bridgettines were invited back to Syon from the Netherlands, with Katherine Palmer as abbess. The restoration was to be short-lived as they were expelled on Elizabeth's accession. In 1594 the Percy family acquired Syon and they are still in residence in their grandiose house. (The Bridgettine community settled in Lisbon and in 1861 returned to England in Dorset. They moved to Chudleigh, Devon, in 1887 and then to their present house at South Brent, Devon, in 1925. Thus the nuns of Syon have the distinction of being the only English religious community that survived the Reformation and has continued in truly unbroken existence until the present time.)

Agnes Jordan was not the only religious superior to remain close to her former nuns. Many other examples can be cited of disbanded sisters trying to maintain some form of community existence. Elizabeth Sackville, the last prioress of Clerkenwell, lived with some of her nuns for a long time. Elizabeth Shelley, the last abbess of St Mary's, Winchester lived with a few of her nuns close by her former convent. Her will, made in 1547, the year of her death, reveals how these women clung to their religious profession. She left twenty shillings each to seven of her nuns whom she names. Morpheta Kingsmill, last abbess of Wherwell, in her will of 1569, left bequests to seven members of her community who it appears were still living with her at the time of her death.

When Westminster Abbey was surrendered in January 1540 the monks removed the body of St Edward the Confessor from its shrine and concealed it. The resting places of other saints had not been so fortunate. From their destruction and the pillaging of their treasures, the King amassed a fortune of immense value. At Canterbury the internationally celebrated shrine of St Thomas Becket was one of the wonders of the religious world. It was covered in gold and smothered with precious stones donated by the faithful over centuries. In the autumn of 1538 St Thomas was retrospectively declared a traitor and all references to him were to be expunged by order of the King. His relics were removed and burned. The treasures, which filled twenty six carts, were plundered when the shrine was demolished. The great jewel, known as the Regal of France, that had been given by Louis VII in 1179 was used to make a ring for Henry. French ambassador Charles de Marillac, describing Henry as 'so covetous that all the riches of the world would not satisfy him', was of the opinion that Becket's posthumous disgrace was an excuse to destroy his shrine in order for Henry to get his hands on its treasures. The ancient pilgrimage shrine of Our Lady at Walsingham, Norfolk, once so revered by the young Henry, was dismantled. The Augustinian priory had been suppressed in 1538, looted and destroyed. The jewels adorning the shrine were removed and the image of Our Lady was taken to London and burned at Chelsea. The plate, the sacred vessels and the treasures accumulated at the shrine of St Alban were prodigious. They were all taken to the royal jewel-house. The destruction of St Swithun's shrine at Winchester took place at 3 a.m. by candlelight. In addition to the precious metals and stones that were removed the King's commissioner took a cross of emeralds. At Lichfield was the marble shrine of St Chad, its feretory adorned with gold and precious gems. Bishop Rowland Lee of Coventry and Lichfield begged Henry VIII to spare the shrine. Likewise he and the mayor and aldermen of Coventry vainly tried to persuade Henry to spare St Mary's, the priory cathedral church of their city. Lee pleaded with Cromwell for his help 'that the church may stand, whereby I may keep my name and the city have commodity and ease to their desire.' Clearly all Lee's personal services to the King in suppressing religious houses cut no ice and his pleas fell on deaf ears. In spite of being a wonderful architectural gem with its three spires, the cathedral roof was removed and the building dismantled for its materials. (Some of St Chad's bones were saved and later preserved by recusants. They are enshrined in St Chad's Catholic Cathedral, Birmingham.)

At Durham in December 1539 Dr Legh and Walter Henley supervised the destruction of the richly adorned shrine of St Cuthbert. The despoilers received a shock when they broke open the sarcophagus and found inside a coffin containing the saint's relics. Instead of the expected bones they found an extraordinarily lifelike whole body clothed in Mass vestments, still incorrupt after 850 years, with the face bare and a growth of beard on it. In the process they broke one of Cuthbert's legs. Nonplussed by their discovery the body was placed in the sacristy while instructions were awaited from London. Cuthbert was later buried under the original site where he still rests. The shrine was robbed of its treasures, including the sumptuously illuminated Lindisfarne Gospels, which were sent to London. Throughout the country, along with the destruction of the shrines of saints, statues and roods were being torn down and burned.

It was inevitable that having destroyed the monasteries Henry would next turn his greedy eyes on the Order of St John of Jerusalem. In the year 600 Pope St Gregory the Great commissioned the Benedictines to build a hospital in Jerusalem on the site of the monastery of St John the Baptist. The monastic Hospitaller order grew from this enterprise. Founded in Jerusalem in the 11th century to provide care for poor or sick pilgrims to the Holy Land it developed into a religious order of fighting military knights, chaplains and brothers who worked with the sick. It gradually spread across Europe. Its special patron was, appropriately, St John the Almsgiver, 7th century Patriarch of Alexandria, who used the wealth of his see to found hospitals and hostels. The Muslim conquests drove the Order from Jerusalem. The headquarters were moved to the island of Rhodes and eventually to Malta. (Its capital, Valletta, is named after a Grand Master of the Order Jean de la Valette.)

The Order was in the vanguard of scientific medicine and its hospitals on Malta and elsewhere were famous as among the finest in the world. The Order was established in England in the 12th century when the knight's were given land in Clerkenwell, London. Here they built their great priory, whose church was consecrated by Heraclius, Latin Patriarch of Jerusalem, in 1185. Over the years the Order established other houses around the country, including one for sisters in Somerset. It acquired property and wealth and was granted many privileges by successive kings. In 1540 an act of Parliament conveyed all the property of the Order to the King and on 10 May the London priory was suppressed. On the same day the last Grand Prior, Sir William Weston, died of a heart attack, brought on by shock and grief. Many of the knights escaped to Malta. (Under Edward VI most of the priory was blown up to provide materials for the Protector to build Somerset House in the Strand. Queen Mary invited the Order to return with Sir Thomas Tresham as Grand Prior. Their return was brief. At the accession of Elizabeth they were banished and the Queen gave the priory church at Clerkenwell to her Master of the Revels from where many of Shakespeare's plays received their performing license. All that remains of the priory is the 12th century crypt and the splendid gatehouse, built in 1504, which now houses the museum of the Order of St John. It was from here in 1877 that the St John Ambulance Brigade was initiated.) Today the Sovereign Military Hospitaller Order of St John of Jerusalem, known as the Military Order of Malta, enjoys observer status at the United Nations. It works in 120 countries and runs hospitals, day care centres and first aid corps with over 20,000 doctors, nurses and paramedics dedicated to the care of the poor, sick and disabled, the homeless, lepers and the terminally ill, as well as helping the victims of natural disasters.

The suppression of the religious houses caused enormous social upheaval, involving not only the loss of the monastic hospitals but also their charitable work in providing help and shelter for the poor. Judging by the surviving records the charitable work was extensive, as the 'Pilgrimage of Grace' leader Robert Aske emphasised. As well as providing hospitality to travellers the religious houses used a significant proportion of their gross annual income on almsgiving. Lancashire monasteries seem to have been exceptionally generous. Cistercian Whalley Abbey gave special payments at Christmas and major feast days, and regularly supported twenty-four poor men in the house. In 1536 the canons of Premonstratensian Cockersand, a much smaller and poorer community, in addition to their alms, provided daily bed and board for fifteen poor, aged men.

The monasteries were the chief sources of learning, education and patronage of the arts. Their suppression resulted in unemployment for all those who worked for them. In July 1536 Eustace Chapuys, the Imperial Ambassador wrote, 'It is a lamentable thing to see a legion of monks and nuns, who having been chased from their monasteries, wandering miserably hither and thither seeking means to live.' While some ex-religious received pensions or benefices most did not, for example, Thomas Catton, the deprived last abbot of St Albans. This was punishment for his obduracy in refusing to surrender his house, declaring that he 'would choose to beg his bread all the days of his life than consent to surrender.' In any case the pensions were mostly too inadequate to enable them to live without finding employment. The fortunate monks were those whose houses were endowed with the benefices of churches, chapels or chantries. At least thirteen of the Lancashire parish churches were served by monks. Those in situ were often allowed to continue serving after the suppression and thus provide a livelihood, but they were expected to pay for secular clerical dress for themselves. (There is a recorded case from Cumberland of a vicar, a former Cistercian of Furness Abbey, paying £4 for a special licence to be allowed to continue wearing his monk's habit underneath his cassock.) Finding employment would have fallen particularly hard on the friars whose houses, unlike many of the abbeys, did not enjoy control of churches. By 1539 finding posts as priests for ex-religious became increasingly difficult because, by then, there were so many of them seeking employment and not enough places available. For example, of the twenty-six Premonstratensian canons of Cockersand only four obtained clerical employment after being expelled from their house. From an examination conducted of the records of over 2,000 ex-monks in England without pensions, it has been calculated that only fifty found employment; the remainder were in poverty. For monks without any pension - by far the great majority - who could not find new clerical employment, life would have been hard. They would have had to try teaching or labouring on the land or be dependent upon the charity of their neighbours.

The rampant greed knew no bounds. None of the wealth accumulated was used for the good of the realm, let alone for any charitable purpose. It was used primarily to help fill the avaricious King's emptying coffers, the monastic lands and the ecclesiastical benefices and other properties being sold on for cash to those who could afford to buy them and aggrandise themselves even further. Cromwell was inundated with importunate demands from the nobility and gentry in a deplorable scramble for a share of the monastic spoils. It was also a means of ensuring that these often *nouveaux riches* gentry were, in their own economic interests, allied to the new Protestant tendency. Many of the lands and possessions of the monasteries were acquired by courtiers and members of the King's household, who hungrily clamoured for some of the booty, taking advantage of their positions for personal gain. Henry must have derived particular satisfaction when the famous Dominican Blackfriars monastery in the City of London was suppressed in 1538. As the venue for Queen Catherine's divorce court hearings it was the scene of his humiliation when the proceedings were adjourned. The monastery was valued at just £104.15s 5d. The church plate was taken to the King's Jewel House and the buildings granted to Sir Thomas Cawarden, Keeper of the Royal Tents and Master of the Revels. Most of the monastery was demolished, including the church. The father and mother of Katherine Parr, Sir Thomas and Lady Maud Parr, had been buried there. History does not record what Henry VIII's sixth wife may have thought of his treatment of her parents' final resting place. Cawarden sold the monks' refectory for use as the Blackfriars Playhouse, which became London's premier theatre.

Thomas Cromwell, the man responsible for the suppressions, profited hugely. As the progress of the suppressions gathered pace Cromwell was overwhelmed with gifts from religious houses in money and kind in an effort to stave off their destruction. This was just as well because his expenditure was lavish. He spent a fortune on goldsmiths and jewellers, including a diamond and a ruby bought by him for the astronomical price of £2,000. His share of the monastic spoils was enormous. It included the Cluniac priory of St Pancras at Lewes - suppressed in November 1537 - whose monks received no pension. Having made alterations to the buildings he allowed his newlywed son and his wife to live there; a residence which the new Mrs Cromwell found 'very commodious.' He also acquired Michelham, Sussex; Modenham, Kent; St Osyth, Essex; Alcester, Warwickshire; Yarmouth, Norfolk and Laund, Leicestershire. Cromwell ensured that members of his family got their share. For example, his nephew, Richard Williams alias Cromwell - the great-grandfather of Oliver Cromwell - was yet another royal commissioner who did well out of the suppressions. He bought Benedictine Ramsey Abbey and all its properties for a song. He also acquired in Huntingdonshire Cistercian Sawtry Abbey and Hinchingbrooke convent for £19.9s.2d; St Helen's Benedictine Priory for nuns, Bishopsgate, London; and Cistercian Neath Abbey, once the largest abbey in Wales. As we have seen with Syon, some monasteries were converted into palatial dwellings whose names even today, with their suffix 'abbey' or 'priory', are a reminder of their former purpose. The acquisition of the spoils from the destruction of the religious houses laid the foundation of the fortunes of many families.

The tenants of these new owners soon found what harsh landlords and taskmasters they turned out to be when compared with the monks. To quote an anonymous contemporary writer unearthed by J E Thorold Rogers: 'All sorts of people were helped and succoured by the abbeys. Yea, happy was that person that was tenant to an abbey, for it was a rare thing to hear that any tenant was removed by taking his farm over his head ... and thus they fulfilled all the works of charity in all the country round about them to the good example of all lay persons that now have taken forth other lessons.' Some monastery churches were used as parish churches; many others were simply left to decay, the stones being re-cycled for new buildings. The metal from the bells that had once called the inhabitants to prayer was used to make guns.

It was not only the glorious religious edifices that were lost. One of the greatest losses, not just to England but to European culture, was the destruction of the monastic libraries. Instead of being preserved, the irreplaceable books were wantonly broken up; their precious bindings ripped off and sold. The scale of the destruction was immense. For example, the Augustinian library at York had 650 volumes, and Worcester Priory over 600. John Bale (1495-1563), the former Carmelite Prior of Ipswich turned aggressive Protestant, who was made Bishop of Ossory in Ireland in the reign of Edward VI, lamented in 1549 that the books had not been saved for the sake of learning and the good of posterity. Their destruction without consideration he said, 'will be unto England for ever a most horrible infamy'. The libraries contained priceless treasures of early Anglo-Saxon manuscripts. Bale spoke of manuscripts and pages of books being used to clean boots, wrap soap or as toilet paper. Illuminated manuscripts from Malmesbury

The Henrician Martyrs

Abbey were used by brewers as stoppers for their casks. The service and medieval music books were also wantonly destroyed. What little has survived offers just a tantalising glimpse of the rich musical heritage of the English religious houses and their choral schools which Erasmus praised so highly for their love of singing with organ accompaniment.

In May 1539 Henry decided to exercise his spiritual supremacy as head of the English Church and self-styled God's own deputy on earth, by introducing in Parliament a bill, later known as the Six Articles Act. His intention was to 'abolish diversity in opinion' about religious doctrine. The Articles reiterated Catholic teaching on transubstantiation and confession; affirmed priestly celibacy and private Masses etc. When the Act became law in June Bishop Hugh Latimer resigned his Worcester see in protest and was placed under house arrest. The Act stipulated that any person, who by any means, denied any of the Articles faced the punishment of traitors: death by hanging, drawing and quartering or burning as a heretic. Cranmer, secretly opposed to the articles, must have been in a bit of a panic so he took the precaution of temporarily sending his wife, Margaret, back to Germany.

The 1539 Act for the Dissolution of the Greater Monasteries (31 Hen.8.c, 13) paved the way for the destruction of the remaining 552 religious houses. The Act confirmed that ' in the reign of our most dread Sovereign Lord ... all other monasteries ... which hereafter shall happen to be dissolved, suppressed ... shall be vested ... in the possession of the King,' Despite the legalised vandalism a hypocritical charade continued to be maintained that the religious willingly surrendered their houses to the King. The learned antiquarian and Garter Principal King of Arms, Sir William Dugdale (1605-86), wrote in his *Monasticon Anglicanum*, a historical survey of the British monasteries, 'What could not be effected by arguments and fair promises was by terror and severe dealing brought to pass. For under pretence of dilapidation in the buildings or negligent administration of their offices as also for breaking the King's injunctions they deprived some abbots and then put others that were more pliant in their room.' The royal instruction was that if any of the heads of the houses that had already been 'appointed to be dissolved' [nota bene] obstinately refused to surrender, the property was to be seized by force. There are myriad examples to be found in the records, that of already-mentioned Waverley Abbey being but one case in point. A few more illustrations selected at random will suffice. From Christ Church, Canterbury, Prior Goldstone wrote to Cromwell begging that the monastery would be spared. He informed Cromwell that the monks will never be

The Henrician Martyrs

constrained to give up their house against their wills, or voluntarily renege on their religious profession as sons of St Benedict. Cromwell visited Canterbury with the King in September 1538 and informed the monks in the chapterhouse that he had already resolved upon suppression. From the Charterhouse at Hinton, Somerset, Prior Horde wrote that he and his brothers would not give up their house, 'a thing which is not ours to give, but dedicated to Almighty God for service to be done to His honour continually with many other good deeds of charity which daily be done in this house to our Christian neighbours. And considering that there is no cause given by us why the house shall be put down, but that the service of God, religious conversation of the brethren, hospitality, alms-deeds, with all other our duties, be as well observed in this poor house as in any religious house in the realm.' John Tregonwell and William Petre, the royal commissioners, arrived at Hinton in January 1539 and set about trying to obtain its surrender. Tregonwell, a Cornishman and lawyer, was another typical Tudor time-server. He had played a part in the condemnation of the Carthusians, Thomas More and Anne Boleyn. He had a major role in the surrender of the religious houses, supplying Cromwell with a list of nine suppressed abbeys, any one of which, he said, he would be happy to acquire. One of those he got his hands on was Milton Abbey, Dorset. In spite of his past he was knighted by Queen Mary and was buried at Milton in 1565. His kneeling effigy under a marble altar tomb can still be seen. William Petre informed Cromwell that, 'Immediately after our coming we entered conversation with the prior there ... and used such means and persuasions unto him ... His answer in effect was that if the king's majesty would take his house, so that it proceeded not of his voluntary surrender he was contented to obey; but otherwise he said his conscience would not suffer him willingly to give over the same.' But after being asked to reconsider overnight he stood firm and the commissioners reported that in conversations with the other twenty-two monks they 'perceived them to be of the same mind as the prior'. One of the monks, Nicholas Balland, boldly spoke out against the royal supremacy, affirming that the Pope was the head of the Church and was prepared to die for that belief. By 31 March the grinding pressure had done its work and the prior and fourteen of the monks signed the surrender document. The property was sold to Sir Walter Hungerford who, three months later, complained that Sir Thomas Arundel had 'despoiled and quite carried away a great part of the church.'

It appears there was an assumption that when royal pressure was brought to bear upon convents the nuns would be easily cowed into compliantly surrendering their houses. The opposition was stiffer than anticipated. Most of the nuns showed heroic resistance. At the Benedictine Abbey of St Mary and St Melor, Amesbury, Wiltshire, founded c.979 by Queen Aelfthryth, the royal commissioners, Tregonwell and Petre came up against the formidable prioress, Florence Bonnewe. They 'could not by any persuasions bring her to any conformity. At all times she resisted.' This went on for four months and it is not difficult to imagine the pressure that was brought to bear until she gave in at the King's command and left 'though I beg my bread; and as for pension I care for none.' Of the many convents suppressed it appears that only three genuine surrender documents exist. It is significant that so many of the 'surrender' documents in the public records bear no signatures or only that of the abbess, such as at Shaftesbury, where Cromwell personally supervised the suppression. Although there were fifty-six nuns only the abbess, Elizabeth Zouche, signed. Some documents are clearly worthless forgeries insofar as the signatures they bear are all in the same handwriting. Other unsigned documents were written out by the royal agents after the event to make it look as if the houses had been voluntarily surrendered.

The ancient and important Benedictine abbey at Romsey, Hampshire, had a community of twenty-five nuns, ruled by their abbess, Elizabeth Ryprose. Two of the nuns were relatives of Sir Thomas Seymour. He was the brother of the late Queen Jane Seymour, and future husband of Henry VIII's widow, Queen Katherine Parr. It seems Seymour coveted Romsey and commissioned a report on the financial status of the house. The report confirmed that the abbey had no debts; that the plate was worth £300; six bells were worth at least £100; the abbey lands, from which it derived its income, were in good shape; and the church 'a great sumptuous thing, all of free stone and covered with lead, which as I esteem it, is worth £300 or £400 or much better.' Powerful as he might be Seymour could not get the nuns to surrender their abbey. No surrender deed was ever signed; no pensions were ever provided for the abbess and her nuns. They were all forcibly ejected. The abbey church lay despoiled and neglected until February 1554 when the townspeople of Romsey saved it from destruction by purchasing it for £100.

A particularly notorious case that provides an insight into the methods used to force compliance concerned the Cistercian monastery of Our Blessed Lady, Vale Royal, at Whitegate, near Nantwich, Cheshire. The exactions made upon the monastery's resources by Cromwell were such that it became impossible for the house to meet any further demands. The abbot, John Harwood, wrote to Cromwell, 'I most humbly beseech your good lordship, for the love of God and our

The Henrician Martyrs

Blessed Lady and for the maintenance of good service and poor hospitality to be kept in the house, to pardon our refusal.' In August 1538 Commissioners Thomas Legh and Thomas Holcroft arrived at the abbey and on 7 September claimed that Vale Royal had been voluntarily surrendered. This claim was strongly repudiated by the abbot who set out for London to reinforce his denial. From Lichfield he wrote to Cromwell, 'The truth is, I nor my said brethren have never consented to surrender our monastery, nor yet do, nor never will do by our good wills ... And if any information be given unto his majesty by your lordship, that we should consent to surrender as is above said, I assure your good lordship upon my fidelity and truth, there was never any such consent made by me or my brethren and no person or persons had authority to do so in our names'. He adds a plea that the King will spare his monastery. The abbot's journey proved fruitless. Cromwell had to find a means to suppress the monastery while maintaining some outward pretence of justice. In 1539 he descended upon Vale Royal in person and charged the abbot with treason. Needless to say, Abbot Harwood was judged guilty, which meant that he faced execution. The price for sparing his life was the surrender of his monastery. As Vale Royal was acquired by none other than commissioner Thomas Holcroft it is obvious why that perjured villain had forged the document claiming the abbey's surrender.

Ostensibly for similar resistance, on Saturday, 15 November 1539 two Benedictine abbots, Blessed Hugh Faringdon of Reading and Blessed Richard Whiting of Glastonbury, were hanged, drawn and quartered. They were followed on 1 December by Blessed John Beche, whose real name was Marshall, Abbot of St John's, Colchester. Many other heads of monasteries resisted the suppression of their houses, but they were not executed. In the case of these three prominent abbots they were clearly singled out because of their outspoken loyalty to Rome. Cromwell had determined well in advance upon the attainder and execution of the three abbots for high treason, with no semblance of judicial procedure being followed. Cromwell acted as 'prosecutor, judge and jury.' (J A Froude, *History of England*, 1856). The seizure of their monasteries was 'against every principle of received law, held to fall by the attainder of their abbots.' (Henry Hallam, *Constitutional History of* England). Even the prejudiced Bishop Gilbert Burnet argued that the proceedings were unjustified because the seizing of the abbeys and their lands, arising from the attainder of the abbots, 'was thought a great stretch of law, since the offence of an ecclesiastical incumbent is a personal thing, and cannot prejudice the church; no more than a secular man, being in office, does by being attainted bring any diminution of the rights of the office on his successors.'

Abbot Hugh Faringdon of Reading, whose real name was Cook - his birthplace was most likely Faringdon - had been educated at Reading Abbey where he became a monk about 1500. He was elected abbot in 1520. Arrested at his manor at Pangbourne he was sent to join Whiting in the Tower. Abbot Cook was particularly vociferous about the royal supremacy saying that 'he would pray for the pope's holiness as long as he lived'. At his trial he was accused of denying that the King was Head of the Church in England. It is difficult to resist the conclusion that Henry was taking his belated revenge, because in 1533 Abbot Hugh had the temerity to argue against the King's divorce of Catherine of Aragon.

Richard Whiting was educated at Glastonbury and then joined the community. He completed his education at Cambridge taking his M.A. degree in 1483. His fellow students at Cambridge at that time included John Houghton, William Exmew and Richard Reynolds. Whiting was ordained priest at Wells in 1501 and in 1505 took his final degree as Doctor in Theology at Cambridge. He became Abbot of St Mary's, Glastonbury in February 1525 in succession to Richard Bere. As a mitred abbot who sat in the House of Lords Whiting had a reputation as both a caring spiritual leader and an efficient manager of his abbey's affairs. Commissioner Layton had earlier found Glastonbury in good order, but this was not to the liking of Cromwell, and Layton had been obliged to make an abject apology for his 'folly' promising that in future he would be 'more circumspect whom I shall commend to his Grace or you.' Without any prior warning and with instructions to find faults to ensure the abbey's suppression, on 19 September 1539 Cromwell's Commissioners, Dr Layton, Richard Pollard and Thomas Moyle, arrived at Glastonbury; by then the only religious house left standing in Somerset. They ransacked eighty-year-old Abbot Whiting's apartments for 'evidence' and interrogated him as to his opinions before sending him to the Tower, despite his 'being a very weak and sickly man'. In his absence the commissioners expelled the monks and pillaged the abbey for its furniture, rich vestments and plate.

John Beche, vere Marshall, of Colchester became a Doctor of Divinity at Oxford in 1515. He was elected Abbot of Colchester 10 June 1533. Marshall soon joined Whiting and Cook in the Tower. One of the witnesses against Abbot Marshall was a cleric, John Seyn, who declared that when Marshall had been informed of the surrender of the nearby Augustinian Abbey of St Osyth he had said, 'I will not say that the King shall never have *my* house, but it will be against my will and against my heart, for I know by my learning that he cannot take it by right and law, wherefore in my conscience I cannot be content, nor shall he ever have it with my heart and will.' Another witness stated that Marshall had claimed that authority was given by Christ to St Peter and to his successors, the bishops of Rome. Others alleged that he had also expressed his sympathy with the 'Pilgrimage of Grace' and said God would take vengeance for the destruction of the religious houses. Furthermore, he had praised the martyrdoms of Thomas More and John Fisher, both of them 'good men'. Under no illusions as to the real cause of his plight and that of his monastery, Marshall was recorded as saying that 'the King and his Council were driven into such inordinate covetousness that if all the water in the Thames were flowing with gold and silver, it were not able to slake their covetousness'. (*Letters and Papers, Foreign and Domestic, of the Reign of Henry VIII*). No details now exist about Marshall's execution at Colchester but his gold and enamelled pectoral cross has survived. Browne Willis in *The Mitred Abbeys,* 1718, wrote of Marshall, 'he had courage enough to maintain his conscience and run the last extremity, being neither prevailed upon by bribery, terror or any dishonourable motives to come into a surrender, or subscribe to the king's supremacy; on which account ... he suffered death.'

Martyred with Richard Whiting at the summit of Glastonbury Tor were two of his priest monks; Blessed John Thorne, the abbey treasurer, and Blessed Roger James, the sacristan, who, in 1534, was listed as the youngest monk at Glastonbury. The executions were supervised by Lord John Russell and Richard Pollard. Whiting's head was displayed over the gate of his deserted abbey and his quarters were sent to Wells, Bath, Ilchester and Bridgwater.

With Hugh Cook died Blessed John Eynon, Benedictine priest at St Giles' church, Reading, and a special friend of the Abbot's, and Blessed John Rugg, a Benedictine prebendary of Chichester Cathedral, in retirement at Reading. He had been indicted for denying the royal supremacy. When asked why he had earlier sworn to the supremacy Rugg replied, 'I added this condition in my mind, to take him for supreme head in temporal things, but not in spiritual things.' Awaiting his execution Cook spoke to the assembled crowd of people. He told them that he and his companions were to die for openly professing fidelity to the See of Rome, which was but the common faith of those who had the best right to declare the true teaching of the English Church. The three of them were martyred before the inner abbey gatehouse. By then the monks had been expelled without any pensions and the abbey had been stripped bare, its contents being sent to London for the 'use of the king's majesty.' At least one of the monks, Dom

The Henrician Martyrs

Roger London, who was a lecturer at Reading, was in the Tower by November 1539. His fate is unknown. Abbot Cook had found a means of sending communications to other abbots by an itinerant blind harpist named William Moore, who proved a trusty agent. In November 1539 Moore appears on the same list of prisoners in the Tower as Roger London and Peter Lawrence, Warden of the Grey Friars at Reading. He seems to be identical with the blind harpist, a Welshman, who was hanged and quartered on 1 July 1540 for allegedly singing songs critical of the King.

As with Glastonbury and Reading, within a few days of Abbot Marshall's death there was wholesale plundering of the monastery at Colchester. The plate, together with mitres and croziers, were all sent to the King's treasury. The lead was stripped from the roofs; the bells melted down. Within six weeks the monastic buildings and the abbey church of St John were dismantled. The abbey lands were given to Thomas Darcy, later 1st Baron Darcy of Chiche. History does not record what happened to the 'many poor people' who lived at the abbey, and of whom the Lord Chancellor, Lord Audley, wrote that they 'had daily relief of the house'. Such sentiments did not stop him from acquiring his share of the monastic plunder in the avaricious scramble that followed the suppressions. Audley secured the property of at least nine religious houses.

In the summer of 1539 several other executions had taken place. Four were hanged, drawn and quartered at St Thomas Waterings, Southwark, on 8 July. They were Venerable John Griffith, Vicar of Wandsworth, a former chaplain to Henry Courtenay, Marquess of Exeter, and his unknown curate. Charles Wriothesley in his *Chronicle* relates that two friars died with them. The historian John Stow in his *Annales of England*, first published in 1580, names one of them as Venerable John Waire, probably a Franciscan. (In 1568 Stow's house was raided and books he possessed 'in defence of papistry' were seized. He was again investigated in 1570 but on both occasions was not prosecuted.) On 9 July two laymen, both Knights Hospitaller of the Order of St John of Jerusalem, were executed by beheading on Tower Hill. The first was Blessed Sir Adrian Fortescue, who was also a Knight of the Bath. 19 He was one of a group of sixteen condemned for treason without any trial or any evidence against him. Their only 'crime' appears to have been their 'adherence to the bishop of Rome' and their hostility towards the King's religious policies. The second was Venerable Sir Thomas Dingley. He came from Lincolnshire and was included in the same bill of attainder passed on Margaret Pole, Countess of Salisbury. No specific charges of a treasonable nature were

The Henrician Martyrs

ever brought against him. On 30 July the priest John Harris was executed.

The following year, 1540, two priests, William Peterson and William Richardson were executed, plus Thomas Abel, Edward Powell and Richard Fetherston, [20] who were executed on a gallows set up at St Bartholomew's Gate, Smithfield. Venerable Edmund Brindholme, parish priest of Our Lady, Calais, and a layman, Venerable Clement Philpot, suffered the same fate at Tyburn on 3 August. In May 1541 Margaret Pole, Countess of Salisbury, was beheaded. [21] On 12 July of that year Blessed Sir David Gunston, a knight of the Order of St John of Jerusalem, was hanged, drawn and quartered at St Thomas Waterings having been attainted for denying the royal supremacy. [22] On 7 March 1544 three priests and a layman suffered together at Tyburn: Robert Singleton, John Larke, John Ireland and German Gardiner. [23]

On the 29th of that month a layman, Venerable Thomas Ashby, was executed for denying the royal supremacy. For the same reason, also that year, two Augustinian monks, Martin de Courdres and Father Paul of St William were executed. At least fifty-two Catholic martyrs suffered death in the last twelve years of Henry's reign, not counting the hundreds whose names are unknown, executed after the 'Pilgrimage of Grace'.

The theory has been advanced that Henry VIII - described by S Hubert Burke (*Historical Portraits of the Tudor Dynasty and the Reformation Period,* 1880) as 'a cruel, relentless, heartless, blaspheming, despotic voluptuary' - suffered from what is now known as Cushing's syndrome, a condition caused by abnormally high levels of the hormone cortisol. His physical symptoms, obesity, 'moon face' and his behaviour, amounting to psychosis, would seem to substantiate this hypothesis. As his death approached, the King can have been under no illusions that Protestants were in the ascendancy at Court. In his final speech to Parliament he described himself as 'I whom God has appointed His Vicar'. He maintained the self-deception that he remained a Catholic to the end of his life. Believing personally in the Real Presence of Christ in the Eucharist, he did not hesitate to have Protestant heretics burned for denying the doctrine; sometimes on the same day that the ruthless tyrant despatched victims to Tyburn for denying the royal supremacy.

In his will Henry commended himself to the prayers of the Blessed Virgin Mary and the saints and asked - surely greatly more in hope than expectation! - that daily Masses be said for his soul in perpetuity. Yet he appointed leading Protestants as the guardians and regents for his son, Edward.

The Henrician Martyrs

Notes to Chapter One

1 Thomas Cranmer was born in Nottinghamshire and was educated at Cambridge, receiving his MA in 1515. Shortly afterwards he married but his wife died in childbirth and Thomas was ordained priest. Appointed Henry's ambassador to the Emperor Charles V he came into contact with German and Swiss Protestants and began to accept Lutheran ideas. He was in Italy with the imperial court when news of his elevation to Canterbury arrived. The Pope, anxious to appease Henry, issued the necessary bulls and Cranmer was consecrated archbishop on 30 March 1533. One of his first tasks was sending John Frith to be burned at the stake in June 1533 for denying the Real Presence in the Eucharist. Cranmer encountered much opposition to his policies from the bishops so in 1535 Thomas Cromwell appointed himself Vice-gerent, making him the head of ecclesiastical affairs, second only to the King, thus relegating Cranmer to a lesser role. Cranmer also had to accept the retention of Catholic doctrines when the *Six Articles* were affirmed by Parliament in 1539. In January 1540 he officiated at the wedding of Henry to Anne of Cleves but obligingly annulled the marriage on 9 July. With the execution of Thomas Cromwell Cranmer's star was in the ascendant as a trusted servant of the King. It was Cranmer who was deputed to inform Henry of the alleged affairs of Queen Catherine Howard. Under Edward VI Cranmer had free reign to pursue his Protestant agenda and he announced his rejection of the Real Presence. He publicly acknowledged his wife and children. In 1548/49 Cranmer compiled, from various sources, the *Book of Common Prayer* and sought to enforce it throughout the parishes. Cranmer then co-operated with the German reformer, Martin Bucer, to produce a new ordinal which rejected the sacrificial nature of priesthood. When Queen Mary came to the throne Cranmer was tried for treason in 1553 and heresy in 1555. During his two year's imprisonment he recanted several times and was reconciled to the Catholic Church accepting all its teachings. But before his execution by burning at Oxford in 1556 he once again declared his Protestantism. He is regarded as a martyr by the Anglican Church.

2 Elizabeth Barton was a nun at St Sepulchre's Benedictine Convent at Canterbury. She was known for her exemplary holy life and she claimed to experience visions. She became acquainted with Archbishop Warham, the Bridgettines at Syon, the Franciscans at Greenwich and the Carthusians at Sheen. She met Bishop Fisher three times and Thomas More once, who told her she had better keep quiet. She and

every one connected with her were in trouble when her prophecy's spilled over into the political sphere and she began to speak ill of the King, predicting his doom because of his divorce and re-marriage. Elizabeth was sent to the Tower but the government wanted to use her to ensnare as many others as possible who were opposed to the divorce. She was hanged at Tyburn on 5 May 1534 with five companions. These were two Benedictines, Dr Edward Bocking - who had been asked by Archbishop Warham to investigate the nun - and John Dering, both of Christ Church, Canterbury; an Observant Franciscan, Father Risby; two secular priests, Richard Masters, parson of Aldington, and Henry Gold who came from St Neots and was a fellow of St John's, Cambridge. Ordained priest in 1520, two years later he was elected university preacher. He then became secretary to Archbishop Warham and in 1526 was appointed to the parish of St Mary Aldermary in the City of London. In the Public Record Office is the only surviving letter of St Richard Reynolds, written in beautiful Latin' script to his friend Henry Gold. A sixth priest, the Franciscan Hugh Rich, had cheated the gallows by dying in prison. The priests were twice offered their lives if they would accept the royal supremacy: all refused. Elizabeth was buried in the Greyfriars Monastery.

3 Thomas Cromwell was born in 1485 at Putney, the son of a drunken brewer and fuller. After studying law he entered the service of Cardinal Wolsey. He became a Member of Parliament in 1523. During the King's divorce crisis, Cromwell made himself invaluable to Henry and by 1533 he was Secretary of State. Time-server Cromwell was conveniently unencumbered by such irksome constraints as morals or deeply held principles. It was most probably Cromwell who first suggested to Henry that he should make himself head of the Church, and he steered the necessary legislation through Parliament. He presided over the suppression of the monasteries and was made a knight of the Order of the Garter in 1537. In 1539 Parliament passed the Act of Precedence in which Cromwell, as the King's Ecclesiastical Vicegerent, was given precedence over all peers and bishops, including the Archbishop of Canterbury. In 1540, he was created Earl of Essex and Lord Great Chamberlain. His downfall came when he arranged for Henry to marry Anne of Cleves. Henry took an immediate dislike to Anne and while Cromwell was in disfavour his enemies closed in, accusing him of heresy by favouring Lutheran ideas; the ostensible reason for his attainder for treason. But the real, underlying reason was his promotion of Henry's fourth disastrous marriage. Henry, ungratefully forgetting all his chief minister's services to him, called

him 'the greatest wretch ever born in England.' Cromwell was executed at the Tower in July 1540. On the very same day Henry married Catherine Howard.

4 Richard Rich was born in London into a wealthy mercer's family. He studied law at the Middle Temple, where he met Thomas More, who had no great opinion of Rich's moral qualities and deplored his ambitious streak. In 1533 Rich was knighted and appointed Solicitor-General. He was a time-server insofar as he always trimmed to the prevailing wind in order to secure further advancement and wealth for himself. Rich prepared the indictment against Elizabeth Barton. He played an odious role in the trial of Thomas More, when he shamefully perjured himself in giving evidence. By 1536, the year he served as Speaker of the Commons, as Chancellor of the Court of Augmentations, he was responsible for disposing of the monastic revenues. In the same year he acquired for himself around one hundred manors in Essex, including Augustinian Leighs Priory near Chelmsford, which he converted into a luxurious residence, and the prior's house at St Bartholomew's, Smithfield as his London home. In 1540 his evidence helped convict Thomas Cromwell. He was an executor of Henry VIII's will and became Lord Chancellor during the reign of Edward VI. He was made a baron in 1548. In spite of Rich's support for the Protestant reforms, when Mary I succeeded to the throne she retained his services in the Privy Council and he played his part in actively persecuting heretics in Essex. One of his daughters became a Bridgettine nun at the re-established Syon Abbey. Rich died in 1567.

5 Richard Whytford came from a well-to-do family in Flintshire. A Fellow of Queen's College, Cambridge, he was a secular priest before joining the Bridgettines at Syon. He was closely connected with Queen Catherine and her circle, as he was for a time chaplain to William Blount, 4th Lord Mountjoy, her chamberlain. One of the great humanist scholars of his day he was, like Thomas More, a close friend of Erasmus. He produced a stream of devotional works intended to help the laity lead a more prayerful life, but modestly never put his name to them. His wonderful translation of the *Imitation of Christ* has stood the test of time. There is no evidence that Whytford ever subscribed to the royal supremacy when, along with the remainder of his community, he was expelled when Syon was suppressed in 1539. He was given refuge by Charles Blount, 5th Lord Mountjoy at his London house, where he remained until his death in 1542.

The Henrician Martyrs

6 Blessed John Haile (or Hale) was perhaps a native of Worcestershire. He was a secular priest and Bachelor of Law from Cambridge, where he was a Fellow of Kings' Hall. In 1505 he was appointed Rector of St Dunstan's, Cranford, Middlesex, and in 1521 he became Vicar of Isleworth. In 1531 he was appointed a Canon of Wrigham, Kent, by Archbishop Warham. He originally came to the attention of the authorities for his forthright and somewhat intemperate condemnation of Henry's repudiation of Queen Catherine and his marriage to Anne Boleyn. A friend of the Bridgettines of Syon, he was an elderly man in poor health and greatly afraid of execution; but remained stalwart in condemning Henry's marriage, his immoral life, his oppression of the Church and his heretical claim to be supreme head of the Church. Robert Feron, a priest from Teddington, was also tried and found guilty with Haile. He was pardoned after turning King's evidence by betraying the conversations that had taken place between him and Haile.

7 Blessed Humphrey Middlemore, a priest, came from one of the most ancient families of Warwickshire. He was the son of Thomas Middlemore of Edgbaston. His mother was Ann Lyttleton of Pillaton Hall, Staffordshire. He was firstly Procurator, then Vicar, of the London Charterhouse.

8 Blessed William Exmew, priest. He was possibly related to a former Lord Mayor of London and educated at Cambridge. He was one of the first members of Christ's College, Cambridge after its foundation by Lady Margaret Beaufort. A fine classical scholar he was proficient in Latin and Greek. He joined the London Charterhouse c.1518 and became Vicar and then Procurator, where he enjoyed a reputation for holiness. He was no more than 30 years old at the time of his execution. Exmew's hand-written manuscript copy of *The Cloud of Unknowing*, the late 14th century English spiritual classic, today belongs to the UK's only Charterhouse; St Hugh's, Parkminster, Sussex.

9 Blessed Sebastian Newdigate came from an ancient family. The seventh of the fourteen children of John Newdigate, Lord of the Manor of Harefield, Middlesex and his wife, Amphyllis Neville. He was born on 7 September 1500. He was educated at Cambridge. He went to Court and became a member of the Privy Chamber. He married Katherine, co-heiress of Sir John Hampden and widow of Henry Ferrers of Baddesley Clinton. By her he had two daughters, Amphyllis and Elizabeth. After his wife's death he entered the Charterhouse as a

The Henrician Martyrs

novice. His sister Jane expressed her concern to Prior William Tynbygh as to Sebastian's suitability for the cloister after his lifestyle at Court. Nonetheless he remained, being ordained deacon 3 June 1531 and later priest. At his trial, the judge reminded Sebastian not only that he belonged to the nobility but also how he had enjoyed the King's favour.

10 Thomas Audley, 1st Baron Audley of Walden was born 1488. He is a classic example, *par excellence,* of a lawyer/politician, subserviently toadying to his royal master apparently without a moral scruple in the world. He supported the King's divorce and was Speaker of the House of Commons, presiding over the Parliament that abolished papal jurisdiction in England. He was the mouthpiece of the King in preparation for the Act of Supremacy. He presided at the trials of John Fisher and Thomas More, whom he succeeded as Chancellor. He tried Anne Boleyn and her alleged lovers and was present at the scaffold at her execution. He condemned to death the 'rebels' following the 'Pilgrimage of Grace' 1536/37. He played a major role in the suppression of the religious houses and personally benefited by being granted the Benedictine Walden Abbey, which he converted into his house; the mansion that became known as Audley End. He presided at two further judicial murder trials; those of Henry Pole, Lord Montague, the son of Margaret Pole, Countess of Salisbury and Henry Courtenay, Marquess of Exeter, a grandson of Edward IV, both executed in January 1539. They had to be disposed of by Henry VIII because they were too close to the legitimate hereditary succession to the throne. He was an instrument of the King's in enforcing religious conformity. In 1540 he achieved the desired attainder and execution of Thomas Cromwell and the annulment of Henry's marriage to Anne of Cleves. He founded Magdalen College, Oxford. He resigned as Lord Chancellor in 1544 and died shortly afterwards. He was buried in the grandiose tomb he had prepared at Saffron Walden.

11 St John Fisher, the son of Robert Fisher, a prosperous merchant and his wife Agnes, was born at Beverley, East Yorkshire, in 1469. John was only eight when his father died and his mother re-married and had a second family. John seems to have remained in close contact with all his siblings throughout his life. He was educated at Beverley Grammar School and then Cambridge becoming MA in 1491. He was appointed vicar of Northallerton, Yorkshire, but in 1494 he resigned his parish to take up the post of University Proctor. He then became chaplain and confessor to Margaret Beaufort, Countess of Richmond, the mother of King Henry VII. She founded Christ's and St John's Colleges at

The Henrician Martyrs

Cambridge. In 1501 John was elected Vice-Chancellor of Cambridge University, which he reformed, attracting leading scholars from around Europe, among them Erasmus. With all these heavy responsibilities he somehow managed to find time to write learned and spiritual books. In October 1504 he was elected Chancellor of Cambridge and, on the recommendation of Henry VII, he was appointed Bishop of Rochester, where he enjoyed a great reputation for erudition, austerity and holiness. In 1509 he officiated at the funerals of both the King and his mother. John was in the forefront of combating Lutheranism and at the command of Henry VIII he preached a famous anti-Luther sermon at St Paul's Cathedral. Henry VIII declared that no other sovereign had such a brilliant prelate. He became confessor to Catherine of Aragon and opposed the King's divorce. Henry never forgave him for this defiance. When the King started to encroach upon the Church John gave a warning that such intrusions would greatly damage the Church. He, together with Nicholas West, Bishop of Ely, incurred the wrath of the King in 1530 when they sent an appeal to Rome against the measures being employed. Henry immediately issued a decree that all appeals to Rome were to be forbidden and John was imprisoned for a few months. He was the only one of the bishops to remain steadfast in opposing the royal supremacy of the Church. After Thomas More had resigned as Chancellor in 1532 John publicly preached against the King's divorce. John was arrested in the same week that Thomas Cranmer was consecrated Archbishop of Canterbury. It seems this may have been a ploy to get him out of the way while Cranmer annulled Henry's marriage to Catherine and performed Anne Boleyn's coronation because shortly afterwards he was released. In March 1534 the affair of the nun Elizabeth Barton presented a good excuse to attack Fisher and he was attainted and sentenced to the forfeiture of all his estate. On 26 April 1534 John was sent to the Tower for refusing the Oath of Succession. Every effort was made to get him to submit but he resolutely refused. In November he was again attainted and deprived of his bishopric. He was held in very severe conditions and all his requests to Thomas Cromwell to be allowed to see a priest were denied. Probably advised by More, John took refuge in silence on the question of the royal supremacy. The ever-ready Richard Rich was called into service to try and entrap John. Rich visited him in the Tower in May 1535 and told him that Henry wished to know in strictest secrecy and confidence what John's true opinion was. Taking Rich at his word Fisher uttered the fatal words that 'the King was not, nor could be, by the Law of God, Supreme head of the Church in England.' Fisher enjoyed widespread esteem throughout Europe and presumably in the hope of helping him Pope Paul III Farnese (1534-49) created John a cardinal, but this only incensed Henry even further. On 17 June, for denying the King's supremacy, John was tried at Westminster Hall on a charge of treason before a specially convened court, including Thomas Cromwell and Anne Boleyn's father. The only prosecution evidence offered was that of Richard Rich. John was sentenced to be hanged, drawn and quartered. There was a public outcry and the King gave way and commuted the sentence to beheading, and conscious of the parallels that might be drawn with the execution of St John the Baptist, Henry ordered the execution to take place before 23 June, the Vigil of the Nativity of John the Baptist. On 22 June 1535, John was martyred by beheading on Tower Hill. As to be expected, he conducted himself with dignity and courage. On Henry's instructions after death John's headless corpse was treated with the greatest disrespect. It was stripped naked and left on the scaffold until evening when it was impaled on pikes and thrown unceremoniously and without any prayers being said into a hole in the churchyard of All-Hallows-by-the-Tower. Two weeks later his body was removed and interred with that of Thomas More in the Tower chapel of St Peter ad Vincula. His head was placed on a pole on London Bridge and later thrown into the River Thames.

12 St Thomas More was born in Milk Street in the City of London on 7 February 1478, the only surviving son of Sir John More, a judge who became Lord Chief Justice of the King's Bench. He was sent to St Anthony's school in Threadneedle Street, where a fellow pupil was John Colet. While a boy he spent some time in the household of John Morton, Cardinal Archbishop of Canterbury and Lord Chancellor. Morton was impressed by More's intellect and predicted a marvellous future for him. At the recommendation of the Cardinal he went to Oxford and studied history, mathematics and French. Here he met another lifelong friend, Thomas Linacre. He also learned to play the flute and viol. Thomas did not take a degree but entered New Inn as a law student, obtaining a place at Lincoln's Inn in 1496. He was called to the Bar in 1501. It was during this period that he took lodgings near the London Charterhouse and while contemplating his religious vocation he took part in the worship at the monastery. It was from this time that he began wearing a hairshirt; a penitential discipline that he secretly kept to the end of his life. Deciding that his vocation lay in the world in 1504 he became a Member of Parliament. Remarking that he would rather be a chaste husband than an incontinent priest, the following year he married 17 year old Jane Colt, daughter of Sir John Colt. Thomas delighted in family life and was a model husband and

father. Jane died in 1511, at the age of twenty-three, leaving four young children. Thomas quickly - and happily - married again to an older widow, Alice Middleton. He was earning a substantial income as a lawyer and from 1510 to 1518 was one of the under-sheriffs of London. Good reports of More reached Cardinal Wolsey who recommended him for the King's service which he entered not without doubt and trepidation. In the next few years he was employed on several diplomatic missions in Europe. He was appointed a Privy Councillor and Master of Requests where he enjoyed a reputation for absolute integrity. Once, at a Council meeting, Thomas's was the only dissenting voice to a proposition of Wolsey's. 'Are you not ashamed, asked the Cardinal, ' to dissent from so many noble and prudent men? You know yourself to be a foolish and stupid councillor!' To which More replied, 'Thanks be to God that the King's Majesty has but one fool on his council.' He soon became the King's trusted advisor, being knighted in 1521. He was appointed Speaker of the House of Commons in 1523 and in 1525 Chancellor of the Duchy of Lancaster. He enjoyed a European-wide reputation as a humanist, wit and man of letters. His most famous work, *Utopia*, was first published in 1516. Despite his public and family duties he remained a man of deep devotion and prayer, but he was not conventionally pious. He was only too well aware of the harm that could be done to the Faith by superstitious nonsense. He once wrote, 'There is scarcely the life of any martyr or virgin in which some falsehood has not been inserted; an act of piety, no doubt, considering the risk that Truth would be insufficient, unless propped up by lies!' He practised great charity, generous in almsgiving to the poor, whom he would personally visit, especially the old and sick. And often he invited poor neighbours to join in family meals. When he built his fine house at Chelsea he also hired a property in which many old and infirm people were cared for at his expense. When Wolsey fell from power in 1529 Thomas was appointed Lord Chancellor; the first layman ever to hold that office. Thomas was greatly loved and respected by all his friends and acquaintances. It was his contemporary, Robert Whittinton, who declared that he knew not his equal, describing him as 'a man for all seasons.' As Chancellor he maintained a dignity befitting his office but remained personally humble. It shocked the Duke of Norfolk that Thomas would don a surplice and serve Mass in his parish church. Norfolk felt that it was demeaning to the King's dignity for his chancellor to behave thus. More answered, 'It cannot be displeasing to my lord the King, that I pay homage to my King's Lord.' When Henry declared himself head of the Church More resigned. He was sent to the Tower for refusing the

Oath of Supremacy. He was willing to swear to the succession to the Crown, that being a matter of civil law, but to the royal supremacy he 'could not swear without the jeopardising of my soul'. It must not be imagined that Thomas found his stand an easy option. On the contrary, it was extremely hard for him. He loved life and enjoyed its pleasures and above all he loved his family. At his trial Thomas asked how, in law, silence could be construed as opposition, and he challenged the prosecution to prove that his silence was in any way malicious as required under the Act. Only when Lord Audley was about to pronounce sentence upon him did Thomas at last give vent to his true feelings telling the court that no temporal prince could be head of the Church. That office belonged to the 'spiritual pre-eminence of the See of Rome' in the person of its bishops as successors of St Peter. No one, small part of the Church, he told them, could make laws in contradiction of Christ's universal Church. Before quitting the court Thomas told his judges that although they had condemned him he heartily prayed that 'we may hereafter in heaven merrily all meet together, to our everlasting salvation.' The day before his execution, writing in coal on scraps of paper for want of better materials, he told his beloved daughter, Margaret Roper, that he longed to go to God and sent her his hairshirt. Thomas was martyred on Tower Hill by beheading 6 July 1535: 'the King's good servant, but God's first'. Europe was aghast at More's execution. Erasmus declared that his 'genius was such that England never had and never again will have its like.' Those two 18th century literary giants, Doctors Samuel Johnson and Jonathan Swift, concurred in the opinion that More was 'the person of the greatest virtue this kingdom ever produced.' The eminent historian Hugh Trevor-Roper wrote that he was 'the most saintly of humanists, the most human of saints.' Thomas was canonized in 1935 and since 2000 he has been named as the patron saint of politicians.

13 **Blessed John Rochester**, a priest, from an ancient family of Terling, Essex. He was the younger brother of Sir Robert Rochester who subsequently became the devoted Comptroller of Queen Mary Tudor's household and a Knight of the Garter. At his death in 1557 Robert left most of his estate to the Carthusian order. John was educated at Cambridge. During the period of oppression in the Charterhouse, John Rochester was summoned to see Archbishop Cranmer but the monk remained immune to his blandishments. His splendid letter defending his beliefs, written in York to the Duke of Norfolk, is extant in the Public Record Office.

The Henrician Martyrs

14 Of these ten members of the community seven starved to death in Newgate between 6 and 16 June 1537. They were: Brother William Greenwood, Deacon John Davy, Brother Robert Salt, Brother Walter Pierson, priest Thomas Green DD, Brother Thomas Scryven and Brother Thomas Reding. Two priests, Richard Bere and Thomas Johnson, were given food and water with the aim of saving them for execution, but this plan was abandoned. Oxford-educated Bere was a nephew of Richard Bere, Abbot of Glastonbury. He became a Carthusian c.1521 and was ordained priest in 1524. Bere survived until 9 August and Johnson until 20 September. Brother William Horne was kept alive only to face execution three years later. All ten have been beatified.

15 Margaret Mercy Clement, née Giggs, 'a gentleman's daughter of Norfolk', was born c.1508 and was the foster-daughter of Thomas More. Her brother, Thomas, was More's godson. Margaret was brought up as part of the More family and appears with them in the famous Holbein painting. In 1526 she married the physician Dr John Clement, also an intimate of the More household. They had four children: a son and three daughters. The family went into voluntary exile under Edward VI, returning on the accession of Queen Mary. They left behind at St Ursula's, Louvain, their daughter, Margaret. Margaret senior died in exile at Mechlin in July 1570. Margaret Clement junior became an Augustinian Canoness and one of the founding English sisters of St Monica's, Louvain. She was elected Prioress of St Ursula's in the same city in 1568 and served in that office for thirty-eight years, going blind in her old age. Among her contemporary English sisters at the convent were many from families mentioned in the book: Margaret and Eleanor Garnet, sisters of Father Henry Garnet SJ; Helen and Catherine Allen, nieces of Cardinal Allen; Mary and Bridget Wiseman; Anne Clitherow and Frances Burrows, q.v. niece and adopted granddaughter of Lord Vaux.

16 Giles Heron was a teenager when his father died and his wardship was granted to Sir Thomas More. In 1525 he married More's daughter, Cecily. When Sir Thomas was Chancellor, ever the honest judge, he gave judgment against his son-in-law in a chancery case. It must have been due to More's patronage that in 1529 Heron secured election as Member of Parliament for Thetford. At the same time one of More's other sons-in-law, William Dauntsey - married to Elizabeth More - was also elected to the Commons. Thomas Cromwell identified the pair of them, along with a third son-in-law, William Roper, as being members

opposed to the Statute in Restraint of Appeals in 1533. This was the key measure that forbade appeals to Rome. Heron's downfall seems to have arisen from a dispute he had with a tenant, one Lyons, whom he had expelled from his farm. In 1539, seeking revenge, Lyons informed Cromwell that Heron had spoken certain treasonable words. What exactly these were is a matter for conjecture, but Heron, as a member of More's family, was sympathetic to his ideals and it is quite likely that he had expressed his opposition to the royal supremacy, *ipso facto* high treason. He was sent to the Tower but as it was unlikely Cromwell could secure a conviction on the strength of the evidence he was never brought to trial. Instead, Cromwell had a bill of attainder passed against him in the Lords in May 1540. Heron's schoolboy sons, Thomas and John, appealed on behalf of their father but it had no effect. It might have been expected that Cromwell's own execution in July 1540 could have saved Heron, but it was not to be, and he was executed in August. Lyon's malice was then turned on Heron's three brothers who he accused of being implicit in his treason. Luckily the accusations against them were dismissed as groundless. In 1554 Queen Mary restored to Giles's elder son, Thomas, part of his father's forfeited lands. The whole story is a stark illustration of the arbitrary application of Tudor "justice". Along with other members of Thomas More's family, William Dauntsey had been imprisoned at the time of his father-in-law's execution in 1535 but escaped with his life. At one time, whether in jest or in complaint, he chided Sir Thomas that his chancellorship had not brought much benefit to his family and friends. Dauntsey remained a Catholic and this cost him dearly, alienating his father who cut him out of his will and left his property instead to his illegitimate son.

[17] These three friars were Anthony Brookby DD, Thomas Belchiam and Thomas Covert. Belchiam, a young priest, had written a book denouncing the King as a heretic and rebuking the bishops for their cowardice. Covert had preached a sermon against the King in St Lawrence's church, London. Covert and Belchiam both died of starvation in Newgate in 1537: Covert on 27 July and Belchiam on 3 August. Anthony Brookby was a distinguished scholar; a lecturer in divinity at Magdalen College, Oxford. Well versed in Greek and Hebrew, he had a reputation as an eloquent preacher. Henry VIII was incensed by a sermon of Brookby's attacking his actions and the friar was arrested. For twenty-five days he was not allowed to lie down nor have any water to wash himself. He was tortured most cruelly on the rack so that he 'could not turn in his bed or lift his hand to his mouth.'

The Henrician Martyrs

A fortnight later, by command of the King, during the night of 19 July 1537, Anthony was strangled to death with his own Franciscan cord. He was buried privately in St Sepulchre's church and a kind woman named Margaret Herbert placed a stone over his grave.

18 Blessed John Forest was born c.1471, probably at Oxford, of which university he was a theology graduate. When he was twenty he joined the Observant Franciscan Order at Greenwich Friary. He became one of Queen Catherine's chaplains and was appointed her confessor. Along with his brethren, he was a strong supporter of Queen Catherine and opposed the divorce. The friars incurred the wrath of the King in 1531 because of their outspoken opposition. In 1533 John had to leave London as it was no longer considered safe, the King being so furious with him. He was imprisoned in 1534 at Newgate, where he wrote a treatise against Henry and his policies. He was released from prison and incarcerated in the ancient Greyfriars Monastery in Newgate Street, London. In April 1538, probably coinciding with the suppression of Greyfriars, he was called before Archbishop Cranmer at Lambeth to make an act of abjuration of his views and to accept the royal supremacy. This he refused to do and was re-arrested and sent back to Newgate Prison. He was condemned to death and was taken to Smithfield for execution on 22 May. After its suppression Greyfriars and its magnificent Christ Church, was used as a store for war spoils captured from the French, while other parts of the monastery were turned into private houses. The King's Printer set up his presses in the nave. In 1547 all the tombs were destroyed, including the many royal tombs, and the marble, alabaster and brass from them was sold.

19 Blessed Adrian Fortescue, the son of Sir John Fortescue was born at Punsbourne Park, Hertfordshire, c.1476. His mother was Alice Boleyn, the aunt of Queen Anne Boleyn. Adrian married Anne Stonor in 1499 and had seven children. He was made a Knight of the Bath in 1503 and served with Henry VIII in the wars in France in 1513. He was present at the legendary Field of the Cloth of Gold in 1520 and again served in France in 1523. He was close to Queen Catherine. Now a widower, he married secondly Anne Rede in 1530. He attended the coronation of his cousin Anne in 1533. He was a devout man, a Dominican tertiary, who led the quiet life of a country landowner and became a Knight of the Hospitaller Order of St John of Jerusalem. This led to his fall from royal favour. As part of his destruction of the religious houses the King had seized all the property of the Order and Adrian was summoned to take the Oath of Succession. Presumably he refused because in August

The Henrician Martyrs

1534 he was imprisoned in the Marshalsea where he remained for several months and was then released. On 14 February 1539 he was arrested and sent to the Tower and an inventory of his property was drawn up. His estates and possessions were then confiscated by the King. Along with sixteen others, at the behest of Thomas Cromwell, Adrian was attainted by Parliament for high treason for refusing to recognise Henry as head of the Church. He was beheaded on Tower Hill on 9 July. By then the Order of St John of Jerusalem had been wiped out in England. Adrian's Book of Hours, which contains his handwritten pious maxims and proverbs, survived with his descendants and is now in the possession of the Grand Priory of England. The Sovereign Military Order of Malta greatly venerates Adrian Fortescue and there is a painting of him in their college at Valletta.

[20] **Blessed Thomas Abel DD** was born c.1497. A secular priest, he was chaplain to Queen Catherine, to whom he also taught modern languages and music. In 1532 he published a defence of the Queen's marriage and was sent to the Tower, where he spent a year. In December 1533 he was again imprisoned for encouraging the Queen 'obstinately to persist in her wilful opinion against the divorce,' and for listening to the prophecies of Elizabeth Barton. He was kept a close prisoner and a letter of his to Cromwell has survived in which he begs for some mitigation of his situation; 'license to go to church and say Mass here within the Tower.' He was never tried, but his act of attainder states that he and others had 'most traitorously adhered themselves unto the bishop of Rome.' In the Beauchamp Tower may be seen a rebus he carved on the wall. It shows the picture of a bell with the letter A in front and his name, Thomas, above.

Blessed Edward Powell DD was born in Wales c.1478. He was an MA and fellow of Oriel College, Oxford; headmaster of Eton; vicar of St Mary Redcliffe, Bristol and prebendary of Salisbury, among others. He was a court preacher to the King and was asked by Henry to publish a reply to Luther in 1523. Oxford University strongly commended his work and described Edward as 'the glory of the University.' Powell was one of the theologians chosen to defend the legality of Queen Catherine's marriage. In March 1533, Edward was selected to answer Hugh Latimer at Bristol and in the course of the debate was alleged to have disparaged Latimer's moral character. Latimer complained about it to Cromwell. When Powell denounced Henry's marriage to Anne Boleyn he incurred the wrath of the King. He was deprived of his benefices and attainted for high treason.

Blessed Richard Fetherston DD, a secular priest, was educated at

The Henrician Martyrs

Cambridge. He was a chaplain to Queen Catherine and tutor to Princess Mary, as well as being archdeacon of Brecknock. He took part in the Convocation of April 1529, when he was one of the members who refused to sign the Act declaring Henry's marriage to Catherine illegal. In 1534 he refused to take the Oath of Supremacy and was committed to the Tower on 13 December. There he remained until, attainted with Abel and Powell, he was hanged, drawn and quartered at Smithfield 30 July 1540. With the three priests were also executed three Zwinglian's who were burned for heresy. The six condemned were drawn through the streets on hurdles; a Catholic and a heretic to each hurdle. The priests' heads were fixed on poles on London Bridge, their quarters hung about the city.

21 Blessed Margaret Pole, 8th Countess of Salisbury in her own right, was born in 1473. She was the last of the direct Plantagenets, being the daughter of George, Duke of Clarence, and the niece of Edward IV and Richard III. She married Sir Richard Pole and had five children: four sons and one daughter. Her brother, Edward, Earl of Warwick, who had long been a prisoner in the Tower, was executed in 1499. Margaret was widowed in 1505. She became a lady-in-waiting to Catherine of Aragon and was appointed godmother and governess to Princess Mary. After Henry's marriage to Anne Boleyn and her protests about declaring Mary illegitimate she was forced to retire from Court. The Princess, who considered Margaret her 'second mother', felt the separation keenly. In 1536 when her son Reginald published his *Defence of Church Unity* opposing the royal supremacy Margaret had written to reprove him for his 'folly'. This, however, did not reflect her true views as she had written to satisfy the Council, which read and dispatched the letter. One of Margaret's granddaughters was a Bridgettine nun at Syon. In 1538, along with the rest of her family, Margaret was arrested and sent to the Tower. In 1539 her eldest son, Henry, Lord Montague, was executed. Even if his nearness to the throne had not been judged sufficient excuse to kill him his opposition to Henry's religious policies would have been enough to seal his fate. He made known how 'deeply grieved' he was at the suppression of the monasteries and the severing of ties with the papacy. Partly in belated revenge for her son Reginald's opposition, Margaret was attainted for treason. Under the sweeping Bill of Attainder, Cromwell produced as 'evidence' a white silk tunic embroidered with the Five Wounds of Christ, which had been used as a symbol in the 'Pilgrimage of Grace'. He claimed it had been found in her house, which was probably a lie. Margaret was never brought to trial but remained a prisoner, short of clothing and other necessities.

The Henrician Martyrs

On the morning of 27 May 1541, aged 68, Margaret was given one hour's notice that she was to die. Protesting that no crime had ever been imputed to her she was taken to a place in the precincts of the Tower where a group of about one hundred had assembled to witness her execution. There was no scaffold, only a low wooden block. She specially commended Princess Mary, her god-daughter, to the prayers of the onlookers. Refusing to lay her head on the block she was forced down. The executioner, a clumsy novice, hideously hacked her neck and shoulders and had to use several more blows before her head was severed. She was buried in the chapel of St Peter ad Vincula within the Tower. Initiated by his father, the avaricious usurper Henry VII, it was Tudor policy to ruthlessly, systematically eliminate every rival for the throne, especially the heirs of the legitimate House of York. With Margaret Henry VIII successfully disposed of the last of them.

22 Blessed David Gunston, or Gonson, came from a naval family. William, his father, was Vice-Admiral of Norfolk and Suffolk and subsequently Paymaster of the Royal Navy. David joined the Order of Malta in 1533 and served on ships of the Order in the Mediterranean until October 1540 when he returned to England. He was imprisoned in the Tower for the treason of 'persistently' denying the King's supremacy.

23 Robert Singleton came from Lancashire and studied at Oxford. He was arrested on a trumped-up charge of speaking treasonable words. Blessed John Larke, a secular priest, was rector of St Ethelburga's, Bishopsgate, London, for twenty-six years. From March 1530 he was rector of Chelsea, Thomas More's parish church, and became a close friend of More. On 15 February 1544 he was indicted with Blessed John Ireland, and two laymen. Ireland, a secular priest, was chaplain to the Roper Chantry, St Dunstan's, Canterbury, before becoming vicar of Eltham, the parish of William Roper, More's son-in-law. The first of the laymen, Blessed German Gardiner, was educated at Cambridge. He lived at Southwark and was secretary to his uncle Stephen Gardiner, Bishop of Winchester. He was executed for depriving 'the King of his dignity, title and name of Supreme Head' of the Church. Cranmer played a direct part in his condemnation. The second layman was John Heywood of London. The five were condemned, but while on the hurdle Heywood recanted, and later made his recantation public at Paul's Cross. The remaining four were hanged, drawn and quartered at Tyburn 7 March 1544.

Chapter Two

Edward VI and Mary Tudor

By education most have been misled; so they believe, because they were so bred.
The Hind and the Panther, John Dryden, 1631-1700

On 28 January 1547 a delicate, sickly nine-year-old boy not only became King but also Supreme Head of the Church of England, which was now a hereditary office along with the Crown. The obstinate, bookish Edward shared the Lutheran beliefs of those who were now his masters, most notably the Lord Protector, his uncle Edward Seymour, Duke of Somerset 1 and the Regent, John Dudley, later Duke of Northumberland. 2 Together with Archbishop Cranmer they immediately set about turning England into a Protestant nation on the model of the Continental Reformation, knowing full well that their power base hinged upon their success in achieving this aim. Doctrines and practices were introduced for which adherents would have been burned by Cranmer as heretics in the previous reign.

Protestantism on any scale was still mainly confined to London and other larger towns and cities in the south of England. In rural areas the people carried on as before attending Mass in their parish churches until new doctrines and liturgical innovations were forced on them by legislation. As history demonstrates, revolutions are always made by minorities: this one was no exception. Royal commissioners were sent around the country with the task of removing every vestige of Catholic piety. Remaining shrines, chapels and chantries were destroyed and then came the despoiling of the parish churches. Their altars, denoting sacrifice, were dismantled and replaced with communion tables, as at St Paul's Cathedral. Sacred vessels and vestments were sold off for the personal profit of the ruling elite. Wall paintings were whitewashed over, stained glass windows were smashed and crucifixes were thrown out. Church feasts such as Palm Sunday were abolished.

Disturbances broke out in the disaffected West Country, protesting about the changes in worship and the abolition of holy water, rosaries, votive candles, making the sign of the Cross and prayers for the departed. The people of Devon and Cornwall were in ferment that led to bloodshed in a number of places. In April 1548, while destroying the statues in the parish church at Helston, William Body, Archdeacon of Cornwall and royal commissioner, had been attacked and killed by an

Edward VI and Mary Tudor

angry crowd of townspeople. Retribution was swift, and dozens of Cornishmen who resisted the sacrilegious depredations of the commissioners were executed in various locations, including Father Martin Geoffrey, the parish priest of St Keverne, who was hanged, drawn and quartered at Smithfield, London, on 7 June, his severed head being displayed on London Bridge.

The progress of the Reformation in England was by no means inevitable or inexorable. It had largely come about piecemeal, each step dictated by the current political or personal interests of the monarch and his advisers. It started with the rejection of the papacy; followed by the subjection of the clergy to the royal will; the destruction of the religious houses; the denial of Purgatory and prayers for the dead and the consequent abolition of chantries. Although his father had paved the way, the deliberate attempt at a Protestant Reformation began under Edward VI. It was an entirely destructive process. Slowly but surely, more aspects of Protestantism were introduced. In 1549 clerical marriage was officially legalised. The numbers of clergy who took advantage of this proviso varied enormously according to location. As might be expected London saw the greatest take-up, whereas in Lancashire less than one in twenty of the parish clergy married and the county continued to show hostility towards married ministers to the end of the boy King's reign. There was also a great shortage of clergy as new ordinands were not forthcoming. All these changes culminated in the complete abolition of the traditional Catholic liturgy. Even the possession of Catholic service books was a crime punishable by imprisonment.

The 1549 Act of Uniformity which came into effect on Whit Sunday abolished the Mass and substituted a Protestant communion service in English in accordance with the first *Book of Common Prayer*. This provoked serious disturbances in various locations. There were risings in East Yorkshire, Warwickshire, Oxfordshire and elsewhere demanding the restoration of the Mass. William Grey, 13th Baron Grey de Wilton, in command of his mercenary force was charged with suppressing the Oxfordshire rebellion; which he did with great brutality. At least a dozen of the rebels were executed at Oxford and other locations in the county, including four priests.

In Devon and Cornwall, with support from Somerset and Dorset, many parishes refused to allow their priests to read the new service, which they derided as 'a Christmas game', and magistrates were sent out to enforce the changes. The West Country disturbances, referred to as the Prayer Book Rebellion, became a widespread revolt, attracting the support of thousands of ordinary citizens on the march.

Edward VI and Mary Tudor

As explained by Philip Caraman SJ in *The Western Rising 1549* (1994), the rebels demanded that the Latin Mass be restored, with prayers for the souls in Purgatory; that the Blessed Sacrament should once more be reserved in a pyx over the high altar, there 'to be worshipped'; that palms and ashes and saints' statues be reinstated along with 'all other ancient ceremonies used heretofore by our holy mother Church'. They also asked that abbeys be restored in those places where once major religious houses had stood. To quote Dr Samuel Gardiner again, 'The reformers had gone much further than the mass of the people were prepared to follow'. The underlying cause of the opposition of country and clergy, as exemplified by the Devonshire peasants, was the proof which the Prayer Book seemed to give that all the changes of the last few years were likely to end in a permanent cleavage between the past and the present; the traditional and familiar was to give way to something strange, foreign, imposed. And Bishop Gilbert Burnet acknowledges that 'the bulk of the people of England could not be depended upon' because they clung to the faith of their fathers, or 'the old superstition', as Burnet describes it.

With the banner of the Five Wounds of Christ carried before them [as in the 1536 'Pilgrimage of Grace'] and the Blessed Sacrament borne under a rich canopy, thousands of rebel farmers and labourers of Devon and Cornwall, naïvely pitting themselves against the whole might of the Tudor state, marched on Exeter, singing hymns as they advanced.

Sir Peter Carew, Sheriff of Devonshire, was instructed by the Council to use all ways and means of appeasing the rebellion. Carew, whose brother had been the captain of the *Mary Rose*, had a reputation for ruthlessness. Exeter was soon besieged by the rebels. The Bishop, John Vesey, and his cathedral clergy, although opposed to the religious changes, were not going to support armed rebellion and the gates of the city were closed to the insurgents. (Bishop Vesey was deprived of his see in 1551. He was restored under Queen Mary.) Their numbers swollen to many thousands, the rebels surrounded Exeter, which would not be able to hold out for long because of food shortages. The government of Lord Protector Somerset was in a panic, believing that the rebels might next march on London. The Council even reproached Princess Mary with encouraging the rebellion by continuing to have Mass celebrated in her household. Somerset now appointed Lord John Russell to suppress the rebellion, but he seemed to be taking his time in relieving Exeter.

By now thoroughly alarmed, the government mobilised an army of mostly German and other foreign mercenaries under Russell's command and by August the uprising was swiftly and mercilessly quashed, with heavy loss of life. The decisive confrontation took place at Clyst St Mary, near Exeter. About one thousand of the rebels were killed; others drowned while trying to escape and Russell ordered that every house in the village should be burned. Nine hundred rebels were taken captive at Clyst St Mary. Lord Grey de Wilton, sent from Oxfordshire to join forces with Russell, gave orders that they should all be killed, so this group of defenceless, bound, captured prisoners had their throats cut in little more than ten minutes.

Devon-born James Anthony Froude was a polemical and controversial, rather than a scientific historian, indeed he was deplorably careless about accuracy in many instances. Although he was a propagandist for the religious changes under the Tudor's, in his *History of England* (1856) he had the following to say of the 1549 rebellion. 'Never before had English rulers used the arms of strangers against English subjects ... The half-armed Devonshire peasants were poorly matched against trained and disciplined troops. Few who went up the hill came back again; they fell in the summer gloaming, like stout-hearted, valiant men, for their hearths and altars; and Miles Coverdale, translator of the Bible, and future Bishop of Exeter, preached a thanksgiving sermon among their bodies as they lay with stiffening limbs, their faces to the stars.' (It is satisfying to note that Coverdale was deeply unpopular in his diocese and when he was deprived under Queen Mary there was general rejoicing.)

Archbishop Cranmer was furious that his Prayer Book had been spurned. Determined to exact the last ounce of revenge on those who had dared to rebel he issued orders that everyone involved should be hunted down. The gentry, along with many of the rebels, were sent to London for execution. The bloodshed continued, with many public executions, at Tyburn and in Devon and Cornwall, of those who had been involved, including at least nine priests. At Exeter the greatly respected parish priest of St Thomas's church was hanged in chains from the church tower while in his vestments and with 'popish trash', such as a sacring bell and rosary, attached to him. His name was Robert Welsh. Froude comments, 'And there he hung, till the clothes rotted away, and the carrion crows had pecked him into a skeleton - and down below in St Thomas's ... a new vicar read the English liturgy.'

As an answer to the religious demands of the West Country rebels, Cranmer published a vitriolic pamphlet on behalf of the Council, contemptuously referring to the 'superstitions' of those 'ignorant men of Devon and Cornwall'. Lord Russell was amply rewarded: he was created Earl of Bedford for his services in promoting the new religion. He received enormous property in London and was granted the former

Edward VI and Mary Tudor

Cistercian abbey at Woburn, Bedfordshire.

The Protestants were divided into many opposing sects, all hating each other's guts. Cranmer, who had sent Zwinglians to be burned at Smithfield under Henry VIII for denying the doctrine of the Real Presence in the Eucharist, in a volte-face now decided that this teaching was not scriptural. But this freedom of opinion was not extended to others whom he condemned to be burned at the stake at Smithfield, such as the Anabaptist Joan Bocher in May 1550. Convicted as a heretic in 1549 she refused to recant. John Foxe - he of the *Book of Martyrs* fame - asked the royal chaplain, John Rogers, to intervene to save Joan but Rogers refused on the grounds that burning was a 'mild' punishment for grave heresy. (Rogers himself was burned in 1555 under Queen Mary.) Another victim was the naturalised English, Dutch-born Arian, George van Parris, burned in 1551. His judges were Cranmer, Nicholas Ridley and Miles Coverdale. It seems the only factor the warring Protestant sects had in common was their even more virulent hatred of the Catholic Church. But the zealous Protestants said the newly imposed services were too Catholic, while the Catholics did not believe them to be Catholic in any way, shape or form.

The Church of England under Edward was nothing to boast about, as its own clerics complained. It did nothing to raise the morality of the people. Bishop Latimer, preaching before the King declared that, 'never was there so much adultery ... lechery is now a trifle'. And he bemoaned the fact that the dioceses were notorious for 'unparalleled immorality'. Archbishop Robert Holgate, the first Protestant Archbishop of York (1545-1554), and a former President of the Council of the North, wrote that, 'Adultery, fornication and even incest' seemed to be common among the cathedral clergy.'

What of the Catholics during this period? Apart from the Prayer Book Rebellion at least those who voiced their objections to all the Protestantising were spared execution; but many, including the more conservative bishops, were deprived of their sees and replaced by Protestants under Letters Patent from the King. Others were imprisoned without trial, some for the entire duration of Edward's reign. To replace the Catholic rite with a ceremony more compatible with Protestantism a new Ordinal was introduced in 1550. In 1552 the *Second Book of Common Prayer* was issued by the authority of Parliament; a most significant and revolutionary innovation, as hitherto religious doctrine had been considered the province of the Church. The Real Presence in the Eucharist was explicitly denied as 'idolatry'. Cranmer then produced the *Forty-two Articles of Religion,* in which only two Sacraments were acknowledged. Following the advent of the 1552

Edward VI and Mary Tudor

Book of Common Prayer, the King's Commissioners required the surrender of all the remaining 'Church ornaments of the Catholic times' and there are detailed inventories of what was handed over. One example will serve to illustrate all the rest, that of St Mary Magdalene parish, Bermondsey, London. The list is long, beginning with three gilt chalices and two communion cups, whose weight is specified. It continues with five silk or damask copes and fourteen vestments, whose colours and materials are described. Then come lists of surplices, altar cloths, altar curtains, hearse cloths, pyxes, candlesticks, cruets, the organs and sacring bells. And the inventory concludes with the liturgical books and a large Bible. If this inventory is multiplied thousands of times it will give some idea of the immense volume of plunder that was taken from the parish churches nationwide.

Dying, probably of tuberculosis, in 1553 Edward was persuaded by the Regent Northumberland to remove his half-sisters, Mary and Elizabeth, from the succession. He willed the crown to Northumberland's daughter-in-law, Lady Jane Grey, 3 the granddaughter of Henry VIII's sister, Mary. The fact that Jane's mother was still alive and thereby had a better claim to the throne was immaterial.

Edward died at Greenwich Palace on 6 July 1553. To gain the political advantage, Northumberland did not make the King's death public until two days later, when he declared sixteen-year-old Jane Grey queen. Poor Jane! Forced into marriage with Northumberland's son when it was clear that Edward was dying, she was the victim of a plot to usurp the throne. The only leading Anglican prelates who supported her were Cranmer and Nicholas Ridley, the Bishop of London. Lacking any real support her 'reign' lasted just nine days. She subsequently paid for it with her life. London and the south-east, the fleet - even many of the Protestant zealots - rallied to Princess Mary, the lawful heir, and she was proclaimed Queen amid a spontaneous outburst of tremendous rejoicing.

Mary Tudor and the Reunion with Rome

And there are some, of whom there is no memorial.

Sirach/Ecclesiasticus Chapter 44:9

Few sovereigns can ever have come to the throne on such a tide of popular support as Mary Tudor (1516-58), the first Queen Regnant of England. The citizens of London poured into the streets, singing and dancing, bonfires were lit and the church bells rang incessantly, all day

Edward VI and Mary Tudor

and all night, at her accession in July. Yet over the next five years she alienated most of that goodwill, not least by her ill-advised marriage to King Philip II of Spain. Mary believed it was her divinely given destiny to restore Catholicism. In a hurry to achieve this goal, she tragically misunderstood the public mood, especially in London, and was only too willing to listen to the misguided counsel of some of the more embittered Catholic prelates who had suffered so much at Protestant hands. In many places, especially in the North, there was no lack of enthusiasm for the restoration of Catholic worship, and the church furnishings that had been secreted away quickly reappeared. There was also an impressive resurgence in vocations from men once again attracted to the traditional priesthood. Care was taken by Mary and Archbishop Reginald Pole to appoint only well-qualified men to benefices and bishoprics. Almost all of the twenty new bishops were university graduates in theology; very much in the new Counter-Reformation spirit that Pole was promoting. The new regime faced enormous problems, not least refurbishing the dilapidated and devastated cathedrals and parish churches. The dioceses were in a sorry financial state. The official restoration of Catholicism was begun with moderation and no penalties were imposed for non-attendance at Mass. With the approval of Pope Julius III del Monte (1550-55), assurances were given that those who were in possession of Church property would be able to retain it. If only this spirit of conciliation had been maintained for longer the outcome may have been very different.

At first Mary had to accept the anti-Catholic legislation until Parliament should see fit to repeal it, and she had to proceed with caution, resisting pressure from Rome that she should restore communion with the Holy See without delay. At the outset of her reign she declared that while conscientious Protestants would not be compelled to go to Mass, Catholics must not be denied that opportunity; nor was it her desire to punish 'ignorant people who had been misled'. Mary restored the monastic lands and buildings in the possession of the Crown, including Westminster Abbey, which was re-occupied when John Feckenham was installed as abbot, with fourteen monks. It was the only major abbey to be restored: Mary's example was not followed by any of the nobles. The Abbey church was in a shocking state with its whitewashed walls, denuded of all its beauty. The body of St Edward the Confessor was retrieved and replaced in the broken shrine. In tears, Mary gave her jewels to cover the cost of its repair.

Parliament was usually ready to do the Crown's bidding, as long as its members were not materially disadvantaged. Parliament was now packed with the *nouveaux riches* beneficiaries of the plunder of the

Reformation. To quote Professor William Paul McClure Kennedy in his *Studies in Tudor History* (1916),

The new Parliament ... would do nothing for the Pope or Pole until the secular question of property was settled to their advantage ... Mary found it [Parliament] quite tractable as soon as it became known that the wealth diverted from the Church would not be restored, and that its holders would be confirmed in their possession of it. All this was arranged ... before Pole left Brussels for England. His attainder was hurriedly repealed, and he was received by Parliament with such an expression of joy as relief from the fear of personal loss can produce.

On 30 November 1554 Parliament repealed the Act of Supremacy and formally agreed to restore links with the papacy. Cardinal Reginald Pole, 4 son of the martyred Countess of Salisbury, and Mary's cousin, absolved the nation from schism, and re-union was accomplished. To quote W P M Kennedy again, 'Lords and Commons were quite ready to accept an absolution which did not hurt their pockets in this world, whatever effect it may have had on the next.'

Dom Maurice Chauncy, the chronicler of the martyrdom of his brother monks, had fled overseas and joined the Carthusians of Sheen at Bruges. As the old Charterhouse at Sheen had reverted to the Queen, she invited the Carthusians to return. In November 1556 a group of nineteen monks belonging to various houses re-occupied the derelict monastery and Chauncy was elected prior. It was to be a short-lived restoration, for Chauncy and his monks were again in exile at Bruges by 1559. There they lived with their Flemish brothers until 1569, when they obtained a house of their own with Chauncy still their prior. He died at the old Charterhouse in Bruges in July 1581. The English Carthusian community of Sheen survived abroad until the late eighteenth century.

Parliament repealed all the anti-Catholic legislation dating back to 1529 and also unanimously passed an Act restoring punishments for heretics. This paved the way for the burning of heretics to begin. The burnings commenced in 1555 and continued for the next four years, earning Mary the soubriquet by which she is known to history: 'Bloody Mary'. The death penalty for heretics flies in the face of the teaching of the Doctors and Fathers of the Church. Although St Isidore of Seville (c.560-636) believed that the State had a duty to help the Church suppress heresy, that stopped far short of execution. St Athanasius the Great (c.296-373) said 'fire and sword are not proper instruments wherewith to convince men' and 'it is the business of religion not to compel but to persuade.' St John Chrysostom said that 'To put a heretic to death is an unpardonable crime' and 'God forbids us to put them to

Edward VI and Mary Tudor

death ... but he does not forbid us doing all in our power to prevent ... their preaching false doctrine.' Pope St Leo the Great (d.461) said 'The Church, in the spirit of Christ, ought to denounce heretics, but should never put them to death.'

Notwithstanding this teaching the burning of heretics was very much in keeping with the spirit of the time. Catholicism was so deeply ingrained in European society that states had made heresy a civil crime because heretics were regarded as moral outcasts who threatened the very fabric of that society. It must not be thought that the feelings of horror the burnings arouse in us would necessarily have had the same effect on our sixteenth-century forebears. Every year thousands were publicly executed for all sorts of offences and people were largely inured to it. (Poisoners were executed by being boiled alive in a cauldron at Smithfield!) Catholic and Protestant alike accepted that burning was the punishment prescribed for heresy. The fact is that many of the Protestant victims were quite happy to see their fellow Protestants with whom they disagreed burned. In the reign of Mary's father, heretics had been burned by the score almost as a matter of routine. Few questioned that it was the legitimate and appropriate application of the law of the land. Even under Northumberland's Protectorship, extreme Protestants had been burned and later Elizabeth I had few qualms about burning Anabaptists, Arians and other dissenters, such as Matthew Hammond 1578, John Lewis 1583 and Francis Kett, who was burned in the ditch of Norwich Castle in January 1589. They were still burning Arian heretics at Smithfield by order of Archbishop George Abbot under James I. (In parenthesis, it may be of interest to note that in England's 'green and pleasant land' they were still burning women criminals outside Newgate until 1790, when the law was changed.) So why was there such a different reaction during Mary's reign? And why has such a different historical judgement been made about Mary, as distinct from her bloodthirsty father and her half-sister?

To answer the first question, it was not so much that the heretics were being burned before a public accustomed to violence and executions, rather it was the *scale* of the burnings that was of significance.

The chief source for the Marian persecution is John Foxe (1517-87), the first edition of whose *Acts and Monuments*, more popularly known as the *Book of Martyrs*, was published in 1563. As it contains much invention masquerading as history, it is unreliable. It has been described as 'the most extraordinary compilation of falsehoods ever offered to the public under the guise of history.' Because of its many errors of fact its veracity was immediately challenged by, among others, Father Robert Persons, who subjected the book to detailed criticism. The book has continued to be subject to scepticism ever since. No less an authority than the *Encyclopaedia Britannica* (1911) accused Foxe of 'wilful falsification of evidence'. Another source that did not hold the book in much esteem was the Protestant Professor J S Brewer MA, who in his *Letters and Papers, Foreign and Domestic, of the reign of Henry 8th*, Vol. I published in 1862 wrote:

Had Foxe, the martyrologist, been an honest man, his carelessness and credulity would have incapacitated him from being a trustworthy historian. Unfortunately he was not honest; he tampered with the documents that came into his hands, and freely indulged in those very faults of suppression and equivocation for which he condemned his opponents.

Dr Richard Frederick Littledale (1833-90) was a famous Anglican clergyman and controversialist. In 1868 he wrote:

Two mendacious partisans, the infamous Foxe and the not much more respected [Bishop Gilbert] Burnet, have so overlaid all the history of the Reformation with falsehood …

Whilst all these charges may be true, it is only fair to add that contemporary Catholic historians, such as Professor Eamon Duffy, have tended to somewhat redress the balance about Foxe with regard to his general overview of the Marian persecution. There were 282 burnings over a short period of time. 113 of them were in the diocese of London, embracing Middlesex, Essex and Kent, and 69 in other dioceses. Some areas, for example, Lancashire, saw no burnings. This may be attributed to two factors a) that militant Protestants were thinner on the ground in those areas and b) the episcopal oversight in pursuing alleged heretics was more lenient. That is certainly true of York and Durham whose bishops, Nicholas Heath and Cuthbert Tunstall, strongly disliked persecution. On the other hand London had the formidable Edmund Bonner, and Canterbury Cardinal Reginald Pole, both of whom were assiduous in dealing with those reported to them as heretics. Surprisingly, Foxe treats Pole rather kindly in that he emphasises the number of times he pardoned heretics, which is true, but the fact is that, once launched, Pole was committed to the policy of persecution. On the other hand for 'Bloody Bonner', as Foxe calls him, he had only hatred. Needless to say, Foxe, as usual, greatly exaggerated and falsified the facts when it suited his purposes to vilify Bonner. Even then he concedes that the notoriously hot-tempered and diligent Bishop of London often went to extraordinary lengths of patience and perseverance in seeking to persuade Protestants to be reconciled. James Gairdner pointed out in his article in the *Dictionary of National Biography* (1886) that Bonner had no control over the ultimate fate of those charged once they were declared to be irreclaimable heretics and handed over to the secular power. This is surely a casuistical argument. While it is perfectly true that legally it was the State and not the Church that was directly responsible for the fate of heretics, the bishop was well aware of what that fate would be once he had condemned them for obdurate heresy. Furthermore, even though he was acting strictly in accordance with royal instructions, the bishop supported the persecution policy, which he declared arose from Christian love, charity requiring that those in error had to be corrected. Of the 113 condemned heretics in the London diocese Bonner personally pronounced excommunication against 89 of them, paving the way for them to be handed over to the secular authorities for their horrendous punishment. The condemned were placed on a raised wooden platform and fastened to a stake by a chain. Bundles of faggots were piled high around them and set alight. Death often came quickly. Frequently the victim was rendered insensible before the burning commenced but sometimes the condemned endured appalling suffering.

Among those burned in 1556 were bishops Thomas Cranmer, Hugh Latimer and Nicholas Ridley, who in their ascendancy had been happy to approve of the burning of heretics, and who now met a similar fate themselves. There is little contemporary evidence that their execution had any notable impact on the general populace. (The famous noble words attributed to Latimer, about lighting a candle that would never be put out in England, are, in fact, apocryphal; yet another, much later invention of John Foxe - never a man to let the truth get in the way of a good story.) It was the fact that the majority of the condemned were ordinary, good-living, artisan citizens such as weavers and tanners, most of who went to their terrible deaths with great courage, which caused revulsion. As a result, those who were burned became martyrs in the eyes of their neighbours. Towards the end of the reign, Mary ordered that only the most extreme, pertinacious heretics should suffer, but this had little impact on public opinion in London and the southeast. The burnings inevitably became firmly associated in the minds of many people as the consequence of the reunion with Rome. What is more, the policy was a failure. As any study of history clearly demonstrates, all violence in the cause of religion is futile. Many Protestants, like so many of their fellow citizens, were confused waverers, not knowing what to think any more after all the changes.

Edward VI and Mary Tudor

Most did not take much persuading that doctrines promoted under Edward were erroneous, and with varying degrees of sincerity they recanted and attended Mass. So instead of curing the ills of heresy, which Mary abhorred, the persecution served only to strengthen the resolve of the hard core of Protestants.

The answer to the second of the questions posed earlier can be summed up in one word: prejudice. As the adage has it, the winners write history; and as the winners were the Protestants it was they who determined the perceptions of future generations, perceptions so deeply inculcated that today they still largely hold popular sway, to such an extent that, perversely, even when the truth is presented, people don't want to hear or believe it because it upsets their ingrained, preconceived beliefs too much. Myths are constructed by the victors whose version of history prevails, but as Sir Francis Bacon wrote in his *Novum Organum* (1620) 'Truth is, rightly named, the daughter of time, not of authority.' A classic example is that following the loss of Calais - in reality an economic drain of limited national value, except to pride - Mary is claimed to have said that after her death Calais would be found written in her heart: a canard for which there is no historical authenticity whatsoever. Principally due to the enormous influence of Foxe's book every schoolboy knew about 'bloody' Mary Tudor the persecutor, and all suggestions that her 'tolerant' sister was an even worse oppressor who executed hundreds of Catholics were laughed at scornfully. These stereotypes passed into the national consciousness, even though the 'Good Queen Bess' presiding over an 'Elizabethan golden age' of school history books was a myth. As someone once perceptively observed, people don't believe lies because they have to, but because they want to.

Dr Charles Cox, a late nineteenth-century Anglican clergyman and historian wrote in his *Three Centuries of Derbyshire Annals* (1890):

> A policy of outrageous and long-continued oppression, before which the short-lived Marian persecution absolutely pales in comparison ...This page of our national history has been generally slurred over, through wilful suppression of the truth, by most of our historians. The facts are beyond dispute ... every persecution was resorted to immediately after Elizabeth's accession.

Yet even Mary's most die-hard opponents never questioned her sincerity, the depth of her religious beliefs or the strong moral principles that motivated her actions. She believed she was actually trying to save the souls of those in error from damnation. Foxe himself attributed to Mary the declaration that the souls of her people meant more to her than ten kingdoms. There can be many mitigating factors pleaded in Mary's behalf. Her precarious upbringing with its daily insecurities, together with the privations and humiliations she and her mother suffered, all played a part in the formation of her personality. As a monarch she was impressively dignified and hard-working. On a personal level she led a simple life and was a very kind, charitable woman, especially to the poor and sick, possessing a sensitivity devoid of the overweening selfishness that characterised Henry VIII. She was certainly greatly loved by her Court, and her servants were devoted to her. But even when all this is taken into consideration, the undeniable fact remains that whoever initiated the policy towards heretics, Mary bore ultimate responsibility.

It was not that she lacked advice to pursue a different course. John Feckenham,[5] abbot of the restored Westminster, endured imprisonment in the Tower under Edward VI. He was no friend to Protestantism and opposed Cranmer, Latimer and Ridley, but he disliked the bigotry and the brutal measures being employed. He used all his influence with the Queen to procure pardons or mitigation of the punishment being meted out to Protestants. As Queen, Mary had the authority to change the disastrous policy and halt the burnings; she did not do so, therefore she must be held culpable for this heinous persecution, whose tragic legacy was persecution for Catholics and incalculable damage to the Catholic cause in England for generations to come.

Edward VI and Mary Tudor

Notes to Chapter Two

1 Edward Seymour, Duke of Somerset, born in 1506, was the brother of Jane Seymour, the third wife of Henry VIII. The marriage led to his rapid advancement in royal favour, being created Earl of Hertford. He was appointed Lord Protector of his nephew Edward VI, who made him a duke. Seymour exercised tremendous influence over the boy and was the real ruler of the country. His collaborator, John Dudley, turned against him. Seymour was sent to the Tower in 1549. Cranmer signed his death warrant and Somerset was executed for treason in 1552.

2 John Dudley, Duke of Northumberland. Born c.1502, he was one of the executors of Henry VIII's will. He collaborated with Lord Protector Somerset in governing the country during the reign of Edward VI. He appears to have been devoid of any real religious convictions, but ambitious for power he hedged his bets both politically and in religious matters. He pursued a strongly Protestant agenda, promoting the Reformation when he saw it would suit his aims and increase his power base and influence over the boy King. Having disposed of his rival Somerset, he made himself a duke in 1551. In order to perpetuate his own rule he sought to place his daughter-in-law, Jane Grey, on the throne. In his final days, he presented the Marian government with a huge propaganda coup. He renounced his Protestantism and declared his return to Catholicism. Was this a hypocritical, last minute attempt to evade execution for treason or a genuine conversion? Either way it did not save him. There has been much debate about Dudley's declaration. It is impossible to know the truth, but on the day of his execution, 22 August 1553, he attended Mass in the Tower, and on the scaffold he insisted that his return to the Old Faith was personal and sincere and not the result of government pressure. His son, Robert, created Earl of Leicester, a favourite of Queen Elizabeth, became an important member of her government.

3 Lady Jane Grey, born in 1537, was the daughter of Henry Grey, Marquess of Dorset and Lady Frances Brandon, who was the daughter of Henry VIII's younger sister Mary. Attractive and intelligent, Jane had no desire to be Queen, but with the connivance of her parents she became the pawn of Dudley and the Protestant faction. Dudley and his self-serving hypocrisy disgusted Jane. She and her husband were sent to the Tower when Mary was proclaimed Queen but they were not executed until after Sir Thomas Wyatt's rebellion against the Queen's planned marriage to Philip of Spain had been crushed, when, like

Edward VI and Mary Tudor

Wyatt, they were beheaded for treason in 1554.

4 Cardinal Reginald Pole was born in Staffordshire in 1500, the grandson of George, Duke of Clarence, the brother of Edward IV. A BA of Oxford and Fellow of Corpus Christi College, in 1523 he left to study on the Continent where he came into contact with all the leading Renaissance humanists of the day. He returned to England in 1526 and was eventually offered the Archbishopric of York, if he would promote Henry's divorce from Catherine. Rather than do so, Pole went into exile to continue his studies, acquiring an international reputation. Although not a priest, he was made a cardinal in 1536 and was one of the three papal legates who presided over the Council of Trent. In 1549 Pole was almost elected Pope, falling short by only one or two votes. When Mary succeeded to the throne, Pole returned from exile as Papal Legate. He was appointed Archbishop of Canterbury, ordained priest in March 1556 in the friars' church at Greenwich, and two days later consecrated bishop; the day after the execution of Cranmer. Pole was to be the last Catholic to occupy the Primatial See. He died within hours of Mary on 17 November 1558.

5 John Feckenham (1515-84) was born at Feckenham, Worcestershire, into a well-to-do yeoman family called Howman. He received his first education from his parish priest. As a boy he was sent to the cloister school at Evesham Abbey and from there, at the age of eighteen, he went to Gloucester Hall, Oxford, as a Benedictine student. After gaining an Arts degree he returned to Evesham and took monastic vows. When he entered religion he was known by the name of his birthplace. In 1537 he returned to Oxford to complete his education becoming a Bachelor of Divinity in 1539. He was a monk of Evesham when his abbot, Clement Litchfield - described as 'a man of most chaste living' - was compelled to resign his office because he would not surrender the monastery. Bishop Hugh Latimer hated Litchfield, presumably because he so strongly disagreed with the Bishop's Protestantism. Following Litchfield's resignation, Latimer persuaded Cromwell to appoint the young Philip Harford in his place. The Bishop assured Cromwell that he would find Harford 'a true friend.' That proved to be the case because shortly afterwards, on 27 January 1540, Evesham was suppressed and Harford, having served his purpose, was given a pension of £240. Feckenham was awarded a pension of £10. He became domestic chaplain firstly to John Bell, Bishop of Worcester and secondly to Bishop Bonner of London from 1543 to 1549. He soon established a reputation both as an intellectual and as an eloquent

preacher, as well as a man of great charity. After Bonner was deprived of his see in 1549 Feckenham was sent to the Tower by Cranmer. He was temporarily freed in 1551 in order to take part in public disputations with John Jewel, future Bishop of Salisbury and the Calvinist John Hooper, Bishop of Gloucester. He was released from the Tower in September 1553 to become Queen Mary's chaplain and confessor. In March 1554 he was appointed Dean of St Paul's. Feckenham was chosen to prepare Lady Jane Grey for her execution. His intervention with the Queen to secure the release of the imprisoned Princess Elizabeth after Wyatt's rebellion was not appreciated. In 1556 Oxford made him a Doctor of Divinity, and on 29 November of that year he was installed as abbot of the restored Westminster Abbey, where he re-opened the abbey school. In Parliament he staunchly defended the Old Faith and in 1558 rejected Elizabeth's offer not only of the See of Canterbury but also the preservation of Westminster if he and his monks conformed to the new church. After Westminster was again suppressed in July 1559 Feckenham was sent to the Tower by Archbishop Parker in May 1560 for refusing the Oath of Supremacy and to attend Anglican worship. He spent virtually the rest of his life in confinement. In 1571 he prepared his fellow Tower prisoner, Blessed John Storey, for his execution. Moved to the Marshalsea in 1574, although still a prisoner, for the good of his health he was allowed out on bail to sleep at a house in Holborn, where his charity to the poor was legendary, distributing free milk to the sick every day. He set up a public aqueduct in Holborn and a hospice for the poor at Bath; he took care of orphans and encouraged the youth to take up sports pastimes. In 1577 he was once more strictly confined in the charge of Richard Cox, Bishop of Ely, who said that 'he was a gentle person' whose only fault was his obstinacy 'in the popish religion.' In 1579 John was sent to join Bishop Watson of Lincoln and others in Wisbech Castle: the first of many Catholics to be incarcerated in that place. Here he was revered as a moderating influence among his fellow prisoners. Having suffered for twenty-four years for his beliefs, he died in the prison in 1584 and was buried in an unknown grave at Wisbech parish church.

Chapter Three

The Elizabethan Persecution

What a rocky-hearted perfidious Succubus was that Queen Elizabeth! Judas Iscariot was a sad dog to be sure, but still his demerits sink to insignificance, compared with the doings of the infernal Bess Tudor.

Letters to Dr John Moore, Robert Burns, 1759-96

Elizabeth I (1533-1603) seems to have held no strong religious convictions whatever. As Arnold Oskar Meyer wrote in *England and the Catholic Church under Queen Elizabeth,* (1915) 'Her soul was scarcely ever touched by anything of the nature of religious enthusiasm'. Skilled as she had become in cunning and dissimulation, no one was fooled or doubted where her sympathies lay, and any argument that at the time of her accession Elizabeth had not made up her mind in which religious direction she wished to go is untenable. She ignored the provisions of Mary's will but gave her a Catholic funeral in Westminster Abbey in December 1558, which was followed by the house arrest of Bishop John White of Winchester, who had delivered the eulogy, as it contained remarks considered to be critical of the new monarch. It was a portent of things to come. The Calvinists returned from their self-imposed exile in Switzerland and Germany, and in the first few weeks of the reign William Cecil, 1 the newly appointed Secretary of State, made a written submission to the Queen in which he set out the pros and cons of either a Catholic or Protestant future for England. Cecil concluded that it would be politically expedient to opt for Protestantism. Although she gave instructions that nothing was to be changed immediately, it was a judgement that Elizabeth was happy to accept; after all, she was hardly likely to favour the religion of those who regarded her as Anne Boleyn's bastard daughter, which legally she indeed was, Parliament never having repealed the Act declaring her illegitimate.

The Queen's behaviour at Mass on Christmas Day presaged what was in store when she left the royal chapel after the Gospel. Elizabeth's first major problem was finding someone to perform her coronation. The death of Cardinal Pole on the same day as Queen Mary had left the See of Canterbury vacant. Several other deaths had occurred, so at the beginning of 1559 the hierarchy consisted of just sixteen bishops. They were asked, in order of seniority, if they would perform the ceremony: they declined to do so. The duty therefore fell to Bishop Owen

The Elizabethan Persecution

Oglethorpe of Carlisle, who somewhat naïvely agreed - providing it was a Catholic ceremony. He lived to bitterly regret his action. So the usually parsimonious Elizabeth spared no expense for her lavish coronation which took place on the date chosen by her personal occultist and astrologer, Dr John Dee, later to be Warden of the Collegiate Church, Manchester. Elizabeth was crowned and anointed as a Catholic sovereign but during the celebration of Mass she absented herself. Notwithstanding the solemn oath she had taken to defend the Catholic Faith, a few days later she began the task of bringing about a permanent religious settlement designed to end the upheavals of the last twenty-five years, an object that could only be achieved by compromise and by enforcing religious uniformity and conformity. The Anglican Church, as conceived by Elizabeth, was a political instrument to achieve political ends. Thus the Church of England, as established by law, came into being. * The *Book of Common Prayer* of Edward VI was re-introduced. Priests who refused to use it in public worship incurred the loss of a year's income and six month's in prison. A second refusal meant deprivation of benefice and imprisonment for a year. Clergy who risked a third refusal faced life imprisonment.

As the majority of the population remained Catholic at heart, especially in the rural areas, they were not simply going to change their religion overnight. At Elizabeth's accession, Protestants were in a small minority nationwide, in some areas virtually non-existent, but significant in London and other cities, particularly seaports. Given that London and the south and east coast ports had contacts with Continental Protestant merchants, who were able to influence those with whom they traded, this is not surprising. The most reliable estimate of numbers indicates that Catholics may still have accounted for nearly two-thirds of the total population. It is only through relatively recent scholarly research that some of the 'received' history familiar from State school textbooks has been revised and assumptions discounted.

Notable examples of this can be found in the work of historians such as Professors Eamon Duffy, J J Scarisbrick, and Christopher Haigh.

---

* This Erastianism ultimately led inexorably to the bizarre situation whereby Parliament dictated the beliefs of the Church of England and its liturgical practices. MPs who were of all faiths and none, including militant atheists, became responsible for legislating about the doctrine of the Church. As John Henry Newman wrote, the Church of England 'has always been in the closest dependence on the civil power and has always gloried in this ... The great principle of the Anglican Church is confidence in the protection of the civil power and its docility in serving it.' Still today, the decisions of the C of E Synod have to be ratified by Parliament to become effective and its bishops and other senior clergy are appointed by the government.

The Elizabethan Persecution

The attachment to the old religion was far more tenacious than we had Been led to believe from our school history lessons. In fact, all the evidence now available leads to the conclusion that the survival of Catholic piety has been greatly underestimated. For example, Professor Duffy maintains:

... Late mediaeval Catholicism exerted an enormously strong, diverse and vigorous hold over the imagination and the loyalty of the people up to the very moment of the Reformation. Traditional religion had about it no particular marks of exhaustion or decay and indeed in a whole host of ways, from the multiplication of vernacular books to adaptations within the national and regional cult of the saints was showing itself well able to meet new needs and new conditions.

From *The Stripping of the Altars* by Eamon Duffy [*]

It surely cannot be without significance, as the eminent Protestant historian Lord Macaulay observed in his *Essay on Burleigh and his Times*, that the greatest and most popular dramatists and poets of the Elizabethan age showed great regard in their works for priests and monks and treated the vow of celibacy with great respect. He points out that every member of a religious order that they introduce is a holy and venerable man. He contrasts this with the 'coarse ridicule' of later times in which 'the Catholic religion and its ministers were assailed' with literary caricatures. Indeed, it is remarkable that the alleged evil repute of monks and friars of popular imagination dates mainly from the time of Bishop Burnet and his ilk. It suited their biased agenda to lend credence to the reports of Henry VIII's commissioners without questioning the credibility or motivation of men whom modern historians would categorise as perjured robbers.

So how was it then that the change of religion was apparently assented to by so many? How was it that the faith that had been established in England for a thousand years, had been firmly rooted in the land, had inspired its art and architecture, should, in the space of a few years, have apparently been almost swept away? The truth is that, contrary to the myth that used to be peddled, it wasn't! Today it is impossible to appreciate the power enjoyed - or abused - by absolute monarchy in the sixteenth century. The coercive power of the Tudor monarchy was very formidable, especially when directed by such

---

[*] Copyright © 1992 by Yale University Press. Reproduced by permission of Professor Eamon Duffy and Yale University Press, London

The Elizabethan Persecution

ruthlessly efficient men as Thomas Cromwell or William Cecil. It has to be recalled that the nation had already been asked to change its religion three times in a dozen years in obedience to its rulers i.e. Henry VIII, Edward VI and Mary. This habit of conformity no doubt bred carelessness and indifference and many - probably most - people either wondered just how permanent the latest alteration would turn out to be, or were simply unable to comprehend what was happening, which, in turn, explains how relatively few of them were prepared to put their lives on the line in defence of the Old Faith. Familiar piety may well be the keyword. People were attached to the old, traditional, devotional ways - but how deep or shallow was their understanding of real Catholic beliefs? There is much truth in the assertion that clergy and laity had become detached. The Mass was celebrated by the priest mostly *sotto voce*, without much active participation by the congregation; indeed the more devout worshippers were probably saying their rosaries or reading some spiritual tract, only taking any notice at the Elevation when the sacring bell caught their attention!

As Professor Frederic Seebohm recognised in his, *The Era of the Protestant Revolution* (1911), as well as religious motives there were political, social and economic aspects to the revolt against Rome that emanated from Germany in the sixteenth century. There was also a significant nationalistic element in the equation that cannot be discounted. However familiar the cadences of the Latin Mass had become, even to illiterate worshippers, the Established Church offered prayers and scripture readings in their own language. This was something for which many Catholics had long sought permission in vain from Rome and it may have been an incentive to many to attend Anglican worship. (English-speaking Roman Catholics had to wait another 400 years to have their liturgy in the vernacular.)

Having said all that, and taking every factor into consideration, it remains the case that the only way the new religion could be imposed on a largely unwilling people was through the employment of the massive machinery of State repression; a sustained offensive of coercion and propaganda, backed by an extensive degree of brute force. The facts, however much disguised or suppressed, cannot be denied. It is always an advantage to know the truth and to learn how to face it.

Anyone reading this book will be left in no doubt as to why thousands yielded, attended the Protestant Church, and were mostly lost to the Catholic Faith. The wonder is not that so many conformed, but that in the face of such unremitting persecution there were any Catholics left. All the more reason, therefore, to recall and honour those who courageously remained steadfast. The persecution policy was cold

The Elizabethan Persecution

and calculating and merciless in its execution. Under Elizabeth - and her successor James I - no pity was extended to the old, the sick or to children, who were often arrested when caught attending Mass and thrown into prison along with their mothers.

Elizabeth could count upon the support of the *nouveaux riches* who had profited from the spoliation of the Church and the religious houses. As Lord Macaulay observed, most of them were place-seekers; political adventurers whose self-preservation became the prime object of their existence. And that meant they now had a vested interest in maintaining the Anglican settlement.

In 1559, in the teeth of opposition from the bishops and clergy in Convocation, a new Act of Supremacy (1 Eliz. I, c.1) was passed. The Act made it high treason to acknowledge the Pope's authority in England and bestowed upon Elizabeth the title 'Supreme Governess' of the Church in all spiritual as well as temporal matters. This was presumably felt to be less emotive than 'Head' of the Church, but for all practical purposes it meant exactly the same. The Oath of Supremacy assenting to the Act read:

I do truly testify and declare, in my conscience, the Queen to be supreme governess both of this realm of England and of all her Majesty's other dominions, no less in all spiritual and ecclesiastical matters and causes, as in temporals. And that no foreign prince, person, prelate, state or potentate, either *de facto* or *de jure*, hath any jurisdiction, power, superiority, pre-eminence, or authority, ecclesiastical or spiritual, in this realm. And, therefore, I do fully renounce and repudiate all external jurisdictions, powers, superiorities and authorities.

It fell to Archbishop Nicholas Heath of York, head of the hierarchy with Canterbury vacant, to present to the House of Lords the unanimous decision of Convocation, upholding the primacy of the See of Rome in spiritual matters. He was supported by Cuthbert Scott of Chester and Thomas Thirlby, Bishop of Ely, who declared that he would rather die than consent to a change of religion. Notwithstanding these protests, the House of Lords, albeit only by a small majority, passed the bill. To their eternal credit, unlike their timorous counterparts in the time of Henry VIII, all the bishops, with the solitary exception of Anthony Kitchin of Llandaff, remained true. Kitchin had been a monk of Westminster Abbey before becoming abbot of Eynsham in 1530. When his abbey was suppressed in 1539 he was given a pension. In 1545 he was appointed Bishop of Llandaff. A classic time-server he managed to hang onto his see under both Edward VI and Mary, dying in 1566.

The Elizabethan Persecution

Within months of her accession Elizabeth had deprived the bishops of their sees. They were imprisoned, placed under house arrest or exiled. Twelve of them eventually died in confinement. 2 A huge number of the higher clergy - deans, archdeacons and prebendaries - following their bishops' lead were deprived. For example, Richard Petre, Archdeacon of Buckingham, brother of Sir William Petre, was deprived and in Yorkshire Archdeacons John Hanson of Richmond and George Palmes of the West Riding were deprived in January 1560. * Palmes was later imprisoned. The vicars of Arncliffe, Bingley, Doncaster, Kildwick, Otley, Guiseley, Whiston, Burnsall, Sedbergh, Tickhill and Ripon were among those deprived. Without any bishops, the Catholics were left without leaders and Elizabeth had to appoint a new Protestant hierarchy, men for whom she barely bothered to disguise her disdain. It was widely believed that Elizabeth, in a private interview, first offered the See of Canterbury to Abbot John Feckenham of Westminster, if he conformed: an offer he certainly refused. He was the last mitred abbot to sit in the House of Lords, where he opposed all the religious changes and was imprisoned by Matthew Parker, the new Anglican Archbishop of Canterbury. 3

Queen Mary and Cardinal Pole have been criticised for the number of dioceses that were vacant (5) at the time of their deaths. With hindsight it is easy to see how this certainly made it much simpler for Elizabeth to get her new religious settlement established. Mary and Pole were faced with so many problems, not least of finding exactly the right men for the posts, which led them to proceed with caution. They were anxious to appoint men of proven pastoral experience rather than administrators. Elizabeth also moved slowly in appointing new bishops. This was partly due to the difficulty she had finding acceptable candidates, but mainly it was because she deliberately chose to leave many dioceses vacant after she had removed the Marian bishops. She did this not only to save money but to take advantage of the revenues of the vacant dioceses which the Crown enjoyed. Archbishop Matthew Parker remonstrated with Cecil, recognising the dangers to the new religious settlement inherent in the policy if, for the sake of short term

---

* In addition other archdeacons deprived included: John Blaxton, Brecknock, John Boxall, Ely, John Bridgewater, Rochester, Matthew Carew, Norfolk, William Carter, Northumberland, Thomas Darbyshire, Essex, James Dugdale, St Albans, Michael Dunning, Bedford, Humphrey Edwards, St Asaph, John Fitzjames, Taunton, John Glazier, Hereford, Edward Gregory, Bangor, John Harrison, Stowe, Nicholas Harpsfield, Canterbury, Owen Hodgson, Lincoln, Alban Langdale, Chichester, John Lawrence, Wiltshire, Edmund Mervyn, Surrey, Robert Pursglove, Nottingham, John Rambridge, Derby, Griffith Roberts, Anglesey, Thomas Robertson, Leicester, John Standish, Chester, Thomas Taylor, Lewes, Nicholas Wendon, Suffolk.

The Elizabethan Persecution

monetary gain, there was no bishop in place to enforce conformity.

By the end of 1559 sixteen dioceses - out of twenty-two - were without bishops. There was a two-year delay in making an appointment to York when Thomas Young took up the office in May 1561. Archbishop Young succeeded the Earl of Rutland as President of the Council of the North in 1564, a post he held until his death in 1568. York again had to wait over two years for a new archbishop, Edmund Grindal being sent North in 1570. Oxford diocese had to wait nine years - until 1567 - for a bishop and Ely was kept vacant for eighteen years.

In 1559 the Act of Uniformity (1Eliz.I,c.2), abolished Mass and restored the 1549 *Second Book of Common Prayer* as the only permissible, indeed compulsory, form of worship. The wording of most of the Act is devoted to setting out the details of the penalties by which it was to be enforced. The House of Lords passed the bill by a majority of just three votes. Here it is relevant to quote James A Froude again. 'We are told that the Church of England reformed herself, meaning by the Church not the laity who alone did the work, but the bishops and clergy, who never consented as a body to any measure of Reformation except under judicious compulsion'. The Reformation which Elizabeth sought to complete did not create a united Protestant England: it resulted in a deeply divided nation. To quote David Starkey, a contemporary historian, Elizabeth 'created a kind of hybrid church'. Thus, the Erastianism of Henry VIII was carried to its logical conclusion under his daughter and a subservient, national State church, the Church of England as by law established, was invented and imposed by intimidation. The compromise settlement was unacceptable to both Catholics and Protestants. As Father Godfrey Anstruther OP in *Vaux of Harrowden* (1953) put it so aptly, 'The religion of nobody imposed upon everybody'.

Elizabeth undoubtedly saw the Act in the context of consolidating her power and the domination of every aspect, including spiritual, of her subjects' lives, which she believed she had a right to demand. Her attitude may be gleaned from a speech she made to one of her later Parliaments, 'I was never so much delighted that God had made me His instrument to maintain His truth and glory.' Elizabeth's 'halfway-house' church was designed to try and make Protestantism acceptable. Fourteen of the men Elizabeth appointed bishops between 1559 and 1562 had been voluntary exiles in Germany and Switzerland under Queen Mary, among them Edmund Grindal, Bishop of London and Edwin Sandys, Bishop of Worcester. Calvinists were dominant in the

The Elizabethan Persecution

Queen's Established Church. Writing of the newly-appointed State Church hierarchy a percipient Froude wrote,

A Catholic bishop holds his office by a tenure untouched by the accidents of time. Dynasties may change - nations may lose their liberties - the Catholic bishop remains at his post; when he dies another takes his place ... the person perhaps changed - the thing itself rooted like a rock on the adamantine basements of the world. The Anglican hierarchy, far unlike its rival, was a child of convulsion and compromise: it drew its life from Elizabeth's throne, and had Elizabeth fallen, it would have crumbled into sand. The Church of England was as a limb lopped off from the parent trunk ... and the life of it as an independent and corporate existence was gone for ever. But it had been taken up and grafted upon the State. If not what it had been, it could retain the form of what it had been - the form which made it respectable. The image in its outward aspect could be made to correspond with the parent tree; and to sustain the illusion it was necessary to create bishops who could appear to have inherited their powers by the approved method, as successors of the Apostles.

At first only higher ecclesiastics and those holding public office were obliged to take the Oath of Supremacy, but in 1562 this was extended to include all those in holy orders, members of Parliament, university graduates, lawyers and schoolmasters - in practice all educated Catholics.

Dr Augustus Jessop, nineteenth-century Anglican clergyman and former headmaster of King Edward's School, Norwich, spent many years carrying out important research into original sources for his fascinating book about the Walpole family, *One Generation of a Norfolk House* (1879). He wrote:

As my book has proceeded the England of Queen Elizabeth's days has become to me an altogether different land from the England I had formerly imagined it to be: the conflict with Rome had gradually unfolded itself as a problem which must remain unintelligible to the merely political historian ...The real value of the [Walpole] story lies rather in this, that it is one which, mutatis mutandis, might be told of fifty families in England which were rich and prosperous in the first half of the 16th century and were simply reduced to beggary for conscience' sake.

At the accession of Elizabeth there were not wanting many men of conscientious convictions who would have boldly faced the scaffold rather than acknowledge the claim of the spiritual supremacy of the sovereign ...The oath in its new form became the cause of deep and widespread offence. A large proportion of the English gentry refused to swear allegiance in the terms prescribed. But the Act of Uniformity was one which touched Catholics in a different way. The re-establishment of the Mass in Queen Mary's reign had caused immense joy throughout the land, now it was enacted that the *Book of Common Prayer* alone should be used and to 'sing or say any common or open prayer, or to administer any sacrament otherwise ... than is mentioned in the said book ... in any cathedral, parish church or chapel, or in any other place' subjected the offender to forfeiture of his goods and on repetition of his offence, to imprisonment for life. The Mass ... was known to be the one great and precious mystery which every devout Catholic clung to with unspeakable awe and fervour and to rob him of that was to rob him of the one thing on which his religious life depended; that gone, it was imagined that all else would go with it.

The consequences of the new Anglican Church on the Catholic community were dire. Catholic Faith and worship was now illegal. Attendance at Protestant services was compulsory. Just how did the educated Catholic laity react? We have an illuminating example in the form of a letter dated 23 November 1569 from Sir Thomas Copley, lord of the Manor of Gatton, to Sir Henry Weston, High Sheriff of Surrey, and his fellow justices at Dorking. Copley, who claimed the extinct barony of Hoo, had been a member of parliament from 1554 to 1563. In Queen Mary's reign he had favoured Protestantism, but was reconciled to the Catholic Church in 1562 and had a spell in prison for recusancy. His letter, as it appears in *Letters of Sir Thomas Copley*, edited by Richard Copley Christie, 1897, is worth quoting at length.

> For that the true knowledge of God should be served, and the true order of the administration of the Sacraments was known, practised and established in the Church of God long before the Act of Parliament was made whereunto I should now subscribe and that the referring as it were of the original and true setting forth thereof, to the said Act so lately made, would seem a great derogation to the Christian faith, and a great slander and discredit to the Church of God, that the same should be so many ages either ignorant how God should be served, or a false teacher of his people (which cannot be, since the Apostle saith that the same is columna et firmamentum veritatis) and because without a faithless mistrust in God it may not (in my opinion) in word or thought be doubted, that God (who being Truth itself) and promising that He would be with His Church, not after fifteen hundred years only, but by all days to the world's end, and to instruct the same into all truth, which words permit no intermission, would contrary to that His divine promise, suffer such long and general error and blindness in his Church as is by some imagined. For these and divers other great causes I cannot yet by any search find sufficient matter to persuade me with safe conscience to that which is at this present required of me, amongst others ... Neither am I so senseless or stony but that I feel the grief thereof, and gladly would avoid the same and do with all my heart as others do ... if I could do it without fear of danger and by offense of God and my conscience in this case.

Copley's plea to be allowed his freedom of conscience and not participate in Protestant services was denied and he was summoned

The Elizabethan Persecution

before the justices. They never had the satisfaction of dealing with him. He escaped to France in 1570. His estate was confiscated and came into the Queen's possession. Copley wrote many letters from exile to the Queen and prominent members of her government protesting his loyalty which he maintained was not in conflict with his faith. He declared that he loved his country and asked why his adherence to 'the religion holden and practised by the universal church ever since His ascension' was now such a heinous crime. His pleas fell on deaf ears and he died in Flanders in 1584. His heir was his nineteen-year-old son, William. On returning to England to claim his inheritance William Copley found that, being legally a minor, he was subject to the Court of Wards, whose Master was William Cecil, Lord Burleigh. William was required to take the Oath of Supremacy, but refused and went into exile in Spain. He married and had four children. He moved to the Netherlands and, having no income from his forfeited English property, he lived on a pension paid by the Spanish Regent. On the accession of James I he was able to return to England and regain possession of part of his estate. His eldest son, another Thomas, became a Jesuit priest, using the alias Philip Fisher q.v. and two of his daughters became nuns at Louvain. Sadly, most Catholics did not have the strength of conviction of the Copley family, or the courage to openly resist, and they stretched their consciences to breaking point.

Penalties for both priests and laity who did not conform to the new services ranged from fines to life imprisonment. As the Elizabethan Anglican calendar required obligatory attendance at church on seventy days in the year, the basic shilling fine for non-attendance imposed on every member of a recusant household would have been crippling for poor Catholics, if it had been consistently and rigorously applied. Fines extended to those who came to church late, left early, walked about and talked during services. Anyone who spoke against the Prayer Book or interrupted the minister faced a fine of 100 marks. Unlike their bishops, the majority of the parish clergy, however reluctantly, docilely conformed, and their congregations mostly followed their example even though many were church papists - that is, they conformed outwardly.

Throughout England and Wales the Anglican bishops were confronted with huge difficulties trying to enforce conformity to the new services. Available evidence indicates that attendance at church was poor. Yorkshire, as usual, was obstinately resistant to the new liturgy. Professor Christopher Haigh, quoting contemporary sources, relates that at Tickhill, near Doncaster in 1569 many of the congregation had abandoned the church and attended Mass in a nearby chapel. In a parish near York in the 1570's the parishioners had withdrawn from attendance at church services and the minister regularly locked up the church and left when no one turned up in response to the bell. In the Fylde district of Lancashire in 1580 the bishop complained that no more than fourteen or fifteen parishioners had regularly attended each of its parish churches for years past, whereas the number of recusants increased in Lancashire year by year.

The Ecclesiastical Commissioners complained that 'many undutifully and unchristianly abstain and refrain from church ... while a great number superstitiously given do still solemnly keep holy days and fasting ... long since abrogated and forbidden.' Many church papist priests performed the new services in church, and then secretly celebrated Mass and provided the Sacraments to their parishioners. This practice, evidence for which is overwhelming, continued for many years, to the horror and condemnation of the Catholic exiles. In 1575 a Lancashire vicar publicly said the Church of England was a defiled church and encouraged his parishioners to pray 'according to the doctrine of the Pope of Rome.' In 1580 a rector in Lincolnshire told his congregation that only those who frequented Catholic Sacraments would be saved. As late as 1584, a Suffolk vicar was saying Mass secretly for his parishioners in his house. It can be argued, with hindsight, that such clerics made an invaluable contribution to the preservation of Catholicism in continuing to foster as much of the Old Faith as they could get away with among their parishioners, many of whom subsequently became full-blooded recusants. But it had its down side. Often recusants would go to church just before the assizes were due in order to avoid prosecution. Father John Gerard SJ records that he was at Mass in Lancashire attended by as many as two hundred people. Such large gatherings could surely only have taken place if sympathetic local justices were prepared to turn a blind eye. Gerard believed that in the 1590's Lancashire Catholics were very numerous. If the number of out-and-out recusants is added to the number of church papists, Gerard's assessment was probably correct, but he complained that they only practised their religion when they thought it was safe to do so.

This compromise with conscience led to a religious indifference as many sought to justify their conduct. After all, if the Anglican Communion service offered only bread, where was the harm in receiving it? Under the new religious settlement parishes were required to destroy all surviving remnants of Catholic piety, although many items such as vestments and images were hidden. This new spoliation of the Church was attacked not only by Catholics; many Protestants also spoke out against such sacrilege. They pointed out that materials given for the glory of God and His worship were profaned just as much

The Elizabethan Persecution

by greedy, acquisitive laymen as they were by being used in popish ceremonies. John Jewel, Bishop of Salisbury (1559-71), a virulent opponent of Catholics and chief apologist for the Anglican settlement, declared - as had John Bale q.v. and others before him - that he hung his head in shame that the Protestant Reformation had failed to make use of its acquired Church wealth for good purposes. Rather it had fostered greed and selfishness and lack of concern for the poor. Even Bishop Hugh Latimer compared unfavourably the opportunities that had been offered by the monasteries to scholars and the situation in his own day when, 'no man helpeth to maintain them'. In a sermon he said, 'It is a pitiful thing to see schools so neglected; every true Christian ought to lament the same to consider what has been plucked from abbeys and chantries;' it was a marvel that none of it had been used to help scholars.

As the parishes were denuded of their beauty it seems that the indifference this bred led to a diminished respect for the desecrated church buildings themselves. What incentive did congregations have to maintain churches built to celebrate the Mass that had become desolate whitewashed meeting halls, where they were expected to sit and listen to interminable sermons? As the reign progressed the reports on the neglected and dilapidated state of the fabric of the nation's churches makes sorry reading. The lead had been stripped from the roofs for profit; birds flew in freely through the smashed windows. Since the chancels of the churches were not used in services by the Anglicans - to disassociate them from the idea of the altar at which was offered the sacrificial Mass - they were allowed to fall into such neglect that many of them collapsed. When the historian and antiquary William Camden visited Luton, Bedfordshire in 1586 he reported that the choir of the 14th century St Mary's parish church was roofless and overgrown with weeds. It remained in this sad state until 1603. Furthermore, the Elizabethan Church was hardly held in respect; far from it. A great Elizabethan scholar, Dr Hubert Hall, Litt.D., F.R.Hist.S, F.S.A. (1857-1944), wrote, 'The state of society was the worst that had ever before been in the land. And where all this time was the influence of the Church at work? There was no pretence even at such an influence.' The numbers of the poor had greatly increased, and soon poverty came to be viewed as a crime. As has already been demonstrated, at the suppression of the monasteries many estates were acquired by absentee landlords, who proved hard masters, while the poor were deprived of the charitable relief that had once been provided by the religious houses. Sir Thomas Wilson, a contemporary, wrote a book, *The State of England,* in 1600. In it he speaks of the old clergy, who 'never raised

The Elizabethan Persecution

nor racked their rents nor put out tenants as the noblemen and gentlemen do to the utmost penny.' He castigates the Elizabethan clergy as being 'over rich, for that order of men have most damnified England by their profuse spending upon their pleasures.'

The royal commissioners continued to report on the inveterate obstinacy that was found among the priests in still practising the old Catholic ways. From the start the Elizabethan bishops constantly complained about the way in which the old 'Mass priests' still functioned. As has already been quoted from Dr Charles Cox, 'every persecution was resorted to immediately after Elizabeth's accession.' And confirming the truth of this statement examples abound of the treatment meted out to priests who would not conform. Berkshire-born Thomas Slythurst was a Bachelor of Divinity of Oxford, rector of Chalfont St Peter, Canon of Windsor and first President of Trinity College, Oxford. Deprived in 1559 he died in the Tower the following year. Father Henry Cole, born c.1500, was fined 500 marks and deprived of his preferments. On 20 May 1560 he was sent to the Tower and then moved to the Fleet where he remained for the next twenty years, dying in February 1579. William Chedsey, a Doctor of Divinity of Oxford, came from Somerset. He was a prebendary of St Paul's Cathedral. Under Edward VI he was imprisoned in the Marshalsea in 1551. Released under Queen Mary he was appointed a canon of St George's Chapel, Windsor and archdeacon of Middlesex. In 1558 he became President of Corpus Christi College but was deprived of all his offices in 1559 and sent to the Fleet. Anthony Draycott, son of Sir John Draycott, was Chancellor of Lichfield diocese. Deprived and imprisoned in 1560 he spent ten years in the Fleet until released just a few weeks before his death. The tentacles of persecution also extended widely to the laity. Edward Waldegrave was the nephew of Sir Robert Rochester q.v. A member of Princess Mary's household, in 1551 he was sent to the Tower with his uncle for refusing to implement the ban imposed on saying Mass in Mary's house. A married man with five children, Edward was knighted by Queen Mary and became Master of the Wardrobe and a Member of Parliament until he succeeded Rochester as Chancellor of the Duchy of Lancaster. On Elizabeth's accession he was dismissed for having Mass in his house and sent to the Tower where he died in 1561. And in the prisons of York men and women were already dying in the early 1560's for refusal to conform.

Edmund Grindal of London was particularly assiduous in pursuing non-conforming priests and urging upon Cecil 'extraordinary punishments' for them, recommending that 'priests be put to torment.' In 1562 he interrogated a number of 'popish' prisoners, among them a priest named Harvard. The priest refused to betray anyone, so the Bishop suggested to the Council that he might divulge more if put to the torture. This might make him disclose numbers of recusants who heard Mass who could be fined and make a 'good mass of money for the Queen's Majesty'. Such statements lead one to conclude that torture was being used much earlier in the reign than generally thought. John Scory was a former Dominican friar, appointed Bishop of Chichester. Having turned Protestant, he was deprived by Mary, and then appointed Bishop of Hereford by Elizabeth. In 1564 he provided a list of a dozen priests who were travelling around in his diocese, 'mortal and deadly enemies to this religion.' Edwin Sandys, Bishop of Worcester, lamented that 'popish priests which, misliking religion have forsaken the ministry, yet lie in corners, are kept in gentlemen's houses and are had in great estimation with the people'. John Jewel of Salisbury urged that greater action should be taken against priests who 'had liberty to stay at their pleasures within this realm and who do much hurt secretly'. In 1565 Archbishop Thomas Young of York wrote about the 'inconstancy and murmuring of the people in the North touching the alteration of religion'. By 1570 Grindal had been moved to York and was shocked to find that his archdiocese was still strongly imbued with Catholic traditions, so much so that he described it as more like 'another church, rather than a member of the rest'. Given that around 65% of the Yorkshire gentry were still Catholic at this time, and allowing for the influence they wielded on their local populations, Grindal should not have been so surprised. He teamed up with the President of the Council of the North, Henry Hastings, Earl of Huntingdon, in launching an all-out assault on Catholicism. The somewhat fanatical Richard Curteys, Bishop of Chichester (1570-82), had a hard task trying to enforce conformity in Sussex, including the local justices, on whom he depended for apprehending recusants. He bit off more than he could chew when he attacked the JP's and provoked them to unite against him, regardless of their shades of religious opinion. In 1574 the Privy Council complained that Lancashire was 'the very sink of popery', with many unlawful persons secretly hidden. Bishop John Aylmer of London complained in 1577 that the 'papists do marvellously increase both in number and in obstinate withdrawing of themselves from the church'.

We know that hundreds of priests resigned or were deprived of their parishes, were imprisoned or exiled, rather than conform to the accommodating worldliness of the Established Church. From the records of the royal visitation to the Province of York in 1559, we see that ninety priests were summoned to take the oath at York: only

The Elizabethan Persecution

twenty-one of them did so. A similar situation was replicated in Lancashire, where many clergy resigned their benefices and the majority of them did not take the oath. The Bishop of Chester, whose diocese covered the county, behaved very leniently towards them. In reality he did not have a great deal of choice: if he had acted against them the churches and chapels would have been denuded of clergy, and the true level of support for the new religious settlement would have been exposed. Many priests, deprived of their means of livelihood, wandered in disguise around the country, ministering secretly to Catholics, particularly in the North and Wales. By abandoning their livings many chose to put themselves into poverty for the sake of conscience. In some areas there were nearly as many recusant priests as those serving the Established Church. They were able to minister successfully with the active connivance of a significant 'fifth-column' of Catholic sympathisers within the Anglican Church. This is borne out by the extraordinary entry in the baptismal register of Whitchurch Canonicorum, Dorset. On 4 June 1582 John Warham was baptised by (sic) 'The Roman priest'.* Many areas of the country ignored the new arrangements and continued to celebrate Mass in the parish churches.

The recusant clergy, ordained in the reigns of Henry VIII and Queen Mary, a great many of whom died in prisons, were known by the authorities as 'old priests'. Many of them were men of considerable ability who after being deprived of their posts conducted a wandering ministry. Priests such as Thomas Bailey, Master of Clare College, Cambridge; Dr Thomas Robertson, Dean of Durham; Dr Francis Babington, Rector of Lincoln College, Oxford and Thomas Marshall, Dean of Christ Church, Oxford. Thomas Sedgwick DD became Regius Professor of Divinity at Cambridge in 1557 and in 1558 rector of Stanhope, Co. Durham. Deprived by Elizabeth he was confined to an area within ten miles of Richmond, Yorkshire, until sent to prison in 1570, dying in jail in 1573. In 1580 an old Marian priest, Thomas Briggs of Pateley Bridge, Yorkshire, was hauled before the Commissioners at Ripon and interrogated. When he would not yield he was committed to York Castle for 'an indefinite term'. James Stonnes

---

* John Warham was ordained priest at Tournai in 1610 and served with his older priest brother, George, on the mission in the West Country becoming Vicar General of Cornwall in 1649. Whitchurch Canonicorum still possesses uniquely intact the unpretentious shrine containing the bones of the Saxon St Whyte or Witta, after whom the village takes its name. Thomas More ironically mentioned the quaint custom of offering cakes or cheese at her shrine on 1 June, her feast day. Her lead coffin, containing the skeleton of a woman aged about forty, was opened in 1900.

was born 1513. At Elizabeth's accession he refused to conform and wandered about Yorkshire and Durham ministering secretly. He was arrested by the Earl of Derby on 19 November 1585 in the parish of Ormskirk, Lancashire. He refused to acknowledge the royal supremacy and was committed to the New Fleet prison, Manchester. He was seventy-two and died in the jail the following year. Stephen Hemsworth was a fellow prisoner in Hull Blockhouse with Thomas Mudd and John Almond q.v. After many years in prison he died there in August 1585.

William Fieldsend, Vicar of Tideswell, Derbyshire, died in Hull blockhouse in 1585. Thomas Rudall, committed to York Castle, fell sick and died there 11 April 1587. William Bandersby MA, deprived fellow of Christ's College, Cambridge, lived in disguise for many years with the Dowager Lady Wharton in Yorkshire. He was arrested at a house in York and committed to the Castle. Falling sick and leaving all he possessed to his fellow Catholic prisoners, he died there 21 April 1587. Richard Bowes was one of the clergy of Ripon Cathedral and took part in the restored Catholic services during the 1569 Northern Rising. Refusing to conform, the old man was driven from pillar to post for many years before being sent to York Castle where he died 31 August 1590.

Some 'old priests' perished on the gallows, such as Blessed James Bell from Warrington. Ordained under Queen Mary, he had been a conformer for twenty years, but left the Anglican Church in 1579 and was reconciled. He became an itinerant priest serving the recusant community of Lancashire. Arrested in 1584 he was committed to Manchester jail. He was tried at Lancaster with Fathers Thomas Williamson and Richard Hutton. They were all condemned but Williamson and Hutton were sentenced to perpetual imprisonment and *praemunire*. The sixty-four-year-old Bell was hanged, drawn and quartered at Lancaster on 10 April, together with Blessed John Finch, a thirty-six-year-old yeoman farmer from Eccleston condemned for being reconciled and aiding priests. When arrested with Father George Ostcliff q.v. Finch had long been well-known to the authorities as a shelterer of priests. When he would not provide any information he was sent to prison in Manchester where he was treated with great brutality. On one occasion when he refused to go to church he was literally dragged there by the feet, his head beating against the cobbles. After suffering three years in dreadful prison conditions he was sent for trial and condemned.

In the same year at least a dozen 'old priests' were in jail at Salford. The vital part these priests played in sustaining the Catholic community until help arrived from the overseas seminaries has never received the

The Elizabethan Persecution

recognition it deserves. Edmund Campion acknowledged not only the assistance given to him by these priests but also that they had 'cultivated this vineyard for many years before his coming'. Father Henry Garnet, later Jesuit Superior in England, paid tribute to the important work of the 'old priests'. Some of the priests, who had gone into exile at Elizabeth's accession, later returned and secretly resumed their pastoral work. They included priests such as the Welshman, George Morris, who was being hunted by William Blethyn, Bishop of Llandaff, in 1579 or Oliver Heywood who had been ordained under Henry VIII and died in prison in 1586. The problem they posed for the government was nationwide, as is confirmed in a letter, written from Hatfield in September 1578 by Robert Dudley, Earl of Leicester and Lord Burghley to the sheriff and justices of Surrey. It states that the Queen's Majesty is not best pleased that not only in Surrey but 'in divers parts of the realm, there be certain lewd and evil disposed persons which do remain obscurely in secret places or else very secretly go from place to place disguised in apparel after the manner of serving men or artificers, whereas they be indeed popish massing priests, and do under that visor, in whispering manner hold and maintain sundry of her majesty's subjects in superstition and error ...' There follows detailed instructions as to how such priests should be apprehended by searches and the seizure of all 'popish' materials. However, the fact remains that a great many Catholics, before the advent of the seminary priests, must have been bereft of spiritual guidance and sacramental sustenance. Indeed many must have felt abandoned by their Church and had to fend for themselves, wrestling with their consciences as best they could about what course to follow. Many of those priests who remained in the State Church were the time-servers such as Aleyn, the proverbial Vicar of Bray, whose 'principle' was to live and die in possession of his post, or Robert Parkyn of Yorkshire who reluctantly conformed under Edward VI, enthusiastically welcomed the return to Catholicism under Mary, and conformed again in 1559, retaining his vicarage until 1570.

As a result of the priestly defections large numbers of parishes were left without pastors. John Gwynneth remained parish priest of Luton under Henry VIII and Edward VI. A Catholic at heart he welcomed the restoration of Catholicism under Queen Mary but when Elizabeth acceded he had had enough and absented himself from the parish. In the first years of Elizabeth's reign we are told that the Established Church was desperately short of clergy and had to resort to co-opting laymen who could barely read through the new services. During the first few months of the reign the universities of Oxford and Cambridge were relatively free from pressure, and they associated themselves with the declaration of the bishops early in 1559 upholding the spiritual supremacy of the Pope. But too much was at stake for many of the fellows and professors whose livelihood depended upon their 'toeing the line'. It is also true that many of them were 'hedging their bets': having had so many changes of religion, how were they to know that there would not be a reversion to the Old Faith in the near future? By pressure and the removal of key men, a majority for Protestant conformity was achieved at Cambridge. Oxford was a tougher nut to crack. The university virtually ceased to function because most of the best and brightest tutors, fellows and students in the various colleges were Catholics who were expelled on Elizabeth's orders. Many of those who did not go abroad opted for places at the Inns of Court, always centres of Catholicism throughout the reign. Despite all the best efforts of the government Catholicism always maintained a foothold in the universities for the duration of the reign. There are constant complaints about the number of church papists they housed and the amount of Catholic literature that circulated was still causing alarm to the Vice-Chancellor of Cambridge in 1595.

Elizabeth's accession coincided with the election of Pius IV Medici (1559-1565) as Pope. He recognised Elizabeth's accession, and in spite of all the provocation from England, he showed remarkable forbearance and patience, continuing to try and reach an understanding with the regime, even when all his overtures and attempts to send nuncios from Rome - blocked by William Cecil - were rudely rejected. He even invited Elizabeth to send delegates to the Council of Trent. The traditional attitude, adopted by early Protestant historians, that England was from the outset acting in self-defence against Roman claims, is a self-justification that cannot be sustained. From the start the Elizabethan government believed its best method of defence was to pursue a policy of aggression and this it did most successfully. To quote A O Meyer again, 'The government wanted no reconciliation with Rome, but rather to oppress or, if possible, destroy Catholicism'.

During the first three years of the reign the laws against Catholics were not as rigorously enforced everywhere, especially as it tended to be the extreme Protestants who caused more problems for the government: Elizabeth particularly hated the Puritans. A sea change came about in 1563. A more active and vigorous persecution was launched, when the penalties for refusing to conform were made more stringent. (5 Eliz.c.1). To refuse to take the Oath of Supremacy from henceforward entailed not only fines and imprisonment but also disbarment from all office or employment. A second refusal carried

The Elizabethan Persecution

with it the death penalty.

Catholics who attended Mass in the chapels of the foreign embassies in London were imprisoned and, flouting all diplomatic conventions, foreign nationals worshipping at their own embassies were also imprisoned, their ambassadors having to pay bail to secure their release. State documents reveal, in hideous details that do not bear thinking about, the appalling, insanitary conditions in the prisons. Prisoners were treated like animals, given foul water to drink and scanty amounts of rotten food. The report on Richard Fulwood the servant of the Jesuit, John Gerard, makes harrowing reading. Kept in solitary confinement, 'He had hardly enough black bread to keep him from starving. His abode was a narrow, strongly built cell, in which there was no bed, so that he had to sleep sitting on the window sill, and was months without taking off his clothes. There was a little straw in the place, but it was so trodden down and swarming with vermin that he could not lie on it'. Only those wealthy enough to pay their jailers received anything that approximated to decent conditions. The significantly large numbers of Catholics who died in prisons sadly testify to this inhumane regime.

With the encouragement of the Dominican Pope, St Pius V Ghislieri (1566-72), in the late autumn of 1569 came the Northern Rising. Instigated by Sir Leonard Dacre and other prominent North Yorkshire gentlemen, it came under the leadership of Thomas Percy, 7th Earl of Northumberland and Charles Neville, 6th Earl of Westmorland. The people of Yorkshire and Durham rose up in their thousands in protest at the change in religion and to demand the release from captivity of Mary, Queen of Scots, the heir to the throne. The Queen's representative in Yorkshire, the trusted Sir Ralph Sadler, wrote to Secretary Cecil, 'There are not ten gentlemen in all this county who favour the new proceedings in religion'. Under an old banner from the 'Pilgrimage of Grace' depicting the Five Wounds of Christ, the people's army were on the march. The Earls manifesto protested their loyalty to Queen Elizabeth as 'true and faithful subjects' but they 'promised our Faith to the furtherance of this our good meaning. Forasmuch as divers disordered persons about the Queen's Majesty, have, by their subtle and crafty dealings to advance themselves, overcome in this realm, the true and Catholic religion towards God ... We, therefore, have gathered ourselves together ... to see the redress of these things amiss, with the restoring of all ancient customs and liberties to God's Church.'

Leading a force of armed horsemen, the Earls', accompanied by their wives, occupied Durham. Entering the cathedral the rebels destroyed the Protestant prayer books and threw out the Communion

The Elizabethan Persecution

table. The people of Durham came to the cathedral and helped set up an altar again, retrieving one of the old stone altar slabs from a rubbish tip. On 30 November Mass was celebrated again in the cathedral and in the parish churches of the city. After ten days the insurgents marched southwards and Mass was celebrated at Staindrop, Darlington, Richmond and in the cathedrals of Ripon and York. By the time the rebels reached Bramham, near Tadcaster, they numbered four thousand foot and seventeen hundred horsemen. Two hundred years later, inspired by a visit to Bolton Priory ruins in 1807, William Wordsworth commemorated the event in his poem *The White Doe of Rylstone:*

> It was the time when England's Queen
> Twelve years had reigned, a sovereign dread;
> Nor yet the restless crown had been
> Disturbed upon her virgin head;
> But now the inly-working North
> Was ripe to send its thousands forth,
> A potent vassalage to fight
> In Percy's and Neville's right ...
> And boldly urged a general plea,
> The rites of ancient piety
> To be triumphantly restored.

Because it was so badly organised and ill-equipped, the rising was doomed to failure. Even though it never posed any real military threat to the regime, it was crushed without mercy, with the help of the Scots, by the Queen's lieutenant-general in the North, her cousin - and half-brother - Henry Carey, Baron Hunsdon. Elizabeth insisted that not only its leaders be punished but also 700 ordinary working men were condemned to death as a warning to others. Although not all of them were hanged there were 230 executions at Ripon and hangings at Boroughbridge, Hanlith, Threshfield, Spofforth and Tadcaster, one of the chief centres for the Rising. The prisons were filled with totally innocent Catholics who had played no part in the abortive uprising. After the failure of the Northern Rising Northumberland had escaped over the border, where he was captured by the Scots, who sold him to the English Government. On 22 August 1572 forty-four-year-old Blessed Thomas Percy, Earl of Northumberland, refusing to abandon his religion, was beheaded at York. A direct consequence of the Rising was that the Oath of Uniformity was made obligatory on everyone in any official position.

The election of Pope Pius V saw a hardening of attitude to the Elizabethan government in Rome. The ascetic and zealous former

The Elizabethan Persecution

Inquisitor concluded - perhaps surprisingly for a man of such intelligence and integrity - that after ten fruitless years enough was enough and he decided to act. Apparently coinciding with the Northern Rising he had prepared a papal bull, but months before it was finally published in February 1570 the Rising had been crushed. Pope Pius employed a defunct medieval device and issued the bull *Regnans in excelsis* (He that reigneth on high), not only excommunicating Elizabeth as a heretic, but also purporting to release her subjects from their allegiance. 'We charge and command', reads the bull, 'the nobles, subjects and peoples ... that they do not dare obey her orders, mandates and laws'. The bull was brought into England by an Italian nobleman named Roberto di Ridolfi; ostensibly a papal agent. *

Pius sincerely hoped that publishing the bull would assist the oppressed English Catholics, and from his viewpoint Elizabeth's conduct justified his action. But Rome, badly advised, had misjudged the situation and in reality it was a futile gesture, one which was deeply regretted by some of Pius's successors. According to Father John Hungerford Pollen SJ in *The Politics of the English Catholics during the reign of Queen Elizabeth* (1902), Pius himself came to regret his decision, not necessarily because of the harmful consequences for English Catholics, but because no one was willing to take action to implement the bull, so it was ineffectual. King Philip II and the Emperor Maximilian both opposed the bull. But whatever his subsequent misgivings Pius would not retract the bull. Replying to Maximilian's request to revoke it Pius said he could not understand why Elizabeth was so troubled by the sentence. 'If she thinks so much of it, and the excommunication, why does she not return to the bosom of the Church she has abandoned? If she thinks nothing of it, why does she make so much fuss about it?' There were scholars who judged the bull to be uncanonical and this flaw was seized upon by many in England seeking to find reasons to circumvent the 'Roman thunderbolt' and thereby palliate their consciences.

In spite of the opposition to the bull by the great majority of English Catholics, simply because of their allegiance to Rome, they were now seen as potential traitors. It played directly into the hands of Secretary

---

* Ridolfi was a double agent and *agent provocateur*. For many years he had known and been trusted by William Cecil who made use of Ridolfi in various capacities. So although acting for the papacy he was also employed by Francis Walsingham and Cecil. The latter exercised direct influence on the publication of the bull in England. It clearly suited Burghley to make it appear that the Queen's excommunication was timed to assist the Northern Rising, whereas the bull had, in fact, been issued too late to have any real effect on the Rising.

The Elizabethan Persecution

Cecil, and presented him with the ammunition he needed. There can be no doubt that from the outset the complete destruction of Catholicism in England and Wales was Cecil's object, and all his policies and legislation were framed with this object in view.

The executions began in 1570, shortly after the papal bull. Thomas Plumtree [4] was executed at Durham for acting as a chaplain to the Northern Rising and John Felton [5] was executed at St Paul's churchyard, London, for publishing the bull. Felton's execution was followed by that of John Storey [6] in 1571. Two Acts were passed in 1571 (Eliz.13, c. 1 and 2) the first making it high treason to deny the Queen's right to the Crown or to declare her a heretic or schismatic. The second made it treason to bring papal bulls into England and to absolve or reconcile any person to the Catholic Church or to be so reconciled. A third Act (13 Eliz.c.3) was designed to prevent Catholics from seeking refuge overseas. It declared that any who were already abroad had to return and conform or forfeit their property. Anyone leaving the country without the Queen's licence, and not returning within six months, should forfeit their property and all their goods and chattels.

That there were genuine plots, usually originating abroad, to 'dispose' of Elizabeth in favour of the Catholic Queen of Scots is indisputable. Most notorious is the so-called Ridolfi Plot of 1571. Roberto di Ridolfi was a Florentine banker who travelled widely and was often in England. As has been mentioned, it was Ridolfi who brought the papal bull excommunicating Elizabeth into England. He hatched a conspiracy, which received the approval and financial backing of Pope Pius V, to rescue Mary, who would then marry the Duke of Norfolk; they would replace Elizabeth on the throne and restore Catholicism with Spanish military assistance. It seems to have been tacitly understood that the only effective way to 'dispose' of Elizabeth was to assassinate her. In the absence of documentary proof the level of Mary Stuart's personal involvement in the conspiracy remains an open question. Ridolfi co-ordinated the financing of the plan and purportedly acted as papal agent and intermediary with Mary and her supporters. If Ridolfi was indeed a double agent the likelihood is that Cecil knew of the plot well in advance. So when the conspiracy was officially discovered Burghley made the most of it, using it for his personal and political advantage. Norfolk paid for his involvement with his life and Mary was more strictly confined. It does not take much imagination to understand the effect of all this on Elizabeth and her attitude to her Scottish cousin, who had become the focus of conspiracies by her Catholic adherents. It is beyond reasonable doubt

The Elizabethan Persecution

that Gregory XIII, the successor of Pius V, favoured schemes to assassinate Elizabeth, the 'English Jezebel'. The 'justification' for this seems to have been Pius's bull of excommunication. Father J H Pollen SJ in *The Politics of the English Catholics during the reign of Queen Elizabeth*, while trying his best to be fair and just, nonetheless concludes that there was indeed papal toleration of political assassination. Written evidence, which has come to light since Father Pollen reached that conclusion, demonstrates that political murder was not simply tolerated, but tacitly encouraged in Rome. It is recorded that two Englishmen in Madrid asked the papal nuncio if killing Elizabeth would be a mortal sin. The nuncio referred the matter to the Vatican and received the reply from the Cardinal Secretary that, 'Since that guilty woman of England causes so much injury to the Faith, there is no doubt that who send her out of this world with the pious intention of doing God's service not only does not sin but gains merit.' It was in the knowledge of such blood-chilling views that some were foolishly misled into assassination schemes, such as John Somerville of Warwickshire. Somerville, whom many regarded as unhinged, was the son-in-law of Edward Arden, a recusant who lived at Castle Bromwich and kept a Marian priest named Hugh Hall disguised as a gardener. Arden's father was a cousin of Mary Arden, William Shakespeare's mother. Hall seems to have held extremist views and influenced Somerville who planned to kill the Queen. Somerville was soon sent to the Tower and after his trial committed suicide. But his relationship to Edward Arden proved fateful. Although Arden was not involved in Somerville's plan he was executed in 1583.

Increasingly ferocious penal laws were introduced against those who refused to conform to the Established Church. In his ten-volume, *The History of England from the First invasion of the Romans to the Accession of William and Mary in 1688*, originally published in the first half of the nineteenth century, the Catholic John Lingard, writing of the reign of Elizabeth commented:

All her subjects were required to submit to the superior judgement of their sovereign and to practise that religious worship which she practised. Every other form of service ... was strictly forbidden; and both the Catholic and the Puritan were subject to the severest penalties if they presumed to worship God according to the dictates of their conscience. It must appear singular that so intolerant a system should be enforced by men who loudly condemned the proceedings of the last reign, but in its defence they alleged ... the Queen 'would not delve into consciences'. Internally her subjects might believe ... what they pleased. All that she required was external conformity to the law. That she had a right to exact. If any man refused, the fault was his own; he suffered not for conscience sake, but for his obstinacy and his disobedience.

The Elizabethan Persecution

That this miserable sophism should have satisfied the judgement of those who employed it can hardly be credited.

An illustration of this government sophistry and cant is the story of Blessed Robert Anderton and Blessed William Marsden. Anderton was born in 1560 in the Isle of Man and educated at Oxford, where he became an inseparable friend of Marsden who came from Goosnargh, Lancashire. Together they were reconciled to the Church at Douai and on 10 July 1580 both were admitted to the English College at Rheims. Anderton, a Hebrew scholar, was ordained in 1584 and Marsden the following year. They were described as 'most unassuming but full of life and spirits, and they were remarkable for their piety and zeal for sacred things.' Together they set out from Rheims on 4 February 1586 but on the voyage to England there was a storm which forced their ship to take refuge in the Isle of Wight. The two young priests were arrested and taken to Winchester, examined by Bishop Cooper, and tried before the Lord Chief Justice, Sir Edmund Anderson. After their condemnation they protested their loyalty to the Queen and were sent to the Marshalsea in London to be examined by the Privy Council. They were then returned to Winchester on 21 April and from there delivered into the custody of Sir George Carey, Captain of the Isle of Wight, in readiness for execution. This took place, probably at Newport, on 25 April 1586.

The Privy Council issued a self-justifying declaration to be read and published at the time of their execution. Once more trying to deny and refute the claim that priests were being executed for their religion it contained the following astounding piece of monumental hypocrisy: 'Her Majesty minding nothing less than that any of her subjects, though disagreeing from her in religion, should die for the same, as by them and their companions hath been most falsely and slanderously published and affirmed.' The Elizabethan government had an obsession with Catholicism. Its ministers were constantly preoccupied in seeking ways to repress it. Arnold Pritchard writes in *Catholic Loyalism in Elizabethan England* about the conclusions of some other authors:

Others, much taken with Elizabeth's alleged desire not to open windows into men's souls, write as if Elizabeth's government was entirely uninterested in the religious beliefs of her subjects unless they became active traitors ...The persecution was very real and its long-range goal was the suppression of Catholicism per se, regardless of the political loyalty of any particular Catholic. [*]

---

[*] Copyright © 1979 by the University of North Carolina Press. Used by permission of the publisher.

The Elizabethan Persecution

As the reign progressed, a succession of Acts of Parliament ever more firmly established state persecution of those who adhered to the Old Faith. Under 13 Eliz.c. 2 of 1571, the penalties of *praemunire* were imposed on recusants and those reconciled to the Catholic Church. *Praemunire* involved the confiscation of all property and imprisonment at the government's pleasure, as happened to Thomas Williamson of Scarborough, who was caught importing Catholic items such as vestments, rosaries and crucifixes. This savage measure remained the law for the next ten years until even more draconian legislation was introduced.

Commissioners were appointed by the government in every shire. The records contain reams of accounts of their proceedings. The time and energy that must have been expended by commissioners, bishops, JP's and the courts in summoning recusants is absolutely extraordinary. The commissions comprised eight members for each parish, including the minister. At least once every week the commissioners were supposed to visit every house in order to question each inhabitant about their beliefs, and their attendance, or not, at church. If the parish commissioners were not satisfied those concerned were referred to the county commissioners for further examination and punishment by the magistrates, if they remained obstinate in their recusancy. It is astonishing the distances recusants were sent after being arraigned, as lists of lay prisoners in the Marshalsea demonstrate showing that they came from as far afield as Devon, Cornwall and Norfolk. That so many ordinary citizens, in all parts of the country, did resist the oppression is quite remarkable. Their 'Roll of Honour' is not writ large but is hidden in the public records. Take the case of Mrs Parkins, a poor Hampshire woman of great age. She would not conform and could not afford the fines, so at the instigation of the Bishop of Winchester she was sent to prison in the White Lion, Southwark, where she was kept for several years. Magdalen Browne, Viscountess Montague, (1538-1608) daughter of William, 4th Lord Dacre of Gilsland, a fervent Catholic who kept her own chaplain, * heard of her plight and in July 1573 wrote from her home at Cowdray Park, Sussex to Sir William More of Loseley, a county commissioner, urging him to use his influence to get the old lady released as an act of charity.

---

* Viscountess Montague had her own chapel where Mass was regularly sung. It was said that so many Catholics resided at or visited Cowdray it was known as 'Little Rome'. Her chaplain from 1594 was Thomas More, the great-grandson of Sir Thomas More. He was ordained at Rome and returned to England in 1592. In 1609 he went to Rome with Richard Smith, the future Bishop of Chalcedon, as agents of the Archpriest George Birket. Thomas died in Rome in 1625.

The Elizabethan Persecution

Under the 1581 Act of Persuasion 'to retain the Queen's Majesty's subjects in their obedience' (23 Eliz.I, c.1) it became high reason to reconcile anyone or be reconciled to Catholicism, or to shelter a reconciled Catholic. A fine of two hundred marks was imposed and one year's imprisonment on a priest for saying Mass, with a fine of one hundred marks and one year's imprisonment for anyone attending Mass. It was this Act that increased the fine for not attending Anglican services to £20 per month or imprisonment if the fine was not paid. A further £10 per month was imposed on anyone keeping a schoolmaster who did not conform, and the schoolmaster himself faced one year's imprisonment. In March 1585 a retrospective Act was passed (27 Eliz. I, c.2) against 'Jesuits and seminary priests and such like disobedient persons'. There was no other proof of any crime required: under the Act it became treason simply to have been ordained priest overseas from the time of Elizabeth's accession. While the Bill was being debated in Parliament, a group of prominent Catholics, believing or wanting to believe that the policy did not have the Queen's full approbation, drafted a supplication to the Queen, pleading to be allowed some freedom of conscience.

Perusing the text today it is heart-rending to read the lamentations of the petitioners describing how they were persecuted. But the (no doubt obligatory) terms of grovelling, obsequious self-abasement in which it is couched make very uncomfortable reading. A gentleman by the name of Richard Shelley of Michelgrove, Sussex, undertook to deliver the petition personally to the Queen as she walked in her park at Greenwich. Shelley came from a family whose various branches had suffered greatly for their Faith. They gave priests to the Church as well as confessors who died in prison. Richard's brother, Edward, whom we shall meet again later, was martyred. After presenting the petition Richard Shelley was arrested on the orders of Sir Francis Walsingham 7 and incarcerated in the Marshalsea 15 March 1585. As he was unable to pay to provide for himself (prisoners were expected to pay for their food, drink, bedding, etc or go without) he endured a miserable winter and soon became ill. He died in the Marshalsea early in 1586. His son, William, became a priest. It is perhaps superfluous to add that Elizabeth and her ministers completely ignored the petition, not deigning to respond. This notorious statute, 27. Eliz.I c.2, claimed the lives of over 150 innocent priests and their helpers.

The imprisoned Mary, Queen of Scots, continued to be a thorn in Elizabeth's side and a magnet for opposition. This led some Catholics to contemplate wildly unrealistic plots to depose Elizabeth, rescue Mary and place her on the throne. Such was the so-called Babington

The Elizabethan Persecution

Plot of 1586. To what extent the conspirators were serious is a matter for conjecture. Anthony Babington and his cronies were rich dilettantes and the madcap affair began as youthful posturing on their part. The most significant content was provided by the government infiltrators and spies. Father Anthony Tyrell alleged at the behest of Lord Burghley that the idea originated with the priest John Ballard, whom he first met in the Gatehouse prison and they struck up a friendship, a friendship, which, as Tyrell confessed, he repaid with the most monstrous lies. Ballard is alleged to have played upon the romantic fantasies of the vain Babington for rescuing the desperate Queen of Scots from imprisonment.

Burghley supplied Tyrell with a list of names of 'divers gentlemen' and required Tyrell to supply him with incriminating evidence against them. Tyrell accordingly obliged, only later to recant and declare that not only were they all innocent of everything he had accused them but also that he had never even met some of them. Anthony Tyrell [8] was a priest we shall unfortunately encounter several times in our narrative. As in any totalitarian state with an efficient spy network, the government was well informed as to what was happening from an early stage. Sir Francis Walsingham instituted a system for 'secret' messages to be passed to Mary, all of which he could intercept and decipher as part of his objective to bring about the ruin of the Queen of Scots.

The conspirators' every move was closely observed by spies. One of these was the treacherous Gilbert Gifford [9] who, even from his time in the seminary, was acting as a spy for the government. This shameful man went ahead with receiving holy orders for no other reason than to be in a better position to betray Catholics. It also illustrates the immoral depths the government was prepared to plumb to attain its ends. Gifford, already ordained deacon, acted as a double agent, purportedly serving Mary's interests by smuggling letters to and from her while spying for Walsingham. It is clear that Walsingham nurtured and manipulated those involved in the plot so it encompassed the assassination of Elizabeth, then chose the most propitious moment to pounce. At every stage Walsingham was fully aware of everything that was going on, not least because Babington had been suborned to supply him with information, so the plot never posed any real threat to Elizabeth. Nonetheless, everyone thought to be connected to the plot was executed in a particularly bloodthirsty fashion, including Father Ballard. He came from Cambridgeshire, attaining BA at King's College, Cambridge in 1574. Ordained at Châlons in 1581 he returned to England. He seems to have been a somewhat shady character who worked under the alias Captain Fortescue and liked to pretend he was influential. While staying at the Red Lion, Holborn, London at Christmas 1582 he reconciled John Hambley q.v. to the Church. His friendship with Anthony Tyrell was to prove fatal. Ballard, always a worldly man, appeared for his execution at Tyburn on 20 September 1586 accompanied by a servant and flamboyantly dressed 'in a grey cloak laid with gold lace, in velvet hose, a cut satin doublet, a fair hat of the newest fashion, the band being set with silver buttons.'

Justice Richard Young enlisted the help of Tyrell to send other Catholics to their deaths. Tyrell once again obliged by providing him with the false information he required, and within days of the executions of Ballard and his companions, three more victims of the lies of Anthony Tyrell were martyred on 8 October 1586. They were Blessed John Adams, Blessed Robert Dibdale, and Blessed John Lowe, who was born in London in 1553, the son of Simon Lowe, a merchant tailor. His family were Catholics, for he was educated at Douai and was a servant at Benedictine Anchin Abbey, near Douai, for a year. He entered the English College, Rome in 1581 and was ordained in 1582. He worked in London, a close friend of Father William Weston, and was known to frequent the house of Mr Trewayne in Clerkenwell. He was arrested near London Bridge in May 1586 and sent to the Clink.

John Adams was born c.1543 at Winterbourne St Martin, Dorset. He became the vicar of his home parish in the Established Church. After his conversion he went to Rheims in 1579 and was ordained at Soissons in December 1580. He was described as 'of average height with a dark beard, a sprightly look and black eyes. He was a good conversationalist, very straightforward, very pious and pre-eminently a man of hard work'. He had first been apprehended at Rye, Sussex, and sent a prisoner to Francis Walsingham in London. With the help of friends he escaped. He worked in Hampshire for the next three years and was recaptured at Winchester in March 1584 and sent to the Marshalsea. He was banished in 1585 but he must have returned from Rheims immediately as he was in the Clink by December 1585.

Robert Dibdale was born c.1558 at the hamlet of Shottery, Stratford-upon-Avon, and was sent to be educated at Louvain as a boy. He returned to England in 1580 and was arrested on arrival at Dover and committed to the Gatehouse. He had entrusted Thomas Cottam q.v. with a letter for his parents and small gifts of religious items for them and his siblings. When Cottam was apprehended at Dover these items were confiscated from him. The records relate that in November Robert's father, John, sent him by carrier two cheeses, a loaf of bread and five shillings. He was released from the Gatehouse in September 1582 and returned to Rheims where he completed his studies and was ordained there in the cathedral on 31 March 1584. In August of that year he was sent back to England. For a time he acted as chaplain to Sir Edmund Peckham at Denham, Buckinghamshire. Sir Edmund's wife was the sister of Father John Gerard. On 24 July 1586, Robert was arrested in a London Street and committed to the Counter, Wood Street, then moved to Newgate.

Anthony Tyrell had been installed in the Clink prison, Southwark, to preserve the pretence that he was a prisoner, while facilitating his spying activities. There he met John Lowe whom he calls 'a most blessed man and godly priest'. He admitted that he went to 'confession hypocritically' to Father Lowe in order to deceive him with his lies. He committed the further sacrilege of saying Mass in the prison the next day. Lowe's widowed mother, Margaret, lived on London Bridge, and one shudders to think that, following the usual custom, her son's severed head may have been impaled there after his execution, following which Tyrell was full of remorse. He later confessed his wickedness, declaring the priests 'three glorious and worthy martyrs' innocent of any offence, and he asked for the prayers of these and other martyrs for whose deaths he was responsible. Tyrell informs us that he was 'continually sending letters to my Lord Treasurer' [Lord Burghley] and to Justice Young, 'heaping up most horrible and shameful lies' about fellow priests in custody in the Clink.

One reply from Burghley to Tyrell is illuminating. It tells him that his 'dissimulation is to a good end and therefore both tolerable and commendable'. He gave Tyrell the authority to continue acting as a Catholic priest, going to confession and celebrating Mass, all in the cause of obtaining information with which to ruin his fellow Catholics. Burghley signs the letter 'Your loving friend'. Tyrell believed that the wily Burghley knew that most of the time he was lying, but it suited the Lord Treasurer's purposes to treat the information Tyrell supplied as true. Shortly afterwards, Justice Young wrote to Tyrell confirming that Burghley was acting upon the authority of the Queen. Having had a meeting with Elizabeth, Young declared that Her Majesty's pleasure was to 'employ you in finding out those traitors and would have you keep your credit with them to the end that you may better decipher them'.

Cecil and Walsingham, having successfully contrived to bring about the downfall of the Queen of Scots, Elizabeth then wrote to ask Sir Amias Paulet to quietly arrange for the murder of his royal prisoner. The harsh Paulet, a former diplomat and fanatical Puritan, who had replaced Sir Ralph Sadler in 1585 as Queen Mary's jailer, honourably declined. Elizabeth was always paranoid about settling the question of the succession during her lifetime and a statute of 1581 actually made punishable by death all predictions concerning her likely successor. So Elizabeth signed the death warrant and Mary was beheaded at Fotheringhay Castle in February 1587. By that stroke of the axe - or several as it happened - Elizabeth had disposed of the rival for her throne and deprived the Catholics of a focus for conspiracies. Mary Stuart was not the only Catholic victim that year. Within weeks of her execution four priests were martyred in four different locations: Thomas Pilcher, 10 Stephen Rowsham, 11 John Hambley 12 and Edmund Sykes, 13 followed by the Scotsman, George Douglas 14 in September. Some of the 'luckier' priests were committed to Wisbech Castle where, Challoner relates, there were thirty-three incarcerated together with Thomas Pound, a layman whose nickname was the 'lay Jesuit'. *

If 1587 was a dreadful year for English Catholics 1588 was to be absolutely horrendous. In spite of the way they were treated, the vast majority of the Catholics in England were very loyal and opposed any projected invasion by Spain. The priests on the mission had always emphatically rejected any idea of trying to restore Catholicism by force of arms. No evidence whatever exists to indicate that the mission had anything to do with any political schemes. The prevailing attitude of Catholics can best be summed up by one of the many poems written after the martyrdom of Edmund Campion:

> God knows it is not force nor might,
> Not war nor warlike band,
> Not shield and spear, not dint of sword,
> That must convert the land.
> It is the blood of martyrs shed,
> It is that noble train,
> That fight with word and not with sword
> And Christ their capitaine.

---

* Pound, whose brother, John was a priest, was the son of William Pound and Anne Wriothesley, sister of Thomas Wriothesley, Earl of Southampton. A handsome, cultured young man he became one of the Queen's favourite courtiers. In 1571 he became a Catholic and renounced the Court. In 1574 he was arrested as he was about to leave England to join the Society of Jesus. Pound did not cease to speak and write against the royal supremacy. Bishop Aylmer of London had him imprisoned at Bishops Stortford castle where he was kept in leg irons with an iron collar around his neck. After six years he was sent to the Marshalsea where he spent four years and for nine months he had the company there of Francis Tregian. He suffered long years of incarceration in various prisons, including seven years in the Tower, before being moved to Wisbech for ten years. His final three years were at Framlingham from where he was released in 1603 by King James. Having spent thirty years a prisoner he died at home in London in 1616 aged seventy-six.

The Elizabethan Persecution

From their base in Rome, Cardinal William Allen and Father Robert Persons SJ both enthusiastically supported the Spanish Armada plans. In doing so they demonstrated that they were totally out of touch with the attitude of the overwhelming majority of their co-religionists in England. Without any justification whatsoever Persons was writing utterly misleading messages to Philip II claiming that, 'All the Catholics of the country will join your Majesty's troops and will persuade their relations and friends to do likewise'. Nothing could have been further from the truth. National loyalty was one of the striking features of Elizabethan England, and English Catholics proved themselves to be as patriotic as their Protestant neighbours in opposing foreign invasion. It would be stretching credulity beyond breaking point to claim that the Catholics loved their Queen, but she was their legal sovereign in an age when obedience to absolute monarchy was virtually unquestioned. Those priests who prayed for Elizabeth on the gallows and cried God save the Queen were far more representative of English Catholic opinion than the exiles in Rome and Spain plotting invasion.

When the government got wind of the Spanish naval preparations it rounded-up all prominent Catholics, who were imprisoned or placed under house arrest and made to pay huge fines. The fact that Catholics had demonstrated their loyalty by offering their services to the armed forces and by donating funds to the defence efforts was ignored. Anthony Browne, 1st Viscount Montague, (1528-92) was one of the leading Catholics of the reign. He had been imprisoned under Edward VI in 1551 for continuing to attend Mass. He rose to prominence under Mary, from whom he received his peerage. In 1559 he was the only lay peer to oppose the Act of Supremacy in the House of Lords, and he made his opposition known again in 1562, when he spoke against the act making it compulsory to take the Oath of Supremacy. At Cowdray Park, his home in Sussex, he and his second wife, Magdalen, maintained a Catholic household and kept their own chaplain. In spite of all this he was conspicuously loyal to the Crown and seems to have been tolerated by Elizabeth. Montague rode with his sons and grandsons and a large troop of horsemen to the pre-invasion muster before the Queen at Tilbury. The failed Spanish Armada of July/August 1588 brought even greater misery and repression to Catholics, who were now suspected of being in league with foreign powers to destroy the Elizabethan regime. It resulted in the executions of over thirty priests and laypeople, all of whom have been beatified.

By this time the number of Catholics in jail was so great that new prisons had to be opened, utilising buildings such as castles. There were several such detention centres around the country, most notably the fifteenth-century Wisbech Castle in the Fens, which was used specifically for priests. Surrounded by a forty-feet-wide moat, the only access via a drawbridge, it was in a ruinous condition by the time priests were sent there. In 1596 the keeper, William Medeley, wrote to inform Sir Robert Cecil that on the night of 28 February the priest Francis Tilletson q.v. 'by a cord of a bed let himself down over the castle wall and so is escaped. I have laid very great wait for him both by water and land round about me, far and near, and yet I hear not of him, but am in good hope.' Tilletson - who seems to have been a somewhat obstreperous character - came from Richmond, North Yorkshire, and was ordained at Rheims in 1585. While returning to England he had been captured at sea off the Suffolk coast and was sent to the Marshalsea and then to Wisbech. Tilletson's own account of his escape is too good not to relate. It sounds as if it had been well planned. When he went over the castle wall at midnight he was met by a Mr Ellis, the husband of the priest's laundrywoman. Ellis rowed him in a boat to Willingham, Cambridgeshire, from where he walked to Rampton and was provided with a horse by Mrs Alcock. He rode to the home of Mr Scroggs, two miles from Bedford, but Scroggs was too afraid to take him in so he was forced to ride on through the night to Mrs Willows' house three miles north of Bedford where he was given shelter. Medeley must have been on his trail because the next day Tilletson was re-captured.

In 1597 Medeley again wrote to Cecil complaining that because of the expense he was out of pocket and he asked that more priests should be sent to him. Some had recently died and others, he says, 'at this instant are in extreme peril of death.' He also told Cecil that during his absence in London two of the priests 'having beaten out great iron bars of their windows by breaking the freestone whereunto they were let two inches at the least, by their bed cords let themselves down and so escaped. I will spare no cost for their apprehension.' The priests' involved were George Stransham q.v. and William Parry. Wisbech continued to be used as a concentration camp for clergy until 1618.

Other prisons were reserved especially for the gentry. In this latter category can be cited the apparently mindless treatment meted out to John Towneley, from a prominent and very wealthy Lancashire gentry family. No doubt hoping to make an example of him, he was arrested and imprisoned at Chester Castle and was then sent to the Marshalsea in London. In 1571 he was called to York to answer charges of recusancy and was bound over. His failure to conform led to his being imprisoned in York Castle. Once again he was sent to London to see if his half-brother, then Dean of St Paul's, could persuade him. That ploy

The Elizabethan Persecution

obviously failed because John was imprisoned again at York in 1573. Released into private custody in 1574 he was back in jail later that year. In the summer of 1576 the Privy Council ordered that he be released into private custody in Lancashire, but by the autumn he was returned to prison in York and transferred to the Hull blockhouses. In 1578 he was sent to London in the custody of his half-brother. From there he went to the Gatehouse; then to a camp near Ely. Aged seventy-three, blind and disabled, he was finally released on condition that he never travelled more than five miles from his home and continued to pay the extortionate monthly fines. Although his case was exceptional it was by no means an isolated one: other gentry families suffered similar penalties. The fact that so many resisted for so long the intense pressure on them to conform, indicates the strength of their convictions and the failure of the authorities' efforts to 'break' them.

It is easy to blame families who conformed, but the fines imposed for non-attendance at the Protestant services were so crippling that it meant absolute beggary for all except the wealthiest. Even keeping a known Catholic servant was an offence for which a fine had to be paid. By the end of the reign only sixteen Catholics were left still able to pay the full, annual £260 in fines for recusancy, among them the Arundells of Lanherne, Cornwall. The rest, like the Cornish Becket family, who had been imprisoned for non-payment, had forfeited most of their estates. Recusants' goods - even their homes - were confiscated and sold to pay the fines. The Queen made use of the iniquitous system to reward members of her entourage; presumably to keep them loyal. Many of the goods and properties confiscated from recusants were granted to members of her household. (Vide the case of Joshua Pulleyn cited in the Preface.) Among the beneficiaries can be found 'gentlemen of the Chapel', waiters, cooks and Yeomen of the Guard. Even the Queen's laundress, Ann Twist, benefited handsomely. As the reign progressed, many Catholics who had Protestant relatives or friends arranged to transfer property to them in trust to protect it from the predations of the government. I would like to give an illustration by telling the story of the downfall of the Fitzherbert family because it is a classic example of the tragedy that engulfed so many families and graphically epitomises what Dr Augustus Jessop was referring to in his book about the Walpole's of Norfolk.

The Fitzherbert's were a prominent and ancient family whose estates were spread over Derbyshire and Staffordshire. Sir Anthony Fitzherbert (1470-1538), a famous lawyer and high court judge, was obliged to assist in the trial of the Carthusian priors and Richard Reynolds, and the tribunals that tried John Fisher and Thomas More.

The Elizabethan Persecution

His three sons, Thomas, John and Richard, survived him. Sir Thomas, the eldest, succeeded his father as fifteenth Lord of Norbury. He was Sheriff of Staffordshire under Queen Mary. He inherited the manor of Padley through his marriage to Anne Eyre and handed over the tenancy to his younger brother, John and his wife, Catherine. Under the Elizabethan penal laws Sir Thomas was made to pay a huge £260 a year for recusancy, which was more than his yearly rents. He had already been imprisoned many times for his refusal to conform. In 1561,when he was in the Fleet, among his fellow captives were the last Catholic Bishop of Chester and the last Catholic Dean of St Paul's. In 1568, while still in the Fleet, he witnessed the will of Dr Poole, the last Catholic Bishop of Peterborough.

In the Armada summer of 1588 a special search of the Peak District was undertaken for papists. Sir Thomas's brother, John, who had also served many terms of imprisonment, was caught hiding two priests at Padley Hall - Blessed Robert Ludlam and Blessed Nicholas Garlick. 15 George Talbot, 6th Earl of Shrewsbury, Lord Lieutenant of Derbyshire - and for fourteen years the jailer of Mary, Queen of Scots - seized the hall and all its contents on 12 July, together with many acres of surrounding land occupied by rent paying tenants. John Fitzherbert's sons, John and Anthony, and his three married daughters, Matilda, Mary and Jane, together with their servants, were arrested.

John Fitzherbert was sent first to Sheffield and then to Derby jail, along with his son Anthony and ten servants. John and the priests Ludlam and Garlick were condemned to death, but John's life was saved by his son-in-law, who sold his manor and with the help of friends raised the enormous sum of £10,000 to purchase a reprieve. However John was kept in Derby prison for two years before being transferred to the Fleet, where he died on 8 November 1590 of jail fever, the common name for epidemic typhus, to which so many succumbed.*

Sir Anthony Fitzherbert's third son, Richard, had escaped to the continent and later returned to Norbury, where he was arrested by order of the Privy Council in 1590. Despite falling ill in prison, he was transferred to London with his brother John, and there he too died.

Meanwhile their elder brother, Sir Thomas Fitzherbert, still languished in the Tower, where he was tortured by the infamous

---

* Father John Gerard SJ relates that in one of the jails he was imprisoned the cell door 'was so low that I had to enter, not on my feet, but on my knees, and even then I was forced to stoop; however, I reckoned this rather an advantage, inasmuch as it helped to keep out the strong and pestilential stench that came from the common place close to my door, that was used by the prisoners. I was often kept awake by the bad smell to say nothing of the injury to health.'

Richard Topcliffe. ₁₆ The shackles they placed on him were so heavy and tight that he lost the use of his legs. He was left in close confinement for three years and died in the Tower on 2 October 1591 aged seventy-four, having spent over thirty years of his life in various prisons. With the connivance of Sir Thomas's wicked nephew, Topcliffe managed to get his hands on the Padley estate for himself after the deaths of Sir Thomas and John Fitzherbert but had to forfeit it in 1603 when James I granted it to Henry Butler.

Of John Fitzherbert's two surviving sons the younger, Anthony, who had been arrested at Padley with his father, endured three years' imprisonment in Derby followed by a spell in a London jail. He continued to be harassed and convicted for recusancy for the rest of his life. The elder, Nicholas, was educated at Exeter College, Oxford, but because of his religion did not take a degree. He went abroad and matriculated at Douai University, going on to study law at Bologna University. In his absence he was found guilty of treason on 1 January 1580, particularly on account of his activities in raising funds for the English College. He settled in Rome on a pension from Pope Gregory XIII. When William Allen was appointed a Cardinal Nicholas became his secretary and lived with Allen until the latter's death. This is significant because Nicholas strongly and publicly opposed the policies advocated by Father Robert Persons SJ with regard to foreign intervention in English affairs. When Padley Hall was raided in 1588 and the priests' captured, Nicholas was attainted for treason. Although he was recommended for ecclesiastical office he never took holy orders. Nicholas Fitzherbert, while on his way back to Rome, was drowned attempting to cross a river near Florence on 6 November 1612. He was buried in the Benedictine Abbey at Florence. We shall meet Nicholas's first cousin, Thomas Fitzherbert, elsewhere in our narrative. Padley Hall fell into ruin, but the gatehouse, with its original chapel, was restored in 1933 and Mass is regularly celebrated.

Writing in the 1590's, Father Henry Garnet, Jesuit Superior in England, relates the following story to illustrate how desperate the persecution had become. A recusant nobleman and his eight-months pregnant wife, hiding from the authorities, lived for six weeks in an underground shelter that they had constructed under a large oak tree in their own park. They dared emerge from the narrow entrance, concealed by grass sods, only at night when food was secretly brought to them from the house. When it rained and snowed the whole edifice collapsed in on them. Father Garnet also recounts the treatment of the Trollope family of Co. Durham. The Earl of Huntingdon, President of the Council of the North, brought a posse into Co. Durham in order to

The Elizabethan Persecution

make a search of the home of John Trollope. This was most likely the raid that took place in 1594, which is also described by Father Richard Holtby SJ, who evaded capture at the time. John Trollope and his wife, his son, a thirteen-year-old niece, and two servants went into an underground hiding-place, leaving one maid to answer any questions. When the searchers failed to find John they began to violently ransack the house, forcing locks and tearing down partitions. They helped themselves to whatever took their fancy, taking away silverware, clothes, linen, saddles and anything else that appeared to be of value. All this time, for two nights and days, John and his family remained concealed without either food or drink, terrified lest one of them should cough or make some other noise that would betray their whereabouts. When the searchers departed they emerged in a shocking state from their ordeal. Father Garnet also mentions groups of Catholics who banded together in comradeship, living in the ruins of old buildings to escape the pursuivants and avoid being forced to attend church or pay heavy fines. The contemporary accounts of how Catholics lived and worshipped call to mind the days of the primitive Church: small groups assembling in secret to hear Mass and receive the Sacraments, never quite sure if a traitor might have infiltrated their company. Most were resigned to longing for better days and hoped that at their deaths they would have the ministrations of a priest. Amongst the more active Catholics there was remarkable cohesion and mutual helpfulness and love.

In this context it is most apposite to here include the story of Margaret Ashton, not only because of its connection with Blessed Nicholas Garlick but also for the rare, moving and illuminating insight it provides of the intimate lives of his contemporary Catholics. In 1911, in an old grey stone farmhouse at remote Long Kirby in the Derbyshire Peak Forest, an amazing discovery was made: a yellowed diary from Elizabethan times written in a fine hand by Margaret Ashton. The Ashton family were recusants who were probably relatively safe in their remote home. One of William Cecil's priest-hunters wrote that the Peak was difficult country to search 'for the recusants keep scouts day and night, and they ride armed.' With the caves and rugged terrain they would not have been short of hiding places. Margaret, the daughter of a yeoman, was born in 1558 and at the time of the discovery of her diary her portrait, painted in 1583 and stating her age as twenty-five, still hung in the parlour of the farmhouse. On the back of the picture was inscribed the words, 'Only those who endure to the end shall be saved.' The diary commenced in 1584 and clearly inscribed at the top of the first page was the name of Margaret Ashton. Much of the diary was

The Elizabethan Persecution

concerned with Richard Ingham, who it soon emerged, was Margaret's sweetheart and she records every one of his visits to her home, even down to the exact time of his arrival and departure. Richard was also a recusant and Margaret feared for his safety. On Easter Sunday 1584 Margaret wrote:

> It is Easter Day. My heart misgives me when I think how very long it is since any of us poor Catholics have seen a priest. We have had no Mass these many weary days and have not received the Body of the Lord for nigh upon two years. We are starving. Richard Ingham came this day. I fear me he is no longer so brave a Catholic. He thinks no more of our great need for spiritual food. I do pray God not to try him over much.

The diary continues throughout the summer of 1584:

4 July. Richard Ingham rode over this forenoon. He seemed ill at ease and then told us that late last night a fugitive priest came, asking for shelter, not telling his name. Would to God he had come to Long Kirby. I warrant me we could have housed him secretly and got him off. But Richard is half-hearted in this affair. I fear the worst.

5 July. Ingham came this morning. He asked to speak with me alone. His face was drawn and haggard. He asked for my help and counsel. I told him that most assuredly I would give all the help I could. Then he said - and how it should have gladdened me to hear this: You know, Mistress Margaret, why I come for at least you know I love you, though you cannot know how much. I am not a coward. I would die cheerfully in a fair quarrel, but to be caught like a rat and buried alive within the four walls of Derby prison! There is a heavy penalty for priest-harbouring - imprisonment for life - it would be easier to die. Dear love, I said, and caught his hands, it is easier to die than to betray God's servant. It is easier to suffer torture and long imprisonment. Be strong, hold up your head. The Queen's men have not yet found us out. Tomorrow we will have Mass. It will give us strength and we shall have no more of these fears.

6 July. We set out at sunrise for Ingham's house. [Margaret does not record where that was located.] Walking by untrodden ways through the hills. Arrived we did knock upon the side door and were admitted. None speaking any word. In the upper room right in the roof we found a table spread over with a linen cloth, and lights burning. Richard stood by the door to admit each one to confession, and there were many there. Later in the big room Mass was said. Richard Ingham served, and I did note with joy that he already looked a new man and held his head as one proud in the service of the Lord. With beating hearts we saw the strange priest - his very name unknown to us standing before the altar of God. Time seemed a little thing besides these great mysteries which for hundreds of years have brought strength to faint hearts. We could

The Elizabethan Persecution

have sung for joy. The face of the priest will never pass from my remembrance if I live many years - though it may be that we shall all most happily suffer for this day's work, and God grant it be so. The priest was of most excellent countenance, strong, yet full of gentleness, and though some weeks unshorn of beard he bore himself with all the manner of a prince, and showed no sign of fear. We knew not his name nor whence he came, only from his papers that he was known to my Lord Bishop of Lincoln before he was committed to the Tower. But for his voice and that of Master Ingham we did hear naught save the wind in the trees near the house, and once I did think a sound as of a horse galloping. When we all drew near to receive the Bread of life the very wind seemed hushed, but towards the end of Mass a clamour of voices broke out along the hill road, and a rattle of horses' feet. Then we knew that the Queen's men had come and all raised their heads to listen, all that is save the priest, who did not seem to hear. Quietly he moved about the altar-table and read the final prayers with voice unshaken. Richard too remained as one who heard nothing but the voice of the priest. Then loud blows fell upon the door below, and a voice called to open in the Queen's name. Mass being ended we all waited and then Ingham went down and let the men come in, for they would have burst the door. Then we heard them call the priest's name. And it was Nicholas Garlick.

We had long known of this holy man, for he was sometime master of Bishop Pursglove's school at Tideswell, many miles southward from this place, and he was known to be full of learning and virtue. This then was he who with his head lifted and eyes aflame waited without a tremor for his arrest. I cannot write of what followed nor of the rough usage he got, but he bore it all right manfully like the brave gentleman he is. Richard too was taken, and then I felt my heart would burst, and I did beg and pray of the Queen's officer that he would take me too. But he pushed me away when I went forward, and even when I knelt to him he would not hear me. And now here at Long Kirby I wait for tidings, while those who have gone to the foul fever den at Derby, there to stand trial with other recusants. And I know how heavy is the trial which I must bear alone. And yet to know that Richard Ingham did not fail, and will not, God helping him, and that he loves me, is enough for any woman's happiness.

The following diary entries tell of tears and sorrow thinking about what Ingham was suffering in Derby jail. Then came the news that Ingham had been banished along with Garlick and seventy-two other priests and recusants. Only two months later Nicholas Garlick was back in Derbyshire bringing with him Richard Ingham. Father Garlick performed the marriage ceremony of Margaret and Richard in the parlour at Long Kirby. Unlike the fate of Nicholas, what subsequently happened to the brave couple is unknown. One hopes it was a happy future together.

It was not only the gentry who suffered; recusants of every class

The Elizabethan Persecution

were caught in the clutches of the police state, which spied upon, examined and recorded every minute detail of their lives. Schoolmasters were always a prime target. Blessed John Slade came from Dorset. He was educated at New College, Oxford, from which he was expelled for religion. Blessed John Bodey was born at Wells, Somerset in 1549. He was educated at Winchester and New College, Oxford, becoming a Fellow in 1568. He too was expelled in 1576 and went to Douai to study civil law. He returned to England in 1578 and became a schoolmaster at a house of the Shelley family in Sussex where one of his pupils was Benjamin Norton who became a priest, being ordained in Rome in 1591. In 1580 John was arrested near Petersfield, Hampshire, and committed to Winchester jail where several priests and nuns were his fellow prisoners. Two years later he was joined by John Slade. At the Spring Assizes in 1583 both were tried for denying the royal supremacy. For some obscure reason - perhaps a flaw in the legal proceedings - the pair of them were re-tried at Andover on 19 August and once more condemned. Slade was hanged, drawn and quartered at Winchester 30 October 1583 and Bodey suffered at Andover 2 November. On the scaffold he declared, 'Understand good people, that I suffer death for denying her Majesty to be supreme head of Christ's Church in England ... other treasons, except they make the Holy Mass, or saying the Ave Maria treason, I have committed none.' On the day of her son's execution his mother threw a party for all her friends and neighbours to celebrate his martyrdom. Shortly afterwards a Mr Hardy of Farnham was arrested and committed to jail for daring to speak publicly in defence of the two martyrs.

Blessed Thomas Watkinson was a yeoman and a widower with a family living quietly at Menthorpe, in the East Riding of Yorkshire. On the Saturday night before Palm Sunday, 28 March 1591, Blessed Robert Thorpe arrived at his home in readiness for saying Mass the following day. Father Thorpe, also a Yorkshireman, had been ordained at Rheims in April 1585. A nosy neighbour, having seen greenery being gathered, became suspicious and informed the Justice of the Peace, John Gates at Howden. In the early hours of Sunday Gates, with a great company, descended on Watkinson's house and arrested Thorpe in bed. The searchers rampaged through the house, taking whatever they liked before marching Thorpe and Watkinson off to prison in York Castle. They were both condemned, and in spite of reportedly being of a timorous disposition, as well as being offered their lives if they would conform, they were martyred together at York on 31 May.

Father Henry Garnet was in Winchester in 1592 and a witness to the outbreak of persecution that occurred. Blessed James Bird, who it appears was personally known to Garnet, was born at Winchester. As a boy he converted to Catholicism and because he refused to attend church he was imprisoned and suffered 'many whippings'. Accompanied by Henry Wells, brother of Swithun, he went to Rheims to study. After returning home he became a servant to Mr Jerome Heath. In 1592 the house was searched looking for Winchester-born Father Benjamin Norton. The priest evaded capture but James was apprehended, accused of being reconciled to the Church and was arrested and imprisoned. He was tried before Sir Edmund Anderson and offered his liberty if he agreed to go to church and acknowledge the royal supremacy. This he refused and was condemned. James, aged nineteen, was hanged, drawn and quartered outside the West Gate, Winchester on 25 March 1592. His head was displayed over the gate. Perhaps it was not fastened too securely because as his father passed below the head seemed to nod at him. 'Ah, son Jemmy', he said, 'living you were always dutiful and obedient and now in death you pay reverence to your father.' Another layman, John Thomas, a convert Calvinist reader, was condemned at the same assizes. Faced with execution he recanted and promised to go to church. Returned to prison he regretted his weakness and informed the judges. 'Why is he in such haste to go to the gallows,' they asked. He was executed in August.

On 23 June 1592 a Lancashire man, Venerable Roger (or Robert) Ashton, was hanged, drawn and quartered at Tyburn for the crime of having obtained a dispensation from Rome to marry his cousin. Robert Jebb was a poor Yorkshire farmer who sheltered priests. His own little home being both inadequate and spied upon by the authorities, he decided to build out in his fields, amongst a copse of bushes, a little house. It was ten feet long, seven feet wide and eight feet high. Here he secretly met priests. When his house was searched and he was arrested and carted off to prison, he told a relative of the secret little dwelling, in case priests came there for shelter. The information was betrayed to the authorities. Ralph, 3rd Lord Eure, Vice-President of the Council of the North, went to find the place and destroyed it.

Ordinary labourers were made destitute by crippling fines. Bear in mind that the fine for non-attendance at church was equivalent to two days' wages. Those recusants who could not pay were whipped in the market places, were put in the pillory, had their ears cut off, or were imprisoned until they yielded. Many recusants spent years perpetually in and out of prison for being unable to pay the fines or endured life imprisonment rather than take the oath.

For example, the Hampshire prison records show that most of the recusants held were poor people; labourers and spinners and suchlike.

The Elizabethan Persecution

At Slackstead lived Blessed Ralph Milner. He was a poor, illiterate husbandman with a wife and ten children. He regularly sheltered priests and for this spent many years in and out of Winchester jail. He was a constant companion to Father Thomas Stanney in his travels. In his memoirs the priest tells us that on one occasion Ralph came to him ready to make another journey around the Hampshire villages. Father Stanney was very fatigued from his recent missionary labours. But the uneducated Ralph gently chided him, 'But master, we have still a great many hungry souls that want bread and there is no one to give it to them; many also would be glad ... to embrace the Catholic faith, and I can find none to help them and receive them into the Church. What then must I say to them?' Stanney decided that he needed assistance and asked that Father Roger Dickenson or Dicconson be sent back to Winchester. Blessed Roger Dickenson came from Lincolnshire and was ordained at Laon in 1583. He had served terms of imprisonment in the Bridewell and the Gatehouse. He laboured for several years in Winchester, assisting Father Stanney in his work among the poor and the prisoners. In 1591 Ralph and Roger were arrested, bound hand and foot and sent to London on the orders of Bishop Thomas Cooper of Winchester. The servants of the Bishop who escorted them were paid £8 for their trouble. After time in jail, when Roger was tortured, they were returned to Winchester for trial at the summer Assizes. Both were condemned to death. Ralph asked the judge to be good to his wife and children and received the response, 'Go to church you fool, and look to thy children yourself.' At the same trial eight or nine Catholic women were condemned for attending Father Dickenson's Mass, but not executed. Ralph and Roger were martyred on 7 July 1591.

Also in Winchester lived a young man called Laurence Humphrey. An earnest Protestant, he began to have doubts after reading some Catholic books and sought out a priest. He met Father Thomas Stanney and became a Catholic. Within the next couple of years he fell extremely ill and in his fever he referred to the Queen as a heretic. This was overheard and, in spite of his sickness, he was arrested for treason and committed to Winchester jail. He was fettered to one of the common felons, who Laurence begged to remain quiet and still while he stood to say his prayers each day. He was tried at the next assizes, where he was shown a rosary that had been taken from him at the time of his arrest. Laurence reverently kissed the crucifix hanging from the beads. 'So you take this for your God', said the judge. 'Not so, my lord', Laurence replied, 'but for a remembrance of the death which my Saviour suffered for me.' He was found guilty of treason for the words uttered in his delirium, and upon being urged to confess what he had said he declared that to his knowledge he had never spoken them, but if the witnesses said that he did, he would not dispute it. Sentenced to be hanged, drawn and quartered he responded, 'All this is but one thing.' 'What thing?', asked the judge. 'One death.' While awaiting execution he was continually harassed by the ministers until they gave up, realising that they were not going to change his mind. At the gallows the hangman hurled insults at him. 'You hold with the Pope', he sneered, 'but he has brought you to the rope, and the hangman shall have your coat.' At this Laurence just smiled, at which the hangman cuffed his ear, saying, 'What! Dare you laugh at me?' Laurence responded, 'Why do you strike me? I have given you no occasion'. He had hardly got the words out of his mouth when he was turned off the ladder. Blessed Laurence Humphrey, who was just twenty years of age, suffered at Winchester in 1591.

There was also a whole class of numerous vagrant recusants who spent their lives 'on the run', constantly moving from place to place to avoid seizure by the authorities. The better-off gentry, who probably had several houses, were accustomed to moving around their scattered residences. Thus Gilbert Leigh of Leeds in the 1590's was presented for recusancy in four different places in quick succession. And the well-known Anne family as well as their houses in Yorkshire held property in Lincolnshire to which they could escape from the jurisdiction of the Earl of Huntingdon. Sir William Ingleby of the recusant family of Ripley - thanks to them a strong Catholic centre - and his numerous children regularly moved around between their homes in the East, West and North Ridings. One incredible story is worth relating in detail; that of Blessed John Bretton, from the place of that name in Sandal Magna parish, near Wakefield, in the West Riding of Yorkshire. John was a gentleman farmer who came from an ancient, landowning family. In 1543 he married Frances Wentworth, from the family owning Bretton Hall, and they had five children. He and his wife appear in the 1577 list of recusants compiled for Archbishop Edwin Sandys of York, where they are described as 'most obstinate and perverse'. John had suffered constant harassment and in order to avoid imprisonment, in 1577, he left his family, living as a fugitive for sixteen years, although he clearly made secret visits to his home at various times.

In August 1580 there was a meeting of Sandys, the Earl of Huntingdon and various commissioners at Wakefield. They placed Matthew Wentworth of Bretton Hall, under bond not only to attend church, but also to bring his wife before the commissioners at York, to apprehend Romish priests and, 'to apprehend John Bretton if at any time he meet with him and bring him to York'. At the same meeting

The Elizabethan Persecution

Robert Bretton, John's younger brother, protested his conformity but was instructed, under bond, to bring his mother, Agnes, to York, to answer charges of recusancy by January next. Robert failed to comply and forfeited his bond. In August 1582 Robert, who was clearly running the farm in John's absence, was summoned to York and being taken before Archbishop Sandys at his residence at Bishopthorpe, was bound over to 'bring John Bretton, his brother, the first day after Michaelmas next, or else yield himself personally in the Castle'. Three days later he was hauled before the Dean of York and placed on bond 'to bring John Bretton on Monday before Martinmas next following or else that day to yield himself personally in the castle and remain there according to the order taken in that behalf, and a warrant was sent to the gaoler for his delivery forth of the prison for this.' Robert was summoned again in October 1582 and in January, February and April 1583 to answer why he had not produced his brother. In November 1583, having lost patience with him, Robert was summoned to York once more. The decision was that Robert 'shall have a warrant to apprehend John Bretton, his brother' and condemned Robert to a fine of £20 for contempt of court in not complying with his earlier instructions. When summoned in January 1584 Robert failed to appear, but was forced to do so in March, when he was commanded to pay forty shillings to one Anthony Darrell, a pursuivant, and amazingly was then discharged from his bond.

From this it can be surmised that Robert had probably provided information as to his brother's whereabouts. In October 1585 Sir John Hotham, Sheriff of Yorkshire, wrote to Sir Francis Walsingham that John Bretton was in Salford jail, Manchester, where one of his fellow prisoners was Sir John Southworth of Samlesbury. Walsingham instructed Thomas Preston, Sheriff of Lancashire, to ask Bretton to contribute either a horse or £25 in cash as a contribution towards the expenses of the Earl of Leicester's proposed expedition to the Spanish Netherlands. Preston said that he had already made the request to John who had replied that he was a minor gentleman, 'not able to find neither horse, money or furniture, but one that lives off the charity and relief of others'. It appears that John was released in November and went into hiding. In February 1589 orders were issued under patent by Lord Burghley, for an assessment and seizure for the benefit of the Queen of two-thirds of all John's property. By April the assessment had taken place and the details appear alongside those of forty-five other recusants. John's lands comprised approximately 120 acres. The assessment reads that

John Bretton and Frances, his wife, are seized or that John Bretton is seized, of

certain lands in Bretton of the yearly rent of £4 and of certain lands in Dewsbury, of the yearly rent of £3.6s.8d: and that they are possessed of four oxen, price £8: two stutts [?] price £3, four kine, price £5, six young beasts, price £4; twelve acres of oaks, price £6'
making a grand total of £30.

John was ordered to pay a yearly rent to the Queen of £4.17s.9d. He ignored the order. On 25 March 1590 the seized portion of his lands was granted to Cuthbert Stillingfleet 'an usher of the Chamber Royal'. John's debt of £30 remained, but he never paid it. In July 1594 he was ordered to pay a further £6. It was never paid. In July 1596, on top of the annual rent he was supposed to be paying, an additional charge of £10.13s.4d was imposed. It was never paid.

The 1593 Act (35 Eliz.c.2) forced all recusants to return to their homes and not travel more than five miles without incurring the loss of all their property. By 1594 John was back at Bretton with his wife and three of their children, Luke, Mark and seventeen-year-old Dorothy, because they were listed by the churchwardens as 'obstinate recusants'. They appear as such again in 1595, this time with an additional son, Richard, and once more in 1597, when they are recorded as 'All recusants'. By now they were virtually under house arrest. In March 1598 John was charged with the following offences a) because he was reconciled to the Catholic Church b) urged others to embrace the same religion and c) denied the spiritual supremacy of the Queen. He was also accused of saying that 'he hoped to see the crown on the head of a Catholic monarch'. On 31 March John was tried under 23.Eliz.cap.2, 'An Act against seditious words and rumours against the Queen' and condemned. He was offered his life if he would conform. He refused and was hanged at York 1 April 1598. He was seventy years old.

Not content with this the authorities continued to pursue his widow, Frances. She must have found herself in deep trouble, being now responsible for her husband's unpaid fines - which would have amounted to £760 - and with no one to turn to, especially as so many of her relatives had by now yielded and conformed. In 1599 she engaged a lawyer to plead her case for retaining her property. She found that the law demanded her to conform. In 1601 her resistance gave way and she agreed to put in an appearance at the parish church at Sandal Magna. Even this did not satisfy the persecutors. Nothing less than a public act of submission would do. So on 15 June 1601 Frances was summoned before Archbishop Matthew Hutton of York. In his chapel at Bishopthorpe she made her submission, and received a certificate from him confirming the fact. The certificate refers to Frances as 'very aged and troubled with much infirmity and weakness'. Her lawyer argued,

The Elizabethan Persecution

ipso facto, that her debts were now legally invalid. Judgement was given by Attorney-General Coke in favour of the plea and Frances was discharged. Thus what remained of her property was saved for her eldest son. However, the records show that Frances and her daughter, Dorothy, were listed amongst a large group of recusants convicted on 11 March 1604 and again in 1607. She was alive in 1615; still listed as a recusant in Sandal parish. Two of her sons, Matthew and Richard, became seminary priests. Matthew, who was born in 1564, was ordained at the Lateran, Rome, in 1586. In 1593 he was appointed a tutor at Douai College until he was sent back to England in 1604. He served on the mission mainly in Lancashire, becoming Archdeacon of Westmorland and Cumberland. His younger brother, Richard, entered Douai in 1599. From there he went to Seville and was ordained in 1610. He worked in England for about one year and later may have joined the Franciscans.

Yorkshire was recognised as the greatest centre of resistance to the Elizabethan settlement. From 1573 to the very end of the reign there was a whole series of letters sent in the Queen's name to the mayor and aldermen of York, issuing detailed instructions how the rigours of the law be applied against recusants. The authorities responded by sending amazingly detailed reports back to London about known Catholics, their opinions and activities. These include tradesmen such as weavers, millers, locksmiths, butchers, carpenters, innkeepers and braziers. John Gibson was a poor tailor of little learning, but for refusing to attend church he was imprisoned for seven years at Ousebridge and died shortly after being moved to Durham. Ralph Cowling, a shoemaker, was arrested in 1586, treated abominably and died in York Castle 1 August 1587. William Chalner and his sister Bridget were prisoners for religion for eight years, both dying in York Castle, where their parents, John and Isabel, had perished before them in 1582. John and Margaret Stable died in the Castle respectively on the 26th and 27th July 1584. Margaret had been born in the prison where both her parents had died religious prisoners. The names were recorded of scores of Catholic women who suffered years of imprisonment in the most dreadful conditions in the York prisons, particularly the ghastly, disease-ridden Kidcote on Ousebridge. The dreaded lower Kidcote was regularly inundated by the river, so the inmates were in permanent damp and mud. So notorious were the appalling prison conditions that there are many touching bequests in the wills of Catholics from the 1580's onwards leaving money specifically to help prisoners in York Castle and the Kidcote.

The long lists of those who died in the prisons of York and Hull make pitiful reading. Recusant prisoners were expected to pay for the 'privilege' of incarceration. For example, at York Castle, on being committed, everyone of yeoman status had to pay ten shillings for his fetters; every gentleman twenty shillings. Priests were placed in the latter category. In order to be fed yeomen paid six shillings and eight pence per week; gentlemen ten shillings and fourpence. These charges did not include cooking the food; that was extra. Few recusants were able to afford these fees and they often went hungry. Sometimes it was cheaper for prisoners to pay the jailers at York and Hull chamber-rents, and then try and provide for themselves. Typical chamber-rents started at twelve pence for the very worst, rising to sixteen and twenty pence for 'better' accommodation. For the 'best' rooms the charges were three or four shillings, the prisoners providing all necessities for themselves. That did not guarantee any privacy, of course; often each chamber was crowded with as many people as could be crammed in. No wonder infections spread like wildfire in the jails.

No mercy was shown - not even to pregnant women such as Isabella Foster. She was the second wife of William Foster of Earswick, York, and daughter of Blessed Richard Langley 17 of Ousethorpe, Pocklington, who was hanged at York in 1586 for harbouring priests. Mrs Foster was in the habit of visiting the Catholic prisoners to take them food and alms and was arrested for her charity. As she left the jail she was apprehended and taken before Dean Hutton who, when she refused to attend church, committed her to York Castle. She died a victim of disease as a close prisoner in the Castle on 3 December 1587. (Her husband, William Foster, married for a third time and conformed in spite of having a recusant family. His parents, John Foster and Agnes Lascelles, had suffered imprisonment in York Castle. His younger brother Seth was educated at Douai and Rome. He was ordained at the Lateran in 1581 and in 1584 he joined the Bridgettines. He moved with the community to Lisbon as their chaplain; a post he held until his death in 1628. One of William's own sons, Thomas, became a priest. He was ordained by St Robert Bellarmine in 1614 and returned to England in 1616, shortly afterwards joining the Society of Jesus. He died at Lincoln in 1648. William Foster was reconciled to the Church later in life by Father Richard Holtby SJ. He went into exile for religion and died at Antwerp.)

Another York prisoner was Isabel Whitehead, who had been a nun at Arthington Priory, Yorkshire, until her convent was closed. Arthington had been founded in 1241 and was one of only two Cluniac nunneries in England. The priory had been surrendered on 26 November 1540. The report made at the time of the suppression states that the forty-five-year-old prioress, Elizabeth Hall, and her nine nuns aged between twenty-five and seventy-two, 'be of good religious living' and wished to continue in their vows. The property was given to Archbishop Thomas Cranmer but he could not have made much profit from it as the annual value of the priory and its lands was given as just £17. Sister Isabel spent the rest of her life in charitable work, especially visiting Catholic prisoners. She was given a home by Lady Middleton at Stockeld and after her benefactor's death she went to live with a Mrs Ardington. When the house was searched Isabel was violently taken into custody while lying on her sickbed. She refused to reveal the names of priests or their whereabouts and was imprisoned and treated cruelly at York. Sister Isabel died a very old woman in 1587 and was buried under the castle walls. She was perhaps one of the last surviving members of the suppressed religious orders.

There were many women who courageously flouted the law in order to hide priests. One example is Mrs Eleanor Hunt. (We shall meet some of her counterparts - the Vaux sisters, Anne and Eleanor, Mrs Alice Wells, Mrs Jane Wiseman and others - in the lives of the martyrs.) Mrs Hunt was a Yorkshire widow who regularly sheltered priests, the last of whom was Blessed Christopher Wharton. He was born c.1540 at Middleton in the West Riding, of Yorkshire, the son of Henry Wharton and Agnes Warcop, and the younger brother of Thomas, 1st Baron Wharton. He was educated at Trinity College, Oxford, where he graduated MA in 1564 and later became a Fellow. He went to Rheims in 1583 and was ordained there in March 1584 by Cardinal de Guise. He did not return to England until 1586 in the company of another destined for martyrdom, Father Edward Burden q.v. Christopher was arrested by Sir Stephen Proctor of Fountains in 1599 at Mrs Hunt's house on the Ripley Castle estate of Sir William Ingleby. Proctor, a fanatical Puritan, had virtually built his career upon anti-Catholic activities, pursuing vendettas against his recusant neighbours. Christopher Wharton and his hostess were confined in York Castle, where, on the orders of the Lord President, Thomas Burghley, they were among the group of Catholic prisoners forcibly taken in chains and with physical violence, to hear Protestant sermons: a strategy that utterly failed. Wharton and Mrs Hunt were tried together before Baron Savile at the Lent Assizes 1600: both were condemned to death and both refused life and liberty at the price of conformity. Christopher - who declared at his trial that he 'had no breach of charity with any person' - was hanged, drawn and quartered at York 28 March 1600. Later that year, having forfeited all she possessed, Mrs Eleanor Hunt died in prison.

Mrs Dorothy Brown, a widow with five children, was frequently arraigned at the assizes for refusing to attend church and each time was committed to Ousebridge and other prisons. To get her released, her friends rallied round to pay her fines, she being too poor to be able to do so. She eked out her living by brewing in a small way, but in an act of petty revenge was forbidden by the Lord Mayor to carry on the trade and had her children taken from her unless she agreed to go to church. While Dorothy was in prison one of her neighbours took her children to the Lord Mayor, begging him for their sake, to have pity on their mother. The Lord Mayor was furious with the poor man, asking how he dared to bring the children before him. 'Their mother doth deserve no favour, nor none shall have'. Cases such as these can be multiplied many times over year upon year.

The conspicuous part played by women in maintaining the Faith deserves deep study on its own, notwithstanding Father Roland Connelly's most valuable 1997 book on the subject, *Women of the Catholic Resistance: 1540-1680*. The records show that in the prisons it was the women who were in the majority for refusing to pay the fines. Father John Mush commented that 'the gents were much fallen off, but the gentlewomen stood steadfastly'.

Typical is the case of Anne Killingale. She was the wife of Henry Killingale of Sadbery, Co. Durham. Henry was denounced as a recusant by his own brother, for having been married and having his child baptised by a Catholic priest. Under pressure he conformed, but Anne remained steadfast. She was arrested and imprisoned in the bishop's jail at Bishop Auckland. When she refused to attend church she was compelled every day for six weeks to listen to the Protestant service read in her cell. Interrogated by the Ecclesiastical Commissioners in September 1582 she refused the Oath of Supremacy when offered it by Lord Huntingdon. When she saw the dangerous drift of the questions they were asking her she would not be drawn into their entrapment, and refused to answer any further questions. She was pregnant, but they sent her to Sadbery jail, which was in a ruinous state. Here she gave birth to her child in terrible conditions She was then removed to Durham jail and finally to York Castle.

In families, the influence of the women is most apparent by the numbers of their children and servants who were recusants. It also perhaps reveals the true nature of their husbands' religious convictions. The authorities frequently adopted a policy of threatening punishment for husbands whose wives refused to conform. And completely ignoring the Pauline injunction that they should obey their husbands and submit to them, there are innumerable instances where husbands

The Elizabethan Persecution

pleaded in mitigation that their obstinate wives persisted in their recusancy and they could do nothing about it. There were so many women recusants that special prisons had to be allocated to accommodate them all, such as the one at Sheriff Hutton Castle, Yorkshire. A great number of women were incarcerated in this royal castle in the 1590's, among them some of the most prominent Yorkshire ladies. They included Lady Constable and Lady Grace Babthorpe, wife of Sir Ralph Babthorpe, from one of the staunchest recusant families. They were kept here for two years at their own expense. As a widow, in 1617 Lady Babthorpe became a nun at St. Monica's, Louvain, together with her granddaughter, Frances.

Any lawyer who was courageous enough to attempt to put in a defence on behalf of these women soon found himself in dire trouble. Mr Leonard Babthorpe, solicitor, and Mr Launder, attorney, pleading the law on behalf of their Catholic wives, were committed to prison by order of Lord Huntingdon. They were heavily fined and disbarred from practising, and when Launder expressed his outrage he was sent to the Clink in London and sentenced to the pillory. He wrote to his wife, Anne, a prisoner in Ousebridge, York, asking her to conform to save him from the ignominy of such punishment. After many tears and much heart-searching, Anne wrote back telling him that she could not yield and encouraging her husband to bear the punishment; and so he suffered the pillory. In 1579 Anne was moved to York Castle and later to Hull Castle, where she spent six years. She was then removed to the Clink to join her husband and there they both died.

Everyone over the age of sixteen who did not attend the Established Church was fined £20 per month, and in addition if the 'crime' persisted for a year a further fine of £200 was imposed. The statute expressly states that illness was not acceptable as an excuse for non-attendance. Those who could not pay were imprisoned without bail until they either paid or conformed. Even young children were incarcerated to force them to incriminate their parents. Indeed, the cruelty towards children by the regime would be difficult to believe were it not so well documented. Take the case of the four Worthington brothers from an ancient and staunchly recusant family at Blainscough, Lancashire. The brothers were staying with their uncle, Father Thomas Worthington, q.v. at Great Sankey, near Warrington. At 3 a.m. on 12 February 1584 the house was raided and the four boys - Thomas (16), Robert (15), Richard (13) and John (11) - were arrested. They were interrogated at various locations by the Earl of Derby and the Bishop of Chester to get them to reveal what they knew. They were taken to the House of Correction at Manchester and every effort was made to get them to go to church. They were deprived of food and sleep and the two eldest were beaten with rods. The two youngest were stripped naked ready for a beating but were spared. Despite the taunts and insults that 'such little boys' refused to conform, they bravely remained constant. They were eventually taken to house imprisonment with the Bishop of Chester with orders that they be strictly confined. Even so Thomas, the oldest, and John the youngest of the brothers escaped. As a revenge punishment their brother, Robert, was ordered to be incarcerated in Chester Castle. En route he was rescued by a group of horsemen. The three brothers now at liberty were taken into Staffordshire where they met up with their uncle, Father Thomas, who conducted them to London. While staying at an inn at Islington they were betrayed and Thomas and his nephews were arrested by Richard Topcliffe. Two of the brothers managed to escape but Father Thomas and the eldest boy, Thomas, were sent to the Gatehouse. Father Thomas was moved to the Tower where he was accused by Topcliffe of 'stealing' his nephews from the Bishop of Chester. Thomas remained in the Tower until banished in 1585. The young Thomas was held in the Gatehouse for over two years. He later went abroad and married Mary Allen, a niece of Cardinal Allen, the daughter of his brother George. Thomas died at Louvain in 1619. Robert, Richard and John went to Rheims in 1584. Their health having been undermined by their treatment Robert and Richard died within a few months of each other in 1586. John q.v. became a Jesuit priest and was the founder of the Lancashire St Aloysius district. He was destined to die a prisoner for his faith.

A particularly wicked piece of legislation was that of 1593 which provided for the statutory removal of children from recusant parents. From the age of seven the children of such stubborn Catholics could be forcibly removed and given into the care of Protestant families. Not surprisingly, it caused significant numbers of the gentry to conform rather than lose their children. Those who had their children baptised by priests rather than in the local church were heavily fined - or worse. Living at North Stanley, Yorkshire, William Reynold, a webster, was committed to York Castle for not having his child baptised in the Protestant church. He was then sent to Hull Castle, transferred to Hull Blockhouse and then sent back to York. Having spent years in jail he died in the Kidcote 4 February 1587 and was buried at Toft Green..

Marriages were invalid unless conducted by a Protestant minister. Catholics who married secretly before a priest were punished by huge fines or imprisonment. They were regarded as 'living in sin' and their children as illegitimate. Prosecutions of Catholic couples for contracting such marriages continued until the 1630s. To protect

The Elizabethan Persecution

themselves it later became the practice for Catholics to have a secret Catholic marriage and then undergo a ceremony in a Protestant church. Under the Statute of Confinement, Catholics were not permitted to travel more than five miles from their homes without obtaining a licence from two magistrates and the bishop of the diocese to certify that their journey was bona fide. Failure to observe this requirement meant forfeiture of property for life. Recusants were caught in the web of the State on all sides, subject to repeated, wearisome attendance at a multiplicity of courts, with all the trouble and fees that entailed. And when they were excommunicated by the Established Church they lost all rights to any form of legal redress.

Priests who had conformed to the Anglican services were punished for continuing to say the *Ave Maria*. The cult of the Blessed Virgin Mary, the *Mater Gloriosa*, was to be replaced with the nauseating cult of Gloriana, the 'Virgin Queen': a myth created about the callous Elizabeth by her political spin doctors.

Catholic books were proscribed, confiscated and burned. Smuggling Catholic literature was a very dangerous task. There was a well organised network for supplying books, but those who printed or distributed them were severely punished. Trade with Europe was used as a cover for transporting Catholic books. Cloth exports from Leeds through the port of Hull were a regular means of conveying literature to and from the Continent. One Leeds man, Richard Hargrave, was reconciled to the Church at Douai and posing as a cloth merchant he then embarked upon a series of regular smuggling journeys between Leeds and Paris, also taking money collected by West Riding Catholics for the support of the seminaries. On one occasion he conveyed the future martyr Edmund Sykes to the seminary. In 1577 a bookseller in Oxford was sentenced to having his ears nailed to the pillory; the only way for him to be released was for him to cut off his own ears. John Cooper was a book smuggler. Captured on arrival at Dover he was sent to the Tower where he died of 'cold, hunger and the stench' in 1580. Anyone printing Catholic literature was running a terrible risk. William Wrench, a noted City of London printer and recusant was sentenced to death but managed to secure a pardon. (His son, Bernard, became a priest in 1627 and died in London in 1629.) Others were executed, such as Blessed William Carter, [18] a printer who was hanged, drawn and quartered at Tyburn in 1584. William Roper, son-in-law of Sir Thomas More and like him a famous lawyer, got into trouble with the Council for sending money abroad for printing books. In the 1590's a Sheffield cutler by the name of Simon Knowles q.v. also used his craft as a cover for smuggling books as well as priests to and from Saint-Omer. Later in

The Elizabethan Persecution

the narrative we shall meet Jesuit lay-brother Ralph Emerson, companion of Edmund Campion. Ralph was long occupied in book smuggling and when finally caught served twenty years in prison.

A modern historian, referring to the united and powerful assault on Catholicism in the North that took place from 1571 onwards, in a memorable phrase calls it the 'machine of repression', into which every organ and official of the Elizabethan local government was pressed into service. (*Northern Catholics*, Hugh Aveling, 1966). 1571 was the year in which Archbishop Grindal of York issued his injunctions against going to Confession, lighting candles, making the sign of the Cross, possessing a rosary or Catholic prayer book, genuflecting and every other remnant of Catholic devotional piety. Groups of commissioners were sent out to enforce the injunctions. Those caught disobeying them - such as those apprehended at Leeds and Skipton - were reported to the authorities and suffered the consequences.

In an age when torture was shockingly widespread the Elizabethan government carried it to new extremes. Even one of the rack-masters complained that it was cruel and barbarous. Used as a means of extracting factual information, it was now extended to matters of conscience. In 1583 Lord Burghley published a justification of torture for priests - whom he described as 'venomous vipers' and 'vermin' - in which he did not deny the use of torture but argued that it had been used 'moderately', pointing out that, where the rack had been used more than once on prisoners, they were usually still able to walk afterwards! Torture was also sanctioned by the Anglican establishment. The last of Elizabeth's Archbishops of Canterbury, the ostentatious, Calvinistic John Whitgift (c1530-1604), vigorously enforced the penal laws and defended the use of the rack against Catholics, as well as persecuting Puritans, hatred of whom he shared with the Queen.

Even in death, Catholics continued to be persecuted. As recusants were excommunicated by the Established Church - the fact that they may never have belonged to that Church was a nicety that could be ignored - they were not permitted church funerals but were usually interred in common ground, often secretly at night without any rites or ceremonies. The dates of death and place of burial are unrecorded even for prominent members of the recusant community such as Anne Vaux and Eleanor Brooksby, the daughters of William, 3rd Baron Vaux of Harrowden.

The Catholic decline was a slow and gradual process, but by the end of Elizabeth's reign of forty-four years those attached to the Old Faith were in a minority, albeit still a substantial minority. In addition to the hundreds who suffered imprisonment and penury in the reign of 'Good

The Elizabethan Persecution

Queen Bess', 128 priests and 63 lay people were executed for their Catholic faith, not including those who were executed after the Northern Rising. As the reign drew to a close there was no let up in the persecution. In addition to those whose narratives appear in the course of this book, during Elizabeth's last three years those martyred included three hanged, drawn and quartered in 1599: Father Matthew or Matthias Harrison from Yorkshire who was executed at York; Venerable John Lion, a layman, executed at Oakham, Rutland and Venerable James Dowdall, a layman, executed in August at Exeter. He was born at Drogheda, Ireland and was a merchant travelling regularly to France on business. On one return sailing bad weather forced his ship onto the Devon coast. He was arrested and imprisoned for about a year. When he refused to take the Oath of Supremacy he was executed on 20 September. Others martyrs were Thomas Sprott and Thomas Hunt, [19] Thomas Palaser, John Norton and John Talbot, [20] John Pibush, [21] Robert Middleton, [22] Thurstan Hunt, [23] James Harrison and Anthony Battie, [24] and James Duckett. [25] The executions continued right to the bitter end: the last martyr of the reign, the Yorkshire priest William Richardson, [26] was executed at Tyburn in February 1603, just a month before the Queen died, terrified of the bloody phantoms with which she imagined she was surrounded.

The Elizabethan government anticipated - wrongly - that as the older priests, who had been ordained in the reigns of Henry VIII and Mary, eventually died out, the Catholic Church in England and Wales would simply cease to exist. In 1571 there was a new statute (13 Eliz.cap.12) aimed directly at the Henrician and Marian clergy. By the Act such priests were required to subscribe to thirty-nine very Protestant Synodal Articles. This proved to be the last straw and many priests who had hitherto appeared to conform resigned; such as Leonard Bateson, Rector of Spofforth. As has already been shown earlier in this chapter many of these 'old priests' continued their ministries, often for much longer than has been realised. So much attention has been paid to the seminary priests that the vital role of the 'old priests' has tended to be overlooked. These men provided the continuity between the ancient Catholic Church in England and Wales and the Counter-Reformation Catholicism represented by the seminary priests. Especially in the North the records are full of details of recusant priests who were still serving in the 1590's. Hugh Aveling, in his *Catholic Recusants of the West Riding,* states that in 1580 the 'old priests' working in Lancashire outnumbered those from the seminaries by two to one, and in 1590 a quarter of the priests in the county were Marian priests. Similar numbers existed in Yorkshire. By 1593 Huntingdon had captured at

The Elizabethan Persecution

least twenty-two Marian priests, nine of whom died in York Castle or Hull Blockhouse. In 1596 the Jesuits reckoned that there were still as many as fifty Marian priests in England. There were some extraordinary survivors. Francis Smith, late Vicar of Crowle, Lincolnshire, was still active in Yorkshire in 1606. Harry Stapper, ordained in 1558, was being sheltered by a widow at Kettlewell, Yorkshire in 1581. He was arrested in Richmond in 1593 but escaped. He was still working in the West Riding in 1612 when he must have been at least eighty-years-old. Hugh Ile had been ordained by Bishop Cuthbert Tunstall during his last days as Bishop of Durham in 1559. Ile, then a very old man, was recorded in the Douai Diaries as working in North Yorkshire in 1611. Another was Roger Venise, ordained in Durham Cathedral by Tunstall 25 March 1559, two months after Elizabeth's coronation. He was appointed vicar of Mitford, Northumberland, but in 1570 he was reported to be absent from his parish. By 1579 he was at Rheims and Paris. He was arrested at the house of Sir Thomas Tresham in London in 1585. He was still alive in 1588 when he was reported as an 'old priest'. Yet another priest was Valentine Taylor, who was still active on the mission in 1616.

It was against this background of persecution that it was felt necessary to set up seminaries on the Continent to train courageous new priests prepared to undertake the dangerous task of continuing a ministry to the remaining faithful. A few English priests had already been ordained on the Continent before the establishment of the new seminaries. The Yorkshire records, for example, show a number of ordinations in the 1560's, such as Lancelot Blackburne, who was ordained at Cambrai in 1561 and was captured in Derbyshire in 1587. Without the approval and funding that Rome was to provide the dream of an English seminary could not, of course, have been realised, but the momentous step owed nothing to any plan of action of Rome: it was the English exiles themselves who, trusting to providence, took the initiative.

The first of the seminaries was established by William Allen [27] on 28 September 1568 in a hired house at Douai in Flanders. Located on the River Scarpe, about twenty miles south of Lille, since 1677 Douai has been part of northern France, but in Allen's time it was in the territory of the Spanish Netherlands, under the rule of Philip II. Douai was a new university opened in 1562 with the aim of combating Protestantism. It was modelled on Louvain University, from which most of its early teaching staff was drawn; but there was a strong English presence and Englishmen held some of the chief posts in the early years. The first chancellor was Richard Smith, formerly Fellow of

The Elizabethan Persecution

Merton College and Regius Professor of Divinity at Oxford. Dr Owen Lewis was Regius Professor of Canon Law, having held the same post at Oxford, so many of the old Oxford traditions were maintained at Douai. It was thus a most congenial place for the Fellow of Oriel and former Principal of St Mary's Hall, William Allen, to set up his new college, which, in old age, he described as the dearly loved work of his life.

It attracted many students of the highest calibre and published a stream of polemical works and Catholic literature. First among them was the English translation of the Bible - 'Douai-Rheims' - so named because, following the unstable political situation in Flanders, the English College resided at Rheims in France from 1578 to 1593. The project to translate the Latin Vulgate into English was of long gestation, until undertaken by Gregory Martin [28] at the behest of William Allen. The New Testament was published in 1582 and the Old Testament in 1609. For a nation whose Protestant masters purported to be so keen on having the Bible in English the reception afforded to the Douai-Rheims version was the height of hypocrisy. A contemporary account of the arrival of the New Testament in England states that, 'Every corner of the realm was searched for those books ... Paul's Cross is witness of burning many of them, the Prince's proclamation was procured against them; in the universities by sovereign authority colleges, chambers, studies, closets, coffers and desks were ransacked for them ... ancient men and students of divinity were imprisoned for having them.' The debt owed by the translators of the later Authorised Version under James I to the Douai-Rheims Bible has never received the recognition it deserves. Douai College was suppressed in 1792 during the French Revolution and re-founded at Ware, Hertfordshire, in 1793 and Ushaw, Durham, 1808. (Sadly, Ushaw College closed as a seminary in 2011.)

The lasting work of Douai on which rests its fame was the training of priests for the English mission: the only means by which Catholicism in England could be saved from extinction. It would not be entirely hyperbolic to claim that Catholicism in England and Wales today is as historically indebted to one little town in Flanders as it ever was to the Eternal City herself, from whence Pope St Gregory the Great (590-604) sent the monk Augustine as apostle to the Angles, nearly a thousand years before. This sentiment echoes that of Allen himself, who before his death referred to Douai as 'the ground of all good and salvation which is wrought in England'. In 1581 Allen, writing to former Douai students in prison awaiting execution, summed up the spirit of his college.

The Elizabethan Persecution

This is it that gives us so great hope of the conversion of our country ... Blood so yielded makes the most forcible means to procure mercy that can be. Every time that you confess Christ's name, every wrench of any joint for it, every opprobrious scoff and scorn given by the populace when you be carried in the sacred vestments through the streets (for that also some of our brethren have borne), every villainy and sacrilege done to your priesthood, every one of your sore sorrows and sighs, every one of your wants and necessities make a stronger intercession for our country and afflicted Church than any prayers lightly said in this world. This is the way by which we hope to win our nation to God again.

The first Douai seminary priests to return to England in 1574 were the Welshman, Lewis Barlow, [29] who worked mainly in Suffolk; two Yorkshiremen, Thomas Metham [30] and Martin Nelson; [31] and from Chester diocese, Henry Shaw. [32] These four were the precursors of hundreds of Douai-trained priests, nearly 170 of whom were executed and a great many more suffered imprisonment and torture. As a result of the Elizabethan government's crackdown, the old English Hospice of the Most Holy Trinity and St Thomas of Canterbury, founded in 1362 to house the many thousands of English pilgrims to the Eternal City, had become little more than a retirement home for exiled clergy. In 1576 Allen converted the Hospice into a seminary named the English College. The first students moved into the college in 1577. Pope Gregory XIII, who proved a generous patron, giving the new institution property and an annual grant, issued the papal bull of foundation in 1579. The college, whose motto, quoting Christ in Chapter 12 of Luke's Gospel, was *Ignem veni mittere in terram (I have come to bring fire to the earth)*, continued to be administered by the Jesuits until 1773. From the early 18th century it received the epithet *Venerabile*, in recognition not only of its antiquity but also the number of martyrs it had nurtured. In 1589 Allen co-operated with Robert Persons and the Jesuits in establishing the English College of St Alban at Valladolid, Spain, which they continued to administer until 1767. The Royal English and Welsh College, Valladolid - to give its official title - can boast among its students six canonized and sixteen beatified martyrs. Valladolid still continues to be a place of formation for English students considering their vocation to the priesthood.

Other colleges under the Jesuits were later set up at Seville in 1592 and Lisbon in 1628, a college that survived until 1971. The later seminaries were opened because the number of students was too great to be accommodated at Douai or Rome. The course of studies at Douai was tailored to the requirements of Counter-Reformation Catholicism. It was probably the first seminary geared specifically to the reforms of

The Elizabethan Persecution

the Council of Trent. The packed college day began at 5 a.m. and ended after night prayers at 9 p.m. Heavy emphasis was placed on Bible study. The New Testament was read through sixteen times each year and the Old Testament twelve times. William Allen laid down that it was 'of the utmost importance that the missionary priest shall be thoroughly familiar with the whole of the Bible.' He stipulated that a priest must have 'at his fingers' ends' those passages of scripture disputed by Protestants. Every week there were disputations, in which the students were trained, not only to present the Catholic teaching, but also to understand the Protestant interpretations to the extent of speaking in defence of them. To meet these needs there were daily lectures on the New Testament and running commentaries on chapters from the New and Old Testaments at dinner and supper. The training regime in these seminaries was severe in the extreme. It was strictly disciplined and spartan, everything being geared towards equipping the students intellectually and spiritually for their future in the dangerous English mission. All self-pride was to be driven out and replaced by humility and the spirit of loving self-sacrifice: a conscious preparation for the likelihood of martyrdom, and that likelihood was high given that one in every three of the seminary priests were executed. All the more amazing then that among the oppressed Catholics there was never any shortage of young men willing to give up home and family to undergo this austere education. To quote from A O Meyer again, 'Seldom has education won a grander triumph over human nature.' No other European country at the time could compare with the calibre of the little band of Catholic priests that worked in England, carrying out their duties with such dedication. It would require a separate volume to recall the great number of those priests who suffered and died in prisons.

The Elizabethan government employed spies who entered the seminaries with the purpose of informing on their brethren. For instance, there was Richard Baines, who arrived at Rheims in 1579 and was ordained at Soissons in 1581. It soon emerged that he was an English government spy who planned to destroy William Allen and the whole of Douai College by poisoning their food one evening. Baines was imprisoned at Rheims in 1582 where he made a confession and recantation.

The Public Record Office contains scores of reports from government spies. One example will suffice of the wicked perfidy of these reprobates; a long letter written in 1584 by a Samuel Pettingat to Sir Francis Walsingham. In the letter he tells how he and his companions arrived at the English College, Rome, claiming to be young scholars 'in necessity' seeking instruction in the Catholic religion. Although eight days was the normal maximum permitted stay, for six weeks they received hospitality from the college during which they were given Catholic books to read and Pettingat, after - blasphemously - making his confession, was absolved and received into the Church. Pettingat writes, 'Whereas your honour commanded me to set down the names of all such as I did know beyond the seas ... although I cannot remember all the names those which I did know I will rehearse unto your honour'. He then proceeds to provide a long list of names of students and priests and relates detailed stories about many of them. Several of the names are familiar as they later died as martyrs or prisoners. He also gives the names of others who, like him, 'live among them under a shadow of mere devotion' and are willing to act as spies. The moral calibre of such men can be gleaned from Pettingat's own assessment of one of them, John Brigosa, who will spy for money 'because this man lives the life of a hypocrite and is therefore more easily to be persuaded to serve the Protestant cause'. The adage 'it takes one to know one' springs to mind!

It is the case that by no means were all the seminary priests as faithful or courageous as our martyrs. Sad to relate, many priests saved themselves by agreeing Judas-like to become government spies, some being planted in the prisons. From these renegades the government was able to obtain authentic information about the seminaries and who frequented them. Because they were able to identify priests, the traitors were responsible for causing the imprisonment or death of a great many colleagues and imperilled the Catholics who had risked their lives to shelter them. One example is that of James Younger, sometimes called Young. Born in 1563 in Co. Durham he was ordained in 1587 and arrived in London in 1590. He found lodging with Mr Lawrence Mompesson in Clerkenwell where he said Mass every Sunday. On 12 December 1590 he was joined at the house by fellow Durham-born priest, William Patteson, also ordained in 1587. After saying Mass the two priests joined their host for dinner when the house was raided by pursuivants. Younger managed to escape by a back door but Patteson was arrested and sent to Newgate. Tried and condemned at the Old Bailey, Blessed William Patteson was hanged, drawn and quartered at Tyburn 22 January 1592, having converted three of the four thieves who occupied the condemned cell with him. Younger went into hiding in Holborn but was captured in the summer when he provided immensely damaging information about all those who had risked their lives to offer him shelter and details about many fellow priests. To secure his release he offered to act as a spy, with the proviso that it must be made to appear that he had escaped from custody. Some years

The Elizabethan Persecution

later he turned up at Douai and Dr Worthington, the President, generously found him work to do.

Another example is that of Thomas Clark, born in Kent in 1555 and educated at Winchester School. He went to Rheims in 1588 and was ordained at Laon September 1590. In October that year he returned to England with newly-ordained Francis Clayton. They sailed in a French ship, landing at South Shields. They found shelter with the Trollope family at Thornley, Co. Durham. Clark was next at the house of Sir Henry Constable at Burton Constable, Flamborough when Lady Margaret was arrested for sheltering him. Clark was captured in 1593 and provided ample information about his co-religionists. He apostatised and received a pardon. On 30 September 1594 he was responsible for the arrest of Blessed Edward Osbaldeston. Edward, the son of Thomas and nephew of Edward, of Osbaldeston Hall, near Blackburn, was ordained at Rheims 21 September 1585 but only came back to England in 1589. Edward's own account relates that he and Abraham Sayer came to the inn at Tollerton, near York. While they were having supper Clark arrived and 'I looked earnestly at him and thought it was he, and yet I still persuaded myself that he knew me not, and if he should know me he would do me no harm.' Osbaldeston's trust was misplaced. As Edward was retiring to bed Clark called the curate and the constable who apprehended him. He was held at the inn overnight before being taken to York the following morning accompanied by Clark, who 'stood by when I was examined before the Council.' Edward was imprisoned in York Castle and was martyred on 16 November 1594. The letter which he wrote to his fellow prisoners before his execution reveals a man of great humility and serene trust in God. Clark repented of his actions and died reconciled to the Church.

Some apostate priests were rewarded with parishes or positions in the Established Church. A couple are known to have died on the gallows as common criminals. One of these was the Northamptonshire priest, Alexander Bowker who apostatised and was executed at Tyburn 23 April 1618 for the capital offence of coining.

With the benefit of charitable hindsight, most of these priests should be pitied for their weakness rather than condemned for their treachery. The marvel is not that some of them fell by the wayside, but that the vast majority manfully persevered through to the end. They knew only too well, particularly in the later years of Elizabeth's reign, that they could expect no mercy if captured. The case of Yorkshireman, Thomas Bell, affords an example of the kind of treatment to which they were subjected. Bell was born in 1551 and became an Anglican minister. He served a prison term in York Castle before he entered the English

The Elizabethan Persecution

College, Rome, and was ordained in 1580. He returned to England in 1582 and often acted as assistant to Father John Mush. An audacious man he boldly managed to infiltrate York Castle. For fourteen days he remained undetected while saying Mass and hearing confessions. Four other priests were persuaded to join Bell, and when this became known on the 'Catholic grapevine,' a large number of York Catholics went to the Castle at night to take part in the High Mass that was celebrated. Needless to say, this hardly escaped the notice of the Warden, who alerted the pursuivants and as a result two of the priests, William Hart and William Lacey q.v. were captured and martyred. Bell managed to escape and moved to Lancashire, where he served diligently, often in great danger. Father Robert Persons reported that the house in which Bell was staying was raided in the night and, barefoot, he had to make a run for it in his night clothes. He was ill for a month afterwards. Back in York, he was captured and committed to Ousebridge, where he remained several years. We are told that one exceptionally freezing cold winter he was kept in the stocks day after day while harangued by Protestant ministers. In 1592, he was sent by the Council of the North to Archbishop Whitgift of Canterbury, when he offered to conform. Notwithstanding his earlier heroic labours, he was obviously no longer able to withstand the pressures, and by 1594 he had apostatised and become a spy, writing anti-Catholic pamphlets.

The seminary priests lived lonely, hunted lives, rarely daring to relax their vigilance, placing their trust in those brave enough to offer them shelter, and in perpetual anxiety that they and their hosts, who were constantly under surveillance, may be captured at any time. The comfort of contact with their families was denied to them, as that would expose not only themselves but also their relatives to great danger. The pursuivants who hunted them were nothing but bandits plying their vile government-sanctioned trade for profit and sadistic satisfaction. They behaved with impunity, raiding and ransacking houses without warning at any time, night or day, smashing up the property, plundering possessions and livestock and physically mistreating the occupants in their lucrative search for priests or evidence of a Catholic presence. Recusants were not spared such treatment even when in custody. Father Richard Holtby SJ describes in great detail the treatment of Catholic prisoners in York Castle at Christmas-time 1593 when they were suspected of hiding a priest among them. A great company of men descended upon the Castle, and for three days and nights ransacked the place, breaking through walls and ceilings. Prayer books were confiscated and anything of value that the prisoners had in their possession was stolen. The prisoners, including the children, were shut

The Elizabethan Persecution

up in confined spaces where they were so squashed together there was only room to stand. Prisoners were called into the Castle yard at all times of the day and night; groups of them were taken away for interrogation, including a ten-year-old girl who was threatened with a beating if she did not confess that there was a priest hidden in the Castle. No priest was found and the search was finally abandoned.

In urban areas, priests for the most part lived shut away in attics or cellars, as remote as possible from observation, afraid to have a light that might attract attention and unable to move around too much for fear of making a noise that would alert the servants. At certain hours of the day all movement was prohibited. If the room they occupied had a window even greater caution had to be exercised and rarely was it possible to open a window. They might spend weeks or even months at a time in oppressive isolation, venturing out only in the dead of night to perform some priestly function or meet up with a fellow priest. Their meals were brought in by one trusted servant who immediately left. In rural areas they were able to travel around either on foot or, if lucky, on horseback. They were constantly on the move from place to place, reliant upon a farm, a cottage or a secluded country house which they would stealthily enter late in the evening to spend a restless night. They would head off again before dawn, often having changed their dress or appearance in some way in order to put off the scent any who were following them. Failing that they would spend their nights in barns or under the hedgerows. Particularly active missioners were exposed to greater danger to themselves and any who gave them shelter.

The Calendar of State Papers, 1581-90, records the case of a priest whose hiding place, and meeting place for his little flock, was a sea cave on the North Wales coast. That was Blessed William Davies, or Dai in Welsh, who was born in Denbighshire, North Wales. Father Davies was hanged, drawn and quartered at Beaumaris on the Isle of Anglesey 27 July 1593. [33]

The more fortunate priests - if such a term may be used in the context - were those who obtained rare, semi-permanent places in the houses of the nobility or gentry. Here they would enjoy greater liberty and be able to carry on a fruitful ministry within the household and to the neighbourhood. Father John Gerard SJ [34] described the houses of the Catholic country gentry as the churches of the time. In all but a few of the larger towns and cities, Catholicism depended upon them for its survival.

Since necessity required that they lived in secrecy, disguised and under false names, all too little is recorded about the hundreds of seminary priests who lived and died in obscurity. The fate of a few of

The Elizabethan Persecution

them is known to us from prison records because they died as confessors for the Faith. 35 There are some seminary priests whose real names have never been discovered. They are known to us only by the aliases they adopted. Father Gerard tells us that when a priest died it was imperative that his identity be kept secret, as he was in the country illegally. Those who died in towns had to be buried on the properties they occupied, sometimes in gardens or even basements. Such was the fate of the Cornishman Father John Curry. Ordained in 1577, he joined the Jesuits in 1583 and returned to England with Father Richard Holtby in January 1590. He was closely associated with many martyrs. He helped St Edmund Campion distribute his books and shared a room with St Ralph Sherwin. He moved to Dorset and became chaplain to Lady Arundell at Chideock, at whose house also lived Blessed John Cornelius SJ, martyred at Dorchester in 1594, along with three Blessed laymen: Thomas Bosgrave, John Carey and Patrick Salmon. 36

Father Curry moved back to London and was described by a spy as being 'about forty years old, long, slender-faced, black hair and a little black beard'. Father Gerard records that he died in the house kept by St Anne Line and was buried there secretly. All the information about Father Curry's movements comes from informers. It is an irony of history that so much information about our martyrs, including their physical descriptions and the clothes they wore, comes via reports from the efficient network of spies and informers who infiltrated the Catholic community.

The lengths to which the informers went to ingratiate themselves with Catholics can be illustrated by the case of Nicholas Berden, one of the best - if one can use that adjective pejoratively - of Francis Walsingham's spies. Berden was given the special task by Walsingham of keeping surveillance on Philip Howard. In 1586, for sordid gain, Berden wrote to Thomas Phelippes, the government forger-in-chief, asking him to intercede with his master, Walsingham, to procure the release of two priests: Ralph Bickley, the friend of St Ralph Sherwin, who had been in the Gatehouse for a year; and Richard Sherwood, alias Carleton, then in the Counter, Wood Street. (We shall meet Richard again in the story of St Edmund Gennings.) The mercenary Berden said the two priests were worth £20 and £30 to him respectively, as someone would go surety for their release. It would also make them more beholden to Berden. Phelippes passed on the request to Walsingham, but it was not granted as Sherwood was banished later that year. After three years in the Gatehouse, Ralph Bickley, who had been ordained at Rome in October 1580 and returned to England in 1583, was sent to Wisbech Castle where he remained until 1618, having been admitted

The Elizabethan Persecution

into the Society of Jesus by Father Henry Garnet in 1597.

Undeterred, Berden soon tried again. He wrote directly to Walsingham, thanking him for sparing the life of Father Christopher Dryland q.v. at Berden's request because it had 'much increased my credit amongst the Papists' if they thought that it was by his endeavour that the priest's life had been saved. He declared how much he abhorred the priest but asked Walsingham the favour of releasing Dryland from prison, as that would further increase the trust the Papists had in him. Berden clearly had great influence: one wonders just how many more like him there were. The State Papers contain his comments to Walsingham on captured priests as to whether they should be executed or kept in prison. Were it not there in black and white as proof it would be unthinkable that the lives of priests might have depended upon the whim such a squalid villain. He was instrumental in deciding to which prisons some priests were directed. Working in league with the prison keepers, from whom he received back-handers, he produced lists of the names of priests in various jails, arranging for the 'best priests' i.e. those who could afford to pay most for their custody, to be sent to them, enabling the keepers to make a bigger profit. When Anthony Tyrell's inventive fabrications had run their course he asked to be released from the Clink and was party to a similar subterfuge. In an attempt at allaying suspicion he asked Justice Young to also release Father Nicholas Gellebrand, a Marian priest.

George Orwell did not invent 'Big Brother' or the thought police in his novel *1984*. Nor did that dubious distinction belong to the Stalinist system Orwell was satirising: Elizabeth I and her merciless ministers had beaten Stalin to it 350 years earlier. The ruthless activities of the Elizabethan government against the Catholic community may be justifiably compared with identical methods used against the Church by the totalitarian regimes of Russia and Eastern Europe in the twentieth century. These closely mirrored the techniques used by their Elizabethan counterparts: torture, lying propaganda and sham show trials, such as those of Cardinal Jozsef Mindszenty in Hungary or the martyred Metropolitan of Petrograd, Saint Benjamin Kazansky. Such sustained, unrelenting repression is the only rationale that satisfactorily explains why the majority of the population of England and Wales eventually became Protestant. But, just as under those later totalitarian regimes, the Faith was not extinguished. Despite all that the machinery of repression could throw at it, State persecution proved incapable of destroying Catholicism. Sustained by the brave seminary priests, the true heroes of the Elizabethan age, it survived its catacomb existence.

The Elizabethan Persecution

Notes to Chapter Three

1 William Cecil, 1st Baron Burghley, was born in 1520. He served in various capacities during the Lord Protectorship of Somerset, and under the Duke of Northumberland he was made Secretary of State. He managed to avoid getting involved in Northumberland's attempt to usurp the throne and suffered no consequences during Mary's reign, when he sat in Parliament. He came to prominence under Elizabeth whom he served as secretary and Lord Treasurer and as her chief adviser for forty years. He was to all intents and purposes what today would be the Prime Minister. His personal religious views were Puritan - he was a friend of the fanatical John Knox - but he recognised that he had to support the Anglican Establishment. He was uncompromisingly harsh towards Catholics, whose continuing presence he did all in his power to crush. Created a baron in 1571, he died in 1598.

2 Edmund Bonner of London deprived May 1559 and sent to the Marshalsea where he spent ten years, dying 5 September 1569; Ralph Bayne of Lichfield, deprived June, died 18 November 1559; Owen Oglethorpe of Carlisle, deprived June, died in prison 31 December 1559; Henry Morgan of St David's, deprived June, died December 1559; John White of Winchester, deprived June 1559, died in prison 12 January 1560; Cuthbert Scott of Chester, deprived June 1559, died 1565; Richard Pate of Worcester, deprived June 1559, died in prison 23 November 1565; Thomas Watson of Lincoln, deprived June 1559, died in Wisbech Castle in September 1584 at the age of seventy-one having spent twenty-five years in prison. Thomas Thirlby of Ely, deprived July 1559, died 26 August 1570; Nicholas Heath of York, deprived July 1559, died 1579; Gilbert Bourne of Bath and Wells, deprived October 1559, died in prison 10 September 1569; Cuthbert Tunstall of Durham, deprived September and died 18 November 1559 aged eighty-five; David Poole of Peterborough, deprived November 1559, died in prison May 1568; James Turberville of Exeter, deprived November 1559, died in prison 1 November 1570. In addition Thomas Reynolds, bishop-elect of Hereford, was set aside by Elizabeth before his consecration and died a prisoner in jail. The last survivor of the hierarchy, Thomas Goldwell of St Asaph, was deprived July 1559 and fled to Rome. After the Bishop's escape his servant, John Thomas, was arrested and died in the Counter, London. Goldwell spent most of the rest of his life in Rome and died there in 1585 at the age of eighty-five. As a footnote of history, in addition to ordaining many English priests, he it was who ordained St Camillus de Lellis (1550-1614) the founder of the Ministers

The Elizabethan Persecution

of the Sick, the forerunner of the Red Cross.

3 Matthew Parker, the first Anglican Archbishop of Canterbury, was born at Norwich 1504. After achieving BA at Cambridge, he was ordained priest in 1527. He became the favourite chaplain of Queen Anne Boleyn before becoming Vice-Chancellor of Cambridge University on the nomination of Henry VIII. Within a short time of the accession of Edward VI, he 'jumped the gun' by taking a wife prior to the legalisation of clergy marriages. By this time he had aligned himself firmly in the Protestant camp and in 1552 was made Dean of Lincoln. Under Mary, Parker was deprived of his appointments. When Elizabeth succeeded to the throne she chose Parker to be her Archbishop of Canterbury. He had to wait five months for his consecration because it proved difficult to find the four bishops required to ordain him to the episcopate. One reason why the depositions of the Catholic bishops was spread out over a number of months was in the hope that some of them would consent to consecrate Parker. None did so. Four married former bishops, William Barlow, Miles Coverdale, John Hodgkins and John Scory, who had been deprived as Protestants under Mary, two of whom had been excommunicated, performed the task, for which purpose the Edwardine Ordinal was used. This was not legal at the time as it had been abolished by Parliament under Mary, so Parker's claim to validity as archbishop rested entirely upon the will of Elizabeth as Supreme Governor of the Church of England. Contemporary Catholics derided the validity of Anglican orders and from the outset consistently referred to Church of England clerics as 'pretended bishops and false priests'. The Catholic Church has always maintained that Parker's consecration was invalid because it was defective both in form and intention, and therefore neither he nor any whom he subsequently ordained were in the Apostolic Succession; their orders were null and void. Parker, who with Cranmer was arguably the co-founder of Anglicanism, was a moderate man who never involved himself in government affairs although he implemented its religious policy. For example, he kept confined in his own house in Kent John Boxall DD, who had been Dean of Windsor and Secretary of State under Queen Mary. Boxall, for whom Elizabeth harboured a particular hatred for no apparent reason, was sent to the Tower in 1560. It is easy to imagine what Parker's reaction must have been when Boxall converted his secretary, Richard Stevens. Stevens later became a priest. Boxall died still under house arrest in 1571. Parker died in 1575.

4 Blessed Thomas Plumtree was educated at Corpus Christi, Oxford. He

The Elizabethan Persecution

was Rector of Stubton in his native Lincolnshire. He resigned his parish with the accession of Elizabeth and became a schoolmaster, only to have to give up his post because he would not conform. Having acted as a chaplain in the Northern Rising and celebrated Mass in the cathedral, he was hanged, drawn and quartered at Durham on 4 January 1570.

5 Blessed John Felton, a married man, came from a wealthy Norfolk family but was born at Bermondsey in London. He was condemned for publishing the bull of Pope Pius V excommunicating Elizabeth by nailing it to the door of the Bishop of London. Even though he admitted his 'crime' he was tortured in the Tower before being hanged, drawn and quartered in St Paul's Churchyard, London, on 8 August 1570. His daughter was present at his execution.

6 Blessed John Storey was born at Salisbury and educated at Oxford, becoming a Doctor of Law. Under Queen Mary he was Regius Professor of Canon Law at Oxford and served as a Member of Parliament for various constituencies. He was also a commissioner for heresy and had a reputation for severity in interrogating any suspect who came before him. He was one of the Queen's proctors at the trial of Cranmer at Oxford in 1555. With the accession of Elizabeth he fled abroad and was employed in the Spanish Netherlands as a book censor. In 1570 he was abducted by government agents and taken aboard a ship at Antwerp. Returned to England, he was imprisoned in the Tower. Here he was charged with treason and repeatedly tortured and without any evidence was condemned. It is clear that the real reason for his capture was not treason but long-delayed retaliation for his role as a heresy commissioner. Before he was hanged, drawn and quartered at Tyburn on 1 June 1571 Storey made a plea for his wife and four children to be taken care of. (Storey's grandson, Edward Weston, q.v. was a priest.) The first permanent, triangular gallows was erected at Tyburn specially for Storey's execution. The later gallows was so large that twenty-one people could be hanged from it at the same time.

7 Sir Francis Walsingham (d.1590) was born at Chislehurst, Kent. He studied at Cambridge and in 1552 he enrolled at Gray's Inn. On Mary's accession he went abroad, returning when Elizabeth succeeded. A protégé of William Cecil, he was elected to Parliament in 1559. He became the chief spy master of the Elizabethan government, organising one of the most efficient European-wide spy networks in history, indulging in deceptions and fabrications against all those thought

suspect in loyalty. His spies were skilled at forging documents and he was adept at concocting scams to entrap his victims, including Mary, Queen of Scots. Along with William Cecil, Walsingham was the chief proponent of the persecution. Blinded by his hatred of Rome, his conduct betrayed his brutality and fanaticism in his treatment of priests. The wily, cunning character of the man is well captured in his portrait. As the historian William Camden wrote in his *Annales* of the reign of Queen Elizabeth, Walsingham 'well understood how to win over men's minds and exploit them for his own purposes.' He must have 'turned in his grave' when his daughter, Frances, became a Catholic convert!

8 Anthony Tyrell is archetypical of the damage that an apostate priest could inflict on Catholics. Born in 1552, he came from an Essex recusant family who fled abroad early in Elizabeth's reign. Educated probably at Louvain University, Anthony paid a visit to England in 1574 and was arrested on arrival in Kent. He served nearly two years in prison before returning to the Continent. He was one of the original band of students at the English College, Rome, and was ordained in 1580. Having returned to England he was captured in a London street in April 1581 and sent to the Gatehouse, from where he escaped early in 1582. He spent two years abroad with Father John Ballard doing precisely no one knows what before returning to England with Ballard, landing at Southampton on Christmas Eve 1584. At the time of the supposed discovery of the Babington Plot, Tyrell was arrested on 4 July 1586 and imprisoned in the Counter, Wood Street. He was examined by Walsingham, Topcliffe and Justice Young. The nature of the pressures that may have been exerted upon him is unclear, but by his own testimony they seem to have been more in the form of subtle persuasion rather than physical threats, although he was shown the crippled Ballard after his tortures. He was moved to St Catherine's in the company of another waverer, Father William Tedder. Nonetheless he proceeded to incriminate Father Ballard, by now also a prisoner, and many others. He then issued a long recantation, confessing that it was all lies. It did not save the fourteen who were executed for their supposed part in the Babington Plot. He also wrote to the relatives of those whom he had falsely accused asking their forgiveness, as well as composing a long missive to the Queen craving her pardon for all the lying information he had supplied, which he attributes to 'sin and the devil'. Tyrell apostatised and recanted at least three more times. A pathological liar, it is impossible to know which, if indeed any, of his statements are true. Later in life he wrote an excruciatingly long and exaggerated account of his 'lamentable fall' in which he listed forty-seven people, including the

Pope, the Queen of Scots and St Philip Howard and his wife, all of whom he had maliciously accused with his abominable lies. He retracted everything he had said about them and begged their forgiveness. In February 1589 Tyrell was granted a pardon for his services and made rector of Dengie, Essex. He was deprived of this living but became vicar of Southminster, Essex, in 1591. Now married, he went through yet another reversion to Catholicism and was sent to the Marshalsea in 1593, from where he wrote a grovelling letter to Robert Cecil. He continued as a Protestant minister, acting as chaplain to Lady Bindon, and gave anti-Catholic evidence before Bishop Bancroft in 1602. Once more claiming to be a repentant Catholic he planned to flee abroad but was caught and sent to the Marshalsea from where he wrote yet another abject plea to Sir Robert Cecil. What then happened to him is unsure but it appears he retired to Flanders, where his Catholic brother lived. As all bad pennies have a habit of doing, he finally turned up again in Naples where he died in 1615 - allegedly reconciled to the Church to which his treachery had done so much harm.

9 Gilbert Gifford, born 1560, came from a Staffordshire recusant family and was a second cousin of Father John Gerard. He went to Douai in 1577, later transferring to the English College, Rome. He was expelled but given a second chance by William Allen and was finally ordained deacon in 1585. Later that year he returned to England, where he was arrested and examined by Francis Walsingham. This resulted in Gifford agreeing to act as a double agent. His actions ensured the downfall of Anthony Babington and all associated with him. He left England after the executions and despite Allen's misgivings was inexplicably ordained priest in March 1587. In December of that year he was arrested in a Paris brothel. He continued sending information to the British government about his co-religionists until his trial. He died in a Paris prison in 1590.

10 Blessed Thomas Pilcher (sometimes referred to as Pilchard), was born at Battle, Sussex, c.1557 and educated at Balliol College, Oxford, becoming MA in 1579. He arrived at Rheims in 1581 and was ordained at Laon 5 March 1583. Two months later he returned to England and was based for a time with Lady Mary West of Winchester, widow of Sir Owen, at her house in Buckinghamshire. (Lady Mary spent around eighteen years in prison for her recusancy. Her nephew, Peter Warnford was a Benedictine priest.) Arrested in Fleet Street, London, Thomas was exiled in 1585, but came back early in 1586. He worked in Dorset,

The Elizabethan Persecution

until apprehended at Dorchester with his great friend John Jessop. He was hanged, drawn and quartered there on 21 March 1587. The rope was cut so quickly that Thomas was able to stand erect under the gallows. 'Is this then your justice?' he exclaimed to the sheriff before being pulled down to suffer the butchery. He was described as of 'a most gentle disposition, more than moderately learned, a remarkable pattern of priestly life. He was above middle height and had a cast in his eyes which made him easily recognised. His countenance was modest and sedate; he wore a small beard round the mouth and chin.'

As a corollary it is appropriate that the martyrdom of Blessed William Pike, four years later, can be added. He was a Dorset-born layman, a carpenter by trade. He was either a Protestant convert or a former Catholic who had conformed. He was reconciled to the Church by Thomas Pilcher and was charged for this offence. It appears he was arrested with Father Pilcher and John Jessop and may have been kept in prison until 1591 when he was charged with proselytising amongst his fellow prisoners. When offered his life if he would conform he responded that it did not 'become a son of Father Pilcher to do so'. William was hanged, drawn and quartered at Dorchester in December.

11 Blessed Stephen Rowsham was born c.1555 in Oxfordshire and was educated at Oriel College, Oxford. In 1578 he became an Anglican curate at St Mary's, Oxford. Having converted, he travelled to Rheims in 1581, was ordained at Soissons on 29 September of that year, and returned to England in April 1582. By May he had been captured and was in the Tower, where he spent over eighteen months in the appalling conditions of 'Little Ease'. Why he was not selected, as he anticipated, for trial and execution with the batch of priests who were martyred in that year, is unexplained. In 1584 he was moved to the Marshalsea, before being exiled in 1585. While abroad he made a pilgrimage to Rome before returning to England. He was captured at the house of Mrs Strange, a widow of Gloucester, who was arrested with him, and they were imprisoned in Gloucester Castle. While in the castle he worked hard at reconciling as many of the prisoners as he could, to the consternation of some of his fellow Catholics, who urged him to be more cautious, but Stephen declared that by now he was past fear of the laws. Mrs Strange is described as a resolute Catholic who had long been 'chased into many shires by persecution.' Stephen was tried at the next assizes and condemned to death. The exact date of his martyrdom is unclear, but it was some time in March 1587. He was described as of a pleasant and manly countenance, with a brown beard and a full and sweet voice. He was low in stature and a 'little crooked due to an

inequality of his shoulders'.

12 Blessed John Hambley was born c.1560 at St Mabyn, near Bodmin, Cornwall. A convert, he went to Rheims in 1582 and was ordained at Laon in September 1584. He returned to England in April 1585 landing on the Suffolk coast near Ipswich. At Easter 1586 he was arrested at Chard, Somerset, and after his trial at Taunton was condemned. He promised to conform and promptly escaped from prison, being re-taken near Salisbury in August. He then made a detailed confession in which, unfortunately, he implicated some of his fellow priests. Notwithstanding, he refused to honour his promise to conform and was martyred at Salisbury in March 1587.

13 Blessed Edmund Sykes was born c.1550 at Kirkgate, Leeds, Yorkshire, into a family of clothiers. He studied at Rheims, where he was ordained priest 21 February 1581, returning to England on 5 June. He worked around Ledsham but was arrested in the town of his birth having been betrayed by an apostate. He was imprisoned at York Kidcote and Hull Castle in August 1585. He agreed to attend a Protestant service, but repented of it immediately. The following month he was exiled. He arrived at Rome in 1586, where he hoped to join a religious order, but he believed that his duty lay on the English mission, to which he soon returned. It was not long before he was re-captured at Wath - having been betrayed by his own brother - and committed to York Castle. Challoner reports that while in prison Edmund suffered from grievous temptations to abandon his religion, believing them to come from the Devil. He overcame them by prayer for which he rejoiced and thanked God. He was hanged, drawn and quartered at York 23 March 1587.

14 Blessed George Douglas was born in Edinburgh and served as a schoolmaster in the county of Rutland, England. He studied in Paris and was ordained priest at Notre Dame Cathedral about 1574. He returned to Scotland in 1584, but having lost his passport, he made his way to Rutland to seek out his friends. There he was arrested, but was soon released. He moved to Yorkshire and was arrested again at Ripon in 1587 and hanged, drawn and quartered at York on 9 September.

15 Ludlam and Garlick: Blessed Robert Ludlam was born at Radbourne, Derbyshire, c.1551 He studied at St John's College, Oxford, but took no degree. He worked for a time as a schoolmaster before going to Rheims in 1580. He was ordained at Soissons 23 September 1581. He

returned to England in 1582 and worked on the mission for about six years. Arrested at Padley Hall, he was sent to Derby jail, where he met Father Richard Simpson, who had already been tried and condemned but reprieved because he was wavering. Tried at Derby on 23 July 1588, Robert was hanged, drawn and quartered the next day at St Mary's Bridge, Derby.

Blessed Nicholas Garlick was born near Glossop, Derbyshire c.1555. He studied at Gloucester Hall, Oxford, for a short time. For about seven years he was a master at Tideswell Grammar School. Three of his pupils became priests, two of whom were martyred, including Christopher Buxton, executed at Canterbury in 1588. Nicholas went to Rheims in 1581, was ordained at Châlons 31 March 1582, and returned to work on the English Mission in his native county. In 1584, a Catholic resident of Tideswell, who was then a prisoner in the Bridewell, was prevailed upon to confess what he knew about priests. He named Nicholas as sometimes staying in Staffordshire with a Mr Waterton, who regularly sheltered priests. Nicholas was arrested and banished, staying just two days at Rheims before returning to England. He was captured with Ludlam at Padley and executed with him and Simpson.

Blessed Richard Simpson was born near Ripon, Yorkshire, c.1553. He was a schoolmaster in Lancashire, and may have been a convert minister, before going to Douai. He was ordained at Brussels in August 1577, only three months after his arrival. Within days he returned to England. He was arrested in January 1588 while on a journey from Lancashire to Derby. Sharing the company of Ludlam and Garlick in prison strengthened his resolve. Father Henry Garnet SJ wrote an account of Richard's temporary fall from grace after his condemnation and his penitence afterwards. He recorded that Richard managed to live on tuppence a day, and that when he was captured and stripped he was found to be wearing a hair shirt.

A popular ballad composed about the three martyrs read:

When Garlick did the ladder kiss
And Simpson after hie,
Methought that there Saint Andrew was
Desirous for to die.
When Ludlam looked smilingly
And joyful did remain,
It seemed Saint Stephen standing by
For to be stoned again.

16 Richard Topcliffe (1532-1604) came from a landed Lincolnshire family. He was orphaned at a young age and studied law at Gray's Inn.

He was a Member of Parliament in the service of William Cecil and worked closely with Francis Walsingham. His precise official status remains a mystery but he was a favourite of Elizabeth's. Known as 'Her Majesty's Servant' he seems to have derived his authority directly from the Queen. He held a commission to hunt down priests and a licence to torture them in the private torture chamber installed at his home. In a letter to Queen Elizabeth he boasted that he had been responsible for sending more priests to Tyburn than anyone else. Without the Queen's approval he could not have practised his inhuman conduct, in which he took perverted pleasure in inflicting pain. Were it not so well attested by eye-witnesses his unspeakable brutality would be unimaginable. There are no words adequate to convey the depraved nature of this cruel, vicious, evil, sadistic monster who today would be classed as a psychopath. Evidence that he was close to the Queen is furnished by his being one of the royal party that was entertained by Edward Rookwood at Euston Hall, Suffolk, in 1578. Topcliffe recorded the Queen's appalling treatment of Edward. After spending three days at his house being lavishly entertained the Queen thanked Rookwood, and then immediately ordered his arrest. A recusant, he died after twenty years in jail at Bury St Edmunds in 1598. (His youngest son, Robert Rookwood, on his way to Saint-Omer in 1617 was arrested and imprisoned in Newgate from which he escaped. He was ordained at Rome in 1621.)

17 Blessed Richard Langley was born at Grinthorpe, Yorkshire, according to Challoner. The son of Richard Langley, of Rathorp Hall, North Dalton in the East Riding, and his wife, Jane Beaumont. He married Agnes Hansby of Malton. Richard was known as a 'notorious entertainer of seminaries' and Lord Huntingdon sent a group of justices and ministers to search his houses in the autumn of 1586. They discovered two priests, one of whom was John Mush. Richard and the priests were taken the short distance to York and committed to the Castle. Father Mush managed to escape. Richard was brought to trial at the November Assizes with captured priest, Alexander Crow. Upon coming into court Richard knelt down and asked the priest for his blessing. He told the court that he would never repent that he had harboured priests, and was only sorry that he had not been able to give shelter to more of them. Richard was a well-known gentleman in the area and the jury that had been impanelled consisted mostly of his neighbours. Huntingdon, anxious that they might acquit Richard, had them dismissed and a new jury appointed. When he was condemned Richard thanked God that he might die in such a good cause. His brother interceded with Huntingdon, who promised him that Richard

The Elizabethan Persecution

would be reprieved until the Lent Assizes. But he reneged on his promise and Richard was hanged at York on 1 December 1586. Richard's daughter, Anne, married Robert Hodgson of Hebburn, Jarrow. She had two sons, John and Edmund, who both became priests and were working on the English mission in the 1630's.

Blessed Alexander Crow was born c.1550 at Howden, in the East Riding of Yorkshire. For a time he worked as a shoemaker in York. On 30 April 1581 he arrived at Rheims and was ordained at Laon 17 December 1583. The following February he was sent to England. We may assume that he ministered in the area of his birthplace because at the time of Langley's arrest, Alexander was apprehended at South Duffield in the East Riding, while en route to baptise a child. Imprisoned in York Castle he was tried with Langley and condemned. He was martyred on 30 November 1586: the day before Langley's execution. Alexander was said to be a 'simple man ... undeterred by danger. He was of more than medium height, with a serious countenance and black beard; well grown and strongly made.' The story is related that the night before his execution he was greatly agitated and could not rest. He seems to have been hallucinating, claiming to see a horrible monster who was threatening him with hell. He prayed loudly that this anguish be lifted from him, begging the prayers of his fellow prisoners. Suddenly he became calm and joyful and afterwards explained that when he found himself in the greatest distress he saw a light come in at the door, and in the light were the Virgin Mary and St John, who comforted and consoled him, promising him that he would enter into heaven.

18 Blessed William Carter, born in London c.1550 was apprenticed in 1563 to John Cawood, a printer. Because of his trade, William was constantly under surveillance. He was arrested in 1578 and spent time in prison. Arrested again, and committed to the Gatehouse in 1579 for recusancy, he was released in 1581. He married but his wife, Jane, died in 1582. He was discovered printing Catholic books, in particular Father Gregory Martin's *A Treatise of Schism*, and also storing vestments and sacred vessels. Arrested in 1582 by Topcliffe, he was sent to the Tower and tortured but he refused to reveal information about his fellow Catholics. His trial, presided over by John Aylmer, Bishop of London, was a travesty. He was violently insulted and abused by the prosecution and the judges joined in urging his guilt. He was hanged, drawn and quartered at Tyburn on 11 January 1584.

19 Blessed Thomas Sprott and Blessed Thomas Hunt. Sprott was born in

The Elizabethan Persecution

1571 at Skelsmergh, near Kendal, Westmorland, and baptised in the parish church there. He studied at Rheims but, because of a gap in the records at that time, the dates of his sojourn have not been traced. He was ordained in the spring of 1596. In May of that year he was arrested by Captain Turner at Brielle* in the western Netherlands. This ancient, fortified seaport, situated on the island of Voorne-Putten, became an English possession in 1585. It was one of four towns captured by Dutch rebels that were acquired by Elizabeth I, under the Treaty of Nonsuch, as security of payment for the services of 5000 English soldiers, used by the Dutch in their war against the Spanish. Thomas Sprott was shipped from Holland to England, and by July was a prisoner in the Bridewell. He managed to escape and was given shelter by Father Henry Garnet, the Jesuit Superior. He stayed with Garnet for nearly four years.

Thomas Hunt, whose real name was Benstead, was born in Norfolk in 1574. He entered the English College, Valladolid, 12 May 1592. From there he went to Seville, where he was ordained. He returned to England in 1595 and by December 1599 he was a prisoner in the Clink, from where he was sent to Wisbech Castle in 1600. During the night of 10 March, together with five companions, he escaped. He made his way to the house called White Webbs at Enfield Chase where he too found refuge with Father Garnet, who recommended both of the priests to friends in Lincolnshire, where they could continue their ministry. Journeying together, Sprott and Hunt arrived at Lincoln, and were staying at the Saracen's Head inn. Unfortunately for them, a search was taking place for an escaped criminal and when the two priests were questioned they were unable to give satisfactory answers. When their belongings were searched holy oils and breviaries were discovered, so they were arrested and examined by the mayor on suspicion of being priests. The Summer Assizes happened to be in session and here they were tried. At no point did they admit to being priests, and no evidence to that effect was produced, but the judge, Sir John Glanville, instructed the hesitant jury to find them guilty. The two priests were martyred at Lincoln in mid-July 1600. We know for certain that the date was before 27 July because on that date Judge Glanville, riding away from the assizes, was killed in a fall from his horse. Father Rivers SJ, secretary to Father Garnet, wrote that Glanville broke his neck in the

---

* Brielle has long been a Catholic pilgrimage centre, commemorating the Martys of Gorkum. These were a group of nineteen religious – including eleven Franciscans – who, when Gorkum was captured from the Spaniards by the rebels in 1572, were forcibly shipped, half-naked to Brielle. Asked to deny their faith they refused and were hanged by militant Calvinists. Their mutilated bodies were dumped in a ditch. They were canonized in 1867.

The Elizabethan Persecution

fall. Challoner, quoting Dr Thomas Worthington, President of Douai, reports that it was a head injury that caused his death.

20 Blessed Thomas Palaser was born c.1570 at either Ellerton-upon-Swale or Kirby Wiske in the North Riding of Yorkshire. He arrived at Rheims in July 1592 and was transferred to Valladolid in January 1593. He was ordained there in 1596 and returned to England. On 12 May 1597 he was a prisoner in the Gatehouse, from which, on the 29th, he escaped with two other priests, Francis Tilletson and Robert Hawkesworth. As he had promised not to escape his scruples led him to leave behind a letter to the Keeper, Hugh Parlour, justifying his conduct on the grounds that as his promise had not been freely given but had been forced upon him in order to avoid being manacled twenty-fours hours a day, he did not feel bound, in conscience, by the promise. He moved north to Durham and served on the mission for three years. In the summer of 1600 he was staying with John Norton at Lamesley, Co. Durham, when the house was raided by a pursuivant named Henry Sanderson. Thomas, Norton and his wife Margaret, and two other gentlemen who were present, John Talbot, from Thornton-le-Street, and Richard Sayer, were all arrested. They were taken to Durham together with "massing stuff and prohibited books'. Tried at the Summer Assizes they were all sentenced to death, but were offered pardons if they conformed. Mr Sayer agreed to do so and secured his liberty. Blessed John Talbot, a married man, was a well-known recusant, having already been convicted in 1588. He and Blessed John Norton were executed on 8 September with Father Palaser. Mrs Norton was reprieved, being thought to be pregnant, and was given a special pardon in 1601.

21 Blessed John Pibush, the son of Thomas Pibush of Great Fencote and Jane Danby, was born at Thirsk, Yorkshire, in 1557. Having studied at Rheims he was ordained 14 March 1587 and sent to the English mission in January 1589. He was apprehended at the Hart inn at Moreton-in-Marsh, Gloucestershire, in summer 1593. His captor received £6.13.4p for apprehending him and for escorting him to Lord Chandos, Lord Lieutenant of Gloucestershire, who sent him to London. He was returned to Gloucester in September 1594 and on 19 February 1595 there was a mass break-out from Gloucester jail. There seems to be some disparity in the account of what exactly happened. Challoner states that it was the common felons who breached the walls and Father Pibush simply took advantage of this to abscond. But the vile Richard Topcliffe - who ought to know - claims that John was responsible for

the break-out and the twenty other prisoners followed his lead. Unfortunately John, on foot, got no further than about two miles before he was re-captured. Once more he was sent to London and committed to the King's Bench prison. On 26 June he was tried and condemned to death, but inexplicably was left in prison for six years. His constitution, which had been strong and robust until then, was ruined not only by the dreadful insanitary conditions of the prison but also the treatment he had to endure from the common criminals. In a long letter to Father Henry Garnet, whom he refers to as 'the first and best friend I have ever met since my return to my country' John describes how friends coming to visit him in jail did not recognise him he was so changed. He suffered from jaundice for which Father Garnet managed to provide medicine to give him some relief. He contracted a lung disease, and having gained the sympathy of the jailer, he was allowed to make a separate cell for himself. In 1599 his name appeared on a list of prisoners to be transferred to Wisbech Castle, but for some unknown - perhaps entirely arbitrary - reason Lord Chief Justice Popham crossed out his name. John was accused of reconciling fellow prisoners to the Church and on 17 February 1601 he was brought back to court before Popham and his death sentence was confirmed. The very next day, 18 February, he was taken to St Thomas Waterings, Southwark, and hanged, drawn and quartered. Father Henry Garnet wrote an account of his trial and martyrdom. It is just possible that he was present at his execution. In extant letters John refers to Anne Vaux and her sister Eleanor and to Father John Gerard, all of whom he clearly knew.

22 Blessed Robert Middleton was born at York in 1570. (What relation may he have been to Margaret Clitherow, née Middleton?) He was educated in his native city, and until the age of eighteen he conformed to the Established Church, at which point he converted to Catholicism, apparently as a result of his reading. He spent the next few years in London and Hull, where he lived with a merchant. It was from Hull that he sailed to Calais on a coal boat and made his way to Douai, where he stayed for three years. In 1597 he was sent to Rome and in 1598 was ordained at the German College returning to England three months later. At Christmas 1599, together with Father Martin Nelson, he was arrested by Thomas, 2nd Lord Burghley at Ripon. How Robert secured his liberty is unknown but he was re-arrested on the public highway in the Fylde by Sir Richard Houghton on 30 September 1600. The following day, while he was being taken under armed escort to Lancaster, somewhere near Garstang an attempt was made by Father Thurstan Hunt and three lay Catholics to rescue him. The attempt failed

The Elizabethan Persecution

and Thurstan was imprisoned with Robert at Lancaster Castle. In November both were sent to London to the Gatehouse. There they remained until March 1601 when they were ordered back to Lancaster tied to their horses and Robert faced intensive interrogations about his life and work. Both priests were martyred at Lancaster. The exact date is in doubt but it was probably 3 April. A contemporary account claims that Robert's sister was present at his execution and that he reproached her when she offered £100 for his life and the promise that he would talk to a minister with a view to persuading him to conform.

23 Blessed Thurstan Hunt, son of Gilbert Hunt and Dorothy Mallet, was born in 1555 at Carlton Hall, Leeds. He went to Rheims in 1583, was ordained by the Cardinal Archbishop of Rheims 20 April 1585 and sent to England. For fifteen years he served on the mission until he was captured near Garstang in 1600 attempting to rescue Father Middleton and suffered with him at Lancaster. In the British Museum is a copy of a sung ballad that circulated in Lancashire following the martyrdoms of Robert Nutter, Edward Thwing, Robert Middleton and Thurstan Hunt. It is entitled '*A song of four priests that suffered death at Lancaster*':

In this our English coast
Much blessed blood is shed.
Two hundred priests almost
In our time martered.
And manie lay men die
With joyful sufferance.
Manie moe in prison lye
God's cause for to advance.
Amongst this gratious troupe,
That follow Christ his traine,
To cause the devil stoupe,
Four priests were latlie slaine,
Nutter's bould constantie
With his sweete fellow Thwing
Of whose meeke modestie
Angels and Saints may singe.

Hunt's hawtie corage staut,
With godlie zeale soe true
Myld Middleton, Oh what
Tonge can halfe thy virtue shew:
At Lancaster lovingly
These martyrs tooke their end.
In glorious victorie

Their faith for to defend.
And thus hath Lancashire
Offered you sacrifice
To daunt their lewde desyre
And please our Saviour's eies,
For by his meanes I trust,
Truth shall have victorie,
When as that number just
Of such saints compleat bee.

24 Venerable James Harrison came from Derbyshire and was ordained at Rheims in 1583. He returned to England in 1585 and was arrested at the home of Thomas Heath in Staffordshire in April 1588 and sent to the Tower. Heath was committed to Newgate and indicted in the King's Bench for sheltering Harrison, but there is no record that he was condemned. James was still in the Tower in 1590 when he was transferred to the Marshalsea. At some point he secured his liberty: how is not known. He was re-captured in March 1602 by Sir Stephen Proctor of Fountains in Nidderdale, Yorkshire, at the home of Venerable Anthony Battie, who was a smallholder at Masham, owning a poor cottage and a few sheep. The two of them were martyred together at York 22 March 1602.

25 Blessed James Duckett was born at Gilfortrigs, Skelsmergh, Westmorland. He was raised as a Protestant and became an apprentice in the City of London. As a result of reading Catholic books he ceased attending church. He was taken to task for this by the minister of St Edmund's, Lombard Street, and when he refused to go to church he was committed to the Bridewell. His master obtained his freedom but soon afterwards he was questioned again about his non-attendance at church and sent to the Compter. Once more his master secured his release, but nervous of his troublesome apprentice, who might put him in danger, James was forced to buy out the remainder of his apprenticeship. He sought out an old priest, Father Weeks, then a prisoner in the Gatehouse, who received him into the Church. After a couple of years he married a Catholic widow and earned his living as a book dealer, many of them Catholic books, which exposed him to danger. He was arrested several times and imprisoned for this activity. Challoner states that of twelve years of Duckett's married life, nine of them were spent in various prisons. A bookbinder named Peter Bullock was sentenced to a year in prison, and in the hope of securing a pardon he informed Lord Chief Justice Popham that James had published copies of Robert Southwell's *Humble Supplication* to the Queen. In

The Elizabethan Persecution

March 1602 Duckett's home was raided at midnight and Catholic literature was found, so he was committed to Newgate. He was tried before Popham alongside the very ill Father Robert Watkinson and James did his best to support the young priest. Bullock was the only witness against James and the jury returned a 'not guilty' verdict, which infuriated Popham, who urged them to reconsider and sent them out again. This time they found him guilty, as well as three priests: Robert Watkinson, Francis Page and Thomas Tichborne. James was appointed the first to die on the following Monday, 19 April. His wife was allowed to visit him that morning and as he was taken out for his execution he was given a cup of wine which he drank and asked his wife to also drink to Bullock as a sign of her forgiveness. Bullock's betrayal availed him nothing: he was taken to Tyburn in the cart with James who, with the rope around his neck, kissed Bullock and forgave him. The martyrdom of the three priests took place the next day.

26 Blessed William Richardson, alias Anderson, was born at Wales, near Sheffield, Yorkshire, in 1572. He was received at Rheims 16 July 1592 and the following year was sent to Valladolid, where he arrived 23 December. On 1 October 1594 he was sent to the College of St Gregory, Seville, where he was ordained. Betrayed by a false Catholic, he was captured at St Clements Inn, one of the Inns of Court, and sent to Newgate on 12 February 1603. After a week as a close prisoner he was brought to trial at the Old Bailey. Lord Chief Justice Popham, hearing of William's arrest, interrupted a case being heard by the Recorder of London and demanded that William be immediately brought before him. No evidence was presented, no witnesses called. Popham, acting both as the prosecutor and judge, conducted the trial in shocking haste. William confessed that he was a priest, but denied that he was a Jesuit or knew Father Garnet. William was condemned to death for his priesthood, thanking God and telling Popham that he was a bloodthirsty man. Popham vacated the court and left sentence to be pronounced by the Recorder. The next day, cheerful and courageous, William was hanged, drawn and quartered at Tyburn on 17 February, accompanied by a throng of Catholics who crowded around him until the end.

27 William Allen was born at Rossall in the parish of Poulton-le-Fylde, Lancashire in 1532, the son of John Allen and Jane Lister. A BA and MA of Oriel College, Oxford, in 1556 he became principal of St Mary's Hall and two years later, while still a layman, a canon of the cathedral chapter at York. On the accession of Elizabeth in 1558 he had

to resign all his posts and went to live in Flanders. He returned to England for about three years but left the country permanently in 1565 and was ordained at Malines where he lectured on theology. Convinced that the future of Catholicism depended upon a supply of well-trained priests in tune with the Counter-Reformation spirit of the Council of Trent, in 1568 he established the college at Douai to send clergy to the English Mission. In 1570 he was made a Doctor of Divinity. He was president of Douai for seventeen years. In 1585 he was called to serve in Rome, where, in 1576, he had helped create the second English College. He was appointed cardinal in August 1587, the first Englishman to be elevated since Cardinal Pole. In his ten-month reign (1590-91) Pope Gregory XIV Sfondrati named him Prefect of the Vatican Library and commissioned him to oversee the revision of the Latin Vulgate Bible. He published many works in defence of Catholicism. He became involved in political intrigues with Spain, which was not at all in accordance with the views of most Catholics in England. Nonetheless Allen deserved the gratitude of English Catholics for his lifelong labours in preserving the Faith in their country. He died in Rome 1594 and was buried in the chapel of the English College. In the late 18th century his tomb was destroyed by the French occupiers of Rome. Two of his nieces, Helen and Catherine Allen, became nuns at St Monica's, Louvain, under Mother Margaret Clement. They were professed in 1594 and 1595 respectively.

28 Gregory Martin was born in Sussex. A BA of Oxford he spent thirteen years at the university and acquired a reputation as a brilliant scholar and linguist. He was ordained deacon in the Anglican Church, but being Catholic at heart he left the university and for a time was tutor to Philip Howard, Earl of Arundel, the future martyr. When Philip's father, Thomas, 4th Duke of Norfolk, was arrested in 1569 Gregory went to Douai and was ordained priest at Brussels in March 1573. He led the first group of students to Rome at the opening of the new college. When he returned to Rheims he devoted the remainder of his life to teaching and to the work on which rests his lasting fame: the translation of the Bible into English from the Vulgate, which he began in October 1578. It was published in spring 1582. Although the translation lacks the harmonious cadences of the later Authorised Version, its value lies in its accuracy, a fact recognised by all modern translations. Worn out by his labours, Gregory died of consumption at Rheims in 1582. The Old Testament, which was also largely recognised as his work, was not published until 1609.

The Elizabethan Persecution

29 Lewis Barlow was born in Pembrokeshire, South Wales. He entered the Middle Temple in 1567, followed by exile in Flanders in 1571. Ordained 1574, he returned to England and worked mainly in Suffolk, often based at Euston Hall. Arrested in 1587, thanks to the treachery of Anthony Tyrell, he was imprisoned in the Counter, Wood Street, London. He was moved to the Marshalsea, where he sent for Tyrell to admonish him very lovingly for his anti-Catholic activities, urging him to repentance. Barlow was moved to Wisbech Castle in 1588 before being banished in 1603. He returned to England later that same year and died in Oxfordshire in 1610.

30 Thomas Metham, born 1532, was the son of Sir Thomas Metham and his wife Dorothy, the daughter of George, Lord Darcy. He matriculated from Louvain in 1566. He was sent to England from Douai in 1574 and was again at Douai in 1577. By 1579 he was a prisoner in the King's Bench and on 4 May that year, while still in jail, he joined the Society of Jesus. He was moved to Wisbech Castle where he died and was buried 1 April 1592.

31 Martin Nelson was born at Skelton, Overton, near York and was the brother of John q.v. and Thomas Nelson, both seminary priests. Martin arrived at Douai in 1574 and was ordained the same year. Although he returned to Douai for visits in 1576 and Rheims in 1578, the rest of his life was spent on the mission in England and Wales. In 1591 he was chaplain to Lord Scrope at Whitby. In 1594 he was arrested and by January 1595 had agreed to conform, as a result of which he was granted a pardon. Such pardons did not come cheap; they were expensive to purchase. However, he soon resumed his priestly activities and in January 1600 Thomas Cecil, 2nd Lord Burghley, President of the Council of the North, and future Earl of Exeter, wrote to his half-brother, Sir Robert Cecil, that at Christmas he had captured two priests at Ripon: Robert Middleton and Martin Nelson. Stating that Nelson was timorous, Burghley anticipated getting lots of information from him on the promise that his pardon would be renewed, in spite of his relapse. Just what information Nelson divulged is unknown but in 1601 he received his pardon. Once more he took up his priestly activities and was in South Wales in 1610. He died at Sutton, Herefordshire in 1625. His brother, Thomas, was ordained at Cateau Cambresis 23 March 1577 and returned to England in July. He seems constantly to have divided his work between England and the Continent. He was recorded in England in 1603 and 1623. He died at Antwerp in 1625.

32 Henry Shaw was listed in the Douai diary as of the diocese of Chester. He was educated at St John's College, Oxford, where he matriculated MA in 1570. In 1573 he went to Douai and was ordained the following year and sent to England. In 1598 he was appointed an assistant to the Archpriest Blackwell and died in 1608.

33 Blessed William Davies was born c.1557 at Groes-yn-Eirias, now part of Colwyn Bay in Denbighshire. It is likely that he was the student who matriculated at St Edmund Hall, Oxford in 1575 and took his degree in 1578. He arrived at Rheims 6 April 1582 with a number of other Welsh students and served at the first Mass of the future martyr, Nicholas Garlick. He was ordained April 1585 and came to England in June and made his way to North Wales. His base was at Plas Penrhyn, the home of Robert Pugh and his family. (Known today as Penrhyn Old Hall the house, much altered, still stands in the suburbs of Llandudno.) In 1586 the Council of the Marches was reprimanded for its laxity and was ordered to crack down on recusants. William and his host were warned and they fled into hiding. The sea cave, which William Davies occupied for nine months, was in the Rhiwledyn cliffs on Little Orme's Head, Llandudno. It was eighteen feet deep and here small groups of Catholics would secretly assemble. They even had a printing press on which - to quote the authorities - to print 'popish and traitorous books in Welsh'. The cave and its contents, including a decorated wooden altar, were discovered on 14 April 1587 by a Justice of the Peace. But William Davies and his companions had escaped. He carried on his ministry until 1592. On 15 March that year he and Robert Pugh were at Holyhead making arrangements for a group of four students for the priesthood to sail to Ireland and from there to Spain. Their presence aroused suspicion and an attempt was made to arrest them, only Pugh managing to escape. The arrest caused riotous dissension among the people at Holyhead, most of who were clearly opposed to the action. The prisoners were removed to Beaumaris for imprisonment and examination. Davies confessed he was a priest and was kept in solitary confinement. He and the students refused to attend the Protestant church. In a letter to a fellow priest William related how, in an effort to get him to conform, the ministers 'laid siege to me for the space of four or five days together.' The five of them were put on trial before Mr Justice Leighton and Mr Justice Philips. Davies's own account of the trial has survived. It was almost certainly written to Father John Bennet. Judge Philips 'gave very fair words, wishing me to look to myself, saying it was come to that now, that a thread divided between my life and death. I said I never made other account of my life.' The youngest

of the four students, named Robert, was eighteen-years-old and he was specially targeted and intimidated, 'threatening to whip him, to set him in the pillory, to cut off his ears and nose', unless he agreed to conform. 'But no persuasion would serve.' William and the students were all found guilty, the priest of treason and his companions of recusancy: when condemned William intoned the *Te Deum*. Beaumaris was still a Catholic stronghold and there was uproar in the court so the judge ordered that all five should be imprisoned until the wishes of the Privy Council were known. (One of the students, William Robins, managed to escape custody. He eventually found his way to Valladolid where he was ordained in 1602 and returned to work in England.) William was transferred to Ludlow Castle, Shropshire, headquarters of the Council of the Marches. Every effort was made to get him to conform, including taking him to church, but when the service began William began to recite the Latin Vespers in such a loud voice that he drowned out the minister. He was then moved to Bewdley, Worcestershire, being made to walk all the way. Ill and weary he was kept in a foul cellar among the common criminals who treated him with respect. As nothing was achieved William was sent back to Beaumaris. After six months he was taken to court again and once more offered his life if he conformed. When the death sentence was pronounced he gave thanks to the Lord 'who had shown great mercy in enabling him to shed his blood for love of Him.' On 27 July 1593, after sixteen months in prison, William was taken to Beaumaris Castle for execution. His address to the sympathetic crowd of silent people, who stood with heads uncovered, was cut short. Taking hold of the rope he kissed it saying, 'Thy yoke, O Lord, is sweet and Thy burden light.' These were his last audible words. William Robins bought the martyr's cassock stained with his blood and took it with him to Spain as a precious relic. Today there is a chapel on Anglesey as a memorial to William Davies.

34 John Gerard SJ was born 4 October 1564 in Derbyshire. His father was Sir Thomas Gerard of Bryn, Lancashire, who was imprisoned in the Tower for plotting to rescue Mary, Queen of Scots from her captivity at Tutbury and take her to the Isle of Man. His mother was Elizabeth Port, daughter and heiress of Sir John Port. John Gerard is one of the most fascinating and charismatic of all the priests who worked in England. His two books, the *Narrative of the Gunpowder Plot* and his *Autobiography*, provide a vivid insight into the lives of the English Catholic community. The books are invaluable sources of contemporary information. Aged fifteen he entered Exeter College, Oxford, but was forced to leave on religious grounds. He was then

tutored at home by William Sutton q.v. In August 1577 he went to Paris and studied philosophy at Clermont College but contracted a serious illness. When he recovered he went with Father Thomas Darbyshire, his spiritual director, to find Father Robert Persons who advised him to go home to fully recover. He returned to England and on 5 March 1584 was imprisoned in the Marshalsea and released at Easter 1585. He made his way to Rome and was ordained at the Lateran 17 July 1588 under a special dispensation as he was under the canonical age. Just a month later he joined the Jesuits and returned to England. He made many notable converts in his apostolate. Among them was Sir Oliver Manners, son of the 4th Earl of Rutland, and a Member of Parliament, who was ordained in Rome in 1611 by St Robert Bellarmine. Sadly, Manners returned to England seriously ill. He died in 1613 and was buried at Belvoir Castle. Another Gerard convert worth recalling is John Good, an Anglican minister who literally left his bride-to-be at the church door and went into hiding. He was captured and spent nine months in prison before escaping abroad. He was ordained at Rome in 1612 and returned to work in England in 1615. Gerard avoided capture on many occasions but at the time of the Gunpowder Plot he also suffered imprisonment and torture, primarily in an attempt to make him reveal the whereabouts of Father Henry Garnet. In spite of his weakness from torture while awaiting trial, with the aid of friends outside, by means of a rope attached to a tower and stretched across the moat he made a dare-devil escape from the Tower of London in 1597. He carried on his ministry, a wanted man, until 3 May 1606, when he embarked at Dover and crossed the Channel disguised in the livery of the Spanish ambassador on the very day that his Superior, Father Henry Garnet was executed. He died at the English College, Rome, in July 1637 aged seventy-three. To quote the nineteenth-century Anglican, Dr Jessop, writing in 1881:

The extent of Gerard's influence was nothing less than marvellous. His powers of endurance of fatigue and pain were almost superhuman ... his autobiography ... recent research has proved to be absolutely correct. As a literary effort merely the autobiography is marvellous.

35 As well as the countless laymen and women Confessors for the Faith among the many priests who died in prison were:

Roger Wakeman came from Worcestershire. A student at Douai he was ordained at Binche in 1576 and returned to England. He is known to have been based at Rowington, Warwickshire for several years. He was arrested in London in 1581 and committed to Newgate. His cell was next to the place where the prison sewage was dumped and where

The Elizabethan Persecution

the corpses of quartered traitors were burned. He died there 16 November 1582.

William Chaplain, born probably in London. He went to Rheims in 1579 and was ordained in March 1581. He died in prison in 1583.

James Lomax was educated at Cambridge and went to Rheims in 1579. In 1580 he entered the English College, Rome, where he was ordained in August 1582. When he arrived in England in July 1583 he was in bad health and was arrested on disembarking. Aged twenty-eight he died in prison February 1584.

Edward Pole was born at Coventry and was ordained deacon under Queen Mary. He was advanced in years when ordained priest at Soissons in May 1580 and shortly afterwards returned to England. Captured on landing at Dover he was sent to the Gatehouse where he died in July 1584 and was buried at St Margaret's, Westminster.

Thomas Crowther came from Ludlow, Shropshire and was educated at Oxford. He went to Douai in 1571 and was ordained in 1575. He was arrested by a pursuivant in Smithfield, London and committed to the Marshalsea in March 1582 where he remained until condemned to death in February 1584 but was not executed. He died in the prison in January 1585.

Laurence Vaux, born in Lancashire in 1519. As Warden of the Collegiate Church, Manchester he went into exile at Louvain in 1559. He published an influential and popular catechism in 1567. In 1572 he became a Canon Regular. In 1580 he returned to England for the last time, was arrested at Rochester and sent to the Gatehouse and examined by Bishop Aylmer of London. In 1583 he was transferred to the Clink where he was very ill but received harsh treatment. He died of starvation in the prison in 1585.

John Harrison from Peterborough diocese was educated at Rome and Rheims where he was ordained in April 1585. He returned to England in October of that year but must have been speedily captured as he died in prison in 1586.

John Brushford was born in Cornwall in 1559. He was ordained at Rome in 1584. In London he was one of the priests sheltered by Blessed Alexander Blake q.v. at his home in Gray's Inn Lane. He then moved about a great deal and was recorded at Amesbury and Monmouth. In 1590 he returned to France hoping to joint the Jesuits but this plan was thwarted due to sickness. While returning to England he was captured off the Scilly Isles and imprisoned at Launceston. Moved to London he died in prison in March 1593 aged thirty four. He left a moving account of his work on the mission.

The Elizabethan Persecution

36 Blessed John Cornelius alias Mohun and O'Mahony, was born into a poor Irish family at Bodmin, Cornwall, in 1554. The records of the Society of Jesus state that he was baptised as John Conor O'Mahony and called himself by the Latinised form of his middle name; hence Cornelius. His education at Exeter College, Oxford, was funded by Sir John Arundell of Lanherne. John became a Fellow of his college in 1575 but, following an examination by the Commissioners of his religious beliefs, he was expelled on 3 August 1578. He went to Rheims in September 1579 and the following year was sent to the English College, Rome. He was ordained deacon 10 October 1581 and gave a Latin oration in front of Pope Gregory XIII on St Stephen's Day. Very animated in his speech he was said to have been loved by all who knew him. He was ordained in 1583, shortly afterwards returning to England. He seems to have been based with Sir John and Lady Arundell at their houses in Muswell Hill, London, and Lanherne, Cornwall, at least until Sir John died in January 1591. He then moved with Lady Anne Arundell to her home at Chideock Castle, Dorset, from where he conducted a wide-ranging apostolate. He was notable for the intensity of his personal prayer-life and often wore an undergarment of coarse sacking as well as fasting rigorously. He was close to Father Henry Garnet who greatly esteemed John's holiness. Cornelius repeatedly asked to be admitted to the Jesuits. John's activities were betrayed by a servant to the High Sheriff of Dorset, Sir George Morton. On the second Sunday after Easter, 14 April 1594, he said Mass as usual at 5 a.m. and as it ended sheriff Sir George Trenchard of Wolfeton and Justice Ralph Horsey, with swords in hand, broke into the house. John managed to get into a hiding place where he remained undetected for five hours until the justices sent for the traitorous servant who led them to the priest-hole and John was discovered. Taken with him were two Irish serving men, Patrick Salmon, who had been serving the Mass, and John Terence Carey, together with Thomas Bosgrave, son of Leonard Bosgrave and grandson of Sir John Arundell, who was present. Bosgrave upbraided the raiders for their lack of respect towards the priest. After spending a fortnight in custody with Trenchard at Wolfeton Cornelius and his three companions were ordered to be taken to London where he was examined before the Privy Council at Greenwich - the Court being in residence there - by Lord Treasurer Burghley and John Whitgift, Archbishop of Canterbury. While in the Marshalsea he was visited by Sir Walter Raleigh with whom he had a long discussion. Raleigh promised John to try and use his good offices with the Queen for him. Having extracted no useful information from him they sent John back to Dorset to be tried. On 2 July, when the

sentence had been pronounced on them by Judge Walmsley, his three companions knelt at his feet for his blessing. The judge, who treated Cornelius with courtesy, assured them that if they would conform their lives would be spared; an offer they refused. At 2 p.m. on 4 July John was taken on a hurdle to his place of execution at Gallows Hill, Dorchester; his companions, who were to be hanged, walked behind him. The gallows consisted of two uprights with a crossbeam connecting them. The space below was wide enough for a two-wheeled cart conveying prisoners to pass under. Before he had left the prison John had written a letter to Dorothy Arundell, daughter of his benefactor. Dorothy, the dedicatee of St Robert Southwell's *Mary Magdalen's Funeral Tears*, had vowed to become a Bridgettine nun. 'He that loveth his life in this world shall lose it; and he that hateth it, shall find it. If I find it, by the grace and infinite mercy of God (though very unworthy and miserable) with exceeding great satisfaction and never-ending pleasure, I shall remember you. In the meantime, while the soul remains in this body, pray you for me; for I have great confidence that we shall see one another in heaven if you keep inviolable the word you have given me, first to God and then to St Bridget ... I do not forget those whom I do not name. God be your keeper. Yours, John, who is going to die for a moment that he may live forever.' Carey was the first to die, kissing the rope, which he called a 'precious collar'. He was followed by Salmon who exhorted the spectators to embrace the Catholic faith. Then came Bosgrave, who made an eloquent speech. Cornelius kissed the feet of his three dead companions. Finally it was John's turn, but he was allowed to give only a short discourse. He prayed for the Queen and for his executioners before, kissing the rope, he placed the noose around his own neck. He was cut down while alive and lay writhing and gasping, trying to make the sign of the Cross, as he was ripped open. His severed head was nailed to the gibbet but soon removed and placed on top of the town gates. After the martyrs remains were exposed on poles for the remainder of the day they were taken down and buried together. John is counted among the martyrs of the Society of Jesus because while in prison he made his profession as a member of their order.

At Gallows Hill, Dorchester, there is a memorial sculpture by Dame Elizabeth Frink. Consisting of bronze figures it commemorates in particular the seven Catholic martyrs who suffered there.

Chapter Four

The Elizabethan Martyrs, 1577-1601

Cuthbert Mayne

Tyrants seldom want pretexts.

Edmund Burke, 1729-97

The first martyr of the seminaries was the son of William Mayne of Youlston in the parish of Sherwell, near Barnstaple, Devon. He was baptised on St Cuthbert's Day, 20 March 1544. His uncle was a priest who had conformed to the Established Church in order to keep his benefice. Hoping that his nephew would succeed him in his comfortable living, he had Cuthbert educated at Barnstaple Grammar School. On 6 December 1561, at the age of seventeen, Cuthbert was inducted as rector of the village of Huntshaw, south of Barnstaple. He soon went to Oxford to prepare for ordination, firstly to St Alban's Hall (since re-named Merton College) and then to St John's College. He took the Oath of Supremacy and orders in the Anglican Church and became chaplain of St John's College. He graduated BA 1566 and MA 1570.

At Oxford University he found that there was still a strong attachment to Catholicism and he became friends with several staunch Catholics. He also met the two men who were to influence the whole direction of his life: the convinced Catholic Gregory Martin and the wavering Edmund Campion. Cuthbert gradually became uneasy about his own religious position, watching as one after another men were forced to resign or were deprived of their teaching posts because of their Catholic sympathies. Francis Walsingham, Elizabeth's spymaster in chief, wrote, 'Those who are seminary priests learnt not their papistry abroad but carried it with them from their Oxford colleges'.

Martin and Campion kept up a frequent correspondence with Mayne, trying to persuade him to join them at Douai. In 1570 a letter to him from Gregory Martin on matters of faith, was intercepted by the authorities and given to the Bishop of London. The letter contained the names of Catholic sympathisers at Oxford and the bishop deduced from it that Mayne was a suspect papist and sent a pursuivant to Oxford to

The Elizabethan Martyrs, 1577-1601

apprehend him. Warned of his imminent arrest by a fellow Devonian student, Thomas Ford, 1 Cuthbert had already left Oxford for Devon and when this was learned an order was made by the Privy Council for his arrest. In the West Country Cuthbert made contact with Catholics, including old Marian priests, as he made his way into Cornwall. After three years of spiritual struggle his mind was at last made up. He took ship, probably from Padstow, directly to France and made his way to Douai, where he was received into the Catholic Church. In 1575 he was ordained priest and on 7 February 1576 he graduated from Douai University.

On 24 April 1576, at his own request, he set out for England in the company of another future martyr, John Paine. Strictly enjoined not to engage in any political activity, they were equipped with the bare necessities to carry out their priestly functions: a Mass kit, a small crucifix, a stole suitable for all seasons, vestments and copies of the Scriptures. Cuthbert also carried with him a printed copy of an outdated papal bull announcing the Jubilee year in 1575, which he had bought in Douai, probably as a souvenir. After a stormy crossing, the two priests landed in England and were detained on suspicion and examined. Their baggage was searched and their papers scrutinised by port officers. Their luggage contained many religious items such as books and rosaries. These were held by the authorities but Cuthbert and Paine were allowed to proceed. Surprisingly the religious artefacts were later recovered for them by a former Catholic student of Douai named Richard Evingham. How he achieved this we are not told. Perhaps by bribery is the answer. Cuthbert made his way to London, where he is believed to have stayed at the house of the Arundell's in Clerkenwell; it was they no doubt who arranged for him to go to the Tregians in Cornwall. Cuthbert was taken in by the long-suffering Francis Tregian (pronounced Trudgian) at his home, Golden Manor, at Probus, near Tregony, a few miles east of Truro. Francis, born 1548, was the son of Thomas Tregian of Wolveden and Catherine Arundell. He inherited substantial property estimated as worth £3,000 per year. Cuthbert acted as steward on the extensive Tregian estates.

Almost nothing is known of Cuthbert's year-long apostolate but it is not difficult to imagine the form it took: saying Mass for the family and neighbours, administering the Sacraments and reconciling those who had conformed. He would have ridden about the country lanes visiting Catholic families while ostensibly keeping an eye on the widespread Tregian farms and properties. He made friends with a number of families who were later to suffer for their loyalty. It is known that he visited Sir John Arundell's house, Lanherne, at St Mawgan on a number of occasions. The Arundells were among the leading West Country families, and were connected to the royal family by marriage. Despite enduring many vicissitudes they had remained faithful Catholics. Francis Tregian's mother being an Arundell, they were closely allied to the Tregian's by marriage. In this lay the seeds of the downfall of Cuthbert and his protectors.

The subsequently famous Richard Grenville had been made Sheriff of Cornwall in 1576. He was a member of an old Cornish seafaring family whose father had lost his life in the sinking of the *Mary Rose* in 1545. He had twice been a Member of Parliament but, currently out of favour at Court, Grenville, a cousin of both Francis Drake and Walter Raleigh, was anxious to ingratiate himself once more. He had been a violent youth and we can still read in the State Papers a contemporary assessment of his character. A man of 'intolerable pride and insatiable ambition, unquiet in his mind ... of nature very severe, so that his own people hated him for his fierceness and spoke hardly of him'.

The fanatically anti-Catholic Grenville was envious of the wealth and influence of the Arundells and Tregians. In 1570 he had made a great display of his declaration accepting the Act of Uniformity. He harboured a personal hatred for Francis Tregian and Sir John Arundell. He must have been aware for some time that a priest was operating from Golden Manor, but he bided his time. From the evidence now available, it appears that the government was watching Tregian and intended to make an example of him. The Queen authorised her Boleyn cousin, Sir George Carey, to proceed against Tregian, applying the statute of *praemunire*, under which it was a felony to recognise the authority of the Pope in England. If found guilty the penalty was forfeiture of all goods and perpetual imprisonment. Carey's prize for a successful outcome would be the possession of Tregian's valuable estates. Carey, later 2nd Baron Hunsdon, enlisted the help of Richard Grenville.

On 8 June 1577, which happened to be Corpus Christi that year, came the pretext he needed to act. A prisoner had escaped and efforts were being made to recapture him. There was never any suggestion that he might have found his way onto the Tregian estates, but as Bishop William Bradbridge of Exeter was on a visitation to Truro at the time he was persuaded by Grenville to agree to a search of Golden Manor. Bradbridge, a land speculator, was heavily in debt and may well have thought it politically prudent to go along with Grenville's wishes. The legality of the proposed raid was extremely doubtful; nonetheless Grenville assembled a formidable armed posse of over one hundred for the purpose, which descended en masse upon Golden Manor. The house was surrounded as Tregian met Grenville in the courtyard, protesting at the unwarranted intrusion and denying any knowledge of the escaped convict. Grenville forced his way in. Cuthbert had been in the garden, but hearing the commotion had re-entered his chamber from outside. Grenville, presumably having been tipped-off, made his way straight to the room and hammered on the door. He must have been nonplussed when Cuthbert himself opened the door. Seizing Cuthbert he shouted, 'What have we here? Who are you?' To which Mayne simply, if somewhat ironically, replied, 'A man, sir'.

While Cuthbert was securely held, Grenville ripped off the priest's doublet revealing a thin cord from which was suspended a little wax Agnus Dei medallion. He snatched the image from Mayne's neck. Cuthbert's room was then thoroughly ransacked and all his books, papers and his 'massing stuff' seized as evidence. Grenville ordered the arrest of Cuthbert and Tregian along with eight others. Their hands tied behind their backs, they were carried off to Truro.

The elderly Bishop Bradbridge, not feeling up to interrogating a popish priest, was given the uncomfortable task of examining Francis Tregian, one of the wealthiest leaders of Cornish society. He found that Tregian, rock solid in his Faith, had no patience with theological niceties and appeared rather unconcerned with the affairs of the world, so the bishop threw in the towel. As a symbol of his power and authority, following an unprecedented ransacking of homes, by August Grenville had ordered the arrest of thirty-one other leading Cornish Catholics for recusancy, including Sir John Arundell. Grenville had been thorough; hardly any family among the Catholic gentry of Cornwall had been left untouched.

Tregian and Arundell were sent to London, to the Fleet prison and the Tower of London respectively, in readiness for their trial before the Council. Anthony Tyrell was called into service to provide 'evidence' against Arundell. He claimed to have visited him at his house and heard Sir John and his family indulge in 'treasonable' talk, when in truth he had never met Arundell. Cuthbert, loaded with iron chains, was dragged in stages the forty miles from Truro to Launceston Castle, where he was incarcerated in solitary confinement, chained to his bed in a dark and filthy dungeon to await trial.

On 23 September 1577, he and his eight companions were indicted for treason at the assizes. Cuthbert faced six indictments, including bringing in the papal bull and the Agnus Dei, for saying Mass and for upholding the authority of the Pope. Tregian was named as the procurer of the priest's services and Arundell was indicted for refusing to go to church. Of the eight others all were charged with aiding and abetting the priest. They had accompanied Cuthbert on some of his journeys and delivered messages for him. John Kempe, Richard Tremayne, Thomas Harris and Richard Hore were all persons of social standing in the county. Hore was cited as being in possession of a rosary. John Williams, a schoolmaster, had brought his child to Golden to be baptised. John Hodge was a tailor who supervised all the household sewing requirements, while John Philips and James Humphreys were yeomen farmers.

Prosecuting was Sir John Popham, soon to become Solicitor-General and a future Attorney-General and Lord Chief Justice. Hearing the case were Sir Roger Manwood, an ardent Protestant and a harsh and cruel judge, and Sir John Jeffreys. There was a flaw in the proceedings insofar as the laws that were to make the trial a mere formality had not yet been passed, but there was enough anti-Catholic legislation to make a charge stick: after all it was treasonable to bring any papal bull into the country. Jeffreys was satisfied that the bull was no longer in force. But Manwood told the jury to ignore this fact, calling Cuthbert a 'traitor to the Queen's realm'. Jeffreys, who was clearly unhappy with the whole proceedings, also felt that the evidence for saying Mass was entirely circumstantial; but again he was overruled. Grenville, anxious to ensure that it was established Mayne had said Mass at Golden, was allowed to harangue the jury. Manwood instructed the jury that 'where plain proofs were wanting, strong presumptions ought to take place.'

As the Whig politician and historian, Thomas Babington, Lord Macaulay (1800-59) wrote in his *Essay on the History of the Reformation*:

> The trials of the accused Catholics were exactly like all state trials of those days; that is to say, as infamous as they could be. A state trial was merely a murder preceded by the uttering of certain gibberish and the performance of certain mummeries.

Thus it was with Mayne; thus it was with all those priests who suffered after him.

After such a blatantly sham propaganda trial, they were all found guilty on every point of their indictment. Cuthbert and Francis Tregian were sentenced to death. When passing sentence, Manwood agreed that 'Though the bull be out of date we never did nor do account any such thing to be of force or to be worth a straw. Yet the same is by the law of this realm treason and thou therefore have deserved to die'. Cuthbert received his sentence with a happy countenance, raised his eyes and said '*Deo gratias.*'

The Elizabethan Martyrs, 1577-1601

Judge John Jeffreys was uneasy that a man was to be executed just because of his religion. He thought it a poor advertisement for the justice system of a Queen who had allegedly declared she would not 'open windows into men's souls'. He successfully had the case referred to the whole bench of judges in London. On balance, the majority shared Jeffreys' view, but the final decision rested with the Privy Council. As a result Mayne was made to wait three months before the sentence was carried out.

Grenville in the meantime had hurried off to London, fearful that the death sentence would not be upheld. He found the Council split in their opinions, while expressing approval of the measures he had taken against the Catholics in his jurisdiction. The Council finally upheld the sentence on the grounds that 'we need to make a terror for these papists'. Grenville visited the Queen at Windsor, where she bestowed a knighthood on him for his services in dealing with 'a matter of religion'. Having obtained confirmation of the sentence, Grenville, presumably enjoying his reinstatement at Court, surprisingly lingered on in London rather than hurrying back to Launceston for the execution.

Cuthbert was given three days' notice of his execution. He was offered life and liberty if he would take the Oath of Supremacy but he refused. When the jailer told him the day on which he was to die, he replied, 'I wish I had something valuable to give you for the good news you bring me'.

The following day he was taken to the Assize Hall and made to stand for seven hours with fetters on his ankles and wrists while being questioned by a group of Protestant ministers and officials. Their threats and promises could not shake his resolve. Full details of his examination may still be read in the Public Record Office. While admitting his priesthood, he refused to disclose any information about his contacts or where he had said Mass. Calling for a Bible and kissing it, he stoutly maintained that 'the Queen neither ever was, nor is, nor ever shall be, head of the Church in England,' and upheld the conscientious right of Catholics to refuse to attend the Established Church. He also asked for clemency to be shown to those convicted with him. The written statements of his replies bear Cuthbert's signature: 'These things affirmed by me Cuthbert Mayne I think to be trewe'.

On 30 November 1577 he was placed on a hurdle and led out to suffer the full agony of his sentence in Launceston market place. The deputy sheriff, George Grenville, presided over the execution. On the scaffold Cuthbert was pressed to incriminate Tregian and Arundell, but he defended their reputation saying only that he knew them to be 'good and godly gentlemen'. As a final indignity he was made to ascend the ladder backwards so that he faced the crowd of spectators. This he accomplished with great difficulty, his feet slipping off the rungs as the hangman supported him up to the platform from where he began a brief speech. He said that the law had judged him worthy of death but he asserted his innocence as God would shortly be his judge. He was interrupted by one of the magistrates, who called on the hangman to make haste and place the rope around his neck. As he was quickly turned off the ladder he was heard to exclaim, '*In manus tuas, Domine*'.

They had built an exceptionally high gallows and Cuthbert swung widely from the gibbet, his head violently striking the side of the scaffold, severely bruising his face and damaging his eye, while the executioner wildly slashed at the rope. As he fell to the ground the executioner tore off his clothes, straddling his body as he carried out the bloody butchery. His head was hung on Launceston Castle and his quarters sent to Bodmin, Wadebridge, Tregony and to Barnstaple as a warning to all. Father Gregory Martin wrote to inform Edmund Campion of Cuthbert's martyrdom. 'The novice has outdistanced me,' was Edmund's reaction. 'May he be favourable to his old friend and tutor. I shall boast of these titles now more than ever.'

Cuthbert's martyrdom and the wholesale round-up of Catholics associated with him had far greater significance than the death of one priest. It was tantamount to an acknowledgment by the government that its policy had failed and that far more brutal measures would have to be employed if Catholicism was to be eradicated. This was especially so with the influx of zealous young priests now coming in from the Continent, who were strengthening the resolve of the Catholic community and instilling in them a renewed ardour for their faith.

Grenville obtained his revenge in full measure. After Cuthbert's execution the other weary prisoners were dragged to London and brought before the court, which ordered them to be returned to Cornwall. The evidence presented against them was proved to be perjured, but this was blatantly ignored by Justice Manwood. He pronounced them guilty under the statute of *praemunire* to lose land and goods and to endure perpetual imprisonment at the Queen's pleasure. Sir John Arundell was regularly in and out of prison. His home, Lanherne, was given in the eighteenth century to the nuns of the Carmelite Order and is the oldest Carmelite House in England. Fittingly, the nuns are the proud possessors of the main relics of Cuthbert Mayne, including his skull.

Francis Tregian was reprieved but condemned to life imprisonment

The Elizabethan Martyrs, 1577-1601

and forfeiture of all his goods. As previously promised to him by the Queen, her cousin, George Carey, Lord Hunsdon, received Tregian's lands. Carey travelled to Cornwall to evict Tregian's mother and family from Golden Manor. Tregian and his wife, Mary, daughter of Charles, 7th Lord Stourton, had eighteen children. She was allowed to join Francis in the Fleet, coming and going as she pleased. She never ceased to petition Elizabeth on behalf of her husband who endured over twenty year's imprisonment. While in prison, Francis managed to convert several of his fellow inmates. Released on condition of going into exile on the accession of James I, he retired to Madrid. He died at the Jesuit hospice Lisbon in 1608 and was buried in the church of São Roque. Seventeen years later his grave was opened and his body was found to be incorrupt, in a remarkable state of preservation, complete with hair and beard, his limbs flexible. The Franciscan habit, in which he had been buried, had completely rotted away. The doctors who examined the body were stunned and could offer no medical explanation.

Tregian's body was moved into an upright tomb beneath the west pulpit between the chapels of St Anthony and Our Lady of Pity. It is inscribed with an epitaph detailing his life and sufferings for the Faith which reads:

Here stands the body of Francis Tregian, a very eminent English gentleman who - after the confiscation of his wealth and having suffered much during the 28 years he spent in prison for defending the Catholic faith in England during the persecution under Queen Elizabeth - died in this city of Lisbon with great fame and saintliness on December 25th 1608. On April 25th 1625, after being buried for 17 years in this church of São Roque which belongs to the Society of Jesus, his body was found perfect and incorrupt and he was reburied here by the English Catholics resident in this city on April 25th 1626.

Tregian wrote, 'Let prayer be your practice; let prayer be your play ... Let prayer be your stay. Let prayer be your chief delight by day and by night.' The cause for Tregian's beatification is still actively pending.

His son, the younger Francis, born 1574, was educated at Douai and served as chamberlain to Cardinal William Allen for a time in Rome. In 1594 he returned home to claim his father's estates in Cornwall. In 1609 he was arrested as a recusant, his estates were seized and he was imprisoned in the Fleet, London, where he died ten years later, in 1619 and was buried at St Bride's, Fleet Street. He was a fine scholar and musician to whom we owe a special debt of gratitude. Without his efforts in collecting and copying Elizabethan music, including one of England's greatest composers, the Catholic William Byrd, much of our

The Elizabethan Martyrs, 1577-1601

musical heritage would have been lost.

Two months after Cuthbert Mayne's death there were two other martyrdoms. On 3 February 1578 Blessed John Nelson was butchered at Tyburn. One of three priest brothers he came from Skelton, Overton, near York. He must have been about forty-years-old when he arrived at Douai in 1573. Ordained at Binche 16 June 1576 he returned to England in November that year. He was arrested in London on 1 December 1577, the day after Mayne's execution. Imprisoned in Newgate, he was condemned on 1 February 1578 for refusing the Oath of Supremacy and suffered two days later. He was soon followed at Tyburn by a twenty-seven-year-old layman, Blessed Thomas Sherwood. Born in London, Thomas, a draper, went to Douai as a student in 1576. He returned to London intending to settle his affairs but before he could return to Douai he was betrayed, accused of hearing Mass and refusing to acknowledge the Queen's supremacy. He was sent to the Tower by the Ecclesiastical Commissioners and spent several months in a filthy cell where he suffered much from cold and hunger. On 17 November 1577 the Attorney-General gave orders for him to be placed in the dungeon 'among the rats'. This was a dreaded place below the Thames high water mark. It was totally dark and as the tide flowed scores of rats were driven into the dungeon. The horror that this induced in those incarcerated was part of the torture. When Sherwood's constancy was still not broken, on 4 December the Privy Council instructed that he be cruelly racked to make him divulge whose houses he had frequented. William Roper, son-in-law of Thomas More, hearing of his plight arranged for some money to be used for his relief, but this was refused by the Lieutenant of the Tower. Sherwood was martyred at Tyburn 7 February 1578.

Edmund Campion

Always to be best and distinguished above others.

Homer, Iliad, c.1000BC

He was born in London on 25 January 1540 and named after his father, a bookseller and printer in St Paul's churchyard. Edmund senior later conformed to the Established Church under Queen Elizabeth. It was intended that Edmund would follow his father's trade, but he was obviously such a gifted boy that from the age of ten his education at

The Elizabethan Martyrs, 1577-1601

Christ's Hospital was sponsored by the Grocers' Company, one of the City of London Livery Companies. As a 'bluecoat boy' he was so precocious that at the age of thirteen he was chosen to deliver a speech of welcome when Queen Mary entered London in 1553.

The Catholic Lord Mayor of London, Sir Thomas White, had established St John's College, Oxford, to which Edmund won a scholarship. In 1557 at seventeen-years-old he became a Junior Fellow of St John's. Edmund completed his degree and became a tutor and junior proctor. A charismatic personality at the centre of an admiring group his mannerisms were imitated by his fellows and his exceptional brilliance, eloquence and great popularity made him a person of outstanding importance; one of the most notable men of his time. It won him the patronage of the Queen's favourite, Robert Dudley, Earl of Leicester, who was chancellor of the university, as well as attracting the notice of William Cecil. Edmund was chosen to deliver the orations at the funerals of Leicester's wife, Amy Robsart, who had accidentally died in unexplained circumstances, and Sir Thomas White. When the Queen, amidst scenes of incredible pomp, visited Oxford University in 1566, Campion was the natural choice to deliver the speech of welcome and then, for entertainment, held a debate with four other scholars. Elizabeth was greatly impressed and told Leicester to see that Campion received anything he should ask for. A golden future clearly lay ahead.

Having already taken the Oath of Supremacy, he was ordained deacon in the Anglican Church in 1568/69 by Bishop Richard Cheney of Gloucester, but remained uncertain of his religious position. His studies made him increasingly uneasy, as he realised that the doctrine of the Established Church could not be identified or reconciled with that of the Fathers of the Church. Nor could he accept the premise inherent in the Protestant position that for 1500 years God had allowed his Church to promulgate false teaching, until suddenly men had appeared on the scene to enlighten mankind as to the iniquitous error of their ways. He began to openly show signs of sympathy with the Catholic cause, and this cost him the support of the Grocers' Company, which insisted that he come to London to publicly express his confidence in the Established Church. When Edmund declined, they withdrew their financial support from him. He was compensated for this loss by being presented with a benefice, the vicarage of Sherborne, by his friend Bishop Cheney. The much maligned Cheney was eventually to be excommunicated by the Anglican Church for his Catholic beliefs, although there is no conclusive evidence that he was ever reconciled to the Catholic Church before he died.

Full of remorse for having accepted Anglican Orders, at the

invitation of the Stanihurst family in 1569 Edmund travelled to Ireland to act as tutor to their children. Sir James Stanihurst was Speaker of the Irish House of Commons. It was hoped that Edmund would play a part in trying to revive a university in Dublin. He attracted favourable attention from Sir Philip Sidney, the Lord Deputy in the process. While in Ireland Edmund began writing *A History of Ireland*, which he graciously dedicated to the Earl of Leicester in gratitude for his patronage. But his religious views brought him under suspicion, especially in the wake of Pius V's excommunication of Elizabeth. He had to go into hiding in friendly houses to avoid the pursuivants. (The Primate of Ireland, Richard Creagh, Archbishop of Armagh, in spite of his unwavering loyalty to the English Crown, had been arrested in 1567 and sent to the Tower of London. Equally steadfast in his Catholicism he remained a prisoner until his death in 1585, probably from poison. Throughout the period covered by this book, from the reign of Henry VIII through to the first Hanoverians, Catholics in Ireland suffered horrendous persecution. Bishops, priests, religious and lay people were slaughtered and martyred in great numbers.)

Urged on by Gregory Martin, who had already gone to Douai in 1570, Edmund finally gave in and acknowledged that he was a Catholic. Still he delayed joining Martin at Douai. He returned to England in disguise and under an assumed name in May 1571. The executions in retaliation for the papal bull had already begun, and while in London Edmund witnessed the trial and condemnation of Blessed John Storey in Westminster Hall. Despite his powerful friends and scholarly reputation, Edmund realised that he had no choice but to respond to the sacrifice that was being asked of him. Acting upon his convictions he left all behind him and on 1 June - the day of Storey's execution - he secretly took a boat to cross to Douai. The vessel was stopped in the Channel and he was put aboard the *Hare,* an English frigate and taken back to Dover. It seems Edmund bribed the captain by handing over his purse and he was let go. Edmund raised money from friends in Kent and once more took ship to Calais. He made his way to Douai and was reconciled to the Catholic Church. When his departure became known - which would not have taken long, given the efficient spy system - William Cecil, now Baron Burghley, expressed his regret at the loss of 'one of the diamonds of England'.

Edmund studied theology at Douai and was ordained subdeacon. In order to join the Jesuits, in January 1573 he set out for Rome on foot, arriving at the end of February. 'Make the most of Rome.' he wrote to Gregory Martin, 'Do you see the dead corpse of that Imperial City? What can be glorious in life, if such wealth and beauty has come to

The Elizabethan Martyrs, 1577-1601

nothing? But who has stood firm in these wretched changes - what survives? The relics of the Saints and the chair of the Fisherman.' The General of the Society of Jesus, the great St Francis Borgia, had died in 1572 and members of the Order were assembled in Rome to choose his successor. On 23 April they elected a Fleming, Everard Mercurian. Edmund was eagerly accepted as a new recruit to the Society.

It was in Rome that Edmund received the news of the martyrdom of Blessed Thomas Woodhouse. Thomas had been ordained in Mary's reign and served as rector of a parish in Lincolnshire for a year. Presumably he left on Elizabeth's accession and became a private tutor in Wales. On 14 May 1561 he was arrested while saying Mass and committed to the Fleet prison. He remained in jail for the next twelve years, managing to say Mass and making no secret of his religious opinions. In November 1572 he wrote a letter to Lord Burghley which he gave to the prison washerwoman to deliver. In the letter Thomas urges Burghley to seek reconciliation with Rome and to 'persuade the Lady Elizabeth, who for her own great disobedience is most justly deposed, to submit herself to her spiritual father.' This led to a personal interview with Burghley in which he expressed himself forcefully. This resulted in his being placed in solitary confinement. He occupied his time writing notes about the 'true faith and obedience' which he threw from his window into the street. Repeatedly examined, on one occasion, when he had denied the Queen's supreme governorship, someone said to him, 'If you saw her Majesty you would not say so, for her Majesty is great.' To which he responded, 'But the majesty of God is greater.' He was tried at the Guildhall and condemned. Sent to Newgate he became a member of the Society of Jesus in prison. He was hanged, drawn and quartered at Tyburn 19 June 1573. The news of the martyrdom caused Edmund to reflect on the deplorable state of his afflicted native land. But his sorrow and depression only intensified his yearning to be part of the remedy for England's woes.

As there was no English province of the Jesuits, Edmund was assigned to the province of Bohemia and, along with five other novices, was sent to the novitiate at Brno, the capital of Moravia. Here he remained until 1574 when he was moved to Prague. He spent six years in Prague, where he taught rhetoric in the Jesuit school and was ordained priest in September 1578. The following year the Pope agreed to William Allen's request to send Jesuits to the English mission and Edmund and Father Robert Persons [2] were chosen as the vanguard. The night before he left Prague a fellow priest prophetically wrote over Edmund's door, P.Edmundus Campianus, Martyr. At first Edmund does not seem to have been over-enthusiastic about leaving his work in

Prague. Furthermore, he asked for, but did not get, a mitigation for English Catholics of the papal bull *Regnans in Excelsis*.

Edmund set off in 1580 on his journey home, travelling via Rome and Milan. As we learn from Campion's letter to Everard Mercurian, Father Persons made his way to Saint-Omer and then to Calais from where he made a night sailing. He was excellently disguised as a soldier and accompanied by his brother George, Persons arrived at Dover on 16 June 1580 and reached London without encountering any problems. It was hardly an auspicious time to be embarking upon the Jesuit mission. Although there were no executions that year the prisons were full of Catholics, many of whom died in captivity. They included the laymen Robert Dimock, John Cooper, the brothers Robert and William Tyrwhit as well as Christopher Watson who, together with about twenty other Catholics, perished in York Castle.

While Persons was on his way to England Edmund waited at Saint-Omer to make sure it was safe for him to follow. 'I am getting myself fitted out with Ralph as my companion,' he wrote to Mercurian on 20 June. 'What do you think all this will cost? ... As we wish to disguise ourselves and imitate the vain fashions of life around us, many trifles which we think altogether silly had to be bought for us. The money for our journey, these clothes and four horses which we shall have to buy on the spot in England, will account for our funds. These must come from the same kind of providence whereby loaves were multiplied in the wilderness ... Today the wind is dropping so I shall move off quickly for the sea ... I have waited a further day but as there is still no news either way of Father Robert, I persuade myself he got through safely.'

Accompanied by the Jesuit lay brother Ralph Emerson, Edmund found a ship but they had to wait four days for a favourable wind. They set sail on the evening of 24 June, making an overnight crossing, and landed at Dover before daylight on 25 June. On arrival Campion posed as 'Mr Edmunds', a merchant in precious stones with Ralph as his servant. At the same time a search was taking place for an exiled Catholic named Allen who was said to be coming to visit his family. Edmund was detained by the authorities on suspicion and the mayor decided to send him to London, but while waiting for horses he suddenly changed his mind and Campion was released. Making his way to London, he made contact with a secret network of young Catholic gentlemen dedicated to assisting priests. One of the members of this 'club' was the future priest, Thomas Fitzherbert q.v. Edmund was kitted out by them with new clothes, a horse and money. He was lodged at the house of Thomas, 3rd Baron Paget of Beaudesert. Paget and his family

The Elizabethan Martyrs, 1577-1601

remained zealous Catholics. (Paget was attainted in 1587 and died an exile at Brussels in 1590.) At first Edmund's reception by his co-religionists was by no means universally welcoming. The beleaguered Catholics were fearful that the arrival of the Jesuits would only bring further troubles upon them, especially as it unfortunately coincided with another piece of papal politicking when Gregory XIII funded an unsuccessful Spanish expeditionary force to Ireland. Although Gregory had been a worldly man - he fathered an illegitimate son before his ordination - he was an able administrator who served the Church well, trying to put into effect the reforms of the Council of Trent. After his election as Pope he led a faultless life of great simplicity. He is famous for commissioning the reform of the calendar which bears his name. But he was inevitably caught up in the politics of his time and with the connivance of William Allen, the Pope had engaged Sir Thomas Stukeley (on whom he had bestowed the title Marquess of Leinster) to launch an invasion in Ireland as a "back door" diversion against England. Devon-born Stukeley was basically a mercenary who had commanded galleys at the legendary Battle of Lepanto. Having interested himself in Irish affairs, he was equipped with arms and troops and in March 1578 set sail from Italy. The exiled Father Nicholas Sander, one of the most important and learned English Catholics of the time, was appointed papal nuncio to Ireland where he arrived in July 1579. The whole expedition was a fiasco which Stukeley abandoned midway. Few of the papal-sponsored soldiers reached Ireland and the small number of Spanish and Italian troops who did land were quickly slaughtered. The propaganda value to the Elizabethan government was enormous and English Catholics, yet again, paid a heavy price for this piece of papal folly. Notwithstanding their initial misgivings, through his forceful personality, his holiness and cheerfulness, Edmund won them over and put new heart and hope into the disconsolate Catholics.

Five months after his arrival in England, in a letter to Everard Mercurian Campion writes:

> I came to London and my good angel guided me into the same house that had harboured Father Robert before, whither young gentlemen came to me on every hand ... they reapparel me, furnish me, weapon me and convey me out of the city. I ride about some piece of the country every day. The harvest is wonderful great. On horseback I meditate my sermon; when I come to the house I polish it. Then I talk with such as come to speak with me, or hear their confessions. In the morning, after Mass, I preach; they hear with exceeding greediness and very often receive the Sacrament ... I dare scarcely touch the exceeding reverence all Catholics do unto us ... we are ever well assisted by

the priests, whom we find in every place ... I cannot long escape the hands of the heretics; the enemies have so many eyes, so many tongues, so many spies ... I am in apparel to myself very ridiculous; I often change it and my name also ... My soul is in my own hands ever ... Let those who are coming to help us think about this. Certainly, the consolations arising from the work make up not only for the fear of the consequences but would compensate for any sort of pain with infinite satisfaction. ... Among the Protestants ... there is no race of men less worthy or more unsound than their own ministers. Not unreasonably, we get angry that in this lost cause men so unlearned, so reprehensible, so divided among themselves, and so little worthy of esteem, should be in a position to lord it over the minds and spirits of the very flower of the nation. Threatening proclamations accompany us on all sides. Nevertheless, through caution, the prayers of good people, and most important, by God's help, we have safely covered a good portion of the island. All the jails are crammed with Catholics and new ones are being set up ... There will never want in England men that will have a care of their own salvation, nor such as shall advance other men's. Neither shall this Church here ever fail; so long as priests and pastors shall be found to their sheep, rage man or devil never so much.

It was while staying with Sir Thomas Tresham at Hoxton near London that Campion was asked to write a testament setting out the spiritual intentions of the Jesuit mission. Robert Persons recorded that Edmund 'arose from the company ... and taking a pen in his hand wrote presently upon the end of a table that stood by in less I suppose than half an hour this declaration.' Edmund wrote his open letter to 'The Lords of Her Majestie's Privy Council', subsequently known by the derogatory title given to it by his Protestant opponents as 'Campion's Brag'. It set out the purpose of his mission 'of free cost to preach the Gospel, to minister the Sacraments, to instruct the simple, to reform sinners' and generally reclaim Catholics from error. The letter set out a challenge to the government.

Touching the Society, be it known that we have made a league ... cheerfully to carry the cross you lay upon us, and never to despair your recovery, while we have a man left to enjoy your Tyburn, or be racked with your torments, or consumed with your prisons. The expense is reckoned, the enterprise is begun; it is of God, it cannot be withstood. So the faith was planted: so it must be restored.

The letter was not intended for publication but was to be held in readiness should he be captured. When it was prematurely published, Edmund became the object of an intensive manhunt, so on the advice of Persons he left London for Berkshire. In February 1581 William, 3rd Baron Vaux of Harrowden and Sir Thomas Tresham were fined and imprisoned for sheltering Campion. (Tresham was a wealthy landowner, but as a result of the crippling fines he had been required to pay for his recusancy he was hugely in debt by the time of his death in 1605.)

Robert Persons spent the summer visiting Northamptonshire, Derbyshire, Worcestershire, Gloucestershire and Herefordshire. During the course of a year Edmund worked secretly in various parts of the country, incessantly travelling, rarely stopping more than one night at any house to keep one step ahead of the spies who relentlessly pursued him. As well as covering much of the Home Counties he visited Oxfordshire and Northamptonshire. He found many of his recusant hosts greatly impoverished and had many hairbreadth escapes from the priest hunters. 'Everyone talks of death, prison, fines or the ruin of friends', he wrote. The secular priest, William Watts, was sent North to prepare the way for Campion who was in Derbyshire in January 1581. From there he was escorted via Nottinghamshire into Yorkshire by a Mr Tempest. Campion's arrival in Yorkshire coincided with a great drive against recusants many of whom were conforming as a result. Among those Edmund stayed with was a close relative of Cardinal Allen's, William Hawksworth of Hawksworth, Otley. Hawksworth paid for his hospitality by being sent to the Fleet in London. By January 28th Edmund was in the North Riding at the home of Blessed Ralph Grimston at Nidd. Ralph, a married 'gentleman' with a family, was described as someone who was an 'aider of papists beyond the seas'. Like Thomas Warcop, q.v. he ran one of Father Holtby's safe houses for priests. He made quarterly payments to help support the training of seminary priests. He too was a relative of William Allen and regularly harboured priests for which he suffered the confiscation of most of his estate and imprisonment in York Castle. In 1594 he was convicted on the evidence of the apostate Yorkshire priest, William Hardesty, whom he had sheltered. (Hardesty, who was born at Hampsthwaite in 1559 and ordained at the Lateran 1586, returned to England in 1588 and was arrested in 1592. He was given a special pardon in exchange for becoming a government spy.) In 1598 Grimston was caught with Blessed Peter Snow, who came from a prominent Ripon family. Peter had been ordained at Soissons in 1591 and worked on the mission over a wide area of Yorkshire under the alias of Sharp. He was apprehended while being escorted to York by Ralph, who tried to thwart the priest's arrest. They were martyred together at York on 15 June 1598.

In mid-Lent Edmund was the guest of the Harrington family at Mount St John, an isolated house in the parish of Felixkirk. It was here over a period of twelve days that Edmund wrote his famous book,

The Elizabethan Martyrs, 1577-1601

Decem Rationes: *Ten Reasons for the confidence with which Edmund Campion offered his adversaries to dispute on behalf of our Faith, set before the famous men of our Universities.*

Campion made such an impression on fifteen-year-old William Harrington that the following year he entered the English College at Rheims. William wrote, 'Campion I desired to imitate whom only love of country and zeal for the house of God consumed before his time'. Because of ill-health and other vicissitudes William was unable to join the Jesuits as he had wished and had to return home. An apostate Catholic spy named Ralph Miller, who had been a tailor at Rheims, reported him as lodging at the White Horse in Holborn, and being at Mass with eighteen others at the home of Lord Vaux at Hackney. William was sent back to his father at Felixkirk where he lived for the next seven years. In 1591 he returned to Rheims and was ordained in March 1592. He ministered partly in the West Country for a year before being captured in London at the chambers of Henry Donne. Sent first to the Bridewell and then to Newgate, he was condemned but his execution was delayed in the hope of persuading him to become a government informant. William wrote from prison that betraying his friends could not serve his prince or country. (Donne, the brother of poet and cleric John Donne, died a prisoner in the Clink in 1593.) On 18 February 1594 Blessed William Harrington achieved his wish to imitate his hero, being martyred at Tyburn aged twenty-seven.

From Felixkirk Edmund was handed over to a new guide, Edward More, an ex-pupil of his at Oxford who was then living with his family near Sheffield. Mr More escorted Edmund into Lancashire where he spent Easter before returning south. In the spring of 1581 Edmund was at Stonor Park, Oxfordshire, the guest of Dame Cecily Stonor. Here a rather primitive, but effective, secret printing press had been set up under the eaves to print *Decem Rationes*. The book was written in the spirited style of his earlier 'Brag'. He challenged the Protestants to debate with him. 'I did fervently demand the combat,' he wrote, 'not that jocular and sportful skirmish, which the vulgar perform in their public streets; but that severe and grave conflict, by which we may encounter in the schools of your own Universities.' Beginning with the sovereign authority of Scripture, through the Fathers and Ecumenical Councils and the apostolic traditions Campion succinctly set out the arguments for Catholicism. 'Witnesses are all things whatsoever,' he wrote, 'great or small, contained within the circumference of this vast universe, that no other religion than ours did ever take any deep root and plantation ... Catholicism is the Christianity of history and fact.'

He launches sweeping attacks on Luther, Calvin and Zwingli and

The Elizabethan Martyrs, 1577-1601

their heresies. In withering, scornful language he especially castigated Protestants for their mistranslation, manipulation and distortion of the Bible, and for excising those parts that did not conform to their teaching so as to prevent their followers from discovering the truth. He takes outrageous quotations from some of the leading Protestants of the day and throws them back in their teeth: for example, that God is the author and cause of sin. If evidence were needed to demonstrate Edmund's outstanding scholarship, one need look no further than this extraordinary little book. It is remarkable for its myriad quotations from scripture, the Fathers and saints of the Church, all of which was done from memory, as Campion did not have access to any library. The proof was sent to Father Persons, the Jesuit Superior who was amazed by it. His prudence would not allow him to authorise its publication without first having all the quotations checked. Thomas Fitzherbert, the future priest, undertook that task scouring various libraries. He was able to verify the accuracy of all the references and copies of the book were accordingly printed. The future Tyburn martyr William Hartley, [3] who with Father Arthur Pitts had already established clandestine contacts at Oxford University, secretly distributed 400 copies of the book around the University in June 1581. This caused quite a stir, galvanising the government to redouble its efforts to capture Edmund. During the first week of August Stonor was raided and Father Hartley, Stephen Brinkley, the printer and his four assistants were arrested and sent to the Tower, along with Dame Cecily's younger son, John, who took the blame for sheltering the priests at Stonor. After eight months in the Tower John was released on bail with the proviso that he conform within three months. He jumped bail and fled to Flanders. Dame Cecily escaped imprisonment, but she was placed under house arrest in the custody of her elder son, Francis, where she remained for the rest of her life. Brinkley served eighteen months and then went to live in Normandy where he continued printing Catholic books.

Meanwhile, in July, Campion and Persons had enjoyed a brief reunion. Persons wanted Edmund as far removed from London as possible so Campion planned to return to Lancashire to collect some of his books and papers, which he had left at Park Hall, the home of Richard Houghton, and then move into Norfolk. Before embarking upon the journey he received an invitation to visit the home of Mr Francis Yate at Lyford Grange, a moated manor house situated in the Vale of the White Horse near Wantage, Berkshire. As a recusant, Mr Yate was in prison at the time. He had previously asked Campion to visit Lyford and his request had been declined, but now that he was in the vicinity Edmund did not feel able to refuse again. The house was quite unique in that it was also home to a group of eight Bridgettine nuns. They were the remnant of the reconstituted Syon community under Queen Mary. They had returned from exile following upheavals in Belgium. Among them were sisters Julian Harman, Catherine Kingsmill, Joan Lowe, Elizabeth Sanders and Elizabeth Yate, a cousin of Francis Yate. There were also two chaplains, Fathers John Colleton and Thomas Ford. Because Lyford Grange was such a well-known refuge for Catholics, Father Persons only very reluctantly gave his consent for Edmund's visit, placing him under obedience to the presumably more cautious Brother Ralph Emerson, 4 who was to accompany him to Norfolk. Campion and Persons then parted, exchanging hats as a friendly gesture. Edmund duly went to Lyford on 15 July where he was ecstatically received. He stayed overnight, saying Mass the following morning. Afterwards he and Father Colleton quietly departed.

Those 'in the know' about Campion's visit could not resist telling their fellow Catholics about it, who were upset at not having had the opportunity of meeting the famous Jesuit. Father Ford was asked to go after Edmund and persuade him and Colleton to return. He caught up with them at an inn near Oxford where they were engaged in a debate with some university students. He entreated them to come back to Lyford. Brother Ralph was unhappy with the idea, but finally gave in when Edmund promised he would stay just over the weekend. It was agreed that Ralph would ride into Lancashire, collect the missing books and papers and then meet up with Edmund at the arranged rendezvous in Norfolk. It was not to be.

Campion spent a pleasant weekend in the company of the group of Catholics. On Sunday morning, 17 July, after Mass he would depart for Norfolk. Father Ford planned to say Mass first for the sizeable gathering of over forty people, consisting of the members of the household and neighbours. While Father Ford was still at the altar, it was reported by the watchman that two visitors had arrived at the outer gates. They were George Eliot and David Jenkins. Both were priest hunters in the pay of the government. Eliot was a low-lifer who had ingratiated himself by claiming to be a Catholic, being formerly employed as a servant with the Roper family in Kent and Lady Petre at Ingatestone. He was arrested for embezzlement, rape and murder and to save his skin had written from prison to the Earl of Leicester offering his services to the government informing on Catholics. Secretary Cecil and spymaster Walsingham were very interested, and Eliot was offered his freedom in return for a government commission to find and arrest as many priests as he could.

The Elizabethan Martyrs, 1577-1601

Eliot may have been unaware that Campion was at Lyford and presumably had no idea what a prize catch was awaiting him. He was sure that the house was an important recusant centre and had called in expectation of finding a Mass that Sunday morning and thus capturing a priest. As it happened Eliot was acquainted with one of the servants, Cooper, who was the cook at Lyford Grange. He had also been employed by the Ropers and Eliot asked to speak to him. The wary watchman made them wait on the drawbridge while he went in to fetch Cooper, who came out, recognised Eliot and invited him to stay for dinner. Leaving Jenkins down in the kitchen, Eliot was taken to the room where Campion was about to say Mass. No doubt Eliot could not believe his luck when he heard Campion's name but containing himself and feigning piety Eliot joined with the congregation. After Mass Edmund distributed blessed bread and water to all present, including Eliot, before sitting down to give a sermon lasting about an hour. Immediately afterwards, excusing himself from dinner, Eliot rejoined Jenkins, and the two of them rode off post-haste to alert the local authorities.

A number of Catholics had stayed for dinner and it was around one o'clock that the watchman raised the alarm that the house was surrounded by armed men. Eliot and Jenkins, with the local magistrate, Justice Bessels Fettiplace, and a large posse of soldiers from the Berkshire militia, demanded admission. Campion was all for trying to escape, if only to spare everyone else from the consequences if he was found in the house. The nuns quickly put on lay dress while Mrs Jane Yate (née Tichborne) insisted that the three priests take something to eat and drink and get into one of the hiding places in the wall above the gateway, which they managed to do, having just enough room to lay side-by-side when the panelling was closed. When all the incriminating religious evidence had also been hidden away, the magistrate was admitted. Accused of hearing Mass that morning, the whole company denied it and Justice Fettiplace, who was related to the Yate family and embarrassed at invading her privacy, seemed prepared to take the word of Mrs Yate and her gentlemen guests. However, Eliot insisted that the house be thoroughly searched; but nothing was found. Justice Fettiplace and his men left the house and those inside breathed a sigh of relief - but not for long. Persuaded by Eliot, making great play with his royal commission, and warning Fettiplace of the consequences if he failed in his duty, the party returned and conducted a thorough search, smashing through walls and panelling and overturning beds in the process. By now the soldiers were tired of the whole business and their officer apologised to Mrs Yate for the loutishness of Eliot. But brandishing his royal warrant, Eliot sent for reinforcements in the person of a second magistrate, Justice Edmund Wiseman, who arrived around dusk with a gang of his own servants. Still no sign of the priests was found. So a guard of around sixty men was placed around the house overnight and Mrs Yate arranged for them to have supper.

Campion, Colleton and Ford were still squashed together in a secret chamber at the top of the house. Early in the morning the search was renewed, as Eliot was convinced that the priests had to be hidden somewhere on the premises. Just when the officer once again gave orders to depart, thinking the priests might have escaped after all, a beam of light was spotted coming from a narrow gap in the stairwell. Using a crowbar Jenkins broke open the false wall at the head of the stairs and called out 'I've found the traitors!' They then discovered the secret compartment, revealing the priests, who quietly surrendered themselves.

The High Sheriff of Berkshire, Sir Humphrey Forster, also a relation of Francis Yate, was summoned from Aldermaston and, giving instructions that the prisoners be treated courteously, he sent a messenger to the Court to ask for instructions. But Eliot had rushed to London to claim the credit and armed with authority he returned to Lyford Grange to escort the priests to London under guard. A fourth priest, William Filby [5] had the ill-luck to choose that fateful day to call at Lyford Grange, knowing he could expect a warm welcome. The welcome he got was from those now in control of the house and he was promptly arrested along with seven gentlemen, including Edward Yate, Francis's brother, and neighbours John Doe and William Hildesley. (The Bridgettine sisters, Julian Harman and Catherine Kingsmill, were taken to Reading jail where they most probably died. Sister Joan Lowe died in the White Lion, Southwark after eight years imprisonment. Hildesley was banished but embarked on a career of smuggling in Catholic books, for which he was again arrested.)

The journey to London via Abingdon, Henley and Colnbrook, took two full days, during which Campion managed to charm his guards, who clearly despised and ignored the exultant Eliot. Finally he said to Edmund, 'Mr Campion, you look cheerfully on everyone but me. I know you are angry with me for this work'. Edmund replied, 'God forgive thee, Eliot, for so judging me. I forgive thee', and raising his cup he drank to the health of his captor whom he begged to repent.

Forster's honourable treatment of his prisoners came to an end when, en route, he received orders from the Council that they were to be publicly humiliated. Their hands tied behind their backs, their feet strapped under the horses' bellies, on 22 July Campion and his

The Elizabethan Martyrs, 1577-1601

companions arrived in London and were ignominiously paraded through the streets. Attached to Edmund's hat was a label reading 'Campion the seditious Jesuit'. The four priests were all committed to the Tower. Edmund was shut in a cell which can still be seen today, known as 'Little Ease' because it is too small for a man to either lie or stand in it.

Four days before Edmund and his fellow captives arrived in London the trial had taken place on 18 July of Blessed Everard Hanse. He was born in Northamptonshire and his brother William had preceded him into the priesthood in 1579. Everard had been a minister in the Established Church for two years but after consulting his brother he converted and went to Rheims, where he was ordained with William Filby on 25 March 1581. A few weeks later he arrived in England and was arrested while visiting Catholic prisoners in the Marshalsea and jailed at Newgate. At his trial the spiritual supremacy of the pope and his power to excommunicate the Queen formed the central arguments for the prosecution. The account of the trial relates that Everard's attempt to explain the nature of the papal primacy was drowned by derisive laughter from the court. The government was in something of a panic following the arrival of the first Jesuits on the mission, and Everard, cut down while fully conscious, was executed at Tyburn with exceptional barbarity on 31 July 1581. There are probably more extant contemporary accounts of Everard's execution than any other Elizabethan martyr. For instance, Father Persons wrote a long account of his martyrdom to the Jesuit Superior General. Campion and his fellow prisoners got to hear of Everard's death while languishing in the Tower.

The government was willing to go to any lengths to get Campion to conform. After four days crouching in his dark cell, he was rowed secretly up river to the house of Sir Thomas Bromley, the Lord Chancellor. Awaiting him there, with Bromley, were his former patron, the Earl of Leicester, and Sir Christopher Hatton, who courteously put questions to him on behalf of the Queen. Closely questioned about his motives and his loyalty to the Queen, Edmund acknowledged Elizabeth as his lawful sovereign in all temporal matters, but quoted Christ: 'Render unto Caesar the things that are Caesar's'. It is probably fair to say that Elizabeth had no particular desire to see Edmund executed, but he could not be allowed to defy the law. He was promised that he could expect an Anglican bishopric if he would publicly abjure his Catholicism and conform. Campion refused the offer and was sent back to the Tower.

As no useful information could be extracted from him, five days

The Elizabethan Martyrs, 1577-1601

later Burghley issued the order that he be tortured. The register of the Tower of London in a most revealing slip of the pen contains the instruction, 'In case he continues to wilfully tell the truth, then to deal with him by the rack'. After being racked a third time, Edmund was asked how he felt, 'Not ill', he replied, 'because not at all'.

He lost most of his fingernails by having iron spikes thrust down them. In order to disgrace Edmund in the eyes of the Catholic community, the government repeatedly claimed that under torture he had revealed the names of some of the people who had sheltered him, yet no written evidence was ever produced to substantiate the allegation. That he betrayed those who had been his friends is highly unlikely. The State Papers show that Burghley was already in possession of many details about people and places where Edmund had stayed; information no doubt supplied by spies. If there is any shred of truth in the government propaganda, it is that confronted with the evidence Edmund perhaps admitted that it was correct. There was little point in denying it at that stage, as those identified were already in deep trouble. When it was clear they had obtained all the information they were likely to get from him, Edmund was kept in the Tower in solitary confinement for the next four months, during which the government fostered many lying statements about him.

On the orders of the Privy Council, anxious to discredit him in any way they could, he was brought from his cell on four occasions to face public disputations with different groups and academics. At one of these sessions Edmund explicitly denied that he had betrayed anyone. Refuting the claim that he had been tortured for matters of state, rather than for religion, he was reported as saying his punishment was because 'he would not betray the places and persons with whom he had conversed and dealt with concerning the Catholic cause'. He cited the example of the early Christians who had suffered martyrdom rather than yield up the sacred books and vessels to the pagan authorities.

'Much more I ought to suffer anything rather than to betray the bodies of those who ministered necessaries to supply my lack'. His opponents, deciding they were on shaky ground chose not to pursue the matter, but were especially eager to respond to his *Ten Reasons*.

Stands had been erected for members of the Court to enjoy the spectacle. Disoriented and weak from torture, given no prior warning, and therefore unable to prepare for the confrontations, without notes Campion endeavoured to rebut the arguments put to him, despite the obvious unfairness and inequality of the proceedings. He was constantly interrupted, insulted and refused access to books. The disputations lasted several hours at a time and Catholic witnesses

The Elizabethan Martyrs, 1577-1601

reported that Edmund looked deathly pale, exhibiting signs of confusion at times by getting his quotations mixed up. Nonetheless it was generally conceded that he emerged from the ordeals with integrity. As they could not demonstrably get the better of him, the Council put an end to the farce and left Edmund alone in his cell to await trial.

For propaganda purposes the government had to destroy the perception that Campion was being indicted purely for spiritual reasons: they had had to impugn his motives, calling into question his loyalty. The government must have been fully aware of the instructions given by the Society of Jesus to its members embarking upon the mission in 1580. Priests were strictly forbidden to involve themselves in politics but to confine themselves to the salvation of souls. They were enjoined 'not to mix themselves up with affairs of state, nor write to Rome about political matters, nor speak, nor allow others to speak in their presence against the queen'. This was the defence Edmund boldly presented at his trial. Echoing his instructions he declared, 'I am straitly forbidden by our fathers that sent me, to deal in any respect with matters of state or policy of the realm'

Having questioned dozens of witnesses under duress, they failed to establish that Edmund had been involved in any treasonable activity. So in the absence of evidence they fabricated an entirely fictitious conspiracy to assassinate the Queen, in which he and several priests had been allegedly involved at Rheims and Rome. Planning to kill many birds with one stone, the government took the opportunity of adding to the charge the names of nearly every priest they held in custody in London. William Camden, who had first hand evidence both from State papers and interviews, wrote in his *Annales*, with its honest absence of anti-Catholic rhetoric, that the Queen knew 'most of these wretched little priests' were not guilty, but lay the blame on their superiors for sending them.

On 14 November 1581 Edmund was arraigned in Westminster Hall with fellow priests Ralph Sherwin, Luke Kirby, Thomas Cottam [6] and Robert Johnson, [7] all of whom were also destined for martyrdom. Another priest, Dr Richard Bristow, who had been ordained with Thomas Ford in 1573, was also one of those arraigned with Campion. Bristow came from Worcestershire and was educated at Exeter College, Oxford, as a nominee of Sir William Petre. He joined William Allen at Douai and became his assistant in establishing the College. He was ordained at Brussels in 1573 and remained on the teaching staff at Douai. He collaborated with Gregory Martin on the English translation of the Bible. As he was suffering from tuberculosis he returned to

The Elizabethan Martyrs, 1577-1601

England in September 1581 and lodged with the Bellamy family at Uxendon Hall, Harrow. Asked why he had come to England, Richard told the Court that his widowed mother had written many letters begging him to return home after the death of his brother, which had deprived her of help, otherwise he would not have returned, 'as God is my witness'. Bristow was not brought to trial with Campion. He died in prison during the week before that took place on 20 November, when Edmund asked incredulously if it would be possible to find twelve men so wicked and lacking in conscience that they would find the priests guilty. Edmund's hands were tucked into the sleeves of his gown but were so crippled by torture that he was unable to hold a Bible or raise his right arm to take the oath. One of his companions pulled back the sleeve, kissed his hand and raised his arm for him. 'I protest before God and his holy angels, before heaven and earth, before the world and this bar whereat I stand ... that I am not guilty of any part of the treason contained in the indictment or of any other treason whatever'.

No fair trial was possible; the verdict had been pre-determined by the Privy Council. The jury was rigged; the foreman was a Calvinist and a government informer. Three men refused to serve and were replaced by others more likely to produce the required guilty verdict. False witnesses were suborned to testify against the priests, most of whom were unknown to each other. As the historian Henry Hallam FRS (1777-1859) wrote in his immensely influential *Constitutional History of England*, 'The prosecution was as unfairly conducted as any in our books.' Among the unsavoury bunch of witnesses, in addition to Eliot, were Charles Sledd, a notorious spy, and Anthony Munday, a government informer who had once been at the English College, Rome, and ingratiated himself with the Catholics in order to spy on them. It was he who perjured himself by claiming to know of the pretended plot to assassinate the Queen.

A large group of priests, nineteen in all, were taken by river to Westminster Hall for trial with Campion before Sir Christopher Wray, the Lord Chief Justice, whose wife, mother and elder brother were recusants, and his nephew a priest. The group included Alexander Briant, Thomas Cottam, William Filby, John Hart, [8] Robert Johnson, Luke Kirby, Lawrence Richardson (real name Johnson), [9] Edward Rishton, [10] Ralph Sherwin, John Shert, [11] John Colleton, [12] James Bosgrave [13] Thomas Ford and George Ostcliff. (Ostcliff, who came from Felkirk, York and was ordained in 1579, was condemned but not executed. He spent five years in prison, part of the time in Lancaster Castle from where he was banished in June 1586.) On trial with the priests was Henry Orton, a law student, who had been apprehended by

The Elizabethan Martyrs, 1577-1601

Sledd. Orton was condemned but banished. Prosecuting were the Attorney-General, John Popham, Solicitor-General, Thomas Egerton, and Mr Anderson QC. Prisoners were allowed no defence counsel so they had to defend themselves. Campion inevitably became the spokesman for all the accused. He asked that they be given individual trials and Wray showed some sympathy with the request but it had to be refused on the grounds that time did not permit it. Among those present to observe the trial was Edmund Plowden, the famous Catholic lawyer who, on being spotted by one of the judges, was ordered to leave the court. Ever a moderate he thought it prudent to obey. *

Popham employed disingenuous and scornful invective against Edmund. Why had he entered the country secretly, disguised as a merchant? Why did he dress like a gentleman? 'What should a messenger of Christ, as you like to think yourself, be doing with feathers and silken doublets? What should a priest do with a sword? What has the light of the Gospel to do with the things you pursued in the shadows? If you love your country or any good purpose had brought you back to England, there was no need to hide.' Campion put up an impressive defence, ably refuting the allegations, although on the principal charge of treasonably plotting to kill the Queen no evidence against him was actually offered. The dates on which he was supposed to be in Rheims or Rome are demonstrably impossible, but that seems to have been irrelevant. 'Our laws' he said 'as I understand them, have been passed with much foresight and caution that they do not intend to rob any man of his life on the mere conjectures of any orator whatsoever. Nor do they intend to put him at the mercy of anyone who can make a violent speech. The matter should be decided either on irrefutable evidence or on most certain testimony of men beyond reproach. Hence I fail to see the purpose of so much bitterness on the part of the Crown prosecution.' One of the charges against him was that he had corresponded with the imprisoned Thomas Pound. Edmund was careful to distinguish between the spiritual and temporal authority of

---

* Edmund Plowden (c.1518-1585) was the most distinguished lawyer of the late Tudor age. His religion prevented him from the promotion that was his due. He refused to take the Oath of Uniformity and was a byword for integrity. Queen Elizabeth at one time offered Plowden the Lord Chancellorship with the proviso that he conformed to the Established Church. Plowden's brave reply was, 'Hold me, dread Sovereign, excused. Your Majesty well knows, I find no reason to swerve from the Catholic Faith, in which you and I were brought up. I can never, therefore, countenance the persecution of its professors. I should not have in charge Your Majesty's conscience one week, before I should incur your displeasure, if it be Your Majesty's intent to continue the system of persecuting the retainer's of the Catholic Faith.' It says something for Elizabeth's judgement that this bold rebuke did not alter her opinion of Plowden's abilities and she continued to use his legal services.

the pope and he expressed doubts about the legitimacy of Pius V's bull. Some of the accusations made by Eliot and Munday against his co-defendants were ludicrous. For example, Munday told the court that Father Rishton planned to use fireworks to burn the Queen, and Father Cottam was accused of possessing an objectionable book.

The proceedings had taken about three hours and Edmund was allowed to address the jury before they retired. He asked them what truth might be expected from the likes of Eliot, a murderer, and Munday, a professed atheist; men devoid of any honesty who had betrayed both God and man. How could such men be believed? And he made a somewhat forlorn final appeal to their consciences, as they were to 'render at the dreadful Day of Judgement'. While waiting for the jury to return Edmund was offered and drank a glass of beer.

The jury was not long in reaching the expected verdict which was announced by the foreman, Lee. Wray asked Edmund if he had anything to say before sentence was pronounced.

It is obvious to everyone that we have been found guilty not for any offence against the throne, but simply for our religion ... If all the things alleged against us were true, the crime would be so enormous that it could not be expiated simply by going to one of your churches. We die therefore for religion. There can be no more honourable cause in the eyes of God or man ... It was not our death that we ever feared. But we knew we were not lords of our own lives and therefore for want of an answer would not be guilty of our deaths. The only thing that we now have to say is, that if our religion do make us traitors, we are worthy to be condemned; but otherwise are, and have been, as good subjects as ever the Queen had. In condemning us you condemn all your own ancestors - all the ancient priests, bishops and kings - all that was once the glory of England, the island of saints and the most devoted child of the See of Peter. For what have we taught, however you may qualify it with the odious name of treason, that they did not uniformly teach? To be condemned with these lights - not of England only, but of the world - by their degenerate descendants, is both gladness and glory to us. God lives: posterity will live: their judgement is not so liable to corruption as that of those who are now going to sentence us to death.

When the dreadful sentence was pronounced, the priests spontaneously sang the *Te Deum*. The next day a further seven priests were condemned, including Fathers Colleton and Ford, neither of whom had ever set foot in either Rheims or Rome. Both of them produced alibis that they were elsewhere on the dates when they were alleged to have been plotting at Rheims. Ford's alibi was rejected, but as Father Colleton could bring a witness to prove he was in London he was acquitted of the treason charge but still kept in prison.

The Elizabethan Martyrs, 1577-1601

Many popular ballads were composed about the notorious trial. One read:
> They packed the jury that cried guilty straight,
> You bloody jury, Lee and all the eleven,
> Take heed your verdict, which was given in haste,
> Do not exclude you from the joys of heaven.

For a further eleven days Edmund lay in chains in the Tower. Even at this late stage attempts were still made to persuade him to conform, making him promises of rewards. For the first time we hear of him having a sister who was allowed to visit him, offering a lucrative benefice in the Established Church on behalf of the government. One of his visitors was none other than George Eliot, claiming that when he had betrayed him he had not thought it would lead to his execution, only imprisonment. It seems that Eliot was motivated by fear of reprisals, as he had already been called 'Judas' by passers-by in the street. Campion gave him the benefit of the doubt, treated him courteously and begged him to confess his crime and repent. Sadly the counsel fell on deaf ears; Eliot continued his spying career. But Edmund made one last convert: his jailer, who much moved and impressed by his prisoner, became a Catholic.

On 1 December 1581 Campion was strapped to a hurdle, while Alexander Briant and Ralph Sherwin were bound together on a second hurdle. 'God bless you and make you all good Catholics', Edmund called out to the bystanders. They were dragged through the muddy streets to be hanged, drawn and quartered at Tyburn. All along the route people called out asking for a blessing. In spite of the awful weather, there was huge crowd which included many of the leading members of the Court. The eyewitnesses noted that the mud-spattered Edmund and his companions were laughing together and did not seem to care at all that they were about to die.

Standing in the cart, the rope around his neck, Edmund tried to make himself heard above the noise. He began his address quoting from St Paul's first letter to the Corinthians, 'We are made a spectacle to the world, to angels and to men ... As to the treasons which have been laid to my charge, and for which I come here to suffer, I desire you all to bear witness with me that I am thereto altogether innocent. I am a Catholic man and a priest; in that Faith I have lived and in that Faith do I intend to die. If you esteem my religion treason, then I am guilty; as for the other treason, I never committed any, God is my judge'.

All the while he had to endure taunts and heckling from the dignitaries present. He forgave his persecutors and asked pardon of any he might have harmed. The courtiers demanded that he ask the Queen's forgiveness and pray for her. 'Wherein have I offended her?' he asked, 'In this I am innocent. I do pray for her ... Elizabeth your Queen and my Queen, unto whom I wish a long quiet reign with all prosperity'.

These were his last audible words as the cart was pulled from under him and he was left hanging from the gibbet. Thankfully he appears to have been unconscious before the dismembering began. His quarters were displayed on each of the four City gates.

In the crowd to witness the martyrdom of Edmund and his companions was Father Thomas Alfield [14] who wrote *A true report of the death and martyrdome of Mr Campion, Jesuit and priest, and Mr Sherwin and Mr Bryant priests,* which was secretly printed in London by Richard Verstegan. His printing press was seized and Verstegan was imprisoned but escaped to France in 1582. He settled in Antwerp from where he continued to produce accounts and engravings of Campion's martyrdom which circulated all over Europe, much to the chagrin of the Queen and the Privy Council. (In February 1582 Richard Topcliffe searched Symon's Inn for copies of Alfield's book when Father Edward Osborn happened to walk in. Seeing Topcliffe the priest beat a hasty retreat but was pursued and arrested. Threatened with torture Osborn talked, betraying those who had sheltered him. He named several houses where he had said Mass as well as in the prison cell of Lord Vaux in the Fleet when Sir Thomas Tresham and others had been present. He gave evidence against Vaux and his companions at their trial at the Guildhall when they were convicted, heavily fined and returned to prison. Osborn later repented.)

All shades of religious and political opinion have never been in any doubt that the trial of Campion and his companions was an appalling travesty - judicial murder at its worst. There is likewise unanimous concurrence that with Campion this country lost a brilliant thinker and writer, a man of genius, not just a great Elizabethan but a great Englishman. Let Evelyn Waugh have the last word:

He was one of a host of martyrs ... some performed more sensational feats of adventure ... many suffered crueller tortures, but to his own and to each succeeding generation, Campion's fame has burned with unique warmth and brilliance; it was his genius to express, in sentences that have resounded across the centuries, the spirit of chivalry in which they suffered, to typify in his zeal, his innocence, his inflexible purpose, the pattern which they followed.

From *Edmund Campion* by Evelyn Waugh [*]

---

[*] Copyright © The Estate of Evelyn Waugh, reproduced by permission of PFD on behalf of the estate of Evelyn Waugh.

The Elizabethan Martyrs, 1577-1601

Ralph Sherwin

Must they fall? The young ... the brave, to swell one bloated chief's unwholesome reign.

Childe Harold' Pilgrimage, Lord Byron, 1788-1824

He was born at Rodsley, near Ashbourne, Derbyshire in 1549/50. Raised as a Protestant, he was educated at Exeter College, Oxford. The College had been founded in 1314 by Walter de Stapeldon, Bishop of Exeter, under the patronage of the Virgin Mary, St Peter and St Thomas of Canterbury. In the sixteenth century it was transformed and expanded with generous donations by a graduate of the College, Sir William Petre of Ingatestone, Essex, and became one of the leading colleges of the University. Devonshire-born Sir William, whom we have met several times in the narrative of the destruction of the monasteries, held public office in the royal service for many years, being knighted in 1543. As Cromwell's deputy he had got rich by profiting from the suppression of the religious houses, notwithstanding that in later life he disapproved of Elizabeth's religious policy and was a secret Catholic sympathiser, although he did not let that stand in the way of his material and political advancement. Certainly his wives were Catholic and priests were sheltered at Ingatestone Hall by his second wife, Anne.

Sir William's descendants, the Petres of Ingatestone, were to become one of the staunchest Catholic families of England giving many priests and two bishops to the Church. The son of Sir William, John, created 1st Baron Petre, was the patron and protector of the great William Byrd who lived nearby at Stondon Massey and often brought companies of musicians to perform at Ingatestone Hall. Father Henry More SJ (1586-1661), the great-grandson of Sir Thomas More, was chaplain to William, 2nd Baron Petre (1573-1637) and to his son Robert, the third baron (1599-1638) and his wife Mary Browne, the daughter of Anthony-Maria, 2nd Viscount Montague. William, 13th Baron Petre (1847-1893) was himself a priest.

Ralph's uncle was a Marian priest, Father John Woodward, who had been rector at Ingatestone and then acted as chaplain to the Petres. It was through his influence that Sir William nominated Ralph for an Exeter fellowship in 1568. This was unusual because, unlike most of his fellow students, Ralph did not come from the West Country. Exeter

The Elizabethan Martyrs, 1577-1601

College was notable for its Catholic sympathies. In the 1570's the Royal Commissioners paid visits to the college to purge it of papists and as result the Rector, John Neale, the Sub-Rector, William Wyatt, and the Dean, John Brereblock, were forced to leave. Ralph took his MA with honours in 1574, and became noted as a Greek and Hebrew scholar as well as a philosopher. He had a great zest for life and adventure; vivacious and impulsive, he accumulated a large circle of good friends. He saw friends, such as Nicholas Roscarrock, depart before him because of their religion but he stayed on. He loved his life at Oxford, pursuing a highly successful academic career, and a public disputation brought him to the favourable notice of the Earl of Leicester.

He seems to have been very close to his priest uncle and what role Father Woodward may have played in his conversion and subsequent vocation is unknown, but in 1574/75 Ralph became a Catholic. In that latter year he was given leave to study abroad. He gave up the prospect of a brilliant career and with two friends, Martin Array and John Curry, q.v. he travelled to Douai. He was ordained priest at Cateau-Cambresis on 23 March 1577 together with the future martyrs, Lawrence Richardson (vere Johnson) and William Andleby q.v. In August of that year, in the company of newly-ordained Fathers Martin Array and Edward Rishton, he was transferred to Rome to continue his theological studies at the newly established English College, converted from the old English Pilgrims' Hospice. Of the fifty students who took the college oath on 23 April 1579, his name stands first in the register. The fourteenth name in the list was that of the future apostate Anthony Tyrell. The college students were required to swear an oath that they were prepared to serve on the English mission. When it was Ralph's turn to swear it is recorded that he added, 'Potius hodie quam cras' (Rather today than tomorrow). Thus Ralph became the proto-martyr of the English College, Rome.

All was not well at the new Roman College. There was discord between the Welsh and English students, the latter justifiably claiming that the Welsh received preferential treatment from their superiors. The rector of the college, the former rector of the hospice, was the Welshman, Dr Maurice Clynnog, one of whose students, Morgan Clynnog, was his nephew. Dr Clynnog was chaplain to Cardinal Pole and had been named Bishop of Bangor by Queen Mary but she died before he could be consecrated. With the accession of Elizabeth he had gone into exile. The dispute at the college went much deeper than trivial national rivalries. There was a fundamental difference of approach to their studies and objectives between many of the students

208

coming from Douai and the older, more conservative priests who had been placed in charge of the college. They had not yet fully grasped the reality of the situation in England and fondly imagined that before long there would once more be a reversion to the Old Faith. They conducted the college as a place of genteel higher education in preparation for the restitution of Catholicism. The students, on the other hand, knew that a re-conversion of their country was now required and were fired with zeal for the English mission which was their goal. The dispute turned into a full-scale revolt, in which Ralph appears to have been one of the vociferous leaders, making full use of his oratorical skills. Sherwin was somewhat uncharitably forthright in referring to the Welsh nation as barbarous savages. 'Many of us,' he said, 'wish ourselves Welshmen, because we would gladly have so good a provision as they.' He composed a petition to the Cardinal Protector of the college, the eminent elder statesman, Giovanni Morone, explaining that the only reason for their being there was to acquire sufficient knowledge to better equip them to return to England.

Dr Clynnog enjoyed the support of his countryman, the influential Archdeacon Owen Lewis who was *persona grata* at the papal court. At first the Pope and Cardinal Morone were inclined to dismiss the students' rebellion, but after a meeting with Ralph and his companions Morone became more sympathetic. The campaign gathered momentum and in 1579 Dr Clynogg had no choice but to resign. The students made it clear that they wished to have the college under the direction of the Jesuits, but not even appeals to the Pope had any effect. A story was spread that gained widespread credence that the Jesuits themselves had fomented the students' rebellion in order to take control of the college. As a result the Superior General of the Society, Everard Mercurian, declined to have anything to do with the college and Dr Clynnog was reappointed. The students were threatened with expulsion unless they agreed to obey the reappointed Rector. Sherwin and Martin Array decided to approach Pope Gregory XIII directly and they tracked him down on his way from Civitavecchia to Rome, but he told them he did not have time to listen to them. Sherwin, Array, Edward Rishton and Arthur Pitts were summoned to see Cardinal Morone who told them that either they obeyed Dr Clynnog or left the college and they were given twenty-four hours to make up their minds. Things began to get ugly with the English and Welsh students collecting signatures for rival petitions. Instead of waiting, with typical student defiance, on Ash Wednesday thirty-three of the students, including many of the Welsh, walked out and were offered accommodation elsewhere. The students' revolt became the talk of Rome and there is no doubt that the students had the sympathy of the Romans on their side. Recognising that the intolerable situation was causing scandal Pope Gregory gave in to their demands. Dr Clynnog, who was not in any way a bad man, just deficient, left Rome and the Jesuits were placed in charge of the college with Father Alfonso Agazarri as rector.

Ralph spent a further year in Rome studying hard and when he left the *Annals* of the English College had nothing but praise for him. On 18 April 1580, he set off on foot from Rome to begin the journey to England in the company of Edmund Campion, Robert Persons, Luke Kirby, Edward Rishton, four old Marian priests and two laymen, Thomas Briscoe and John Paschal, the latter being a pupil and friend of Ralph's from his Exeter College days. Also in the party was the Jesuit brother, Ralph Emerson, who was carrying Catholic books. Before leaving Rome the group called on St Philip Neri, founder of the Oratorians, who gave them his blessing. Describing their journey in a letter to a friend, Campion wrote: 'I see them all so prodigal of blood and life that I am ashamed of my backwardness'.

The party travelled by way of Bologna and Milan, where they stayed for several days with the Archbishop, St Charles Borromeo, and Ralph was asked to preach. From there they reached Turin but instead of crossing directly into France, because of political and military problems they opted for continuing their journey through Switzerland via Geneva. Writing to his friend, Ralph Bickley, a former Exeter College member who had been studying for the priesthood back in Rome since 1579, Sherwin described his journey and arrival at Geneva.

Before we arrived at this sink of heresy every man disguised himself, and Mr Campion dissembled his personage in the form of a poor Irishman, and waited on Mr Paschal; which sight, if you had seen how naturally he played his part, the remembrance of it would have made you merry. Well, thus disfigured, we represented ourselves to the gates of Geneva, and there by the soldiers were demanded from whence we were and whither we went. After answer was made, a captain commanded one of his soldiers to conduct us to the magistrate. He asked what countrymen we were, and it was answered some English, some brought up in Ireland, and here Mr Campion was called Patrick. After this he enquired whether we were of their religion, and Mr Paschal answered, no: and one other of our company boldly told that from the first to the last we were all Catholics ... After this he commanded a soldier to guide us to our inn, and gave charge that we should be well used. All this while, above in chambers looking out, we saw the long-bearded ministers of Geneva who laughed at us.

During their stay Sherwin, Paschal, Persons and Campion sought out the famous Theodore Beza, the successor of Calvin and one of the leading figures of Protestantism. They disputed with him about religious matters. Sherwin does not seem to have been impressed with Beza, judging by the rude comments he wrote about him, calling him an 'old doting heretical fool' and 'reprobate apostate'. Before leaving they also had some reckless fun, arguing in the street until nearly midnight with one of the nine Calvinist leaders of the city. Ralph wrote that they had sparred with the minister so long 'we almost made the fellow mad'.

Many of the group fell ill which slowed down their progress. On 31 May the group arrived at Rheims, where Douai College was then located. The Pope had agreed that a bishop was needed for England and the octogenarian Thomas Goldwell, Bishop of St Asaph, the only surviving member of the old Catholic hierarchy, had volunteered to return. The Bishop had arrived at Rheims from Rome a few days before and Ralph and John Paschal were chosen to accompany him to England. Although the Bishop attempted the journey to Paris, ill-health forced his return to Rheims - which was just as well because spies had reported his intentions to the English Government, whose agents were waiting to arrest him should he try to set foot in England.

In a letter sent from Rheims to Father Agazzari at the English College in Rome Ralph wrote,

> They say here that our names are betrayed to the enemy; but let them say and plot what they like, we shall take our lives in our hands and break through the ranks of our foes. The nearer we get to the labours and perils of England, the more eagerly we advance upon the country commended to our zeal.

Ralph's presumption was only too true. Before he had even left Rome a spy's report was on its way to London in which Sherwin was described as being aged about thirty, 'tall of stature and slender, his face lean, his beard of a flaxen colour cut short'.

Bidding farewell to Bishop Goldwell, Sherwin and Paschal set out on the final leg of their journey home. In his long letter to Ralph Bickley, which was finally sent from Paris on 11 June 1580, Sherwin wrote self-mockingly of how foppish he looked in his French garb, disguised as a man about town in silk doublet and hose.

'You'll never be handsome', Paschal told him, 'not even in that colourful attire', to which Sherwin replied, 'There was never a priest handsome in this attire. Thus for Christ we put ourselves in colours'.

By 3 July, Rouen was reached and Ralph was able to visit his priest uncle, then living in retirement, to say goodbye. Paschal was taken ill at Rouen, which delayed their journey for several weeks. In a letter to

Father Alfonso Agazzari Ralph mentions that he left Rouen on the feast of St Peter's Chains, which would have been 1 August. He asks his correspondent to 'say his beads' for him 'so that in humility and constancy, with perseverance to the end, I may know God in this vocation whereunto though unworthy I am called'.

From where the two travellers embarked or at what place they landed in England is unknown, but they must have arrived in late August. Ralph made an immediate impression. In a letter to Father Agazzari, Robert Persons wrote in praise of Ralph's 'ardour of spirit' when preaching. Sherwin's apostolate lasted barely three months. In November Ralph visited Father Persons and told him that the spies were so close on his heels that he expected to be captured at any time; later that day he was taken while preaching at the house of his old university friend, Nicholas Roscarrock, in London. The Roscarrocks were a Cornish family, allied by marriage to the Arundells, and had been closely associated with Cuthbert Mayne, for which they were made to suffer. Ralph was imprisoned in the Marshalsea in heavy chains that rattled loudly whenever he moved. This greatly amused Ralph, to the consternation of his fellow religious prisoners. These two men, who belonged to a Protestant sect, thought Ralph must be a madman. Under Ralph's guidance and influence they both became Catholics. Writing to Father Persons to thank him for the money he had sent him to buy food, he remarked,

I have on my feet some little bells that remind me, when I walk, who I am and to whom I belong. I have never heard sweeter harmony than this. Pray for me that I may finish my course with courage.

He added that when the money was spent he would
go down to my brothers the thieves in the pit and subsist on the common basket of alms; and I shall go to it with more alacrity than ever to a banquet; for that bread of charity, for my Lord's sake, will be sweeter to me than honey or all kinds of dainties.

By this he literally meant that he was prepared to subsist on the charitable offerings put into the 'beggar's basket' of the prison, the only means by which prisoners unable to pay would get something to eat.

Shortly afterwards, his friend John Paschal was sent to join him in prison. John had always been full of zealous speeches for which Ralph often reproved him, telling him that it was one thing to be brave now, but what will you do when put to the test? It was almost prophetic, for unlike Ralph, Paschal did not have the inner steel to withstand the threats of torture; out of fear, a few months later, in January 1581, he conformed and publicly apostatised at the Guildhall. In later life he returned to the Church and remained a much persecuted recusant. During the month Ralph spent in the Marshalsea a message was

The Elizabethan Martyrs, 1577-1601

received asking if there were any papists in the prison who were prepared to enter into disputations. Sherwin volunteered along with Father James Bosgrave and Father John Hart. But before the debate could take place on 4 December he was sent to the Tower with Luke Kirby, Robert Johnson, Thomas Cottam and Nicholas Roscarrock. On two successive days Ralph was cruelly tortured on the rack while undergoing intensive interrogation to make him reveal the names of his converts and to incriminate Campion, but he did not utter a word. He was put into solitary confinement and starved for five days and nights, and then left chained in the snow to make him divulge information. Roscarrock, who was also racked, could hear him groaning. Sherwin's brother, John, managed to get in to visit him and reported on his condition. It is from him that we learn of the offer made to Ralph - whether seriously or not - that he would be offered an Anglican bishopric if he would conform.

Three times in the new year Ralph, Roscarrock and the others were forcibly taken to a Protestant church to listen to a sermon, but they protested so much that the farce was not repeated. Roscarrock was sent to the Fleet to join his fellow Cornishman, Francis Tregian. In June 1581 Sherwin, Kirby and Cottam were asked if they would voluntarily go to the Protestant church. When they refused they were told that they would be charged under the new recusancy law. This is significant because it proves that the later allegations of treasonable plotting against the Queen, under which they were brought to trial, had not yet been invented by the government.

Ralph spent a whole weary year suffering in prison during which time he engaged in disputes with Protestant ministers. He knew that his execution was inevitable and wished it would come soon, and he prepared himself with much prayer and meditation, especially upon Christ's Passion. His ardent prayer life and meagre diet earned him the respect of his jailer who called him a true man of God and the most devout priest he had ever met. A letter Ralph wrote to a friend is quoted in Cardinal Allen's *Briefe History of the Glorious Martyrdom of Twelve Reverend Priests*.

Delay of our death doth somewhat dull me. It was not without cause that our Master himself said, *Quod facis fac cito* (What you do, do quickly.) Truth it is I hope ere this, casting off this body of death, to have kissed the precious glorified wounds of my sweet Saviour, sitting in the throne of his father's own glory. Which desire, as I trust descending from above, has so quieted my mind that since the judicial sentence proceeded against us, neither the sharpness of the death has much terrified me, nor the shortness of life much troubled me. My sins are great I confess but I flee to God's mercy ... I have no boldness but in his blood; His bitter passion is my only consolation ... Our Lord perfect us to that end whereunto we were created, that leaving this world, we may live in Him and of Him. World without end ... God grant us humility, that we following His footsteps may obtain the victory.

Arraigned with Campion and others before Sir Christopher Wray on 14 November 1581, Ralph declared boldly, 'The plain reason for our standing here is religion and not treason'. To show that this was true, Campion pointed out that Ralph's friend, John Paschal, had been given his freedom because he had agreed to conform. Sherwin was specifically accused by the prosecution of unlawfully persuading the Queen's subjects to the Catholic Faith, against her injunctions as to what they ought to believe and profess. His answer was to appeal to the Apostles and Fathers of the early Church in whose footsteps he was following.

He regarded his death sentence as a victory achieved. Returning to the Tower, Ralph pointed to the shining sun and said, 'Father Campion, I shall soon be above yonder fellow'. From his cell on 30 November he wrote a final, loving letter to his uncle, Father Woodward:

This very morning, which is the festival day of St Andrew, I was advertised by superior authority, that tomorrow I was to end the course of my life. God grant that I may do it to the imitation of this noble Apostle and servant of God ... After many conflicts ... mixed with spiritual consolations and Christian comforts, it hath pleased God of his unspeakable mercy to call me out of this vale of misery. To him therefore ... be all praise and glory. Your tender care always had over me and cost bestowed on me I trust in heaven shall be rewarded. Innocence is my only comfort against all the forged villainy which is fathered on my fellow priests and me ...When by the High Judge, God himself, this false visage of treason shall be removed from true Catholic men's faces, then shall it appear who they be that carry a well meaning and who an evil murdering mind. In the meantime God forgive all injustice; and if it be His blessed will to convert our persecutors, that they may become professors of the truth.

He asked for his uncle's prayers and said he was never quieter in mind nor less troubled.

I bid you farewell once again to the lovingest uncle that ever kinsman had in this world. God grant us both His grace and blessing until the end that living in His fear and dying in His favour we may enjoy one another for ever.

Taken to Tyburn the thirty-one-year-old Ralph watched his fellow priest die. 'Come Sherwin, take thy wages', said the hangman. Ralph then kissed the hands of the executioner covered in Campion's blood before climbing into the cart. Ralph tried to speak but was interrupted by the officials. Sir Francis Knollys urged him to confess his treason. He protested his innocence of any treasonable crime.

'I have no occasion to lie', he insisted, 'for so doing I should condemn my own soul; and although in this short time of mortal life I am to undergo the infamy and punishment of a traitor, I make no doubt of my future happiness, through Jesus Christ, in whose death, passion and blood I only trust'.

Knollys persisted to which Ralph replied, 'You and I shall answer before another Judge where my innocence shall be known, and you will see that I am guiltless. If to be a Catholic only ... be to be a traitor, then I am a traitor'. As they placed the noose around his neck and drew away the cart, he kept on repeating the name of Jesus. Someone in the crowd called out, 'Good Mr Sherwin, God receive your soul'.

A postscript may be added concerning Ralph's parents. From a letter written by William Knyveton to George Talbot, 6th Earl of Shrewsbury in February 1587, six years after Ralph's death, we learn that following instructions from the Earl, Constance, the wife of John Sherwin of Rodsley, had been committed to jail for persistent recusancy. She begged to be released, promising to attend church, in order to look after her blind, incontinent, bedridden husband. The letter goes on to state that 'we dare not, for doubt of his sudden death thereby, commit him to jail, neither yet remove his body out of the house. If his wife be from him for any time it is thought he cannot live'. Knyveton concludes, '... of which two persons we beseech your honour for their cause to have pity.'

Alexander Briant

I have fought a good fight: I have finished my course: I have kept the faith.
St Paul, *Second Letter to Timothy*

Alexander was born into a yeoman family in Somerset in 1556 and may well have been raised a Catholic. While a teenager, he was sent to Oxford where, because of his purity and handsome face, he was known as 'the beautiful youth'. He studied at Hart Hall, where he matriculated in 1574, the year he was reconciled to the Catholic Church. He moved to Balliol College, where another Somersetshire man, Robert Persons was his tutor. Although Persons left Oxford just a few months later, his influence on Alexander was profound. Persons was later to describe Briant as his disciple and pupil. Another tutor was Richard Holtby, who left the University for Douai, arriving there on 3 August 1577. Eight days later he was joined at the college by Briant. They were ordained priests in the same ceremony at Cambrai on Holy Saturday, 29 March 1578. Alexander set out to return to England 3 August 1579.

He went home to Somerset and visited his mother. He reconciled many to the Church, including Robert Persons' father. Persons wrote that Briant never willingly left his side. It was this attachment that caused his capture. Two years later, Alexander was living in London close to Father Persons' secret lodgings near St Bride's church in the Strand. Another resident in the house was Roland Jenks, a Catholic book publisher, who produced Father Persons' books. In 1577 Jenks had been condemned at the Oxford Assizes and sentenced to the pillory for his printing activities. They only way he could free himself was to cut off one of his ears. Father Persons rented the house from a Protestant bookseller, and used it for meetings and to store religious artefacts. A servant of Jenks', named Wilks, had unwisely been allowed to see the stock of rosaries, crosses and pictures, and he reported his find to the authorities. On the evening of 28 April 1581 a large party of priest-hunters, led by Thomas Norton, the rack-master of the Tower, searching for Father Persons raided the house, but the Jesuit had been forewarned and had got out of London. So the pursuivants decided to search the adjoining house, where they discovered Alexander and finding him in possession of a silver chalice, among other things, they suspected he was a priest and took him into custody.

He was taken first to the Compter or Counter, one of the sheriff's prisons in Wood Street, off Cheapside. He was kept in solitary confinement and left without food or drink for forty-eight hours. He was so thirsty that he tried to catch the rainwater falling from the prison eaves in his hat. Someone showed pity by giving him a little piece of bread and cheese and some beer, and this is all he had for six days. As he refused to reveal the whereabouts of Father Persons and his fellow priests, by order of the Privy Council on 25 March he was taken to the Tower with instructions that he be tortured. He arrived in such a wretched weak state that he could barely stand. In spite of that, he was loaded with heavy chains. He was tortured for the first time on 27 March. The Public Record Office has a list of the questions he was persistently asked in order to extract information about Persons' and Briant's attitudes towards the Queen and her authority. The only answers that are recorded are those he gave on 6th and 7th May when he was content to affirm Elizabeth as his sovereign lady, but he would not be drawn into the question of whether the Pope had authority to withdraw subjects from obedience to her.

The Elizabethan Martyrs, 1577-1601

Alexander adamantly refused to reveal anything about Father Persons which infuriated his interrogators. They used the thumbscrews on him and resorted to the 'pricking' torture which involved thrusting needles or iron spikes under his fingernails. Through it all he recited the *Miserere* psalm and asked God to forgive them. He was then racked, but throughout his excruciating ordeals he seemed to remain unmoved. Alexander later revealed that under torture he fixed his mind on the Passion of Christ and became so absorbed that he felt no pain. Only when the torture was stopped did the agonising pain start. Dr Hammond, one of his tormentors, raged that they were unable to make Alexander give them any information. He was later reported as saying that, 'This is an evident miracle, but it is a miracle of indomitable pertinacity in the popish priest; otherwise from the very pain of the torture he was bound to confess not only facts but cognizance of them, nay even his inmost thoughts'. And he expressed the opinion that it was just as well that only convinced Protestants were present otherwise the priest's fortitude might well convert them. 'I would not on any account', he said, 'that anyone were here present who was not well and solidly grounded in our faith.'

Alexander was cast into the Pit, a subterranean dungeon some twenty feet deep. He was kept in the dark in this vermin-ridden hole for eight days, only to be brought out to face more torture on the rack. This was a large wooden frame on which the prisoner was laid. Cords were tied around his ankles and wrists, and the cords were attached to wooden rollers at either end of the frame. As the levers were pulled, rotating the rollers, the prisoner's body was stretched; the more turns of the rollers the harder the stretching. Prolonged racking caused permanent dislocation of the limbs as well as internal damage. In spite of the pains that affected his whole body, and his congealed blood - an effect of racking - the following day Alexander was racked yet again. He endured it for three hours when spikes were also thrust under his toenails. He thought he was going to die but was resolved to make no answer that might betray anyone. Repeatedly asked whether the Queen was head of the Church in England, Alexander responded, 'I am a Catholic and I believe as a Catholic should do'. Thomas Norton, 15 the barbaric rack-master, countered, 'And they say the pope is,' to which came the reply, 'And so say I'.

Each time he lost consciousness cold water was thrown on his face to revive him and he was stretched even harder. His body became so disjointed that Norton boasted he had made him a foot longer than God intended. Sir Owen Hopton, the Lieutenant of the Tower, behaved appallingly to him, reviling him and slapping him in the face. (Hopton's

217

daughter, Cecily, became a Catholic and acted as a messenger between prisoners in the Tower and their fellow Catholics in the Marshalsea.)

He was consigned to an underground chamber known as Walesbourne where, barely able to move as a result of the racking, he was left semi-naked in the dark for two weeks. Some reports claim that he was also subjected to the Scavenger's Daughter. When details of Briant's tortures became known, the public revulsion was so great that the government made Norton a scapegoat by going through the motions of having him confined to prison for a few days so as to appear not to have sanctioned the atrocities. Lord Burghley later felt obliged to issue a pamphlet entitled *A Declaration of the favourable Dealing* seeking to exonerate the government, by placing all the blame for his sufferings on Alexander himself. 'Whatsoever Briant suffered, in want of food, he suffered the same wilfully and of extreme impudent obstinacy', because of his refusal to ask his jailers in writing for food and drink.

Alexander's importance to the government is revealed in the State Papers. In a letter written on 3 May 1581 from the Council to Sir Owen Hopton, more than a month after Alexander was first tortured, they graphically refer to subjecting him to 'torture, pain and terror' to 'wring from him the knowledge of things as shall appertain'. The letter candidly reveals that the government was not interested in the truth but only in making him confess to anything incriminating, however false. Incredibly, throughout all these sufferings, he stalwartly revealed nothing. Bishop Richard Challoner in his *Memoirs* compares Alexander to the martyrs of the early Church. Briant very much wanted to join the Society of Jesus and he wrote a hasty letter asking to be admitted. In his letter he explained how he had resolved to join the Society while on the rack.

More than two years ago I resolved, if it were God's will that I should return to foreign parts, that I would embrace the mode of life of congregations dedicated to God, and seek admission among the Fathers of the Society. But because I hoped that my labour and industry in the harvest of the Lord would not be altogether useless, I deferred the proposal, though I have very frequently renewed my resolution during these two years which I have lived in England. Yet now since I am by the appointment of God deprived of liberty, so as I cannot any longer employ myself in this profitable exercise, my desire is hereby revived, my spirit waxes fervent hot, and at the last I have made a vow and promise to God, not rashly (as I hope) but in the fear of God, not to any other end than I might thereby more devoutly and more acceptably serve God, to my more certain salvation, and to a more glorious triumph over my ghostly enemy. I have made a vow (I say) that whensoever it shall please God to deliver me ... I will, within one year then next following, assign myself wholly to the fathers of the society, and that (if God inspire their hearts to admit me) I

The Elizabethan Martyrs, 1577-1601

will gladly and with exceeding joy thoroughly and from the bottom of my heart give up and surrender all my will to the service of God, and in all obedience under them.

This vow was to me a passing great joy and consolation in the midst of all my distress and tribulations ...The same day that I was first tormented on the rack before I came to the place, giving my mind to prayer and commending myself and all mine to our Lord, I was replenished and filled up with a kind of supernatural sweetness of spirit. And even while I was calling upon the holy name of Jesus and upon the Blessed Virgin Mary, my mind was cheerfully disposed, well comforted and readily prepared and bent to suffer and endure those torments which I most certainly looked for. At length my former purpose to become a Jesuit came to my mind ... In my afflictions and torments God himself of his infinite goodness, mercifully and tenderly did stand by and assist me, comforting me ...Whether this be miraculous or no, God knoweth: but true it is ... in the end of the torture, though my hands and feet were violently stretched and racked ... yet notwithstanding, I was without sense and feeling well nigh of all grief and pain ... and continued still with perfect and present senses, in quietness of heart and tranquillity of mind. The commissioners ... gave orders to rack me again the next day ... Now when I heard them say so... I did verily believe and trust, that with the help of God I should be able to bear and suffer it patiently. In the meantime I did meditate upon the most bitter passion of our Saviour.

The letter was smuggled out of the Tower for him and safely reached its destination. Although his situation meant that he could not be formally inducted to the Order he expressed his intentions so clearly that the Jesuits were proud to claim him as one of their own.

On 15 November Alexander was arraigned with six other priests. The trial took place on the 21st, the day after Campion and his companions. Alexander came into Westminster Hall having tonsured his head to indicate he was a priest. In prison he had made a rough wooden cross on which he had drawn in charcoal a picture of the Crucified Christ. He clasped the cross in his hand and kept gazing at it during the trial. One of the Protestant ministers told him to throw the cross away, but he answered, 'Never. I am a soldier of the cross and this is my standard unto death'. When the cross was snatched from his hands he replied, 'You may tear this cross from my hands but not from my heart ... until I shall shed my blood for him who for my sake poured out his upon the cross of Calvary'. The cross was later acquired by some Catholics and is now among the relics at the English College, Rome.

Few details of the trial are known. Alexander had never set foot in Rome and had left Rheims many months before the date when the alleged plot was supposed to have been concocted. It obviously made no difference to the proceedings which, no doubt, followed a similar pattern to that of Campion and Sherwin. Munday and Sledd once again gave 'evidence' for the prosecution. Despite going through the legal motions of questioning and cross-questioning, the verdict was in no doubt. When it was delivered Briant, his face radiant with peace and serenity, recited Psalm 42: 'Judge me, O God and distinguish my cause from the nation that is not holy ... I will go unto the altar of God: to God who giveth joy to my youth'.

Briant was returned to the Tower and loaded with chains awaiting his execution. Early in the morning of 1 December, he and Sherwin stood by the Coldharbour Tower waiting for Campion to be brought to join them. When he arrived they all embraced. Dragged from the Tower to Tyburn with Campion and Sherwin, Alexander had to watch while both of them were executed. Perhaps this was a deliberate ploy by the authorities to see if it would shake his resolve. If so, the stratagem failed. The crowd was greatly moved at the sight of Alexander's handsome, young face. He was described as a man of angelic beauty, both of body and soul, and of obvious simplicity, which despite all his sufferings had not been dimmed. He did not say very much except to protest his innocence of any wrongdoing, not only in deed but also in thought. He professed his faith and greatly rejoiced that God had found him worthy to die in the company of Father Campion, whom he revered with all his heart. While he said the *Miserere* psalm the cart was pulled away. Due to either the malice or the carelessness of the executioner, the rope slipped, and instead of being rendered insensible Alexander was fully conscious when cut down to endure the disembowelling. He was just twenty-six years old.

John Paine

Fear no more the frown o' the great; thou art past the tyrant's stroke.

Cymbeline, William Shakespeare, 1564-1616

John Paine or Payne was born at Peterborough, Northamptonshire, perhaps as early as 1532, but nothing else is known of his earlier life. As he mentions his 'very earnest Protestant brother', it has been inferred that John was a convert, although there is no evidence for this, and when or where he may have become a Catholic is unknown. He entered the English College at Douai as a mature student in 1574 and served as the College bursar which suggests that he may have held a

The Elizabethan Martyrs, 1577-1601

position in charge of financial/business affairs. This supposition is reinforced by the later, most plausible, claim that John served the Shelley family at Stondon Hall, Stondon Massey, near Chipping Ongar, Essex. Sir William Shelley, a Justice of the Common Pleas, inherited the manor of Stondon in 1521. His son, John, and his grandson, William, remained steadfast recusants and Mass was celebrated at Stondon throughout the penal times. The younger William was imprisoned in 1580 and spent most of the rest of his life in jail, forfeiting his estates in 1584 after being implicated in the Throckmorton Plot of 1583: yet another attempt to depose Elizabeth and replace her with Mary, Queen of Scots. William was sentenced to death, but reprieved and died in 1597, shortly after being released from prison due to his failing health. (The second manor house was Stondon Place and it was here that the composer William Byrd later lived and he and his family were several times presented as recusants.)

The fact that John Paine was ordained priest so soon at Cambrai on 7 April 1576, suggests he was already advanced in his studies. He spent the two weeks after his ordination following the *Spiritual Exercises* of Saint Ignatius Loyola before setting out to return to England on 24 April with Cuthbert Mayne and Henry Shaw. They were delayed for several days by stormy weather in the English Channel but finally made the crossing safely.

Although John's apostolate ranged over a wide area, including visits to London, he made his headquarters at Ingatestone Hall, Essex, the home of Lady Anne Petre, the second wife and widow of Sir William Petre, whom we have already briefly met in the life of Ralph Sherwin. John's name appears in a list of recusants at Ingatestone prepared for Bishop John Aylmer of London in 1577. Aylmer, enjoyed something of a reputation as a Greek scholar, but his inadequacies as a prelate rendered him the butt of satirists in his time, not least by the great poet, Edmund Spenser. Aylmer had lived in Switzerland in Queen Mary's reign and became notorious for his harsh treatment of all non-conformists, Catholic or Puritan.

As Secretary of State under Henry VIII, Sir William Petre, a capable, ambitious man, had been responsible for visiting and suppressing religious houses. In 1538 he procured the surrender of twenty monasteries and in the first quarter of 1539 he succeeded in suppressing thirteen more. Almost single-handedly he was responsible for the destruction of the twenty-six houses of the Gilbertines. This was the only indigenous English religious order of nuns and canons, founded in the 12th century by yet another wonderful saint who now suffers the neglect of his countrymen; Gilbert of Sempringham. Sir

The Elizabethan Martyrs, 1577-1601

William was a personal friend of Dorothy Barley, the last abbess of Barking, who was godmother to his daughter. It was Petre the royal commissioner who, on 14 November 1539, received the forced surrender of the ancient and illustrious Benedictine abbey from the abbess and her thirty nuns. It was a valuable prize yielding much parcel gilt plate and a large bejewelled monstrance. The copes and other vestments of cloth of gold were reserved for the use of the King. Yet when the goods of the abbey were sold they fetched less than £200: an indication of the poverty observed by the nuns. Barking Abbey had a manor at Yenge-atte-Stone (hence Ingatestone), and Sir William purchased this property when the abbey was suppressed. Petre was a great survivor. He served as Secretary of State under Edward VI and Queen Mary and obtained a papal bull exonerating him from wrongdoing in his acquisition and confirming him in possession of the former Church properties. He then built the house, Ingatestone Hall, which still stands today, and after his death his staunchly Catholic widow, Anne, continued to live there. Anne was the daughter of Sir William Browne, who died during his term of office as Lord Mayor of London. She first married John Tyrell and the notorious apostate priest, Anthony Tyrell, was her nephew by marriage. Ingatestone Hall possessed a tiny secret chapel accessible through the back of a cupboard in an alcove, and a priests' hiding place some fourteen feet long by two feet wide and ten feet high. The entrance to it was beneath the flooring.

John Paine acted the part of estate steward while ministering to the scattered Catholic community. Details of his movements are sketchy, but he was clearly a very active missionary. He was first arrested at Ingatestone around June 1576 but had certainly been released before March 1577, perhaps because of the influence of the Petre family. He was at Douai in November 1577 accompanied by three students, who he later conducted to Paris. He was back at Ingatestone by June 1578 because he was one of the witnesses to Lady Petre's first will in which she stated that she would die as she had ever lived; a true member of the Catholic Church. Among the bequests in the will, preserved in the Essex Record Office, is one 'unto my servant John Paine ten pounds.' Lady Anne's will also set up a trust to administer her property and John was named as one of the trustees. Some years later, when she re-wrote her will, John's name was entirely omitted. As he was a prisoner in the Tower at the time this is hardly surprising.

In January 1579 John was lodging with a Catholic woman in London for a time. If the evidence of George 'Judas' Eliot, capturer of Campion, is to be believed, John was at Ingatestone for Christmas, which is where he claimed to have met him for the first time. Eliot, who pretended to be a good Catholic, was employed for a time as a servant at Ingatestone.

We next hear of John at Haddon in Oxfordshire, where he stayed at the house of William Moore, together with Father George Godsalf. Here, Eliot alleged, John celebrated Mass on 2 July 1581 and provided the names of those present. Godsalf had been ordained deacon during the reign of Queen Mary but had then developed Protestant sympathies. He was befriended by John who, three months after his arrival in Essex, reconciled him to the Church and recommended him to Douai in 1576. Godsalf carried with him a letter from Paine which read:

> On all sides, in daily increasing numbers, a great many are reconciled to the Catholic Faith, to the amazement of many of the heretics. And when any of them as does happen fall into the hands of the raging heretics, with such fortitude, with such courage and constancy do they publicly confess the Catholic Faith (especially those who are of the gentry) that the heretics are dumbfounded with astonishment and already begin to give up hope of putting them down by violence. Greatly also are they troubled by the very name of the Douai priests ... which on the other hand fills all Catholics with consolation and the greatest hope of the recovery of the Catholic religion. They lay snares therefore for all priests, but especially and most eagerly for those sent from thence.

Priests were urgently needed and John begged that more be sent. He beseeches that he and his priestly colleagues be daily remembered in the prayers of Douai that they may persevere in their work.

Godsalf was ordained at Cambrai on 22 December 1576 and returned to England the following June. He and John were betrayed by Eliot and captured in Warwickshire in July 1581 by the under-sheriff who received £12 for apprehending them and sending them to the court at Greenwich. Here they were examined by Sir Francis Walsingham. On 14 July Walsingham wrote to William Cecil, 'My very good Lord, I have been all this day by her Majesty's express commandment set at work about the examining of certain persons charged to have conspired to have attempted somewhat against her own person. But as far as I can gather by the examination that I have already taken, I think it will prove nothing. And yet it is happy that the parties charged are taken for they be runagate priests such as have been bred up at Rome and Douai and seek to corrupt her Majesty's subjects within this realm.' John, Godsalf and Father John Shert were sent to the Tower that same day. Although no one was in any doubt that John was a Douai priest, the law making this fact treason was not yet on the statute book, so a new charge would have to be devised. Here Eliot proved his usefulness. He alleged that Paine had conspired to kill the Queen and tried to involve him in the plan. Walsingham felt that the accusation was too general and could not be sustained. Eliot accordingly obliged by supplying much greater detail elaborating the alleged conspiracy. Fifty armed men were involved, to be paid for by the Pope. For good measure the plan now also included assassinating the Earl of Leicester, Walsingham and Burghley, as well as Elizabeth, whom Paine would personally stab to death.

Imprisoned in the Tower for nine months, John was repeatedly tortured by order of the Privy Council. The Tower diary for 31 August records that 'John Paine, priest was most violently tormented on the rack'. He suffered again on 31 October. Some of the accounts of the Tower that have survived include the claims of Sir Owen Hopton, the Lieutenant of the Tower, for his expenses in holding John which amounted to thirteen shillings and fourpence per week, plus four shillings for fuel and candles. Hopton told John to write a confession revealing those who had sheltered him and what he had plotted against the Queen and State. If he failed to do so he would answer at his utmost peril. Unable to use his hands after being racked, John dictated his response, which he signed off as 'Her Majesty's faithful subject and Your worship's humble prisoner':

Right Worshipful, My duty remembered, being not able to write without better hands, I have by your appointment used the help of your servant. For answer to your interrogations I have already said sufficient for a man that regardeth his own salvation, and that with such advised assentations uttered, as amongst Christian men ought to be believed. Yet once again briefly for obedience sake. First, touching Her Majesty, I pray God to preserve her Highness to His honour and her heart's desire; unto whom I always have and during life will wish no worse than to my own soul. If her pleasure be not that I shall live and serve her as my Sovereign Prince, then will I willingly die her faithful subject, and I trust God's true servant.

Touching the State I protest that I am and ever have been free from the knowledge of any practice whatever, either within or without the realm, intended against the same. For the verity whereof, as I have often before you and the rest of her Grace's commissioners called God to witness, so do I now again; and one day before His Majesty the truth, now not credited, will then be revealed.

For Eliot I forgive his monstrous wickedness and defy his malicious inventions; wishing that his former behaviour towards others, being well known, as hereafter it will be, were not a sufficient proof of these devised slanders.

For host or other person living, in London or elsewhere, unless they be by subornation of my bloody enemy corrupted, I know they can neither for word, deed nor any disloyalty, justly touch me. And so before the seat of God, as also before the sight of men, I will answer at my utmost peril.

At the same time Campion, Sherwin, Briant and others were held in the Tower, tried and condemned on similarly perjured 'evidence'. As Paine was equally a victim with them of Eliot's lying concoctions why he was not included with them remains a mystery. On 12 March the Privy Council issued orders to the Lieutenant and the Sheriff of Essex to make preparations for Paine's trial at Chelmsford.

During the night of 20 March 1582 John was abruptly roused by the Lieutenant of the Tower. Denied the opportunity to dress, gather his belongings or retrieve his purse, he was handed over to officers and hurried away to Chelmsford to be tried at the assizes. As the jail lists show, John was held in Colchester Castle. In spite of the nine months' delay affording the government the opportunity to gather further evidence, none was forthcoming, so John was charged solely on the perjured testimony of Eliot, who received the enormous sum of £100 as a 'free gift.'

John was taken to court on the evening of Thursday, 22 March to hear his indictment read. The document, which is in the Public Record Office, is similarly worded to that of Campion and his companions, with the necessary changes to fit John's case.

'The jury presents on behalf of the Queen that John Paine, lately of Ingerstone [sic] in the county aforesaid, a cleric, acting as a false traitor against our most illustrious and glorious Princess and Lady Elizabeth, by the grace of God, Queen of England, France and Ireland, defender of the Faith, not having the fear of God in his heart nor weighing his due allegiance but led away by the devil, with malice aforethought, did on the 7th day of January in the 21st year of the reign of the said Lady Elizabeth, Queen, and on divers other days before and after at Ingerstone, falsely, maliciously, wickedly and traitorously conspire, imagine, contrive and compass by force and arms to kill the said supreme and gracious lady the Queen and to bring her to final destruction. And the said John Paine at Ingerstone as aforesaid on the 7th day of January in the aforesaid year and on divers other days and occasions before and after at Ingerstone did traitorously and maliciously by express words move and persuade a certain George Eliot that the said George should assist and aid the said John Paine to kill the said lady the Queen and bring her to death and final destruction, contrary to his due allegiance and against the peace of the said Queen, her crown and dignity, and in manifest contempt of the laws of the realm.'

At the trial on 23 March Mr Morris, the prosecuting counsel, told the jury that they should presume the truth of Eliot's accusation because John had committed the crime of 'going beyond the seas' to be ordained priest. Despite knowing the hopelessness of his situation,

The Elizabethan Martyrs, 1577-1601

John vigorously defended himself, vehemently denying the charges and protesting his innocence declaring that men could not be made traitors just because they were ordained priests. He pointed out that it was totally unjust and against all natural law that he should be condemned on the uncorroborated evidence of one man, especially such a notoriously infamous character as Eliot. He accused Eliot of being an evil man, of embezzling money from Lady Petre, of lewd acts with women and guilty of personal malice towards himself.

The jury delivered the guilty verdict expected of them. The following day, being Saturday, Judge Gawdy asked Paine if had anything further to say. John replied that he had said all he could in his defence. The judge retorted that if he were innocent the jury would have found in his favour. To this John responded that he excused the jury for being 'poor, simple men, nothing at all understanding what treason is'. He accepted his sentence calmly, and his comment, 'If it please the Queen and her Council that I shall die, I refer my case to God', revealed that he was under no illusions that his condemnation had been engineered and by whom. He asked what day was appointed for him to suffer and was told the following Monday. He was returned to a dungeon at Colchester Castle. On the Sunday, the day before his execution he had to endure the unwanted attentions of two Puritan ministers, who greatly vexed and troubled him 'by their foolish babbling'. He was offered a pardon if he agreed to conform, leaving no one, then or since, in any doubt that he was to die purely for his religion.

Paine was a meek and gentle man, greatly loved by all who knew him. An anonymous contemporary account, probably by a fellow priest, published in Allen's *Briefe History of ... Twelve Reverend Priests*, states:

> All the town loved him exceedingly and so did the keepers. No man seemed to dislike him, but much sorrowed and lamented his death. I, amongst many, coming to him about ten of the clock with the officers, he most comfortably and meekly uttered words of constancy to me and with a loving kiss took leave of me.

At Chelmsford on Monday, 2 April 1582 at 8 a.m. John was laid on the hurdle and taken outside the town to the gallows. On the scaffold he was offered a pardon if he would conform, but he courteously refused. He asked forgiveness of anyone he had wronged, forgiving everyone who had harmed him, including Eliot whom he named and prayed for. Despite being harangued by the ministers who insisted he pray in English, not Latin, he knelt in prayer then ascended the ladder a smile on his face. He kissed the gallows and was allowed to speak to the crowd. He protested his innocence. 'My feet never did tread, my hands never did write, nor my wit ever invent any treason against her Majesty, but always wished unto her as my own soul, desiring God to give her a prosperous reign and afterwards eternal happiness.'

Robert, 3rd Baron Rich, immensely wealthy, radical Puritan grandson of the infamous Richard Rich, and later to be created Earl of Warwick, was in the crowd. He called out to John to confess his guilt and repent. Paine replied that to confess a lie was to condemn his own soul and repeated that he was to die simply for being a Catholic priest. *'Sweet my Lord,"* he said, 'certify Her Majesty thereof, that she suffer not hereafter innocent blood to be cast away which is a great sin'. When one of the ministers claimed that John's brother had confirmed the charge of conspiracy, he temporarily lost his composure. *"Bone Deus!* My brother is, and always has been, a very earnest Protestant; yet I know he will not say so falsely of me'. John said he believed his brother was in Chelmsford and they should send to the town for him.

If this Protestant brother is the one named Jerome, he was not present to speak for himself and if the statement were true, why did the government not summon him to give evidence at the trial to that effect? In fact when he heard about the matter, the brother completely denied it, saying it was all a fabrication as he would inform Lord Rich. Jerome Paine had been arrested in 1586 as he was then a servant to one of those suspected of involvement in the Babington Plot and he spent two years in the Tower.

John said the *Miserere* and then the Lord's Prayer in English. The Spanish Ambassador, Don Bernardino de Mendoza, wrote that Paine died with the greatest fortitude. When John was turned off the ladder, he hung without moving hand or foot, repeating the name of Jesus. He was so well liked in the neighbourhood that some men in the crowd 'courteously' hung onto his feet and made sure that he was dead before he was cut down to suffer the barbarities, much to the annoyance of Simon Bull, the hangman of Newgate, who had been specially brought to Essex for the execution.

Father George Godsalf remained in the Tower until the end of 1583. In February 1584 he was transferred to the Marshalsea, where he was kept until banished in September 1585. He died in Paris about six years later.

There remains in existence an interesting reminder of an episode in John Paine's life: the 'Bosworth Burse'. Around the border of the burse is embroidered an inscription bearing John's name. The centre of the burse has an embroidered image of Christ appearing from the chalice, an image well-known in ikonography; but in this instance it commemorates a vision of Christ rising from the chalice claimed to have been seen by John while at Mass at Douai.

Luke Kirby

We step from days of sour division into the grandeur of our fate.

The Fourth of August, Laurence Binyon, 1869-1943

According to Bishop Challoner, Luke was born at Bedale, North Yorkshire, in 1548. Other sources claim Richmond, a little further north, as his birthplace. It is believed he was a graduate of Cambridge University, yet the records of Louvain University, Brabant, show that Kirby matriculated there in August 1566 having, one assumes, taken his MA. It is said he was a convert; if that is so his attendance at Louvain suggests that he became a Catholic there or as a teenager rather than later. Luke is said to have arrived at Douai in 1576. What he was doing or where he lived in the intervening ten years is unknown. While at Douai we are told he suffered from 'the stone' - whether kidney or bladder is not disclosed - but it was extremely painful. Luke submitted to the gruesome surgery for its removal, but afterwards his health was always rather frail.

He was ordained at Cambrai on 21 September 1577, choosing to wait to say his first Mass until 18 October, the feast day of his patron, St Luke. On 3 May 1578 he was sent to England but was back in Douai by July, when it was decided to send him to Rome for further study. He left Douai for the English College, Rome, on 17 August and spent the next two years there, taking the missionary oath on 23 April 1579, the same day as Ralph Sherwin. An observant English spy mentions him in a report as being thirty-two years of age, of reasonable stature and well-built, his beard cut short, of a brown colour, having prominent teeth and a little stutter. In Rome he was noted for his charity towards all, ever ready to empty his purse, and once literally gave the shirt off his back to a beggar. He spent Lent of 1580 preparing himself with great fervour for his return to England. In April, in company with Robert Persons, Edmund Campion and Ralph Sherwin, he set off for home. He particularly enjoyed the encounter they had with Beza in Geneva. Making his way to Dunkirk, it is believed he may have crossed over to Dover in June 1580.

The Elizabethan Martyrs, 1577-1601

Wherever it was he landed, he was arrested immediately on arrival. He was sent to the Gatehouse Prison in London where he found many other Catholics. On 4 December he was moved to the Tower where six days later he was cruelly tortured with the Scavenger's Daughter. The name was a corruption of that of its inventor, Sir William Skevington, Lieutenant of the Tower under Henry VIII. The instrument was a hinged hoop of iron in which the victim's whole body was rolled into a ball and compressed into the hoop which was placed under his legs and over his back and then fastened. It caused nosebleeds and blood to flow from under the finger and toenails. Luke was left in this agonising state for hours.

He was arraigned with Campion and his companions on 14 November and tried and condemned with them on 20 November. One of the suborned witnesses, Sledd, gave evidence against him, alleging that Kirby had talked of the great day when there would be an invasion of England by the King of Spain and the Pope. Luke's answer was, 'As I hope to be saved at the last doom, there is not one word of this that ... is either true or credible. Neither at any time made I the least mention of that alleged day ... I always bore as true and faithful a heart to her Majesty as any subject whatsoever did in England ... I defended her cause and always spoke the best of her highness'.

Luke was not executed with Campion: his execution was delayed until 1582. While in prison in January of that year he wrote a long letter to friends from which the following extracts are taken. The John Nichols to whom he refers was a well-known Calvinist minister who had converted to Catholicism while living in France but had reverted to Protestantism on his return to England. He made an uncharitable habit of haranguing and annoying Catholic prisoners. On the day after Alexander Briant's arrest, the apostate Nichols had spotted Anthony Tyrell in the street and had him arrested. Tyrell was sent to the Gatehouse, from which he soon contrived to escape. Richardson, Filby and Hart were, of course, Luke's fellow priest prisoners.

My most hearty commendations to you and the rest of my dearest friends. If you send anything to me you must make haste because we look to suffer death very shortly, as already it is signified to us. John Nichols came to my chamber window with humble submission, to crave mercy and pardon for all his wickedness and treacheries committed against us and to acknowledge his books, sermons and infamous speeches to our infamy and discredit, to be wicked, false and most execrable before God and man which he had indulged in for favour and hope of promotion. He knoweth in conscience our accusations and the evidence brought against us to be false and to have no colour of truth, but only out of malice forged by our enemies. As for Sledd and

The Elizabethan Martyrs, 1577-1601

Munday, he is himself to accuse them of this wicked treachery and falsehood and of their naughty and abominable life ... for which cause he hath forsaken his ministry and is minded to teach a school ... in Norfolk. I wished him to make amends for his sins and go to a place of penance ... He offered to go to ... Mr Secretary Walsingham and declare how injuriously I and the rest were condemned, that he might be free from shedding innocent blood. He was afraid to show himself in London where already he had declared our innocent behaviour ... To give my censure and judgement of him, certain I think he will within a short time fall into infidelity, except God of His goodness in the meantime be merciful to him ... yet it would seem he hath not lost all good gifts of nature, when as in conscience he was pricked to open the truth in our defence ... I am minded to signify to Sir Francis Walsingham this his submission to us, except in the meantime I shall learn that he has, as he promised faithfully to me, already opened the same. Mr Richardson and Mr Filby have now obtained some bedding, who since their condemnation have laid upon the boards. Mr Hart hath had many great conflicts with his adversaries. This morning ... he was committed to the dungeon where he now remaineth. God comfort him; he taketh it very quietly and patiently ... Thus beseeching you to assist us with your good prayers whereof now especially we stand in need, as we by God's grace shall not be unmindful of you.

John Nichols did honour his promise. He confessed to the Lieutenant of the Tower, who ignored him. He then confessed to Burghley, who admitted that they all knew Nichols was a liar but it made no difference. Nichols later returned to France.

On 30 May 1582 Luke suffered with three other priests, William Filby, Laurence Richardson and Thomas Cottam. Even on the scaffold, on behalf of the Queen, the Sheriff offered them their lives and liberty; but Luke and his companions refused to deny their faith. Standing in the cart Luke declared his innocence and the fact that he was to die for his religion. A group of ministers constantly importuned him so that he had to struggle to prepare himself amidst the harassment. Finally they offered to pray with him, suggesting that they say the words and if he did not find them objectionable he could repeat them. Luke told them he preferred to pray on his own and saying the Pater Noster and Ave Maria, he was turned off the ladder. Unusually, the quartered bodies of the four priests were not displayed but were buried in the common grave by the Tyburn gallows and relics of Luke were obtained. While in prison materials were smuggled in to him to enable him to say Mass. The linen corporal that he used was given by him to another priest prisoner who was later exiled. It has survived and along with the other relics it now rests at Stonyhurst College.

The Elizabethan Martyrs, 1577-1601

Richard Gwyn

He that hath left life's vain joys and vain care ... hath got an house where many mansions are and keeps his soul unto eternal mirth.

The Timber, Henry Vaughan, 1622-95

Wales had long remained a bastion of Catholicism, but Richard, who it is believed was raised as a Protestant, was the first Welshman to die for the Faith under Elizabeth. He was born c.1537 at Llanidloes, then in Montgomeryshire, but now in Powys. At the age of twenty he went to Oxford, where he studied for a time before moving to St John's College, Cambridge, where he lived largely on the charity of Dr George Bullock, the Master.

Dr Bullock had left England during Edward VI's reign but returned at the accession of Queen Mary. When Elizabeth came to the throne he had to resign his Mastership for refusing the Oath of Supremacy and went to spend the rest of his life abroad. The loss of his benefactor made life very difficult for Richard, and to earn money he took pupils. After leaving the university he returned to Wales in 1562 and became a schoolmaster, teaching at Overton and Gresford, both close to Wrexham, while continuing his own studies in theology and history. It must have been sometime during this period that he became a Catholic, presumably reconciled by a seminary priest. He was fascinated by the rich folklore of his country, and being fluent in Welsh wrote songs and poetry in the language. He married a girl from Overton called Catherine and they had six children, three of whom survived.

As a recusant in a small community, Richard's absence from church was very noticeable. He tried by all means, frequently moving around, to avoid taking the Oath of Supremacy and was threatened with fines or imprisonment if he did not conform. What is more, he was not one to keep his opinions to himself, exhorting his neighbours to return to the Catholic Church. The Anglican bishops were told to be more vigilant against recusants, especially schoolmasters, who exercised great influence. William Downham, who had been a Catholic chaplain to Princess Elizabeth in her sister's reign, was appointed Bishop of Chester in 1561. He was regarded as ineffectual in suppressing Catholics and it may have been the case that the Council leaned on him particularly heavily in this respect prompting him to take action. Within a month Richard had been arrested by the Bishop's officers. Threatened

The Elizabethan Martyrs, 1577-1601

with imprisonment Richard was concerned about the welfare of his family and after much bullying he very reluctantly agreed to go to church at Overton the following Sunday. As he left church a strange thing happened; a great flock of crows and kites swooped down and began to peck at his face and head. Richard took this as an omen and resolved never again to violate his conscience by attending the Protestant church.

Incensed at Richard's refusal, the Bishop made life so unbearable for him that he and his family packed up and left Overton on foot. Arriving at Erbistock, they found an old deserted barn where they made their home. Richard set up a secret school for the local Catholic children, but while visiting Wrexham cattle market he was recognised by the vicar, an apostate priest, who had him arrested and imprisoned. Told he was to appear before the magistrates next day, he escaped during the night. Now he was really a marked man. He was at liberty for eighteen months.

Richard was stopped on the public highway by a fanatical Puritan cloth merchant called David Edwards, who without any legal authority had him dragged to his house and chained up while the magistrates were summoned. Richard was taken to Wrexham prison and locked in a horrible underground dungeon, known as the Black Chamber, for two days. Brought before the magistrate, he was sent back to prison on suspicion of treason. Within a month Richard had been moved to Ruthin Castle, where he was harshly treated. On his repeated refusal to conform he was put in heavy manacles. At the Michaelmas Assizes he was asked to betray the people whose children he had taught. This he refused to do, nor would he consent to go to church so he was returned to prison. About Christmas-time he was sent back to Wrexham jail, his hands and legs heavily loaded with irons. Brought once more before the magistrates, he refused to conform.

At the May Assizes the magistrates ordered that Richard be forcibly taken to the magnificent parish church of St Giles, one of the finest churches in the Principality, whose richly decorated 135-feet high, 16th century tower is one of the 'Seven Wonders of Wales'. Carried in by six of the sheriff's men he was laid under the pulpit to hear the minister preach. Richard rattled his chains so loudly that no one could hear a word of the sermon. Furious, the magistrates ordered him to be put in the stocks from 10am until 8pm - 'vexed all the time with a rabble of ministers'. Taken back to his cell, he was visited by some of the ministers. One of them, who had a very large purple nose, wanted to dispute with Richard about the keys of the Kingdom of Heaven, asserting that God had given those keys also to him and not only to St

The Elizabethan Martyrs, 1577-1601

Peter.

'There is a difference", said Richard, 'St Peter was entrusted with the keys of the Kingdom of Heaven, while the keys entrusted to you appear to be those of the beer cellar!'

Brought to court, the only new charge they could make against him was for causing a disturbance in church, for which he was heavily fined. In September 1581 he was moved from Wrexham to Denbigh Castle. Tried before Sir George Bromley, he was fined £140 for refusing to go to church. That was an absolutely enormous sum for the time. When asked how he was going to pay, he told the magistrate that he had something towards it.

'How much?' Sir George asked, to which Richard replied, 'Sixpence'. Angrily the judge ordered him to be sent back to prison in extra irons. He was soon joined by two other recusants, John Hughes and Robert Morris. In readiness for the Spring Assizes of 1582, they were moved back to Wrexham. When brought to court they found that the judge had engaged a minister to come and preach to them. The three prisoners responded by haranguing the preacher, one in Welsh, one in English and one in Latin, until he gave up.

They next appeared at the Assize at Holt. David Edwards had tried to bribe two other prisoners, Wynne and Thomas, into giving evidence that Richard had been persuading them not to attend church. The plan failed because when Wynne and Thomas were called they told the court it was a lie, and that they had been bribed to give false witness. In May 1583 Richard was sent before the Council of the Marches in company with three other recusants and a Welsh priest, from Flintshire, Father John Bennet, who was born c.1548 and served the chapel at St Winefride's Well, Holywell. Bennet had been ordained at Cambrai on 29 March 1578, one of a group of thirteen ordained that day, immediately before the transfer of Douai College to Rheims. When sent to the Council, all the prisoners were brutally tortured at Bewdley and Ludlow to make them reveal the names and whereabouts of other Catholics. Richard was put in the manacles, that is he was hung up by his wrists to a post while being interrogated.

Despite the agony he refused to reveal anything and only spoke in prayer for himself and his tormentors, which angered the judge. 'There is no more pity to be had on thee than on a mad dog', he retorted, 'Wretches like you should all be hanged'. Richard's answer was, 'I pray you put me to death ... and therein you shall do me greater pleasure than to kill me continually with these tortures', after which he continued to pray in silence.

(When Father Bennet was eventually tried he was not condemned to

The Elizabethan Martyrs, 1577-1601

death. He was later moved to a jail in London and sent into exile in 1585. The following year he joined the Society of Jesus. He returned to Wales and Holywell and ministered for many years before dying of the plague in London on Christmas Day 1625.)

On 9 October 1584 Gwyn, Hughes and Morris were tried for high treason before Sir George Bromley, the Chief Justice of Chester, at Wrexham. No one wished to sit on the jury so a collection of the local anti-Catholic riff-raff had to be paid to do jury service. Richard was accused of reconciling a man called Gronow to the Church, of making up satirical verses against married priests, and for maintaining the papal supremacy. Richard denied ever having met Gronow. John Hughes called in a witness of his own who could testify that the prosecution evidence had been obtained by bribery. The jury were understandably disturbed by this revelation, but the trial continued. It was later shown that the witnesses had indeed been bribed at the instigation of the vicar of Wrexham. As Richard refused to go to church or acknowledge Elizabeth as head of the Church there were plenty of grounds on which to convict him of treason.

The jurymen were clearly unhappy with the evidence they had heard. Sir George threatened them with dire consequences if they did not bring in a guilty verdict and they retired for the night. Unable to reach a decision they sent a delegation to the judge to seek his advice. Whom, they asked, should we convict and whom acquit? So Bromley told them. Next morning the verdicts were announced: Richard and John Hughes were found guilty of treason and Robert Morris discharged; poor Morris wept. Then the judge announced that Hughes was to be reprieved but Richard was to be hanged, drawn and quartered.

Seemingly unperturbed Richard accepted his sentence calmly: 'What is all this? Is it any more than one death?' he asked.

Mrs Gwyn and Mrs Hughes were in court holding their babies. Richard and Hughes had been granted an unauthorised parole by the sympathetic jailer, Coytmore, the result of which was now all too obvious to the authorities who were not best pleased at this breach. The judge admonished the two wives not to follow the bad example of their husbands. Unfazed, Mrs Gwyn responded: 'If it is blood you want, you may take my life as well as my husband's. Fetch the witnesses and give them a little bribe and they will bear evidence against me as well as they did against him'. For thus speaking up the two women were sent to prison for a few days.

Two days before his execution Richard was visited by the sheriff with the offer that if he would accept the Queen as head of the church he would even now go free. The offer was refused. Catherine was allowed to join her husband in jail and the next day he asked her to purchase for him two dozen silk ribbons. These he kissed and asked his wife to distribute to twelve priests. His personal belongings, including his signet ring, he also asked to be sent to close friends as keepsakes. Thursday was the day appointed for the execution and in the morning they caught sight of David Edwards. Catherine shouted after him, 'God be a righteous judge between thee and me'.

Richard gently rebuked her telling her that if they did not now freely forgive him all their sufferings would have been in vain. Shortly afterwards they heard loud weeping and discovered it was the jailer's wife. She and her husband had become fond of Richard and now - perhaps as a punishment, for his earlier act of clemency - Coytmore had been designated as hangman. Richard sent Catherine to comfort Mrs Coytmore before going down into the part of the jail where common thieves were kept to say farewell to them.

As he left the jail a crowd of sympathisers greeted him, many of them in tears, including some of his former pupils. To one young man Richard said: 'Weep not for me, for I do but pay the rent before the rent day'. Someone had sent him five shillings in small pieces of silver, and this he distributed to the poor people. To Catherine, who was carrying their month-old baby son, he gave his rosary and his remaining money, then he kissed her and she knelt for his blessing, all the while being harassed by the sheriff. He was tied to the hurdle and dragged to the market place, all the time saying the rosary using his chains.

It was pouring with rain and when Richard reached the scaffold he remarked: 'God is merciful to us; even the elements shed tears for our sins'. The hangman knelt down to ask his forgiveness which Richard gladly gave him saying, 'I do forgive thee before God and I wish thee no more harm than I wish my own heart'.

The sheriff asked him if he repented of his treason against the Queen: 'I have never committed any treason against her any more than your father or grandfather, unless it be treason to pray', his way of signifying that unlike their forebears it was now treason to be a Catholic. The vicar of Wrexham pressed him whether he acknowledged the Queen to be head of the Church. Richard indicated that he held her to be the lawful Queen, but not head of the Church. He declared, 'Na all fod Vn ffydd onyd y wir Ffydd.' There can be no other Faith than the true faith.

Climbing the ladder, Richard spoke to the crowd: 'My dear countrymen, remember your souls and do not lose them for this vile transitory muck which Christ hath so dearly bought. This is but one hour's pain to me, and what is that in respect of the torments in hell which shall never have an end?'

The hangman was so overcome with emotion that Richard had to help him put the rope around his neck and a handkerchief was tied across his eyes. He asked forgiveness of any whom he had offended. As he was saying 'God be merciful to me a sinner,' he was turned off the ladder. He hung from the rope some considerable time, beating his breast crying, 'Jesus, have mercy on me'. As the crowd called out that he should be allowed to die before dismemberment, the hangman hung onto his legs hoping to hasten the end. When Richard appeared to be insensible he was cut down, but revived as he was being disembowelled. He cried out in Welsh in his pain: 'Holy God, what is this?' His last words before his head was severed were, 'Jesus, have mercy on me'. The Catholic Cathedral of Our Lady of Sorrows, Wrexham, appropriately possesses a relic of Richard Gwyn.

Margaret Clitherow

No coward soul is mine ... I see heaven's glories shine and faith shines equal, arming me from fear.

Last Lines, Emily Bronte, 1818-38

Popularly known as 'the Pearl of York', Margaret was born in Davygate, York in 1553, the year of Queen Mary's accession. She was the second daughter and the youngest child of four of Thomas and Jane Middleton neé Turner. Her older siblings were Thomas, George and Alice. The father of Jane Turner was the successful landlord of the Angel inn and her brother Robert was a priest. The Middletons were a prominent and very prosperous York family. Thomas, who came from Ripon, was a wax chandler and a churchwarden of St Martin's, Coney Street. He later served a term as sheriff of York and was elected to its Privy Council.

For the early years of her life, Margaret would have experienced the Mass and Catholic liturgy, but the full impact of the Elizabethan settlement hit St Martin's in 1561. The high altar and side altars were dismantled and the statues destroyed. Thomas knew 'on which side his bread was buttered' and conformed, at least outwardly. In this he seems to have been following his parish priest, Thomas Grayson, who was also a close friend. In 1567 Grayson was summoned before the

The Elizabethan Martyrs, 1577-1601

Ecclesiastical Commissioners for possessing Catholic books which should have been burned.

Margaret would have seen all around her evidence of the destruction of York's religious heritage. The two beautifully carved shrines of St William in the Minster had been dismantled and the pieces buried. (His stone coffin survived and is still in the Minster crypt.) The great Benedictine abbey of St Mary's, founded 1089, whose church once rivalled the Minster in grandeur, had fallen into ruin, its walled grounds in the possession of the Crown. The former abbot's house, recently much extended, served as the headquarters of the dreaded Council of the North. The abbey's fine library and its boarding school for fifty poor scholars had both long since been lost. The ruins of the infirmary chapel bore testimony to the closure of St Leonard's Hospital, once the largest medieval hospital in the north of England. A quasi-monastic institution permanently staffed by 13 brothers and 8 sisters, it had beds for 206 poor, sick and elderly; it offered convalescent facilities and a refuge for pregnant women and the homeless. It distributed daily alms to the poor and to prisoners in the city and provided an education for 30 choristers. Its dissolution had caused massive unemployment for its large staff and left a gap in the care of the sick and elderly which lasted for centuries. (York did not have another hospital until 1740.) All that remained of the Benedictine Priory of the Holy Trinity - suppressed in 1538 - was the tower and nave, which had survived because it served as a parish church.

Margaret, having been raised in the Established Church, was fourteen when her father Thomas died in May 1567. His true religious feelings may be gathered from his bequest of money to the poor on condition that they prayed for the repose of his soul. He was buried in St Martin's, Coney Street, and his will, written in 1560, and witnessed by Thomas Grayson, clearly reveals his wealth, owning extensive property and land not only in York but also Ripon. He left bequests to his servants and to Margaret he left a silver goblet and six silver spoons as well as his house in Davygate after his widow's death.

Barely four months later, Margaret's mother remarried. Her new husband, Henry May, who came from the South of England, was an ambitious but penniless social climber and a rich widow - even one twenty years his senior - was just what he needed to help him achieve his ambitions. He succeeded insofar as he rose to be Lord Mayor, but proved no friend either to his stepdaughter or the Catholics of York. May soon converted the large house in Davygate into a flourishing inn and as a teenager Margaret was very much involved in its busy social life. His new-found connections soon began to pay off; within months of marrying May was elected a chamberlain of York and was granted trading privileges. He became a churchwarden at St Martin's, with the responsibility of eliminating any remaining traces of Catholicism. This included selling off the chalices and patens, removing the Rood screen and loft and paying for an anti-Catholic pamphlet. In 1570 May became one of the two Sheriffs of York.

As well as being very attractive, Margaret was an intelligent and sharp-witted young woman. On 1 July 1571 at St Martin's, Coney Street, she was married to John Clitherow, son of Richard Clitherow, a former Chamberlain of York. Margaret was John's second wife, his first wife Maud or Matilda Mudd having died, leaving him a widower with two young sons. John was a grazier and butcher by trade, a hard-nosed, ambitious businessman who was the bridgemaster and became a chamberlain of York in 1574 and one of the richest citizens of the city. The Clitherow's home in Christ's parish was in The Shambles, the meat market of York from where John conducted his trade, and they 'lived over the shop'. Margaret was invaluable, helping her husband run his business and we are told how he liked to show off his lovely young wife at York's social gatherings. Their reputed house at No. 36 in the well-preserved medieval street with its overhanging timber-framed houses still stands and is a chapel shrine. John's family remained Catholic, although John, who does not appear to have had any deep religious beliefs, had conformed. His brother, William, born 1542, after working as a lawyer's clerk, became a seminary priest, being ordained at Soissons 9 June 1582. He became a Carthusian monk at Louvain in 1589. John Clitherow in 1572 was asked to participate with his parish officials in enforcing newly issued orders from the Council of the North. These instructions required every person who was an upright citizen to spy upon and report all recusants to the authorities.

In 1574, apparently quite suddenly, Margaret decided to become reconciled to the Catholic Church. Margaret's spiritual director for the last two years of her life was Father John Mush, [16] who clearly admired and revered her for her holiness. 'This golden woman,' he calls her in the emotional biography he wrote in the summer of 1586, *A True Report of the Life and Martyrdom of Mrs Margaret Clitherow*. Mush tells us that 'to her beautiful and gracious soul God gave her a body with comely face and beauty correspondent'. We can forgive him his irascibility, his verboseness and his antipathy towards the Jesuits for leaving us this priceless record of Margaret.

Mush writes that Margaret converted because
she found no substance, truth nor Christian comfort in the ministers of the new church, nor in their doctrine itself, and hearing also many priests and lay

The Elizabethan Martyrs, 1577-1601

people to suffer for the defence of the ancient Catholic Faith.

She knew she was playing with fire and can have been under no illusion about the dangerous step she had taken. She could see persecution all around her in York, where the prisons were constantly full of Catholics, such as Margaret Webster whose own son, Arthur, reported her and her daughter, Frances, his sister, to the Council of the North and they were committed to different prisons. While in jail Frances learned that in the dark dungeon below was a priest, Father John Fingley. She found a little grating which she could open and speak to the priest. Through the grating she passed him a gown to wear to keep out the cold and also serve as a cover to lie on as he had no bed. When her 'crime' was discovered she was moved to York Castle to join her mother, who died there on 27 May 1585. After falling sick, Frances was not long in following her, dying on 29 June. Blessed John Fingley was born at Barmby, near Howden in the East Riding in 1553. He was educated at Cambridge, ordained at Rheims in 1581 and was martyred at York 8 August 1586.

Close to home in Margaret's street and parish there were prominent recusants such as Janet Geldard, another butcher's wife, and the courageous physician Dr Thomas Vavasour and Dorothy his wife. Janet had converted her husband and she and Dorothy were among the first women of York to be imprisoned for recusancy. There were also cousins such as Anne and Agnes Weddell and family friends suffering for their faith. The records of their examinations and the fines imposed before the Lord Mayor and aldermen are extant.

Dorothy Vavasour, wife of Thomas Vavasour, doctor of physic, sayeth she cometh not to the church because her conscience will not serve her to do so ... As for the substance of the same Thomas, we think it little or nothing worth, and he hath no lands.

Janet Geldard, wife of Lancelot Geldard, butcher, says she cometh not to the church, for her conscience will not serve her to do so. And the same Lancelot hath small substance or none to our knowledge.

Agnes Weddell (in prison) wife of John Weddell, butcher, sayeth she cometh not to the church, for her conscience will not serve her, because there is neither altar, priest, nor Sacrifice. The same John sayeth that he is worth in clear goods £3, and so we think.

And so the list goes on, page after page, parish by parish, with millers, tailors, drapers, butchers, milliners, locksmiths, bakers, felt-makers, servants, widows all declaring that as there is no priest and no valid Sacraments they will not go to church; and all being assessed for their worth to decide upon the level of fine to impose. In June 1578 a letter was sent by Hugh Graves, Lord Mayor of York, to the churchwardens of the City instructing them to 'levy of the goods of Thomas Vavasour, William Hutton, Percival Geldard, Lancelot Geldard, John Weddell, John Clitherow' and a list of others named, because their wives 'wilfully absented themselves from their parish church.' For every absence they were to be fined twelve pence.

When Margaret's conversion became known her family were deeply displeased, to put it mildly. What engendered her conversion is unknown: we can only speculate; we will never know. Maybe she was influenced by her Catholic in-laws or perhaps recusant neighbours, such as Mrs Vavasour, introduced her to a seminary priest. Father Mush gives us no clue because writing so contemporaneously with the events he described he had to be very circumspect; but there are a number of possibilities. Margaret may have been taken to visit priests imprisoned in the Ousebridge Kidcote such as Father Henry Comberford, a fellow of St John's College, Cambridge and precentor of Lichfield until deprived by Elizabeth and imprisoned in March 1559. He was freed on bond in 1561 but was rearrested at Sheffield with several other priests at the home of the Dowager Countess of Northumberland. Outspoken on behalf of the papal claims and denial of the Queen's supremacy he spent over sixteen years in jail in York and Hull, greatly angering Archbishop Edwin Sandys by the number of converts he made amongst his fellow prisoners. He died in Hull Blockhouse. Margaret and Mrs Vavasour became good friends. The doctor's wife was an excellent midwife whose home, as well as being a refuge for priests, was a place where women could deliver their babies in safety. Often several women were summoned to help with a confinement, and this served as an excellent cover, when necessary, for Margaret and others to meet together to receive the Sacraments from a visiting priest without arousing suspicion.

Margaret possessed great tranquillity of soul and humility. 'In her own eyes she thought herself nobody but an unprofitable servant to God and man.' As became her social status, she had servants; but 'there was nothing to be done in the house so base that she would not be most ready to do or take in hand herself'. She would not disdain to make the fire or sweep the house or wash the dishes. 'God forbid,' she would say, 'that I should will any to do that in my house which I would not willingly do myself first'. Yet she could be demanding of her servants who she sometimes sharply corrected if any were slacking or negligent. Father Mush wondered how she dared do this when they could put her in great danger if, taking offence, they revealed her activities to the authorities. 'God defend', said Margaret, 'that for my Christian liberty

The Elizabethan Martyrs, 1577-1601

in serving Him in my house I should neglect my duty to my servants, or not correct them as they deserve.' But she need have no anxiety because her servants loved her. Margaret had a highly developed sensitive conscience, and Father Mush records that after hearing her confession of her small imperfections he was 'cast into some extraordinary sense of joy of mind' and always felt humbled and more conscious of his own sins and failings, hoping to 'emulate some little part of that virtue and purity' with which she was endowed.

John and Margaret seem to have had a happy marriage, despite the fact that over the next ten years she was in and out of jail many times. John once said that Margaret had only two faults: she fasted too much and would not accompany him to church. In fact, she kept a strict fast every Friday. And Margaret declared that she loved her husband next only to God. In spite of her worldly responsibilities she found time to lead a very devout life. Every morning she would spend over an hour in prayer and meditation on her knees in her room, after which she would attend Mass in the secret chamber if a priest was in the house.

The priest's chamber was actually a room in her neighbour's house which she had hired, and it was connected to Margaret's attic. The concealed exit enabling the priest to escape without detection led through the neighbour's property. Who had the skill to carry out the work is unknown; it had to be constructed in great secrecy - presumably without the knowledge of John Clitherow. This may have been possible because the neighbour's on one side were John's sister and her husband, Millicent and William Calvert; on the other side were relatives of John's first wife, Michael Mudd and his wife, all of whom were Catholics. Margaret would again devote time to prayer after completing the day's household duties late in the evening. She was also much engaged in charitable work, frequently visiting the jails to bring material comfort to the poor prisoners.

Margaret's home became one of the chief secret Mass centres of York. Her easy-going husband seems to have turned a blind eye to her activities, although he must surely have known what was going on in his own house. However, at no time in his life does he seem to have felt any desire to become a Catholic, although Margaret declared how much it grieved her heart that he would not convert. As well as being a good wife and a loving if rather strict mother, it was said of Margaret that 'everyone loved her and would run to her for help, comfort and counsel in distress'.

Margaret was always kind and charitable towards her neighbours who regarded her as a 'jewel' in their midst. It is a testament to her goodness and popularity that none of her Protestant neighbours, who

241

were well aware of what was going on under their noses, ever betrayed her. Indeed, she enjoyed such good will amongst her neighbours that they would warn her of any likely danger. Margaret's prudence and 'discretion was marvellous,' but the only criticism that Father Mush makes of her is that in her fervent desire to serve God and the Church she tended to 'adventure more than in these ungracious times' was wise. It greatly concerned him that she let her children and their schoolmates into the secrets of the house, including the location of the priest's chamber. Yet he declares he dare not condemn her for this indiscretion because her intention was sincere and good.

In 1576 a crackdown was ordered on the recusants of York. As an active Catholic, Margaret was soon in trouble, and by June of that year her name appears for the first time in the lists of recusants, where she was described as heavily pregnant. On 2 August 1577 Margaret and John were summoned before Archbishop Edwin Sandys and the Ecclesiastical Commissioners. This resulted in John being imprisoned in the Kidcote for three days for refusing to pay more fines, although he promised to try and persuade his wife to attend church.

Margaret refused to consider the idea and was sent to York Castle in the company of several other women, including Anne Weddell and Janet Geldard, who were judged to be particularly dangerous for the influence they might have on others. The great numbers of Catholics in York Castle formed a real community. The priest prisoners were sometimes able to hear confessions and say Mass and Margaret had many opportunities to nurture her spiritual life. 'The prison she accounted a most happy and profitable school,' and it was while in prison that she learned to read. As a result she came to know Thomas à Kempis's *Imitation of Christ* and later the Douai-Rheims New Testament which was her delight when she had leisure time for reading. She was released in February 1578 but ordered to present herself at the Castle on 8 April. She duly reported and was sent home to be confined to her house except for attending church; for every non-appearance John was to be fined two shillings. Needless to say, Margaret had no intention of attending the Protestant church and appeared before the Ecclesiastical Commissioners on 3 October 1580. When she refused to take the oath she was committed a close prisoner to the Castle. She was freed on 24 April 1581 in order to give birth, on condition that six weeks later she returned to jail. She must have been bitterly disappointed to learn that while in prison she had missed the opportunity of meeting Father Edmund Campion, who had celebrated Mass at the home of the Vavasours.

Henry May became an Alderman and Justice of the Peace in March

The Elizabethan Martyrs, 1577-1601

1581. He could have tried to protect Margaret but he did just the opposite. His attitude to Catholics may be gauged from two events. Early in 1581 he had presented to the Ecclesiastical Commission a list of the names of twenty-five recusants. It must have been galling for Margaret to learn that on the Feast of the Assumption 1581 he took part in the raid on Dr Thomas Vavasour's house in Christ's parish and arrested him at Mass with his wife and daughters, the old Marian priest, Father William Wilkinson, and eleven others including William Hutton, a draper, who also lived in Christ's parish, and his wife Mary. Father Wilkinson was dragged through the streets of York still wearing his vestments while being mocked and spat upon. The whole group was committed to the New Counter prison at Ousebridge.

There is a York Council record of February 1583 complaining that the children of the Hutton's - still imprisoned in the Kidcote - were free to carry messages between their parents and 'all such prisoners as there are for religion.' As a result, the children, who were examined and threatened by the magistrates, were denied all access to their father and ordered to be locked up with their mother because there was nowhere else for them to go. William Hutton left a detailed account of the sufferings of the prisoners in York, as well as a memoir of Margaret Clitherow. After a long painful illness Dr Vavasour died a prisoner at Hull Blockhouse on 12 May 1585 and was buried at Drypoole, within the garrison walls of Hull. His wife Dorothy had been moved to the Lower Kidcote in 1587 but was so ill that she was returned to the New Counter where she died on 26 October 1587, the day after the death of Mary Hutton. Along with another recusant prisoner, Alice Oldcorne, whose husband, Thomas, was in prison at Hull, the women were buried together without any ceremony at Toft Green, a common near Micklegate Bar. The Vavasour's son, James, who was born in 1561, studied at Douai and Rheims. In 1581 he was sent to Rome. He was ordained at the Lateran 7 September 1586 and afterwards returned to Rheims. He never came back to England but was occupied as a theology teacher at Rheims from January 1589. While the college was making preparations for the move back to Douai in 1593, James was named as Vice-President at Rheims but died within days of his appointment on 6 July. There is a report from the Lord Mayor to the Earl of Huntingdon in 1593 that Peter Hutton, son of William, who was still alive, had gone abroad to be educated. Peter, who was born 1573, arrived at Rheims in January 1589. He was sent to the college at Eu, Normandy, for further studies but was captured en route and served two years in prison. He finally made it to Eu and in 1593 he went to Valladolid and to Seville the following year. What subsequently happened to him is unknown. His brother, John, also escaped abroad and arrived at Valladolid in 1598. He was one of the students who ran away to join the Benedictines with St John Roberts. John Hutton was professed at Santiago de Compostela as Brother John of St Thomas.

In August 1582 Margaret was convicted of recusancy at the Quarter Sessions. Convicted again in early March 1583 she was sent to the Castle and was released on bond for two months in May 1584, but must have returned to prison because she was released on bond that autumn. On each occasion it was John who was summoned to pay the recently increased heavy fines and put up the large amounts demanded in bond money. The terms of these bonds meant that for long periods she was confined to her own house.

Some time in 1584 Margaret took a great risk by sending her eldest son Henry to Douai to be educated and hopefully train for the priesthood. What her husband thought of this when he found out is not recorded. In spite of his mercenary pre-occupation with accumulating wealth and getting on in the world he was an indulgent husband. Margaret, aware that she was being closely watched, had to be extra careful. In addition to Henry, born 1572 and named after his godfather Henry May, she had three other children: Anne, born 1574; a second daughter whose name is unknown and a second son (John?), probably the child born in 1581. From the generous allowance given to her by her husband, Margaret committed the criminal offence of paying for a private Catholic schoolmaster for her own children and those of her neighbours. He was a former prisoner whom she had met in York Castle and when he managed to escape after seven years incarceration she hid him in her house. Priests were also constantly sheltered in her home; just how many priests we will never know. Margaret provided beautiful vestments for them, the finest altar linen and sacred vessels.

Father Mush informs us that many of the priests who suffered martyrdom at York had passed through Margaret's house. They included William Lacey, [17] Richard Kirkman, [18] James Thompson, [19] William Hart, [20] Richard Thirkeld [21] and Francis Ingleby. [22] Margaret would often recall with joy the conversations she had with these holy priests and the spiritual profit she had derived from them. We learn that when her husband was away on business it was her practice to go boldly barefooted to visit the York Tyburn at the Knavesmire to pray. This was the hallowed place where forty-nine Catholic martyrs were executed; so many that it was only surpassed by the London Tyburn. The Knavesmire was, and still is, a marshy area to the south-west of the city, outside its historic walls. It was a place of public executions since 1379. Today a large part of the Knavesmire is occupied by York

244

The Elizabethan Martyrs, 1577-1601

Racecourse.

In March 1585 the Act was passed making it an offence punishable by death to receive a Catholic priest. Margaret's Catholic friends begged her not to offer priests hospitality any more. Being such an audacious Catholic she was rather shocked by this pusillanimous attitude. Her answer was that 'I will not be afraid to serve God and do well. If God's priests dare to venture to my house I will never refuse them'.

Following the death of her mother in June 1585 she inherited the inn at Davygate. Although Henry May now possessed property of his own, he must have been aggrieved at being deprived of the inn by his recalcitrant stepdaughter. She may well have used the property as a Catholic centre. In February 1586 Henry May remarried in a splendid ceremony, having by then achieved the summit of his ambitions by becoming Lord Mayor. Margaret did not attend the wedding. One can imagine the scandalous gossip in the city when the Lord Mayor's recusant stepdaughter was arrested.

The Council of the North set about implementing the 1585 Act in earnest and raids on the homes of recusants were carried out. Blessed Marmaduke Bowes, who lived at Ingram Grange, near Welbury in the North Riding, was a married gentleman of substance. To safeguard his property he had occasionally attended the Protestant church, but he employed a Catholic schoolmaster for his children. While travelling one day the schoolmaster was apprehended by John Barnes, brother of Richard Barnes, Bishop of Durham. Under torture, the schoolmaster accused many Catholics, including Marmaduke, of harbouring priests; in particular the Durham-born priest, Blessed Hugh Taylor. Father Taylor, born c.1560, had been ordained at Soissons in June 1584. Soon after returning home he was apprehended and tried at York on Friday, 25 November 1585. The next morning he was hanged, drawn and quartered, and on the following day, the 27th, Mr Bowes, who had been summoned before Lord Eure and members of the Council, was hanged: the first execution under the new Act for harbouring a priest. In the same week, over twenty 'old priests' and six seminary priests held prisoner in York and Hull were permanently banished to the Continent. And another twenty-two lay people were arrested and imprisoned for harbouring.

On 10 March 1586 John Clitherow was summoned for a second time before Lord Eure and others to explain his missing son's whereabouts. His explanations proving unsatisfactory, he was arrested and confined to York Castle. While he was absent his house was raided and thoroughly searched by the two sheriffs and their constables

245

looking for Father Francis Ingleby. What part Henry May played in his step-daughter's arrest is unclear but he must surely have had a hand in it considering what a huge embarrassment she must have been to him and to the civic authorities. Margaret was at home and although Mass had been celebrated that morning no priest was found. He had safely exited via the small door, an awkward task because it was only 'large enough for a boy', and made his escape through the house next door.

Mr Stapleton, the schoolmaster, knowing that he too was in danger, remained with his pupils locked in an attic room. When he was discovered the searcher, armed with a sword, assumed he was a priest, and while he was calling for reinforcements Stapleton managed to get away through the priest's chamber into the neighbour's house, which left only the children to face the interrogators. The searchers had still not discovered the secret entrance into the priest's chamber and despite the bullying tactics they were unable to extract anything incriminating from the servants or the children. Among them was a Flemish boy aged about ten years old who, stripped naked and threatened with a whipping, revealed to them the priest's chamber where vestments and altar utensils were discovered.

That was proof enough; Margaret was arrested and her servants and the children were sent to various prisons. She never saw her children again. Brought before Lord Eure and members of the Council of the North, she was questioned for hours but maintained her composure and conceded nothing. About 7 p.m. in the evening she was imprisoned in York Castle. The poor Flemish boy had by then named Father Ingleby and Father Mush and supplied the names of those who attended Mass in the Shambles, among them Mrs Anne Tesh, who was also arrested and sent to the Castle where she and Margaret occupied the same chamber over the weekend. Anne was the wife of Edward Tesh, gentleman, who had been hauled before the authorities in York for non-attendance at church. At the time of Anne's arrest Edward was in London and the Commissioners assessed him as worth £5. Mrs Tesh was tried before Mr Justice Francis Rodes (or Rhodes), who abused her most shockingly and accused her of sheltering priests. 'Find her guilty!', was his angry instruction to the jury. John Clitherow was still in detention and was brought to see Margaret in the hope that he would persuade her to recant. If that was the object it did not succeed. It was to be John and Margaret's last meeting.

On the afternoon of 14 March 1586 Margaret was arraigned at the Common Hall, charged specifically with sheltering Francis Ingleby, the charge being brought under the Act against 'Jesuits and Seminary priests'. John Clench (or Clinch) and Francis Rodes, two Assize judges, presided, accompanied by members of the Council of the North, watched by Lord Mayor Henry May. When asked how she pleaded, guilty or not guilty, Margaret answered that she knew of no offence which she had committed requiring her to plead one way or the other. The judge insisted that she had maintained enemies of Her Majesty, to which Margaret forthrightly responded that she had never harboured traitors. Moving on, the judge then asked her, as required by law, how she would be tried, anticipating the stock answer, by the country; meaning by a jury. Instead Margaret replied, 'Having made no offence, I need no trial,' and despite all the attempts of the judge she refused to plead. The most she would concede was 'If you say I have offended and must be tried, I will be tried by none but God and your own consciences'.

Even by the standards of Elizabethan courts of law, what followed was deeply offensive. The vestments taken from Margaret's house were brought into court, two men dressed themselves in them and holding up the altar wafers and chalices lampooned the actions of the priest at Mass in a sacrilegious travesty. Asked how she liked the vestments, Margaret answered that she liked them well enough if they had been on the backs of those that were fit to use them in God's honour, as they were intended. Every means was used to persuade her to plead but she resolutely refused.

Father Mush relates that later Margaret privately explained her reasons. Her refusal to plead, and thereby avoid a trial, was to save the jurymen, several of whom were known to her, from being complicit in her condemnation; her in-laws, friends, servants and neighbours from incriminating themselves; and she from incriminating them, and above all her children, from having to give evidence against her - or if they did so, from perjuring themselves in order to save her. 'If I had put myself to the country evidence must needs have come against me which I know none could give but only my children and servants. It would have been more grievous to me than a thousand deaths if I should have seen any of them brought forth before me to give evidence against me'. Losing patience the judges reminded her that the law imposed a terrible penalty for refusing to plead. 'God's will be done. I think I may suffer any death for this good cause'.

Yet it is doubtful if Margaret fully understood at this stage just what the penalty for refusing to plead involved. The law demanded that such a person be crushed to death; the *peine forte et dure*.

Accompanied by a troop of men with halberds, Margaret, smiling and serene, was taken from the Common Hall. The judges ordered that she be detained overnight at the New Counter Prison on Ousebridge, known as John Trewe's house. John Trewe was a shoemaker who owned chambers on Ousebridge which were used as a private jail. Prisoners in the Kidcote could transfer there provided they paid enough. From his profits Trewe paid a surety to the mayor and sheriffs of York. By the time Margaret was held there the tenancy of the prison had been acquired by Christopher Fordam who paid an annual fee of £13.6s.8d to the York corporation. Here Margaret was locked up in a close parlour with a Protestant couple, Mr and Mrs Yoward, who were in prison for debt. That evening Margaret was visited by Giles Wigginton, a Puritan minister, but Margaret sent him rather curtly away having no wish to converse with him. To counteract the sympathy that the city had for Margaret, the Council spread vile slanders accusing her of having adulterous relationships with the priests she sheltered. Council member Hurleston called out in court that 'it was not for religion that thou harbourest priests but for harlotries.' 'God forgive you for these forged tales', was Margaret's response.

At 8 a.m. the following morning she was taken back to court and asked yet again if she would plead and be tried, bearing in mind that the only real evidence against her was the word of one small boy.

'Indeed, I think you have no witness against me but children, which with an apple and a rod you can make to say what you will,' was her somewhat sardonic reply. Margaret then engaged in an argument with the judges about the true purpose of the seminary priests. 'I know no cause why I should refuse them as long as I live. They come only to do good to me and others,' she declared. 'I know them for virtuous men sent by God'.

Mr Justice Clench *again reminded her of the punishment that she faced. Mr Wigginton was present in the court and he shouted out, 'You sit here to do justice; this woman's case is a matter of life and death: you ought not, either by God's law or man's, judge her to die upon the slender witness of a boy, unless you have two or three men of good credit to also give evidence against her.' Angry at the interruption Judge Clench retorted: 'I may do it by law.' At which Mr Wigginton asked, 'By what law?'

By the Queen's law,' came the answer, to which Wigginton responded, 'That may well be, but you cannot do it by God's law.' Mr Justice Rodes was a coarse man who seems to have resented and felt

---

* John Clench was born in Essex, but his grandfather came from Leeds, Yorkshire. He worked mainly in the northern circuit and the bulk of the criminal cases he tried consisted of ecclesiastical recusancy. He is said to have been a special favourite of Queen Elizabeth's but does not appear to have been knighted, although he is often given the title 'Sir'. He died in 1607.

The Elizabethan Martyrs, 1577-1601

intimidated by the presence of members of the Council of the North sitting with him on the bench. He angrily asked why the court was wasting its time with such a wilful woman and demanded that sentence be passed. Clench, who clearly was anxious to spare her, even now delayed and once again urged Margaret to plead; but to no avail, and in the end he was overruled by the members of the Council present and pronounced the dreadful sentence.

This came as a shock to Margaret, especially the knowledge that she would be stripped naked, but she retained her composure saying, 'If this judgement be according to your conscience, I pray God send you a better judgement before Him. I thank God heartily for this.'

Even after pronouncing sentence Clench said it was still not too late for her to save her life by agreeing to plead. He asked her to think of her husband and children and not needlessly throw her life away.

'I would to God that my husband might suffer with me for such a good cause', was her response. In spite of the judge's urging, Margaret remained resolute. 'Whatever God sends shall be welcome to me. I am not worthy of so good a death as this.'

So with her arms bound and with a smiling countenance, she was escorted back to prison. When the news of Margaret's condemnation was broken to John Clitherow, he suffered a profuse nosebleed, broke down and wept violently like a man out of his wits. 'Let them take all I have and save her for she is the best wife in all England.'

As the judge had ordered a delay in carrying out the sentence, for the remaining ten days of her life Margaret was confined in the prison on the bridge. During this time Sir Thomas Fairfax and other members of the Council came to urge her to go to church with them. They told her that Father Henry Comberford had renounced his faith before his death. (Why would they do this unless they believed this was indeed the priest who had reconciled her to the Church?) Then they claimed that Father William Hart had declared it was lawful for unlearned women to attend church. 'Father Hart would not say such a thing and if he had said it I would not have believed him. This is not the first lie that has been made of dead men, which are not here to answer, but such talk as this will get you small credit,' was Margaret's rejoinder. Protestant ministers were then sent to harangue and pester her incessantly in an effort to convert her. Margaret's answer to them was, 'I am fully resolved in all things touching my faith, which I ground upon Jesus Christ and by Him I steadfastly believe to be saved, which faith I acknowledge to be the same that He left to His Apostles and they to their successors ... and is taught in the Catholic Church throughout Christendom, and promised to remain with her unto the world's end ... and by God's assistance I mean to live and die in the same faith, for if an angel came from heaven and preached any other doctrine than we have received the Apostle biddeth us not to believe him. Therefore if I should follow your doctrine I would disobey the Apostle's commandment. Wherefore I pray you, take this for an answer and trouble me no more for my conscience.'

The only one she received kindly was Mr Wigginton, who visited her twice; they discussed their religious differences at great length, but the minister went away regretting that he had been unable to persuade Margaret.

Some of her friends and relations tried to obtain a stay of execution by claiming that she was pregnant. Margaret herself was questioned on the subject, but she could only answer that it was possible but if so only in the very early stages. Mr Justice Clench asked that the claim be investigated, as he was not prepared to sanction her execution and be responsible for the death of an unborn infant if it was true.

'You are too merciful, Brother Clench,' said Mr Justice Rodes, urging that Margaret had to be executed regardless. * None of this cut much ice with Council member Hurleston who insisted to Clench that even if she were pregnant she still had to die, if only to make of her an example to others who might be tempted to flout the law.

Margaret was also visited by her stepfather, Henry May, who with 'a great show of sorrow and affection' claimed he could use his influence to obtain a pardon for her if she would renounce her Catholicism. He then asked Margaret to give him custody of her daughter, Anne, which she refused. Having thus been rebuffed Henry made his real, unsympathetic feelings plain, accusing her of immorality and courting suicide; later he tried to blacken her memory.

She was urged to confess that she had offended her husband. 'If I have offended my husband in anything but for my conscience, I ask God and him forgiveness,' she replied. 'I beseech you let me speak with him before I die,' she begged; but her request to meet John having been refused, she knew she would never see him again. Margaret realised that her death would not be long delayed when she learned that

---

* Cambridge educated Sir Francis Rodes came from an ancient family. He was called to the Bar in 1552 and made a fortune from his legal practice. In 1582 he was made Queen's Serjeant. Raised to the bench in 1585, in 1586 he took part in the trial of Mary, Queen of Scots at Fotheringhay. His principal seat was in Derbyshire where he engaged Robert Smythson to build the palatial Barlborough Hall, near Chesterfield. He died 1588. By one of those delicious ironies of history the Hall became a Jesuit-run Catholic school in 1939. It is now a co-educational Preparatory School and the names of the houses are those of Jesuit saints Campion, Loyola and Xavier.

The Elizabethan Martyrs, 1577-1601

her husband had been released from prison and banished from York for five days until after her execution had taken place.

From Father Mush's biography we know a great deal about her final days in prison. On Tuesday she was informed by the sheriffs that she was to die on Friday. After they had left she admitted, 'Now I feel the frailty of mine own flesh, which trembleth at these news, although my spirit greatly rejoiceth. Therefore for God's sake pray for me and desire all good folks to do the same.'

She then began a strict fast. She also got someone to obtain some white linen and with it she made a short, loose-fitting habit 'like to an alb' to wear for her execution. Father Mush's account of Margaret's last hours in prison was taken from the details given to him by Mrs Yoward, the Protestant lady imprisoned for debt, who befriended Margaret and spent the last night with her to keep her company. Margaret was clearly very disturbed and could not rest. She asked her fellow prisoner to see her die. Mrs Yoward said she would not see her die such a cruel death for all York but she would 'procure some friends to lay weights on you that you may be quickly despatched from your pain.' Margaret replied, 'No, good Mrs Yoward. God defend that I should procure any to be guilty of my death and blood.' She spent a long time kneeling in prayer, needing to summon up all her strength and courage to face her ordeal. At midnight she undressed and put on the linen habit and continued praying until 3 a.m. before finally going to bed. She left her hat for her husband as a sign of her loving duty to him as to her head. To her daughter, Anne, she sent her shoes hoping that she would serve God and follow in her mother's steps.

Margaret rose by 6 a.m. to prepare herself. At 8 a.m. on the morning of Friday, 25 March 1586, the Feast of the Annunciation, Roland Fawcet, the Sheriff of York, came to lead the thirty-three-year-old, barefooted, bareheaded Margaret from the Ousebridge prison to the Tollbooth for her execution. Carrying her linen garment over her arm, she appeared smiling and cheerful and spoke of going to her marriage. It was only six or seven yards' distance to the Tollbooth and as she walked across the crowded street she gave out alms. Entering the Tollbooth, she knelt and prayed for the Church, the Pope and the Queen 'that God turn her to the Catholic Faith and that after this life she may receive the joys of heaven. For I wish as much good to her majesty's soul as to mine own.'

The Protestant ministers continued to pester her and announced they would pray with her. In common with other martyrs, Margaret replied, 'I will not pray with you, nor shall you pray with me: neither will I say amen to your prayers, nor you to mine.'

The Elizabethan Martyrs, 1577-1601

In our so-called more enlightened, ecumenical age on the face of it this sounds harsh; but in the circumstances of the time, when Catholics and their Church were literally fighting for survival amidst bloody persecution from the Protestant Establishment, it is not to be wondered at. William Gibson, the Under-Sheriff of York, was deeply distressed and stood weeping by the doorway. When the Sheriff himself remarked, 'Remember Mrs Clitherow, you die for treason,' Margaret replied in a loud voice, 'No, Master Sheriff I die for the love of my Lord Jesus.'

The sentence was that she be stripped naked, laid down with a large, sharp stone placed under her back and weights placed upon her until she was crushed to death. Margaret was very distressed about being stripped in front of everyone and begged on her knees that it be omitted. This request was refused, the Sheriff insisting that she must die naked, exactly as she had been sentenced. The four women friends accompanying her gathered around to shield her. When they had undressed her she quickly lay down naked, her face covered by a handkerchief and the linen habit was placed over her as far as it would reach. A door was placed on top of her and in these last moments, with death imminent, Margaret experienced a very human fear. She firstly clasped her hands tightly in front of her face and then over the door but the sheriff told her that she must have her hands bound so they were pulled apart and her arms were stretched out in the form of a cross and her wrists tied to stakes in the ground. Weights were then placed on the door. As she felt the weights pressing down on her she cried out, 'Jesu! Jesu! Jesu! have mercy on me!'

These were her last words. The weights they piled on her were so great - about 800 pounds - that her ribs burst out through her skin. For a quarter of an hour she moaned in agony and then all was quiet. It was 9 a.m. and Margaret Clitherow's crushed body was left in the press until 3 p.m that afternoon.

By order of the sheriffs, Margaret was buried in secrecy at night beside a dunghill; 'a filthy place', as a contemporary chronicler describes it. It is reported that Father Mush was able to discover the place and six weeks later he and others exhumed the remains, which although broken and bruised showed no sign of corruption. Two weeks later he had the remains re-buried, far away from York. Where that was is unknown, but Margaret's right hand is preserved in a reliquary over the altar at St Mary's, the Bar Convent, York. It is the only relic to have survived.

Father Mush tells us that the next day 'the heretics railed against her from their pulpits with shameful lies and slanders'. He concludes his

The Elizabethan Martyrs, 1577-1601

True Report of Margaret as follows:

But now, O sacred martyr, letting go thy enemies, I turn to thee. Remember me, I beseech thy perfect charity, whom thou hast left miserable behind thee, in times past thy unworthy Father, and now thy most unworthy servant, made ever joyful by thy virtuous life, and comfortable by lamenting thy death, lamenting thy absence, and yet rejoicing in thy glory ... I was not so able to help thee as thou art now to procure mercy and grace for me; for thou art now all washed in thy sacred blood from all spots of frailty, securely possessing God Himself ... Be not wanting, therefore, my glorious mother, in the perfection of thy charity, which was not little towards me in thy mortality, to obtain mercy and procure the plenties of such graces for me, thy miserable son, as thou knowest to be most needful for me, and acceptable in the sight of our Lord, which hath thus glorified thee; that I may honour Him by imitation of thy happy life, and by any death which he will give me, to be a partaker with thee and all holy saints of His kingdom.

After Margaret's death John Clitherow married for a third time. In 1603 he was described as one 'of the best citizens and inhabitants of this city' and he was provided at public expense with a 'comely gown' in which to welcome King James I when he passed through York. Margaret's two eldest children remained faithful. Henry was educated at the English Colleges at Rheims and Rome. In 1592 he joined the Capuchin Franciscans but later transferred to the Dominican Order and died at Viterbo, Italy. There is no record of his ever being ordained. Anne was twelve years old at the time of her mother's martyrdom. As a teenager she left home and at the age of eighteen or nineteen she suffered imprisonment at Lancaster in July 1593 for refusing to conform. Her father asked Robert Askwith, Lord Mayor of York, to write on his behalf to the Earl of Derby to obtain his daughter's release. She made her way to the Continent and became a nun of the order of Augustinian Canonesses at St Ursula's, Louvain in 1596. A contemporary of Mother Margaret Clement, Anne died there 3 August 1622, bequeathing to her order her copy of Father Mush's *True Report*. If John Clitherow was Margaret's second son, as seems likely, he too was a butcher. He died in 1614. He married and had three children, the youngest of whom, another John, was still living at the Shambles in 1628.

Margaret must have had a lasting influence on her two stepsons - the children of John Clitherow and his first wife Maud - who were also constant. Thomas, the youngest, suffered in York Castle and died a prisoner for religion at Hull in 1603. William, his brother, often mistakenly referred to as Margaret's son instead of stepson, visited his half-sister Anne at Louvain before entering Douai in 1604. Ordained

22 March 1604 and sent to England in July 1608, William ministered in Yorkshire and was first arrested in 1610. Amazingly, his uncle, James Mudd, in 1611 left £200 for the mayor of York to provide an annuity of £20 for William. In 1618 he was a prisoner in York Castle and again in 1621 and 1624. He died in 1636 and was said to be seventy-three years of age. There seems every reason to believe that the Brian Stapleton of York who arrived at Rheims in 1586 and was ordained priest in 1589 was none other than the schoolmaster engaged by Margaret. He returned to England and was ministering in the north in 1593.

Mrs Anne Tesh was constantly in and out of prison for recusancy and hearing Mass. She told the Commissioners that her conscience would not allow her to attend church because 'there is neither priest, altar, nor sacrament'. In 1596, together with another of Margaret's friends, Mrs Bridget Maskew, she was sentenced to be burned to death, the penalty for women convicted of treason. Bridget was the wife of Thomas Maskew, merchant to the sheriffs of York. In 1592, along with several others, she had been committed by John Piers, Archbishop of York, to Ousebridge prison. Condemned with the two women were three laymen, Blessed George Errington, Blessed William Knight and Blessed William Gibson, 23 who were hanged, drawn and quartered at York on 29 November. Anne and Bridget were reprieved, their sentence being commuted to life imprisonment. They remained in York Castle until the end of the reign, being brought out on occasions and taken forcibly to listen to Protestant sermons.

Margaret Ward

The martyr does not see the hooting throng. Their eyes are fixed on the eternities.

Benjamin N Cardozo, 1870-1938

Our second Margaret reputedly came from a gentleman's family at Congleton in Cheshire. Beyond that we know nothing of her early life. At a young age she went into service in London as maid/companion to a well-to-do Catholic lady, Mrs Whittle, who often sheltered priests. It was presumably this involvement that led to the exploit for which Margaret is principally known: her part in the escape of the priest William Watson from the Bridewell Prison. In retrospect it is to be regretted that Margaret forfeited her life helping a priest so unworthy of her as Watson. It was, perhaps, a blessing that she did not live to see his subsequent ignominious career, although charity requires us to accord him a measure of sympathy if he was suffering from some form of mental illness.

The Bridewell, situated by the Fleet River, had started life as one of Henry VIII's palaces. It was a rambling brick edifice built around three courtyards and was the scene of many famous historical occurrences. Under Edward VI it became a reception centre for vagrants and orphans. In 1556 the City of London took it over and turned it into a prison. Flogging was a regular feature of Bridewell's function, and public flogging sessions took place twice a week.

Father Watson unfortunately seems to have had few attractive characteristics. Born in Durham in 1558, he had a violent streak, manifested in his vituperative and vociferous calumnies against the Jesuits. Even the autobiography he wrote in 1598 is highly suspect, as it is so full of inconsistencies and lies. For example, he claimed to have studied at Oxford, when in truth he was there in the capacity of servant to a future martyr, St John Boste. Ordained at Laon 4 April 1586, he returned to England that year. A few months later he was captured and served about five months in the Marshalsea. He obtained his freedom by agreeing to attend the Established Church. According to his account he had been released pending banishment but was re-taken after abjuring his apostasy.

He was committed to the Bridewell, kept in terrible conditions and inhumanely treated by Richard Topcliffe; at least that part is not difficult to believe. He was later moved to a cell high up in the building but got no peace from wearisome, pestering Protestants anxious to get him to apostatise once more. As a result he was said to be suffering greatly, and in his mentally unstable condition in need of help and support. Whether this was a naturally occurring deterioration or had been brought on by his treatment we cannot know.

Margaret, obviously a girl of spirit and courage, resolved to help him. By making friends with the jailer's wife she succeeded, after much difficulty, in obtaining permission to visit the priest. At first she was carefully watched and searched on entering and leaving the prison and was only allowed to speak to the priest in the jailer's presence. But in time the jailer's vigilance gradually relaxed and Margaret, in addition to comforting the priest, managed to smuggle in various items, one of them a rope concealed under a basket of food. In the meantime she had arranged with an Irish waterman, John Roche, alias Neale, to procure a boat and to wait below the prison wall in the early hours of the next morning. The priest was confined in a cell on the top floor of the prison. At the appointed time, Father Watson let himself down by the rope, but it was either not long enough or he had not tied it correctly because he had to jump the remaining distance, badly injuring himself in the fall. John Roche, waiting below helped the priest get away and exchanged clothes with him. As the rope was left hanging from the window the jailer immediately guessed that Margaret was responsible and the following morning she and John Roche were arrested.

There could not have been a more fateful time for a Catholic to fall into the hands of the authorities. The Spanish Armada had sailed in May 1588 and finally appeared off the Cornish coast in late July. A great many myths have been perpetuated by the British about the Armada. Its main purpose was to punish England for encouraging its privateers to attack Spanish treasure ships and colonies in the New World and for sending troops to support the Dutch rebels: an action that was tantamount to an act of war on Spain by England. As a by-product it was also hoped that it would curtail or even reverse the Protestant ascendancy in England.

With the aim of achieving all these objectives, an army from the Spanish Netherlands was to affect a landing in south-east England. Pope Sixtus V Perretti (1585-1590) supported the Spanish expedition and promised a large papal subsidy if a landing was successful. As matters turned out, it was the atrocious weather as much as English and Dutch naval action that saved England from invasion. The English nonetheless hailed it as a great victory, claiming it showed that God, who had blown His Protestant winds to scatter the Spanish fleet, was on their side. An ungrateful Elizabeth left hundreds of English sailors to die of hunger and the typhus that ravaged the fleet. Lord Admiral Howard of Effingham spoke of his grief to see them die so miserably, some in the streets. He used his own money to clothe and feed the discharged sailors. The other victims who suffered most horrendously as a consequence of His Catholic Majesty Philip II's projected invasion were the English Catholics.

The Armada was either still in the English Channel or seeking a way of escape sailing around Scotland when Margaret Ward was arrested. She was treated with incredible brutality, kept in heavy irons for eight days and severely flogged. She was hung up by the wrists for hours, the tips of her toes barely touching the ground. As a result of this ill-treatment she was crippled and partially paralysed. She and John Roche were taken to the Old Bailey for trial on 26 August. She admitted that she had helped Father Watson escape, but in spite of threats of more torture she resolutely refused to disclose his whereabouts. Directed to ask the Queen's pardon she declined on the grounds that she had not committed any offence against her. In the face of such danger Margaret

The Elizabethan Martyrs, 1577-1601

boldly told the court that never in her life had she done anything which she less regretted than rescuing Father Watson from the hands of bloodthirsty wolves. She declared that if the Queen was a woman of any compassion she would understand. Both she and John Roche were promised their freedom if they would conform to the Established Church. They expressed their position very clearly: it was not lawful for them as Catholics to do so. Margaret said she was prepared to lay down many lives if she possessed them rather than go against her conscientious beliefs, thereby offending God and His Church. John declared he had done nothing to offend the Queen but it was against his conscience to attend her church William Fleetwood, the Recorder of London, was reluctant to condemn Margaret to death but he was undermined by Justice Richard Young who had intimidated the jury into finding her guilty. Margaret and John were sentenced to be hanged for rescuing Watson. Fleetwood, either from disgust or an attempt to salve his conscience, made representations to the Queen about Margaret and urged that women should not be subjected to such barbarous treatment.

With the country in ferment following the threat of the Armada, the government were determined to seek revenge by executing many of the priests they held in custody. Designed to form part of the entertainment for the Armada victory celebrations, Catholics were martyred in greater numbers than ever. The first victim of these brutal reprisals was Robert Sutton at Stafford in July. [24] On 28 August alone, a total of eight were martyred at different locations in and around London, where new gibbets had been erected for the purpose, in order to make a wider impact by spreading the terror. They were William Dean; [25] Henry Webley; [26] William Gunter; [29] Robert Morton; [30] Hugh More; [31] James Claxton; [32] Thomas Felton; [33]; and Thomas Holford. [49]

The news had reached London on 24 August that the danger from the Armada was over. It would have been a great propaganda coup for the government to have tried those in custody on the grounds of supporting the invasion, thereby discrediting the loyalist protestations of Catholics. The government did not do so; because there was no evidence to sustain such a charge, therefore, there was no pretence that all those executed in the aftermath of the Armada died for anything other than being priests or for sheltering them.

Why some imprisoned priests were selected for execution and others managed to survive the fury is difficult to fathom. Among the survivors were two Cornishmen. The first, John Vivian, was a former Protestant rector of St Just, Cornwall, who was ordained in 1579. He seems to have worked in Suffolk, being based at Long Melford. Arrested in 1585 he was sent to the Marshalsea before being banished. In 1586 he was back at Long Melford and was re-arrested and returned to the Marshalsea. The second was David Kemp, who was ordained at Rheims in 1581 and returned to England in 1582. He was known to be staying at the Red Lion, Holborn, London, at Christmas that year. He was imprisoned at York and banished in 1585 but in 1586 he took ship to return to England. He was captured on the voyage, which technically meant that he had not fallen foul again of 27 Elizabeth. He was sent to the Marshalsea in April 1587 with Vivian. A third priest was John Marsh, ordained in 1579. In 1585 he was committed to Hull Castle and then banished. By 1586 he had returned and was sent to the Marshalsea with Vivian and Kemp. All three were still prisoners in September 1588. Their unbelievable luck in escaping death during the Armada crisis remains a mystery; as does the time of their release. Later they all joined the English Bridgettine community at Rouen and moved with them to Lisbon where Kemp became chaplain to the exiled Syon community. Other priest prisoners escaped only because death cheated the executioner. For instance, the Yorkshireman John Baldwin, who was ordained at Laon 22 September 1584 with John Hambley q.v. On his return to England in 1585 he was imprisoned in the Gatehouse where he died in 1588. Or his fellow Yorkshireman, Martin Sherson, who was born 1563 in the East Riding. Ordained at Laon in April 1586 by October of that year he was in the Marshalsea and died there in 1588. Sheffield-born Father James Clayton, crossed to England with John Hambley in April 1585. At Christmas 1588 he was arrested while visiting Catholic prisoners in Derby. Condemned to death he died in Derby prison of jail fever on 22 July 1589. Then there were those who saved themselves by apostatising, such as William Tedder. He had been ordained in 1582 but on his return to England was committed to the Marshalsea. In 1585 he was banished but returned later that year. In September 1588 he was arrested at the house of Mrs Dorothy White in Westminster and sent to St Catherine's where a fellow prisoner was Anthony Tyrell. Mrs White was sentenced to death for sheltering Tedder. Dr William Allen had expressed misgivings about Tedder; doubts that proved to be only too well-founded. Tedder wrote to Walsingham offering to conform and on Sunday, 1 December 1588 he made a public recantation of his Catholicism at Paul's Cross. On the following Sunday Anthony Tyrell did likewise. Tedder was kept in prison for several months but was eventually granted a pardon and became an Anglican vicar.

On 30 August 1588 Margaret Ward was executed at Tyburn with her helper, Blessed John Roche, and four others: a twenty-seven-year-

The Elizabethan Martyrs, 1577-1601

old priest, Blessed Richard Leigh, [34] who was another victim of Anthony Tyrell's betrayal, and three Blessed laymen. The first was Edward Shelley, a relative of Robert Southwell's from the famous recusant family from Sussex. He had been sent to the Clink by Bishop Aylmer of London on 5 July 1581 for 'receiving, aiding and comforting' Father William Dean. After eighteen months he was removed to the Counter in Wood Street. The other two were Shropshire-born, and Oxford-educated, Richard Martin; and twenty-two year-old Richard Flower, or more correctly, Floyd, from Anglesey; all condemned for sheltering priests, Floyd specifically for harbouring Lincolnshire-born, Father William Horner, in the parish of St Dunstan, London. Floyd's much older brother, Owen, was a seminary priest. Ordained at Cambrai in 1578, he worked in England from 1581 until his death in 1591. Margaret and her companions sang the *Te Deum* and hymns as they were carted off to their execution. As they were drawn through the streets a lady of fashion forced her way through the crowd and kneeling down, asked for Father Leigh's blessing, whereupon she was immediately arrested and committed to prison. They had to suffer filthy abuse from Topcliffe as they waited to die. Father Leigh, who was the last to suffer, blessed each of his companions in turn as they climbed onto the scaffold. Except for Father Leigh, they were all forbidden to speak to the crowd, presumably because of the impact that the last words of a group of young people going courageously to their deaths might have on their hearers. Robert Southwell, who was present at their martyrdom, described Margaret, as 'a maiden among a thousand, in whose frail sex shone a courage hard to parallel.'

The Catholics could be forgiven for thinking that God had abandoned them as the vengeful executions continued throughout the summer and autumn of 1588. A simple glove-maker of Gloucester, Blessed William Lampley, was hanged, drawn and quartered in his home city. He had been betrayed by a member of his own family for 'persuading to popery.' The relative in question had even informed on his own recusant wife, who was imprisoned. Lampley appeared before Sir Roger Manwood, who offered him a pardon if he promised to go to church. The offer was refused. It was renewed on the scaffold, but William Lampley remained steadfast.

On 23 September, Father Willam Way [35] was martyred at Kingston-upon-Thames. He was followed by seven others on 1 October: Robert Wilcox; [36] Edward Campion; [37] Christopher Buxton; [38] Robert Widmerpool; [39] Ralph Crockett; [40] Edward James: [41] and John Robinson. [42] On 5 October, three more met their deaths: William Hartley; [3] Robert Sutton; [43] and John Hewett. [44] And finally, Edward

Burden 45 was executed on 29 November. The fall-out from the Armada folly continued unabated into 1589, when eight more were martyred. 46

As for Father Watson, after his rescue he claimed to have spent the next two years at Liège and returned to England in 1590. By May 1597 he was once more in the Bridewell but managed to escape. He turns up next in the Gatehouse in 1598 and while there he wrote his supposed autobiography before escaping in June 1599. Escapology seems to have been the one talent for which he had a real aptitude. In the same year he submitted to the Attorney-General a wholesale denunciation of the Jesuits working in England, supplying their names and whereabouts, and the names of those who sheltered them. According to his literary effort of 1601, the treatment by Queen Elizabeth of her Catholic subjects had been 'both mild and merciful'. His attempts to ingratiate himself with the government, by issuing yet more pamphlets attacking his co-religionists, do not seem to have borne much fruit. As evidence of the 'mild and merciful' treatment he then served a term in the Clink, but was caught with other priests preparing to say Mass for the large number of Catholic prisoners and confined to the Kings Bench prison in April 1602, being released on the accession of James I.

In 1603 he teamed up with another priest, William Clark, and they became involved with others in the so-called Bye-Plot against the King. By no means were the plotters exclusively Catholics; some were Puritans who, like the Catholics, were seeking religious toleration and the removal of penal laws. From what little evidence there is available, it is difficult to decide if the plot was real or if it only germinated in the fevered imagination of Watson. Certainly it seems never to have got further than far-fetched discussions. The plan was to kidnap James, imprison him in the Tower, force him to dismiss his ministers and appoint Catholics in their place. In this coup Watson had allocated to himself the post of Lord Chancellor! Someone tried to recruit Father John Gerard into the madcap scheme and he alerted Henry Garnet, the Jesuit Superior, who, fearing the consequences to the Catholic community, found means to tip-off off the government. Sir Robert Cecil was already aware of Watson's crazy conspiracy. A warrant was issued for Watson's arrest in which he was described as 'a man of the lowest sort, about the age of 36, [he was actually 45] his hair betwixt a brown and flaxen. He looketh asquint and very purblind, so as if he read anything he puts the paper near to his eyes. He did wear his beard at length, of the same coloured hair as his head, but information is given that now his beard is cut.' Watson was captured near Hay-on-Wye and on 10 August 1603 he was committed to the Tower.

The Elizabethan Martyrs, 1577-1601

Clark came from Walsall where his father was master of the grammar school. He went to Rheims in 1587 and moved on to Rome where he was ordained at the Lateran in 1592. He returned to England that year and by February 1601 was a prisoner in the Clink. He strongly opposed the Archpriest, George Blackwell who, in a monumental exercise of bad judgement, asked Fathers Anthony Rouse q.v. and Robert Barwise q.v. to examine him. As a result Clark was suspended by Blackwell. In the proclamation ordering his arrest in 1603 Clark was described as, 'a man of middle stature but inclining to the lower sort, about 36. His hair is betwixt red and yellow.' He was caught at Worcester on 13 August and sent to join Watson in the Tower. They were both taken to Winchester for trial and on 29 November 1603 they were hanged in the market place. On the scaffold Watson partially redeemed himself by asking the forgiveness of the Jesuits he had so gravely abused.

Edmund Gennings

Dying has made us rarer gifts than gold ... poured out the red sweet wine of youth.

The Dead, Rupert Brooke, 1887-1915

Edmund was the son of John Gennings, an innkeeper at Lichfield, Staffordshire. He was born in 1567 and raised in the Established Church. He was always a boy of a serious frame of mind and he loved contemplating the night sky. He attended Lichfield Grammar School and then at the age of sixteen was recommended as page in the Sherwood household, a family of London drapers who were staunch Catholics. Mr Richard Sherwood senior died in prison and Elizabeth, his widow, also suffered long prison terms in the Marshalsea and White Lion. There were three sons, John, Henry and Richard, who had also been imprisoned for recusancy and who all became seminary priests.

John Sherwood went to Rheims in 1580 and was ordained at Laon 5 March 1583. Having returned to England he became chaplain to Sir John Arundell at Isleworth and continued as chaplain to his widow at Chideock, Dorset, where he died in 1593. Henry Sherwood arrived at Rheims in 1587, his health ruined by seven years' imprisonment. He was ordained three years later on 11 June 1588. Richard Sherwood junior left England for Rheims in 1583 and was ordained at Soissons 13

The Elizabethan Martyrs, 1577-1601

June 1584. He was sent to England later that year in the company of Oxford-born John Clinch, who was ordained at Rheims in March 1581; and a future martyr, Father Robert Dibdale q.v. Using the alias Carleton, Richard ministered in London for about a year before being imprisoned in Wood Street Counter in 1585 and was banished in December 1586, never to return to England.

Under his employer's influence, Edmund became a Catholic and following his master's example on 12 August 1583 entered the English College, then at Rheims. His health was poor and he was found to be suffering from tuberculosis. After some time spent by the sea at Havre-de-Grace, Normandy, he recovered sufficiently to resume his studies. On 18 March 1590, he was ordained at Soissons by special dispensation because he was under the canonical age. He greatly hoped he would be sent to England as a missionary and less than a month later his wish was granted. He set off from Rheims on 9 April 1590 in the company of three other new priests: Alexander Rawlins, with whom he had been ordained, Polydore Plasden and Hugo Sewell, a former Anglican minister and Canon of Carlisle. En route they were waylaid by a party of Huguenots, robbed and kept in prison for three days. They were later joined by Father William Mush, the recently ordained younger brother of Father John Mush, and Father William Singleton. They all eventually embarked from Tréport, Normandy, and were landed secretly at night on the Yorkshire coast near Whitby. The following morning Gennings and Plasden were nearly caught at an inn near Whitby by an infamous Yorkshire pursuivant called Ratcliffe. Managing to give him the slip they made their way to a Catholic gentleman's house a few miles away, where they parted. (William Mush worked in Yorkshire for several years until he was captured in 1608 and sentenced to death. With the help of the keeper, William Wharton, he escaped from York Castle, for which Wharton was fined £250.)

After working for some months in the North, Edmund made his way to Lichfield to find his family. He was told that his parents had died but his younger brother, John, was in London. He spent a month searching for his brother until one day he met him quite by chance on Ludgate Hill. They had not seen one another for over eight years, but Edmund felt sure it was his brother and speaking to him so it turned out. But Edmund was bitterly disappointed: his brother was rabidly anti-Catholic and urged Edmund to leave the country.

He left London for a time and worked in the countryside, but on his return to the capital he met up with his former companion, Polydore Plasden, and they arranged to say Mass at the house of Swithun Wells

The Elizabethan Martyrs, 1577-1601

in Gray's Inn Lane. The day appointed was 28 November 1591, the first Sunday of Advent. Early in the morning, Edmund was saying Mass in an upstairs room for a small group of ten Catholics when there was banging on the front door below. When the door was opened it revealed a posse of officers; leading them was Richard Topcliffe - 'this most sordid of men'- as Henry Garnet described him. They forced their way in, but some of the gentlemen drew their swords and forcibly kept Topcliffe from entering the room where Mass was in progress. He was seized and held by John Mason, and in the scuffle that ensued Topcliffe fell downstairs, injuring his head. After much argument and to avoid further force being used against him, Topcliffe agreed to let the Mass proceed to its conclusion, provided they all undertook to surrender themselves to him. As soon as Mass was over Topcliffe rushed in and arrested Edmund, still in his vestments. He was dressed in a fool's coat to make him look ridiculous as he was led through the streets. He was taken to the Gatehouse prison, examined by Justice Young, and committed for trial. The same day Topcliffe received a letter from the Council commissioning him to carry out an examination of Gennings and those apprehended with him.

On 4 December they were all tried at Newgate, the jury having been instructed in advance to find them guilty. For celebrating Mass the priests were condemned for treason and the laymen and women for the felony of assisting priests. They were offered their liberty if they conformed but refused. Edmund's response was, 'I will live and die in the true Roman Catholic Faith which ... all antiquity had ever professed and would by no means go to the Protestant church or ever think that the Queen could be head of the Church in spiritual matters'.

On 10 December 1591 Edmund and Swithun Wells were taken back to Gray's Inn Lane, where a gallows had been erected outside Mr Wells's house. 'Confess your popish treason', said Topcliffe. Edmund replied: 'If to return to England a priest or to say Mass be popish treason, I here confess that I am a traitor; but I think not so and therefore I acknowledge myself guilty of those things, not with repentance, but with an open protestation of inward joy'.

Topcliffe was furious at the priest's attitude and in his rage he ordered the hangman to turn the ladder, and then immediately had the rope cut so that Edmund was fully conscious when he fell and was able to stand up. The hangman pushed him to the ground and began his butchery. Edmund screamed in agony, 'Oh, it hurts!' while Swithun encouraged him to be brave, 'Alas, sweet soul, thy pain is great indeed, but almost past; pray for me now, most holy saint, that mine may come.' While Bull, the executioner, was groping for his heart Edmund was heard to say, 'St Gregory, pray for me.' This elicited the hangman's callous riposte, 'See his heart is in my hand, yet St Gregory is in his mouth'.

Edmund Gennings is the youngest of the Forty Martyrs. He was just twenty-four years of age. No wonder the judges sometimes spoke disparagingly of these 'Romish boy priests'. John Gennings at first 'rejoiced rather than bewailed the untimely and bloody end' of his brother, but ten days after Edmund's execution a change came over him. He began to dwell on the manner of his death and to compare his own worldly life with that of his martyred brother. Full of remorse, he prayed for guidance and concluded that he should become a Catholic. He went to the English College, Rome, and was ordained priest in 1600.

In 1601 he was sent to England where he ministered until 1611, when he was imprisoned for a time at Newgate. In 1614 he published a biography of his brother and Swithun Wells. Shortly afterwards he entered the Franciscan Order, being received by William Stanney, the last representative of the Greenwich Marian friars. John became eager to restore the English Province of the Franciscan Observants. He obtained a house for English Franciscan sisters at Gravelines and then established St Bonaventure's Friary at Douai. In 1618 he was formally commissioned to re-establish the English Province. By 1625 the number of English friars had considerably grown and Rome was requested to canonically set up an English Province. John became the first Minister Provincial in 1629 and died at Douai in 1660.

Swithun Wells

We'll to the woods no more.

Last Poems, Alfred E Houseman, 1859-1936

Swithun or Swithin Wells, who came from a wealthy family, was born at Brambridge, near Winchester, Hampshire c.1536. Obviously named after the great Saxon bishop of Winchester, he was the youngest of the six sons of Thomas Wells and Mary, daughter of Sir John Mompesson. We know that two of his brothers were called Gilbert and Henry. Gilbert suffered much for his faith. He had a house in Holborn where, like Swithun, he sheltered priests. One of these was Father Robert Holmes, who went to Rheims in 1579, was ordained in 1580 and had

The Elizabethan Martyrs, 1577-1601

worked in England since 1581. He was captured at Gilbert's house on 27 August 1584 and was taken with all his Mass equipment to Newgate, where he died of hunger and ill-treatment within the year. Henry, who studied at Winchester College and Oxford, also remained true.

Swithun was a cultured, witty, well-educated man of many pursuits; a poet and musician as well as country sportsman. He travelled widely, visiting Italy, and after spending some years in Rome could speak Italian well. For a time he was tutor to Henry Wriothesley, heir of the Catholic Earl of Southampton; a post he held until his marriage to Alice Morin or Morren, a Catholic lady. He outwardly conformed to the Established Church becoming a church papist for a time, while living a peaceful country gentleman's life until middle age.

About 1576 he set up his own school for young gentlemen at Monkton Farleigh in Wiltshire. One of the masters was the future priest and martyr, Nicholas Woodfen. 47 In May 1582 Swithun came under suspicion for his Catholic sympathies and the Privy Council ordered the sheriff of Wiltshire to investigate 'Wells the schoolmaster.' As a result he had to give up the school, but it was about this time that he was formally reconciled to the Church. As well as being involved in Catholic book smuggling Swithun played a key role actively supported priests, organising their dangerous journeys from one safe house to another. Father Thomas Stanney relates how upon his arrival in England, he had been conducted by Swithun into the West of England, where he found refuge. (Father Stanney was born at Purbeck, Dorset, in 1558. He went to Rheims in May 1581 and entered the English College, Rome, in October. He was ordained in May 1585 and came back to England in 1586 where he worked in Hampshire. He joined the Society of Jesus in 1597. In 1605 he was arrested near Reading and imprisoned in the Gatehouse. He was suffering from measles and severe fatigue and his mental condition was cause for concern, but he soon recovered.) Swithun became so well known for helping priests that it was not safe for any of them to be seen in his company. When this work became too hazardous, Swithun, by now somewhat impoverished, decided in 1585 to move his family to London.

In 1586 Swithun moved to a little house in Gray's Inn Lane, which quickly became a place of hospitality for priests. In June he was arrested with Father Christopher Dryland 48 and the future priest and martyr, Alexander Rawlins, and committed to Newgate by Justice Young. He was bailed by his nephew, Francis Perkins, on 4 July. He was then arrested on 9 August and interrogated in the Fleet about his knowledge of the Babington Plot. He was released on 30 November.

The Elizabethan Martyrs, 1577-1601

Some time afterwards he undertook a mission about which we tantalisingly know little. No doubt it came about because of his earlier connection and the fact that he knew Rome and spoke Italian, but he travelled to Rome in the service of his former pupil, Henry Wriothesley, 3rd Earl of Southampton. The Earl was not only one of the richest and most fashionable young noblemen in England but also a Catholic.

Southampton's father, the second earl, was an active Catholic as was his wife, Mary Browne, daughter of 1st Viscount Montague. In 1570 the Earl was summoned to Kingston-upon-Thames to give 'proof of his submission to Her Majesty's Council'. He obviously failed to meet their requirements because he was placed under house arrest at Loseley Hall, under the care of Sir William More, a reluctant jailer because of what it was costing him. At some point he attended 'common prayer' which caused him to fall 'into that heaviness and pensiveness of mind as there is fear it will ... breed in him some present sickness'. In 1573 the Earl was transferred into the custody of his father-in-law, Viscount Montague, at Cowdray Park, Sussex. To all intents and purposes he outwardly conformed, but remained Catholic at heart until his death in 1581 aged thirty-seven. Proof of this is that he allowed Edmund Campion to stay at his house in Holborn, London, and priests were certainly sheltered by his wife there and at Cowdray. The 3rd Earl, who was born at Cowdray, was acquainted with Robert Southwell. Implicated in the rebellion led by Robert Devereux, Earl of Essex, Southampton was tried with the Earl and condemned to death, but had his sentence commuted to life imprisonment. When his fellow bisexual, James I, came to the throne Southampton was pardoned and returned to Court. Much of Wriothesley's fame rests upon the fact that he was Shakespeare's patron and the dedicatee of some of his works.

Swithun could not have been absent in Italy for long because by the spring of 1587 he underwent further questioning, from which we learn that his cousin was George Cotton, of the strongly recusant family at Warblington, Hampshire. Mr Cotton was well-known to the authorities. The government was aware that he had given shelter to Lancashire-born, Father Thomas Lister SJ, who was also at Hindlip Hall, Worcester for a time, with Father Edward Oldcorne. From 1587 until 1607 Cotton and his wife appear in the Recusant Rolls. Each year he paid the full £260 for his recusancy; a staggering £5,200 over the twenty years. In order to obtain some easement from continued harassment, he offered to pay an additional £30 a year to Her Majesty, later increased to £40. The result was inevitable. His wealth spent, and no longer able to pay, his remaining goods were seized and he was sent

The Elizabethan Martyrs, 1577-1601

to prison. Here he spent several years in filth and misery, which led to a chronic illness. According to the *Records of the Society of Jesus*, when he died in 1614 he was not permitted a Christian burial in any churchyard. His corpse was deposited unceremoniously 'in an open field'.

In the fateful summer of 1588 Swithun spent some months in Newgate following the capture of Thomas Holford 49 when leaving his house after saying Mass. Father Holford was 'on the run', having escaped from his captors almost a year earlier, and being a wanted man, was recognised by a pursuivant in the street.

In November 1591 when Edmund Jennings and Polydore Plasden were arrested after saying Mass in Swithun's house, his wife, their servants and all those present were apprehended with the priests. Swithun was not in the house at the time, but when he returned home he found the house ransacked and his wife arrested. He went straight to Justice Young to demand his wife's release. Young quipped, 'though he had missed the feast, he should taste of the sauce' and promptly arrested Swithun and sent him to Newgate in chains. When examined he declared that although he had not been present at the celebration of Mass he believed his house to have been greatly honoured that the divine sacrifice had been offered there. While in prison he wrote to his brother-in-law, Gerard Morin:

The comforts which captivity brings are so manifold that I have rather cause to thank God highly for his fatherly correction, than to complain of any worldly misery whatsoever. God send me withal, the prayers of all good folks to obtain some end of all miseries, such as to his holy will and pleasure shall be most agreeable. I have been a long time in durance and endured much pain; but the many future rewards in the heavenly payment, make all pains seem to me a pleasure ... desiring nothing more than solitariness, but rather rejoice that thereby I have the better occasion, with prayer, to prepare myself to that happy end for which I was created and placed here by God ... He is not alone who has Christ in his company. When I pray I talk with God, when I read he talks to me, so that I am never alone. He is my chiefest companion and only comfort.

I have no cause to complain of the hardness of prison, considering the effects thereof, and the rather because I fasten not my affection upon worldly vanities, whereof I have had my fill to my great grief and sorrow. I renounced the world before ever I tasted of imprisonment, even in my baptism: which promise and profession, however slenderly soever I have kept heretofore, I purpose for the time to come, God assisting me, to continue to my life's end. The world is crucified to me and I to the world. God forbid that I should glory in anything but the cross of Christ. 'Vanity of vanities, all is vanity' besides loving God. I am bound, yet I am loose and unbound towards God; and far better account it to have the body bound, than the soul to be in bondage ...

The Elizabethan Martyrs, 1577-1601

God send me his grace and then I weigh not what flesh and blood can do to me.

The whole group was indicted at Westminster on 4 December, tried alongside the priests on the 5th, and condemned to death. Taken from prison with her husband on the day of execution, to her great sorrow Mrs Alice Wells was told she had been reprieved and was not to die. She was returned to Newgate, sentenced to life imprisonment. She died in prison ten years later in 1602. Her daughter, Margaret, later became a nun.

As already related, on 10 December Swithun was executed with Edmund Gennings on a gallows specially erected outside his own house. Seeing an old friend in the crowd Swithun cheerfully called out to him, 'Goodbye dear friend. Farewell all hunting parties and old pastimes; I am now going a better way'. Topcliffe told Swithun to look upon Gennings. Swithun said, 'I see him well and I thank God that ever I did know him.' Topcliffe retorted that he should 'rather reprehend him for having brought you to this shameful end.' To which Swithun responded 'I count it honourable.' He had to watch while Edmund was butchered, and did his best to support him. It was a bitterly cold day and when he was stripped he turned to Topcliffe and said jocularly, 'Hurry up, please Mr Topcliffe. Are you not ashamed to make a poor old man stand in his shirt in this cold? God pardon you and make you of a Saul a Paul, of a bloody persecutor one of the Catholic Church's children; by your malice I am thus to be executed, but you have done me the greatest benefit that ever I could have had. I heartily forgive you.' Topcliffe sneered at him, 'See what your priests have brought you to.' Swithun replied: 'I am happy and thank God to have been so favoured to have so many and such saint-like priests under my roof.' After he had suffered his remains were taken by friends and buried in the churchyard of St Andrew, Holborn.

Polydore Plasden

The white flower of a blameless life.

> *The Idylls of the King,* Alfred, Lord Tennyson, 1809-92

Polydore strikes us as a very unusual name but in the sixteenth century it was not so uncommon. There was at least one other priest of that name, the Welshman Polydore Morgan. Ordained in Paris in 1579, by

The Elizabethan Martyrs, 1577-1601

July 1580 Morgan was a prisoner in the Gatehouse, where he remained for more than two years, without the authorities realising he was a priest. In April 1581 he was prosecuted as a recusant and on 5 November of that year it was recorded that his brother sent him three pies and a bottle of wine and petitioned to have access to him. Permission was granted, for we next learn that on 12 November his brother visited him, and again on 19 November, each time bringing mutton pies. Morgan was released from the Gatehouse in August 1582 and went to Rheims. He reached Rome in 1583, and ended his days as a Capuchin Franciscan at Tours in 1616.

Polydore Plasden was born in 1563 by Fleet Bridge, one of the four bridges which then spanned the Fleet River. The bridge linked Fleet Street and Ludgate Hill, London. His father was a musical instrument maker, 'a horner' and retailer at Ludgate Circus. Polydore was educated at Rheims, where he is recorded under his alias of Oliver Palmer. The extant examples of his signature read both Oliver Plasden and Polydore Plasden. Some sources would have us believe that Palmer was his real name and Polydore Plasden his highly improbable alias. What is more, as his father was well known, there does not seem to be any doubt that Plasden was his name. He entered the English College, Rome, on 25 April 1585 and was among the group of fifty students who signed the petition in August requesting that the Jesuits should be retained to run the College.

He was ordained priest at the basilica of St John Lateran, the cathedral of Rome, on 7 December 1586. (St John's, dedicated in 324AD, is first in rank of all the Catholic churches of the world; even above St Peter's.) He returned to Rheims in April 1588. The college diary shows that he left again on 2 September 1588, but where he spent the next eighteen months is uncertain. As there is a mention of him working in Sussex it is possible to speculate that he came to England in 1588 and then beat a hasty retreat to Rheims. As this was the year of the Spanish Armada, it was an especially dangerous time for any priest to be in the country. On 9 April 1590 he again left Rheims for England in company with Edmund Gennings, landing with him under cover of darkness at Whitby, where they separated at midnight. For the next four years he ministered in and around Holborn, in the very area of London in which he had been born.

Polydore met Edmund Gennings again by chance one evening in November 1591. They said matins together and arranged to say Mass the next day at Swithun Wells's house. When the house was raided by Topcliffe it was Polydore, concerned about the safety of the Blessed Sacrament, who promised him that they would surrender themselves if he let the Mass proceed. Arrested with Gennings and the Wells's household, he was tried and condemned with them at Westminster before the Lord Chief Justice and William Fleetwood, Recorder of London. After the guilty verdict was delivered Plasden was asked if he had anything to say: 'These twelve simple men find us guilty of treason for exercising our priestly function. But you, learned in the law and in history, know very well that the priesthood was in all ages an honourable calling if yet you dare speak the truth.' Mr Recorder Fleetwood made a tasteless joke at Polydore's expense. Alluding to his father's trade, he said: 'Plasden, dost thou talk so? Methinks thou wouldst better wind a horn, for I think thy father is a horner at Fleet Bridge' - which the court found highly amusing.

On 10 December Polydore was taken to Tyburn with Father Eustace White and three Blessed laymen, all to die for relieving priests. The first two were Sidney Hodgson, who was a servant of the Wells', and Kendal-born John Mason who was, or had been, a servant in London to a Mr Owen of Oxfordshire. It seems highly likely that this was either the father or the brother of St Nicholas Owen. The third was Brian Lacey of Brockdish, Norfolk. Brian had first been arrested in 1586 for aiding priests and acting as a carrier of messages. He was imprisoned in Newgate by Justice Richard Young. Lacey had experienced at first-hand the full force of the machinery of repression. After his cousin, Blessed Montford Scott, [50] had been arrested Brian was again apprehended having been betrayed by his own brother, Richard Lacey. Committed to the Bridewell Brian had been cruelly tortured by Topcliffe. He was tried at the Old Bailey before the Lord Mayor, condemned and sent for execution just five months after his cousin.

As Polydore stood on the scaffold he prayed aloud for the Queen. Sir Walter Raleigh was in the crowd and he asked Polydore if he sincerely meant his prayers. 'Yes', answered Plasden, 'otherwise I could expect no salvation'. Raleigh questioned him further, asking if he acknowledged Elizabeth as his lawful Queen, and would he defend her against foreign enemies.

When Plasden replied in the affirmative, Raleigh declared he was no traitor and could see no cause why such an honest man should die. He offered to go immediately to the Court to plead with the Queen herself for a reprieve, if the sheriff would delay the execution. But Richard Topcliffe, who had dashed from the execution of Gennings and Wells at Gray's Inn Lane, intervened. He asked Plasden if he thought the Queen had any right to impose her religion and forbid Catholicism, to which Polydore answered no. He then wanted to know, if the Pope came to establish Catholicism, would Plasden defend the Queen against the Pope? 'I would never fight nor counsel others to fight against my religion, for that were to deny my faith'.

Topcliffe demanded confirmation that Polydore was a Catholic priest and this he confessed, kissing the rope and saying he would rather forfeit a thousand lives than deny Christ. After this Raleigh allowed the execution to proceed, but he insisted that Polydore be allowed to hang until he was dead.

Eustace White

Truth put down by persecution.
On Liberty, John Stuart Mill, 1806-73

Eustace was born at Louth, Lincolnshire, in 1560, the son of William White and Anne Booth. They were a prominent Protestant family and William White was involved in the town corporation and the management of the grammar school. When Eustace became a Catholic in 1584 his father laid a curse on him. Eustace must have known about the recent religious history of his native town. Louth was, and is, dominated by the hexagonal spire of the 15th century St James's Church. At 295 feet it is reputedly the highest spire of any parish church in England. Begun in 1501 the spire was completed in 1515. The forerunner of the 'Pilgrimage of Grace' in 1536 the Lincolnshire revolt started at the church following the suppression of the nearby Louth Park Cistercian abbey, which had been founded in 1139. At the closure it had an abbot and eleven monks whose annual income was just £147. Thomas Kendall, parish priest of Louth since 1534, urged his congregation to resist the King's commissioners. In 1537 Kendall was hanged, drawn and quartered at Tyburn, as was William Moreland, a monk of Louth Park, and many of the townsfolk were hanged in Louth market place.

Eustace arrived at Rheims on 31 October 1584 and transferred to the English College, Rome, on 24 October 1586. He was ordained deacon on 16 April 1588. It is presumed that he was ordained priest in Rome later in the same year as he was sent back to Rheims that autumn, leaving for England on 2 November.

On his return to England he ministered to the Catholics in the West Country for almost three years. One day when on a journey he met a lawyer. They rode along together for some time and as his companion seemed friendly Eustace conversed about religion. It was 1 September

1591 when they reached Blandford in Dorset. The lawyer insisted that Eustace join him for breakfast at the inn. Eustace removed his saddle bag from his mount and took it into the inn with him. After breakfast Eustace left, but suspecting that he was a seminary priest, the lawyer informed the local officers, advising them which road to take to catch up with him. In the meantime, having realised he had left behind at the inn his bag containing his breviary, Eustace retraced his steps and actually passed the officers on the road before returning to the inn to collect his bag. Here, when arrested, he admitted that he was a priest. The local minister, Dr Houel, was sent for to make White see the error of his ways. During their disputation Eustace, to support a Catholic doctrine, used a quotation from the Gospels which the minister insisted did not exist and accused him of lying.

'Bring me your own Bible', said White, 'and I will show you that it exists in your own version. If you are right and the passage does not exist I will go with you to the Protestant church'. The minister retorted, 'If you can show me that the text exists to support your view, I will become a papist'.

News of this spread all over the town and the next day a large crowd assembled to hear the continuation of the debate. When asked to show the disputed text, the minister refused and clutched his Bible tightly under his arm, trying to turn the debate onto other subjects. Eustace insisted that the Bible be given to him but the minister refused. White then turned to the crowd and explained what had happened. They demanded that the Bible be handed over to be checked if the disputed text existed. Despite all efforts, to the jeers of the crowd, the minister clung onto the Bible, refusing to relinquish it and refusing to admit that he was wrong. Eustace cautioned them to beware of the erroneous religious teaching they were being given that included the falsification of the scriptures. The townspeople were so impressed with Eustace - who was described as a fine gentleman-like man of good conversation - that they organised a petition for his release. He must have had musical abilities too, as a silver flute was listed amongst his possessions when he was arrested. He was sent to the Council at Basing before being taken to London and put in the Bridewell on 18 September; the following month his torture was authorised in a letter dated 25 October to Topcliffe from the Privy Council. It stated that Eustace should 'be put to the manacles and such other tortures as are used in Bridewell'.

The sadistic Topcliffe tortured him with the greatest savagery. He was racked seven times and once was hung up by his wrists in manacles for eight hours while remorselessly interrogated to reveal in whose houses he had said Mass or who had helped him in his mission.

The Elizabethan Martyrs, 1577-1601

Eyewitnesses testified that White poured so much with sweat from his ordeal that it ran from his clothes and lay in a pool on the ground beneath him. They could extract no information from him. 'Lord, more pain if you please and more patience', was White's prayer. We have a vivid first-hand account of what this torture was like from Father John Gerard, who had to endure it twice a day. In his autobiography he tells us:

They took me to a big upright pillar, one of the wooden posts which held the roof ... Driven into the top of it were iron staples for supporting heavy weights. Then they put my wrists into iron gauntlets and ordered me to climb two or three wicker steps. My arms were then lifted up and an iron bar was passed through the rings of one gauntlet, then through the staple and rings of the second gauntlet. This done ... removing the wicker steps ... they left me hanging by my hands and arms fastened above my head ... Such a gripping pain came over me. It was worst in my chest and belly, my hands and arms. All the blood in my body seemed to rush up into my arms and hands and I thought that blood was oozing out from the ends of my fingers and the pores of my skin. But it was only a sensation caused by my flesh swelling above the irons holding them. The pain was so intense that I thought I could not possibly endure it ... the perspiration ran in drops continuously down my face and body ... I fell into a faint ... the men held my body up ... until I came to ... I fainted eight or nine times that day ... they took me down ... it was a great effort to stand upright.

The second day Gerard was hung up once again just as before, fainting and being revived before being taken back to his cell by the warder who had to feed him.

For many days after I could not hold a knife in my hands - that day I could not even move my fingers or help myself in the smallest way. He had to do everything for me.

A modern medical expert has likened the effects of this torture to that of crucifixion. After undergoing similar torture Eustace told Topcliffe, 'I am not angry with you for all this, but I shall pray to God for your salvation'. Topcliffe furiously replied that he did not want the prayers of a traitor who he would see hanged. 'Then', said White, 'I shall pray for you even on the gallows for you are in great need of prayers'.

On 23 November Eustace managed to smuggle out a letter to Father Henry Garnet by a good man who had been a servant of Sir Thomas Fitzherbert and who now tried to help Eustace. The letter, which reveals the appalling conditions in which he was kept reads:

This bearer, late and last servant unto the good Sir Thomas Fitzherbert for he attended on him ... his death in the Tower, can partly relate unto you mine estate ... He hath spared from himself to relieve me with victuals as he could through a little hole and with other such necessaries as he could by that means do, whom truly I did never see in my life but through a hole. Nothing was too dear to him that he could convey unto me, for whom as I am bound so will I daily pray while I live. I have been a close prisoner [solitary confinement] since the 18th day of September, where for forty-six days together I lay upon a little straw in my boots, my hands continually manacled in irons for one month together never once taken off.

Tried with Gennings, Plasden, Wells and their companions, he was condemned. Moved to Newgate to await execution, on 10 December 1591 Eustace was taken to Tyburn, together with Plasden and the three laymen tried with them. Not wanting to miss the culmination of his handiwork Topcliffe rushed from Gray's Inn Lane to be present.

Eustace spoke to the spectators. 'Christian people, I was condemned as a traitor for being a priest and coming into this country to reconcile and use other of my priestly functions, all which I confess I have done in sundry places of this realm for some years together. I thank God that it hath pleased Him to bless my labours with this happy end, when I now am to die for my faith and my priesthood. Other treasons I have not committed. If I had ever so many lives I would think them very few to bestow upon your Tyburns to defend my religion. I wish I had a great many more than one, you should have them all one after another'.

He was cut down while still alive and tried to rise to his feet. Two men held him down by standing on his arms while he suffered the butchery.

John Boste

We wrestle against ... the rulers of the darkness of this world, against spiritual wickedness in high places.

St Paul, Letter to the Ephesians

John, the son of Nicholas Boste, was born c.1543 at Dufton, just north of Appleby in Westmorland. The religious affiliation of his family is unknown, but there are several pointers in his later life that at least his mother may have been a Catholic. She belonged to the Hutton family of Hutton Hall, many of whom remained Catholics. It is known that she gave to her relation, Andrew Hilton, a copy of the Douai-Rheims New Testament; not the action of a woman at odds with the Catholic Church. As a boy John attended Appleby Grammar School which had long-established connections with Queen's College, Oxford, and John was given a scholarship to the college. He graduated BA in 1569 and then MA in June 1572 and was elected a Fellow of the college. It must have been around this time that he was ordained in the Anglican Church. John's brother, Laurence, was also a minister of the Established Church. By January 1574 John had resigned his fellowship and was recorded as being the schoolmaster at Appleby, probably on the recommendation of Queen's College.

By 1578 he was back at Queens College, Oxford, as master of the college junior school so we may be fairly certain that up until this time he was not suspected of being a secret Catholic. He began to doubt the validity of his orders in the Established Church and before long he was expelled for being absent without leave. What brought about his conversion to the Catholic Faith is unknown. Perhaps it was the result of his reading or contacts with Catholics at the University. Some sources state he was converted as early as 1576. This seems very doubtful as it does not readily fit in with his known movements and career during that period.

He left England and is recorded as acting as school teacher to Gerard Clibburn, one of his former Oxford pupils, at Louvain. Together with Clibburn, John was admitted to the English College (then at Rheims) on 4 August 1580. He progressed rapidly through his studies and within a year was ordained priest at Châlons on 4 March 1581. (His protégé, Clibburn, was ordained in 1587 and returned to England the following year.) On 11 April 1581 John left for England, landing at Hartlepool after dark under the alias of John Harckley or Hartley. Perhaps abiding by a prior arrangement, he made his way to Norfolk, where he stayed with an Anglican minister called James Warcop who came from Appleby. Escorted by Warcop, John set off for London and then pushed on westwards along the Thames Valley, meeting up with a relative of his mother's, Andrew Hilton, who was to severely suffer for his faith. Hilton had a house at Barton, Westmorland where he sheltered priests. For a time John took on the role of servant to the Catholic Anthony Browne, 1st Viscount Montague. This cover enabled him to travel reasonably freely and John made his way northwards. A description by Andrew Hilton of Boste's appearance at this time says he dressed in a brown cloak, a white wool jerkin laced with blue and a pair of leather breeches and rode with a cloak bag behind him containing his priestly equipment.

Because of the coal boats plying their trade between the Continent and Newcastle, that port was used for smuggling in not only priests but also Catholic literature. There is ample evidence that Boste was involved in the distribution of these contraband books, and we read in

The Elizabethan Martyrs, 1577-1601

one of his letters how he regrets not having more time to engage in this work. Certainly some Catholic books were later found in his mother's house. He also appears to have supplied information about shipping to those charged with securing safe passages for priests or young men going abroad to be educated.

Boste spent nearly twelve years in a very active ministry, covering a wide area of the north of England and the Scottish borders. It is known that he visited Edinburgh more than once and that he stayed with George, 5th Lord Seton, former Master of the Household to Mary, Queen of Scots. John was so successful that he was the most wanted priest in the North.

Given the widespread survival of Catholicism in Yorkshire and the other northern counties, an effective organisation was needed to keep its adherents ruthlessly subdued. That role was undertaken by the Council of the North based in York at the former house of the abbots of St Mary's, later known as the King's Manor. The Council composed several knights and landed gentry under the Presidency, since 1572, of the viciously anti-Catholic Henry Hastings, 3rd Earl of Huntingdon. Hastings was the grandson of Henry Pole, Lord Montague, and great-grandson of the martyred Blessed Margaret Pole therefore he had Plantagenet royal blood, but as a confirmed Protestant he did not share the Pole's faith. Under Edward VI Hastings was a political ally of John Dudley, Duke of Northumberland, and married his daughter, Katherine. In spite of his Calvinism he was loyal to Queen Mary and actually served in the household of his great-uncle, Cardinal Pole, for a time. He succeeded to the earldom on the death of his father in 1560. Although it was said that the Queen did not entirely trust him, as a possible Protestant claimant to the throne, nonetheless Hastings was committed to the Elizabethan regime. He ruthlessly presided over the Council of the North for over twenty years, during which 'the Tyrant', as they termed him, earned the hatred of the Catholics for his unrelenting, malicious treatment of them.

Huntingdon offered a special reward for John's capture. He must have been in Hull at some time because there is a letter from Huntingdon ordering a search for him in that town. It is a tribute to the brave people who sheltered him that he was able to evade capture for so long. Many of them paid a heavy penalty for their compassion, for example, John Carr, the postmaster of Newcastle, who was arrested and tried for sheltering Boste. It is also indicative of how closely Boste's whereabouts were monitored by the spies.

Another of those who gave him assistance was Blessed Robert Bickerdike, who came from a staunchly recusant family at Farnham,

The Elizabethan Martyrs, 1577-1601

near Knaresborough, and was an apprentice in York. Two Puritan merchants of the city, knowing Robert was a Catholic, maliciously accused him of various offences. Tried in the Common Hall, he was acquitted of the charges, but he was soon imprisoned again in Ousebridge as a recusant. He was brought to trial before Mr Justice Clench and Mr Justice Rodes, but once again the jury returned a 'Not guilty' verdict. Furious, Birkhead, the prosecuting attorney, had him committed to York Castle, determined to have him convicted. At the time when Francis Ingleby was being drawn to his execution, Robert overhead a conversation between a minister's wife and her sister, in which she had remarked that they should go and see the traitor coming over the Ousebridge on the hurdle. Robert had protested to her that the priest was no traitor but as true as she was.

The altercation was reported and used as the excuse to bring him to trial for a third time. He was accused of harbouring priests because he had been seen in the company of Father Boste, for whom he had bought a pot of ale. He was asked whose part he would take if the Pope made war against the Queen. He replied that he would react as God would put him in mind at the time. The judges demanded he be found guilty of treason, and this time the jury obliged. Robert was hanged, drawn and quartered at York in August 1586.

Huntingdon was so desperate to capture John that he engaged a spy called Francis Ecclesfield specifically for the task. In common with other priests in the area, John often said Mass at Waterhouse, the small thatched house of William Clapton who had endured long imprisonment for his religion. (Many sources - following Challoner - call him Claxton but contemporary documents, including the account of Father Richard Holtby, clearly name him Clapton).Waterhouse was an isolated house among dense woodland. It stood near Brancepeth, not far from Durham on what was formerly the estate of Charles Neville, 6th Earl of Westmorland, now in exile following the abortive Northern Rising of 1569.

Amongst those who attended Mass at Waterhouse were the future martyr, George Errington and Lady Margaret Neville and her married sister, Lady Catherine Gray, daughters of the disgraced Earl. Ecclesfield, pretending to be a Catholic, somehow ingratiated himself with this little recusant community and gained their trust. He was present at a Mass celebrated by Boste in August 1593 and learned that he was due to return in September. A former Marian priest, Anthony Atkinson, had also turned informer, and between him and Ecclesfield the Council was kept supplied with the names of those who both celebrated and attended Mass at Waterhouse.

The Elizabethan Martyrs, 1577-1601

On 10 September John returned to Waterhouse as planned. While Mass was in progress the house was surrounded. When Mass was over John made ready to leave, when Ecclesfield knelt and asked for his blessing - no doubt the Judas-like pre-arranged signal to identify the priest to those watching. Perhaps having the intuition to read the man's true character, John immediately retreated into the house and climbed into the hiding place over the chimney breast. The pursuivants ransacked the house, smashing through walls and taking up the floorboards. They found vestments and altar utensils but no priest. They also discovered an empty hiding place in the bottom of a cupboard and supposed that John had somehow escaped. Ecclesfield told them to try the chimney breast and there they finally found Boste. John was strapped to a horse and with his arms bound was led through the woods. At the time William Clapton was once again in prison, but they arrested his wife Grace and his daughter, together with Lady Margaret Neville who were made to follow on foot. When the news of John's capture was relayed to him, Huntingdon exclaimed that he had caught one of the biggest stags of the forest.

The prisoners were taken to Durham and detained in the Northgate, one of the city gatehouses. John was put in chains and the next day was examined by Huntingdon and Dean Tobie Matthew. 51 The future Bishop of Durham and Archbishop of York had once debated with the imprisoned Edmund Campion and had been at Oxford with Boste. Huntingdon could not conceal his delight that after so many years they had at last captured a notorious traitor. With a jocular pun on his own name, John said: 'After all this search, my Lord, at last you have got your Boast'.

John confessed to all that we know of his career and was said to be 'resolute, bold, joyful and pleasant'. He was sent under heavy guard to York, where he was lodged in the Manor, the former house of the abbots, which was now Huntingdon's headquarters. A few days later a letter arrived conveying the Queen's congratulations and instructions to send Boste to London. Strapped to a horse and under strict guard, he was transferred to the Tower, where he was interrogated by Burghley. In a letter describing the event, Topcliffe, who was present, stated that he had been commanded by Her Majesty to attend John's examination. He opined that 'Never since they were born had they heard a more resolute traitor' when John asserted that he was sorry there were not twenty for every one popish priest in England and that he had not won twenty Catholics for every one he had converted.

John was examined fifteen times and tortured on five occasions; four on the rack and once hung up by the manacles, which he said was the worst of all. We are told in a contemporary account preserved by Father Christopher Grene that he was so badly crippled that he was never again able to stand upright but 'walked all double, very slowly with the aid of a stick. When he sat down as he usually did on his heels, he was all on a heap, as if he had been all in pieces.' In spite of the pain he was always cheerful and received any visitors courteously. The Council were only too well aware that with his active ministry John must be privy to most of the secrets of the Catholics in the North, and therefore in possession of invaluable information. Yet he disclosed nothing that was not already available to the government.

Once while being racked he spotted a familiar face watching the savagery: Anthony Major. Born in London in 1565, he was a nephew of Dr Humphrey Ely q.v. by whom he was converted. He had been ordained at Laon in June 1590 and returned to England the following year. He was arrested in 1593 and after some months in prison at York, lacking the courage to resist, he apostatised and was taken into the household of the Earl of Huntingdon. He agreed to inform on his brethren, which cost the lives of several priests. Major was pardoned and rewarded for his services with a benefice in the Established Church in Nottinghamshire; which he still held in 1626. Major named a number of places in the North where he had been with Boste and John admitted it was true, there being little point in denying it. The other apostate, Anthony Atkinson, asked Burghley to let him speak to John to try and obtain information from him by more subtle means than torture. At one point John was sent to Windsor to be examined by the Privy Council and to enable the Queen to have a look at him. The warrant of payment for the guards who escorted him to and from Windsor is extant in the Exchequer Records.

Having failed for so many months to extract from John any information of which the government was not already aware, there was little point in holding him any longer in the Tower. As his ministry had been in the area, it was decided to send Boste back to Durham via York for trial. On his painful ride he was accompanied by Father John Ingram. This twenty-nine-year-old priest was born at Stoke, Herefordshire. Although his parents were not Catholics they must have been sympathisers because John had been sent as a youth to Douai. In 1582 he and three other boys were going from Douai to Rheims but were captured by Calvinists. John managed to escape and made it to Rheims a month later where he arrived 'in rags'. In October 1584 he entered the English College, Rome, and was ordained at the Lateran 3 December 1589. He set off to return home in September 1591 when the English government, well-informed as ever, was advised by a spy that

The Elizabethan Martyrs, 1577-1601

he was on his way. However, John did not come to England. He sailed from Antwerp to Scotland where he remained for several months as chaplain to Sir Walter Lindsay at Balgavies Castle, Forfar. (Lindsay was something of an intriguer against the Protestant Scottish government. For a time he was forced into exile in Spain where he wrote an *Account of the Catholic Religion in Scotland.* In 1605 he was brutally murdered by his kinsman the Earl of Crawford.) On 25 November 1593 some urgent business had brought Ingram across the border into England. After only a few hours he was returning to Scotland at Norham when he was arrested in a boat on the River Tweed and taken to Berwick in the custody of the Governor, John Carew, who treated him courteously. When John was searched they found some relics of the martyrs which they would have burned, but he begged them most earnestly not to take them from him. In February 1594 the Earl of Huntingdon ordered Ingram to be brought to York, where he was identified by the apostates William Hardesty and Anthony Major, with whom he had travelled to Rome in 1584. Like John Boste, Ingram had been sent to the Tower. While incarcerated, John covered the walls of his cell with little poems and Latin epigrams. Many of them were of a humorous nature. One, quoted in translation, will give a flavour of these verses:

Men to the living rock resort
For their sepulchral stones:
A living tomb is mine, unsought -
The crow that picks my bones.

One of the sonnets he composed while a prisoner was entitled *A Sinful Soul to Christ.* It reads:

I lurk, I lour in dungeon deep of mind,
In mourning mood, I run a restless race.
With wounding pangs my soul is pined,
My grief it grows, and death draws on apace.
What life can last except there come release?
Fear threats despair, my sin's infernal wage;
I faint, I fall, most woeful is my case;
Who can help me, who may this storm assuage?
O Lord of life, our peace, our only pledge,
O blissful light, who life of death hast wrought,
Of heavenly love the brightsome beam and badge,
Who by the death, from death and hell us brought
Revive my soul, my sins, my sores redress
That I may live with thee in everlasting bless.

In the Tower Ingram had endured torture at the hands of Topcliffe who, furious that he could get nothing out of him, called him a monster of taciturnity. In his letter of farewell to his fellow prisoners John wrote, 'I take God to record that I neither named a house, man, wife or child in time of, or before, my torments. My bloody Saul, Topcliffe, said I was a monster amongst all other ...'

Boste and Ingram were tied to horses for the long journey north and kept apart so they could not confer. They arrived at York on 13 July and Ingram was placed in solitary confinement for three days. On 16 July Boste was sent to Durham. This time his travelling companion was George Errington whom he had known since their days together at Oxford and Boste must have been party to his work in sheltering and guiding priests. When they arrived at Durham Errington was sent on to Newcastle. The Durham Assizes began on Monday, 22 July, and to set the tone Matthew Hutton, thrice-married Bishop of Durham, future Archbishop of York and eventual successor of Huntingdon as Lord President of the Council of the North, preached an anti-Catholic tirade in which he urged the judges to use all the rigour of the law against seminary priests. The following day the trial of the two priests took place before Sir Francis Beaumont, Lord Huntingdon, Mr Justice Ewings and Hutton. The prosecution was in the hands of Mr Pepper, the Queen's Attorney. Beaumont, a judge of the Queen's Bench, York division, was an interesting representative of his times. He was raised as a Catholic by his devout mother who regularly sheltered priests. She was the aunt of Anne and Eleanor Vaux, her sister having married William, 3rd Lord Vaux. Father Henry Garnet SJ, who calls her 'saintly', knew her well and attended her secretly in her last illness and death. By her request, her son was not informed of her death until after a Requiem Mass had been said for her. Beaumont's wife was also a Catholic. Garnet described Beaumont as a man of honour who did not want to be involved in religious cases, but his weakness was his ambition. His son, another Francis, became a leading poet and playwright of the Jacobean era. In one of his poems he wrote, 'The greatest attribute of Heaven is mercy'. One wonders how much the father may have shared his son's sentiment.

The vivid account of Boste's trial and execution was written by an eyewitness, Blessed Christopher Robinson, [52] a priest who was himself martyred in 1597.

John was brought into court and the charges of his being a priest and having said Mass at Waterhouse were read out. John said, 'Woe be to them that have taught that true obedience to the Queen and true religion cannot stand together well. I do not mean that any of this inquest shall stand charged or be guilty of my blood. I had rather confess the whole

The Elizabethan Martyrs, 1577-1601

indictment'. So to save the jury he declared that as a priest of the Catholic Church he had come to preach the Gospel and administer the Sacraments, and greatly rejoiced that he had done so. Ewings told him that he was an 'obstinate villain'.

No further proceedings were required; his confession was recorded and Beaumont ordered that he be removed from court. When John tried to speak again Ewings ordered him to be silent for being 'impudent.' He was followed on the stand by Father Ingram. He too confessed that he was a priest, but opted for a trial. He acknowledged that he had come into England for about ten hours but had not exercised any priestly function in the country. The evidence of the apostate priest turned spy, William Hardesty, was then produced identifying Ingram. After that Beaumont gave Ingram short shrift, telling him that 'coming into England, even though he no more than set his foot within the land' as a priest was treason and sent him back to prison.

Then George Swallowell, who came from Houghton-le-Spring and was a former Protestant minister and schoolteacher, was indicted for being reconciled to the Church and for persuading others to popery. He had had the courage to announce his conversion from the pulpit at Houghton where he served as curate. He was accused of this and of extolling the virtues of four Blessed priests; twenty-seven-year-old Edmund Duke, and Richard Hill, John Hogg and Richard Holiday, 53 who were all aged twenty-five. Ordained in September 1589, and having been back in England barely two months, they had been martyred at Durham on 27 May 1590.

Later that afternoon Swallowell and Father Ingram were pronounced guilty of treason, Ingram strenuously protesting: 'There is no Christian law in all the world that can make the saying of Mass treason'. He was quickly silenced and returned to his cell.

The following morning, 24 July, John Boste was called back into court with Ingram and Swallowell. Asked if they had anything to say before sentencing, there followed a series of altercations with the bench. Boste said that he was 'glad that God had called him unto that trial of his priesthood and profession, and very sorry that the laws of his beloved country were such as could not concur with the holy Catholic faith.' Beaumont commanded him to be silent. Father Ingram told them he forgave them and all his accusers with all his heart and asked God to give him strength to face what lay ahead. Mr Swallowell however, being very fearful, asked for mercy, even to the extent of indicating that he would take the oath to save his life. When the death sentence was pronounced, the two priests kissed and embraced one another, joyfully bursting into the *Te Deum*, much to the consternation of the court.

The Elizabethan Martyrs, 1577-1601

Seeing the reaction of the priests put new heart into the wavering Swallowell. He called out, 'My lords, I pray you hear me. Let me die with these two blessed martyrs. I will be a Catholic and die as they do; and I here renounce and am sorry for that which I last said ...' He told the court that it had been made out the priests were to die for treason, whereas they were martyrs, 'yet in very truth they die for religion ... and I am content to suffer with them'. He made such vehement protestations that the court fell about laughing. Then Huntingdon said, 'We do laugh at him, but there is much more cause to weep for him.' The bench was nonplussed by this change of heart, but after a hurried consultation the death sentence was confirmed on Swallowell.

At four o'clock that same afternoon Boste was brought out of the Northgate Prison by the under-sheriff. He was laid on his back in a cart, his hands raised towards heaven, and followed by a large crowd, he was taken over Framwellgate Bridge to his execution at Dryburn outside the city. He wore a nightcap on which was embroidered the name of Jesus and an Agnus Dei. John was so popular that special precautions had been taken to prevent a rescue attempt. On arrival at the site John raised himself up and removing his cap thanked the officials for the trouble they had taken in bringing him there. After kneeling in prayer he rose but was denied the chance to speak to the spectators and was ordered to step up the ladder. As he mounted the ladder John made the sign of the Cross and began the Hail Mary, pausing on each step as he continued his prayer. Then almost reaching the top of the ladder he turned around and attempted to address the crowd, but he had no sooner begun than the sheriff commanded the hangman to do his office and the rope was put around John's neck. He said, 'Will you not allow me to thank the ladies and gentlemen who have done me the honour and kindness to accompany me today?' At this point the sheriff told John that now he could speak, but when he tried to deliver the speech he had designed he was told only to say his prayers, to which he replied, 'I hope in God that if you will not suffer me to speak unto you in this world, this my death will speak in your hearts, that which I would have spoken. Suffer me to speak to my soul in the psalms of the prophet David.' Holding up his hands John began Psalm 116, 'I love the Lord because he hears me; he listens to my prayers.' As he recited the psalm in Latin he interposed illuminating comments in English about the contemporary situation between the verses. The sheriff objected to this and told him that if he wanted to continue the psalm it had to be in Latin only.

When called upon to ask the Queen's pardon, he replied, 'I have never offended her. I take it upon my death, I never went about to hurt her. I wish to God that my blood may be in satisfaction for her sins'. At this the sheriff ordered him turned off the ladder. The bystanders heard John say 'Father, into your hands I commend my spirit'.

He was allowed to hang for a few minutes until he lost consciousness. He was cut down from the rope and was caught as he fell by the officers who carried him to the fire prepared under the nearby trees. While his stomach was being ripped open he revived and cried out, 'God forgive thee, go on, go on. Lay not this sin to their charge.' He was still conscious as they cut off his genitals and hurled them into the fire. His body was terribly mangled in the dismemberment. His four quarters were set up on Durham Castle and his head on Framwellgate Bridge.

On 26 July, two days after Boste's martyrdom, Blessed John Ingram was taken from Durham to Gateshead. He wore a cap embroidered in red with the name of Jesus. As he was laid in the cart John said, 'I am led as an innocent lamb to the slaughter.' Once out of Durham they switched him from the cart onto a horse. It was a most uncomfortable ride for him. He had to hold the bridle in his left hand because his right hand was so damaged by racking. They changed horses at Chester-le-Street and so, escorted by Captain Ellis, one of Huntingdon's men, John was conveyed to the Tollbooth at Gateshead. About 3 p.m. that afternoon he was laid in a cart and drawn to the place of execution. Arrived at the gallows he knelt and prayed. As he ascended the ladder he declared, 'I take God and His holy angels to the record that I die only for the holy Catholic faith and religion and I do rejoice and thank God with all my heart that He hath made me worthy to testify my faith by the spending of my blood in this manner'.

A minister protested to the sheriff that John was preaching to the people, so the sheriff interrupted him. As he finished his prayers and made the sign of the Cross he was turned off the ladder. His head was sent to Newcastle and set up on the bridge beside those of two other martyred priests, Joseph Lambton [54] and Edward Waterson. [55] On the same day Blessed George Swallowell was taken to Darlington to be hanged, drawn and quartered. Arrived at the gallows he was disturbed to see so many ministers clustered around. 'Mr Sheriff, you promised me that I would not be troubled; I pray you take them away', he said. He climbed the ladder and the under-sheriff told him he was a traitor and was going to receive his just deserts. He was urged to ask the Queen's forgiveness. Swallowell answered that he had offended God, for he had 'given to Caesar more than was Caesar's due.'

Of those taken with Boste at Waterhouse, Mrs Grace Clapton and Lady Margaret Neville were tried before Lord Huntingdon on 1 February 1594. The Court had a busy day with over eighty recusants

The Elizabethan Martyrs, 1577-1601

indicted, among them Blessed John Speed, said to be a very simple man, aged about twenty-two years, who was convicted of relieving priests; among them almost certainly was John Boste. Refusing to conform he was hanged on 4 February. Mrs Clapton was found guilty but reprieved. She was kept in prison for twenty weeks during which time her children, whom she greatly missed, were used as pawns to get her to eventually conform. Lady Margaret was treated respectfully and was urged by Lord Huntingdon and Tobie Matthew to plead guilty and submit to the Queen's mercy. On her knees, she humbly craved Her Majesty's pardon, and was reprieved. She was put under house arrest, firstly with an under-sheriff, who treated her badly; secondly, with Hutton, Bishop of Durham, at Auckland. He did all in his power to get her to conform. He wrote to Lord Burghley informing him that Margaret had been 'reclaimed from popery'. When she was liberated she married and joined the Established Church. Her father, Charles Neville, attainted in 1571 for his part in the Northern Rising, died a penniless exile in Flanders in1601.

Robert Southwell

God's gift am I and none but God shall have me.

The Nativity of Christ, Robert Southwell, 1561-94

The Southwell's (now pronounced 'Suthell' but in Robert's lifetime the 'w' was pronounced) were an ancient family who took their name from their place of origin. Robert was the third son of Sir Richard Southwell and his first wife, Bridget Copley. Bridget was the sister of Sir Thomas Copley of Gatton, whose story has already been related. Through his mother Robert was related to the Gage, Shelley and Cecil families. Robert's elder brothers were Richard and Thomas and his sisters were Elizabeth, Anne, Frances, Catherine and Mary. Robert was born in late 1561 at what was once an old Benedictine priory at Horsham St Faith, Norfolk. His wealthy grandfather, Sir Richard, Sheriff of Norfolk, had been prominent at the court of Henry VIII and had been called as a witness (a truthful one as it happened!) at the trial of Sir Thomas More. Richard had also been partly responsible, by giving evidence against him, for bringing his distant cousin, the poet Henry Howard, Earl of Surrey, to his death on the block in 1547. (It is ironic that their respective grandsons, Robert Southwell and Philip Howard, were destined to be great friends and martyrs for their faith although they never met.) It was Sir Richard who had acquired the old priory along with other monastic properties after their suppression. Robert's father was a church papist, outwardly conforming to the State religion in order to preserve his status and wealth, although he died in 1600 fully reconciled to the Church. His mother, who had been a companion of the young Princess Elizabeth, remained loyal to the Old Faith and regularly sheltered priests.

As a small child Robert had been stolen from his cradle by a gipsy woman. In adulthood he often speculated what his life might have been like had his nurse not found him in the woods and rescued him. Robert was brought up as a Catholic surrounded by recusant relations. In 1576, at the age of fifteen he was sent to France with his cousin John Cotton to complete his education. He was a pupil of a Jesuit, Leonard Lessius, famous for the austerity of his life. He also studied for a short time at the Clermont College in Paris with another Jesuit, Thomas Darbyshire, who he took as his spiritual director. Darbyshire had once been Archdeacon of Essex under Queen Mary. It was the highly respected Father Darbyshire who, early in Elizabeth's reign, had been deputed by English Catholics to visit the Council of Trent to obtain the opinion of the fathers there assembled as to the lawfulness of attending the Established Church. The answer that he brought back, and which settled the question, was that to do so would be a grave sin. (A nephew of Bishop Edmund Bonner, Darbyshire joined the Jesuits in 1563. He died at Pont à Mousson in 1604, aged eighty-six.)

Robert had thought of becoming a Carthusian but abandoned that idea when at the age of seventeen he decided to join the Society of Jesus. He was refused on account of his youth. He was so determined that he walked all the way to Rome and was accepted by the Jesuits as a novice on 17 October 1578, taking simple vows in 1580. With all the ardour of youth he could, somewhat depressingly, write, 'I must not expect anything throughout my life ... except to suffer and be afflicted by continual tribulations, so as not to have peace even for an hour. Indeed, to be afflicted, I must count among the principal benefits of God, since this is the only way to follow Christ.' He spent his novitiate in France returning to Rome to finish his studies. A brilliant student, his poetry was already beginning to attract attention. He was made Prefect of Studies at the English College and was ordained priest in 1584. He was much influenced by Father Robert Persons and was eager to return home to England to help in the mission even if that meant he was going to his death. He did not have long to wait. In March 1586, on the eve of his departure, he wrote to the young, dynamic Claudio Aquaviva, one of the greatest Superior General's of the Society of Jesus, 'I address you, my Father, from the threshold of death, imploring the aid of your prayers ... that I may either escape the death of the body for further use, or endure it with courage.' Robert declared he wished to give his life to Christ, but before that, to get through a great deal of hard work for the good of souls.

Bidding farewell to Persons on the Milvian Bridge, at the age of twenty-five he set out to return to England in the company of fellow Jesuit Father Henry Garnet, with whom he came to enjoy a close and loving friendship. Spies had alerted the government to their coming, so in July they secretly disembarked on a secluded stretch of the coast between Dover and Folkestone. It was not a propitious time - if there ever was such a time - because it coincided with the fall-out from the so-called Babington Plot.

Fashionably dressed and using the alias of Cotton, Robert travelled to London. Here, he and Garnet made their way to one of the prisons, as this was one place they were sure to find Catholic contacts. As a result they were given temporary shelter with an innkeeper. On being told of their arrival, Father William Weston, the Jesuit Superior, went to the inn to welcome them. Weston was at the time the only Jesuit still at liberty and he managed to get them out of London in the nick of time. He escorted them to Hurleyford House on the Buckinghamshire bank of the River Thames. This was the home of Richard Bold of Prescot, a former sheriff of Lancashire and member of the Earl of Leicester's household. Thanks to Father Weston he had returned to Catholicism. At Hurleyford the priests found sanctuary among a large group of Catholics, among them William Byrd, the great composer and musician who lived nearby at Harlington. (Byrd had been attached to the Chapel Royal but, in spite of writing some marvellous music for the Anglican liturgy, he tired of being forced to compose for the State Church. About 1591 he gave up his position at Court, sacrificing any preferment for his faith. He went to live at Stondon Massey where, aged eighty-three, he died in 1623 declaring in his will that he died a 'true and perfect member of the Holy Catholic Church without which there is no salvation for me.') Arising from this meeting Byrd and Father Garnet, himself a fine musician, became great friends.

They spent over a week at the house and as there was a chapel with an organ, built by Mr Bold himself, we know that they sang Mass. It is not too fanciful to imagine that Southwell and his companions may have taken part in singing some of Byrd's great music. Father Weston wrote 'During these days ... we were very happy and our friends made it apparent how pleased they were to have us.' Acting upon information supplied to them by Father Weston, based on his knowledge of current conditions in England, the opportunity was also taken to work out an organisational plan for the better future deployment of priests on the mission, as well as consolidating the network of safe houses for them.

Walsingham closed in after the Babington Plot had been revealed. His spies must have reported about the Hurleyford House gathering because William Byrd's home was one of those raided and twelve days after his return to London Father Weston was arrested. It was left to Garnet, who succeeded Weston as Superior, to put into effect the plans that had been agreed.

Garnet left London for the Midlands where he was sheltered by Eleanor and Anne, two daughters of Lord Vaux of Harrowden. Robert next found refuge for several months with Lord Vaux at his cultured household in Hackney, London. A great deal of Robert's correspondence has survived and provides valuable insights into the conditions in which he worked and the lives of Catholics. In one letter he asks permission to consecrate chalices and other sacred items - a function normally reserved to bishops - because of the great shortage caused by their confiscations in the raids on the homes of Catholics. Robert was also greatly concerned about the spiritual welfare of his father and siblings, as his letters home reveal. To his brother, Thomas, he wrote, 'Shrine not any longer a dead soul in a living body: bail reason out of senses' prison, that after so long a bondage in sin, you may enjoy your former liberty in God's Church and free your thoughts from servile awe of uncertain perils. Weigh with yourself at how easy a price you rate God, whom you are content to sell for the use of your substance ... Look if you can upon a crucifix without blushing; do not but count the five wounds of Christ once over without a bleeding conscience.' Thomas was reconciled to the Church and later died in exile in the Netherlands.

Robert was lucky in managing to evade capture on several occasions. While staying at the Vaux house he had at least one narrow escape from the pursuivants when the house was raided. Eleanor Brooksby, Lord Vaux's widowed daughter, had adopted her little cousin, Frances Burrows. Aged eleven Frances courageously confronted the searchers and by a quick-witted ruse thwarted them from discovering and capturing Southwell. Robert describes how from behind a partition he heard the searchers smashing the woodwork and sounding all the walls but without finding him. For several nights afterwards he slept in his clothes in a very uncomfortable hiding place.

At first he moved about London fairly freely, often in disguise and one morning he came across a group of Catholics who were being

The Elizabethan Martyrs, 1577-1601

dragged off to prison having been evicted from their homes. He was able to go about the countryside around the capital administering the Sacraments. It was the Jesuit custom for as many of their number as possible to meet up bi-annually to renew their vows and give an account to their Superior. Father John Gerard referring to the meetings wrote, 'It braced my soul to meet all the obligations of my life as a Jesuit and meet all the demands made of a priest on the mission. Apart from the consolation I got from renewing my vows, I experienced a new strength and an ardent zeal'.

In 1591 Robert was at Baddesley Clinton, Warwickshire for one of these meetings with his fellow Jesuits when the moated manor house, which had been leased by the Vaux sisters, Eleanor and Anne, was raided by armed pursuivants at 5 a.m. just as he was preparing to say Mass. Hearing the uproar, Robert pulled off his vestments and hid all the altar furniture. Even the mattresses were turned in case any warmth on them betrayed that the beds had been slept in. While the servants held off the invaders, the priests scrambled down a shaft constructed by Nicholas Owen into an underground tunnel hiding place where they had to stand in water up to their ankles for over four hours. In a letter to a fellow Jesuit Robert described the gathering:

We make progress amid tempestuous waves with no little peril, but in spite of all, our Lord has been pleased to preserve us until now. We meet together to renew our vows according to our custom - a matter of great consolation to us. Indeed, it seems to me that I am witnessing the beginnings of religious life in this island, and albeit amidst tears, ourselves sowing the seed. Thus it may be that others coming after us will carry their sheaves with joy to heaven. All the same our joy was turned to sorrow as sudden alarms sent us packing in all directions. As it turned out the danger was greater than the harm done. We all survived the storm.

Father Gerard, who described Robert as 'so wise and good, gentle and loveable', tells us how he taught Robert the country sporting terms that would enable him to converse in gentlemanly company and so maintain his disguise. Southwell in many ways represented all that was best in the mission priests. Men of cheerful, strong character, unshakeable in their faith, who exercised amazing self-control. As Southwell wrote, 'Our men in prison are happy and cheerful. Those who are free do not expect to remain so for long: but they do not worry much. They are all of them braced up to suffer whatever God's cause may bring. They are more anxious about His glory and the good of souls than any temporal misfortune.' Filled with love, the mission priests exemplified their Saviour's commandment to love their neighbour, though he was their enemy who persecuted them. Men whose spirits, even under the most dreadful torture and in the face of a grisly death, exhibited superhuman courage, and remained unconquered because of their conviction that death would be the gateway to everlasting life. Robert wrote, 'Our vocation is not to be enclosed in cells far from intercourse with men, but to combat openly and while rebuking the irregular devices of others, we must be watchful that we are not overcome by our own. Among the loquacious observe moderation of speech, among the irascible guard the temper, among lovers of pleasure beware of self-indulgence ... The least blot in a religious is a great deformity. Jesu let thy blood run in my mind as water of life, to cleanse the filth of my sins and to bring forth the fruit of everlasting life.'

Robert was of a sweet and gentle disposition and always kept aloof from politics and controversy, but in the intensification of the persecution after the Armada scare in 1588 he had to find new secure lodgings in London. This was provided at Arundel House, in all but name a palace. Situated on the south side of the Strand, with gardens leading down to its River Thames frontage, it was the home of Anne Howard née Dacre, Countess of Arundel, whose husband, Philip, was in the Tower. Martin Array had been the Countess's regular visiting priest until he was captured. Robert took his place. He was able to secretly correspond with Philip and offer him some measure of comfort. With Somerset House and Leicester House for neighbours, Southwell stayed in a secret room of the house by day, going out in disguise at night to minister to Catholics, especially those in the prisons. But his ministry was by no means confined to London. In the dark days following the Armada, encouraged by Father Garnet, he travelled widely for several weeks in Sussex, the Midlands and East Anglia, encouraging the beleaguered Catholics to remain steadfast. He was assisted by the faithful Wiseman brothers, Thomas and John, of Braddocks, near Saffron Walden. In his report of his tour Robert described the plight of the Catholics imprisoned at Ely.

In this way he laboured with great zeal for the next six years. It was at this time that he wrote his many well-known works of poetry and prose, which he managed to publish on a secret printing press funded by the Countess, as well as publishing books of devotion and counterblasts to the anti-Catholic polemical pamphlets. His admired poetry was immediately popular and went through many editions throughout the sixteenth and seventeenth centuries and has been shown to have influenced Shakespeare. Ben Jonson, the dramatist, said of Southwell's *'The Burning Babe'*, that he would readily have destroyed

The Elizabethan Martyrs, 1577-1601

many of his own works if he could only have written that poem.

From his letters it is clear that Robert can have been under no illusions as to the likelihood of his own fate, presaged by the executions of his fellow priests. He wrote admiring accounts to his superiors of martyrs he had helped and befriended, such as Thomas Pormort. 56 Robert was martyred exactly three years later to the day - 21 February - as Thomas. Among Southwell's letters in the Public Record Office is one dated 8 March 1590, four days after he had witnessed the martyrdom of a twenty-five-year-old priest, Blessed Christopher Bales. The same day two laymen, Blessed Nicholas Horner and Blessed Alexander Blake, were executed for assisting priests. Bales was born in 1564 at Conniscliffe, Co. Durham, and educated at Rheims and Rome. For a time he had been a pupil of Robert's. Ordained at Laon 28 March 1587 he returned to England in the Armada year of 1588 travelling with Fathers Henry Garnet and Edward Oldcorne.. The warrant for his arrest, and that of his brother, John, at the home of Henry Thirkell in Gray's Inn Lane, was issued in August 1589 by the Council. Bales was committed a close prisoner to the Bridewell, with the ominous instruction that only Richard Topcliffe should have access to him and permission for torture to be applied 'as is usual.' This was particularly cruel as Christopher was a very frail, sick man, but he disclosed nothing. Nicholas Horner was a tailor by trade. Born at Grantley, near Ripon, Yorkshire, he came to London seeking medical treatment for his leg, which had to be amputated while he was in prison. Referred to as 'a holy old man', he lodged in Smithfield and gave shelter to priests. One of his 'crimes' was making jerkins for priests. Blake, who had formerly been an ostler at an inn, was described as 'a poor man that kept a lodging house'. At his trial, when sentence had been pronounced, Bales answered,' This only do I want to know, whether St Augustine, sent hither by St Gregory the Great, was a traitor or not.' The judge responded that he was not, to which Christopher replied, 'Why then, do you condemn me to death as a traitor. I am sent hither by the same See, and for the same purpose as he was. Nothing is charged against me that could not also be charged against the saint.' This elicited cries from the Court of 'Away with him!' Robert Southwell writes:

As yet we languish in the midst of dangers and we are even now in imminent peril, although for the moment thanks be to God, we are untouched. We have all sworn with one great longing in the renewal of our ancient fealty to be faithful unto the end ... Great joys and deep sorrows succeed each other with startling contrast and no sooner have impending terrors been dispersed as smoke than we experience a sense of relief having suffered less than the danger threatened. I and one other of our companions ... having escaped both

The Elizabethan Martyrs, 1577-1601

dangers through the wonderful goodness of God, we are now securely steering our course to port. Lately, beside others, has been seized a certain priest Christopher Bales ... He was horribly tortured for the space of twenty-four hours, hanging by the hands, his toes scarcely touching the ground. While in this agony they wearied him with incessant questioning. To all this he gave but one answer: he was a Catholic priest, having come to recall souls into the fold of Christ, and he had never entertained in his heart any other design. He was condemned to death ... as he was being drawn to the place of execution he chanted the psalms ... When he ascended the scaffold he said, 'Far be it from me to glory, except in the Cross of our Lord Jesus Christ.' And lifting up his hands to heaven he signed himself with the sign of the Cross as well as the weight of his chains would allow. 'You have come', he said, 'to see a man die, a common spectacle, not less common because that man is a priest; and as you gaze upon the body, would to God that your glance might penetrate deep down into the affections of my heart. Then you might see what is the lot of that soul which is about to take its flight hence. You would then both sympathise and rejoice with me, as even now with unfriendly cry you send me to my doom. From my heart I forgive all and from you all I beg forgiveness...' By such dew is the Church refreshed.

After Bales was hanged, drawn and quartered in Fleet Street the executioner, his hands gory with blood, hurried to Smithfield to hang Nicholas Horner, then to Gray's Inn Lane to perform the same task for Alexander Blake, who was executed outside the inn where he was employed. On the gallows was a sign declaring him to be a traitor. It was Ash Wednesday, 4 March 1590. Southwell concludes his letter, 'Meanwhile, we also as labourers await the advent of our day - always supposing we are not unworthy of so much glory - and this shall be our day of reward.'

While Robert's letter was still on its way the martyrdoms of four other priests - two each on the same day - took place in Rochester and London: Francis Dickenson [57] and Miles Gerard [58] and Edward Jones [59] and Anthony Middleton [60].

In response to the government's abusive proclamation of 1591 against Jesuits and seminary priests, Robert wrote his *An Humble Supplication to Her Majesty*. The book was available in manuscript but was not published in his lifetime. The government did its best to suppress the book when it appeared in 1600, and some of those responsible for its distribution were executed. Robert wrote as if Elizabeth were unaware of what was going on; far removed from the truth, of course. He stressed the religious nature of the persecution of the Church in which the Queen's predecessors and all the saints of England had lived and died. He asked Elizabeth to imagine how amazed all the English of history would be at the final judgement to discover that their faith and charity under the chief pastor, the Pope, was now reckoned as treason. He described what Catholics had to endure and the tortures employed in the prisons and appealed to her 'merciful hand' to alleviate their sufferings. In stark contrast to Pius V's bull Robert contended that Catholics owed obedience to the Queen in everything that did not threaten their eternal salvation, and that active resistance to her could not be justified. Robert emphasized that the Catholic religion 'more than any other, tieth us to a most exact submission to your temporal authority, and to all points of allegiance, that either now in Catholic countries, or even before in Catholic times were acknowledged to be due to any Christian prince.' He contrasted this with the attitude of Calvinists and Puritans and other 'sectaries' who denied the necessity of obeying 'the just laws of their princes'. He went on to say, 'therefore if we were not pressed to that, which by general verdict of allegiance, was judged breach of the law of God: we should never give your majesty the least cause of displeasure, for ... in all other civil and temporal respects, we are so submitted ... as any of your majesty's best beloved subjects.'

Robert often visited the manor house of the Catholic Bellamy family, Uxendon Hall, Harrow. The family was notorious for sheltering priests including Edmund Campion and Father Robert Persons. At the time the house was occupied by Catherine Bellamy, a widow since 1581. She and her son Richard had been indicted for recusancy in 1583. On 2 November 1584 Uxendon Hall suffered one of its regular raids when Father John Bavant, who had been tutor to Edmund Campion at St John's, Oxford, had a lucky escape, although by 1585 he was in prison in London and then sent to Wisbech. Coinciding with the Babington Plot in 1586, for harbouring priests Catherine was imprisoned in the Fleet, later being removed to the Tower. She was a member of the Page family of Harrow, who gave two priest martyrs to the Church. There is an extant, handwritten note of Walsingham's ordering her condemnation before any trial had taken place. Elderly and sickly, Mrs Bellamy never emerged from the Tower; she died there, as did her third son, Bartholomew, who died under torture. Her fifth son, Jerome, was executed for giving food to Babington and some of the escaping alleged plotters who had hidden near Harrow. Her fourth son, Robert, suffered greatly for his religion. Early in 1585 he was committed to Newgate for hearing Mass celebrated by William Thomson, who was martyred 20 April 1586. By December of that year Robert was a prisoner in the Clink. He was in the Marshalsea in 1593, having been in jail for the past seven years.

Catherine's eldest son, Richard Bellamy and his wife, another Catherine, who were Southwell's hosts, moved into Uxendon Hall

The Elizabethan Martyrs, 1577-1601

when his mother was imprisoned. They had five children. Their eldest daughter, aged twenty-eight, was Anne. On a raid of Uxendon in January 1592, as well as taking away a great number of Catholic books, Topcliffe had carried Anne off to the Gatehouse prison. At first she was defiant but she was terrorised and raped by Topcliffe. She became pregnant and was compelled to marry Nicholas Jones, an Under-Keeper at the prison and cohort of Topcliffe's. After Anne had given birth, Topcliffe, seeking to add insult to injury by profiting from his misdeeds, asked her father for a marriage portion and for another of his houses, nearby valuable Preston Manor. Richard Bellamy angrily refused the request. Having been closely confined for months, Anne seems to have been promised that she could obtain a pardon for all her family if she betrayed Southwell, so in her misery she sent a message asking him to meet her at Uxendon Hall. Unsuspecting, Robert agreed, and also arranged to meet his fellow Jesuit, Father Richard Blount, at Harrow. Fortunately for Blount, because of problems with his horse, he was delayed and was thus spared the same fate as Southwell.

On Sunday, 25 June 1592 Robert, accompanied by Thomas Bellamy, Anne's brother, set out for Uxendon. Robert said what was to be his last Mass for the Bellamys and remained overnight. Having been tipped off by Nicholas Jones, Topcliffe arrived in the middle of the night with his large, armed search party and started to violently ransack the house. Topcliffe raved at Mrs Bellamy demanding she surrender Cotton (Robert's alias) to them but she denied knowing such a man. In an effort to save the family from worse trouble, Robert came out of his hiding place and surrendered. Topcliffe compared the description of Robert given by Anne Bellamy and knew he had his man whom he violently abused. Anne was not only the ruin of Robert but also of her whole family. Her parents and her two brothers and two sisters were arrested. On Topcliffe's personal instructions, Mr and Mrs Bellamy - whom he described as 'the old hen that hatched those chicks (the worst that ever was)' - were sent to the Gatehouse, their daughters to the Clink and their sons to St Catharine's. Richard Bellamy remained a prisoner for ten years in harsh conditions. He sold Uxendon Hall and went to live abroad dying in poverty in what is now Belgium. His wife and sons eventually conformed to the extent of attending the Anglican Church but not receiving communion. The two daughters were made of sterner stuff; Audrey, Mrs Wilforde, a widow at nineteen, and Mary declared that their consciences would not allow them to go to church.

Topcliffe was jubilant at capturing Robert and on Monday, 26 June wrote triumphantly to the Queen in his idiosyncratic spelling assuring her that he would extract from the Jesuit all his secrets. 'I never did

The Elizabethan Martyrs, 1577-1601

take such a weighty man ... I have him here within my strong chamber in Westminster churchyard.' 'Her Majesty's Servant' was sure he could break Southwell, describing in detail to the Queen what torture he intended to apply and asking her what it was her pleasure to know from him and he would force Southwell to divulge it. The Queen received the news with 'merriment'. Her Majesty's pleasure was to allow Topcliffe to do whatever he liked with his captive.

Robert was kept prisoner by Topcliffe in atrocious conditions for many weeks during which he was sadistically tortured with unimaginable severity. He underwent the so-called 'wall torture' ten times. He was hung from the wall by his wrists, a sharp circle of iron around each wrist. His legs were bent backwards, his feet tied to his thighs. He was left hanging like this for hours at a time while undergoing questioning. They tried to get him to incriminate Anne Howard, Countess of Arundel, and his fellow Catholics but all he would admit was that he was a Jesuit priest. Each time he appeared to be on the point of death he was taken down, revived and hung up again, despite vomiting large amounts of blood. This barbarity left Robert with permanent internal injuries. Afterwards he was to admit that the pain was so bad death would have been preferable. Lord Burghley's son, Sir Robert Cecil, Secretary of State, [61] who was a relative of Southwell's, witnessed one of these interrogations. Afterwards he wrote, 'We have a new torture thought impossible for a man to bear. And yet I have seen Robert Southwell hanging by it, still as a tree trunk and no one able to drag one word from his mouth.'

His torturers, having failed to extract anything from Robert he was imprisoned in the Gatehouse in a filthy cell where his keepers were Nicholas Jones and his wife, Anne Bellamy. Robert's father was allowed to visit him, and seeing him covered with filth and lice petitioned the Queen that his son should either be brought to trial or at least, as he was a gentleman, that she should order he be treated like one, even though he was a Jesuit. As a result Robert was moved to the Tower and his father was allowed to send clean clothes and bedding. He was left in close confinement in the Tower for nearly three years. Although he found the solitary existence hard to bear at times it was here that many of his most well-known poems were written. Many are on the theme of death, including *Saint Peter's Complaint*. They are very much in the popular style of his day as well as reflecting the nature and character of their author: ascetic, emotional, intense and lyrical; redolent of the sense that he was destined for the path of martyrdom. Hard-hearted Sir Michael Blount, the Lieutenant of the Tower, was captivated by Robert and referred to him as a saint.

The Elizabethan Martyrs, 1577-1601

In his time in the Tower Robert was allowed only one visit, from his father and sister Mary. The Queen had given permission for this providing they tried to persuade him to conform; which, of course, they failed to do. With the complicity of the warders, Robert and Philip Howard were occasionally able to smuggle notes to one another. Robert begged Cecil to bring him to trial. 'If he is in so much hurry to be hanged,' Cecil replied, 'he should quickly have his desire'.

On 18 February 1595, in readiness for his trial, he was moved from the Tower to Newgate, and placed in the underground dungeon known as 'Limbo'. The Catholics sent in food, drink and candles for him. Robert was tried at Westminster Hall on 20 February under Lord Chief Justice Popham, who had come a long way since the trial of Cuthbert Mayne. Henry Garnet was in the street to witness Robert being taken by road from Newgate to Westminster. Popham opened the proceedings with the usual invective against seminary priests and Jesuits in particular. He told the jury how severely men should be punished who 'corrupt the minds of their fellows with a religion that is superstitious.' For good measure he then threw in plots - real or imagined - and the Spanish Armada as 'evidence' of traitorous Catholic activities. Robert's voice had been badly affected and he could only speak in a hoarse whisper. He complained that his memory had been affected by the years of confinement and the tortures he had undergone, and expressed the wish that torturers would stop when it was clear that the victim was not going to reveal anything instead of cruelly carrying on. With quiet dignity he described his tortures to the court - much to the discomfort of Topcliffe, who tried to shout him down. When Topcliffe claimed that he had the permission of the Council to act as he did, Southwell told him: 'You are a bad man' and declared 'upon his soul, as he hoped shortly to answer before God' that what he had said was true. The court seemed genuinely shocked at the revelations.

Having been taken at Harrow, Robert said there was no point in denying the charges. 'I admit,' he said, 'that I was born in England and am the Queen's subject. Neither do I deny that I am an ordained priest; and for this status of mine I return the deepest possible thanks to Almighty God. That I was at Uxendon is plain for all to see since I was led here a captive from that place. I would not have been there, however, if I had not been enticed like a mouse into a trap.' He lodged a formal plea of 'not guilty' and appealed to the judges to hear his case. He was unhappy that the twelve jurymen would be asked to deliver a verdict against him but when Popham insisted Robert acquiesced. 'Seeing that the law so stipulates, and thus I must have those men as my triers, I must obey this unfair condition. Indeed, I must forgive the twelve men; and since I do not know any of them, I am bound by Christian charity not to think unfavourably of any one of them.' Sir Edward Coke, the Attorney-General, prosecuted haranguing the jury with a verbal onslaught. Robert argued his case as best he could despite the constant interruptions, abuse and personalised insults, being repeatedly called 'boy-priest'. Asked his age he replied that he was thirty-three, the same age that Christ had lived on earth. He was then accused of making himself equal to Christ. 'I am ready to give an account of my words and deeds, if you will listen to me. If it is to be a matter of shouting and insults, we have no such usage.' He insisted that he was no traitor; his only crime had been to administer the Sacraments to those willing to receive them. Sad to relate, Anne Jones, neé Bellamy, still believing it could help her family, gave evidence against Robert. While the jury deliberated Robert remained standing, short of breath and in great pain, grasping the dock for support. The jury took just fifteen minutes to return the only verdict they were allowed to deliver and the death sentence was pronounced. Robert responded, 'I pray God from my heart to forgive all of those who are in any way accessories to my death'. Even at this stage of the proceedings Topcliffe mockingly called out, 'I found him hiding under the tiles!' Robert's reply showed that in spite of everything he had still not lost his sense of humour. 'It was time to hide', he said, 'when Mr Topcliffe came.' Popham offered him the services of an Anglican minister but he courteously declined, saying that he would rely upon the grace of God. He was then returned to Newgate and Father Garnet describes how 'at different places along the way' Catholic friends gathered to see him pass by and Robert, insofar as he dared, was able to indicate that that he recognised them. Arrived at Newgate he was incarcerated in 'Limbo'.

The very next morning the keeper of Newgate came to conduct Robert to Tyburn for execution. Embracing him warmly he thanked the keeper, telling him that no one had ever brought him such good news before and gave him his cap as a token of gratitude that being the only thing he had left. It was a freezing cold morning as he lay down on the hurdle. En route a young woman - said to be his cousin - pushed through the guards and fell on her knees in the mud asking for his blessing. Despite his pinioned arms Robert blessed her as best he could, urging her to be careful of the horses' hooves. The woman could only have been Lady Margaret Gage.

On reaching the scaffold, Southwell's face radiated happiness. He used his handkerchief to wipe the mud from his face, then, screwing it up into a ball he threw it to someone in the crowd. It was later given to Father Garnet who wrote that Robert's courage, nobility and gentleness

The Elizabethan Martyrs, 1577-1601

won the hearts of all. There was an enormous crowd and Robert asked if he may speak. When he was refused, the crowd, not wanting to be deprived of the full drama of the event, shouted out that this should be allowed. He began by trying to make the sign of the Cross with his pinioned hands. He spoke on the text from Paul's letter to the Romans, chapter 14: 'If we live, it is for the Lord that we live, and if we die, it is for the Lord that we die. So whether we live or die, we belong to the Lord'.

He prayed for the country and the Queen and for her salvation, denying that he had ever wished her harm saying, 'May she use and enjoy the generous gifts God has given her to the undying glory of His name, the happiness of the whole kingdom, and the eternal welfare of her own soul and body. As for the miserable state of my country, I think I could weep in begging for it the light of truth ... I see they are urging me not to take up too much time and so I surrender this soul of mine into the hands of God my Creator.' He asked pardon for his sins, professed his faith, acknowledged his priesthood and begged his friends to pray for him, hoping that his death, 'though seeming disgraceful, yet I hope in time to come it will be to my eternal glory'. As the hangman placed the noose around his neck, Robert prayed, 'Blessed Mary, ever virgin and all you saints and angels assist me.' Closing his eyes he said, 'Into thy hands O Lord I commend my spirit'. The rope had not been positioned properly and slipped behind his head. The rope was adjusted and Robert opened his eyes. Looking down at the crowd he began reciting the *Miserere*. As he said 'Into thy hands' ... for the third time the cart was pulled away. Robert hung for some time, eyes open, beating his breast. The people loudly insisted that he should not be cut down until dead so the executioner hung onto his legs. And thus Robert attained the desire he had expressed in his poem *Life is but Loss*: 'Free would my soul from mortal body fly'. The words of *Decease-Release*, the ode that Robert penned on the execution of Mary, Queen of Scots were just as apt when applied to himself.

> Rue not my death, rejoice at my repose,
> It was not death to me but to my woe;
> The bud was opened to let out the rose,
> The chain was loosed to let the captive go.

When his head was severed from his body and held up for the crowd to see, instead of the usual shouts there was an eerie silence. Charles Blount, 8th Baron Mountjoy was present along with other nobles from the Court. It is very unlikely that Mountjoy knew Robert's poetic sentiment, 'when he taketh leave of life, then love begins his joys'; but Mountjoy was heard to say, 'I cannot answer for Southwell's religion, but I pray my soul may be with his'. He was, no doubt, echoing feelings shared by many: what was the country coming to when it subjected talented, gentle poets with a mystical turn of mind like Southwell to such barbarity for their religion?

Father Garnet wrote an account of Southwell's martyrdom to Claudio Aquaviva in Rome. 'My sorrow is that I have lost my most dear and loved companion; my gladness that the man I have cherished so much has risen to the throne of God, where he will be given ... peace in return for his cares ... so it is surely more fitting to rejoice and for the Church ... to give solemn thanks to God.'

Henry Walpole

One crowded hour of glorious life.

The Bee, Thomas Mordaunt, 1730-1809

Henry was born at Docking Hall, Norfolk, in October 1558. He was the eldest of the six sons of Christopher Walpole and Margery Beckham, who married at Docking in 1557. The Walpole's could trace their ancestry at Docking and Houghton in North West Norfolk back to at least the early twelfth century. At the time of Henry's birth they were a wealthy, property-owning family with interests in sheep farming. It was the Houghton branch of this same family who, in the eighteenth century, produced Sir Robert Walpole, England's first Prime Minister, and today the family is still prominent amongst the aristocracy and landed gentry of East Anglia. Having been born just weeks before the death of Queen Mary, Henry was baptised a Catholic.

A clever boy, at the age of eight Henry was sent, along with his cousin Edward, heir to the Houghton estate, to Norwich Grammar School where one of their contemporaries was Edward Coke, the future Lord Chief Justice. Henry received the classical education of the period, learning Latin and Greek. The headmaster of the school was a strong Puritan who supported the destruction of Norwich Cathedral organ and opposed its choral services, denouncing them as popish. Henry was expected to attend the Anglican services but he seems to have remained Catholic at heart, even if he did not exhibit any strong religious convictions. Henry matriculated at Cambridge and entered

The Elizabethan Martyrs, 1577-1601

Peterhouse College on 15 January 1575, where he showed great ability as a budding poet. Assenting to the Oath of Supremacy was a pre-requisite of obtaining a university degree. As Henry left Cambridge in April 1578 without taking a degree, the obvious conclusion may be drawn. He decided to study law and took chambers at Gray's Inn, London, whose members had a reputation for their Catholic sympathies. Henry attended one of the public disputations in the Tower between Edmund Campion and the Protestant ministers and was deeply impressed by Campion. He also witnessed the trial of the famous Jesuit and his companions in Westminster Hall and was present at Campion's execution. Standing near the Tyburn gallows some of Campion's blood splashed his clothes; it changed his life. The event made such an impact that he wrote a long, narrative poem, entitled, *An Epitaph of the Life and Death of the most famous and virtuous priest Edmund Campion*. He had the poem privately printed and distributed. It begins:

Why do I use my paper, ink and pen?
or call my wits to counsel what to say?
Such memories were made for mortal men,
I speak of saints whose names cannot decay.
An angel's trumpet were meeter far to sound
their glorious deaths, if such on earth were found.
Their register remaineth safe above.
Campion exceeds the compass of my skill,
yet let me use the measure of my love,
and give me leave in low and homely verse,
his high attempts in England to rehearse.
You thought perhaps when learned Campion dies,
his pen must cease, his sugared tongue be still,
but you forgot how loud his death it cries,
how far beyond the sound of tongue and quill,
you did not know how rare and great a good
it was to write his precious gifts in blood.

England look up, thy soil is stained with blood,
thou hast made martyrs many of thy own,
if thou hast grace their deaths will do thee good,
the seed will take which in such blood is sown,
and Campion's learning fertile so before,
thus watered too, must needs of force be more.
His quartered limbs shall join with joy again,
and rise a body brighter than the sun,
your blinded malice tortured him in vain,
for every wrench some glory hath him won,
and every drop of blood which he did spend,
hath reaped a joy which never shall have end.

The Elizabethan Martyrs, 1577-1601

And concludes:
> Blessed be God which lent him so much grace,
> thanked be Christ which blessed his martyrs so,
> happy is he which sees his Master's face,
> cursed are they that thought to work him woe,
> bounden be we to give eternal praise,
> to Jesus name which such a man did raise.

Henry's poem circulated quickly throughout the country and was seen as effective propaganda for the Catholic cause. The government ordered that all copies of the poem be confiscated and burned. When the printer, Stephen Vallenger, was discovered he was apprehended, but refused to name the author. Vallenger was heavily fined and had his ears cut off in the pillory. It was not only in England that Campion's martyrdom was widely celebrated. Only a few weeks afterwards Sir Henry Cobham, the English Ambassador to France, wrote to Francis Walsingham about a small French book circulating in Paris: 'They have been crying these books in the streets with outcries naming them to be cruelties used by the Queen of England.' William Byrd courageously set some stanzas of Walpole's poem to music in his *Psalms and Songs*, issued in 1588.

Having made his sympathies plain, it appears that Henry was under suspicion, and for a time he returned to his family in Norfolk and kept a low profile. But his mind was made up that he wanted to be a priest. He travelled, usually by night, all the way to Newcastle and from there crossed to Le Havre, France. From there he made his way via Rouen and Paris to Rheims arriving at the English College on 7 July 1582. On 28 April the following year he was sent to the English College, Rome. On 2 February 1584 he joined the Society of Jesus but during his novitiate his health deteriorated with pains in his chest and stomach and he returned to France to continue his studies at Pont à Mousson. Despite his poor health, which no doubt accounted for the delay, he was ordained sub-deacon at Metz, and then deacon and priest at Paris on 17 December 1588.

A cultured man with a captivating personality as well as being a skilful linguist, fluent in French, Italian and Spanish, Henry was sent by Claudio Aquaviva to Brussels to become a chaplain to the many different nationalities of European soldiers fighting in the Spanish army in the Netherlands - then still part of the Spanish Empire - under the command of Alexander Farnese, Duke of Parma. During the winter months Henry was sent to Tournai to complete his Jesuit training. Afterwards, while returning to Bruges, Henry was captured by a Dutch patrol, handed over to the English forces fighting on the side of the rebellious Dutch and sent to Flushing prison. It was intensely cold and having nothing but the clothes he stood up in he was soon experiencing great privation. He managed to send a message of his situation to his family and his brother Michael secretly made his way to Flushing. There, by paying a ransom, Michael secured Henry's release early in January 1590. Henry persuaded Michael not to return to England but to go to Rome with the aim of joining the Jesuits. Henry returned to Brussels stating that as a result of his imprisonment he had come 'to know better both God, the world and myself.'

Henry's younger brother Richard, born at Anmer Hall in October 1564, seems to have followed closely in his footsteps. Also educated at Peterhouse he arrived at Rheims in 1584 and in 1585 was sent to Rome, where he was ordained in 1589. He was sent in 1592 to help establish the English College at Seville. He joined the Jesuits in 1596 and succeeded Father Joseph Cresswell as Superior of the mission in Spain. He died, aged only forty-two, at Valladolid in 1607. Henry was soon joined by two more brothers: Christopher, born in October 1568; Michael, born in September 1570, and their Houghton cousin, Edward, born in January 1560. Richard, Michael, Christopher and Edward all became Jesuits. Christopher had been received into the Church by Father Gerard, who provided him with finance to make the journey to Rome for study. After ordination he joined the Society of Jesus in 1592 but died at Valladolid in 1606. For a time Michael was personal servant to Father Gerard before joining the Jesuits in 1593. He was twice imprisoned and exiled, rose to be Jesuit Superior and acquired a position of influence in England. He died at Seville in 1624. Edward Walpole followed the Calvinist religion of his father but he was converted by his cousin Henry. His parents were so aggrieved that they disowned him as a disgrace to his family and actually complained to the Privy Council about Henry, which may have been what prompted him to escape abroad. Edward arrived at the English College, Rome where he joined his cousin Michael in 1590. He entered the Jesuits in 1593 and two years later returned to England. He died in London in 1637 after forty years on the mission.

In spite of his experience, Henry Walpole continued as a much-loved military chaplain for a further two years, after which he made his final vows in the Society of Jesus at Tournai. He longed to join the English mission and sent frequent letters to Robert Persons asking to be sent home. Instead Claudio Aquaviva summoned Henry to Spain in 1592 to teach in the English Colleges. At Seville he met his brother Richard, whom he had not seen for ten years. Henry was next sent to

The Elizabethan Martyrs, 1577-1601

Valladolid, where he was appointed Vice-Rector. At last Henry got his heart's desire and in June 1593 he was asked to go to England. While in Madrid, acting on behalf of Persons, he had an audience at the Escorial with Philip II, from whom he obtained approval and funding for the newly-founded college at Saint-Omer, then in the Spanish Netherlands.

To Father Peralta, the rector of the English College at Seville Henry wrote from Madrid:

> Being on the point of departing to that perilous country whence come our young men, I could not forbear commending myself to you and all those of the Society who are with you, asking their prayers that God may grant me strength to carry out this voyage of mine successfully and to the glory of Our Lord.

Henry left Madrid on 4 August and arrived at Douai in September. He tried to arrange passage from Calais but there was another outbreak of plague in England and no ship would take the risk of landing at Dover. With his twenty-six-year-old soldier brother, Thomas, as a companion, Henry finally set sail from Dunkirk in November, having paid for his passage on a privateer commanded by a Spanish captain. They had hoped to disembark on the Essex or Norfolk coast but the weather was atrocious and the ship was carried ever further northwards. By the evening of 4 December, the tenth day of the voyage, they were off Flamborough Head on the Yorkshire coast. Henry and Thomas, 'for very weariness of the sea', asked to be put ashore at Bridlington. Unknown to Henry, a spy on board an accompanying ship had already managed to get ashore and report the priest's arrival to the authorities. Henry and Thomas first hid a packet of letters in the sand marked by a stone. They slept in woodland overnight then made their way a few miles inland to Kilham village, arriving at the inn the following morning wet and hungry. Arousing the suspicion of the locals they were arrested by the constable and sent to the Earl of Huntingdon at York where they were imprisoned in the Castle. Under questioning Thomas lost his nerve, confessed all he knew, even revealing the place on the seashore where the letters had been hidden, and was set free. Henry then admitted that he was a Jesuit priest.

At the end of January 1594 the dreaded Richard Topcliffe arrived in York to interrogate Henry, but he provided no useful information. Father Richard Holtby contrived to get in and out of York Castle frequently, and although the two Jesuits never had any personal contact they managed to keep up a smuggled correspondence, which greatly encouraged Henry. In one letter to Father Holtby, Henry wrote:

> I should be overjoyed if I could confer with your reverence by word of mouth about certain concerns of mine. In the meantime, most dear father, I recommend myself to your holy prayers, and those of the rest of our brethren

and friends in Christ Jesus our Lord. I know not as yet what will become of me; but whatever shall happen, by the grace of God, it shall be welcome; for in every place, north or south, east or west, he is at hand, and the wings of his protection and government are stretched forth to every place where they are who truly serve and worship him, and study to promote the glory and honour of his most holy and precious name. I trust that he will be glorified in me, whether in life or death.

And in another letter to Holtby penned after his first examination by Topcliffe he writes:

Your reverence's letters give me great comfort, but if I could but see you, though it were for one hour, it would be of greater service to me than I can express. I hope that what is wanting my sweet Lord Jesus will supply by other means, whose heavenly comfort and assistance has always hitherto stood by me in my greatest necessities, and I am persuaded will continue to do so, since his love for us is everlasting ... In my examination I gave in writing a long account of my life beyond the seas, of the places where I lived, and of my actions and designs; which, I assured them had no other but than the glory of God and the increase of the holy Catholic faith ...To their queries concerning others I refused to answer. When Topcliffe threatened that he would make me answer when he had me in Bridewell or the Tower, I told him, Our Lord I hoped would not permit me, for fear of any torments whatsoever, to do or say things against his divine majesty, or against my own conscience, or to the prejudice of justice and the innocence of others ... I am much astonished that so vile a creature as I am should be so near, as they tell me, to the crown of martyrdom: but this I know for certain, that the blood of my most blessed Saviour and Redeemer, and his most sweet love, is able to make me worthy of it ... I beg your reverence to join your prayers with my poor ones, that I may walk worthy of that high and holy name and profession to which I am called, which I trust in the mercy of our Lord he will grant me, not regarding so much my many imperfections as the fervent labours, prayers and holy sacrifices of so many fathers and my brothers, his servants, who are employed all over the world in his service; and I hope, through the merits of my most sweet Saviour and Lord, that I shall always be ready, whether living or dying, to glorify him, which will be for my eternal happiness ... And if in his mercy our Lord shall grant me now to wash my garments in the blood of the Lamb, I hope to follow him forever, clothed in white.

He spent the winter in prison and plans were discussed by friends on the outside to organise his escape. However Father Holtby advised against such a risky undertaking, especially as it might cause even greater harm to the other Catholic prisoners. Henry accepted the advice with good grace.

I have received your Reverence's letter, and I take the advice it gives me with much pleasure, as from the hand of our Lord God. Similar reasons occurred to me, and I proposed the matter to you only to give satisfaction to

The Elizabethan Martyrs, 1577-1601

others, knowing very well the spirit of our Society on similar consultations ... If St Peter had the help of an angel to escape from prison, it was because he was marked out to be father and universal pastor of Holy Church, and our Lord willed to make him first at Rome, and to place him on his chair. But all this is different with me; and so for me, this prison remains my Rome and my 'Domine quo vadis?' I do not see (even though I had not the hope that I have of attaining that eternal reward to which we run) how I could now be better employed than I am, having here such efficacious means of making profession of that which I am. I give many thanks to Jesus Christ our Lord that courage does not fail me. Since five sheets of paper have been given me, by order of the President, which I am to fill with the motives and reasons of my faith, in the controversies concerning the Church, the Eucharist and the Pope, I am shorter in this letter, and shall be so henceforward.

On 24 February 1594 Henry was transferred to the Tower of London where, brutally treated by the jailers and ill-fed, he was kept in solitary confinement for two months in the middle cell on the first floor of the Salt Tower. Among a great many inscriptions, Walpole's name, carved by himself, along with the names of Jesus and Mary and the pierced heart of Christ can still be seen. The same cell was later occupied by Father John Gerard.

Father Henry Garnet, the Jesuit Superior later wrote:
Father Walpole met in the Tower of London with the greatest misery and poverty, so that the Lieutenant himself, though otherwise a hard-hearted man, was moved to inquire after some of the Father's relations and told them that he was in great and extraordinary want - without bed, without clothes, without anything to cover him, and that at a season when the cold was most sharp and piercing, so that himself, though an enemy, out of pure compassion had given him a little straw to sleep on.

Robert Southwell was a fellow prisoner but it seems most unlikely that he and Henry ever met, though circumstantial evidence suggests they found some means to communicate. Repeatedly asked what he knew about plans to assassinate the Queen Henry replied, 'For mine own part I protest before God, as I have often done, that I abhor to think thereof, and never did nor would not move any man thereunto for all the good in the world. As Jesus is my witness.' Kept in the Tower for over a year, he was horrendously tortured by Topcliffe with the rack, thumbscrews, the Scavenger's Daughter, and hung up in the manacles. Henry Walpole has the dubious distinction of having been subjected to the most atrocious forms of torture more than any other martyr - no less than fourteen times - in an attempt to break him. His hands were crippled, his middle fingers having been torn loose. As a result he could no longer properly sign his name.

Under such torture and relentless questioning some information was obtained from Henry but he never betrayed anyone. For example, he admitted he knew that Father Henry Garnet had stayed at Braddocks, the Essex home of the Wiseman family. In the nineteenth century, documents were discovered in the Public Record Office purporting to be confessions made by Henry under torture. Some of them, countersigned by Richard Topcliffe, are 'confessions' allegedly bearing Henry's signature, abjectly begging the Queen's pardon and mercy and agreeing to join the Protestant Church. Scholars who have subsequently examined these documents are convinced that they are forgeries. Briefly, there are a number of reasons for this conclusion. The first and most overwhelming reason remains that if the 'confessions' were genuine, why were they not produced in evidence at Henry's trial? What an unprecedented coup it would have been for the government to have such 'confessions' read out in court; but they were never even mentioned.

Secondly, if Henry had purportedly renounced his faith, why was it necessary to go on torturing him? Thirdly, there are errors of fact in the 'confessions' that Walpole would never have made. And finally, every piece of contemporary information we have indicates that Henry was unable to write legibly after being tortured. Father John Gerard tells us,

He lost through it the proper use of his fingers. This I can vouch for from the following circumstances. He had a discussion with some ministers which he wrote out with his own hand. A part of this writing was given to me ... these writings, however, I could scarcely read at all ... because the hand of the writer could not form the letters. It seemed more like the first attempts of a child, than the handwriting of a scholar and gentleman such as he was.

Yet the signatures on the 'confessions' are perfectly formed and may be compared with those on letters prior to his torture. It is likely that the counterfeiting was carried out by Thomas Phelippes, who was in the pay of Walsingham and had been responsible for the forgeries to the letters of Mary, Queen of Scots for the benefit of the government. (The government also employed Arthur Gregory, an expert at breaking open and re-sealing intercepted letters without detection.) It has been conjectured that one of the reasons for the forged 'confessions' may have been to deflate and shake the resolve of other priest prisoners, such as Father Southwell, by confronting them with Walpole's alleged submission. Justice Richard Young - who also signed some of the 'confessions' - had already tried a similar ploy with Father John Gerard, swearing to him on the Bible that Southwell had conformed. The trick failed because Gerard, of course, did not believe it.

In spring 1595 Henry, physically a broken man, was sent back to York for trial at the Mid-Lent Assizes under Judges Francis Beaumont, who had presided at the trial of John Boste; Matthew Ewens; William

The Elizabethan Martyrs, 1577-1601

Hillyard, Recorder of York; and the Earl of Huntingdon. Although at first denied by Hillyard any right to be heard in his own defence, Henry, weighed down with leg-irons, successfully appealed against this objection. As a trained lawyer, Henry was able to make a good defence. Pleading 'not guilty', he argued that the priesthood had been instituted by Christ and given by Him to the Apostles and their successors down to the present. The Gospel had been brought to England by priests, therefore, being a priest could not ipso facto constitute treason. He denied any harmful intent towards the Queen or country, but only wished to exercise his functions as a priest.

The judges were forced to concede the point but countered that a priest returning to England was illegal. Beaumont pointed out that the law required any priest entering the country to present himself to a justice within three days and make his submission to the Queen in matters of religion; otherwise he would be deemed a traitor. Henry then made the valid defence plea that he had been in the country less than twenty-four hours before he was apprehended. The period of time allowed under the Statute had not thereby elapsed, so his arrest was not strictly in accordance with the law and he should not have a case to answer.

The Court ignored such technicalities. Judge Ewens told him to 'Stop that double-talk and tell us simply; are you willing to allow the Queen that authority which the laws of England ascribe to her?' Asked if he would now renounce his Catholicism and submit to the Queen in religion, Walpole protested that he prayed for the Queen that God would bless her and fill her with His Holy Spirit. He would most willingly submit to the Queen's authority in all things except his religion, on the conscientious grounds that the submission he owed to the Queen was subordinate to that he owed to the 'Great King of Heaven and earth. You, my lords, sit here at present in judgement as men, and judge as such being subject to error and passion, but know for certain that there is a Sovereign Judge who will judge righteously, whom in all things we must obey in the first place, and then our lawful princes in such things as are lawful and no farther.'

Lord Huntingdon interposed, 'We deal with you very favourably, Mr Walpole, when notwithstanding all these treasons and conspiracies ... we offer you the benefit of the law, if you will but make the submission ordered by the law, which, if you will not accept of, it is proper you should be punished according to the law.' Henry replied, 'There is nothing, my lord, in which I would not most willingly submit myself, provided it be not against God; but may His divine Majesty never suffer me to consent to the least thing by which He might be dishonoured, nor you desire it of me. As to the Queen, I love her as a faithful subject and every day I pray for her to our Lord God that he would bless her with His Holy Spirit, and give her His grace to do her duty in all things in this world, to the end that she may enjoy eternal glory in the world to come; and God is my witness, that all here present and particularly to my accusers and such as desire my death, I wish as to myself the salvation of their souls and to this end they may live in the True Catholic Faith, the only way to eternal happiness.'

After the prosecutor, Sir John Saville, had passionately denounced Henry as a traitor, the jury was directed to find him guilty. As they left to consider their verdict, Henry addressed them: 'Gentlemen of the jury, I confess most willingly that I am a priest and that I am of the Company of Jesus ... that I came over in order to convert my country to the Catholic Faith and to invite sinners to repentance. All this I will never deny; this is the duty of my calling. If you find anything else in me that is not agreeable to my profession, show me no favour. In the meantime act according to your consciences and remember you must give an account to God'.

The outcome was a foregone conclusion. Sentencing was deferred until the following day after which Henry was returned to York Castle to await execution. During his final hours in prison Henry wrote religious verses. Fathers Garnet and Gerard, who saw them, attested that they were barely legible given the damage to Walpole's hands. Henry spent the night before his execution in prayer, standing leaning against a bench to help him to stay awake. His cellmate reported that whenever he opened his eyes he found Walpole at prayer.

In his last letter written to Father Holtby, he said:

I am to be executed tomorrow. I commend myself to your prayers and those of our fathers and brethren. I do not doubt that in this my day of need God's Holy Spirit will have anticipated my letters and moved your hearts at this time, and those of all Catholics in whose fellowship I rejoice, to pray ... that He may help my weakness and strengthen me inwardly with the spirit of endurance ... All the more because my sentence of death was directly on account of my return to England as a Jesuit priest. No cause on earth could be more glorious than this ... I tell you nothing of all that passed during my year's detention in the Tower of London. You will know it in heaven when we shall see each other again. This will do, then, written in haste as it is, but with much affection and heartiest goodwill. The time has come to bid my pen farewell and to pray hard in the presence of Him for whom I battle, until eventually we meet.

On Friday, 7 April 1595, together with Blessed Alexander Rawlins

62 Henry was taken to the Knavesmire. Father Rawlins had refused to lie on the right side of the hurdle, which honour should go to Henry. They were laid head to toe, Henry with his head behind the horses. The crowd numbered around 2,000 and close by the gallows stood Lord Huntingdon. On the scaffold, Father Rawlins asked Henry for his blessing and the two priests warmly embraced. Henry then had to watch his companion being hanged and butchered. They showed the mangled remains of Father Rawlins to Henry and even at that stage he was offered his life if he would conform. When asked to join in prayer with the Protestant ministers for his own peaceful death, he replied that by the grace of God he was in peace with all the world and prayed God for all, particularly those who were the cause of his death. They kept him standing on the ladder for a long time as they harangued him. He said the Pater Noster in a clear voice and was just beginning Ave Maria when he was turned off. Mercifully they allowed him to hang until he was dead. Afterwards his head was stuck on one of the gates of York.

Philip Howard

His trust was with the eternal ... the sum of earthly bliss.

Paradise Lost, John Milton, 1608-74

Philip belonged to two illustrious families. On his Fitzalan mother's side he could trace his ancestry back to 1020 in Brittany, where the family originated. The Howards had been dukes of Norfolk since 1483 and despite their turbulent and troubled history were the most powerful aristocrats in Tudor England. Philip, the eldest son and heir of Thomas Howard, 4th Duke of Norfolk, was born at Arundel House, London at 12 noon on 28 June 1557. His paternal grandfather, Henry, Earl of Surrey, 'the poet Earl', had been attainted and beheaded in 1547. Surrey's two first cousins, the daughters of his aunt Elizabeth and his uncle Edmund respectively, were Anne Boleyn and Catherine Howard, the second and fifth wives of Henry VIII. Surrey's sister, Mary Howard, married Henry Fitzroy, Duke of Richmond, Henry's illegitimate son. Because of the Boleyn connection Philip's father was cousin to Queen Elizabeth. So the family was closely linked to the Tudors.

Most of our information for the details of the life of Philip Howard comes from a contemporary biography written by an anonymous Jesuit priest who served as chaplain to his widow. Philip was heir not only to the premier dukedom and earldom of England but also five baronies. He was baptised on 2 July 1557 in the gold font hitherto reserved for royal babies in the Chapel Royal at Whitehall by Nicholas Heath, Archbishop of York. His godparents were Queen Mary and King Philip of Spain, after whom he was named. His talented sixteen-year-old mother, Mary Fitzalan, daughter and co-heiress of Henry Fitzalan, Earl of Arundel, died only a few weeks after Philip's birth.

The Duke then married the eighteen-year-old widowed Lady Margaret Dudley, daughter and heiress of Lord Chancellor Thomas Audley. She brought the property of Walden to the Howards, and it was Philip's half-brother, Thomas, who magnificently rebuilt Audley End. Margaret died in 1564 following childbirth. In 1567 the Duke took a third wife, Elizabeth Dacre, widow of Thomas, Lord Dacre of Gilsland. She was an immensely wealthy Catholic with four children inheriting huge estates in the north of England. Although supporting the Catholic cause under Mary, the Duke was content to conform to the state religion under Elizabeth. John Foxe, who gained fame as the chronicler of the persecution under Queen Mary, was appointed Philip's tutor and enjoyed the Duke's lifelong patronage. As the son and heir of the richest and most eminent nobleman in the land, Philip was destined for the greatest position after the throne itself.

The Duke had bought the former London Charterhouse in 1564, converted it into his London residence and renamed it Howard House. The Howard coat of arms is still to be seen on the ceiling bosses. It was here that Philip and his brothers and sisters grew up. By all accounts the Duke was a good father. With the aim of keeping their vast wealth and titles in the family, at the age of twelve Philip was betrothed to Anne Dacre, his late stepmother's daughter. In 1571, having both reached the age of consent at fourteen, Philip and Anne were married by order of his father, who was then a prisoner in the Tower. Philip's half-brothers, Thomas, future Earl of Suffolk, and William, Lord Howard, were married respectively to Anne's sisters, Mary and Elizabeth. Despite the Duke's avowed Protestantism, for a time Philip's tutor was 'closet Catholic' Dr Gregory Martin of St John's College, Oxford, the English translator of the Douai-Rheims Bible.

His third wife having died in childbirth in 1567 the Duke's ambition - a fatal failing of his family - got the better of him and he became involved in secret negotiations with the imprisoned Mary, Queen of Scots with a view to a possible marriage with her as his fourth wife. It was his ruin. When his plans were discovered he was sent to the Tower. The teenaged Philip wrote to the Queen protesting his father's loyalty to her but Thomas was deprived of his dukedom, found guilty of high treason and, attended by John Foxe, he was executed on Tower Hill 2 June 1572. The Duke wrote a last, loving letter to his son urging him to 'Beware of the court ... Serve and fear God above all things and love and make much of your wife.' In his will Thomas had selected Lord Burghley to be Philip's guardian; an extraordinarily naïve choice given that Burghley was the architect of the Duke's ruin. Martin was dismissed as Philip's tutor and, in accordance with his father's wishes, he was sent, with his half-brothers, to St John's, Cambridge to complete his education. In November 1576 he was awarded his MA degree by the Vice-Chancellor, John Whitgift, having taken the Oath of Supremacy as required. A handsome, eloquent and gifted young man with a prodigious, photographic memory, Philip, failing to heed his father's warning, went to Court at the age of eighteen and became a favourite of the woman who had signed his father's death warrant. He showered Elizabeth with expensive gifts and organised grand entertainments to mark the anniversaries of her coronation. He lavishly hosted Elizabeth - whose appetite for flattery was insatiable - and her toadying courtiers at several of his houses, including Howard House, and led a worldly and extravagant life of pleasure for six years. By his spendthrift lifestyle he squandered most of his inheritance and fell deeply into debt, being forced to sell Howard lands to pay his creditors. Elizabeth did not like the wives of courtiers around, so Philip left Anne behind at Arundel Castle, not only cruelly neglecting her while spending her Fitzalan inheritance but also being unfaithful with 'immodest young women with which the court did too much abound.'

In spite of all his ostentation, sumptuous living and dissipation Philip took seriously his responsibilities to the poor, to whom he was always generous. He once severely reprimanded another courtier for rudely treating a beggar. 'You have too much forgot yourself, good Sir, in abusing such a poor man in the manner you have done. Far better it had been had you considered that before God there is no difference between the poor and the rich, betwixt the beggar and the gentleman ... Those who are of better birth or higher degree ought not to condemn others, much less insult them, but rather help them.'

The Norfolk dukedom had been forfeited by his father, but in February 1580 Philip inherited his maternal Fitzalan grandfather's title, becoming the 20th (or 13th) Earl of Arundel. This was (and still is) the oldest extant earldom in the English peerage, dating from 1139. With the title came substantial properties, including Arundel Castle. In 1580 his castle at Framlingham, Norfolk, was commandeered by the Queen for use as a place of imprisonment for Catholic priests. He took his place in Parliament as the premier earl of England and began to show signs of taking his duties more seriously. These included his wife who, after her grandfather's death, had come to live with him in London. At first he was rude and resentful towards her, but gradually reconciliation was effected largely because of Anne's loving sweetness towards her husband.

In 1581 Philip had gone out of curiosity to hear a disputation in the Tower between Edmund Campion and the Deans of St Paul's and Windsor. The dirty, dishevelled Campion's solitary defence of the Catholic Faith made a deep impression on him, in contrast to the superficial mockery of his detractors. Philip was also present at Campion's trial and was moved by the priest's holiness and sincerity, contrasting it with his own mode of life. Much to the Queen's annoyance, afterwards he attended court less frequently, spending more time with his wife, whom he came to love dearly. A clever and studious young woman Anne had outwardly conformed insofar as she sometimes attended church. But she was convinced of the truth of the Catholic Faith in which she had been brought up by her mother and grandmother, Lady Mounteagle. Having read Gregory Martin's *Treatise of Schism* she eventually took the step of asking a Marian priest to reconcile her to the Church, in spite of the risks this entailed. A servant, Richard Bailey, secretly brought the priest into Arundel Castle. To her great surprise, when Philip was informed he did not seem to mind. The reason for this was that Philip was confused about his own religious position. He was well aware that members of his own family were converting to Catholicism. They included his beloved half-sister, Margaret, married to Robert Sackville, Earl of Dorset, and his much loved half-brother, William as well as his uncle, Lord Henry Howard, who was imprisoned several times because of unfounded suspicions about his loyalty. Philip also knew that many of his fellow peers dissembled about their faith and that those who openly avowed their Catholicism - such as the Earl of Southampton and Lord Vaux - were in prison as a result.

Anne was expecting a child and when it became known that she was a reconciled Catholic she was presented at Arundel as a recusant. Her Catholic servant, Richard Bailey, fled to Flanders where he was financially supported by Anne. The vindictive and jealous Elizabeth, to show her new hostility to Philip, ordered Anne's arrest. She was placed in the custody of courtier Sir Thomas Shirley at his home, Wiston House, Sussex with strict instructions that she was not to be allowed visitors. In 1583, as a lonely prisoner, Anne gave birth to a daughter who, perhaps as a gesture towards the Queen, was named Elizabeth and

The Elizabethan Martyrs, 1577-1601

baptised in the Established Church. In November 1583 the Throckmorton Plot was revealed, so named after the chief conspirator, Francis Throckmorton, who was executed the following July. Philip's uncle, Lord Henry Howard, was among those arrested in connection with the plot. While ever he was still subserviently toadying to the Queen Philip was safe but the paranoid Elizabeth began to harbour suspicions about him and the Throckmorton Plot provided her with a pretext to chastise him. She invited herself to Howard House where a lavish dinner and entertainment was provided. When she departed she thanked Philip for his hospitality and then coldly informed him that he was under house arrest. Philip was interrogated over Christmas about alleged involvement in the Throckmorton Plot. He was also accused of sheltering Father Jasper Heywood, who had once been a page of honour to the Queen when Princess Elizabeth, and became a Jesuit in 1562 at the age of twenty-seven. As they could find no evidence to use against Philip they left him alone, finally releasing him from house arrest in April 1584. Anne was also freed from custody later that year.

For two years Philip had agonised over his future. He finally made up his mind to become a Catholic. This took enormous courage when he was already suspect and given the likely consequences amidst the bloody persecution. He spoke of his intention to his brother, William, who loaned him one of William Allen's books. In September 1584 he asked one of his Catholic servants to recommend a priest. The servant was well-known to a saintly Jesuit priest recently arrived in England, Father William Weston, alias Edmonds. [63] Weston was brought to Philip at night and had a long, very secret conversation with him. On 30 September Weston returned and, according to the priest's account, 'in the presence of two of his very near relatives' reconciled him to the Church saying Mass and giving him Holy Communion. The Earl's contemporary biographer wrote that henceforward Philip 'lived in such a manner as he seemed changed into another man.' Philip kept a priest at Howard House and often served Mass. It was a torment to him that he now had to dissimulate about his religion, feigning sickness or other excuses to avoid attending the Protestant services at court. But the change that had come over him could not be concealed from the Queen. Meanwhile, united in faith, Philip and Anne drew even closer together.

They found it frustrating not to be able to practise their religion and Philip decided to write to Dr William Allen for advice. Using the alias of Bridges, Father Edward Gratley had become chaplain to Philip and Anne at Arundel House. He had formerly been with Henry Vaux, the poet son of Lord Vaux, but was now working for spymaster Francis Walsingham and was to play a role in the Babington Plot the following year. Gratley was designated to arrange delivery of Philip's letter to Allen, but he handed it over to the government and a plan for the Earl's entrapment was laid. Allen, of course, never received Philip's letter. The gist of the fake answer purporting to come from him was that Philip and Anne should flee to the Continent. Philip ought to have realised that the cautious Allen would never have committed himself to recommending such a course of action, and certainly not in writing. He also sought the advice of Father Weston, who tried hard to dissuade him from leaving, urging him to stay in England where he would be an encouragement to his fellow Catholics. However, Philip attached great weight to Allen's purported answer, coming, as he believed, from the acknowledged leader of the Catholic exiles. As Philip wrote, 'On the one side my native country, friends, wife and kinfolk did invite me to stay; on the other, the misfortune of my house, the power of my adversaries, the remembrances of my former troubles, and the knowledge of my present danger did hasten me to go.'

Philip should have listened to Weston's wise opinion, instead he began arranging his escape, and all the while his plans were being betrayed to the government by Gratley alias Bridges. Anne was pregnant again, so it was decided that Philip would go alone and she would follow later with the children. Twice Philip attempted to take ship from Littlehampton but was told on both occasions that adverse winds prevented the vessel from leaving. This was a lie designed to delay Philip's departure until all the arrangements were in place for his capture. Philip wrote a very long, eloquent letter to the Queen in which he justified the reasons for his conduct ... 'in which he must consent either to the certain destruction of his body or the manifest endangering of his soul'. He wanted to be able to practise his religion in peace and bring up his children as Catholics, none of which he could legally do in England. He told the Queen, 'I found little by little your good opinion declined and your favour somewhat estranged from me. I heard from time to time how your majesty in words took exception to many of my actions and how it pleased you daily in your speeches to betray hard and evil consent of me.' He continued, 'When I considered in what continual danger I did remain here in England, both by laws established and by a new act lately made [27 Elizabeth] I did think it my safest part to depart the realm and abide in some other place where I might live without danger to my conscience, without offence to your majesty, without the servile subjection to mine enemies and without peril to my life.' The letter was left in the keeping of Gratley, to be passed to the Queen only when Philip was safely across the Channel, and to be destroyed should the escape attempt fail.

The Elizabethan Martyrs, 1577-1601

Philip finally embarked at Lymington, Hampshire on the night of 24 April 1585. With him were two servants, one of them William Bray, perhaps not a wise choice as Bray was known to the government as a smuggler of Catholic literature and priests. Also in the company was Father Jonas Meredith. [64] As soon as the boat reached open sea the captain hoisted a lantern on the mast, the pre-arranged signal to the waiting government boarding party. A small warship came alongside and its captain, a villain by the name of Francis Kelloway, came on board. At first he pretended to be a pirate and offered to let Philip continue his voyage if he handed over all the valuables he had with him as well as providing him with £100. Philip, still not grasping the situation, wrote a note to his sister, Margaret, asking her to arrange with Edward Gratley to hand over the money to Kelloway. At which point Kelloway showed Philip his letter of authority from the Council to arrest him, which he proceeded to do. (In 1586 Kelloway got his reward by being made sheriff of Hampshire and in 1587 received a licence from Lord Burghley authorising him to arrest any Catholics on the seas who were seeking to flee to France.)

Having been brought ashore, escorted by a waiting guard, the prisoners spent the night at Guildford en route for London, and on arrival Philip was sent to the Tower where so many members of his family had been before him. His letter to the Queen had been immediately handed over to the government by Gratley and was made public. What Elizabeth thought of the contents of Philip's letter is unknown, but it played into the hands of Walsingham, so that when Philip eventually appeared before the Court of Star Chamber he was accused of libelling the court and disparaging the Queen. His situation was made worse by the totally unfounded lies of Anthony Tyrell, who accused the Earl of supplying Father John Ballard with money for subversive purposes. Tyrell also dragged the Countess into his slanders. Not content with all of this to further incriminate Philip Walsingham resorted to one of his favourite tactics; a forged letter. Purporting to have been sent to William Dix, Philip's steward, it read that the Earl planned to return to England with an army to 'trouble both the queen and state.' The forgery, in handwriting resembling Philip's, was almost certainly the work of Thomas Phelippes. Philip passionately denied he had ever written the letter, protesting that he was as innocent of treason, 'as a new-born child.' The letter was never mentioned again. Philip did admit that he had written to William Allen but declared that he quickly regretted doing so, and believing it had not yet been handed to the messenger, he asked that the letter should be burned. 'What was done with it,' he said, 'I know not, but Bridges told me it was burnt.'

The Elizabethan Martyrs, 1577-1601

Because of the lack of evidence against him Philip was made to wait until May 1586 before he was arraigned in the Court of Star Chamber charged with being reconciled to the Catholic Church, attempting to flee the country and corresponding with Dr Allen. The Attorney-General, John Popham, made great play with Philip's letter to the Queen, alleging that it treated her contemptuously and disparagingly. He was fined £10,000 and sentenced to imprisonment at the Queen's pleasure i.e. indefinitely. Lord William Howard, his half-brother, and his half-sister, Margaret Sackville, Countess of Dorset, were also arrested and committed to prison. Writing to his wife, Philip said the imprisonment of his sister caused him more grief than his own incarceration. Elizabeth's malice against the Howards had to be sated. Edward Gratley openly apostatised and spent several years in the prison of the Inquisition in Rome. He was last heard of in Apulia.

Philip was kept in solitary confinement in a foul-smelling cell in the Beauchamp Tower for nearly two years, after which time he was permitted to have a servant, on condition that he had to share his master's strict imprisonment. The Lieutenant of the Tower, Sir Owen Hopton, having been instructed to make Philip's life as unpleasant as possible, treated him with great discourtesy, but Philip accepted all the petty insults with humility. Elizabeth thought that the spoiled young courtier she had known would soon break down under such treatment. But she had reckoned without the grace of God that was at work in Philip's soul, which enabled him not only to face his weary ordeal but also to grow in holiness. He became devoted to a life of prayer, meditation and mortification. His greatest distress was to be deprived of his wife and family, and he suffered deep remorse for the way he had treated Anne in the past. 'I call our Lord to witness', he said, 'that as no sin grieves me so much as my offences to [Anne], so no worldly things makes me loather to depart hence than that I cannot live to make satisfaction according to my most ardent and affectionate desire. *Afflictio dat intellectum'*. (Affliction gives understanding.) His pitiful requests to the Queen for Anne to be allowed to visit him were consistently refused. Even the news of the safe delivery of his son, Thomas, was kept from him. His jailers were instructed not to confirm whether the child was a son or daughter. Meanwhile the Queen continued to find every opportunity to spitefully insult the Countess who was then living in straitened financial circumstances, all the household servants having been dismissed. Philip's health soon began to suffer from the privation and he was constantly watched, but he was not devoid of spiritual comfort. Father Robert Southwell, who had taken up secret residence at Arundel House, wrote to Philip, and the letters reached him through bribing the warders. The beautiful letters were collected, daringly printed on a secret press and published under the title *An Epistle of Comfort*.

In 1587, for whatever reasons, Philip's conditions of imprisonment were relaxed a little and he was moved to better quarters in the Lanthorn Tower. Here he was able to have contact with other Catholic prisoners, including Richard Shelley of Michelgrove and Sir Thomas Gerard, father of John Gerard SJ. There was also an old priest, Father William Bennett, who, with the connivance of Cecily Hopton, the Catholic convert daughter of Sir Owen Hopton, managed to occasionally say Mass for the three of them in Philip's room. A prisoner by the name of John Snowden, seeking to ingratiate himself with the government, masqueraded as a Catholic and gave information to Walsingham about the clandestine Masses. Father Bennett was removed from the Tower to the Wood Street Counter prison where, after interrogation, he confessed to saying Mass. The renewed persecution that followed the failure of the Spanish Armada in 1588 presented a perfect excuse for attacking Philip. He was accused of having prayed for the success of the invasion, whereas he maintained he had prayed only for the safety of the Catholics, who it was feared - not without justification, as evidenced by Burghley's memorandums - would be massacred by the government if the Spaniards landed.

Philip was interrogated by Lord Burghley, Sir Christopher Hatton and Henry, Lord Hunsdon, who was both nonplussed and angered by his composure. He was charged with treason and brought to trial before his peers in Westminster Hall on 14 April 1589. The trial, presided over by the Lord High Steward, Henry Stanley, 4th Earl of Derby, not surprisingly, attracted a great deal of public interest, but legally it was a farce. Philip, gaunt and emaciated, arrived for his trial dressed in a black satin doublet, beneath a fur-trimmed velvet gown, and a tall black hat which he removed and bowed to the judges, among them Lord Burghley, who did not acknowledge his courtesy. Witnesses described him as a tall man, but with a deathly pallor as a result of his long incarceration. Prosecuting was the Attorney-General, John Popham, whose anti-Catholic credentials were impeccable, as we have already encountered. There was no real evidence to substantiate the charges against Philip, but that did not stop the prosecution from indulging in the usual tirade, throwing in every bit of gossip and slanderous allegation it could muster. The extant State Papers contain a letter from Popham in which he acknowledges that he was well aware that the evidence was fraudulent. 'How do you prove me a traitor?' asked Philip, at which Popham snarled, 'Because you have been reconciled to the Pope, there as a law made in the twenty-seventh year of this queen, what whosoever was reconciled to the Pope from the obedience of the queen's majesty, was in case of treason.'

After enormous pressure had been exerted on him for months Sir Thomas Gerard was broken and called as a witness. He falsely testified that Philip had prayed for the success of the Armada, which caused uproar in the court. Philip reiterated that his prayers were for his fellow Catholics and challenged Gerard to look him in the face and, as he would have to answer before God, to tell the truth. But Gerard could not face Philip. He kept his gaze averted, staring fixedly at Lord Derby. The principal witness was Father William Bennett, who repeated his earlier sworn statement, which had been extorted under threat of torture. He claimed that Philip had asked him to pray for the success of the Spanish fleet, requesting a votive Mass of the Holy Ghost for that purpose. Philip told the court that this was an obvious lie because as a recent convert he was unaware of such Masses. He also informed the court that Bennett had written him a letter asking his pardon for falsely accusing him. The priest denied having done so, but to great consternation Philip produced the letter from the sleeve of his gown and threw it onto the floor. The letter confirmed that Father Bennett admitted to saying anything that his interrogators wished to hear and craving God's and the Earl's forgiveness. Some of the peers agreed that Bennett was 'a false man and no lawful witness.'

With the exposure of the fabricated and perjured evidence, Philip's acquittal seemed assured. The issue revolved around whether or not private prayers could be legally interpreted as treasonable. The twenty-three peers debated the question and called in the judges for advice. The lawyers' opinion was that prayer could not constitute treason, but Lord Burghley, acting as foreman of the jury, assured the peers that only a guilty verdict was sought; the Queen did not intend executing the Earl. As a result the required guilty verdict was pronounced and Philip was sentenced to death. Asked if he had anything to say, Philip replied, *'Sic voluntas Dei'* (God's will be done.)

He then requested that his debts should be paid and asked to see his wife and son, and was promised that the request would be forwarded to the Queen. He also wrote to Burghley asking God to send him all honour and happiness and begging him to take care of his wife and children. Lord Derby later spoke of his grief and the burden on his conscience because the Queen had appointed him to condemn Philip on insufficient and 'counterfeited' evidence.

There was widespread disbelief and indignation when the sentence became known. The general unpopularity of the verdict may have contributed to the endless postponement in carrying out the sentence. Members of Philip's family, such as Lord Howard of Effingham, the Lord High Admiral probably used their influence in his favour. Effingham, a grandson of the 2nd Duke of Norfolk, was a cousin of Anne Boleyn and he married Catherine Carey, the daughter of Elizabeth's cousin/half-brother, Henry, Lord Hunsdon, son of Mary Boleyn. On the other hand, the Queen may indeed never have intended that Philip should be executed. Perhaps she wanted to prolong his misery, and certainly the fact that he was never told she had not signed his death warrant was an added piece of callousness. Returned to the Tower, he was constantly spied upon and his treatment worsened. The Domestic State Papers contain his letter to Lord Burghley of 30 March 1590, in which he wrote that he was 'full of misery and void of almost any comfort'. Soon he became an emaciated shadow of his former self. He lived in daily expectation of death showing great fortitude and resignation to a heroic degree. As Father Henry Garnet expressed it, 'Not a bell that sounded but it might be his knell; not a footstep was heard but it might be the messenger of death. Each morning as he rose, he knew not but that, before night he might be a headless corpse; each night as he lay upon his pillow, he was uncertain whether the morning might not summon him to another world'. In a declaration he had prepared pending his anticipated execution, he wrote, 'The Catholic Faith which I hold is the only cause why either I have been thus long imprisoned or why I am now ready to be executed.'

With his correspondent Robert Southwell, he could equally say: 'I live but such a life as ever dies'. Philip and Southwell wrote to one another frequently, even after Southwell was himself imprisoned in the Tower, but sadly they were never allowed to meet. Philip was inexpressibly grateful to Southwell, especially for his prose elegy *Triumphs over Death*, which was written to console Philip following the early death of his half-sister, Margaret Sackville, Countess of Dorset in August 1591. It was for Margaret that Southwell had written his *Hundred Meditations on the love of God*. Philip wrote to Southwell 'Our Lord, who sees all secrets, sees my goodwill and thankfulness and I doubt not will reward you, among all your other worthy merits, for these bestowed on me his most unworthy servant.' Philip was allowed to keep for company a dog that had belonged to his wife, and one day it followed a warder into Southwell's cell. The Lieutenant of the Tower mockingly quipped that he supposed the dog had gone to get the priest's blessing. Philip responded that he now loved his dog even more. He spent increasingly longer hours in prayer and when not engaged in his devotions he filled his time reading the Fathers of the

The Elizabethan Martyrs, 1577-1601

Church and translating religious works from Latin. He wrote meditations and poetry, including *Fourfold Meditations of the Four Last Things* and a poem: *Verses on Christ Crucified*. He also fasted three days a week; when food was brought to him he asked his servant to eat it. He soon found that this was greatly undermining his health and strength and desisted.

By the time Southwell was executed in 1595, Philip was gravely ill, unable to rise from his bed. He seems to have been struck down suddenly with some dysentery-like disease, perhaps brought on by so many years of unhealthy incarceration, although the possibility of poison cannot be ruled out, which was certainly suspected at the time. He wrote a letter to the Queen which Sir Michael Blount, Lieutenant of the Tower, delivered to the court. In the letter he asked to be allowed to see his wife and children, especially the son whom he had never seen. Blount returned with Elizabeth's answer, which was that if Philip would go just once to church, 'his request shall not only be granted but he shall moreover be restored to his honour and estates with as much favour as I can show.'

It was to be her last vengeful act against him. Sorrowfully, he sent back the message that he could not accept the offer. If his religion, he said, was to be 'the cause in which I am to perish, I am sorry that I have but one life to lose.' Doctors were brought to him but he was now beyond their help. Sir Michael Blount, who had treated him harshly came to ask his forgiveness. Taking the Lieutenant by the hand, Philip said, 'I forgive you in the same sort as I desire myself to be forgiven at the hands of God', adding the advice that in future he should not be so severe with prisoners. They already had enough to bear and he should not add to their sorrows. 'Remember, good Mr Lieutenant, he said, 'that God, who, with his finger, turns the unstable wheel of this variable world, can, in the revolution of a few days, bring you to be a prisoner also and be kept in the same prison where you now keep others.' Philip's words proved to be uncannily prophetic. Blount became involved in discussions as to what action to take about securing the Tower upon the death of the Queen. This was held to be treasonable and within weeks of Philip's death he was arrested and imprisoned in the Tower. Blount's son later became a Catholic.

On the morning of Sunday, 19 October 1595 Philip lay praying the psalms. 'I have almost run my course and come to the end of this miserable and mortal life,' he told his weeping servant. About midday, lying with his emaciated hands across his breast, whispering the names of Jesus and Mary, without any sign of grief or pain, he turned his face aside and quietly died with the words, 'Lord you are my hope'. He was thirty-eight-years old. Suspicions that he had been poisoned were widely voiced, but no proof of this has ever been discovered. Philip bequeathed to Father Weston his breviary, which he passed on to Father Henry Garnet.

For two days after Philip's death his body was left wrapped in a sheet before being taken to the Tower chapel, where a Protestant minister who conducted the service preached a heartless and vindictive sermon against him, declaring, 'We are not come to honour this man or his religion ... God has laid this man's honour in the dust.'

The cost of the funeral was a paltry £4.13s.4d. Philip was buried in his father's grave in the chapel of St Peter ad Vincula and there he remained until 1614, when his widow and son had the body removed and placed in an iron coffin, eventually to rest in the vault in the Fitzalan Chapel, adjoining the parish church at Arundel. Above the tomb was placed an inscription detailing his sufferings.

Philip had made his will in 1588 leaving bequests to the poor of London, to his brothers and sister as well as his wife, including valuable gold crosses. His will was not honoured. All of his property, including his wife's, were taken by the Crown.

Anne Howard, a remarkable lady of courage and great generosity, became an exceptionally good and holy woman who had to suffer many hardships. With her husband in the Tower she lived at Arundel House in three sparsely furnished rooms until Lord Hunsdon decided to move in and she was evicted. She later moved into a house in Spitalfields. Cardinal Basil Hume OSB, Archbishop of Westminster, in a homily given at Arundel Cathedral in 1995, said of her, 'I believe that Anne herself achieved the highest degree of sanctity'. The Countess, who died in 1630 at the age of seventy-three, spent her life in charitable work for the sick and orphans as well as sheltering many priests, including Father Gerard for a time, and when she died she was laid to rest in the vault beside her husband.

In 1971, following his canonization, Philip's remains were removed from the Fitzalan Chapel to a shrine in Arundel Cathedral. The relics are surmounted by a statue of Philip with his dog. In 1973 the dedication of the cathedral was changed to that of Our Lady and St Philip Howard. Philip's daughter, Elizabeth, died at the age of sixteen in 1599. His son, Thomas, who was ten years old at the time of his father's death, succeeded him as Earl of Arundel. Although he conformed he died a Catholic and his son, Blessed William Howard, Viscount Stafford, was to follow in his grandfather's footsteps by dying on the scaffold in 1680, a martyr to the Catholic cause. Philip's great-grandson was Cardinal Philip Howard.

The Elizabethan Martyrs, 1577-1601

If you visit the Tower of London climb the narrow stairs to the middle cell of the thirteenth century Beauchamp Tower, where you will find among a great many other carvings three inscriptions, now protected under glass, incised by Philip Howard's own hand on the walls. One is a small crucifix, another is a quotation from St Ambrose dated 26 May 1587, and over the fireplace is a Latin quotation from St Paul's Letter to the Romans, it reads:

Quanto plus afflictionis pro Christo in hoc saeculo, tanto plus gloriae cum Christo in futuro: Arundell June 22 1587.

This translates as, 'The more suffering endured for Christ in this world, the greater will be the glory with Him in the life to come'. (This same inscription is carved on the shrine step in Arundel Cathedral.) Beneath this inscription you will see another added by the hand of Anthony Tuchiner, 65 who occupied the cell after Philip. Tuchiner, who later became a priest on the English mission, carved a quotation conflated from Psalms 8 and 111: *'Gloria et honore eum coronasti domine in memoria aeterna erit justus'.* ('You have crowned him with glory and honour, Lord; the just man shall be in everlasting remembrance.')

John Jones

A rendezvous with death.

> *I have a rendezvous with death*, Alan Seeger, 1888-1916

John Jones was born into a Catholic family at Clynog Fawr, Caernarvonshire, North Wales. In what year we do not know because nothing is recorded of his early life and nowhere do there seem to be any conclusive clues as to his age. The older sources claim that in his youth he became a Franciscan at the Observant Convent in Greenwich in the short time that it was reconstituted. The friary had been revived by Queen Mary, who had the buildings repaired and the friars - led by William Peto, the former provincial of the Observants who was nominally also Bishop of Salisbury - were reinstated on 7 April 1555 by Maurice Giffin, Bishop of Rochester. It is believed that John took the religious name Godfrey Maurice. In July the friars were complaining to the Queen that there had been an incident when they had been 'beaten with stones which were flung at them by lewd persons as they passed.' On 12 July 1559 the friary was suppressed by

The Elizabethan Martyrs, 1577-1601

Elizabeth and the expelled friars went abroad, mostly to the Netherlands, but some as far afield as Lisbon and to the Ara Coeli convent in Rome. It was then that John, still a novice, had left for northern France, where he joined the Franciscan convent at Pontoise and was professed. His ordination probably took place at Rheims where there was also a friary of English exiles. Other authorities, such as Dr Anthony Champney's manuscript, assert that John did not enter the convent at Pontoise until about 1590, when he was already a priest.

If Champney's claim that John arrived at Pontoise only in 1590 is correct, he remained there for just a year before travelling to Rome in 1591 to enter the famous ancient convent of Santa Maria in Aracoeli (St Mary of the Altar of Heaven), located on the summit of the Capitoline Hill. Could it be that he went there in order to be reunited with some of his Greenwich ex-brethren? Later that same year, having become drawn to their ideals, he left the Conventuals and joined the Stricter Observance of the Roman Province. Perhaps in Rome he came in contact with the students of the English College preparing for the English Mission. Whatever it was that motivated him, he begged his superiors to send him to England and the request was granted. Before leaving Rome he had an audience with Pope Clement VIII Aldobrandini (1592-1605) who embraced him and gave him a special blessing.

He arrived in London in late 1592 and, according to Father John Gerard, with whom he developed a close friendship, Jones went to stay with him. 'I was particularly glad to give him the hospitality of my house in order to foster good relations between his Order and ours. But after a few months he found friends of his own and went to stay with them.'

His fellow Franciscans elected John as their Provincial. This suggests that his membership of their Order was of longer duration than just two years, which would have been the case if the 1590 Champney date of joining it at Pontoise is correct. John ministered in different parts of the country under the alias Buckley and was recorded as working among the Catholic prisoners in the Marshalsea.

Through Father Gerard John may have come to hear about the 'wonderfully good' Mrs Jane Wiseman, née Vaughan. Her husband, Thomas, had died in 1585 leaving her a wealthy widow with four sons and four daughters and an estate and 'fine mansion' called Broadoaks or Braddocks, near Saffron Walden, Essex, which Father Gerard made his base for a considerable time. Mrs Wiseman used her wealth to help poor Catholics, especially those in prison. She was 'a holy soul' who regularly sheltered priests and kept a succession of her own chaplains.

The Elizabethan Martyrs, 1577-1601

These included Richard Jackson, an old Marian priest and Norfolk-born, Bernard Gardiner, first cousin to Father Edward Walpole SJ. (Father Gardiner was arrested in 1599 and committed to Newgate. While still in the prison he was condemned to death in 1602, but what subsequently happened to him is unknown.) Despite being related to the extreme Puritan, Lord Robert Rich, the whole Wiseman family was devoted to the Faith. All of Jane's daughters became nuns: Anne and Barbara joined the Bridgettines in Portugal; Bridget was professed at St Monica's, Louvain in 1595, in the same ceremony as Margaret Garnet, sister of Father Henry Garnet SJ. Two of her sons, John and Thomas, became Jesuits. Her eldest son, the deeply devout William, married Jane Huddlestone of Sawston, the eldest daughter of another famous recusant family, and they had a son, John, and two daughters.

Regrettably, not all of the many priests who frequented Braddocks lived up to their vocations. One such was John Scudamore of Herefordshire, son and heir of Sir John Scudamore of the Holme Lacey branch of that ancient family. The martyr, Thomas Holford, was a tutor to Sir John's children for a time. John Scudamore junior entered the English College, Rome, in 1591 and was ordained in May 1592. On his return to England he actually used the name Wiseman as his alias. He spent the summer of 1593 based at Braddocks, and in the autumn of that year it was Scudamore who escorted Mrs Wiseman's daughters to Louvain when they decided to become nuns. He spent some time in Rome and Florence, before returning to Brabant. There is then a gap in the record of his movements, until he appears in the records again in 1606. Sad to relate, he apostasised, being granted a special pardon for doing so, and took up a position in the household of the Archbishop of Canterbury. A second priest in this category was Robert Barwise. He was ordained at Laon in 1589 and frequented Braddocks before leaving for Tournai in 1593 to try his vocation as a Jesuit novice. This lasted only a few months and he returned to England. On arriving in London he was arrested and sent to the Clink where he became a government informer. He was in and out of various London jails, supplying information, until 1603 when he was banished.

Life at Braddocks was becoming too dangerous, and at the suggestion of Father Gerard, Mrs Wiseman moved to another of her houses, Bullocks near Great Dunmow, leaving her son, William and his wife, Jane, at Braddocks. In December 1593, Bullocks was raided and although the resident priest escaped detection, Mrs Wiseman was thereafter closely watched and it was noted that she visited Wisbech Castle to relieve the many priests imprisoned there, taking with her a rich vestment she had made. During her visit she went to confession to

The Elizabethan Martyrs, 1577-1601

Father William Weston. Closely watched, shortly afterwards she was arrested, taken to London and imprisoned. John Gerard had returned to Braddocks and stayed to celebrate Holy Week with the Wiseman family. On Easter Monday, 1 April 1594, following a tip-off from a traitorous servant called John Frank, a dawn raid took place and Father Gerard was hidden in one of Nicholas Owen's constructions, where, unable to stand up or lie down for several days, he survived without detection on a few biscuits and a little quince jelly supplied by the distraught younger Jane, whose husband William was then a prisoner in London.

For her activities in sheltering and relieving priests, Mrs Jane Wiseman was imprisoned in the Gatehouse, but no direct evidence could be found that would convict her. While in prison she spent her time in prayer and embroidering vestments. Half of the income she received was sent to Father Gerard, while she used much of the remainder in helping poor Catholic prisoners.

Richard Topcliffe suspected that John Jones was a priest and set out to trap both him and Mrs Wiseman. She was well known as a nurse and one of Topcliffe's agents at the Gatehouse, Nicholas Blackwall, persuaded her to allow Jones, who was suffering from an ulcer on his leg, to visit her in prison so that she could apply a poultice. John was brought in and Mrs Wiseman attended to his leg, but Blackwall spied on them; something in their conversation confirmed that Jones was a priest and he was arrested, while Mrs Wiseman was accused of comforting and relieving priests.

She was eventually indicted on 30 June 1598 in the Kings Bench Court, Westminster, with the usual false witnesses produced to testify against her. Indicted with her was a wealthy layman, Robert Barnes of Mapledurham, near Petersfield. He had already spent five years in prison and was also accused of sheltering priests, in particular John Jones and thirty-eight-year-old, Preston-born, George Hothersall, then a prisoner in the Gatehouse who was described by Richard Topcliffe as 'very dangerous.' Barnes fearlessly denounced Topcliffe and his methods to the Court, giving evidence of his first-hand knowledge of the evil scheme of Topcliffe and Nicholas Jones to entrap Robert Southwell by using Anne Bellamy. Barnes was sentenced to death but this was commuted to imprisonment. Like Margaret Clitherow before her, Jane Wiseman refused to plead and was sentenced to be taken to the Marshalsea prison and crushed to death. The Queen and Privy Council got cold feet, afraid of public reaction and so she was reprieved, to spend the next five years in a filthy prison cell - 'deprived of all she possessed', Father Gerard informs us. Robert Barnes also remained in jail until the accession of James I when he was pardoned and most of his lands were restored to him. Hothersall had been apprehended at Flushing, Holland, in 1593 and forcibly shipped to prison in England. Because of this he could not be prosecuted but he seems to have remained in jail until 1603 when he was released and returned to Lancashire where he joined the Benedictines.

After her release in 1603 Mrs Wiseman returned to Bullocks and continued to offer priests hospitality. Her son William, who was complicit in the escape of Father Gerard from the Tower in 1597, also spent years in prison, as did several of his family's faithful servants, in Colchester jail. The magistrate's complained to the Council that none of them would inform on their master. William and his wife never ceased to assist priests. The elder Mrs Wiseman went to live in Louvain, where her daughters were Augustinian nuns, and she died there in 1610.

After his arrest John Jones was stripped and whipped; he was put in the manacles and tortured in Topcliffe's house. He was also subjected to unspeakable physical degradation at the hands of this degenerate. He was kept in prison for nearly two years before being brought to trial on 3 July 1598 on a charge of treason. The treason, according to the indictment, consisted of his having gone overseas during the first year of Her Majesty's reign (i.e.1558/1559) and been made priest by the authority of Rome and then returning to England contrary to 27 Eliz.I, c.2. This charge only makes sense if the 'Greenwich tradition' is correct and Champney is mistaken. It seems to be the case, therefore, that John did indeed join the Observant convent at Greenwich and went abroad when it was suppressed, desirous of continuing his vocation as a Franciscan.

John protested his innocence. He had never plotted against the Queen and he refused to allow the case to go before a jury in order, he said, to save twelve simple men from complicity in his unjust condemnation. He appealed to the judges to hear his case according to their consciences. Mr Justice Clench, presiding, told Jones that it was clear he had never contrived anything against the Queen, but as a priest of the Roman Church by his own admission, that constituted treason under Statute 27. John replied, 'If this be a crime I must own myself guilty; for I am a priest and came over into England to gain as many souls as I could to Christ'. He was condemned, and when sentence was passed John fell on his knees and gave thanks to God.

Perhaps because the populace was growing weary of the public butchery, John's execution had been ordered for 7 a.m. on 12 July 1598. It was the 57th anniversary of the martyrdom of Blessed David Gunston in the same place; St Thomas Waterings. This was a marsh two miles from London near the present Old Kent Road, where common criminals were hanged. The place got its name because it was where pilgrims to the shrine of St Thomas Becket made their first halt to water their horses, and is mentioned by Chaucer in his Prologue to the *Canterbury Tales*. Despite the early hour, a crowd had gathered. It was discovered that the hangman had forgotten the rope, so John was kept standing in the cart waiting until a rope was brought.

He spent the time in prayer and speaking to the crowd. He declared his innocence of all political wrongdoing, saying, 'I have never spoken a word or entertained a thought in my whole life against the Queen or my country, but have daily prayed for their welfare'. He told them his only crime was his religion and his priesthood and the crowd showed their sympathy. He specifically exonerated Mrs Wiseman of any offence, denying he had ever said Mass for her.

After an hour a horseman was seen galloping up pell-mell. The crowd excitedly thought it signalled a last minute reprieve, but it was the man bringing the rope. John was allowed to hang until he was dead. His head was set up on a pole in south London and his four quarters stuck up on trees in St George's Fields, Southwark, and by the roadside to Lambeth and Newington. Father Henry Garnet relates that a young friend of his, a law student and secret Catholic named Christopher Blackall, went to Lambeth Fields at night and removed one of John's quarters from a pike. He was caught and the next day appeared before Lord Chief Justice Popham for his offence. When Popham referred to John as a traitor Blackall protested that he was not a traitor but had been condemned solely for being a priest. Blackall said he had known John in prison and 'loved him' and was not prepared to let the 'crows eat him.' Blackall received a long prison sentence during which he was supported by Garnet with funds raised from his friends. It is good to record that a relic of John Jones did eventually reach the Franciscans at his old convent at Pontoise, where he was professed.

John Rigby

Este vivir ? qué será? Mil muertes se me hará
What serves this life ... except a thousand deaths to give?
St John of the Cross, 1542-91

John was born c.1570 at Harrock Hall, Eccleston, near Wigan. He was either the fifth or sixth son of Nicholas Rigby, an impoverished gentleman, by Mary Breres. As staunch Catholics the family had lost its wealth paying fines for their recusancy. Because of his family's straitened circumstances John had to enter domestic service to earn his living with a Protestant family, with whom he occasionally attended church. Regretting this he sought out Father John Gerard, then a prisoner in the Clink, made his confession and was reconciled to the Church. Contrary to what is asserted by numerous sources, he was ***not*** reconciled by Father John Jones. In his autobiography Father Gerard is absolutely clear on the matter. He tells us that when John Rigby was questioned about his reconciliation, he was asked the name of the priest who had done this and (quote), 'He did not want to implicate me, so he mentioned the name of a priest who had been martyred a short time before'. That priest was John Jones, but Rigby himself also specifically referred to Father Gerard as the priest who brought him back to the Church.

Shortly afterwards Rigby went into service with the staunchly Catholic Sir Edmund Huddlestone at Sawston Hall, some five miles south of Cambridge. At Sawston he got to know Nicholas Owen, whom he greatly admired and expressed a wish to join the Society of Jesus. Two years later on 13 February 1600 he was sent to the Sessions House at the Old Bailey to plead illness as the excuse for the non-appearance of Mrs Isabel Fortescue, one of Sir Edmund's daughters, the widow of Edward Fortescue of Faulkbourne Hall, Essex, and the sister of the younger Mrs Jane Wiseman. Mrs Fortescue had been summoned to the sessions at Newgate on a charge of failing to attend the Protestant church. After he had delivered his testimony, one of the magistrates began questioning Rigby about his own religion. As Father Gerard tells us in his autobiography, John, being a straightforward chap, probably did not see the trap being laid for him and honestly admitted to being a reconciled Catholic - a treasonous offence. John was immediately committed to Newgate prison. He was required to sign a confession of his religious beliefs. When the jailer was putting the chains on him, John quipped that he would not exchange his chain for the Lord Mayor's great chain and gave the jailer sixpence.

Over the next few months John kept a detailed account of his arrest and trials. This was smuggled out of prison by friends and published by Douai College in 1601. Augmented by the narrative of Bishop Challoner, a booklet version was published in 1928 by Father C. Newdigate. Some years ago the trial account was dramatised and presented in London by members of the Catholic Stage Guild.

What follows is substantially what John himself wrote:
By and by my Lord Chief Justice sent me word to provide for myself, for I

The Elizabethan Martyrs, 1577-1601

was to be arraigned forthwith. I bid the messenger tell his lordship, I never heard such good news in my life before; and so I was commanded to the common jail ... the following Tuesday I was removed to the White Lion in Southwark and was there quiet till the 3rd of March. And Wednesday, 3rd of March, in the common sessions, with a number of felons, I was brought to my trial. In the forenoon I was called and appeared; but nothing was said to me. When the justice went to dinner, we also went home to prison; and being at dinner, Justice Gaudy sent his man for me and I went willingly with my keeper: and so coming to them at Justice Dale's house, where the judges dined, Justice Gaudy called me to him and asked my name, which I told him. Were you not committed by the Lord Chief Justice and examined by him? Yea, my lord. You know your own hand? So he showed me my hand; and I said, this is my hand: I pray you give me leave to speak for myself. You shall, said he; I well perceive you have thought better of the matter. I am told ... that you are now sorry for what you have done and willing to become a good subject and go to church ... How say you? Will you go to church now? No, my lord. Good, my lord, whoever informed your lordship, that ever I did yield in any point of my profession, was not my friend, nor ever had any consent thereto. I assure you, my lord, I am a true subject and obedient to her majesty and her laws in any thing which might not hurt my conscience: but to say I will go to church, I never will ...Take my first answer as it is; there is my hand, here is my whole body and most ready and willing I am to seal it with my blood. We were told, said one of the judges, you were a simple young man, and willing to recant; but we see now thou art a resolute, wilful fellow and there is no remedy, but the law must proceed ... Let me have law, in the name of Jesus: God's will be done.

The next day, being Thursday, we went again to the sessions at St Margaret's Hill, where about two in the afternoon I was called to the bar ... My indictment was read, and it was a sharp one. Then my lord bid me speak: and I answered briefly in this manner:

1st. Whereas I am charged in my indictment that I was reconciled; it is very true; to God Almighty so I was ... and as I remember, it is also allowed in your Book of Common Prayer ... that if any man find himself burdened in conscience, he should make his confession to the minister ... and by this humble confession he craveth pardon of his sins, and reconciliation to God again...

2nd. Whereas I am charged that I was reconciled from my obedience to her majesty and to the Romish religion. I will depose the contrary; for I was never reconciled from any obedience to my princess, for I obey her still; nor to any religion, for although I sometimes went to church against my will, yet I was never of any other religion than the Catholic, and therefore needed no reconciliation to religion.

3rd. Whereas, in my former answers, I said I went to church, it is true for fear of temporal punishment I so did, but never minded to fall from the old religion and therefore needed no reconciliation.

4th and lastly. I humbly beseech your good lordships, as you will answer before God, to explain the meaning of the statute to the jury: if the meaning thereof be to make it treason for a man fallen into the displeasure of God, through his sins, to be reconciled to God again by him whom God hath committed the authority of reconciliation? If this be treason, God's will be done.

Then said both judges, it was by a Romish priest and therefore treason. I answered it was by a Catholic priest who had the liberty of the prison, and was free for any man to come to him to relieve him; and therefore by the statute no treason ...Then said Justice Gaudy her majesty and her laws are merciful; if you will yet conform yourself, and say here, before the jury go forth, that you will go to church, we will proceed no further. My lord, said I, if that be all the offence I have committed, as I know it is, and if there be no other I would not wish your lordship to think I have (as I hope) risen this many steps towards heaven, only to let my foot slip now and fall into the bottomless pit of hell. I hope in Jesus, he will strengthen me rather to suffer a thousand deaths if I had so many lives to lose. Let your law take its course. Then, said the judge to the jury ... you must consider of it; you see what is said; you cannot but find it treason by law. And so they went forth, and stood not long upon the matter, but came again, and I was called and bidden again to hold up my hand; they bid the jury look on the prisoner, whether he is guilty or no? Who shall speak for you? They all said the foreman. He spoke so softly that I could not hear him. I willed him to speak up and not be afraid. Then he said, Guilty; to the which I said with a loud voice, laus tibi, Domine! Rex aeternae gloriae (Praise be to thee, O Lord, King of Eternal Glory) ...When judgement was to be given I was called first and Justice Gaudy said, What canst thou say for thyself, wherefore thou should not have judgement of death? I answered, If that which before I have said will not serve I can say no more. Good Rigby, said he, think not I seek your death, will you yet go to church? No, my lord: well then, said he, judgement must pass ...Then he pronounced sentence, as you know the manner is, which, when he had ended I said, Deo gratias, all is but one death and a fleabite in comparison of that which it pleased my sweet Saviour Jesus to suffer for my salvation. I humbly thank your lordship for your great pains, and I freely forgive your lordship and the poor jury, and all other persecutors whatsoever. Well, said he, indeed you show your charity: and then he gave judgement to all the rest, and when he had done he called us together, willing us to send for a minister and provide for death. I desired his lordship to spare my presence and bestow that counsel elsewhere, for I hope I am as well provided as by his exhortation I should be. If you be, said he, it is the better for you; God speed you well, and so we parted. I pray God forgive them all, and emend them, if it be his holy will.

Moved and impressed by John, Mr Justice Gaudy or Gawdy, as it is

The Elizabethan Martyrs, 1577-1601

most commonly spelled, obtained for him a reprieve of three months, in the hope that in time he might change his mind and conform. John got a message to Father Henry Garnet asking to be admitted as a Jesuit brother, but Garnet, bound by his instructions from his superiors in Rome, was regretfully unable to meet his request at the time. He sent John word that he should keep to his desire, which would be met in due course. However, events overtook this intention.

After the three months in prison had elapsed on Thursday, 19 June Rigby was again brought to court before Justice George Kingsmill and Justice Francis Gawdy. Asked by Kingsmill if he would conform he answered, 'I thank God I am the same man that I was. It is not lawful to go to your church. I will not go to it.' 'Then you must die', said the judge, 'for a longer reprieve you cannot have.' Noting that the prisoner did not have irons on his legs, the judge instructed the keeper, who brought a strong pair of shackles and riveted them on fast to both his legs. The next day John was again brought to the sessions house and as he stood in the dock the shackles that had bound his legs inexplicably fell off. Smiling, John asked the keeper to rivet them on more securely, which he did, but in a little while they fell off once more. John asked the keeper's man to try again for, he said, 'I esteem them jewels of too great price to be lost', but they declined to fasten them on for a third time. After much deliberation and arguing among the judges, they overruled Gawdy and concluded that Rigby had to die. Gawdy was seen to wipe away tears from his eyes. When asked what he thought of the irons falling off his legs, John answered that he hoped it was a token that his mortality would shortly be loosed. Returned to prison John was asked how he felt about his approaching death. 'I thank our Lord, in very great comfort and consolation of mind', was his reply.

Awaiting execution, John sent a letter of thanks to Father Gerard for making him a Catholic and enclosed his purse as a keepsake. Father Gerard ever afterwards used the purse in which to carry his reliquary. On the morning of Saturday, 21 June 1600, when he was told that he was to die that day he answered, 'Deo gratias. This is the best tidings that ever was brought to me since I was born'. Between five and six in the afternoon he was called, and taking leave of the Catholic fellow prisoners he asked for their prayers to help him on his journey to his true country. Taken down into the yard where the hurdle was waiting for him he knelt to say a prayer, but was interrupted by Mr More, the sheriff's deputy, so getting up he slapped his hand upon the horse and said, 'Go thy ways, this is the joyfullest day that ever I knew.' Then making the sign of the Cross he lay down on the hurdle. Addressing the bystanders he said, 'Bear witness with me, all good people, that I am now forthwith to give my life only for the Catholic cause.'

Father Gerard informs us that Roger Manners, 5th Earl of Rutland - brother of the future convert and priest, Sir Oliver Manners - with a Captain Whitlock and a group of noblemen, happened to be in the street where John was being dragged along on the hurdle. The Earl asked what was his offence and John himself answered that he was guilty of no offence whatever but died for his Catholic Faith. John was urged by the Earl to conform. Such a handsome young man, he said, was made for a wife and children, not to die for his faith. 'As for a wife', John responded, 'I have never in my life had intercourse with a woman,' whereupon Captain Whitlock asked for his prayers. Father Gerard confirmed that John had indeed kept his virginal purity.

Arrived at the scaffold, John gave the hangman a gold coin, saying, 'Take this in token that I freely forgive thee and all others who have been accessory to my death.' All the eyewitnesses of his execution remarked how handsome he was and upon his fine physique, his outstanding cheerfulness and courage.

'I am a poor gentleman of the House of Harrock in Lancashire', he said, 'My age thirty years and my judgement and condemnation to this death is only for that I answered the judge that I was reconciled and for that I refused to go to church'.

He was treated with exceptional barbarity. After he had been cut down by the hangman he was able to stand upright and was thrown to the ground while one of the officials pressed his foot on John's throat and others grasped his arms and legs to hold him down as he was butchered while still conscious. As they disembowelled him his last words were, 'May God forgive you. Lord Jesus receive my soul'. Bishop Challoner records that the people complained bitterly of the barbarity and bewailed John's death.

Anne Line

A ministering angel shall my sister be.

Hamlet, William Shakespeare, 1564-1616

Anne was the second daughter of William Heigham by Anne Allen. She was born c.1565 at Dunmow in Essex. Her father was a strict Calvinist who owned property that had once belonged to the religious houses. When Anne and her younger brother, William, who was the

The Elizabethan Martyrs, 1577-1601

Heigham's only son, became Catholics as teenagers, their father disinherited them both and used every means of vindictiveness against his own children. Anne married Roger Line when she was nineteen. Roger came from a wealthy, long-established recusant family at Ringwood in the New Forest and was heir to an estate in Hampshire.

Anne's brother, William, had a priest who lodged at his house in London. This was Father William Thomson, who is also mentioned as having been chaplain to Anne. It seems that after their marriage Anne and Roger were living with her brother. In February 1585, not long after his marriage, Roger and his brother-in-law William were arrested while at Mass with Father Thomson at a house 'without Bishopsgate'. Roger was committed to the Compter or Counter in Wood Street, along with the priest and was examined by the vicious Mr Justice Young, who had shown more animosity towards Catholics, committing more of them to prison than any man except Topcliffe. While in prison Roger received a message from his uncle that unless he conformed he would be disinherited by his family. Roger sent back the reply, 'If I must desert either the world or God then I desert the world.' As a result the inheritance from his father and uncle went to Richard, his younger brother.

William Heigham was transferred to the Bridewell and Father John Gerard tells us how he saw him being forced to work the tread-mill in the prison while being lashed. He had to pay a heavy fine for his release. Father Gerard also witnessed twenty-six-year-old Blessed William Thomson's martyrdom at Tyburn on 20 April 1586. 66 William Heigham, whom we are told played the harp skilfully, firstly became a tutor to a Catholic family and then went abroad where he became a Jesuit brother.

Roger Line was sentenced to perpetual imprisonment, but as an alternative he was banished on pain of death and sent into exile in Flanders, where he received a small allowance from the King of Spain, some of which he sent to Anne. Roger died in Flanders in 1594 and Anne was left destitute and homeless. Father Gerard introduced her to Mrs Jane Wiseman, who offered her free board and lodging, while he provided her with whatever else she might need; so for a time she stayed with the Wisemans at Braddocks in Essex.

Father Gerard had established a safe house in London as a refuge for priests and he could think of no better person than Anne to supervise this for him, so he asked her if she was prepared to become his housekeeper. Although frail in health, Anne managed the house very capably. She looked after all the household affairs, kept the accounts, answered inquiries, taught catechism and embroidered vestments. The priests who found shelter under her roof called her 'Mrs Martha'. Father Henry Garnet said of her that he had never known a woman 'who equalled her in prudence.' Young women trying to get abroad to enter convents also stayed with Anne until transport arrangements could be made for them. Father Gerard, who always refers to her as 'saintly', tells us that Anne was 'full of kindness and possessed her soul in great peace'. It is clear that Anne played a vital role in the underground network of sheltering priests. In the period before her arrest she supervised three adjoining houses. These were her own house, where she regularly gave religious instruction to children; a house for a resident chaplain and a larger house where priests were lodged. We are told by Father Gerard that she was a chronic invalid. Father Garnet said, 'I myself have seen her completely exhausted ... in fact her infirmities reduced her almost to the extreme stage of physical weakness.' This is confirmed in an account by another contemporary, Dr Anthony Champney [67] in his manuscript *History of the Reign of Queen Elizabeth*, where it was stated that Anne was always suffering from various ailments, in particular continual headaches. Bishop Challoner, citing this manuscript as his source, records that Anne told her confessor of a vision she had of Christ in the Blessed Sacrament carrying His Cross. She also confided to her confessor that she hoped one day to be found worthy of martyrdom.

When Father Gerard, after years of imprisonment and torture, made his hair-raising escape from the Tower in October 1597, he visited Anne at night. She was well known to so many people that she was under suspicion and it was unsafe for Father Gerard to visit any house she occupied. They agreed she had to move house so she rented apartments. At her new location she continued to shelter priests. In order to make her dedication more complete she took vows of poverty, chastity and obedience.

In July 1599 the new safe house was raided while Father Gerard and his companion, John Lillie, were in residence, together with Father Joshua Pulleyn. Trapped in an upper room with no means of escape Gerard's first reaction was to fight his way out using his sword. On second thoughts he realised that this would impact badly on the owner of the house and make matters much worse for him. The searchers came to the room where Gerard and Lillie were and as the door had no lock the two inside held down the latch as tightly as they could. Anne, keeping her cool, calmly said that the servant whose room it was must have gone off with the key and volunteered to go and find him. The pursuivants were having none of that and said they would accompany her - and off they went without ever noticing that there was no lock on

The Elizabethan Martyrs, 1577-1601

the door! This gave Lillie an opportunity to insist that Gerard get into hiding, reluctant though he was to leave Lillie to face the searchers when they returned. Gerard just had time to get into the hiding place when the searchers broke in assuming Lillie was the priest. He held them off as long as he could but was arrested when he claimed that all books and religious materials found belonged to him. He was sent to the Tower and tortured by hanging in the manacles for hours. He was later transferred to another prison from which he escaped, eventually making his way to Rome where he entered the Society of Jesus. (Sadly, John died in London in 1609, aged only thirty-six.)

On Candlemas Day, 2 February 1601, Anne allowed an unusually large number of Catholics to come to the house for Mass. The neighbours noticed people arriving at an early hour and informed the constables. Everything was ready for Mass when the priest-hunters arrived, rushing upstairs to find a room full of people. The priest, Francis Page, [68] who was in the process of blessing candles, managed to pull off his vestments and mingle with the congregation. The constables found a room full of people and an altar, but no one would admit that a priest was actually in the house, although they could not deny they were waiting for Mass. In all the confusion Father Page managed to slip out of the room and hide before making his escape. Anne and most of those present were arrested. Father Garnet managed to get letters to Anne in prison asking her what she needed. She replied that she was very grateful for the interest he had taken in her but she wanted nothing other than his prayers that she might remain faithful to the end.

On 26 February 1601, Anne was tried at the Sessions House at the Old Bailey on a charge of sheltering Francis Page; a treasonous act under Statute 27. She was so weak and ill that she was bedridden, as the prison keepers testified, but Lord Chief Justice John Popham, who treated her abominably, insisted that she be brought to court. She had to be carried in on a chair by two constables. On trial with her was Lady Margaret Gage, who had been sentenced to death once before for sheltering priests. The prosecution failed to make a case. It produced only one witness who gave the slender testimony that he had seen a man dressed all in white in Anne's house, but as the priest allegedly in question was not in custody he could not be produced.

Nonetheless Popham, who seems to have harboured a venomous, personal hatred against Catholics, told the jury that they should be on their guard 'because the woman commonly received many priests and Jesuits' and Catholic artefacts had been discovered in her house. He instructed the jury to return a guilty verdict. Anne received her sentence

The Elizabethan Martyrs, 1577-1601

with thankfulness. Lady Gage was again reprieved. Three of her four sons became priests; William SJ, George, who was die in prison, and Thomas the Dominican apostate, while the fourth was the famous Colonel Sir Henry Gage. (Margaret Gage, daughter of Sir Thomas Copley of Gatton married as his first wife, Sir John Gage, and with her husband was first condemned to death in 1591 after serving two years in prison for sheltering a priest, Richard Beesley, brother of the martyr, George Beesley. Margaret and her husband, their hands bound, were placed in the cart to be taken to their execution when a letter of reprieve was delivered. Their estate of Haling near Croydon, Surrey, had already been seized and declared forfeit to the Crown. After Margaret's death John Gage married Anne, daughter of William Shelley of Michelgrove, Sussex. By her he had three more sons, two of whom, John and Francis, became priests.)

While awaiting execution in Newgate, Anne wrote a letter to Father Page in which she disposed of her possessions. To Father Gerard she left a gold cross which had belonged to her husband. She also gave verbal instructions that she bequeathed her bed to the priest. Sadly, after her execution the jailers had so ransacked her cell that when Father Gerard went to buy the bed back from them all that was left was the coverlet. Gerard informs us that he always slept under the coverlet whenever he stayed in London and felt protected by it.

Early next morning Anne was told she was to die that day but showed no sign of fear. It also happened to be the day fixed for the execution in the Tower of Robert Devereux, Earl of Essex, for treason as his condemnation was unpopular it was thought that butchering a batch of Catholics would provide a diversion. In a freezing snowstorm, Anne was taken to Tyburn to be executed along with two young priests, Roger Filcock, [69] who had often been her confessor, and Mark Barkworth. [70] The priests loudly sang the paschal anthem, '*Haec dies quam, fecit Dominus exultemus et laetemur in ea*' (This is the day the Lord has made, we rejoice and are glad in it.)

On the scaffold Anne was pestered by the Protestant ministers: 'Away with you, I have nothing in common with any of you,' she said. Speaking boldly to the crowd, Anne said, 'I am sentenced to die for harbouring a Catholic priest and so far am I from repenting of what I have done that I wish with all my soul that where I have entertained one I could have entertained a thousand'. A contemporary manuscript account of her execution, now belonging to the family of the Duke of Rutland, tells that after kneeling to pray, 'She behaved herself most meekly, patiently and virtuously to her last breath. She kissed the gallows and then made the sign of the Cross'.

The Elizabethan Martyrs, 1577-1601

She continued praying as she was hanged but never moved. While Anne hung from the gallows, Father Barkworth, who was the second to die, reverently kissed the hem of her robe saying, 'Sister, you've got ahead of us but we'll follow you to bliss as quickly as we can'. He told the crowd, 'I come here to die being a Catholic priest ... belonging to the Order of St Benedict; it was by this same Order that England was converted'. The rope was cut immediately and Mark was able to stand and made some resistance when held down to be butchered, calling out 'O Lord, O Lord!' Father Filcock called on him to have courage. When it came to his own turn, he said, 'Pray for me blessed Father Mark. Pray for me to our Lord whose presence you now enjoy that I too may faithfully run my course'.

As the crowd dispersed a representative of Father Garnet cut off one of the sleeves of Anne's dress, which he dipped in the blood of the two priests. The martyrs' quartered bodies were buried in the pit close by the gallows and the corpses of several thieves were thrown in on top of them. But their remains were secretly retrieved and a number of relics survived. Anne Line's body was reputedly taken to the Countess of Arundel, who arranged for a fitting burial. Where that took place is unknown.

Shortly after Anne's martyrdom in 1601 Shakespeare's allegorical poem, *The Phoenix and the Turtle*, was published in a collection of poetry entitled *Love's Martyrs*. The turtle of the title refers to the turtle dove. The interpretation of the poem has always presented difficulties. Several eminent scholars have argued, on the basis of Shakespeare being a Catholic sympathiser, that the work contains references to the Catholic liturgy and parallels with the *Dies Irae*, as well as references to William Byrd and Father Henry Garnet. It has been suggested that the poem is a eulogy commemorating Anne Line and her husband, who, like the couple in the poem, were childless. Whatever the interpretation certainly '*Beauty, truth and rarity. Grace in all simplicity*', were apposite descriptions of Anne.

The Elizabethan Martyrs, 1577-1601

Notes to Chapter Four

1 Blessed Thomas Ford came from Devon. He was an MA and Fellow of Trinity College, Oxford. In 1571 he quit his fellowship and went to Douai. In 1573 he was ordained at Brussels, alongside two other ex-Oxford men: Richard Bristow and Gregory Martin. These three were the first from Douai College to be ordained. After taking his degree as Bachelor of Divinity Thomas returned to England in 1576 and worked mainly in Oxfordshire. He was captured with Edmund Campion and sent to the Tower where he was tortured on at least three occasions. Accused by the informers Sledd and Munday 71 of plotting at Rheims and Rome - two places where he had never been in his life - he was condemned to death. He was a tall man with a reddish beard. His execution was postponed until 28 May 1582 when he was hanged, drawn and quartered at Tyburn.

2 Robert Persons SJ was born at Nether Stowey, Somerset, in 1546. He was a Fellow of Balliol College, Oxford, before being received into the Catholic Church in 1575. He joined the Jesuits and was ordained in 1578. It may have been Persons who initiated the idea of the Jesuit mission to England. He arrived in the country shortly before Campion but having narrowly evaded capture many times he escaped when Campion was arrested. He spent the rest of his life indefatigably working for the mission, encouraging the founding of English monasteries and seminaries on the Continent and getting involved in many dubious political schemes to further the Catholic cause. To portray Persons as just an inveterate political intriguer, as so many have sought to do, is too simplistic. He was a complicated character of enormous talents with an incredible capacity for hard work driven by his all-consuming desire for the conversion of England to the Catholic faith. Dr Jessop, in his *One Generation of a Norfolk House,* while deploring his less attractive personality traits, nonetheless describes Persons as, 'one of the Titans of his age'. He was Rector of the English College, Rome, from 1597 until his death. The school Persons founded at Eu moved to Saint-Omer. During the French Revolution in 1794 the College moved to the splendid Stonyhurst Hall in Lancashire.

3 Blessed William Hartley was born near Derby in 1551. He matriculated at St John's, Oxford, from where he was expelled by Tobie Matthew, the Vice-Chancellor. Having gone to Rheims he was ordained at Châlons 26 February 1580 and sent to England. He was sheltered by Dame Cecily Stonor at the same time that the secret

The Elizabethan Martyrs, 1577-1601

printing of Campion's *Ten Reasons* was being undertaken. In June 1581 William took copies to Oxford University and secretly distributed them, including leaving copies on every seat at St Mary's Church at a Commencement service where students seeking degrees defended their theses. Two months later Stonor was searched and he was arrested along with John Stonor and the printer, Stephen Brinkley. They were all sent to the Tower. He was then moved to the Marshalsea where William proved a recalcitrant captive celebrating Mass for his fellow prisoners, who included Lord Vaux. This led to a letter of complaint about him in December 1583 from John Aylmer, Bishop of London, who informed Cecil that he had ordered William to be clapped in irons. Along with eight other priests, on 5 February 1584 William was tried and condemned for a fictitious plot against the Queen. To everyone's surprise William was not amongst those sent to Tyburn for execution. Instead he remained in the Marshalsea until banished in 1585. He was described as a man of the meekest disposition and naturally virtuous, modest and grave, with a sober and peaceful look, a blackish beard and of moderate height. He was soon back in London where he was arrested in December 1587. Statute 27 now being conveniently available, William was tried at the Middlesex Sessions at Newgate on 18 September 1588 and condemned for his priesthood. On 5 October 1588 he was executed at Shoreditch, outside the theatre, the first playhouse ever built in England.

4 Brother Ralph Emerson was born in Durham c.1551. He was firstly the companion of Edmund Campion and then was designated to accompany Father William Weston to England in 1584. Ralph had charge of the baggage, which contained a large number of books. The day after his embarkation, Ralph was left to arrange for the books to be transported by river from Norwich to London. Ralph and the baggage arrived safely in the capital and he met up with Father Weston; but the books, which included copies of the Douai-Rheims New Testament as well as volumes by William Allen, were detained at the inn and it was dangerous to make a fuss about getting them released. On Ralph's return to the inn, the books had been discovered. Ralph was arrested on 26 September 1584 and questioned by Topcliffe and others. He was held prisoner without charge in the Counter in the Poultry for three years. Ralph was described as 'a very slender, brown little fellow ... a great dealer for all the papists.' In 1587 he was transferred to the Clink, where he spent the next six years and where Father John Gerard met him. In 1600 he was transferred to Wisbech Castle and remained a prisoner for the rest of Elizabeth's reign. He was in a bad way, by all

accounts, having suffered a stroke that left him severely paralysed. After serving twenty years he was released on the accession of James I and died at Saint-Omer in 1604.

5 Blessed William Filby, the son of George Filby, a courier, and his wife Alice, was born in the parish of St Mary Magdalen, Oxford c.1555. After his conversion he went to Rheims in October 1579 and was ordained there 25 March 1581 and sent to England. His brother, John, who had been ordained two years earlier, was already working on the mission. Captured with Campion, William was sent to the Tower and tried and condemned with Campion; but the sentence was delayed for six months which he spent loaded with heavy chains before he was hanged, drawn and quartered at Tyburn with his three companions about 7 a.m. on 30 May 1582. William was the first to die and protested his innocence while being abused by Sheriff Martin. It was noticed that he was clutching a handkerchief which was snatched from him to disclose a little wooden cross, for the possession of which he was accused of being a villainous traitor. At this Filby only smiled. While he stood with the rope around his neck William was offered the Queen's mercy. 'I have done nothing to offend her', was his response, at which the hangman was told to proceed. As he hung William struck his breast several times saying, 'Lord receive my soul', until his hands were pulled down. He was just twenty-seven years old. His brother, John, was educated at Lincoln College, Oxford, and went to Douai in 1577. The following year he was ordained at Cambrai and sent to England in February 1579. His apostolate was in Oxfordshire, Berkshire and Buckinghamshire. He was still serving the mission in 1610.

6 Blessed Thomas Cottam, the son of Lawrence Cottam and Ann Brerewere, was born at St Michael's-on-Wyre, Lancashire, in 1549. Educated at Brasenose College, Oxford, after becoming BA in 1568 he worked as a schoolmaster in London before being converted through the influence of Thomas Pound q.v. He went to Douai and was ordained deacon in 1577. He travelled to Rome and became a novice of the Society of Jesus in 1579, but after six months he was asked to leave because of ill health. He was ordained priest at Soissons 28 May 1580, shortly thereafter returning to England with Fathers John Hart and Edward Rishton and Dr Humphrey Ely, at that time still a layman. (He was not ordained until April 1582 and spent the remainder of his life teaching at Pont à Mousson University where he died in 1604.) While at Lyons Thomas had met Charles Sledd, the spy, who travelled with

The Elizabethan Martyrs, 1577-1601

him as far as Rheims. He described Thomas as lean and slender of body, his face full of freckles, his beard red and thin and he had a mole on his right cheek. Spies had warned of their coming, and Thomas was quickly apprehended at Dover. The authorities, not realising who he was, charged Dr Ely with the task of escorting Thomas to London and delivering him to Lord Cobham, Warden of the Cinque Ports. This meant that Thomas was free but he became seriously concerned at the consequences Dr Ely might suffer for failing to carry out his instructions. His scruples about how he had obtained his liberty led him to consult Thomas Pound in prison. Pound told him that he should examine his conscience regarding the manner of his escape. After much heart-searching Thomas decided to give himself up. He surrendered at the Star inn to Thomas Andrews, a deputy of Lord Cobham's, for which Andrew's received one hundred shillings. Thomas was sent to the Marshalsea and then to the Tower where he was brutally tortured in the Scavenger's Daughter, causing severe blood loss. His interrogations were overseen by John Popham and Thomas Egerton who were to be the prosecutors at his trial. He was re-admitted to the Society of Jesus in prison. Tried with Campion and his companions, he was condemned but not executed with them. When told he was to die the next day he cried out, 'Give thanks to God with me, for tomorrow is my day!' He was hanged, drawn and quartered at Tyburn on 30 May 1582. Taking Bull, the hangman, by the sleeve Thomas said to him, "'God forgive you and make you His servant'. He was offered a pardon if he renounced his faith, to which he answered, 'I will not swerve one jot from my faith for anything'. The sheriff ordered his despatch as he was so stubborn. He hanged until he was dead, and when he was stripped it was discovered that under his shirt he was wearing a coarse canvas vest in lieu of a hair shirt. The Protestant ministers found this highly amusing and joked about it.

7 Blessed Robert Johnson, born 1544, came from Shropshire. He was a gentleman's servant before entering the German College, Rome, in 1572 and studied there, apparently finding the work hard, not helped by his poor health. Father Robert Persons, while acknowledging that Robert was not academic, described him as 'a very good and godly little man'. He went to Douai and was ordained at Brussels in 1576 then spent some time with the Jesuits at Louvain undergoing the Spiritual Exercises in preparation for his return to England. He only spent a few months in England in 1579 before visiting Rome, which he left in February 1580. From this visit there is a report of a spy which describes Robert as follows: 'About 40, slender of body, somewhat hard-

The Elizabethan Martyrs, 1577-1601

favoured, his face full of wrinkles, the hair of his beard not cut, a flaxen yellow colour, wanting two teeth on the upper jaw on the right side. He speaketh Italian excellently.' By the summer of 1580 he was in London where he was betrayed by the informer Charles Sleddd, arrested and jailed at the Counter in the Poultry. In December he was sent to the Tower, where he was racked three times before being tried with Campion and his companions. Accused of plotting with them he protested that he had never even met any of them until brought to Court. He was condemned and kept for six months in prison before being hanged, drawn and quartered at Tyburn on 28 May 1582. He was repeatedly urged to acknowledge Elizabeth as supreme head of the church, and accused of being a most obstinate traitor for refusing to do so. Robert responded, 'If I be a traitor for maintaining this faith, then all the kings and queens of this realm heretofore, and all our ancestors were traitors, for they maintained the same'. When the rope was put around his neck he began to say the Lord's Prayer in Latin, at which the ministers present called out to him to pray in English. Robert replied, 'I pray that prayer which Christ taught in a tongue I well understand'. 'Pray it as Christ did', he was told. 'What', he exclaimed, 'do you think that Christ taught in English?' He was allowed to hang until dead.

8 John Hart came from a strongly Catholic family at Eynsham, Oxfordshire. He had two sisters who were Bridgettine nuns. He went to Douai and was ordained at Cambrai 29 March 1578, returning to England in 1580, just two days before Edmund Campion. John was arrested on disembarking at Dover and sent for examination to the court at Nonsuch Palace. Unsuccessful efforts were made by Walsingham to get him to conform. He was sent firstly to the Marshalsea and then to the Tower, where he was left for five days over Christmas with only the bare ground for a bed. On 31 December he was cruelly racked and kept in prison before being tried and condemned to death with Campion in November 1581. His execution was postponed with that of Thomas Ford and his companions until 28 May 1582. On the day of the execution, John's fear got the better of him. He wrote to inform Walsingham that he would conform and offered to act as a spy; so at the last minute a stay of execution was ordered and he was returned to the Tower. All the evidence suggests that his offers were never fulfilled. He was allowed a visit from his mother and this seems to have stiffened his resolve. He converted one of the Tower warders, Samuel Kennet, who went over to Rheims and was ordained at Rome in 1589. Having worked on the English mission he eventually joined the Benedictines. John remained steadfast under continued brutal treatment

The Elizabethan Martyrs, 1577-1601

in prison. He was kept in irons for twenty-one days and regularly incarcerated in the dreaded Pit. His constancy was praised by fellow prisoners Luke Kirby and Edward Rishton. In 1583 he joined the Jesuits and two years later was banished. He went to Rome and ended up at Jarislau, Poland, where he died 19 July 1586.

9 Blessed Lawrence Richardson's real name was Johnson, but he was known on the mission as Richardson, and executed under that name. He was born at Sefton, near Liverpool. He was a fellow of Brasenose College, Oxford, and graduated BA in 1572. In 1573 he went to Douai and in March 1577 was ordained at Cateau Cambresis. He returned to his native Lancashire in July of that year. He went back to Douai in 1579 when it seems he had expressed a desire to go to the Indies as a missionary, however he was sent to England again in 1580. He was arrested in Lancashire in 1581 and committed first to Newgate and then to the Queen's Bench prison. As he pointed out – to no avail – he was actually in prison in England when he was alleged to have been at Rheims and Rome plotting against the Queen. Tried and condemned with Campion, he remained in the Tower from December 1581 until 30 May 1582, when he was executed at Tyburn with Luke Kirby and Thomas Cottam. As he waited in the cart Lawrence was forced to watch while Cottam was being butchered. Standing with the rope around his neck he was pestered by Topcliffe and several ministers who importuned him with questions and demands that he confess his treason, which he, of course, vehemently denied. The sheriff offered him the Queen's pardon if he admitted his guilt, to which he replied, 'I thank her majesty, but I must not confess an untruth or renounce my faith.'

10 Edward Rishton was born in Lancashire in 1550 and after becoming BA at Brasenose College, Oxford, went to Douai in 1573. He was ordained at Cambrai in April 1577 and was sent to Rome in August, from where he began his return journey to England in April 1580 in the company of Robert Persons, Edmund Campion, Ralph Sherwin and Luke Kirby. At this time a spy in Rome described Edward as 'short of stature and thick, his beard yellow, thick and cut short, his face pale of colour.' Edward departed from Rheims on the final leg of his journey home on 5 June, just two days before Campion. Rishton's work on the mission was brief. Robert Persons records that Edward was arrested, along with his brother, at the Red Lion, Holborn, London. He wrote an account of his trial with Campion, at which he was sentenced to death. He wrote, 'It was not thought safe to put Father Campion and the other

343

priests to death merely because they preached the Catholic faith ... Accordingly it was pretended ... that he and others had at Rome and Rheims conspired together to kill the queen. Witnesses are sought and suborned, men out of the very dregs of the people; and though their evidence did not hold together and was most easily shown to be false, nevertheless Father Campion and the others are condemned ...' Edward was not executed but kept in prison in the Kings Bench for three years until banished with twenty others in 1585. They were forcibly put aboard a ship for Normandy, landed on the coast and left there. Among them were James Bosgrave, Robert Nutter, William Dean, William Hartley, Jasper Heywood SJ, William Bishop, afterwards Bishop of Chalcedon, and Thomas Worthington, afterwards third president of Douai. Edward is best remembered for continuing the important work of the learned Father Nicholas Sander, *The Rise and Growth of the Anglican Schism*.

11 Blessed John Shert came from Macclesfield, Cheshire. He was educated at Brasenose, Oxford, taking his BA degree in 1566. He became a schoolmaster in London before going to Douai in 1576. He was sent to Rome as one of the first students in the new college. He was ordained at Rome and left for England via Rheims in August 1578. According to an informers report, in 1580 he was living in Holborn, London. On 14 July 1581 he was captured and sent to the Tower. He was tried and condemned with Campion but not executed until 28 May 1582 with Thomas Ford and Robert Johnson.

12 John Colleton was born at Milverton, Somerset, in 1548 and educated at Oxford, but did not take a degree. We have his own account of much of his life and ministry. In 1573 he joined the Carthusians at Louvain, but spent less than a year with them before concluding that this was not his vocation, partly because of indifferent health to cope with the lifestyle and partly, so he tells us, because he was absolutely tone deaf and utterly incapable of singing a note! John related that his singing teacher stated he could teach a cow to bellow in tune more easily than getting John to do so. He went to Douai in 1576 and was ordained at Binche in June of that year, returning to England a month later. He went home to Somerset and reconciled his father, brothers and sisters to the Church, all of whom endured imprisonment for their recusancy. His father was later to die in prison at Gloucester. Colleton had spent three years at Sutton Courtenay, near Abingdon, with James Braybrooke, a lawyer of the Inner Temple, expelled and imprisoned for his refusal to conform. Colleton was arrested at Lyford with Campion

and sent to the Tower. He was tried with Campion and his companions, charged with complicity in the fictitious plot to kill the Queen. John denied that he had ever been at Rheims or Rome and was able to call a witness, Mr Lancaster, who testified that on the day John was alleged to have been plotting at Rheims, he had been with him at Gray's Inn. It did not secure his release and he remained in the Marshalsea until 1585, when, loudly protesting, he was banished. After a time spent in Rome he returned to England and was recognised in London in 1591. Although he consistently refused to take the oath, he firmly protested his temporal allegiance to Elizabeth and to James: it seems to have done him little good. He spent the next thirteen years in and out of various prisons. At the establishment of the Chapter in 1623 he became its first dean and vicar-general. Left relatively in peace under Charles I, he retired to Kent to live with Mr Roper at Eltham, where he died, aged ninety, 29 October 1637.

13 James Bosgrave came from Dorset and went abroad at an early age. He joined the Jesuits in Rome in 1564 and was ordained at Olmutz, Moravia, in 1572. He taught in Poland for several years before returning to England, where he was taken prisoner as soon as he landed. He was sent to the Marshalsea and in 1580 to the Tower. Although condemned to death he was left in the Tower. In 1583 King Stephen of Poland wrote to Queen Elizabeth begging her to release James. He was kept in prison until 1585, when he was banished. He returned to Poland and died there in 1623, well over seventy years-old.

14 Blessed Thomas Alfield was born at Gloucester in 1552 and educated at Eton, where his father had been a teacher before becoming Master of Gloucester School and then a minister. Thomas was a Fellow of King's College, Cambridge. He visited Douai in 1576 and was presumably converted because he returned to the College in 1580, was ordained at Châlons in March 1581 and was sent to England a few days later. He was betrayed by his own father and arrested on 7 April 1582 with Father William Dean and committed to the Tower. There he was twice tortured but was released in September. In 1583 he was in Gloucester but on 14 June 1585 he was imprisoned at Newgate and arraigned on 5 July together with Fathers Leonard Hide and William Wiggs.

With them was a layman, Venerable Thomas Webley, who with Alfield was condemned for distributing copies of William Allen's book, *A sincere and modest defence of English Catholics*. They were both executed at Tyburn the following day. Venerable Thomas Webley was said to be a dyer's assistant in London. Father Hide was born in

The Elizabethan Martyrs, 1577-1601

Berkshire in 1550. Ordained at Cateau Cambresis in 1577 he had been chaplain at Lordington, Sussex to Sir Geoffrey Pole, nephew of Cardinal Reginald Pole. In 1582 Hide, together with his brother Peter, a servant at Lordington, helped Sir Geoffrey and his seven-year-old son - who feared for their lives not only as Catholics but also because of their royal blood - to escape from England to Rome. After returning to England Hide was captured at Highgate, London in 1585 and sent to the Tower and then Newgate. He was in Wisbech Castle by January 1588 and banished in 1603. Shortly before his death in England in 1608 he entered the Society of Jesus. London-born Father Wiggs had been a great friend of Edmund Campion at Oxford and when he was suspected of assisting Cuthbert Mayne in 1577 he had fled to France, leaving behind his pregnant wife. His wife having died, he was ordained at Rome in 1582 and returned to England the following year. By March 1585 he was in the Tower and was then moved to Newgate. In 1587 he was in the Clink before being sent to Wisbech. In 1601 he was transferred to Framlingham and in a quarrel in 1602 he was stabbed to death!

15 Thomas Norton (1532-1584) was a London-born lawyer and Member of Parliament. He was secretary to Edward Seymour, Protector Somerset. He married Margaret, the daughter of Archbishop Thomas Cranmer. A friend of John Foxe and a rabid Calvinist, Norton seems to have pervertedly enjoyed interrogating Catholic prisoners under torture. He became so fanatical that he was deprived of his office and committed to the Tower at the behest of the Anglican bishops, but was soon released on the orders of Walsingham.

16 John Mush was born into a poor family in Yorkshire in 1552. For a time he was a servant to the famous York physician Dr Thomas Vavasour. Educated by the Jesuits out of charity, he was however deemed unsuitable for the Society of Jesus because of his blunt manners and temper, in which perhaps lay the seeds of his future resentment of that Order. He went to Douai in 1576 and moved to Rome to complete his studies, being one of the first group of students at the English College. He became a favourite student of William Allen's. He was ordained at Rome in 1583. His younger brother was also a priest. John left Rome for England in 1583 after an audience with Pope Gregory XIII and three years later Anthony Tyrell informed the authorities in September 1586 that John was in York. He was arrested at the home of Blessed Richard Langley, described as a 'notorious entertainer of seminaries', who was martyred at York for sheltering

The Elizabethan Martyrs, 1577-1601

priests. Mush escaped from York Castle and was reported working in London and Surrey. In 1593 he visited Rome but returned to England in 1594 and became a prominent figure amongst the Catholic clergy, travelling widely at home and abroad and getting involved in all sorts of controversies, being a strong opponent of Archpriest Blackwell. In 1600 he signed an appeal to Rome against Blackwell, asking for a bishop and in 1601 was a member of the deputation sent to Rome. In 1603 he was one of the thirteen priests who signed a protestation of allegiance to Elizabeth. By 1610 he was back in York and died in the North of England in 1617. It is as the biographer of Margaret Clitherow that he will be chiefly remembered by posterity.

17 Blessed William Lacey was born c.1531 into a gentleman's family at Horton, near Settle. His house was always open to seminary priests. He married the widowed mother of Father Joseph Cresswell SJ, future rector of the English College, Rome. The couple suffered great harassment and regular heavy fines for their recusancy. They became vagrants, constantly on the move, dependent upon the charity of neighbours and friends for shelter. When his wife died, although now advanced in years, William decided to offer himself for the priesthood and went to the seminary at Rheims in June 1580. He must have stood out among his young student companions. He received all his orders within three weeks, culminating in his ordination by Bishop Goldwell of St Asaph on 5 March 1581 in the chapel of the English College, Rome, and shortly afterwards returned to England. He frequently visited the Catholic prisoners in York Castle and was captured leaving the Castle on 22 July 1582. He was examined by the Archbishop and Lord Mayor and returned to the Castle, a solitary prisoner chained in a dungeon. Arraigned on 11 August he was condemned and hanged, drawn and quartered on 22 August when his attempts to address the people were thwarted by the ministers present who urged the hangman to fling him off the ladder.

18 Blessed Richard Kirkman was born into a gentleman's family at Addingham, Skipton. He went to Rheims in 1577 and was ordained 18 April 1579. In August of that year he was sent to England. He worked in Yorkshire, Northumberland and Lincolnshire. On 8 August 1582 while on a journey, he and his servant were stopped near Wakefield by Justice Wortley. His baggage was searched and Mass equipment was found. On being questioned he admitted that he was a priest and was sent first to Tadcaster and then to York where the assizes happened to be in session. He was arraigned with William Lacey on 11 August and

five lay Catholic recusants brought from Hull. One of them agreed to go to church but the others 'do remain obstinate and have judgement to pay £20 for each month's absence.' The Earl of Huntingdon was informed that the crowd at the trial was 'so great that the court was in great disorder and the justices of the assize forced to make room themselves like ushers.' Richard was condemned, thanking God for finding him worthy to be honoured with such a sublime death. On the scaffold he was denied the opportunity to speak to the large crowd of spectators when he was hanged, drawn and quartered with Lacey on 22 August. The flimsiness of the charges brought against priests at this time is demonstrated by the report of the trial sent to Lord Burghley. Kirkman was accused of 'withdrawing traitorously her majesty's poor simple subjects from their natural allegiance to H.M. to the obedience of the Pope and Romish religion.'

19 Blessed James Thompson came from Yorkshire, somewhere to the west of York. He went to Rheims in 1580, was ordained at Soissons in May 1581 and returned to England. He was arrested with a companion at York on 11 August 1582 leaving the house of Stephen Branton, a Catholic, who at the time was a prisoner in the Kidcote. The man who apprehended him, Mr Wortley, was carrying a long pike staff on his shoulders. Overtaking Thompson, he demanded to know where he had lodged the previous night, as he suspected him to be a priest. Wortley was advised that Thompson had left a bag full of vestments at the house of Mr and Mrs Thomas Waterton at Walton. An order was issued for their arrest but by the time the pursuivant arrived they had fled to Staffordshire, where they had relatives. When examined before the Council of the North Thompson admitted that he was a priest. This occasioned some surprise because he had been well known in York only a short time before. He told them that his stay at Rheims had been short because he was in very poor health which had obliged him to return home 'sooner than he had designed'. He asked to be excused from divulging the names of those whom he had reconciled to the Church and refused to acknowledge the royal supremacy. He was returned to prison and loaded with heavy irons for seventeen days before being led through the streets still in his chains, when he was transferred to York Castle, where he was kept among the common felons, some of whom he reconciled. Through the influence of friends he was moved into a chamber in the company of two other priests. Thompson was condemned on 25 November for persuading to popery and was executed on 28 November 1582, along with a group of common criminals. Asked how he was he answered that in all his life

The Elizabethan Martyrs, 1577-1601

he had never been so joyful and had quite forgotten the pains of his disease. As he was flung off the ladder, while hanging, he raised his hands towards heaven, then, to the amazement of the onlookers, with his right hand he struck his breast and made the sign of the Cross.

20 Blessed William Hart was born at Wells, Somerset, in 1558. Educated at Oxford, he went to Douai in 1577 and then to Rome where he was ordained in February 1581. In May of that year he returned to England. A deeply spiritual man, he spent most of his ministry in and around York, where he carried on a secret apostolate for a time amongst the many Catholic prisoners in York Castle, hearing their confessions and saying Mass. On 22 July 1582 he was caught saying Mass but managed to escape by climbing down the walls and wading through chest-high mud in the moat. He was exceedingly in demand in the days prior to Christmas. Having said Mass at the home of William Hutton, then in prison, on the night of Christmas Day he retired to bed but was aroused from sleep, having been betrayed. He was imprisoned in York Castle and on one occasion was dragged in chains to take part in a theological disputation with some Protestant ministers, including Dean Hutton of York. He was kept in prison for three months and many of the letters he wrote during that time are extant. On 10 March he wrote a long letter to his mother.

Most dear and loving Mother

Seeing that by the severity of the laws, by the wickedness of our times, and by God's holy ordinance and appointment my days in this life are cut off: of duty and conscience I am bound (being far from you in body, but in spirit very near to you) not only to crave your daily blessing, but also to write these few words to you. You have been a most loving, natural and careful mother to me ... therefore for these and all your motherly cherishings I give you most humble and hearty thanks ... I had meant this spring to have seen you, if God had granted me health and liberty: but now I shall never see you, or any of yours in this life again; trusting yet in heaven to meet you, to see you and to live everlastingly with you. Alas! sweet mother, why do you weep? Why do you take so heavily my honourable death? Know you not that we are born to die: and that always in this life we may not live ... remember that I am going to a place of all pleasure and felicity. Why do you mourn? ... my sweet mother it is the favourablest, honourablest and happiest death that ever could have chanced to me ... I die only for my faith, for my conscience, for my priesthood, for my blessed Saviour Jesus Christ; and to tell you truth, if I had ten thousand lives, I am as bound to lose them all, rather than break my faith, to lose my soul, to offend my God. Be of good cheer then, most loving mother, and cease from weeping. Tell me would you not be glad to see me a bishop, a king or an emperor? Yes, verily, I dare say you would. How glad then may you be to see me a martyr ... a bright star in heaven. The joy of this life is nothing compared to the joy of life everlasting: and therefore thrice happy may you think yourself that your son William is gone from earth to heaven ... wish I were near to comfort you; but because that cannot be, I beseech you, for Christ Jesus's sake, to comfort yourself. If I had lived I would have helped you in your age as you helped me in my youth. But now I must desire God and my brethren to help you. Good mother be contented with that which God has appointed for my perpetual comfort ... Your most obedient and loving son.

William Hart was hanged, drawn and quartered at York 15 March 1583. He had a winning personality and unbounded charity. His reverence and devotion when saying Mass were impressive. He and Margaret Clitherow seem to have had a particular spiritual affinity, so much so that the authorities tried to blacken his name to her.

21 Blessed Richard Thirkeld came from Coniscliffe, Co.Durham. He was educated at Queen's College, Oxford. He must have been of a mature age when he went to Douai and then Rheims. He was ordained 18 April 1579 and returned to England on 23 May. He worked mainly in and around York. On 25 March 1583, as he was leaving the Kidcote, where he had been visiting a prisoner, he was arrested by one of the sheriff's sergeants on suspicion of being a priest. Taken before the Lord Mayor he admitted he was a priest. Keys were found on him and these turned out to be those of his room and a chest at the house of William Hutton, where he lodged. They took away all his 'Church stuff' and his books were burned in the market place. He was committed to the Kidcote until 27 May, the day of his trial at York Castle, where he appeared wearing his cassock. After being found guilty he was incarcerated among the common felons in the castle. The following morning he was taken back to court to receive his death sentence. There were four Catholic prisoners awaiting trial. They begged his prayers and knelt for his blessing, which he gave them, at which the ministers present inveighed against him. The next day, 29 May, he was hanged drawn and quartered, being cut down alive to suffer disembowelling. The sheriff ordered a great fire to be made to burn all the straw and any other material that might be taken away as relics. Half a dozen of Richard's letters written from prison have survived. To one of his penitents he writes, 'There is no true joy, no object, no agreeable pleasure, that can afford any solid delight, but one alone, and that is Christ. I experience now that the greatest joy and comfort is in conversing with him; that all time thus employed is short, sweet and delightful: and those words that, in this conversation, he speaks to me, so penetrate my soul, so elevate my spirit above itself, so moderate and change all fleshly affections, that this prison of mine seems not a prison, but a paradise: my crosses become light and easy and being

The Elizabethan Martyrs, 1577-1601

deprived of all earthly comfort, affords a heavenly joy and happiness.'

22 Blessed Francis Ingleby was born c.1550 at Ripley Castle, Yorkshire. He was the fourth son of Sir William Ingleby and Anne Mallory. He was educated at Brasenose College, Oxford, and then entered the Inner Temple, London, in 1577 to study law and practised as a barrister in London. He arrived at Rheims 18 August 1582 and was ordained at Laon 17 December 1583, returning to England in April 1584. His work appears to have been in his native county. Although poorly attired, suspicion was aroused when it was noticed with what respect Francis was treated. He was arrested in York and tried before the Council of the North. Every time he tried to speak he was shouted down and interrupted. When condemned he responded, 'I am sure I will see the Lord's goodness in the land of the living.' He was hanged, drawn and quartered at York 3 June 1586. He was described as 'a short man but well made. He was of a light complexion, wore a chestnut beard and had a slight cast in his eyes. In mind he was quick and piercing, ready and facile in speech, of aspect grave and austere and earnest and assiduous in action.' Father Thomas Stanney SJ, who wrote an account of Francis's martyrdom, included a strange occurrence. A Protestant preacher named Frost went into a pulpit in a York church and proceeded to denounce the martyr, and promptly dropped dead.

23 Errington, Knight and Gibson. Blessed George Errington was born near Ashington, Northumberland, in 1554. He was an MA of Trinity College, Oxford. He spent his life in the dangerous work of assisting priests, meeting them on arrival in England, sheltering them at his home and escorting them to safe destinations. He also conducted students to and from the Continent as well as acting as a courier carrying messages. Described as a 'lusty tall gentleman' he ran a reception centre from the home of Ursula Taylor at South Shields for priests coming in from the Continent via Newcastle. He was first arrested in 1585 by the River Tyne and was imprisoned in the Tower until 1587. Captured again in 1591, he was in Durham jail from which he escaped on 4 December with Father George Williams, a Welsh priest.* Offered a pardon if he agreed to conform, Errington declared that he would pray for the Queen

---

* Williams, who was ordained at Laon in 1588, purportedly apostatised by taking the Oath of Allegiance in 1603. How genuine his submission may have been can be adduced from the complaint in 1605 by Robert Bennett, Bishop of Hereford to Robert Cecil that he had found Williams 'a perfidious man ... and a spy for the papists. Williams had not only been of no service but had continued to say Mass and reconcile Catholics so that 'all the increase of priests and recusants here has proceeded from his treachery.'

and serve her with his body and his life, but he could not go to her church as his conscience would not permit him. Re-arrested in 1593 he remained in prison at Durham and York Castle. The wealth of information he possessed about priests and their helpers would have been invaluable to the government had he revealed any of it. In prison he met William Knight and William Gibson. Blessed William Knight, the son of Leonard Knight, was born c.1573 at Hemingbrough or South Duffield, then in the East Riding of Yorkshire. On coming of age William, a tenant farmer, claimed property left to him by his father, then in the possession of his Protestant uncle who denounced him to the authorities. He was arrested in 1593 by a pursuivant named Colyer who treated him with great indignity and severity. William served terms of imprisonment in Hull and York Castle. He was only twenty-three-years old when executed. Blessed William Gibson was born near Ripon. He was a lady's manservant and had spent many years in and out of prison at York for refusing to conform. All three were tried and condemned in 1596 on the same charge of 'persuading to popery'.

24 Blessed Robert Sutton was born at Burton-on-Trent, Staffordshire, in 1544. He was an MA of Christ College, Oxford, and although a layman was given the rectory of Lutterworth, Leicestershire, in 1571. In 1576 he became an Anglican deacon, but resigned his living the following year and went to Douai. He was ordained priest in February 1578 and returned to England. Here he found shelter at the London home of Sir Thomas Gerard, father of John Gerard SJ. In 1588 Robert was arrested at Stafford, along with William Maxfield, who had sheltered him. Robert was sent to London for questioning and then returned to Stafford to be hanged, drawn and quartered. Both of his brothers became priests. Abraham was ordained on the same day as Robert. After his brother's execution he was able to retrieve relics, including a thumb, which he gave to Father John Gerard. The third brother, William, also lived in the Gerard household and taught the young John Greek. William later joined the Society of Jesus and was drowned in 1590 while en route for Spain.

25 Blessed William Dean was born at Linton-in-Craven, Yorkshire, the son of a tenant of the Norton family who had taken part with his masters in the 1569 Northern Rising. He was educated at Leeds, Caius College, Cambridge and Magdalen College, Oxford.. For a time he was a curate in the Established Church at Monk Fryston. He went to Rheims in 1581 and was ordained at Soissons that year in the same ceremony as two other future martyrs, Blessed George Haydock 27 and Blessed

Robert Nutter. 28 He returned to England in 1582 but was captured in London with Father Thomas Alfield, to whom he owed his conversion, and was committed to Newgate. In 1583 he was in the Kings' Bench prison and by July 1584 in the Marshalsea. In January 1585 he was exiled. He soon returned and was arrested in 1588 and imprisoned in the Gatehouse. On 26 August, with five other priests and four laymen, he was tried at the Sessions Hall, Newgate and condemned. On 28 August he was taken for execution to Mile End Green where great violence was employed to prevent him from speaking.

26 Blessed Henry Webley, a layman, born at Gloucester c.1558. He was arrested in Chichester harbour, while attempting to board a ship for France. He was taken to London and imprisoned in the Marshalsea. He was hanged with William Dean for assisting the priest.

27 Blessed George Haydock, born at Cottam Hall, near Preston, was a nephew of Cardinal Allen. His parents were Ewan Haydock and Helen Westby. His mother died in 1558 and in 1573 Ewan disposed of most of his property and went to Douai with his son Richard. They both matriculated at Douai University and Ewan was ordained in 1575. In February 1576 he returned to England and worked on the mission until his death at Mowbreck Hall, Lancashire in 1581. Richard Haydock was ordained in 1577, afterwards moving to Rome to help establish the English College. He served on the mission in Lancashire. By 1594 he was in the service of his uncle the Cardinal in Rome. After visits to Ireland and England he settled in Rome and died there in 1605.

When he was sixteen George was sent to Douai, Rheims and then Rome. He suffered from chronic ill-health in Rome and returned to Rheims and was ordained at Soissons in December 1581. While in London in 1582 visiting imprisoned Catholics from Lancashire he was arrested by the evil pursuivant, Sledd, who robbed him of the money he possessed. He was charged with plotting at Rheims and Rome and tried with thirteen other priests on 5 February 1584. Only five of the group were selected for execution; the others, such as Father Arthur Pitts, who had been in the Tower since 1582, were banished in 1585. Haydock and four companions were all martyred at Tyburn 12 February and were treated with exceptional barbarity, the hangman making sure that each one was still conscious when cut down for the butchery. Haydock, who was twenty-six-years-old, was described as looking even younger because he had no beard. Father Pitts, who was born in 1557 at Iffley, Oxfordshire, had been a chorister at All Souls, Oxford. Ordained in 1580 he had returned to England in 1581. After his banishment he served the Cardinal of Lorraine but returned to England due to ill health. He became one of the original members of the Chapter in 1623 and when he died c.1636 he was buried in the church at Rotherfield Peppard, Oxfordshire.

Haydock's four companions in martyrdom were:

Blessed Thomas Hemerford who was born 1554 in Dorset and educated at St John's College, Oxford. In 1580 he went to Rheims and then to Rome, where he was ordained deacon by Bishop Goldwell. Ordained priest in 1583 he returned to England in June of that year. He was soon arrested in Hampshire and committed to the Marshalsea. After his indictment on 5 February 1584 in the Kings' Bench he was sent to the Tower to await his execution. He was described as a short man, with a dark beard, severe of look but with a sweet disposition.

Blessed John Munden was born at Mapperton, Dorset, in 1543. He was educated at Winchester School and Oxford, where he was a Fellow of New College. He was expelled from Oxford in 1566 because of his religious views and became a schoolmaster in his native county. He went to Rheims in October 1580 and moved to Rome in 1581, not as a student at the English College, but living outside the college at the Pope's expense. Ordained in 1582, he returned to England in August that year. As soon as he landed at Dover he was arrested and escorted to London by the mayor of Dover. He was allowed to escape by paying a bribe of £15. He was re-captured on the road near Hounslow and sent to the Tower. The charges against him were identical to those of Campion and his companions i.e. plotting to kill the Queen at Rheims and Rome and the trial proceedings were just as farcical. John was the last of the five priests to die.

Blessed John Nutter was born at Clitheroe, Lancashire and educated at Cambridge. He went to Rheims with his younger brother in 1579 and was ordained at Laon in 1582. In January 1583 he disembarked at Dunwich, Suffolk, with another priest, Samuel Coniers. John was very ill and when questioned he claimed to be a merchant from York, but as his luggage was found to contain many Catholic books he and Coniers were arrested and sent to the Marshalsea. After their condemnation Coniers was returned to the Marshalsea and John was sent to the Tower. Here, heavily chained, he was incarcerated in the Pit, where he also found his brother, Robert. Samuel Coniers was condemned to death but not executed. He was released from prison in 1585 and banished. He died at Rheims in 1587.

The Elizabethan Martyrs, 1577-1601

Blessed James Fenn was born at Montacute, Somerset. His brothers, John and Robert, were also priests. He was educated at Oxford, where he was a chorister at New College, being admitted to Corpus Christi College in 1554. He was expelled in 1560 for refusing the Oath of Supremacy. He became a private schoolmaster, married and had two children, John and Frances. While visiting his father at Wells James was arrested by the Bishop of Bath and Wells, Gilbert Berkeley, who demanded that he take the oath. Berkeley had returned from voluntary exile in Germany to succeed the deprived Gilbert Bourne in 1560. James refused but was released and returned to Montacute to live. Shortly afterwards the vicar, Thomas Morley, threatened him with arrest for failing to attend church. James decided to leave the village and for two months he moved from place to place during which time he received the news that his wife had died. Following his wife's death he arranged for his children to be cared for and took a position at Iron Acton, Gloucestershire, as business agent for the irascible, wavering Catholic Sir Nicholas Poyntz, whose grandfather had been chancellor to Catherine of Aragon. James was persuaded - probably by Father John Colleton - to become a priest and he went to Rheims in June 1579. Ordained at Châlons 2 April 1580, he returned to his native county and was soon apprehended and imprisoned at Ilchester where, loaded with chains, he was publicly humiliated by being exhibited in the market place which, Challoner tells us, greatly shocked the townspeople. He was sent to London and examined by Walsingham. Committed to the Marshalsea there he remained for over two years showing great compassion and charity towards his fellow prisoners, and reconciling many to the Catholic Church. In February 1584 he was transferred to the Tower and tried with thirteen others for the fictitious plot against the Queen, although he had never been to Rome in his life and was actually a prisoner when the plotting was allegedly taking place. On 12 February as he left the Tower for his execution at Tyburn, his daughter, Frances, took her tearful leave of him. While hanging James's shirt was ripped off him, leaving him naked. He was conscious when he was taken down and dismembered.

His brother John, born 1535, was educated at Winchester and Oxford. He was master of the grammar school at Bury St Edmund's. He matriculated at Louvain University and after his ordination became chaplain to Sir William Stanley's regiment, fighting in the Netherlands for the Spaniards. In 1609 he became chaplain at St Monica's convent, Louvain and died there in 1614. Robert Fenn was also at Winchester and Oxford until expelled in 1562. After ordination he returned to England in 1583 and was arrested on 12 February 1584, the day of his brother's martyrdom, and jailed in the Marshalsea. In 1585 he was banished and died in Paris in 1587.

28 **Blessed Robert Nutter** came from Clitheroe, Lancashire, and was educated at Blackburn Grammar School. He went to Rheims with his elder brother, John, in 1579 and was ordained at Soissons in 1581, returning to England in 1582 with George Haydock. He served the mission in Oxfordshire and Hampshire before being caught at Oxford in 1584, when he was sent to the Tower. Here he was severely tortured and manacled for forty-three days. While in the Tower he learned that his priest brother, John, had been martyred at Tyburn with George Haydock. In 1585 he was banished, but later in that year he and three other priests set sail from Calais for England on a packet boat called *The Mary*. Off the Kent coast the ship was intercepted by an English man-o'-war and the suspicious passengers were arrested and taken ashore at Gravesend on 11 November. Robert was sent to the Marshalsea, then on 30 November to Newgate. Here he was correctly identified by John Barcroft - whose brother, Thomas, was a priest - who had been at school with him at Blackburn. Robert pleaded that he had been brought into England by force. In 1586 he was moved back to the Marshalsea and in 1588 he was sent to Wisbech Castle from which he escaped on 10 March 1600 with six other priests. These included Christopher Southworth, son of Sir John Southworth of Samlesbury. Robert and Christopher made their way to Lancashire where Robert was re-captured and martyred at Lancaster 26 July 1600. While in Wisbech he had become a member of the Dominican Order. (Father Southworth, who had been ordained at the English College, Rome, by Bishop Goldwell of St Asaph in 1583 and had returned to work in England in 1586, managed to evade re-capture and was still working on the mission in 1612.) *Robert Nutter's companion in martyrdom was*

Blessed Edward Thwing who was born at Heworth, York, in 1565. He went to Rheims in 1583 and to Rome in 1587. The climate of Rome did not suit him and he returned to France. He was ordained at Laon in December 1590 and taught at the English College for several years, moving back to Douai with it in 1593. In poor health he returned to England in 1594. By May 1600 he had been arrested and was a prisoner in Lancaster Castle. While there he and his fellow prisoner, Robert Nutter, held a disputation with the vicars of Lancaster and Kendal. The two priests found means to say Mass for their fellow prisoners, continuing the apostolate of Father Richard Taylor. By disguising himself as a tradesman Taylor managed to gain regular access to the

The Elizabethan Martyrs, 1577-1601

Catholic prisoners in the castle. The jailer became suspicious so Taylor smuggled in a rope and at night the prisoners would tie the rope securely and let it down for him to climb up into the castle to say Mass. This went on for several months until Nutter and Thwing arrived when Taylor moved on, his services no longer being required. Edward Thwing was tried and condemned with Nutter. The account of his trial, sent by the Court to Sir Robert Cecil, is extant. A great crowd of Catholics assembled for the execution of the two priests on 26 July and while the hangman was busy quartering the bodies many of them surged forward and seized anything of the martyrs' they could lay their hands on. While the guards were busy trying to quell the riotous behaviour some women snatched the priests' hearts from the blazing fire and ran off with them.

29 Blessed **William Gunter** was a Welshman, born at Raglan and educated at Rheims. He was ordained in 1587. Arrested in London in June 1588 and imprisoned at Newgate, he was condemned. On 26 August he was taken in a cart to Holywell Lane, Shoreditch, and, being prevented from speaking, was hanged on a new gallows specially set up outside the theatre. As he hanged some in the crowd chanted, 'This priest for the Pope is hanged with a rope'. Robert Southwell witnessed his martyrdom.

30 Blessed **Robert Morton** was born at Bawtry, South Yorkshire, in 1548. In 1568 he left England and travelled in Europe, spending some years in Rome with his uncle Nicholas, who was a priest. Another uncle, Thomas Norton, had been prominent in the Northern Rising of 1569. In 1573 he went to Douai but left to return home on the death of his father the following year. He married Ursula Thurland and in 1578 he and his wife sold their property and decided to live abroad. They were captured as they embarked on the ship by none other than Richard Topcliffe and Robert was sent to the Gatehouse. Under instructions from Lord Burghley, he was examined by John Aylmer, Bishop of London. Through the influence of friends at Court Robert's release was procured, but shortly afterwards his wife died and he left for Rome, where he entered the English College in April 1587. Quickly ordained deacon at Rome he then went to Rheims and three months later was ordained priest, almost immediately leaving for England where he worked in Northamptonshire and Nottinghamshire. Richard Topcliffe, obviously on the look-out for him, was tracing his movements and Morton was arrested in London, condemned at Newgate on 26 August and hanged at Lincoln's Inn Fields.

31. Blessed Hugh More, a layman from Grantham, Lincolnshire, was educated at Oxford and Gray's Inn. He was converted at the age of twenty-five by Father Thomas Stevenson. In 1585 he went to Rheims and for a time was a student at the college. On his return to England in May 1587 he was arrested and imprisoned. He was hanged with Morton at Lincoln's Inn for being reconciled. Father Stevenson was born 1552 in Co.Durham. He was ordained at Soissons 23 December 1581 and returned to England in 1583. He only worked for about nine months - during which period he reconciled Hugh More - before he was arrested and sent to the Tower. He was tried and condemned 4 May 1584 but not executed. He was banished in 1585 and joined the Jesuits.

32 Blessed James Claxton (sometimes called Clarkson) came from Yorkshire. He was educated at Rome and Rheims and was ordained at Soissons in 1582 and sent to England. In 1585 he was banished from York. Assuming that he actually left the country, how and when he returned to the mission, and how he was captured, is unknown, but he was tried and condemned at Newgate on 26 August 1588. Tied to a horse he was taken to Isleworth and hanged.

33 Blessed Thomas Felton was born in 1567, in the parish of St Mary Magdalene, Bermondsey, London. He was the son of Blessed John Felton, who was executed in 1570 for publicising the bull of Pius V. For a time Thomas was page to Lady Lovett before going to Rheims. At a very young age, in 1583, he was tonsured as a Friar Minim, but found the strictness of the life taxing on his health, so he decided to return to England for a respite. He was arrested on arrival and sent to the Counter in the Poultry, London. Here he remained prisoner for two years. Released through the efforts of his aunt, he was about to return to France when he was again arrested and committed to the Bridewell. Through the influence of Lady Lovett, at the time a prisoner herself in the Fleet, he was released. He managed to get to a seaport before being apprehended a third time and sent back to the Bridewell. Here he was cruelly treated, being confined in a tiny cell and given only bread and water. He was then attached to the mill to grind; a feature of Bridewell. He was hung up by his hands for hours while under interrogation, the blood flowing from his finger ends. He was tried at Newgate, refused to acknowledge the Queen as head of the Church and was condemned. The very next day he was taken to Isleworth and hanged with James Claxton. He was just twenty years of age.

34 Blessed Richard Leigh, the son of Valentine and Catherine Leigh,

The Elizabethan Martyrs, 1577-1601

was a Londoner, born in 1561. Educated at Douai and Rheims, he arrived at the English College, Rome, November 1582. A pupil of Robert Southwell's he was ordained at the Lateran 11 February 1586 and in June returned to England under the alias Garth. In the wake of the Armada, on 4 July 1588 he was arrested and sent to Bishop John Aylmer of London, who called him a 'papist dog', and had him committed to the Tower. He was condemned for his priesthood and suffered martyrdom with Margaret Ward and his companions on 30 August.

35 Blessed William Way, alias Flower, was born at Exeter, Devon and baptised there in St Kerrian's church on 5 August 1565. He went to Rheims in 1584, was ordained at Laon 20 September 1586, and returned to England in December of that year. Captured at Lambeth, south London, by June 1587 he was in the Clink. He was a man of austerity of life who habitually wore a hair shirt. He was tried at Newgate in September 1588 and was hanged, drawn and quartered with great brutality at Kingston-upon-Thames.

36 Blessed Robert Wilcox was born at Chester in 1558. He went to Rheims in 1583 and was ordained priest at Laon in April 1585. He returned to England in January 1586 with newly-ordained fellow priest, Edmund Calverley, who was born at Calverley, Yorkshire, into a strongly recusant family, most of the members of which suffered imprisonment. The two priests were captured soon after landing at Lydd, Kent, and imprisoned in the Marshalsea, where Robert remained for over two years, until selected for execution after the failed Armada. Taken back to Kent, he was hanged, drawn and quartered at Oaten Hill, Canterbury. Father Calverley spent the whole of his time in England as a priest in various prisons. He was sent first to Wisbech Castle where he was prominent agitator among the anti-Jesuit faction. He was transferred to Framlingham Castle, and finally banished in 1603.

37 Blessed Edward Campion seems always to have been known by his alias, but his real name was probably Gerard Edwards. He was born at Ludlow, Shropshire, in 1552. Educated at Jesus College, Oxford, he entered the service of Lord Dacre of the South where he was reconciled to the Church. Having converted, he went to Rheims in 1586, under his assumed name. Following his ordination at Rheims in March 1587, he immediately returned to England. Within a month, he was arrested at Sittingbourne, Kent, and committed to the Marshalsea. He was taken to

Canterbury with Robert Wilcox, and was hanged, drawn and quartered.

38 Blessed Christopher Buxton was born 1562 in Derbyshire, where he was a pupil of Blessed Nicholas Garlick at Tideswell Grammar School. He went to Rheims in 1581 and transferred to Rome in 1584. Ordained at the Lateran in 1586, his return to England was delayed, and it was not until November 1587 that he landed in Kent. He was arrested almost as soon as he arrived and sent to the Marshalsea. Taken to Canterbury, he was hanged, drawn and quartered with Wilcox and Campion. Being so young, he was left the last to die in the hope that he would break, having seen the gruesome deaths of his colleagues. He was offered his life if he would conform, but declared that he would not purchase a corruptible life at such a price.

39 Blessed Robert Widmerpool came from the town of that name in Nottinghamshire. He was educated at Gloucester Hall, Oxford, and became a schoolmaster. For a time he was tutor to the sons of the 9th Earl of Northumberland. Condemned for helping priests, he was hanged with Campion and Buxton at Canterbury.

40 Blessed Ralph Crockett was born at Barton-on-the-Hill, Cheshire, in 1552. We know the details of his life from the autobiography he provided at his examination in 1586. He was educated firstly at Christ's College, Cambridge. When he left the University he became a schoolmaster at Tibenham, Norfolk. He then spent a year at Gloucester Hall, Oxford, before once more becoming a teacher at Ipswich, Suffolk, for about five years. He then took up a teaching post in his native county for two years. He went to Rheims and asked Dr William Allen for admission to the college. He was ordained at Rheims in 1585 by the Cardinal de Guise and set out to return to England in April 1586, in the company of three other priests: Thomas Bramston, George Stransham, alias Potter, and Edward James. They sailed from Dieppe, on a ship whose master, Daniel, from Newhaven, had been recommended to them by a fellow priest. They paid for their passage on board and were the only passengers. Unknown to Ralph and his companions, a spy's report, dated 22 April, was already on its way to England, advising of their coming. The ship brought them to Arundel Haven, near Littlehampton, and they spent two further nights on board, as the master, who went ashore to survey the situation, told them it was too dangerous for them to disembark. They were all apprehended on board the ship and taken to the local Justice at Arundel. From there Ralph and his companions were committed to the Marshalsea, where they

The Elizabethan Martyrs, 1577-1601

remained for two years without trial. As none of them had set foot in England when apprehended, they were outside the provisions of Statute 27, so their arrest and detention was totally illegal. In 1588, Ralph and Edward James were taken back to Sussex, where Ralph was hanged, drawn and quartered at Broyle Heath, Chichester.

Thomas Bramston, who came from Kent, had been a novice for a short time at Westminster Abbey under Abbot John Feckenham, whom he served for nearly two years when the Abbot was in the Tower. He then became a schoolmaster in the house of Sir Thomas Tresham, until it became illegal for him to act in that capacity without taking the oath. He went to Rheims and was ordained. After his capture in 1586, he was sent from the Marshalsea to Wisbech, being transferred to Framlingham in 1601. In 1603 he was banished, but returned almost immediately, only to be caught again on landing at Dover. By this time Dover was a notoriously anti-Catholic town and priests caught there were treated with great brutality. According to a contemporary account church plunder - chalices, patens, crucifixes, bells, candlesticks, etc. - were widely available in the shops and market. Bramston was sent to Newgate and was only saved from execution because it coincided with King James's coronation, and it was not thought a good public relations exercise to be killing priests at that time. As it happened, the coronation was delayed because of an outbreak of the plague, to which many of Bramston's fellow prisoners succumbed. However, he managed to survive and was banished once more. He died at Douai in 1606.

George Stransham, who also came from Kent, was educated at Cambridge and at Lincoln's Inn, London; during which time he conformed. He went to Rheims in 1583, and then to the English College, Rome, from which he was expelled for opposing the Jesuits. He was ordained at Rheims in 1585. After his return to England and capture in 1586 he was sent to the Marshalsea and then to Wisbech, where he proved to be a rather outspoken and disruptive inmate. He escaped from custody about 1593, but was re-captured and imprisoned at Newgate, before being sent back to Wisbech. In 1597 he again escaped, and it seems this time he was successfully at liberty for several years. At some point he must have been re-taken, because in 1606 he was in custody and banished. He was last heard of at Valladolid in 1610.

41 Blessed Edward James was born at Breaston, Derbyshire, c.1557. He attended Derby Grammar School and St John's College, Oxford, leaving without a degree as he would not take the oath, but he conformed to the extent of sometimes attending church. In 1579 he

The Elizabethan Martyrs, 1577-1601

went to London, and was reconciled to the Church. In the autumn of that year he travelled to Dover, in the company of William Filby, with whom he took ship to Calais, having paid £6 for his passage. With Filby he made his way to Rheims, later going to the English College, Rome, in September 1580. He was ordained in the college chapel on 30 October 1583 by Thomas Goldwell, Bishop of St Asaph. He did not leave Rome until 1585 and travelled to Rheims in the company of Father Edmund Calverley. He commenced his return journey to England in February 1586 with Stephen Rowsham. He took ship from Dieppe with Ralph Crockett, Bramston and Stransham and was captured with them. He was sent to the Clink, where he remained until, with Crockett and two other priests, the Welshman, Francis Edwards, and Oxford-born, John Owen, he was sent from London for trial at Chichester on 30 September 1588. Owen saved himself by taking the Oath of Supremacy, and was reprieved. He later apostatised. Francis Edwards waited until he was at the scaffold before he too recanted and apostatised. Edward James was hanged, drawn and quartered with Crockett.

42 Blessed John Robinson was born at Ferrensby, West Yorkshire. He married, but after his wife's death in 1584 he went to Rheims and was ordained there 20 April 1585. He was captured after landing at Lowestoft, Suffolk, and committed to the Clink on 30 June where he remained for three years. He was so much older than the other priest prisoners that he referred to them as his 'bairns'. In the wake of the Armada he was selected for execution. John was sent back to Suffolk for trial, walking all the way in spite of his age, because there was a problem in finding a horse for him. He was tried at Ipswich and showed such resolve that the judge remarked, 'I think this fellow intendeth to be hanged.' To which John responded, 'For what else did I come hither?' He was hanged, drawn and quartered at Ipswich. His son, Francis, born 1569, became a priest in 1597. He too suffered for his faith, being imprisoned at Framlingham from 1598 to 1603 when he was banished. In 1606 he was in Westmorland and arrested at the house of Andrew Hilton. He was still working in Durham in 1623.

43 Blessed Robert Sutton was born at Kegworth, Leicestershire. He may have been educated at Oxford before becoming an Anglican clergyman. In 1575 he converted, and for a time he was at Douai. After his return to England he was arrested and condemned for being reconciled. Taken to Clerkenwell to be hanged, on the scaffold he affirmed that he would be prepared to fight for the Queen, even against the Pope. Asked if he

would acknowledge the Queen's supremacy, he stood for a time in thought, while a preacher argued with him on the subject at great length. But Robert declared that this he could not do and was turned off the ladder.

44 Blessed John Hewett was the son of William Hewett, a York draper, although a government pamphlet, issued after his execution, gives Tollerton, a few miles north of the city, as his actual birthplace. He was educated at Caius College, Cambridge, but took no degree. In July 1581 he went to Rheims, where he was ordained deacon. He came back to England and in August 1585, with a number of priests, was committed to prison at Hull Castle. He was soon banished and returned to Rheims, and was ordained priest late that year. After returning home once more in January 1586 he was sheltered at Gray's Inn by Mr John Gardener, a Catholic, who kept a priest at his houses in London and Buckinghamshire. Early in 1587 the priest, Father John Green, having been betrayed by Anthony Tyrell, was arrested at the house of a Mrs White. She was sentenced to death for sheltering him and he was sent to Wisbech. Hewett stayed with Mr Gardener in the guise of a servant and was kitted out by his host in the same manner as his other servants. By March 1587, Hewett had been arrested, and was tried at the Middlesex Sessions under the name of John Weldon, his alias. Mr Gardener courageously refused to admit to anything but it seems John promised to conform and was soon released. He was re-captured in October 1587 at Sluys, in Holland, carrying relics of recent martyrs. He was sent back to England and imprisoned in the Bridewell, where he remained until after the Armada. Brought to trial, he vigorously protested that he was only in England because he had been sent there from the Netherlands as a prisoner by the Earl of Leicester. He declared that he would support the Queen against any invasion, but this did not prevent his condemnation on 4 October. He was executed at Mile End Green, where, whether by malice or incompetence, he endured an agonisingly slow and painful death, hanging for a long time trying to make the sign of the Cross, with the blood bursting from his mouth, nose, eyes and ears.

45 Blessed Edward Burden was born c.1540 in Cleveland in the North Riding of Yorkshire, being listed in the Douai diary as of the diocese of Durham. He was an MA and Fellow of Corpus Christi College, Oxford. In June 1583 he went to Rheims, and was ordained at Soissons the following year. In May 1586 he returned to England and worked in Yorkshire. He was apprehended by Mr John Constable while on foot at

The Elizabethan Martyrs, 1577-1601

Skinningrove, on the North Yorkshire coast. His captor took Edward to his house and searched him, taking all his possessions from him, including his money. He was then sent to the Council of the North at York, and was committed to the castle. He was very ill with consumption, but was forced from his sickbed to attend court when summoned. At his trial he steadfastly refused to reveal any of the places where he had been, declaring, 'You enquire things of me for no good and therefore I will not answer'. He was condemned, and shouted down by the Protestant ministers when he tried to speak before he was hanged, drawn and quartered at York on 29 November.

46 The eight who were martyred in 1589 were:

Blessed John Amias, about whose true name there is some confusion. It would appear that Amias was his alias and that his real name was Anne, by which name he is called in some accounts. As it is known that he was born near Wakefield, Yorkshire, it is most probable that he was a member of the ancient gentry family of that name from Frickley, near Wakefield. His occupation was a clothmonger. After his wife's death he went to Rheims in 1580 and was ordained there 25 March 1581 with William Filby, Everard Hanse and Nicholas Woodfen. On 5 June of that year he returned to England with Father Edmund Sykes. At the end of 1588 he was arrested at Melling, Lancashire, and sent to York Castle. He was condemned and executed at York on 16 March with Robert Dalby. (Some sources give 15 March as the date, but Challoner, directly quoting from the account in the manuscript history of Dr Anthony Champney, who, at the age of twenty, was an eyewitness of their martyrdom, gives the 16th.)

Blessed Robert Dalby was born at Hemingbrough in the East Riding. He was an Anglican minister before his conversion. He arrived at Rheims 30 September 1580. He was ordained at Châlons 16 April 1588 and fatefully sent into England in August, at the height of the multiple executions that were being carried out in the wake of the Armada. Robert was arrested immediately after disembarking at Scarborough and imprisoned in York Castle. He was condemned at the Spring Assizes and executed with John Amias. Dr Champney relates that the two priests were drawn about a mile from the city and on arrival at the gallows prostrated themselves in prayer. Amias was called first and he kissed the gallows and the ladder which he ascended with 'a serene countenance'. He attempted to speak to the crowd but was silenced. Raising his hands he recommended his soul to God and was turned off.

The Elizabethan Martyrs, 1577-1601

He was allowed to hang until dead. He was quickly followed by Dalby. The sheriff took extra precautions to try and prevent any relics of the martyrs' being taken.

Blessed George Nichols was born at Oxford and educated there at Brasenose College. For ten years he was a master at St Paul's School, London, but in 1581 he went to Rheims and was ordained there 24 September 1583. He came back to England in 1584 and seems to have worked in his native county. At midnight, on Whit Sunday, 18 May 1589, he was betrayed by a false convert and apprehended at the Catherine Wheel inn, Oxford, with fellow priest Richard Yaxley, and two laymen, Thomas Belson and Humphrey ap Richard. The sheriff and his party hammered at the inn door and Humphrey ap Richard, a servant, opened it to them. The searchers barged into the room of the landlady, a sixty-year-old widow. There was nothing the priests could do except wait for the sheriff to discover them. All four prisoners were brought before the University authorities the next morning and interrogated by Dr Edmund Lilly, the Vice-Chancellor. The priests were committed to the Bocardo prison and the laymen to Oxford Castle. The landlady of the Catherine Wheel suffered the penalties of *praemunire*; her goods confiscated and imprisonment for life. The four prisoners were ordered to be taken to London on horseback. Their legs were tied under the horses' bellies; their elbows were tied together behind their backs and their wrists strapped in front, enabling them to hold the reins. Poor Humphrey fell off, hurting his head. They had to suffer cruelty from their guards and abuse from the crowd. Arrived in London Thomas was sent to the Gatehouse and Humphrey to the Bridewell, along with the priests, where they were all tortured by being hung up by their hands for fifteen hours. George and Richard were confronted by two apostate priests; Edward Gratley and the ubiquitous Anthony Tyrell, who identified them. They were examined by Sir Francis Walsingham who asked Nichols what he was. 'I am a priest an it please God', he answered to which Walsingham retorted, 'Then you are a traitor not only for being a priest but because you teach a faith contrary to Her Majesty's ordinances.' After being questioned by the Privy Council the two priests were sent to the Tower with the ominous instruction that only Richard Topcliffe should have access to them. Yaxley, who had still not admitted to being a priest, was racked several times. Then the two of them were incarcerated in the dreaded, twenty-foot deep, dark, vermin infested, Pit. After a month, on 30 June, the four were sent by wagon back to Oxford. As they were so damaged by their torture this was, presumably, the only means by which they could be transported. During the five days left to him in the jail Nichols converted a condemned highwayman, called Harcot, and he was executed with the four martyrs, reciting aloud the *Miserere* psalm which he had specially learned by heart. Sir Francis Knollys, Privy Councillor and Treasurer of the Royal Household, was sent to Oxford to be present at the prisoners' trial at the Summer Assizes; and no doubt to ensure that the 'correct' verdict was delivered. Charged and condemned under Elizabeth 27, on 5 July 1589 the two priests were taken on the hurdle to their execution with the two laymen walking behind.

Blessed Richard Yaxley was born at Boston, Lincolnshire. He went to Rheims in August 1582 and was ordained there 21 September 1585, returning to England the following January. In 1588 he is known to have been in Cornwall but he seems to have worked mainly in Oxfordshire. He was captured at the Catherine Wheel, Oxford, with George Nichols and suffered with him. Richard was described as youthful and handsome. Nichols being executed first, Richard embraced his body as it hung before climbing the ladder. As soon as he attempted to speak he was thrown off. The priests' quarters were hung over the gates of the city and their heads were mounted on the castle walls where their faces were slashed and hacked about by Protestant zealots.

Blessed Thomas Belson came from a prominent Catholic family of substance. He was born in 1563 at Brill, Buckinghamshire, the son of Augustine Belson, a well-known recusant, although Thomas was baptised in the Oxfordshire parish church of Aston Rowant. The Belson's were related to most of the Catholic landed gentry families of Buckinghamshire and Oxfordshire. Augustine Belson frequently sheltered priests at his isolated house, Ixhill Lodge, including John Filby, brother of the martyred William. Thomas was educated at Oxford University, but did not take a degree. He went to the English College at Rheims in 1583. George Nichols and Richard Yaxley would both have been his fellow students at the College, as was Anthony Tyrell. Thomas stayed at Rheims for less than a year. In April 1584 he set out to return home in the company of Blessed Francis Ingleby. Thomas was carrying letters, including ones from Edward Gratley, and made his way to London to deliver them. By 24 June 1585 Thomas had been arrested and imprisoned in the Tower for 'conveying intelligence between Bridges the priest and others beyond the seas and some in this realm'. Bridges was the alias of Gratley. It would appear that Thomas

The Elizabethan Martyrs, 1577-1601

was acting as a secret courier and it is quite possible that it was he who conveyed the false reply, purporting to come from William Allen, to Philip Howard. Thomas's name appears with that of Philip Howard in the same list of prisoners who had been betrayed by Gratley. Exactly when Thomas was released from the Tower is unknown, but as his name occurs in a prison list dated 30 November 1586, it was most likely in December that he was freed on condition of banishment. Thomas's father would have been responsible for the bond money required, and Thomas visited his parents before going into exile. What he was doing for the next eighteen months is a mystery, but given that one of the charges against him after his arrest at Oxford in 1589 was that he was 'a conveyor of letters from beyond the seas', it is safe to assume that he had continued acting as a courier, although Thomas never provided any information about his activities. At the gallows Thomas was the third to die. Before he was hanged he embraced the bodies of the two priests and commended himself to their prayers, declaring that he accounted himself happy to have been their ghostly child and to suffer with them. Thomas's family remained steadfast Catholics in spite of all that they had to suffer as recusants and they treasured his memory. The following is a surviving poem by Thomas, probably written during his first imprisonment in the Tower in 1586.

> I look about me, sick and faint of soul;
> The dwelling of God's glory is my goal.
> But, though I look about so constantly,
> No answer comes, none turns to rescue me.
> Yet, as I wander through the grassy dale,
> Or higher, as the mountain crags I scale,
> Until alone on lonely peaks I gaze,
> I grieve for having left my Saviour's ways.
> And when I think how gentle is his touch,
> And how his justice could demand so much,
> My mind is changed, my labours seem the less,
> And I regret my former foolishness.
> Why should I rail on fortune or repine?
> Why should I grieve? God's remedy is mine.
> Endure, then, as philosophers maintain
> A brave man should, adversity and pain.

Blessed Humphrey ap Richard was presumably born in Wales. He is called Pritchard in some sources, but the contemporary documents give the Welsh form of his name. He was the serving man at the Catherine Wheel. The fourth of the group to die, he appeared joyful on the scaffold. While standing on the topmost rung of the ladder he declared, 'Masters who are here present, I beg for you to bear me witness in this world, and on the day of judgement, that I die for being a Catholic and a faithful Christian of Holy Church'. One of the ministers called out, 'Poor man, how say that you are a Catholic, when your ignorance does not allow you to know what being a Catholic means?' Humphrey answered, 'Although I cannot explain in words what this name Catholic means, all the same God knows my heart, and He knows that I believe all the Holy Roman Church believes, and what I cannot explain by mouth, I am ready and prepared to explain and testify to you at the cost of my blood'. Eyewitness accounts of the martyrdoms soon reached the Continent and were widely publicised by Richard Verstegan, which generated yet more bad publicity for the English government. A few years ago a simple stone plaque was erected in Oxford commemorating these four martyrs.

Blessed William Spenser was born c.1555 at Gisburn in the West Riding of Yorkshire. He was educated firstly by his Marian priest uncle who had conformed in order to retain his benefice. He then went to Trinity College, Oxford, becoming a Fellow in 1579 and MA in 1580. He went to Rheims in 1582 and was received into the Church. He was ordained 24 September 1583 and sent to England 29 August 1584. His first task was to reconcile his uncle and parents. In January 1585 William was granted a license by the Master-General of the Dominican Order to establish the Confraternity of the Rosary in England. He seems to have had a special apostolate to the prisoners in York Castle but few other details of his work are known until he was captured at Ripon and hanged, drawn and quartered at York 24 September 1589. A contemporary account of William says, 'His countenance like his mind was cheerful, his eyes vivacious, his face was long and freckled; his hands were also covered with freckles. He had a yellowish beard and his cheeks were sparsely covered with hair. In other respects he was robust, squarely built and of moderate height.'

Blessed Robert Hardesty was a Yorkshire layman. While riding a little way ahead of the priest, Robert was arrested at Ripon at the same time as Father Spenser. He was charged with helping him, but given that there was no proof that he was actually accompanying William at the time of his apprehension, the charge was dropped. A new charge was substituted; that Robert took food into York Castle for the priests held prisoner. This was enough to convict him and he was hanged with Father Spenser.

The Elizabethan Martyrs, 1577-1601

47 Blessed Nicholas Woodfen was born c.1550 at Leominster, Herefordshire. His real name, according to Challoner, was Wheeler, but he was always known as Woodfen. A teacher, he was employed by Swithun Wells at his school in Wiltshire. He went to Rheims in December 1579 and was ordained there 25 March 1581, returning to England in June of that year. Scantily dressed, hungry and weary, he arrived in London at the home of Sir Thomas Tresham at Hoxton seeking shelter. For a time he had lodgings in Fleet Street and carried on an apostolate amongst students and lawyers at the Inns of Court. He again had to go into hiding at Hoxton, where he narrowly missed being discovered in an intensive search of the house. He was captured, condemned, and hanged, drawn and quartered on 21 January 1586.

His companion in martyrdom was Blessed Edward Stransham who was born at Oxford in 1555. His elder brother, Thomas, was also a priest, ordained in 1578. Edward was educated at Douai and Rheims and although in bad health, was ordained at Soissons in December 1580. In 1583 he returned to Rheims from England taking with him ten students from Oxford University. He did not come back to England until 1585, travelling with a man named Rogers. This was a false name being used by Nicholas Berden q.v. one of Walsingham's spies. Edward sailed in a French fishing boat, disembarked on the Sussex coast and walked to London where he was arrested at the house of Mr Ferrers in Bishopsgate and sent to the Clink. Condemned on 19 January he was executed with Woodfen two days later.

As a corollary it is appropriate to here commemorate Blessed William Freeman. A Yorkshireman who studied at Magdalen College, Oxford, he was converted by the execution of Edward Stransham. In 1587 he went to Rheims and within four months he was ordained and returned to England in January 1589 in the company of four other priests. As they approached the Kent coast the crew of the ship on which they sailed planned to murder them, but the priests drew their swords and locked most of the crew below deck. They then forced other crewmen to drop them off at Gravesend. From there William made his way to Worcestershire and it was here and in Warwickshire that he worked for the next six years. He was arrested in January 1595 at the house of Dorothy Heath at Alvechurch when his breviary was discovered hidden under his hat. They were both imprisoned at Warwick. As yet there was no proof that William was a priest, but a fellow prisoner betrayed him and he was condemned and hanged, drawn and quartered at Warwick on 13 August 1595.

48 Christopher Dryland came from Kent. He and his elder brother went to Douai in 1576. At the end of that year his brother returned to

The Elizabethan Martyrs, 1577-1601

England and was arrested and imprisoned. Christopher was ordained at Châlons 31 March 1582 and returned to England shortly afterwards. His apostolate seems to have covered London and the surrounding counties. A priest of exemplary life, on 20 June 1586 he was arrested with Swithun Wells and Alexander Rawlins, and committed to the Counter in Wood Street. The spy Berden's request that he be released, in order to boost Berden's credit with the papists, was denied by Walsingham and Dryland was sent to Wisbech in 1588, where he became confessor to Father William Weston. He was moved to Framlingham and in March 1603, after seventeen years imprisonment, he was banished. He made his way to Douai and then to Rome, where he joined the Jesuits.

49 Blessed Thomas Holford came from Aston, Cheshire, where his father was a minister. He was a tutor to the sons of Sir John Scudamore of Holme Lacy, Herefordshire. He was converted by Hereford-born Father Richard Davies. In 1582 Thomas went to Rheims and was ordained at Laon in April 1583, returning to England in May under the alias of Acton. On 2 November 1584, together with Father Davies, he was staying with the Bellamy family, at Uxendon Hall, Harrow-on-the-Hill. The house was raided, but both priests managed to escape. (Father Davies, who spent many years in and out of various prisons, escorted Edmund Campion on some of his journeys. In 1582 Mrs Dorothy White was prosecuted for sheltering him at her house in Westminster. She was frequently in prison for harbouring priests. Richard was still listed as a prisoner in Newgate in 1615.) Thomas returned to Cheshire where he was arrested at Nantwich in May 1585, and imprisoned in Chester Castle, where he contrived to say Mass. Interrogated by Bishop William Chaderton of Chester, he acknowledged that he was a priest. The Bishop sent a report about him to London, which contains a fascinating, detailed description of Thomas: 'Holford is a tall, black, fat, strong man, the crown of his head bald ... his apparel was a black cloak with murrey lace open at the shoulders, a straw-coloured fustion doublet laid on with red lace, the buttons red, cut and laid under with red taffeta, ash-coloured hose laid on with lace trimming, cut and laid under with black taffeta. A little black hat lined with velvet in the brim, a falling band and yellow knitted stockings'. He was sent to London, and was lodged at an inn in the Strand guarded by two pursuivants, who were rather the worse for drink. In the early hours of the morning Thomas arose, pulled a yellow stocking on one leg and a white boot on the other, and paraded up and down the room. By acting the fool in this way he managed to get past the innkeeper - who thought he was a

lunatic - and escape from the inn. He ran in his bare feet all the way to Uxendon Hall, Harrow, where he arrived in a terrible state, his legs and feet bleeding, and was taken in by the Bellamy family. The following day the house was searched, but Thomas managed to evade re-capture until 1588, when he was spotted leaving the house of Swithun Wells, by Hodgkins, a pursuivant, and arrested. Sent to Newgate, he was condemned and hanged at Clerkenwell on 28 August 1588.

50 Blessed Montford Scott was born c.1550 at Hawstead, Suffolk. Educated at Cambridge, he went to Douai in 1574 and commenced theology studies. After being ordained subdeacon he decided to return to England in October 1576, in the company of Father Dominic Vaughan. The two of them were apprehended in Essex on 23 December, but by March 1577 Montford was back at Douai. He was ordained at Brussels and returned to England in June of that year. In 1578 he was caught at Cambridge and sent under escort by the Vice-Chancellor of the University to Bishop Aylmer of London, along with all his books and 'trash' that were in his possession. It is unclear what happened to him, but in 1580 he was named by the Ecclesiastical Commissioners as being free. It is known that he was at Brockdish, Norfolk, where he tried, unsuccessfully, to convert his Protestant cousin, Richard Lacey, Brian's brother. It seems that he spent the following years in East Anglia. Two Catholics were indicted at Norwich in April 1584 for receiving blessed rosary beads from him. In 1587 he is known to have been in Northamptonshire, visiting Thomas Colwell, who later died a prisoner for his religion in the Fleet. Montford may have gone to visit members of his family at Hawstead, his birthplace, where he was arrested at the home of William Kilbeck in mid-December 1590. He was sent to the King's Bench prison, tried and sentenced to death. He was hanged, drawn and quartered in Fleet Street on 1 July 1591.

After his capture in 1576, Father Dominic Vaughan, unfortunately provided the authorities with a great deal of damaging information about his fellow Catholics. Later he expressed his deep remorse, claiming that he was so traumatised by fear when arrested that he did not know what he was saying. He was kept in prison - where he converted the jailer's wife - until freed through the influence of his brother. In 1581 he was living and working in London and in Suffolk in 1584.

Montford Scott's companion in martyrdom was Blessed George Beesley. Like Scott he had suffered genital torture. Born at Goosnargh, Lancashire, in 1562 and educated at Rheims, he was ordained in 1587

The Elizabethan Martyrs, 1577-1601

returning to work in his native county. In 1590 he was in London and recorded as performing the marriage ceremony for Richard Webster, a Catholic schoolmaster, who was a prisoner in the Marshalsea. Was George a prisoner there himself? In December 1590 he was committed to the Tower, and then moved to Newgate to await his execution. While incarcerated in the Martin Tower George carved a long biographical inscription which can still be seen.

51 By one of those ironies of history, Archbishop Matthews' son, Sir Tobie Matthew, became a Catholic. Member of Parliament for St Albans, in 1604 he went travelling on the Continent and was converted by Father Robert Persons. When he returned to England he was imprisoned in the Fleet for six months while every effort was used to make him recant. When released he went to Rome to study for the priesthood and was ordained in 1614 by Cardinal St Robert Bellarmine. In 1617 he was permitted to return to England where he stayed with his close friend Francis Bacon. Tobie was again exiled from 1619 to 1622 but as he proved useful to King James in promoting the Spanish marriage for Prince Charles in Madrid he was back in favour and received a knighthood for his services in 1623. He also enjoyed the favour at Court of Charles I and Henrietta Maria but when the Civil War erupted in 1640 he went into exile with the Jesuits at Ghent where he died in 1655. It is possible that he became a member of the Society before his death.

52 Blessed Christopher Robinson came from Woodside, near Carlisle. He went to Rheims in 1589 and was ordained there in February 1592, returning to England that same year. We have his graphic account of the trial and execution of John Boste, at which he was present. For a time he lived with his brother, Edward, at Woodside. He was caught on 4 March 1597 while sheltering at Johnby Hall, Cumberland, the home of the Catholic Musgrave family. Christopher was martyred that month at Carlisle. As the rope broke twice his execution was particularly barbaric. He was thirty years of age.

53 Blessed Edmund Duke was born in Kent in 1563. He went to Rheims in 1583 and was sent to the English College, Rome, the following year. He was ordained at the Lateran 3 September 1589 and returned to England via Rheims on 22 March 1590.

Blessed Richard Hill, Blessed Richard Holiday and Blessed John Hogg were three Yorkshiremen who went to Rheims in 1587 and were ordained together at Laon in September 1589. They all travelled to

The Elizabethan Martyrs, 1577-1601

England with Duke on 22 March 1590 and landed near the mouth of the River Tyne. They were expecting to find contacts at a reception centre for priests. This was probably the centre run by George Errington at South Shields, but the centre had been discovered and was no longer operating. In the circumstances perhaps they were unsure of what to do next, and maybe for friendship and mutual support, they all stayed together as they made their way through County Durham. They soon aroused suspicion at a village where they were looking for somewhere to stay and were arrested and committed to Durham jail. Tried and condemned, they were all martyred at Dryburn, Durham. There is an extremely rare entry in the burial register at St Oswald's church, Durham which records their executions as 'papists, traitors and rebels to her majesty' who 'were hanged, drawn and quartered for their horrible offences'. Presumably St Oswald's is where their remains were buried.

54 Blessed Joseph Lambton was the second son of Thomas Lambton and Catherine Birket, and nephew of Father George Birket. He was born at Malton in the North Riding in May 1568. At the age of sixteen he went to Rheims, later entering the English College, Rome, in 1589. He was ordained at the Lateran 28 March 1592, for which a dispensation had to be granted, because he was under the canonical age. In April 1592 he returned to England, and about midsummer he was apprehended with Father Waterson in Newcastle-upon-Tyne, by the town clerk, Christopher Lewin. They were imprisoned until the Lammas Assizes, when they were tried before Mr Justice Clench on 20 July. Dean Tobie Matthew harangued and abused the priests who were sentenced to death. On the night before his execution, Joseph said to Father Waterson, 'Brother, let us be merry for tomorrow I hope we shall have a heavenly breakfast'. But early the following morning, Monday, 24 July 1592 only Joseph was taken out by the sheriff. On the scaffold Joseph tried to speak but at first was prevented, so for about fifteen minutes he stood quietly, eyes closed, in prayer. He was then allowed to speak briefly, asking forgiveness of God and any that he might have offended, and thanking God that he had been called to be a priest and to die for it. The description of Joseph's execution is truly horrendous and barbaric in the extreme. The hangman was a condemned prisoner, who to save his life agreed to carry out the execution. Lambton was cut down still alive, and while attempting to disembowel him, the hangman panicked, dropped his knife, and ran away, leaving the priest agonisingly bleeding to death. The sheriff paid a French surgeon twenty shillings to carry out the dismemberment.

The Elizabethan Martyrs, 1577-1601

Joseph Lambton was just twenty-four years of age.

(George Birket, who was born at West Brandon, Co. Durham, in 1549, had a distinguished career. He was ordained at Cambrai in 1577 and was one of the first group of students sent to the English College, Rome. He returned to England in 1580 and was staying with the Bellamy family at Harrow in 1581. From 1605 to 1610 he lived with Anthony-Maria Browne, 2nd Viscount Montague. In 1608 he was appointed Archpriest, a post which he held until his death in 1614.)

55 Blessed Edward Waterson was born in London and raised as a Protestant. He seems to have been a seaman who travelled widely, visiting Rome in 1588. Here he was given hospitality at the English Hospice and received religious instruction from Richard Smith, the future Bishop of Chalcedon. After his reception into the Church he went to Rheims in 1589 and was ordained there in 1592. He returned to England in June of that year. By July he had been captured at Newcastle. The Earl of Huntingdon delayed his execution in the hope of persuading him to talk to ministers, with a view to getting him to conform. As a result of the negligence of the jailer Edward managed to escape, but was quickly re-taken. Tobie Matthew, the Dean of Durham, wrote to Huntingdon to tell him of the 'harm' Waterson had done in Newcastle, converting people and saying Mass. He also suggested that an example should be made of the jailer, from whose custody he had escaped. In an attempt to frighten him one of Lambton's quarters was shown to him in prison. Waterson's response was to kiss it. Edward was loaded with irons and cruelly treated. He had no bed and was continually cold and hungry throughout the winter months. Huntingdon, having lost patience with him, ordered his execution to go ahead. At 6 a.m. on 8 January 1593, he was taken from the prison and put on the hurdle. But on the journey, for some reason, the horse refused to go any further and they could not get it to budge, so Edward had to walk the final distance to the gallows. He was pestered by a particularly obnoxious minister called Balmforth who gave him no peace. 'If I were beyond the seas again,' he said, 'I would willingly come to yield this life for the cause for which I am now suffering.' He was allowed to hang until dead.

56 Blessed Thomas Pormort was born c.1560 at Little Limber, near Brocklesby, on the Lincolnshire side of the Humber. He was educated at Trinity College, Cambridge, before going to Rheims in 1581 and shortly afterwards was sent to the English College, Rome. He was ordained at the Lateran in August 1587. In 1588 he left Rome suffering

The Elizabethan Martyrs, 1577-1601

from an illness and went to serve Anglesey-born Owen Lewis, recently appointed Bishop of Cassano, a diocese in the Kingdom of Naples. (Lewis (1533-1595) had taught civil law at Oxford until expelled because of his religion. In 1568 he became rector of Douai University. He obtained the licence from Pope Gregory XIII to print the Douai-Rheims Bible. In 1579 he was appointed Vicar-General in Milan to St Charles Borromeo and went on to serve the papacy in various high-ranking appointments.) Lewis sent Pormort to Milan and it was from there that he left for the English mission, where he worked in London, becoming a close friend of Robert Southwell. In July 1591 Thomas was arrested in the street by William Tedder, an apostate priest who eventually was rewarded with an Anglican vicarage in Kent. Thomas had been sheltered by John Barwys, a haberdasher from St Gregory's parish near St Paul's Cathedral, whom he had reconciled to the Church. Barwys was also arrested. Thomas managed to escape, but was re-captured in September and held prisoner in Richard Topcliffe's house. Pre-figuring what was to happen to Southwell, Thomas was brutally tortured so that he was disjointed and suffered serious internal ruptures. Topclife had made salacious remarks about his relationship with the Queen which Pormort made known. On 8 February 1592 Thomas was tried with John Barwys and both of them were condemned to death. Barwys received a pardon but Thomas was martyred in St Paul's churchyard on 21 February. He was kept standing on the ladder for two hours while being importuned by the worried Topcliffe to deny what he had said about Elizabeth, which Thomas refused to do. On the same day Venerable Richard Williams was martyred at Tyburn. He was a Marian priest who had conformed but was reconciled to the Church.

57 Blessed Francis Dickenson was born at Otley, Yorkshire, in 1565. He attended the Anglican Church but regretted this and left for Rheims in 1582. He was ordained at Soissons 18 March 1589. He set out with five other priests to return to England but the ship's captain refused to take more than two of them so they drew lots which decided that Francis and Father Miles Gerard were chosen. Neither of them was destined to exercise any priestly ministry in England. On 24 November 1589 there was a terrible storm in the Channel which drove the ship ashore near Dover. The two priests were almost drowned while the townspeople pillaged the wreck. Dickenson and Gerard were taken prisoner and asked to take the Oath of Supremacy. When they refused they were sent to London to the Bridewell where they were examined and Dickenson was tortured by Richard Topcliffe. In 1590 they were both removed to the Gatehouse. As they had come ashore at Dover it would have been

logical for them to have been returned to Canterbury for trial but they were inexplicably sent to Rochester. The date of their trial is unknown but they were hanged, drawn and quartered together at Rochester on 13 April 1590.

58 Blessed Miles Gerard was born at Ince, Wigan, Lancashire in 1549. He had been a schoolmaster before going to Rheims in February 1580 and was ordained at Laon 9 April 1583. Miles, a much older man than his travelling companion, had only one eye.

59 Blessed Edward Jones came from North Wales. He travelled around Europe in Spain and Greece and visited Venice and Rome. Here he was reconciled to the Church by an Italian friar, an English Jesuit called Simon Hunt, acting as the interpreter. Two years later, in 1587, he went to Rheims, was ordained at Laon 11 June 1588 and that autumn returned to England. He was caught at a grocer's house at the junction of Shoe Lane and Fleet Street, London, and imprisoned in the Gatehouse. He was cruelly tortured 'by the private parts' by Topcliffe and was hung by his arms for hours. He was tried with Father Anthony Middleton on 4 May 1590 when he defended himself vigorously before being condemned to death. Two days later he was taken back to Fleet Street to be hanged, drawn and quartered. Above the gibbet was hung a large placard falsely stating that Edward was being executed 'For treason and favouring foreign invasions'. Father Henry Garnet SJ wrote that Edward was a man of deep piety and a powerful preacher who had been betrayed by an apostate.

60 Blessed Anthony Middleton was born at Middleton Tyas in the North Riding of Yorkshire. He went to Rheims in 1582 and was ordained at Laon in May 1586, returning to England two months later. The records show that he was working in Essex for a time, but he seems to have been based in London. He was captured on Sunday, 3 May by Richard Topcliffe at the home of Mr Saunders in Clerkenwell and immediately imprisoned in the Clink. The very next day he was tried at the Old Bailey with Edward Jones and condemned. On 6 May Anthony was taken with Jones to Fleet Street by Topcliffe, and was made to stand close by the scaffold while his companion was butchered, Edward's blood splashing on him. Anthony was then taken to Clerkenwell and martyred on a scaffold that had been erected outside Mr Saunders' house. He asked Topcliffe if he was permitted to speak, to which he received the reply, 'So long as you speak to the good of her majesty.' Realising that he would not be allowed to say all that he wanted,

The Elizabethan Martyrs, 1577-1601

Anthony simply affirmed his priesthood and his innocence, concluding, 'Well, since it is not lawful to speak, behold, the Catholic Roman faith, which by my speech I cannot, by my death I will confirm'. He was cut down and butchered while still alive. Father Garnet tells us that Anthony had managed to evade capture for so long because he was very small in stature and had no beard and looked 'scarcely more than a boy', thus for a long time the authorities had not suspected that he was a priest. Garnet, in his tribute, states that Anthony may have been small but he was 'of indomitable soul'. Watching the execution was a man, mounted on a very good gelding, that belonged to his master. Following Anthony's short speech he had called out, 'Sir, you have spoken well.' He was apprehended on suspicion of being a priest, and when he confirmed that he was a Catholic, he was committed to the Bridewell, where he was forced to work the mill for many days and endure other hardships before being released.

61 **Robert Cecil** (1563-1612) was the son of William Cecil, Baron Burghley, by his second marriage to the bluestocking Mildred Cooke, described by Spanish ambassador Diego de Guzman de Silva as a more 'furious' heretic than her husband. Robert was of dwarf-like stature, with a hump back and Elizabeth referred to him as her pygmy. Cecil was trained in arts of espionage and dissimulation by Francis Walsingham and after the latter's death Cecil succeeded him as Secretary of State in 1590. After the death of his father in 1598 Robert took his place as Elizabeth's, and then James's, first minister whose peaceful accession to the throne he managed after secretly corresponding with him for years. Cecil 'nursed' the Gunpowder Plot to great advantage and his part in its timely 'discovery' remains a murky area for speculation. He was created Viscount Cranborne in 1604 and rewarded with the earldom of Salisbury in 1605.

62 **Blessed Alexander Rawlins** was born at Oxford in 1560 and educated at Winchester and Hart Hall, Oxford. As a young man he worked for a time as an apothecary at Denham, Buckinghamshire. In June 1586 he was arrested with Swithun Wells and Father Christopher Dryland, and was twice committed to Newgate within a few months. By the autumn of that year he was in the Fleet prison, from where he was banished. He arrived at Rheims in December 1587 and was ordained at Soissons 18 March 1590. Three weeks later, with Edmund Gennings, he was sent to England, landing on the North East coast near Whitby. He attached himself to Father Richard Holtby and worked in Yorkshire and Durham until Christmas Day 1594 when, secreted in a hiding place at the house

of Thomas Warcop, at Winston, Co. Durham, he was betrayed by a woman neighbour and after a prolonged search he was captured by pursuivants. He was taken to York with his host and some others present in the house. Of his encounter with the Earl of Huntingdon, President of the Council of the North, he writes that the Earl required him to kneel on both knees before him throughout his examination. 'I said I would give his honour that which was due to his honour, but both my knees were due to God alone; if my prince were in place I for my part would give no more than one knee'. At his trial on 4 April, when asked how he wished to be tried, he asked that the judges, Beaumont and Hillyard, should decide his case, as he was unwilling that his death should be laid at the door of the twelve jurymen. This somewhat delayed the proceedings, but made no difference to the outcome. Alexander was condemned, and having been denied the opportunity to speak to the crowd, suffered with Henry Walpole on 7 April.

Blessed Thomas Warcop, a Richmondshire gentleman, ran a 'safe house' on behalf of Father Holtby and for many years lived a dangerous life as both guide and host to priests. In 1594 he was caught hiding Father Alexander Markland, but escaped from custody. After Alexander Rawlins was caught in his house Thomas managed to escape from York Castle and went 'on the run'. Several of Alexander's extant last letters were written from prison to Thomas and contain details about his wife and family of young children. Echoing - whether consciously or unconsciously - the great martyr of Carthage, St Perpetua (d.203) who declared, 'my prison became a palace to me and I would rather have been there than anywhere else', Alexander addressed his letters from what he termed his 'castle of comfort and palace of pleasure',

In 1595 Mrs Ann Warcop and her family were listed as recusants at Gatenby. Thomas daringly resumed his work of sheltering priests and was finally caught in 1597 hiding Blessed William Andleby, an East Riding priest who had served on the mission in Yorkshire for twenty years. The Cambridge educated Andleby had once been a strong Protestant who, at the age of twenty-five, had gone travelling in Europe. Curious to see Douai College he had paid a visit and there met William Allen, who converted him. He stayed at Douai and was ordained at Cateau Cambresis 23 March 1577 in the same ceremony as Ralph Sherwin and Lawrence Johnson, known as Richardson. In 1578 William joined the English mission working mostly in Yorkshire. At great risk to himself he found means to get access to the Catholic prisoners in Hull Castle and give them comfort. At their martyrdom at York on 4 July 1597 Warcop and Andleby were joined by Blessed

The Elizabethan Martyrs, 1577-1601

Edward Fulthrop, condemned for being reconciled to the Catholic Church, and Blessed Henry Abbot, a layman from Howden in the East Riding. He was a victim of entrapment. When George Errington, William Knight and William Gibson were prisoners in York Castle they were approached by a fellow prisoner, a Protestant minister who pretended he wished to become a Catholic. On his release the three directed him to Henry Abbot as a means of contact to find a priest to reconcile him, whereupon the minister reported Abbot to the magistrate. As a result Henry was condemned for 'persuading to popery'. Mrs Warcop was jailed and was still in York Castle in 1600.

63 William Weston SJ was born at Maidstone, Kent, in 1550. He graduated at Oxford before going to Douai in 1572, where he knew Edmund Campion. In 1575 he travelled to Rome on foot and was received into the Society of Jesus at Sant'Andrea where his fellow novices were Robert Persons and Henry Garnet. He was sent to Andalusia, Spain, in 1576 and spent three years at Cordoba. Proficient in Latin, Greek and Hebrew he acquired a reputation for holiness. In 1579 he was ordained and afterwards served at the Jesuit College, Seville until 1584. In company with Brother Ralph Emerson he sailed from Dieppe to the Norfolk coast. Weston was a zealous missionary; learned, scholarly and intensely spiritual, but he was also somewhat narrow in his outlook and while some found him very attractive others thought him unconciliatory. As the senior Jesuit in England he became Superior. One of his first lodgings was with the Bellamy family at Uxendon Hall, Harrow. At other times he stayed at various inns around Holborn or with Sir Thomas Tresham. He had a number of close shaves evading capture. He was finally betrayed by the priest hunter Nicholas Berden and apprehended in a City of London Street near Bishopsgate in August 1586. Held at first in a private house, he was sent to the Clink where he remained for over a year. As he was acquainted with Anthony Babington every effort was made to make him complicit in the Babington Plot. Anthony Tyrell had a particularly malicious desire to ensnare Weston but never managed to do so. In 1588 he was transferred to Wisbech Castle. Before going he was able to bribe his jailer to allow him some liberty to make a visit to say goodbye to Robert Southwell at Arundel House. His first six years at Wisbech were spent in close confinement, only meeting his fellow prisoners at dinner times, but under a later keeper life became a little more bearable. Weston and the majority wanted to establish a regulated communal life. In the winter of 1594 this led to dissension in the community, known as the 'Wisbech Stirs'. Feelings ran so high that eventually Father John Mush was called

upon to arbitrate and by November 1595 a compromise was amicably reached whereby a prayerful community life was established and Mass was said regularly. The priest prisoners had to provide for themselves, relying upon the generosity of Catholics outside to fund them. Each one paid the keeper twelve shillings a month for food and other necessities which, as there were around thirty priests, provided a profitable sinecure. Towards the end of Elizabeth's reign a more severe regime was reintroduced, and the prisoners struggled to pay for food and bedding and often went hungry. In the winter of 1597 Weston was moved to the Tower, where he spent the next four and a half years, a close prisoner in intolerable conditions, sleeping on the damp floor. When he begged to be let out into the open air his jailer took him up to the roof, locked him up there and left him all day in all weathers. Visiting the Tower one day the Queen's favourite, the Earl of Essex, noticed the priest kneeling motionless in prayer on the roof. After watching him for some considerable time Essex wondered aloud if Weston could really be the great traitor he was made out to be. The strain on his eyes trying to read in the dark cell caused his eyesight to fail. Weston wrote that, 'Shut in my cell, I lay there hourly and daily expecting the sentence of death. The time and place were well suited to prayer, and, had not my eyes failed me, to reading and study also. But the sight of one eye was completely gone and a film, forming over the other, made it more than half blind so that I very nearly suffered complete loss of sight. Moreover, owing to a chronic headache, sleep had become all but impossible. I had, in fact, practically none.' On 13 May 1603, after seventeen years in prison, he was released into banishment, along with several other priests, including John Roberts. A crowd of Catholics waited outside the Tower for the famous priest kissing his hands and begging for his blessing. He was accompanied by his guard as far as Calais and then left. Half blind and prematurely aged, he made his way to Saint-Omer. When his health recovered somewhat he was sent to Seville where his eyesight improved and he was able to resume lecturing in Greek and Hebrew. In 1614 he was appointed Rector of the English College, Valladolid, where he died on 9 April 1615 aged 65.

64 Jonas Meredith was born at Bristol in 1547 and graduated BA at Oxford in 1569 but had been unable to proceed to MA because of his religion. In 1574 he was expelled from the University and travelled to Douai. He was ordained at Binche 16 June 1576. He returned to England the following year and was quickly arrested and sent to the Marshalsea, but soon released. He was among the first batch of students

The Elizabethan Martyrs, 1577-1601

at the English College, Rome, where he spent two years, and supported the minority Welsh party in the disputes. He left Rome in October 1579. A spy named Woodwood reported to the government that Jonas was 'short of stature and well timbered, fat-faced and swarth of countenance, the hair of his head cut short and of a flaxen colour. He is also full of words and about two years past was of St John's College in Oxford.' A priest with some 'dodgy' Government associations he was arrested shortly after returning to England and again released in April 1580. In 1584 he was staying with Lord Vaux at his house at Hackney. After being captured with Philip Howard on board ship he was imprisoned and then banished. After visiting Italy he returned to England when he was arrested for the fourth time and sent to the Gatehouse in August 1586. He was transferred first to Wisbech Castle, where he supported the anti-Jesuit minority, and then to Framlingham. After seventeen years in captivity he was banished in March 1603. He was back in England for a short time in 1605 before returning to France.

65 Anthony Tuchiner came from Wiltshire. While still a layman he was arrested at Winchester and committed to the Tower in August 1586, possibly as a consequence of the Babington Plot. In December orders were issued for him to be put to the torture on the rack. He served five years imprisonment in the Tower. He went to Douai in April 1599 and was ordained at Arras 25 February 1600. He was caught at Oxford in 1604 and banished. He was back in England by October 1607 working in Oxfordshire. By 1625 he had risen to be archdeacon of Oxfordshire and Berkshire and died around 1640.

66 Blessed William Thomson was born c.1560 at Blackburn, Lancashire. He went to Rheims in 1583 and was ordained there 31 March 1584, returning to England that year. For a time he was chaplain to Anne Line in whose house he lived. At the time of the discovery of the Babington Plot he was captured at 'the sign of the Tambourine' in Holborn, which is where Robert Bellamy of Uxendon Hall, Harrow-on-the-Hill usually resided when in the capital. Both William and Robert were sent to Newgate. Bellamy was able to make a daring escape, but William was condemned on 18 April 1586, and martyred at Tyburn on the 20th.

Executed with William was Blessed Richard Sergeant. He was born in Gloucestershire and was educated at Oxford, becoming BA in 1571. He went to Rheims in 1581 and was ordained at Laon in April 1583. He returned to England in September and worked on the mission for three years before being arrested in 1586. He was condemned at the Old Bailey on 18 April and martyred two days later.

67 Anthony Champney was born in 1569 in North Yorkshire. He went to Rheims in 1590 and transferred to the English College, Rome, in 1593. He was ordained at the Lateran 21 September 1596 and the following September returned to England. He worked in Yorkshire until arrested in 1599 and was committed to the Marshalsea. In 1600 he was sent to Wisbech and to Framlingham in 1601. He was one of the thirteen priests who signed the Protestation of Allegiance to Elizabeth in 1603 and was then banished. By 1604 he was back in Yorkshire. In 1606 he went to Rome on clergy business. He became a Doctor of Divinity at the Sorbonne, Paris, and in 1611 was appointed superior of Arras College for English priests. In 1619 he became Vice-President of Douai College. In 1637 he returned to England, where he remained until his death in 1644. His *History of the Reign of Queen Elizabeth* was an important source of information for Challoner.

68 Blessed Francis Page, although born at Antwerp, came from the Harrow family of that name who had already given a martyr to the Church in the person of Blessed Anthony Page. While working as a clerk in London, Francis fell in love with one of his employer's daughters. Her family were Catholics and through them Francis came into contact with Father John Gerard SJ, who was a prisoner in the Clink at the time. He became devoted to Gerard, who mentions him many times in his autobiography. When Gerard was moved to the Tower in 1597 Francis aroused suspicion by his visits to try and see him. He was arrested and after six months imprisonment was able to buy his freedom in October 1597. He went to Douai in February 1598 and was ordained at Arras 1 April 1600 and sent to England in June. On 2 February 1601, while preparing to say Mass, he had to hide when the pursuivants raided Anne Line's house. Page was caught in a London street later that day and held in custody in the parish of St Andrew's, Holborn. He was rescued by a Catholic gentleman named Ralph Slyfield, who was later granted a pardon for his 'crime'. In 1602 Francis was spotted in the street by a lapsed Catholic woman who called out to him. He hurried on quickly but she followed him. He went down a narrow alley and tried to evade capture by stepping into an inn. Closing the door behind him he asked the owner to let him out by the back door. The innkeeper, a Protestant, was minded to comply with the request, when the woman began violently banging on the door and calling out, which attracted a crowd. The innkeeper, fearful of the

The Elizabethan Martyrs, 1577-1601

consequences if he allowed Francis to escape, delivered him into the hands of the constables. He was taken before Lord Chief Justice Popham who, establishing that this was the priest who had escaped from Mrs Line's house, committed him to Newgate where he was confined for a time in Limbo. It was while a prisoner that he was admitted into the Society of Jesus, perhaps by a fellow prisoner, Father Henry Floyd SJ, to whom he made a general confession of his whole life. (Father Floyd had been arrested and condemned to death but kept in prison until 1603 when he was banished. He returned to England and worked in London for many years.) Later Francis was sent to the Tower and in the Beauchamp Tower can be seen the inscription he carved on the wall: *Dieu et mon esperance. F.Page*. After his trial and condemnation he was returned to Newgate to await his execution. The night before he died he experienced great trepidation and was comforted by Father Floyd, but by the time the sheriff came to conduct him to Tyburn he was calm, although his face was of a deathly pallor. With Venerable Thomas Tichborne and Blessed Robert Watkinson he was martyred on 20 April 1602; coincidentally the same date as his kinsman Anthony Page.

A member of the famous Hampshire family, Thomas Tichborne had been ordained at Rome in 1592. Having returned to England in 1594 he worked in his native county, until captured in 1597 in Devon. He was sent prisoner to the Gatehouse, from where he was rescued in 1598 by his brother, Venerable Nicholas Tichborne, also a prisoner in the Gatehouse, who was accused of assaulting the Keeper, Hugh Parlour, during the escape. In 1601 Thomas Tichborne was re-arrested at the home of George Baylie, a glover from Clerkenwell. While being led through the streets he was rescued by 'a stout young man', Venerable Thomas Hackshott, who knocked the keeper to the ground. Nicholas and Hackshott were both martyred at Tyburn 24 August 1601. Thomas Tichborne was finally betrayed by the apostate priest William Atkinson and arrested for the third time. Although Thomas was suffering from well-advanced tuberculosis it did not prevent his trial and condemnation. (Atkinson, who was born at Richmond, North Yorkshire, was ordained at Valladolid and returned to England. He was arrested and imprisoned several times, being taken to the Court, then at Greenwich Palace, in 1596. He was jailed at Lancaster in 1601 and Newgate in 1602. By then he had apostatised and was acting as a government spy from which he made a handsome profit. According to Archpriest George Birket, writing in 1611, he took huge payments from priests he apprehended in order to let them escape.)

Blessed Robert Watkinson was born into a Catholic family at

The Elizabethan Martyrs, 1577-1601

Hemingbrough in the East Riding of Yorkshire in 1579. At eight-years old he made his first confession to the martyr, Father Thomas Atkinson. He attended school firstly at Castleford and then Richmond. In 1598 he went to Douai and the following year was sent to Rome. He had serious health problems, and as a result received all the major orders on three successive days - his ordination taking place on 25 March 1602 - at the age of only twenty-three, before being sent to England to seek medical help. He was betrayed by a youth named John Fawther or Feather who had been a spy at Douai. He supplied Bishop Bancroft of London with the names of priests, including Father Edward Weston [72] and Robert was arrested shortly after arriving in the capital. He was condemned on 17 April and martyred three days later; less than a month after his ordination. He must be the youngest of all the priest martyrs.

[69] Blessed Roger Filcock, the son of Simon Filcock and Margaret Lowe, was born at Sandwich, Kent, in 1572. He arrived at the English College, Rheims, 15 June 1588 and was sent to Valladolid where he joined the college in February 1591. After his ordination he returned to England, via Bilbao and Calais in December 1597. As it left port the French boat on which he was sailing was pursued by Dutch ships. Many passengers, fearful of being captured, jumped overboard and successfully made it back to shore. Filcock was captured but managed to escape and eventually landed on the Kent coast in January 1598. He asked to be received into the Society of Jesus but his request was deferred until he had worked for longer on the mission. In 1600 Father Henry Garnet admitted him to the Society, but while preparing to return to Flanders for his novitiate he was arrested and sent to Newgate. At his trial under Popham at Newgate Sessions on 25 February he refused to either deny or confirm that he was a priest, insisting that evidence should be submitted to prove it. He also requested to be tried without a jury, leaving it to Popham to decide the case. No witnesses were produced; instead he was subjected to vicious verbal attacks from Bishop Bancroft of London who was called to testify against him. Roger challenged all that the bishop had to say for which Bancroft had no answers. Popham, clearly losing patience, ordered the jury to find Roger guilty, which they did and he was condemned, responding simply 'Benedictus Deus'. Together with Mark Barkworth he was incarcerated in the dark, vermin-infested, underground dungeon known as Limbo to await execution.

[70] Blessed Mark Barkworth was born at Searby, Lincolnshire, in 1572. He went to Douai in 1593 and became friendly with the staff at the

college, including Dr Edmund Arrowsmith, the uncle of the martyr. Before long Mark was received into the Church by Father George, a Flemish Jesuit. He matriculated from Douai University on 5 October 1594. In December 1596 there was an outbreak of the plague and Mark was sent to Rome and then Valladolid, where he was ordained, probably in spring 1599. After his ordination he left for England that summer in the company of Thomas Garnet. At Valladolid he had expressed a desire to join the Benedictines, and while on his return journey to England was received as a novice at St Mary's Abbey, Hyrache, Navarre, with permission, if in danger of death, to profess himself as a member of the Order. After the escapade with the Huguenots at La Rochelle he arrived in England but was not long in London before he was arrested and confined in Newgate for six months before being moved to the Bridewell. While there he addressed an appeal to Sir Robert Cecil. The letter reads,

'This petitioner hath been a prisoner in Newgate these six months, as supposed to be a seminary priest, which he protesteth he is not. He has been examined nine several times before my Lord Chief Justice and others; he was brought to the Sessions bar at Newgate four times. And wrote about 3 weeks since to your honour, laying open many distresses and humbly praying in respect of his health to be removed to Bridewell, as to a place of more open air. Whereupon it pleased your honour in consideration to direct your letters to Mr Waad and other high commissioners for his remove there to remain in the same sort as formerly he was in Newgate. But by the practice of one Parrat the warrant was altered and the petitioner detained in Newgate some ten days longer, the said Parrat coming unto him every day and practising for gain or otherwise threatening his further trouble. This suppliant gave him ten shillings and was then presently removed, the warrant naming him to be a seminary priest, which he refuseth to accept, rather chosing to remain in Newgate than to receive a remove by such a name: but he was taken away against his will and brought to Bridewell, where he had the liberty of the prison for two days. In all which time the said Parrat solicited him for more money, affirming that ... unless he would give him more he would cause him to be shut up a close prisoner, which the petitioner in respect of his poor estate refused to do. And was instantly closed up in the lowest room of the house, where he remaineth comfortless, unless by your Lordship he may be relieved, protesting that he is not the man he is supposed for being a priest. Therefore he humbly prayeth your honour in your honourable commiseration to grant your warrant to the keeper of Bridewell that he may have the liberty of the house as he had at Newgate. And that he

may rest at your honour's pleasure only to be disposed of at any time as your honour shall think fit; so shall he hold himself bound in all duty to pray for your honour's happy and honourable estate.'

The man Parrat was a pursuivant and, in spite of Barkworth's objection to him, he was a member of the jury at his trial: an example of the Elizabethan idea of justice. Mark was described as a tall man, well proportioned, the hair of his head brown, with a yellow beard and rather heavy-eyed. As with Filcock, no witnesses were called at his trial. Asked how he wished to be tried Mark replied, 'By Christ and His twelve apostles.' He was condemned solely on the strength of the prosecuting attorney's claim that he was a priest. In a letter to a friend he wrote, 'I offer warmest thanks to the Society of Jesus, and to most deserving men in its ranks. I admire them from the bottom of my heart and always will ... An especially good and intimate friend of mine, both when I was free and now I am in prison, has been Mr Arthur [the alias of Roger Filcock] a pattern on which to shape one's life. He was self-forgetful in the extreme, and a great example of regard for others and dedication. Now he is my companion in chains, and as I suppose, about to die with me. We thought highly of one another in life. Now in death it seems we shall not be divided.' On the scaffold Mark wore the tonsure and Benedictine habit, beneath which was a hair shirt. He was cut down alive and as the executioner ripped open his stomach and fumbled about in his intestines, Mark cried out, 'God have mercy on me!' After his quartering an apprentice in the crowd picked up one of his legs and noticed that the knee was callused by much kneeling. 'Which of you gospellers can show such a knee?' the apprentice called out. Part of Mark's body was discovered in 1613 in a crimson damask reliquary at the recusant home of John Cotton * Warblington, a moated manor near Havant, Hampshire.

71 Anthony Munday (1560-1633) had been an actor in his youth before being apprenticed to a printer. In 1578 he was in Rome, probably already a government spy sent to report on the English College. As the son of a well-known English recusant he was treated

---

* John Cotton was the son of George Cotton q.v. and his wife Mary Shelley of Michelgrove. George was cousin to Bridget Copley, the mother of Robert Southwell. George was in first in prison from 1577 to 1585 and his brother William likewise from 1581 to 1597. When Southwell left England in 1576 to begin his studies he was accompanied by John Cotton. As the two boys took ship from the Hampshire coast it is most likely that Southwell had been staying with his second cousins in preparation for his embarkation. John's elder brother, Richard, was already a pupil at the Jesuit school in Belgium. After completing his studies John returned home and tried to hold onto his family's financially ruined estate where he continued to shelter priests after his father's death.

with great kindness by the rector. Making literary capital out of his betrayal of Catholics he wrote an account in 1582 of his experiences in Rome. As the *Dictionary of National Biography* relates he profited handsomely from his vile career of betrayal and false testimony against Catholics. In 1584 he was rewarded with the post of messenger to Her Majesty's chamber. A modern, prize-winning historian, Charles Nicholl, describes Munday as 'a government thug and gallows-hunter'. He became a voluminous writer and prolific playwright, popularising the legends of Robin Hood as well as producing rabidly anti-Jesuit pamphlets. Today he is regarded as little more than a 'hack'. His contemporaries satirised him personally and poured scorn on his works. Munday was not only a bad person, so it seems was his literary output.

72 Edward Weston was born in London in 1565, the son of William Weston, a lawyer of Lincoln's Inn. His mother was a daughter of the martyred Blessed John Storey. In 1579 Edward was at Lincoln College, Oxford, but continued his education at a private Catholic school in Oxford. He went to Rheims, and then to Rome in 1585, and was ordained at the Lateran on 26 November 1589. He taught at Rheims and Douai until 1602 when the spy, John Fawther, reported that 'Mr Doctor Weston is to come over shortly. A man of person and of all sort of knowledge and learning. They make a comparison betwixt him and Campion.' He worked in Co. Durham until 1612, when he returned to Douai. Here he vigorously resisted all attempts by the President to force college students to reveal the names of any of them who harboured liberal views. In this he was supported by Father William Singleton who had landed in England with St Edmund Gennings. Singleton was arrested and imprisoned in the Bridewell from where he was banished in 1606. From 1609 he taught theology at Douai but in 1618 was summoned by the internuncio to Brussels to answer charges that he was causing disharmony. He died at Liège in 1620. Weston too had been hauled over the coals by the internuncio in 1617 and did not return to the college but went to Rome. The author of several books he later became a canon at Bruges where he died c.1633.

Chapter Five

The Jacobean Martyrs, 1603-25

Put not your trust in princes ... in whom there is no salvation.

Psalm 146

James VI of Scotland, the son of Mary Stuart, succeeded to the throne as James I of England on 24 March 1603, although he was unaware of it until the news was brought to him post-haste two days later. Baptised a Catholic he was raised as a Protestant in the Scottish Kirk. He was memorably described by Archbishop David Mathew (*James I*, 1967) as a 'regal Calvinist', so James easily accommodated himself to the Church of England finding the Calvinist theological views of the majority of its bishops and clergy most congenial. At the Hampton Court Conference, which he called in January 1604 in order to facilitate the religious settlement, James declared that it was for kings 'to take the first course' for establishing both Church doctrine and policy. In response the Anglican bishops 'showed an almost desperate determination to convince the King' that the Church of England was 'entirely in conformity' with the views of Calvin. (Mathew, *James I*). Before his accession, when he was anxious to secure all the support he could muster for a peaceful succession to Elizabeth, James had long been secretly communicating with prominent English Catholics. The fact that the new King was rumoured to have a Catholic convert for a wife fuelled Catholic optimism. There can be no doubt that James did give certain assurances about his benign attitude towards his future Catholic subjects. How genuine those promises were we shall never know, emanating from a man referred to as 'One of the most secret princes of the world'. But then James, with his ever-pliant conscience, would have promised anything to anyone if it helped ensure for him the prize of the English Crown. Just as was the case when he went through the diplomatic motions of making overtures to Elizabeth to get a reprieve for his mother; his foremost consideration was for himself. As Caroline Bingham wrote in *James VI of Scotland* (1979) 'He was ... intensely anxious not to jeopardise his own position'. As a contemporary, Father Robert Abercrombie, wrote of him, 'The single object of his ambition is the crown of England which he would gladly take from the hand of the Devil himself ... so great is his longing for this regal dignity.'

While on his journey from Scotland to London, the uncouth and ungainly James, profligately showering honours on all and sundry, had continued to give promises of toleration, which encouraged the despairing Catholics to believe that at last they would be granted some respite. On the one hand, determined to ingratiate himself with everyone, it suited James to raise the hope of toleration. On the other hand, the Catholics were so desperate for relief that they unrealistically took him at his word and exaggerated his promises because it was what they wanted to hear. Father Henry Garnet wrote, 'The Catholics have great cause to hope [for toleration]... in that the nobility almost all labour for it and we have a good promise thereof from His Majesty.' Why a man as perspicacious and well informed as Garnet should have been so hopeful is difficult to understand at this distance in time. He must have been fully aware of the situation of the persecuted Catholics in Scotland to dispel any false optimism he may have entertained about toleration. However, he was in good company. Monsignor Malvasia, papal agent based at Brussels, writing about Scottish affairs to Pietro Aldobrandini, Cardinal Secretary of State in Rome, said, 'We shall be greatly assisted by the good disposition of the King towards the Catholics which is manifested by many signs.' Yet the contrary evidence was all too plain to see. Together with the wanton destruction by the reformers of friaries and abbeys which began in 1559, penal laws against Catholics, similar to those in England, were enacted from 1560 onwards when papal jurisdiction was abolished and the saying of Mass forbidden. As in England, so in Scotland, the cupidity of a majority of mercenary nobility, eager to possess the Church's accumulated wealth, had conformed to the prevailing Protestantism and, like their counterparts south of the border, they benefited hugely from the dissolution of the religious houses. There had been a short period of respite under Queen Mary when Scotsmen were given freedom to live according to their own religion. But after Mary's deposition the persecution had been intensified and all remaining religious houses were finally suppressed: any other religion than Protestantism was prohibited. Just as in England, the persecution of Catholics in his Scottish kingdom was resolutely maintained throughout the whole of James's reign. 1 In 1597 James declared, 'I must love myself and my own estate better than all the world and think not that I will suffer any professing a contrary religion to dwell in this land.' The Catholics should have taken him at his word.

On the face of it, at the commencement of the new reign Catholic hopes seemed justified. James, declared, 'I acknowledge the Roman Church to be our mother church, though defiled with some corruptions. No more am I enemy to their church because I would have them reform

The Jacobean Martyrs, 1603-25

their errors. My mind was ever so free from persecution'. In a letter intended for Rome James wrote,

In the religion we profess we found so much comfort and peace of conscience, as we could never change ... yet should our constancy to that religion beget no such severity toward those who are otherwise persuaded, but that they may enjoy under us the same fruits of justice, comfort and safety, which others of our people do.

In his first speech to Parliament James, who entertained just as exalted an opinion of himself and his position as Elizabeth had before him, spoke about, 'the blessings which God, in my Person hath bestowed upon you all'. He expatiated on the relationship between himself and the country, blasphemously paraphrasing the Gospel, to draw an obvious comparison between himself and Christ. 'I am the head, and it is my Body; I am the Shepherd, and it is my flock.'

Some Catholics felt confident enough to openly profess their Faith - much to the alarm of the Puritans, for whom James, like his predecessor, had scant sympathy. As an example of that new-found confidence, when James's reputedly Catholic consort, Anne of Denmark, * made her progress from Scotland to London in June 1603, Thomas Cecil, 2nd Lord Burghley, son of William Cecil by his first marriage, who was Lord President of the Council of the North, bitterly complained of the great number of Catholic women who had journeyed from far and wide to greet the Queen at York. (Burghley had succeeded Archbishop Hutton as Lord President and during his tenure of office from 1599 to 1603 the persecution of recusants was greatly intensified.) The Puritans were constantly making demands of the King, not least as regards episcopacy, a matter on which James would not budge. After a time, exasperated with their importuning, he told them, 'If this be all your party has to say, I will make them conform themselves or else I will harry them out of the land or do worse.' Hearing this statement the Anglican Bishops congratulated the King, telling him he was inspired by the Spirit of God, to which Sir John Harrington made the sardonic riposte, 'If that is so, then the Spirit is something foul-mouthed.'

The State Papers containing the official returns for recusants reveal that by the end of the first year of James's reign there were 10,000 more who had acknowledged themselves as Catholics than there were at his

---
* Queen Anne was received into the Church c.1599 by Father Robert Abercrombie, a Scottish Jesuit missionary. Anne wrote to Pope Clement VIII informing him of her conversion. James warned his wife to keep this strictly secret so as not to imperil his crown, but he took advantage of his wife's new religion to ingratiate himself with the European Catholic powers when it suited him. Anne had particular confidence in Thomas Dawson who was introduced at Court in London. He was a Discalced Carmelite friar, whose religious name was Father Simon Stock of St Mary.

accession. There is every indication that Catholics were clearly a strong minority and many priests landed in England in the months following the death of Elizabeth. James relaxed the heavy fines and ordered the release from prison of scores of priests, arranging for them to be shipped to exile in France. In return, the Catholics pledged their loyalty to James. A number of leading Catholics were bold enough to present a petition to the King. In it they extolled the Catholic faith as 'a religion venerable for antiquity, majestical for amplitude, constant for continuance, irreprehensible for doctrine, inducing all kinds of virtue and piety, dissuading from all sin and wickedness. A religion beloved by all primitive pastors, established by all ecumenical councils, upheld by all ancient doctors ... sealed with the blood of millions of martyrs, adorned with the virtues of so many confessors, beautified with the purity of thousands of virgins, so conformable with sense and reason, and finally so agreeable to the sacred text of God's Word and Gospel. The free use of this religion we request, if not in public churches, at least in private houses. We protest, before the majesty of God, and all his holy angels, as loyal obedience and as immaculate allegiance unto your grace, as ever did faithful subjects in England or Scotland unto your highnesses progenitors; and intend as sincerely with our goods and lives to serve you, as ever did the loyalist Israelites King David.'

In response James fulminated that 'If there were forty thousand of them [papists] in arms should present a petition' he would 'rather die in the field than condescend to be false to God.' So the illusory hopes of toleration were soon dashed: the respite was short-lived. The persecution was renewed soon after James' accession. After all, he would not be the first or the last monarch to break his promises to others if he could profit by doing so.

By suspending the extortionate fines, James realised he was losing huge sums of money that he needed to reward his rapacious courtiers. He hit upon a brilliant plan to satisfy their greed that would not cost him. An individual was given permission to seek out as many wealthy recusants as he liked. Once they had been identified James then 'granted' those recusants, known as 'the benefit of recusants', to the individual, who could pursue them for their recusancy fines due to the Crown then or in the future. Alternatively, he could extort from them payments or property in lieu: in short the King 'sold' Catholics to his cronies, leaving them at the mercy of ruthless, mercenary persecutors, for whom they were a source of profit. Many famous members of the Catholic gentry lost two-thirds of their properties in this way and a *nouveau riche* class came into being on the backs of their misery.

In March 1604 Edmund, 3rd Baron Sheffield, Lord Lieutenant of

The Jacobean Martyrs, 1603-25

Yorkshire and President of the Council of the North, wrote to Robert Cecil, 'There are so many recusants in the northern parts that at the last assizes nine hundred of them were indicted at York, and there be many more ... A notable recusant in these parts was condemned for beating a minister and uttering very seditious speeches against the King. He was made to stand in the pillory and lose his ears.' Cecil counselled James to vigorously renew the persecution of Catholics. The King, a bad judge of character, who had never set foot in England before his accession, was out of his depth. He appears not to have fully appreciated the ingrained, mindless, anti-Catholic prejudice in Parliament. When Parliament met in 1604 the Elizabethan penal laws were not only renewed but increased. Anyone going overseas to a seminary was rendered incapable of owning any property or goods in England. Fines were made retrospective and Catholic schoolmasters and their employers were fined forty shillings per day. When Anthony-Maria Browne, 2nd Viscount Montague, had the courage to protest about the legislation he found himself in prison. But now James, known as 'the British Solomon', and by his opponents as, 'the wisest fool in Christendom', felt secure in his possession of the throne and his attitude to his Catholic subjects changed: 'We'll nae need the papists now', he remarked.

A new Act for 'the due execution of the statutes against Jesuits, seminary priests, recusants, etc.' came into force in 1604 (1 Jac.I, c.4) and a fresh wave of persecution began. On 30 April Father Thomas Hill, a former servant to John Gerard, was condemned to death, but was reprieved after the intervention of the Spanish ambassador. Hill later escaped from Newgate and joined the Benedictines at Douai in 1613. At the Summer Assizes in Exeter Father Thomas Laithwait 2 was condemned to death, but the sentence was commuted to banishment. The first martyrs of the reign were the priest Blessed John Sugar and his lay helper Blessed Robert Grissold, 3 who were executed at Warwick in July. In August twenty-seven-year-old, Norfolk-born, Father Thomas Montford was captured in North Yorkshire and condemned to death, but reprieved. (His older priest brother, Francis, had been banished the previous year.) Shortly afterwards a layman, Venerable Laurence Bailey, was hanged at Lancaster. Bailey was well-known for sheltering priests but the immediate cause of his apprehension was his involvement in the rescue of a Lancashire priest, James Gardiner, ordained at Laon in 1582. He lived at the home of William Blundell at Ince Blundell and acted as his schoolmaster. He later served in the same capacity at Rishton Hall with a Mr Massey who appears to have been a relative of Blundell's. Gardiner was captured at

The Jacobean Martyrs, 1603-25

Great Marton on 15 July 1604 but while being conveyed to Lancaster jail the next day he was rescued at Rossall by Venerable Laurence Bailey, Richard Kirkham and James Smith. In 1605 three laymen were executed in Yorkshire. Blessed Thomas Welbourne was a schoolmaster from Hutton Bushel in the North Riding. He was condemned for persuading his neighbours to popery and hanged, drawn and quartered at York on 1 August together with Venerable John Fulthering. Blessed William Browne, born at Northampton, suffered for the same offence and was hanged, drawn and quartered at Ripon on 5 September.

The Catholics felt bitter and betrayed and this renewed repression destroyed all their hopes. There can be no doubt that the reneging of the King on his promises of limited toleration directly provoked the Gunpowder Plot and played into the government's hands. Father John Gerard in his *Narrative* was in no doubt about this. 'What shall we think to have been the state of all Catholic minds when all these hopes did vanish away...? What grief we may imagine they felt generally, when not only no one of these hopes did bring forth the hoped fruit, nor any promise was performed, but when, on the contrary side, his Majesty did suffer himself to be guided ... by those that had so long time inured their hands and hardened their hearts with so violent a persecution; yea, when he did not only confirm the former laws with which we were afflicted, but permitted new and more grievous vexations to fall upon us than before ... and prepared yet more and more heavy whips wherewith to scourge us?'

This is not the place to go into the labyrinthine complexities of the Plot, but it played such a pivotal role in the history of Catholicism in Britain that a brief digression is justified. Today it is generally, though not universally, accepted that there was a genuine conspiracy to blow up Parliament, with the King and his two sons at the same time. Equally, not only today, but also contemporaneously with the Plot itself, there seems to have been no doubt that the government knew about it in advance from a mole; given the efficiency of the intelligence service, that is hardly surprising. How far in advance and who the informer was remains a matter for dispute. Whatever the truth, the conspiracy was carefully monitored and nurtured by Sir Robert Cecil as it was put into operation by the group of inept plotters. The 'cloud cuckoo land' Plot, lacking all pragmatism, was an absurdly unrealistic fantasy masterminded by the hot-headed Robert Catesby, and he drew in some of his relations and friends. Despite his notoriety, Guy Fawkes, the ex-soldier, was only the foolhardy 'front man'.

The catalyst for the official 'discovery' of the Plot was an anonymous letter which William Parker, 4th Baron Monteagle claimed to have received and which he gave to Robert Cecil. The letter warned of what was planned and led to the arrest of Guy Fawkes in the cellars of the Parliament House. Historians have written reams about the letter and indulged in inconclusive speculation as to its author. Could it have been Francis Tresham, son of Sir Thomas Tresham, who was involved at a late stage with the conspirators who asked him for funding? He was arrested and sent to the Tower and confessed but made no reference to any letter before he died there in December. If Francis wrote the letter his motive may have been to save his two Catholic brothers-in-law, Edward Stourton, 10th Baron Stourton and Lord Monteagle, who was married to his sister, Elizabeth. Or was Lord Monteagle, the purported recipient of the letter, actually its author? Monteagle also had close connections to a number of the conspirators. Some modern historians, including Antonia Fraser, are of the opinion that the 'anonymous' letter was indeed written by Lord Monteagle himself, in order to ingratiate himself with the King.

In essence, the Plot aimed at destroying the whole Protestant government, to be followed by a general uprising of the Catholic gentry with the aim of installing a more compliant regime. The fact was that, other than the band of conspirators, the Catholic community at large did not share these aspirations, which shows just how self-deluded the plotters were. Catholics might be faced with denial of civil liberties, financial ruin and their very lives for sheltering priests in order that they might receive spiritual succour from the Sacraments; but they were loyal - loyal not only to their country, but also to the Pope, who urged them to bear their sufferings with patient endurance. Within two days of the 'discovery' of the Plot, on 7 November 1605, Archpriest George Blackwell, head of the secular clergy, issued a statement addressed to the Catholics of England. He condemned the 'intolerable, uncharitable, scandalous and desperate' attempt to harm the King, his heir and Parliament, to 'the utter ruin of our native country and Catholic religion … It is known … that his Holiness has prohibited all such attempts against our King, and has commanded us to bear patiently all extremities offered us for our faith and conscience.' It was for Catholics 'to make a virtue of necessity, and to make our gain and increase by patience and prayer.'

Whatever our sympathies with the desperate plight of seventeenth century Catholics, the conclusion must be drawn that the plotters, who saw themselves as brave idealists striking a blow for their Faith, were in reality would-be mass murderers. In her *Gunpowder Plot: Terror and Treason in 1605* (1996), Antonia Fraser bluntly calls the plotters terrorists. They got their just deserts for their misguided zeal and wicked intentions. But as a direct consequence of their actions, incalculable harm was inflicted on their co-religionists. In the popular consciousness Catholicism became equated as never before with treason, recalled and reinforced with the annual 5 November commemorations.

James himself seems to have been oblivious to the measure of personal responsibility he bore for having raised the hopes of Catholics with his promises, only to callously dash them. He simply felt affronted that his 'tolerance' had been so ungratefully abused and aimed at the complete extirpation of Catholicism in his realms. The Plot unleashed a tempest of even greater oppressive and cruel persecution. Dozens of priests were rounded up and imprisoned. Many, such as Father Thomas Strange SJ, spent long years in prison. Arrested in 1605 en route from Harrowden to join Father Garnet at Coughton Court, Thomas was sent to the Tower where the severe racking caused the permanent dislocation of his limbs. He was kept in the Tower until 1617 then banished. George Abbot, Bishop of London and then Archbishop of Canterbury (1611-33), was reported to have begged the King on his knees to treat Catholics with the utmost severity. Not content with persecuting Catholics, Abbot also had Protestant dissenters burned for heresy.

Historian David Starkey is right in saying that the Plot set back the cause of Catholic Emancipation more than one hundred years. Under James I, Catholics became virtually non-persons, pariahs without any legal rights from the cradle to the grave. For example, Catholics could not serve in the armed forces, practice law, take a degree or vote in elections. It took until 1829 before Catholics were given the right to vote.

In the wake of the Plot two savage statutes were passed: 'An Act for the better discovering and repressing of Popish Recusants' (3 Jac.1.iv) and 'An Act to prevent and avoid dangers which may grow by Popish Recusants' (3 Jac.1.v). The main thrust of this second Act was the new Oath of Allegiance which it imposed. Condemned by Rome, it was an oath that no Catholic could take, which meant that when they refused it they were subject to the penalty of *praemunire*. James tried to justify his policy by publishing in 1607 his *Apologie for the Oath of Allegiance* in which he self-righteously and disingenuously claimed that until the Plot he had treated his Catholic subjects with great leniency. Legislation also sought to resolve the issue of recusant wives of Protestant husbands. Since a wife legally had no property of her own, the judges were adamant that such wives must be imprisoned indefinitely as Crown debtors in an attempt to force their husbands to pay their fines. When a recusant wife was widowed she had no right of inheritance and lost all claim to any part of her husband's goods which were seized. Fines for a Catholic baptism were set at £100 and a similar sum for a Catholic marriage, with the loss by the husband of any of his wife's lands and she the forfeiture of her dowry. For a secret Catholic burial the fine was £20. Those who possessed Catholic books were fined £2 per volume. Recusant heirs who went overseas lost for life their rights of inheritance. Ship owners were to lose their vessels if caught transporting the children of Catholics. Children from nine years old were liable to conviction as recusants. Churchwardens and constables received forty shillings reward for every recusant convicted by their efforts and were subject to a fine of twenty shillings for failing to present recusants in their parish to the Justices.

Richard Bancroft, Whitgift's successor as Archbishop of Canterbury and 'chief overseer' of the translation of the King James Bible, complained in the Court of Star Chamber in 1606 that it was a practice of Catholics to wrap their dead in two winding sheets, the first containing soil blessed by a priest and placed around the corpse so that they would lie in consecrated earth before submitting the corpse for burial by a Protestant minister. This practice must have continued for many years because in 1632 Gregorio Panzani, the Vatican envoy, confirmed that it was still happening. It was also common for the relatives of dead Catholics - 'even tender-minded Catholics' - to 'buy' an absolution from excommunication in retrospect for their loved ones in order to procure for them a dignified funeral and interment close to past generations of the family. As the practice was widespread, presumably it was sufficiently lucrative to compensate the ecclesiastical authorities for their hypocritical connivance. In those rare instances where, through the influence and charity of a local landowner, a Catholic cemetery was established, the graves were usually desecrated. This is illustrated by the situation of William Blundell of Ince Blundell, Crosby, Lancashire. He and his father had been imprisoned at Lancaster Castle for their religion in 1590. Because the local Catholics were refused burial in the parish churchyard but dumped unceremoniously in the local common, for charity's sake he enclosed a piece of ground that belonged to him to enable the Catholics to be buried there. About eighty burials took place until, in 1611, the High Sheriff and a group of men destroyed the place, pulling down the walls and smashing crosses placed over the graves. Mr Blundell was fined £2,000 by the Court of Star Chamber for his charity.

In 1614 a bill - chillingly reminiscent of the 20th century treatment of the Jews by the Nazis - was introduced in Parliament to compel

Catholics to wear a red hat as a means not only of identifying them, but also to make them ridiculous. The bill was defeated. During James's reign, with the exception of a few months when he was negotiating for a marriage between the King of Spain's daughter and his heir, Charles, Prince of Wales, the persecution of Catholics was unremitting. Father Michael Walpole SJ, brother of the martyred Henry, wrote an open letter to King James in which he stated, 'It is too notorious in the world what Catholics suffer for their conscience in your Majesty's dominions, how many things lie hid which would astonish and amaze the world, if they were laid open to the view thereof! What prying into men's secret actions! How many are beaten and often tormented even to death in private houses without any trial! I might add such other particulars as the rods kept in store by some of no small account, for young persons under twenty years of age ... to whip them.' The sweeping powers given to the pursuivants to conduct unannounced raids, day or night, on the homes of recusants who had no redress, can only be compared to the modus operandi of the Nazis or the Stalinist regime. These villains had carte blanche to act with impunity and were given every incentive to be ruthless, as they were able to claim one third of the resulting proceeds from their victims. The penal laws were mercilessly enforced.

Bradford-born Father James Pollard SJ, whose real name was Sharpe, worked on the mission in Yorkshire from 1611 and left a valuable account of his recollections. He told the story of the poor old woman from the Yorkshire wolds who lived with her daughter. They were the only Catholics in their neighbourhood and Pollard often rode thirty miles or more to assist them. As a known recusant the woman was summoned by the justices to the local market town. When examined they found that she was too poor to be able to pay any fines and not suitable to send to prison because she would have to be maintained at their expense. So she was put in the stocks in the market place for the day to face insults and taunts.

Another illustration, the truly piteous story of Father William Davies, may be told. He was born in Cheshire in 1544 and as a recusant had suffered twelve years imprisonment before, at the age of sixty, he went to Douai in June 1604. Ordained at Saint-Omer the following November he returned to England on 1 August 1605; two months before the 'discovery' of the Gunpowder Plot. He was arrested and banished in 1607 but by February 1610 he was again a prisoner in London when he begged to be released because of his age and infirmities. Maybe he was released but was in Newgate from 1613 to March 1615 when he was transferred to Wisbech. In June 1618 he was once more ordered to be banished but pleaded that he was too ill to travel and was sent to the Clink. In 1624 a proclamation ordered all priests to leave the country by 14 June on pain of death. William must have been released from the Clink at some point because the house in which he lived was raided and he was arrested. At the age of eighty, lame, almost blind and very deaf he was indicted before the Recorder of London and imprisoned at Newgate. On 25 June, to the disgust of those present in court, he was sentenced to death for failing to obey the proclamation. In July he was placed on the hurdle to be taken to Tyburn but before they reached the gallows a reprieve arrived from the King. Bitterly disappointed poor Father Davies wept at the thought that God did not believe him to be worthy of the crown of martyrdom.

What is germane to our story is that the Gunpowder Plot resulted in exile for forty-six priests. As a direct consequence, it also cost the lives of twenty-one martyrs 4

Nicholas Owen

Only a life lived for others is worthwhile

Albert Einstein, 1879-1955

Nicholas was born into a Catholic family in Oxford c.1550. It is most likely that he was related to the Owen family of Godstow, a hamlet just north of the city centre. The family was established at Godstow by George Owen. He was a physician to Henry VIII and Edward VI. He witnessed Henry's will and in it received a bequest of £100. He attended at the birth of Edward VI and was present at his death. In 1540 Owen finally acquired Godstow Abbey, a Benedictine nunnery that had been suppressed in 1539. The abbey was famous as the final home and burial place, in 1176, of 'Fair Rosamund' Clifford, long-time mistress of Henry II. Owen had clearly been promised he would have the abbey and in November 1539 commissioner John London descended on Godstow and demanded its surrender. The abbess, Katherine Bulkeley, wrote to Cromwell telling him she would never surrender her house unless by express command of the King. After great pressure had been exerted she agreed to hand over the 'domains and stock' to 'master doctor Owen' but begged, forlornly, that the house be spared. The surrender document was sent to the King, but it was not signed, either by the abbess or any of the fifteen nuns. Owen converted the abbey into Godstow House. He was also given property in Oxford by Henry VIII. He did well under Queen Mary, being elected president of the College of Physicians on her accession. His children married into the leading Catholic families of Oxfordshire. In 1558 he was elected a Member of Parliament for Oxfordshire and died that year a very wealthy man owning extensive estates in the county and beyond. His son, Richard, was a stalwart recusant and priests often said Mass at Godstow House. Richard suffered imprisonment for his faith. Several members of the Owen family became priests. In 1561 the mayor of Oxford complained that 'there were not three houses in the town without papists.'

Exactly where Nicholas fitted into the Owen family tree is unclear. He had three brothers: John, Walter and Henry. John was educated at Oxford, becoming a Fellow of Trinity College. He went to Rheims in 1583 and was ordained the following year. He crossed to England from Dieppe with Lancashire-born Father John Sandys, 5 landing at Rye, Sussex. He spent some months in London but left for Winchester where he was arrested at the house of Mrs Warnford in March 1585. John provided a lot of information about himself and his activities at his examination but drew the line at compromising any of his companions. He was banished in September 1585, returning to England in 1586. He and his travelling companion, London-born Father Ralph Stamford, were captured at Battle, Sussex, and committed to the Marshalsea. John obviously did not possess the faith or courage of his brother, Nicholas. He was kept in jail until 1588 when, sadly, he apostatised. Father Stamford was in and out of London prisons for many years. He was in the Clink in 1611 until 1618 when he was one of the priests taken into exile by the Spanish Ambassador, Count Gondomar.

Walter was certainly already a deacon when he went to the English College, Valladolid, in September 1590. He died there in November 1591, probably after priestly ordination. Henry, the third brother, was a printer of underground Catholic literature and suffered imprisonment for his activities. He even managed to set up a secret printing press while incarcerated in the White Lion prison. It was probably through Henry that Nicholas became known to Father Henry Garnet. It is known that Nicholas's brothers were taught at the house of 'Mr Owen of Godstow' in Holborn, London, by Father Richard Norris. 6

Nicholas Owen followed his father Walter's trade: carpenter and builder, which became his vocation. Sometime before 1580 he was secretly received into the Society of Jesus as one of the first English lay brothers. He spent twenty-six years travelling all over England devising hiding places for priests in country houses with incredible skill and extraordinary ingenuity, disguising their construction in such a way that the access to them was virtually undetectable. Among the houses in which he worked were Harrowden Hall and Rushton Hall,

Northamptonshire; Coughton Court, Baddesley Clinton and Billesley Manor, Warwickshire; Sawston Hall, Cambridgeshire and Oxburgh Hall, Norfolk. Built into the walls, the chimney breasts, underneath staircases and between floors, many examples of his hiding places still survive. Some were only discovered in the nineteenth and twentieth centuries and it is likely that some still remain undiscovered. No two hiding places were exactly alike, so as not to provide any clues that might lead to the discovery of others. Sometimes he made false hiding places to fool the searchers so that, having found the decoy empty, they would depart, leaving the real hiding place undetected. The extraordinary construction at Huddington Court, Worcestershire, is a double hide, with a smaller, second room hidden behind the first. While pretending to be carrying out repairs to the property by day, his real work was carried out single-handedly, in great secrecy, at night. He was nicknamed 'Little John' because of his diminutive stature, which enabled him to get into very small spaces. It is thought Nicholas firstly served Edmund Campion. After Campion's execution, Nicholas was in trouble for speaking out openly and boldly about the Jesuit's innocence, for which he was arrested and imprisoned. When he was released in 1586 he went to serve Father Henry Garnet, the Jesuit Superior in England, and was his faithful companion for twenty years. He also served Father John Gerard. Nicholas transacted business for the two priests, such as renting houses.

At Easter 1594, thanks to Owen's skill, Father Gerard was saved from discovery by the pursuivants when he hid, squashed up for several days, in one of Nicholas's secret hiding places at Braddocks, the home of the Wisemans. Owen had removed the tiles from the Renaissance fireplace, burrowed down into the solid brickwork and constructed a false hearth. It was a close shave because while Gerard was hidden beneath the hearth the searchers lit a fire and ash fell down on him! (Granville Squiers in his *Secret Hiding Places* (1933) describes how he visited Braddocks, only a fraction of which - the right wing of the old house - remained as a farmhouse. He investigated the construction beneath the stone fireplace. It took nearly three days to uncover the hole 'the brickwork of which looked as fresh as if Nicholas Owen had quarried it out only the week before.' Squiers also noted that an old quince tree still stood in the garden. Father Gerard had survived his ordeal on a pot of quince jelly.) Gerard was not to remain much longer at liberty. Deciding it was time to move house, Nicholas found him somewhere suitable in London. While the new house was being prepared Gerard and Owen lodged temporarily at the house of Mr Middleton, a tailor in Golden Lane, Holborn. On 23 April, while they were sharing a bedroom at the house, there was a raid in the middle of the night and both were captured. They had been betrayed by John Frank, a former servant of the Wiseman's at Braddocks.

Nicholas was taken first to the Counter in the Poultry and then moved to Newgate where, along with Gerard's servant, Richard Fulwood, who had been apprehended separately, he was tortured by being hung up in the manacles for three hours at a time. As yet the government was unaware of Nicholas's role and neither man revealed anything incriminating. To the Catholic gentry, Nicholas was indispensable, and the secrets he possessed so far-reaching in their consequences if ever disclosed, that they paid a large sum to have him released. Father Gerard spent three years in the Clink, where Nicholas was able to visit him and act as a go-between for him and Father Garnet. This activity was betrayed by a fellow priest in the jail and Gerard was moved to the Tower.

On the night of 5 October 1597 Father Gerard made his amazing escape from the Tower. Many sources believe that Owen was the mastermind behind the escape. Richard Fulwood and John Lillie, faithful servants of Gerard's who both became Jesuits, directly assisted the priest, rowing him down the Thames and thence to a house used by Father Garnet at Spitalfields, where Nicholas waited for them with horses. He and Gerard quickly mounted and galloped off into the country.

In 1599 Father Gerard and Nicholas were nearly caught again while he was constructing a hiding place at Kirby Hall, Northamptonshire, the planned new residence of the intrepid young widow Elizabeth Vaux, daughter of John Roper, 1st Baron Teynham. She had married George Vaux, son of William, 3rd Baron Vaux. In 1595, at the age of seven, her son, Edward, had succeeded his grandfather William, as 4th Baron Vaux. Father Gerard acted as chaplain at Harrowden Hall where Nicholas had already provided several hiding places so skilfully contrived that one would-be searcher stated that unless the house was pulled down there was little chance of finding anyone. That same year Nicholas suffered a bad accident. A horse fell on him, breaking his leg. The leg was set badly and as a result he ever afterwards walked with a pronounced limp.

In 1605 a large party of about thirty Catholics made a pilgrimage to St Winifred's Well at Holywell in North Wales, partly in thanksgiving for the recovery of Father Edward Oldcorne from mouth cancer. In addition to Oldcorne, the group included Fathers Henry Garnet, John Gerard and Oswald Tesimond, and the daughters of William, Lord Vaux of Harrowden, Anne and her widowed sister, Eleanor Brooksby.

The Jacobean Martyrs, 1603-25

The Vaux sisters had made it their life's work to shelter priests, creating safe houses for them supplied with secret hiding places. Chief among these safe houses was White Webbs, a spacious residence at Enfield Chase which, since 1600, was Father Garnet's headquarters for a long time. Conveniently located on the edge of the forest it was a place of meeting and rest for Jesuits on the mission and could accommodate large groups. Eleanor and Anne, under the alias Mrs Perkins, took care of the housekeeping. It was they who officially rented the house and shared the costs. The house was equipped with an organ, sometimes played by William Byrd, and Mass was frequently sung. No doubt the house had also benefited from the skills of Nicholas Owen. Eleanor had married Edward Brooksby of Shoby, Leicestershire. Her son William married Dorothy, the daughter of William Wiseman of Braddocks and the couple went to live at White Webbs where two of their children were born. Anne Vaux was devoted to and fiercely protective of Henry Garnet and was his faithful helper for twenty years. Nicholas Owen travelled with the pilgrim group. It is said that he took the opportunity to renovate some of his hiding places in the houses they passed or stayed at en route to and from Wales.

After the arrest of Guy Fawkes White Webbs was raided searching for Robert Catesby who had been stupid enough to stay there overnight a few days previously. But only the servants were found, arrested, imprisoned and interrogated. Father Garnet had long since departed for Coughton Court, the home of the Throckmorton's, near Alcester, and it was here, on 6 November, that he first received the news of the failed Gunpowder Plot from Thomas Bates, one of the conspirators. Harrowden Hall was under scrutiny, Lord Edward Vaux and his mother Elizabeth being closely watched. (In 1606 the eighteen-year-old Edward refused the Oath of Allegiance and, like his grandfather before him, was sent to the Fleet prison. He was sentenced to perpetual imprisonment and loss of all his property. He was released from jail in 1615. Few families suffered as much for their faith over several generations as did the Vauxes.) Garnet decided that he had to declare his innocence of any involvement in the Plot and wrote accordingly to Sir Robert Cecil.

On 24 November, Garnet, together with Nicholas, Anne Vaux and her sister Eleanor, set out for Worcestershire knowing that they would find refuge at Hindlip Hall, a great house about three miles north of Worcester. The Hall had been built by John Habington, Treasurer of Queen Elizabeth's household. He, his wife and three children, were all recusants. John died in 1582 and in 1586 his sons, Edward, his heir, and his younger brother Thomas (1560-1647), were accused of being implicated in the Babington Plot. Edward Habington was hanged, drawn and quartered at Tyburn on 30 September 1586, ten days after Father John Ballard, but Thomas, because he was the Queen's godson, was imprisoned in the Tower where he remained until 1593 when he was pardoned and allowed to return to Hindlip. Educated on the Continent Thomas was accounted one of the most cultured men of his day. Just why Garnet and his companions thought that Hindlip was their best place of sanctuary is a puzzle given that a Jacobean Catholic, writing contemporaneously with the Plot, described it as 'the most famous house in England for the entertainment of priests.' Catholics flocked to Hindlip to receive the sacraments. The Hall was full of ingenious hiding places - secret stairs, trap doors and chimney breasts with false flues - eleven hiding places in all, constructed by Nicholas Owen. There was also a secret tunnel, believed to be an escape route from the house, which ran from the cellars out under the gardens.

The priests who served at Hindlip are well documented. Father Edward Oldcorne SJ alias Parker took up residence in 1590. He was a most successful missioner, so much so that shortly afterwards Father Thomas Lister SJ, was sent by Father Garnet to assist him in the area. Unfortunately Lister, a learned priest, suffered from claustrophobia, making it difficult for him to cope with the necessary cooped-up lifestyle. He was replaced by Father Richard Banks SJ. The son of a very anti-Catholic London hosier he was ordained at the Lateran in November 1592. He returned to England in 1594 and joined the Jesuits in 1597. He later moved to the home of the Wiseman's at Braddocks.

News of the Plot had already reached Hindlip on 8 November when Father Oswald Tesimond had arrived and told Sir Thomas Habington and Father Oldcorne that a plot to blow up the King and Parliament had been discovered three days previously. Mary Habington, Sir Thomas's wife, was the sister of William Parker, Lord Monteagle, who had been instrumental in the 'discovery' of the gunpowder plotters. At the time Mary was recovering from giving birth to her son four days earlier on 4 November. Edward Oldcorne and his faithful servant, Brother Ralph Ashley, 6 had both been based at Hindlip Hall for fifteen years and they were always happy to offer sanctuary to newly arrived priests. Oldcorne was later to recount that Tesimond had 'brought them the worse news that they had ever heard, and that they were all undone.' Nicholas, Garnet and the Vaux sisters were met near Evesham by Father Oldcorne and Ashley and they rode together towards Hindlip. About four miles from the house they dismounted and continued their journey on foot.

Six quiet weeks passed at Hindlip during which the visitors were unmolested, Garnet spending most of his time in a secret chamber in daily expectation of a raid by the authorities. During this time he wrote a letter to the Privy Council protesting his loyalty to the King and condemning the Plot, in which he had played no part, but accepting that he had somehow been an unwitting accessory to it by giving Communion to those now known to be conspirators. The letter was probably a serious lapse of judgement.

On 15 January 1606, Fathers Garnet, Tesimond and Gerard were declared traitors and warrants were issued for their arrest. Yet the Privy Council still delayed taking any action. Early in the morning of 20 January Sir Henry Bromley, the local Justice of the Peace and his brother, Sir Edward, finally arrived at Hindlip with a large posse of one hundred armed men to search the house. Henry Bromley was a Puritan who had long sought to indict Sir Thomas Habington for sheltering priests, but on every occasion Habington had thwarted him by categorically denying it. Nicholas and Ashley hid in the wainscoted gallery over the gate and Garnet and Oldcorne in one of the chimney breasts. Thomas Habington was not at home but Bromley told Mary, his wife, that he knew she was hiding priests, which she denied. Given her relationship to Lord Monteagle Bromley had to proceed carefully. When Sir Thomas returned home he too vehemently denied all knowledge of the Jesuits. He was arrested, attainted and later sentenced to death, but thanks to the intercession of his brother-in-law, Lord Monteagle, his sentence was commuted. After his release Sir Thomas was permitted to return home but forbidden ever again to leave Worcestershire. He took to writing the history of the county.

The searchers found Catholic literature and 'popish trash' hidden under floorboards in several places but no sign of their quarry. They also discovered several hiding places and no doubt to their chagrin had to admit they were impressed by the amazing constructions. They recorded that they found 'two cunning and very artificial conveyances in the main brick wall, so ingeniously framed, and with such art, as it cost much labour ere they could be found. Three other secret places, contrived by no less skill and industry, were found in and about the chimneys ... These chimney conveyances being so strangely formed, having the entrances into them so curiously covered over with brick, mortared and made fast to planks of wood, and coloured black, like the other arts of the chimney, that very diligent inquisition might well have passed by, without throwing the least suspicion upon such unsuspicious places.'

The two Jesuit brothers, Nicholas and Ralph, spent four days hidden without any food other than an apple between them. They could hear the searchers taking turns to patrol the gallery, which extended around the house. They waited until they thought the coast was clear, when the searchers were furthest away, and in the silence they stealthily came out from hiding behind the wainscot 'secretly and stilly and shut the place again' so that they were not seen or heard. They made for the door of the gallery, but at that moment the searchers unfortunately turned back and they were caught. At first they tried to bluff their way out of the situation. They claimed to be two men who just happened to be in the house and were about to depart. Admitting when questioned that they were Catholics, they were asked where they had been. They confessed to having hidden themselves in order to avoid being apprehended, but denied all knowledge of other men being hidden.

The searchers thought that they had captured the two priests and Nicholas and Ralph did not disabuse them of their error. That same night Sir Henry Bromley, still believing that he had caught the priests, wrote to Robert Cecil, Lord Salisbury to inform, him that he had never come across such impudent liars as he found at Hindlip: 'all recusants and all resolved to confess nothing, what danger soever they incur'. Bromley might have called off the protracted search at this point but Humphrey Littleton, a Catholic, provided information that he was sure Garnet and Oldcorne were still hidden in the house and the search was violently renewed, with the raiders rampaging all over the house throughout the weekend. Littleton, in whose house at Holbeach some of the fleeing plotters had hidden, no doubt 'spilled the beans' in the hope of saving himself.

There are three relatively contemporary descriptions of the raid at Hindlip: an anonymous account written by one of the searchers some months after the event, a letter from Father Garnet and a slightly later version from Father Gerard. Following the interpretation put on his capture in the anonymous account, some authors have asserted that Nicholas voluntarily surrendered, fearing that the two priests in cramped hiding might starve to death. He hoped that if *he* surrendered the search would be called off. Father Garnet's letter shows that he was also under the impression that this was what had occurred and expressed his regret that the two brothers had come out of hiding so soon. He believed that they could have remained undetected. While not denying that this factor may well have played a part in Nicholas's decision, a careful reading of the accounts indicates that this was not necessarily the case. It seems more likely that Nicholas was attempting to escape, which is borne out by the stealthy manner of his emerging from hiding. Furthermore the two priests had marmalade and other provisions and were given hot drinks by means of a special device of

Nicholas's: a reed placed through a little hole in the back of the false chimney piece that backed onto a chimney breast in the chamber of either Anne Vaux or Dorothy Habington, sister of Sir Thomas.

On Monday, 27 January, day eight of the search, although their hiding place had not been discovered, Garnet and Oldcorne surrendered. They emerged, according to Garnet, 'looking like two ghosts'. They had been forced to crouch, unable to stretch their legs, which were very swollen as a result. The two priests were in danger of asphyxiation in the fetid confined space. There were no toilet facilities and the lack of hygiene and stench in those awful conditions must have been unbearable to someone of Garnet's sensitivities. Bromley had no problem identifying Oldcorne, but was unsure about Garnet until on 30 January a former priest Anthony Sherlock turned up. He made a statement identifying Henry Garnet.

He gave Sir Henry Bromley and his fellow Justice of the Peace, John Fleet, an account of his life, stating that he had studied at Oxford and had been ordained at Rouen. He named those with whom he had lodged, including three years spent with Lady Stonor near Henley-on-Thames, and provided details of where he had said Mass. He claimed to have been apprehended and imprisoned in Warwickshire and at that point, tired of living a 'harbourless and comfortless life', renounced his popery. The man is something of a mystery. No trace of Sherlock has been found at Oxford and there is no record of a person of that name being ordained anywhere. What was his real identity?

Bromley carried off his captives - Garnet, Oldcorne, Owen, Ashley, Thomas Habington and two of his servants, Edward Jarret and William Glandish - in his coach. They were detained at his birthplace, Holt Castle, just a few miles away, which was then occupied by his widowed mother. Here he awaited instructions from the Council. Salisbury made sure he left the prisoners in Bromley's care until after the executions of the eight gunpowder plotters had taken place. This appears to have been a deliberate ploy on Salisbury's part in order to achieve his ends. Under torture, the plotters had exonerated the Jesuits of any involvement in their plans. But that did not suit Salisbury's purpose; with the plotters dead it would be far easier for him to implicate the Jesuit's - whom he particularly detested - in the Plot, as there would be no one left able to corroborate their denials that they had been involved.

Bromley and his family seem to have been captivated by Garnet's winning personality and he and Oldcorne were treated in a friendly manner by the whole household with whom they regularly ate dinner. Bromley declared that never in his life had he met a man like Garnet either for modesty, wisdom or learning. In early February Bromley at last received orders to bring his prisoners to London. Garnet was ill and still suffering badly with swollen legs, the after-effect of his incarceration at Hindlip. He was treated courteously and provided with a good horse, and Bromley, out of consideration for his prisoner, took his time in getting to London.

Arriving on 12 February, Garnet and Oldcorne were sent to the Gatehouse where Henry's nephew, Thomas Garnet, was then also a prisoner. Nicholas Owen was first imprisoned in the Marshalsea before being removed to the Tower, to which Garnet and Oldcorne had already been transferred. The Council gave orders for Ralph Ashley, Father Oldcorne and Nicholas to be tortured following their incarceration in the Salt Tower. By then the Council had fully realised the value of their little captive and the importance of the information he could disclose. Salisbury wrote: 'It is incredible how great was the joy caused by his arrest ... knowing the great skill of Owen in constructing hiding places and the innumerable quantity of dark holes which he had schemed for hiding priests all through England.' Salisbury's instruction was that 'If he will not confess, he shall be pressed by exquisite torture and we will wring the secret from him by the severity of his torments.'

Nicholas was first tortured mercilessly on 26 February, during which he uttered nothing but 'Jesus' and 'Mary'. Legally Nicholas should have been exempt from torture, not only because of his leg injury but also because he was already a sick man, suffering from a serious hernia. This may have been caused by his construction work or have been the result of earlier torture. For the second torture session, his persecutors took the cruel precaution of encasing him tightly in an iron girdle to prevent rupture while he was hung up by the wrists for hours at a time with heavy weights attached to his feet. Under this excruciating torture he admitted nothing except that he had worked for Father Henry Garnet at certain locations, facts already known to the government.

On 2 March 1606 the torture proved too much. A report on his death stated: 'They tortured him with such inhuman ferocity that his stomach burst open and his intestines burst out.' He died in terrible agony. To have literally tortured a prisoner to death reflected badly on the government, to say the least. So to hide their guilt the calumny was wickedly put out that Nicholas had committed suicide by stabbing himself in the stomach. Father Gerard pointed out that Owen's hands were so crippled he could not feed himself, let alone wield a knife - even if he had managed to obtain the weapon.

This slander was so improbable that even his enemies did not believe it, much less his friends that were so well acquainted with his innocent life and long-continued practice in virtue.

In his *Narrative of the Gunpowder Plot* Gerard recounts that the jailer had admitted that Nicholas 'died in our hands'. The precise date of Nicholas's death has been questioned because of the emergence of later circumstantial evidence suggesting that it may have taken place on the 12th but the traditional 2 March date seems most likely.

Ralph Ashley and Edward Oldcorne were also severely tortured, the latter for up to five hours a day for as many days, so that he could no longer sign his name. They were then returned to Worcester, where they were martyred together on 7 April 1607. Ralph kissed Father Oldcorne, thanking him for all his kindness and he blessed God for granting him such a happy end to his life in such good company as his 'sweet father.' Executed with them were Humphrey Littleton, who publicly begged Father Oldcorne's forgiveness, and John Wintour, half-brother of two of the conspirators, Robert and Thomas Wintour, with whom he had unwittingly become involved.

Both Father Garnet and Father Gerard wrote eulogies on 'Little John'. Gerard paid this tribute to his work for the English mission:

> I verily think no man can be said to have done more good of all those who laboured in the English vineyard ... he was the immediate occasion of saving the lives of many hundreds of persons, both ecclesiastical and secular ... How many priests then may we think this man did save by his endeavours...

Nicholas Owen may have been a small man but he was great in heart and soul.

Which leaves us with Father Henry Garnet. Protestant imagination turned him into a stereotypical, sinister, scheming Jesuit. Nothing could be further from the truth. Garnet was a devout, gentle scholar, kind-hearted and courteous; violence was abhorrent to him. He was born at Heanor, Derbyshire in 1555, the son of Brian Garnet, headmaster of Nottingham Free Grammar School. He was educated at Winchester College, where he excelled. His musical skills, including playing the lute and singing, attracted admiring praise. It would be expected that he would progress to Oxford, but as a Catholic this was barred to him. His elder brother had already been expelled from the university because of his Faith. Henry became apprenticed to Richard Tottel, the most prominent legal printer in London, before going to Rome, where he entered the novitiate of the Society of Jesus in 1575 where one of his fellow students and close friends was William Weston. After his ordination in 1577, Henry became a professor of philosophy and Hebrew. In company with Robert Southwell he returned to England in

The Jacobean Martyrs, 1603-25

1586 and the following year succeeded Weston as the Jesuit Superior. Fearless and indefatigable, he served in that capacity for eighteen years with conspicuous success.

Garnet was not a conspirator. His misfortune was to learn the bare outlines of the Gunpowder Plot from Father Oswald Tesimond SJ, [7] under the seal of the confessional. Robert Catesby, one of the conspirators, had revealed to Tesimond in confession that some violent plan was afoot and the priest had tried to persuade his penitent to abandon the idea realising what a catastrophic effect it would have on the Catholic community. Tesimond asked Catesby's permission to inform his superior of the plans. Catesby agreed providing that it was done only in confession. When Tesimond, in confession, relayed all this to Garnet, he was horrified. As Caroline Bingham wrote in *James I of England* (1981) 'There was one man in England to whom the Gunpowder Plot was as abhorrent as it was to the King: he was Father Henry Garnet.' Garnet tried at second-hand to dissuade those involved from proceeding. He wrote to his superiors in Rome urging them to issue urgent warnings to English Catholics against attempting any use of force. Faithful to his calling, he was agonisingly unable to divulge what he had heard. 'I could never sleep quietly afterwards,' he said at his trial.

His critics allege that having got wind of the Plot under the seal of the confessional he should have found some way of learning about it outside of confession. That is surely easier said than done; he was in a no-win situation. Firstly the conspirators were hardly likely to start voluntarily blabbing about their secret intentions, and secondly he was in no position to raise the matter with any of them given that the knowledge he had acquired had been imparted in confession, of which he had to maintain the seal. Given the magnitude of the intended crime, one can argue from the moral imperative that this outweighed revealing information gained in confession, and that he should have disclosed what he had learned regardless of the confessional seal; but Garnet did not see it that way. Based on his belief that the seal was so absolute the Church required him to maintain it inviolate, rightly or wrongly he made his conscientious judgement. It was a view that was supported by most of his Catholic contemporaries. (See Appendix 4)

Although he was rigorously interrogated on twenty-three occasions by Robert Cecil and the leading members of the government and judiciary, Garnet was treated courteously in relatively comfortable lodgings. Filthy lies were spread abroad to impugn Henry's morality. He was especially anguished when they accused him of keeping Anne Vaux - who had been arrested - as his long-time mistress, and on the scaffold he made a point of praising his helper and stressing the purity of their relationship. He was tortured once on the rack but maintained his innocence. Garnet was tried at the Guildhall on 28 March 1606 for misprision of treason. The eminent men on the Bench included Robert Cecil, Lord Salisbury. Presiding was Chief Justice Sir John Popham, Thirty-five years previously, when a legal printer's apprentice, Garnet had known Popham who not only came to his employer's offices but also dined with him. King James himself attended the trial, hidden behind a screen. The King sent a note to Salisbury telling him that Garnet should be allowed to speak without interruption: an instruction that was ignored with the result that James afterwards expressed his dissatisfaction with the proceedings. The trial lasted all day but no real incriminating evidence was produced. There was none. As Father Gerard wrote, the judges were perfectly aware that Garnet was innocent of involvement in the Plot, so the prosecution case, conducted by Sir Edward Coke, had to rest upon lies and prejudice against the Jesuits. It would have been simpler just to indict Henry with being a priest. That fact was unchallenged, but this did not satisfy the government which wanted a propaganda coup, branding him a traitor by pinning involvement in the Gunpowder Plot on him. One of the judges, Charles Howard, Earl of Nottingham, put the question, 'Mr Garnet, if a man should tell you in confession that he would stab the King with a dagger tomorrow, are you not bound to reveal it?' Garnet's candid reply, which caused much laughter in the court was, 'My lord, unless I could know it by some other means, I might not.' All he could do in such a situation, he said, was to dissuade the person from doing it and refuse him absolution. Found guilty Popham pronounced the sentence of hanging, drawing and quartering.

At his execution Henry protested that he had never approved the Plot, and that the plotters had not acted as true Catholics because the horrible crime that they had intended was contrary to the teaching of the Pope. He was executed in St Paul's Cathedral churchyard on 3 May 1606, when stands were erected for the spectators who paid for their seats! He prayed 'Lord, fix thy cross in my heart.' Having finished his prayers Henry told the hangman that he was ready. As a result of the loud protests of the crowd, some of whom pulled on his legs, he was allowed to hang until he was dead. Eyewitnesses reported that he crossed his arms over his breast and hung motionless without any sign of struggle. As for what they thought of the affair, no one responded when his heart was held up; there was just discontented muttering. His head, which remained amazingly life-like for weeks afterwards, was stuck on a pole on London Bridge. There is no doubt that Garnet was

The Jacobean Martyrs, 1603-25

seen as a victim and venerated as a true martyr by his contemporaries.

The Church's attitude to him remains a puzzle; she has canonized priests who suffered death rather than break the confessional seal. For example Garnet's contemporary Jesuit, St John Sarkander (1576-1620) who at Olmutz, Moravia, was racked, branded, covered with pitch and feathers and set alight by angry Protestant zealots, but he would not breach the seal. Contrary to a widespread misconception, the saints are not perfect people; they were not, by some special dispensation of divine grace, exempted from sinning. They are just human beings like the rest of us, subject to the same temptations, from which they are not immune, but they strove heroically to overcome their imperfections in order to become more Christ-like.

Historians today generally apply the rule *altri tempi, altri costumi* - other times, other customs - meaning that everyone must be judged by the moral/ethical standards of their own time. But even allowing that completely reasonable principle, in Christian tradition there are certain moral standards that are held to apply to all people for all time. The fact cannot be avoided that the Church recognises as saints men and women who by today's moral judgements may not be regarded as 'whiter than white'. Take, for example, St Bernard (died 1153) who for all his beautiful writings on the love of God and his tender devotion to the Blessed Virgin, thrived on conflict, resorting to violently vituperative language and uncharitably partisan interference. Or the indefatigable St John of Capistrano (1386-1456) patron saint of military chaplains: a fiery preacher, but rabidly anti-Semitic and a ruthless persecutor of the Hussite heretics in Bohemia. Or St Pius V, personally ascetic and reforming, but a harsh and fanatically intolerant pope who expelled the Jews from the Papal State and countenanced plots against the life of Elizabeth I. Or the extraordinary Italian-American foundress, St Frances Xavier Cabrini (1850-1917), whose limitations led her to exclude innocent illegitimate children from her schools. Closer to home is the incomparable 'man for all seasons' St Thomas More who, for all his everlasting, luminous qualities of universal greatness, nonetheless pursued and interrogated heretics. He was also, inescapably, a man of his own time and in common with his contemporaries he approved of the burning of recalcitrant heretics as a punishment of last resort.

It therefore remains pertinent to ask, why the double standards apparently employed in Garnet's case? His name was included amongst those submitted to Rome as martyrs by the English hierarchy in 1880, but his cause made no further progress. One can only conclude that this was due to timidity in the face of anti-Catholic propaganda; but it has resulted in a great injustice to the memory of a good, holy man who died because of his faithfulness to his priesthood.

Thomas Garnet

Where life was slain and truth was slandered.

> *To F C in Memoriam Palestine*, Gilbert Keith Chesterton, 1874-1936

Thomas was born in Southwark, London, in 1574/75, the son of Richard Garnet who had been a fellow of Balliol College, Oxford, where he had been persecuted for his adherence to the old religion. Richard had been intended for the priesthood but married. He was in and out of prisons for about forty years and lost all his property. His son, prophetically named after St Thomas Becket, was educated at Horsham Grammar School. His uncle was Father Henry Garnet. Thomas became page to Lord William Howard, one of Philip Howard's half-brothers, before entering the newly opened Jesuit College at Saint-Omer at the age of sixteen.

In 1595 it was decided to send him with five other students - John Copley, William Worthington, John Ivreson, James Thomson and Henry Mompesson - to train for the priesthood at the English College, Valladolid. The students were accompanied by the Jesuit, Father William Baldwin who was travelling to Spain in disguise. The party set sail from Calais for Spain but encountered terrible weather in the Channel and the ship's captain decided to make for shelter in The Downs, the roadstead between Deal on the East Kent coast and the Goodwin Sands. When the weather calmed the vessel was boarded and searched and Thomas and his companions were discovered sheltering in the hold. Father Baldwin maintained his disguise as an Italian merchant who spoke no English, but he and the students were placed under arrest and the ship was escorted round The Nore, into the Thames Estuary and up to London, where they were examined by, Charles, Lord Howard of Effingham, the Lord High Admiral.

Father Baldwin was sent to the Bridewell where he met Venerable James Atkinson, who was a servant to Robert Barnes q.v. of Mapledurham. Atkinson had been arrested in the hope that he would incriminate Mr Barnes of sheltering priests, among them St John Jones. Under torture in the manacles he had divulged information to Topcliffe but stricken with guilt he was desperate to confess and receive absolution. Learning from a fellow prisoner that Baldwin was a priest

Atkinson asked him to hear his confession. The Jesuit was unsure what to do. If Atkinson was a government spy then Baldwin was placing himself in great danger by revealing himself as a priest. In the end he gave Mr Atkinson absolution after which he was tortured again and died two hours later as a direct result of the injuries inflicted. As Father Baldwin's real identity could not be established he was eventually released. He served as Rector at Saint-Omer 1621-1632.

The students were given into the custody of Archbishop Whitgift of Canterbury at Lambeth, who in turn sent them separately to different Protestant clergy with the object of converting them. Mompesson was the only one who agreed to conform. Thomas seems to have been confined in the house of Dr Richard Edes, Dean of Worcester and chaplain to James I, who resided at Oxford. Thomas was taken ill and sent home to recuperate under a bond to return to custody at Oxford on a specified date. But Thomas escaped and had to keep away from his family to avoid causing them further trouble. Taking ship, Thomas returned to Saint-Omer and made the journey to Valladolid, where he finally arrived on 7 March 1596, over a year since he had first set out.

Like so many other English students, Thomas experienced health problems in the Spanish climate. Having only just reached the canonical age, he completed his studies and was ordained priest in 1599. In August of that year, in the company of the future martyr, Father Mark Barkworth, q.v. he was sent to England apparently primarily for the good of his health. Travelling via Hyrache in Navarre, the two priests took ship to La Rochelle, where they had a brush with the Huguenots and the Puritan English merchants who plied their trade there. Finally the opportunity came to cross the Channel. Thomas tells us that having returned he wandered 'from place to place to recover souls which had gone astray and were in error as to the knowledge of the true Catholic Church.' For a time he was chaplain to Ambrose Rookwood at Coldham Hall, Suffolk. On 29 September 1604 Thomas was received into the Society of Jesus by his uncle Henry. He planned to go to Flanders for his novitiate but his plans were thwarted by the Gunpowder Plot.

In the witch-hunt after the Plot in 1605 Thomas was arrested near Warwick under the unfortunately chosen alias of Rookwood. By then it was known to the authorities that Ambrose Rookwood was involved in the Plot. Thomas was imprisoned in the Gatehouse and then in the Tower. Given that he had been staying with Rookwood and that his uncle was Henry Garnet, it was hardly surprising that the Council believed he possessed important information. He was roughly treated and rigorously interrogated by Secretary of State Salisbury, who

The Jacobean Martyrs, 1603-25

threatened him with the rack and other tortures. Another ploy was then tried: a letter alleged to have been written by his uncle was handed to him, but Thomas denounced it as a forgery. Sir William Wade, or Waad, Lieutenant of the Tower, had authorised Carey, Henry Garnet's jailer, to convey letters between him and his nephew in the hope that their communications might disclose something incriminating. Wade, of course, intercepted the letters and informed Salisbury of their contents, which were completely innocent. Thomas could not provide any information about the Plot because he did not have any to give. He was left in a damp cell in the Tower for eight months with only the bare ground for a bed, which caused him to suffer from back pain for the remainder of his life.

In the meantime the conspirators had all been executed. Ambrose Rookwood, who expressed his repentance for his part in the conspiracy, was executed with them on 31 January 1606 in Old Palace Yard, Westminster. Since the authorities were unable to extract anything incriminating from Thomas or to produce a shred of evidence against him, he was banished by the Council together with forty-six other priests in 1606. On board the ship that was taking them into exile, a royal proclamation was read to them declaring that they faced execution if they ever returned. They were taken across the Channel and set ashore in Flanders.

Thomas made his way to the college at Saint-Omer and then to Brussels, where he visited his old mentor, the Jesuit Superior, Father Baldwin, who directed him to the newly opened English Jesuit novitiate of St John at Louvain in February 1607. In September he returned to England. Just six weeks later, while ministering in Warwickshire, he was petitioned for by the Catholics of Cornwall, desperate for a priest. Setting off for Cornwall in November 1607, he ran into Anthony Rouse, a Suffolk-born, Eton-educated priest who had been sent into exile with him. A convert of Father Gerard's, Rouse had been ordained at Douai in 1592. When he returned to England he was imprisoned on a number of occasions between 1593 and 1605, before travelling to Douai after his banishment. Up to that time he had not given any indication that he was untrustworthy, but when he returned to England he apostatised. Rouse betrayed Thomas, who was escorted back to London. There he was first examined by the notoriously intolerant and authoritarian pluralist Thomas Ravis, Bishop of London on 17 November 1607. Thomas neither denied nor admitted being a priest, but he was offered the Oath of Allegiance, which he refused. After further examinations by Sir William Wade, he was sent to Newgate.

He was tried at the Old Bailey, charged with treason under Elizabeth

27, having been ordained priest overseas and had defiantly returned from exile. He was offered his life if he would take the oath but again refused. He suggested alternative wording of his own: 'I, Thomas Garnet, sincerely heartily profess that I will pay to my rightful King James all fidelity and obedience due to him by the law of nature and the divine law of the true Church of Christ'.

His offer was treated with derision. Thomas was found guilty and sentenced to death, the judge insisting that he was condemned not for his religion but for refusing allegiance to the King. Thomas answered, 'He who is obedient to his prince is not faithless. The prince issues a command: "If any priest returns to England, let him be slain." I have returned here and I consent to be put to death; thus I give my body to Caesar and my soul to God.'

On 23 June 1608 he was taken to Tyburn, where an immense crowd had assembled, including many noblemen astride their horses or in their coaches. On the scaffold Thomas declared himself 'the happiest man alive this day' and forgave by name everyone who had persecuted him, including Anthony Rouse, the priest who had betrayed him, the Bishop of London who had him imprisoned, Sir William Wade who solicited his death and the Attorney-General who had invented so many lies against him. 'May they all attain salvation and with me reach heaven.' He declared that he was a Jesuit priest and explained that he had not admitted this at his trial, as that would have meant he was his own accuser. Thomas was urged to save his life by taking the oath but he remained steadfast, maintaining that the oath was so worded that no Catholic could, with a safe conscience, swear to it. He prayed that God would turn away His wrath from the nation, and not lay his death to their charge. He said the Lord's Prayer and the Hail Mary, and as he was saying the hymn *Veni Creator Spiritus* the cart was pulled away. The crowd insisted that he be allowed to hang until they were sure he was dead. Thomas is the protomartyr of Saint-Omer, the first of many martyrs of that College, of which Stonyhurst is the proud successor. Some of his relics were preserved at Saint-Omer but were destroyed during the French Revolution.

(Suffolk born, Eton educated Anthony Rouse, was admitted to the Inner Temple in 1582. Reconciled by Father John Gerard he studied at Douai and Rheims and was ordained in 1592. He suffered terms of imprisonment in London. Justice requires that a note be added to the effect that Rouse deeply repented. He returned to Flanders in 1613 and was hospitably received and absolved by the Jesuits at Louvain, where Father John Gerard was then rector. He wrote a letter addressed to all the Catholics in England expressing his sorrow for what he had done.)

The Jacobean Martyrs, 1603-25

John Roberts

Put nothing before the love of Christ.

Rule of St Benedict, Chapter Four

The life of the remarkable Welshman John Roberts is one of the most fascinating and adventurous amongst the martyrs. The eldest of the three sons of John and Anna Roberts, he was born in 1575/76 at Trawsfynydd. This ancient Welsh-speaking village, on the shores of the lake (*llyn*) of the same name, was then in the county of Merioneth, now in Gwynedd and part of the Snowdonia National Park. Nearby are the remains of a Roman fort and amphitheatre.

Although John's father was a merchant his family could claim descent from the princes of North Wales. John stated that his parents were sympathetic to Catholicism but had conformed to protect their property, and John was baptised in the little Gothic parish church of St Madryn. Nonetheless he received his first education from an old, presumably Marian, priest. At the age of nineteen he matriculated at St John's College, Oxford, in February 1595/6. St John's was Edmund Campion's old college, and housed many Catholic sympathisers. John left Oxford two years later without taking his degree. Perhaps he would not take the Oath of Supremacy? He moved to London and was admitted to Furnivall's Inn, one of the Inns of Court. However, his law career was brief because in 1598, wanting to see something of the world, he secured permission to travel on the continent.

While in Paris he met an exiled English Catholic gentleman named Mr More, who was in the service of the Cardinal Archbishop of Bordeaux. More (was he related to Thomas More's family?) seems to have been instrumental in bringing about John's conversion. He was received into the Church by Canon Louis Godebert at Notre Dame Cathedral. Various introductions were then given to John, one of whom was Father John Cecil, 8 a relative of Sir Robert Cecil. Long before he met John Roberts, Cecil had been treacherously working as a secret agent for the English government, supplying it with information about fellow priests. Advised by Cecil and carrying letters of introduction from him, John decided to enter the English College of St Alban, Valladolid. Travelling via Madrid, John arrived at Valladolid on 15 September 1598. After only a few months he conceived a desire to join the Benedictine Order, but obstacles were put in his way. His Jesuit

The Jacobean Martyrs, 1603-25

superiors at the college felt that the cloistered Benedictine way of life was not conducive to missionary work and that by joining the Order outstanding young men like him would be lost to England. In the end John and five other students literally ran away to enter St Benedict's Abbey, Valladolid, where they received the habit. He was then sent to the novitiate at the great abbey of St Martin in the renowned pilgrimage city of Santiago de Compostela, reputed resting place of the relics of the proto-martyr of the Apostles, St James. Here he was known as Brother John of Merioneth. At the end of 1600 he was professed and sent to Salamanca, where the Benedictines had a college attached to the famous university. We do not know the date of his ordination but it seems to have taken place at Salamanca in 1602.

On 5 December 1602 Pope Clement VIII granted permission for the English Benedictines in Spain to work on the English Mission. Despite suffering ill-health from the climate of Spain and the austerities of his monastic regime, losing no time, on 26 December 1602 John set out to return to England with a companion, Dom Augustine Bradshaw who's real name was John White. [9] Making their way through Northern Spain, they arrived at Bordeaux and from there went to Paris. Here John met Father John Cecil again who, true to form, passed the information of John's return to an English spy; he in turn alerted the government. Although his movements were observed, John safely arrived in April 1603, having paid £3 for his passage across the Channel at night, and was put ashore while the rest of the passengers were asleep. He was the first Benedictine missionary to work in England since the suppression of the monasteries.

John made his way to London and made contact with two priests imprisoned in the Clink: Francis Barnaby and Thomas Bluet. They both enjoyed considerable freedom at the Clink, but unknown to John they were 'plants' amongst the numerous Catholics in the prison, supplying information to the government and the Bishop of London over many years. It was Francis Barnaby, [10] a malcontent anti-Jesuit agitator, who provided information about Fathers William Watson and William Clark that led to their executions after the discovery of the so-called Bye-Plot. Thomas Bluet was born in Monmouthshire in 1539. He became a Calvinist minister in Sussex but went to Douai in 1577, studying at the university. He was ordained in 1578 and came to England. Arrested in Berkshire he was sent to the Marshalsea, being moved in 1580 to Wisbech and then to Framlingham. After travelling to Rome under a government safe-conduct in 1602, he returned to London where he ended his days in the service of Bishop Bancroft.

A third person, a relative by marriage of John's, joined the conversation with the priests at the Clink and it is believed that this was none other than Lewis Owen. Some sources claim he was John's brother-in-law, married to John's sister, Blanche. But the name of Blanche's husband was Cadwallador Owen, a Protestant propagandist who later specialised in calumniating Catholics. It seems most likely that Lewis was the brother of Cadwallador. Lewis Owen had been acting as a pursuivant for at least two years before he met up with John Roberts. For a time Owen insincerely pretended to be a Catholic. Ironically, it is to Owen that we owe so much detailed knowledge about John Roberts. Owen informs us that John 'became very famous among the English Papists and many resorted to him, some of them out of curiosity to see a Benedictine monk once again in England.'

The outcome of the meeting was that John was arrested having been in the country only a short time. However, following King James's arrival in London, John was released into perpetual banishment on 13 May along with a large group of priests, among who was the almost blind Jesuit William Weston q.v.

John arrived at Douai on 24 May but soon returned to England, where the plague was once again raging that summer. Tens of thousands of people died and the coronation had to be postponed. John ministered to the sick and dying with incredible compassion, receiving the plaudits of his contemporaries for his heroic and selfless devotion and the number of those he reconciled to the Church.

He made a special point of actively encouraging young men with potential vocations. One of his most notable converts was William Scott of Chigwell, the future Benedictine martyr Dom Maurus Scott. 11 John's fame spread amongst the Catholics and he received many donations towards his work. In February 1604, King James issued a proclamation banishing all priests on pain of death. This coincided with John's attempt to return to Spain to attend the General Chapter of his Congregation. He was taking with him four young postulants, but they were all apprehended at the port of embarkation and John was imprisoned. Not knowing he was a priest, he was released after a few months. During the course of 1604 many priests were sent into exile and some sources claim that John was banished with them, but there seems to be no supporting evidence. The claim is surely refuted by the fact that so soon afterwards he was known to be working in London, and in 1606 John himself refers to his 'second exile', which seems to settle the matter

Using the alias Richard Browne, John lodged with Master Knight, a lawyer's clerk at a house in Holborn on the corner of Chancery Lane. We are told of his going out at times gaily apparelled in buff-coloured hose and a black silk doublet slashed with red taffeta and trimmed with silver lace, a sword at his side which, when they heard about it, somewhat scandalised his Benedictine brethren safe and secure in their Spanish monastery.

On 5 November 1605, the very day the Gunpowder Plot was 'discovered', John was arrested for the third time. It would appear that the actual owner of Master Knight's house was none other than the abandoned wife of Thomas Percy, one of the conspirators. She earned her living by teaching and she and John were good friends. Mr Justice Grange came to search her apartment for any evidence against Percy and John had the misfortune to return home while this was taking place. He admitted he was a Catholic and was detained by the constables. A great deal of his correspondence was seized in the hope of implicating him in the Plot. Some of the documents may still be read in the Public Record Office. The searchers must have been disappointed to find that they contained nothing of a political nature.

John was consigned by Archbishop Bancroft to close imprisonment in the Gatehouse, where he remained for nearly eight months. A fellow prisoner in the Gatehouse was Thomas Garnet, with whom John was able to regularly communicate in the later stages of his detention. By one of those quirks of fate, another prisoner was the Benedictine, Sigebert Buckley, [12] the last surviving monk of Westminster Abbey who, following the Plot scare, was again arrested and confined in the prison within the precincts of the Abbey. Dom Sigebert was eighty-eight years old and had spent forty years in and out of various prisons. At the end of July 1606 John, cleared of any complicity in the Plot, was released and banished following the intervention of Antoine Le Fèvre de la Boderie, the French Ambassador. Along with forty-six other priests, including Thomas Garnet, he was shipped to Dunkirk.

During his enforced exile of fourteen months, he was very active, visiting Paris, Valladolid, Salamanca, Santiago de Compostela and Douai. John and his companion, Dom Augustine Bradshaw, wished to establish a Benedictine house for the exiled English monks who belonged to Spanish monasteries. As so often with such enterprises, he encountered a great deal of opposition, much of it fuelled by pettiness, jealousy and rivalry. Sad to recall much of this came from the Jesuits who, for reasons best known to themselves, were still trying to discourage the Benedictines from working on the English Mission. Thanks largely to the generosity of the abbeys of Flanders and Abbot Philip de Caverel of St Vedast at Arras in particular - who provided the buildings - the house of St Gregory was established at Douai in 1606 with John as its first prior. By 1617 English Catholic boys were being sent there to be educated. (The school enjoyed such a high reputation by the beginning of the 18th century that Queen Anne told the Duke of Marlborough to spare it when he stormed Douai in 1710. During the French Revolution the abbey and school was plundered. The monks and boys escaped to England. In 1814 St Gregory's Abbey was re-located at Downside, near Bath, where it has remained.)

John Roberts returned to England in October 1607. In December he was arrested by a priest catcher close by St Dunstan's in Fleet Street and was sent to the Gatehouse, where he was rigorously examined by the Bishop of London, Thomas Ravis. It is from the extant record of that examination that much of our information about John can be corroborated. Once again his fellow prisoner was Thomas Garnet. John refused to take the oath and was left for some months in prison. But with the help of Francis Miles, a sixteen-year-old convert he had received into the Church during his last sojourn in the prison, he escaped from the Gatehouse by cutting through the window bars of his cell and climbing down with a rope.

A year after his conversion London-born Miles was one of thirty people who were arrested at Mass in Newgate but was later released. He spent a year studying with Thomas Garnet while the priest was in the Gatehouse. John managed to remain at liberty by staying hidden for nearly a year, despite the intense efforts that were being made to recapture him. By May 1609 he had been caught and was again in the Gatehouse, from where he was transferred to Newgate preparatory to his execution. He was again saved by the intervention of the French Ambassador and banished for the third time, along with a fellow Benedictine, Mark Broughton, and Francis Miles. The young convert went to Saint-Omer. After John's death he went to the English College, Rome, and was ordained by St Robert Bellarmine in December 1616. He returned to England in 1619 and worked on the Mission where he joined the Society of Jesus. He died in England in 1650.

While abroad, John again visited Spain and Douai, where he was able to set in motion plans to build a proper monastery for the community of St Gregory. Within a year John had returned to London, where the usual summer plague was raging, and his courageous ministrations were soon in demand. His final arrest was on 2 December 1610, when he was taken at a house on the first Sunday of Advent. He had just finished saying Mass in the presence of five other priests when the pursuivants broke in, and they all had to hide in the cellar of the house. Soon discovered, John was carried off, still wearing his vestments, and dragged through the streets to Newgate. On 5 December he was tried in the Justice Hall of Newgate prison before the Lord Chief

The Jacobean Martyrs, 1603-25

Justice, Sir Edward Coke, the Recorder of London and Dr Abbot, Bishop of London. On trial with John was a fellow priest, Thomas Somers,[13] who had been captured by Lewis Owen in the summer, sent into exile and was newly returned. Somers was first asked by Abbot if he would take the Oath of Allegiance. He replied that he would not take it in the form that it appeared in the Statute book.

Abbot then turned to John saying, 'Mr Roberts, you know how often you have been brought before me; what trouble I have taken for you, and with what kindness I have treated you, all in order to persuade you to become a good subject to the king's majesty, who has shown you such mercy.' From the extant accounts of the trial it is clear that John defended himself vigorously, protesting that the Bishop could not be his accuser and judge at the same time, nor should a man who calls himself a bishop be sitting with judges in life and death cases. Using the opportunity to bear witness to the Faith, he disputed at length with the Bishop and put the Catholic case convincingly. John strongly objected when the bishop introduced the subject of the Plot. 'It would be better for you to say not more about the Plot,' he remonstrated, 'as no one knows better than you do how entirely I established my innocence at the time before the Privy Council. So clearly was I justified that they declared me to be a man of good repute and in liberating me testified that no imputation whatever rested on me.' This the Bishop had to acknowledge.

In the hope of saving the jurymen from having to find them guilty, John and Father Somers acknowledged that they were priests, but refused to take the oath.

'I am bound", John declared, 'by my priesthood to do the duty of a priest and the reason I have returned to this country is to work for the salvation of souls.' Accused by the Bishop of deceiving the people, John responded, 'I do not deceive but try to lead back to the right path those ... whom you have led astray ... If I deceive then were our ancestors deceived by St Augustine, the Apostle of the English, who was sent here by the Pope of Rome, St Gregory the Great and who converted this country ... the same faith which he professed I now teach. Nay, I am of the same religious order ... as St Augustine.'

The Recorder told the jury, 'You have heard that he confesses he is a priest and this is enough for you to find him guilty.' To which John replied, 'If being a priest is equivalent to being a traitor then that would make Christ Himself a traitor.'

There were murmurings of discontent in the court, and John was ordered to be silent. He refused to be silenced: 'I must speak ... St Matthew says go teach all nations, baptising them and teaching them to observe all that I have commanded you. I am here to speak in defence of my faith and I demand to be heard.'

The Bishop of London proposed the Oath of Allegiance to John. 'What say you Mr Roberts? Will you take this oath or not?' John replied, 'Sir, you know very well what I think about this oath. I have not refused, nor shall I ever refuse to take any oath of allegiance offered me, which shall in truth be only such, but this oath contains other matters besides allegiance. I have before offered to prove this to you, and to point out what part concerns matters of Faith. If these parts be expunged, I was willing then, as I am now, to swear to the rest, which only concerns allegiance to my sovereign.'

The cut and thrust went on but it was of no avail. After a short time the jury returned the guilty verdict.

Three days later on Saturday, 8 December, the priests returned to court to receive their sentence. The Recorder made a violent attack on John calling him the most dangerous priest in England, who had seduced more people to popery and reconciled more of His Majesty's subjects than any other priest for years. When the death sentence was pronounced, John responded by forgiving his persecutors and promising to pray for them, not only in the time left to him in this life but also after his death. John was taken back to prison amongst the thieves and murderers.

Doña Luisa Carvajal y Mendoza [14] was a devout Spanish lady who had been living in London since 1605. Doña Luisa regularly visited imprisoned priests and had twice suffered imprisonment herself. Her confessor was Father Michael Walpole SJ, brother of Henry. Early in 1610 he was caught and imprisoned, but Doña Luisa, persuaded the Spanish Ambassador, Don Pedro de Zuñiga, Marques de Villa Flores et Avila, to intervene and after great difficulty Michael was released and expelled from the country. On the night before their execution, Doña Luisa bribed Simon Houghton the keeper of Newgate to transfer John and Father Somers from the condemned cell into the company of other Catholic prisoners. Houghton's wife had been converted by a priest prisoner and influenced her husband to be more lenient towards his charges. That evening Doña Luisa gave a dinner for more than twenty prisoners, at which she sat at the head of the table between the two priests. They were waited on by two young Catholic servant women from the prison: Margaret Ashe, a laundress, and Christian Darne. The eyewitness testimony relates that in a symbolic gesture the young women washed John's feet, then those of his fellow priests, several of them future martyrs, including John's convert, Dom Maurus Scott.

'Do you think', asked John, 'that my feasting in this way may be a cause of disedification? Should I not withdraw myself for prayer?' Doña Luisa replied, 'No, let them all see with what cheerful courage you are about to die for Christ.'

This episode caused a great stir. For some weird reason Bishop Abbot seems to have been obsessed by the pear tarts supplied for the dinner by Doña Luisa! King James wrathfully fulminated about the 'idolatrous' goings-on at such length that an official government enquiry was held. Its findings, containing detailed descriptions of all that had taken place at the dinner, can be read in the State Papers. Everyone involved was severely punished. Simon Houghton, Keeper of Newgate and his servant, Abraham Reynolds, lost their jobs and Doña Luisa was threatened with banishment; but this was not carried out after the intercession of the Spanish Ambassador, Don Alonso de Velasco.

On 10 December 1610, on a foggy morning, John, along with Thomas Somers and a group of sixteen thieves, was taken to Tyburn to die, before a dense throng. There are several eyewitness accounts of the martyrdom, one of them from a Protestant school teacher who had followed the hurdle on horseback to Tyburn and then stood close by the gallows. He recalled that 'Mr Somers had a sad, settled countenance as in strong meditation, for I marked him much and long ... sometimes seen to pray softly, his hands for the most part hid, and fingers indented one with the other; but spoke to no man, nor seemed to be moved with the company nor anything on the way.' Roberts showed 'a most cheerful countenance, almost always smiling when he looked up or talked, for sometimes he would lie with his eyes shut and his hat pulled down. After they came to the gallows, they stayed on the hurdle till the other sixteen had the ropes about their necks (which was more than half-an-hour), in which time one Mr Williams (to wit a minister) came to him - I stood close by them - and entreated him, now setting aside all controversies, to settle his thoughts on that main point, his faith in Christ for the salvation of his soul. He took the counsel very kindly and answered that he did so.' The crowd was so dense that it was impossible for the Sheriff of Middlesex to get the hurdle closer so the two priests were untied from the hurdle and walked up to the gallows. John, whose face was bright and joyous, was weak and ill and had not the strength to climb into the cart by himself and had to be lifted into it. He then asked the Protestant ministers to kindly desist from troubling him. 'You only trouble me and do not profit yourselves in the least' he told them.

Noting that he was to be hanged among thieves, just like his Master, he stretched out his manacled hands and tried to bless the thieves who were already on the gibbet waiting to be hanged, urging them to repent as it was not too late and to embrace the Catholic Church. The executioner began to pull off his gown and John asked the sheriff's permission to speak to the people and this was granted, but as soon as he began the ministers started loudly singing psalms. He turned to the sheriff saying, 'In courtesy, sir, remember I cannot be heard through that singing.' The sheriff commanded them to be silent. John's voice was so weak from his illness that someone in the crowd offered him a little aqua vitae which he gratefully accepted and drank a few drops. He began with *'Audite coeli quae loquor, audiat terra verba oris mei'* which he repeated in English: 'Hark ye heavens to that which I say, and let the earth hearken to the words of my mouth'. As the crowd listened in silence he continued, 'My lords here present, and all you others who enjoy with me the honour and the happiness to be natives of this kingdom of England, our sweet country, may it please you to hear that I stand now in this place ready to suffer the death to which I am condemned, for no other reason but that, being a priest, I must die ... I have not committed any other crime but this one; whence it is clear that I die for the cause of religion, the religion, I say, which is the same as that brought here in the days of old by St Augustine, Apostle of England, who was sent hither in the year 596 by the great Pope St Gregory ... He was a monk of the Order of St Benedict; I am one likewise. The vows of my Order, and the habit I wear, are the same as his, and I observe the same Rule as he did ... It is for these reasons that I have been treated as a criminal and condemned to death.'

The hangman began to bind him as customary and John called out in a loud voice *'Extra ecclesiam nulla salus'*, repeating in English, 'Outside the true Church there is no salvation. One God, one Faith, without that Faith it is impossible to please God.' One of the sergeants rebuked him for such words but the sheriff intervened saying that as long as he did not speak to the prejudice of the king he could not be forbidden to say what he wished.

Father Somers was then brought forward and John gave him a helping hand into the cart greeting him with: 'Welcome, brother and companion in the same glorious triumph.' They embraced and blessed one another with great affection, and they were allowed to exchange a few words secretly, no doubt to impart absolution to each other. As he looked at the fire that was being prepared to burn his entrails John cheerfully joked, 'I see you prepare a hot breakfast for us in the cold weather.'

A kindly spectator offered him a cap with which to cover his head as he had been standing in the cold so long in just his loose gown. 'Do not trouble yourself, sir', said John, 'Hereafter I shall never suffer from

The Jacobean Martyrs, 1603-25

headache.'

Father Somers then spoke briefly, maintaining his loyalty to the King but not in matters of faith. 'Outside the Catholic Church there is no salvation: out of Noah's Ark not one was saved,' he concluded. Suddenly they were simultaneously turned off the cart and left to hang amongst the thieves.

Due to the protestations of the crowd they were allowed to hang until they were dead. It was now after noon, and when the barbarities had been carried out on the corpses the severed heads were taken to be displayed on London Bridge. The quartered remains were thrown into a pit near the gallows along with the criminals. Two nights later, a small group of Catholics undertook the ghastly task of retrieving the remains, taking them to the house of Doña Luisa, who had prepared fine linen shrouds to receive them. The relics were taken across the Channel. Portions were given to Valladolid and Santiago de Compostela. The largest relics were kept at St Gregory's, Douai, where they remained until the French Revolution when they disappeared; but, most fittingly, Downside, the successor of John's foundation, still possesses a finger of Dom John Roberts, as well as a relic of Thomas Somers.

Why does the Church so preciously preserve relics of her martyrs and saints? Purely on a human level it is perfectly natural to want to have keepsakes of a departed loved one; perhaps a lock of hair or an article belonging to them. St Jerome (c.341-420), writing about the early Christian martyrs, said, 'We venerate the relics of the martyrs in order the better to adore Him whose martyrs they are.' And St John Chrysostom encouraged the faithful to kiss the relics of the martyrs 'confident that we shall receive some blessing' from those who are able to intercede with the King of Heaven, 'for they can be bolder of speech in death than when they lived.'

John Almond

Love is a greater law.

The Knight's Tale, The Canterbury Tales, Geoffrey Chaucer, c.1340-1400

John was born into a recusant family at Allerton near Liverpool in 1577, although Bishop Challoner claimed it was ten years earlier. His father had been heavily fined for years for his refusal to conform. John first went to school at Much Woolton with his brother Henry, but while still a boy, about 1585, he was sent to Ireland to be educated. Interestingly, John had an earlier namesake who also died for the Faith.

The first John Almond was a Cistercian monk in the time of Henry VIII. Under Elizabeth he was tried at York for his priesthood and imprisoned in Hull Castle, where he suffered greatly. He went blind and by all accounts became rather senile; yet was treated inhumanely by his keepers who just left him. Two Yorkshire Catholic laymen, John Fletcher a former York grammar school master, and Michael Tyrye, a BA of Oxford, who both served over twenty years in prison, performed the charitable task of looking after sick prisoners. They had already cared for Thomas Mudd, an old Cistercian priest monk of Jervaulx Abbey. Expelled under Henry VIII, Mudd had gone to Scotland, but during Queen Mary's reign he returned to Yorkshire where he taught children at Knaresborough. Under Edward VI he had served as a chaplain to Thomas Percy, Earl of Northumberland. For ten years from 1569 he had moved from house to house, sheltered by friends, until arrested at Boroughbridge in 1579 together with John Wright, another 'old priest' returned from exile at Douai. Edwin Sandys, Archbishop of York, had him committed to prison at York and from there he was sent to Hull Castle, with five other priests, where he died on 7 September 1583.

Fletcher and Tyrye also tended the Cistercian Almond as best they could in the appalling conditions. He died in prison on 18 April 1585 in extreme old age. As he came from Cheshire it would be fascinating to know if he was distantly related to our martyr.

Michael Tyrye was born in Wensleydale. He had conformed at university and it was not until 1573, at the age of forty, that he was reconciled by the future apostate, Father Thomas Bell, in York Castle. When this was discovered Archbishop Grindal had him committed to the lower Kidcote, in a vile, stinking cell were he spent sixteen weeks before being transferred to the higher Kidcote. Twice a week Dean Matthew Hutton would send for him to try and persuade him to conform. When this did not succeed he was moved to York Castle in 1576. In January 1577 he was transferred to the North Blockhouse, Hull, where, unable to pay the extortionate fees demanded by the keeper, with John Fletcher he was kept in a dark, damp cell, separated from all other prisoners, for four years.

Fletcher left an account of his long imprisonment. He was first committed to prison in April 1574 by Archbishop Grindal. He was moved around various prisons before being sent to Hull Castle, and then to the North Blockhouse. He said that the greatest cross he had to bear was the knowledge that his wife, who had been a prisoner in York

The Jacobean Martyrs, 1603-25

Castle for nine years, had secured her freedom by agreeing to conform.

There is some dispute amongst sources as to whether or not John Almond studied at the English College, Rheims. There may have been a confusion of identity between him and another priest called Almond, but there can be no dispute that John arrived at the English College, Rome, on 14 April 1597. The college records state that he was twenty years old at the time, thus disproving Challoner's dating. John proved to be an outstanding student. On 21 April 1601 he was ordained priest at St John Lateran. He publicly defended his theses - the 'Grand Act' - covering the whole course of theology and philosophy, to much acclaim, before two Oratorian cardinals, Francesco Tarugi, nephew of two Popes, and Cesare Baronius, the great Church historian. Because of his theological brilliance he was awarded a doctorate in divinity. On 16 September 1602 he left Rome for Douai, from where he departed on 10 November for England.

He worked in London using the aliases of Latham and Molineux. In 1607 we find him visiting George Blackwell in the Clink prison. Blackwell was born in Middlesex in 1547 and educated at Trinity College, Oxford, where he converted. He went to Douai in 1574 and was ordained the following year at Arras. Sent to England in 1576, he was in prison within two years but released. He then travelled widely, spending some time with the Gerard family in Lancashire. On 7 March 1598 Pope Clement VIII appointed him the first Superior of the secular clergy in England with the odd title of Archpriest. In the absence of any other ecclesiastical authority the Scottish secular clergy were also placed under his jurisdiction. It was a highly controversial and divisive appointment and some of the clergy refused to accept his authority, appealing to Rome against him. One must feel some sympathy for the man trying to cope with an impossible situation, albeit not very successfully. He exercised his authority harshly and censoriously and was described as severe, indiscreet and immodest. After the Gunpowder Plot, Blackwell was one of a group of priests who publicly defended the permissibility of taking the new Oath of Allegiance, in spite of the oath having been condemned by Rome. This put him into conflict with the Jesuits. Blackwell was arrested in June 1607 and imprisoned in the Gatehouse, where he took the oath in July. He was then moved to the Clink, where John Almond is recorded as giving him absolution in August. Blackwell's action in taking the oath was seen as a betrayal. It proved to be the last straw and on 1 February 1608 he was deposed. He remained a prisoner in the Clink, where he died in January 1612.

John Almond was arrested in February 1608 and imprisoned in the Gatehouse. He was freed sometime in 1609 and worked mainly in

The Jacobean Martyrs, 1603-25

Staffordshire for the next few years. He was back in the London district in 1611, proving to be an energetic and successful missionary, stiffening the resolve of wavering Catholics and making many converts. He was so highly regarded that the government was determined to capture him. He was arrested again on 22 March 1612. Described as, 'of stature neither high nor low but indifferent; a body lean either by nature or through ghostly discipline; a face lean; his head blackish brown.' It is recorded that his hair was streaked with grey, which is perhaps what led some to conjecture that he was older than his thirty-five years.

He was imprisoned at Newgate in appalling conditions. For twenty-four hours he was given nothing to eat or drink, and then only bread and water. Because of his reputation for learning and holiness the Anglican bishops especially wanted to obtain a recantation from him. Archbishop Abbot of Canterbury and Dr John King, Bishop of London since 1611, both interrogated John; but while declaring his allegiance to King James, he refused to conform in matters of religion. 'I do bear in my heart and soul so much allegiance to King James (whom I pray God to bless now and evermore) as he or any Christian king could expect by the law of nature, the law of God, or the positive law of the true Church.'

Dr King seems to have had a particular grudge against John and pursued him relentlessly. The record of his examination of John is so puerile and pettifogging that one marvels how he ever managed to attain his position. When asked his name John, giving one of his aliases, replied Francis Latham, to which the Bishop retorted, 'Your name is Molyneux.' John said, 'I think not', whereupon the Bishop said, 'I will prove it so.' One cannot help feeling that John may have had a wry smile on his face when he countered, 'You will have more to do than ever you had to do in your life' to prove that. The Bishop then questioned John about the circumstances of his birth, sarcastically asking him if he could not remember being born in a house. Turning the question back on him, John asked, 'Can you?' The Bishop replied that his mother had told him so, to which John responded, 'Then you remember not that you were born in a house, but only that your mother told you so; so much I too remember.'

Conditions in Newgate had gone from bad to worse and because of the severe treatment the priests in custody refused to give their word that they would not try to escape. On 10 November 1612 seven of them did just that. One of them was London-born Richard Cooper who had been ordained at Cambrai in 1608 and returned to England in 1609. By December 1610 he was in Newgate from where he escaped. He was said to have been the priest who converted the wife of Houghton, the keeper of Newgate, and it was believed that it was with her help that he had founds means to escape. It may be conjectured if he was the brains behind the 1612 break-out. Richard was back in Newgate from August 1613 to January 1615 when he again escaped with Father John Capes, who was also named in the proclamation for Cooper's re-capture. Richard was described as 'a short man, somewhat thick set with a camlet doublet of grey colour, laid on with black lace, with a pair of breeches of grey colour, having a brownish beard cut with a peak, round-faced, his nose bending downwards.' Capes came from Somerset and was ordained in 1612. He had already made one escape from Wisbech, was re-captured and imprisoned in Lincoln Castle from where he contrived to escape. Re-arrested again he was sent to Newgate, from where he absconded a third time in 1615. By July 1618 he was in the New Prison and that month was one of seventy priests the Spanish Ambassador, Count Gondomar, was allowed to take out of the country into exile. Nothing daunted, Capes was soon back in England and was in prison by October 1618. King James had made it clear that any priest who escaped from jail or who returned from banishment could expect no mercy but face the full rigour of the law. Given Capes record it is no surprise that he was sentenced to death. However, he was lucky given that at the time the negotiations were opening for the Spanish marriage and he was not executed. He died in London in 1628. Richard Cooper, who had also been quickly re-taken after his last escape, was back in Newgate in June 1618 awaiting banishment.

Among his six escapee companions in 1612 were Thomas Cornforth SJ, Henry Mayler and Francis Greaves alias Green. Mayler was raised in Spain and became a Doctor of Divinity at the Sorbonne. Where and when he was ordained is unknown. On 19 February 1612 he was prosecuted with Elizabeth Vaux for refusing the oath of allegiance. Elizabeth was sentenced to life imprisonment but released a year later due to ill health. At the trial Mayler is said to have 'run rings round' the Bishop of London with his arguments, challenging him to prove he was a priest. After his escape from Newgate he went to Douai where he became a professor of theology. In 1623 he was back in Spain taking part in the negotiations for the marriage of Prince Charles. In 1628 he left Douai for Lisbon to assist with the new seminary. Francis Greaves came from Yorkshire. He was ordained at Cambrai in April 1611 and sent to England but was soon captured. He was swiftly re-arrested after his escape and was still in Newgate in January 1615 when he was sent to Wisbech. He was banished in 1618 and served as a confessor at Douai until 1621 when he returned to England. It is known he served

The Jacobean Martyrs, 1603-25

the mission in Norfolk and he died in Holborn, London in 1673. The frequent re-arrests of apprehended priests suggests that they could simply be arrested at will once they had been in custody.

Poor John Almond appears to have borne the brunt of Bishop King's anger following the escape of the seven priests. He was incarcerated in a filthy dungeon, loaded with chains in total darkness and had only the damp ground to lie on. After nine months in prison John was brought to trial, a long and detailed account of which has survived. Sir Edward Coke presided. Almond comes across as courageous and prudent in his own defence. Dr King was one of the judges, and although John never admitted to being a priest and no proof was offered, he was, nonetheless, condemned for his priesthood. On 5 December 1612 John was dragged to Tyburn. On the scaffold he answered the arguments of the assembled ministers. One of them asked how he, being a priest, could come into the country against the King's laws. John told him, 'Christ is the greater King. Laws made against Christ's laws are not binding. In case I were a priest, which has not been proved, I should have a commission derived from Christ who said, "Go and teach all nations", to come and teach in England.'

John told the crowd of the continuous ill treatment he had endured in Newgate. He threw the remaining coins in his pocket, about three pounds in silver, to the crowd and addressed them: 'One hour overtaketh another and though never so long cometh death. And yet not death; for death is the gate of life for us, whereby we enter into everlasting blessedness. And life is death to those who do not provide for death for they are tossed and troubled with vexations, miseries and wickedness. To use this life well is the pathway through death to everlasting life.'

Although the day was cold and frosty, John was stripped to his breeches. With the rope around his neck, he knelt to pray, giving thanks to God who had strengthened him by his grace to shed his blood for the Catholic faith. All the while he was interrupted and harassed by the ministers present. He asked if it was not customary to have a handkerchief over his eyes, whereupon someone offered him a dirty handkerchief which he refused, but another handed him a clean one which he tied over his face. He asked that the executioner tell him when the cart was to be drawn away that he might die with the name of Jesus on his lips. At the signal he repeated 'Jesu, Jesu, Jesu' and hung for some time while the spectators pulled on his legs to hasten his end before he was cut down to be quartered.

His remains were retrieved at night and put in acid at the house of the Spanish Ambassador, Don Diego Sarmiento de Acuña, who served in London 1613 to 1622 and was created Count of Gondomar in 1617. Later John's bones were smuggled out of England, together with those of Blessed Thomas Maxfield q.v. They were deposited in the Franciscan convent of Saint Simon, on the island of Rondonela, off the North West coast of Spain, within sight of Gondomar Castle on the Galician mainland. Danger from marauding pirates, including Francis Drake, caused the removal of the relics to the mainland. Re-discovered in 1912, with full authenticating documentation, they were re-buried by the Count's descendants in the Gondomar Castle chapel. Some of the bones have since been given to Downside Abbey. Dr King is said to have later regretted his treatment of John but Catholic reports claiming that he was reconciled to the Church on his deathbed seem to be totally unfounded. King James had been misled by Archbishop Abbot into believing that John Almond was a rough, unlearned man and when he discovered the truth he was angry. Perhaps this was one reason why no other priest was executed for another three years; the longest period of relief since Cuthbert Mayne.

The Jacobean Martyrs, 1603-25

Notes to Chapter Five

1 The outstanding Scottish martyr of the Reformation period was St John Ogilvie. He was born into a Calvinist family at Drum-na-Keith, Banffshire in 1579. The son of a wealthy laird, Sir Walter Ogilvie, and Agnes Elphinstone, although there were Catholic connections as his mother's brother, George, was a priest. Sent to complete his education on the Continent he was received into the Catholic Church at Louvain in 1596. This was followed by study with the Benedictines at Regensburg. He joined the Society of Jesus at Brno in 1599 and for the next ten years served in Austria. He then worked in the French province and was ordained at Paris in 1610. He served at Rouen, Normandy but made repeated entreaties to be allowed to return to Scotland. He finally got his wish in 1613. Because of the penal laws he arrived disguised as a horse trader under the alias John Watson. He had hoped that he might find some Catholic nobles willing to assist him but he found that most of them had conformed, at least outwardly. He ministered in Glasgow and Edinburgh, making a point of visiting imprisoned Catholics. In 1614 he was betrayed and arrested in Glasgow. King James, to the mortification of the Presbyterians, had introduced a Protestant episcopate and the Archbishop of Glasgow at the time was John Spottiswoode. When brought to Ogilvie he gave the priest a stunning punch in the face. John responded, 'You act like a hangman and not a bishop in striking me.' Spottiswoode's servants thereupon savagely attacked Ogilvie and submitted him to sexual abuse. Under interrogation, while acknowledging James as his sovereign and condemning the Gunpowder Plot, he refused to incriminate himself. Every effort was made to get him to conform. In an uncanny echo of the questioning by Dr King of Blessed William Scott in London two years before, Ogilvie, when confronted by Andrew Knox, Bishop of the Isles, asked him if he were a priest, which Knox denied that he was. 'Then you are not a bishop', said John. He suffered terrible tortures, being deprived of food and sleep for nine days and nights by retainers of the Archbishop who jabbed him with their daggers every time he appeared to be falling asleep. His hair was torn out and he was repeatedly thrown violently onto the floor. Throughout it all he would not divulge any information about his fellow Catholics. The doctors, fearing that the continuation of the tortures would prove fatal, finally put an end to them. He was tried in Edinburgh for high treason and a set of questions relating to matters of church and state, composed by James himself, was put to him. John answered them truthfully according to his conscience. He was offered a rich benefice in the Protestant church if

432

he would conform. He managed to smuggle out of prison an account of his arrest and ill treatment. At his trial he declared his willingness to shed his blood for James, but could not accept the King's spiritual jurisdiction, which belonged to the Pope. He was condemned and on 10 March 1615 he was taken to Glasgow Cross for execution. On the gallows he vehemently and indignantly refuted any suggestion that he was condemned for anything other than his religion. He was asked if he was afraid to die, 'In so good a cause,' he replied, 'I am not more afraid to die than you are of the dishes when you go to supper.' He asked for the prayers of any Catholics among the crowd and threw down his rosary, which the Catholics scrambled to possess. With his arms pinioned behind his back he was ordered to mount the ladder, which he climbed with difficulty. In a loud voice he began reciting the Litany of the Saints. While saying 'Lord have mercy on me, Lord receive my soul,' he was pushed off the ladder and while he was slowly strangulating the hangman grasped his legs and pulled hard. Although he had been sentenced to be disembowelled and quartered, the reaction of the crowd led the authorities to omit this final barbarity. Placed in a coffin the body was buried two hours later outside the city in the graveyard reserved for plague victims. After John's arrest there was a wholesale round-up of his friends and followers who suffered heavy fines, forfeiture, imprisonment and exile. John was canonized in 1976.

2 Thomas Laithwait was born at Wigan in 1577. He went to Douai in 1598 and in 1601 was sent to Seville where he was ordained. He set off for England in 1604. He was arrested on arrival at Plymouth, imprisoned at Exeter and condemned but the sentence was commuted to banishment. In 1605 a storm drove the ship taking him into exile ashore near Lymington, Hampshire, and Thomas escaped. By then the country was in a ferment following the discovery of the Gunpowder Plot and he was soon re-captured in Bedfordshire and held at the George inn, Dunstable. He removed his cloak and sword and went to the stable on the pretext of watering his horse. Instead he led his horse into a stream and they swam across. It was some time before his jailers realised he was gone. Thomas made for Harrowden Hall, Northamptonshire, hoping to make contact with Father Henry Garnet, but when he got there on 15 November the house was surrounded and he was arrested. His captors complained that he was 'insufferably insolent.' He was sent to the Tower and in June 1606 Sir William Wade, the lieutenant, was instructed to put him to the torture in the manacles. By 1607 he had been released and joined the Jesuits at Louvain. He returned to the English mission and died in London in

June 1655.

3 Blessed John Sugar and Blessed Robert Grissold. John was born at Wombourne, Staffordshire, c.1558. After studying at Merton College, Oxford, he became a minister in the Anglican Church but in 1599 he went to Douai. He was ordained at Tournai 21 April 1601 and returned to England, where he served the mission in Staffordshire, Warwickshire and Worcestershire. Robert was born at Rowington, Warwickshire, and had been employed by a gentleman at Broadway, Worcestershire, before becoming Sugar's faithful servant. He had several unmarried brothers, all faithful Catholics; one of them, John, was a servant to Father Henry Garnet and following Garnet's capture in the aftermath of the Gunpowder Plot he had been arrested and almost tortured to death. On 8 July 1603, while on the highway near Rowington, John and Robert were apprehended by a constable named Richard Smith, accompanied by Clement Grissold, Robert's cousin. Clement told Robert that he was willing to let him go, but Robert said he would not escape unless he could take Father Sugar with him. This was refused and the pair were brought before Justice Burgoyne who, having examined them, had them committed to prison at Warwick. At the assizes held on 14 July 1603 they were tried before Judges Kingsmill and Anderson and condemned to death. The judge asked Robert if he would go to church and when he refused he was sentenced to be hanged for assisting a seminary priest. The two of them were left in prison for a year before being brought once again before the same two judges at the Summer Assizes, when the death sentences were confirmed. On 16 July 1604 they were summoned for execution. On that morning friends came to visit John who told them, 'We have not occasion for sorrow, but of joy; for although I shall have a sharp dinner, yet I trust in Jesus Christ I shall have a most sweet supper.' Seeing a Catholic woman prisoner in the jail weeping Robert said to her, 'Why do you weep? Here is no place for weeping, but of rejoicing: for you must come into the bridegroom's chamber not with tears but with rejoicing.' They were led out for execution, Robert insisting on walking through the mud behind the hurdle dragging John to the gallows saying, 'I have not followed him thus far to leave him now for a little mire.' The executioner was only about eighteen years old, and when he asked for the priest's forgiveness John replied, 'I forgive thee, boy, with all my heart.' Emphasising that he died purely for conscience's sake he prayed to be dissolved with Christ. He was cut down before he was dead to suffer disembowelling. His quarters were set up on the gates of Warwick. Robert protested that he was kept waiting so long after Father

The Jacobean Martyrs, 1603-25

Sugar to die because he wanted to have suffered with him. Before he was hanged Robert declared, 'I die here not for theft, nor for felony, but for my conscience.' The rope was dipped in Father Sugar's blood before it was placed around Robert's neck, the hangman calling him a fool for not saving himself by going to church. By the under-sheriff's permission he was buried near the gallows.

4 In addition to those martyrs numbered among the Forty, and those mentioned separately in the text, the twelve others who suffered as a consequence of the Plot were:

Blessed Robert Drury, born c.1568, came from a Buckinghamshire gentleman's family. He studied at Rheims and Valladolid and was ordained in 1595 by the Bishop of Leon. In 1595 he was at Seville before returning to England. He made his way to London and was found refuge by Father John Gerard in the house kept by St Anne Line. As his ministry was in and around the capital the house remained his headquarters until at least 1598 and perhaps longer. In January 1603 he was one of a group of priests, which included William Bishop, the future Bishop of Chalcedon and John Mush, Margaret Clitherow's biographer, who signed a declaration of loyalty to Elizabeth, while confirming that they acknowledged the Bishop of Rome to be the head of the Church. Drury managed to avoid capture until 1607, when he was apprehended with a seventy-year-old fellow priest, William Davies from Shropshire. They were caught at the house of John Stanesby in the Whitefriars area of the City. Mr Stanesby, his wife and servants were all arrested and examined by the strongly Calvinist Welshman, Bishop Richard Vaughan of London. Loaded with irons the two priests were sent to Newgate by the Bishop. Robert wrote an account of his arrest, imprisonment and trial. He asked the court's permission to shave off his beard and wear a cassock at his trial on 25 February, but this was denied. When the priests refused the oath they were condemned. William Davies, ordained at Valladolid in 1593, became music master at the English College, Rome. He was sent to England in 1603 and worked in Hampshire. Father Davies was taken to Tyburn with Drury but reprieved at the last minute and banished. Robert had the comfort of making his confession to a fellow priest-prisoner Anthony Hebburn, the night before his execution. (Hebburn, born 1567 in Co. Durham, was ordained at the Lateran in 1592. He was known to have been with the Clapton's at Waterhouse in July 1593. He was a prisoner in the Clink in 1608 and was still there in August 1611.) Wearing his cassock Robert was hanged, drawn and quartered 26 February 1607.

The Jacobean Martyrs, 1603-25

Blessed Matthew Flathers was born at Weston, Otley, Yorkshire, c.1564, the son of John and Agnes Flathers of Leeds. He was educated at Oxford, matriculating BA in 1590, when he was described as the 'son of a commoner'. He must have been forty-years-old when went he went to Douai in August 1604 with seven boys escorted by a Welsh priest, Father James Morris, q.v. and was ordained at Arras 25 March 1606. In company with Blessed Thomas Somers he was sent to England in June of that year and worked in Yorkshire. In 1607 he was arrested at Upsall Castle, North Yorkshire, together with Father William Mush, the younger brother of John, and the widow who was sheltering them. All three were tried and condemned, but only Matthew was executed. He was hanged, drawn and quartered outside Micklegate, York, on 21 March 1608. He was butchered in the most barbarous manner. They cut him down while he was fully conscious and he attempted to stand up at which one of the sheriff's men struck him on the head with his halberd and beat him to the ground while another held him down as the executioner ripped open his breast and tore out his heart. His execution caused such revulsion that even members of the Council of the North expressed the hope that no more blood would be shed in this way for religion's sake.

Blessed George Gervase was born in 1569, the son of John Gervase and Frances Shelley, a Catholic family of Bosham, Sussex. He was orphaned at the age of fifteen and there is an established story, repeated in many sources, that not long afterwards he was captured by pirates and was held by them for about twelve years, spending time in the Indies, when he completely lost his religion. This does not fit in with either George's own account of his life or the known chronology. George certainly went to the Indies on the final voyage of Sir Francis Drake which left Plymouth in 1595. Drake died in January 1596 off Porto Bello so the earliest that George could have returned to England and then become a student at Douai would be the spring of 1596. He was ordained at Cambrai in June 1603. His brother, Henry, who was living in Flanders in exile, obtained for George a benefice near Lille but he turned it down and in August 1604 was sent to the English mission. In 1606 he was captured at Haggerston Castle, near Berwick-on-Tweed, imprisoned at Durham and banished. While in exile he visited Rome, where he asked to join the Jesuits, but this was not permitted. He returned to England from Douai in 1607 but was soon apprehended. Having refused the oath he was hanged, drawn and quartered at Tyburn 11 April 1608. While in prison he had been professed into the Benedictine Order, to which he was probably admitted at Douai.

The Jacobean Martyrs, 1603-25

Blessed Roger Cadwallador was born into a yeoman family c.1566 at Stretton Sugwas, Herefordshire. He went to Rheims in 1590 and was ordained deacon in February 1592. In August he was sent to Valladolid, where he was ordained priest and returned to England in the autumn of 1593, serving the mission in his native county and Monmouth. He was a learned man and translated Theodoret's *Ecclesiastical History* from the Greek. He was unsympathetic towards the Jesuits and was a signatory to the declaration of allegiance to Elizabeth in January 1603. In the summer of 1605 he and Father James Morris became involved in the pro-Catholic demonstrations that took place in Monmouthshire and the borders; evidence of the scale of the survival of Catholicism in that part of the country. Morris had been married and had several children but became a priest after his wife's death, being ordained at Arras in 1600. By 1605 he was acting as chaplain at Garway, Herefordshire. Roger was arrested at the house of a widow, Mrs Winifred Scroope, near Hereford on Easter Sunday, 8 April 1610 and examined by Robert Bennett, Bishop of Hereford. He was brutally treated in prison being heavily shackled, even though he was ill. Because of an outbreak of plague at Hereford he was moved to Leominster, walking the whole way, still in his shackles. His sister-in-law attempted to visit him and was refused, but two Jesuit priests did manage to gain access to Roger, one of whom, Robert Jones, wrote an account of his trial and martyrdom. In gratitude for the Jesuits' kindness to him he left his books to the Society. Condemned for his priesthood he had to wait some months in prison before his execution which took place at Leominster on 27 August 1610 at around 4 p.m. in the afternoon. Because of the incompetence of the hangman, Roger hung for a great length of time, making the sign of the Cross in his pain. The bystanders tried pulling on his legs and when it was thought he was dead he was cut down. However, as he was being stripped ready for quartering he revived. When his head was lifted up on a halberd there was no applause from the onlookers.

Blessed George Napper was born into a Catholic family at Holywell Manor, Oxford, in 1550. Educated at Corpus Christi, Oxford, he was expelled in 1568 because of his religion. In 1580, at the time of the arrest of Ralph Sherwin and John Paschal, George was also apprehended for recusancy. There is a document dated early 1589 in which George Napper is listed among the recusant prisoners in the Counter, Wood Street, Cheapside. It seems probable that he had been a prisoner for the whole eight years. There is also a paper preserved in the Public Record Office, written in George's own hand, in which he professes his complete loyalty to the Queen and proclaims his intention of defending her with his blood if necessary, while stopping short of acknowledging her as Supreme Governor. His declaration must have had some effect because he was freed shortly afterwards. In 1594 he went to Douai and was ordained in 1596. He spent the next seven years teaching at Douai and Antwerp, returning to England in 1603 where he served the mission in Oxfordshire, sometimes staying with his family at Holywell. He was arrested on 19 July 1610 at Kirklington and being found in possession of a breviary and other materials was committed to Oxford jail. A long account of his arrest, trial, final imprisonment and execution written by a fellow prisoner is extant. The trial, at which his brother, William, was present, was the usual travesty. Through William's efforts it is probable that George would have been reprieved and banished but Dr John King, then Vice-Chancellor of Christ Church and future Bishop of London, intervened to prevent this. King examined George at Christ Church and when George refused the oath he was left to his fate. On his last day he gave away his possessions and money to the common prisoners, keeping only a silver half-crown to give to the hangman. His sister was present at his execution when he was hanged, drawn and quartered at Oxford, most likely in the castle yard, on Friday, 9 November 1610. The crowd prevented the hangman from cutting him down before he was dead and pulled on his legs to make sure that he had expired before the butchery began.

Blessed Richard Newport was the fifth son of John Newport and Anne Barlow. He was born at Ashby St Legers, Northamptonshire, in 1572. He was converted by witnessing the martyrdom of a priest at Tyburn. He went to Rome in September 1595 and was ordained at the Lateran 10th April 1599 but only returned to England in 1602. His elder brother, Charles, was also a priest and after the Gunpowder Plot a spy recorded that the brothers were hidden at Drayton House, near Lowick, Northamptonshire, the home of Henry, 4th Baron Mordaunt, who at the time was in the Tower suspected of complicity in the Plot. In 1606 the brothers were banished and returned to Douai. Richard was soon back in England and was arrested in 1611 and spent seven months in Newgate. At his joint trial with William (Maurus) Scott OSB Richard admitted that he was a priest who had twice returned from banishment and was convicted of treason. The next morning, 30 May 1612, which was the Saturday before Whit Sunday, between five and six in the morning, Richard and his companion were taken to Tyburn. One of Richard's Protestant brothers accompanied him. In spite of the early hour a great crowd had assembled with many noblemen in coaches,

The Jacobean Martyrs, 1603-25

including Anthony-Maria Browne, 2nd Viscount Montague and Thomas Howard, Earl of Arundel - son of Philip Howard - accompanied by his four-year-old son, Henry! Richard had to wait until William Scott was executed. He thanked God that 'he was come to the same place to suffer the same death' as the priest whose martyrdom had led him to the Catholic Faith and declared he was willing to lay down 'as many lives as he had hairs on his head.' He was cut down and butchered while fully conscious to the obvious disapproval of the spectators, indeed, the executions aroused general indignation both in England and abroad. There were many published accounts in various languages of the martyrdoms, which did great harm to the reputation of the English government.

Blessed Thomas Maxfield was the son of William Maxfield and Ursula Roos of Maer Hall, Stafford. Thomas was born in prison at Stafford c.1585, as both his parents were in jail for recusancy. In 1588 his father, William, was condemned to death for assisting priests, including his own brother, Humphrey, and Father Robert Sutton, who was martyred at Stafford in July. William spent almost twenty years in prison before buying his release in 1606. He was still under sentence of death when he died at his home in 1610. Thomas went to Douai in March 1603, but had to return to England shortly afterwards, having been judged an unsuitable candidate for the priesthood. He returned to Douai in 1612, but later that year there was a recommendation that he be expelled from the College for 'sedition'. That cannot have happened, because he was ordained at Arras in March 1614, returning to England in July 1615. He was arrested in November, in a London suburb, by a pursuivant called Wragg, who, in 1611, had been stabbed by a Catholic gentleman in Holborn, while trying to arrest a priest. Thomas, while admitting his priesthood, refused to take the oath before Bishop King of London, and was sent to the Gatehouse. On the night of 14 June 1616 he made an escape bid from prison by climbing down from a high window, but as he landed in the street the alarm was raised, and he was violently recaptured and put in heavy chains in an underground cell. On the 17th he was moved to Newgate in a terrible state of health and on 26 June he was condemned to death. The pleas of Count Gondomar, the Spanish Ambassador, on behalf of Thomas fell on deaf ears. The night before Thomas's execution Gondomar ordered solemn exposition of the Blessed Sacrament in his chapel to pray for the priest. Accompanied by the Ambassador and his household, Thomas was taken to Tyburn on 1 July 1616, to be hanged, drawn and quartered; little more than one year after his ordination. When Thomas arrived at the gallows he found that the gibbet had been decorated with garlands of flowers and the floor strewn with sweet smelling herbs and Gondomar's staff formed a guard of honour. The sheriff demanded that he be cut down alive, but the crowd protested so much that he was allowed to hang until he was at least unconscious. Anxious to prevent any relics being taken, the sheriff had a deep pit dug near the gallows into which Thomas's remains were thrown, and on top of them he dumped the bodies of thirteen felons who had also been executed that day. During the night his remains were salvaged by English and Spanish Catholics, put in acid, and eventually found their way to Spain with the relics of John Almond. Some of Thomas's relics now reside at Downside Abbey.

Blessed Thomas Atkinson was born in Yorkshire, probably at Leeds, c.1545. He was a 'late vocation' and after studying at Douai he was ordained in 1588 at Laon. He served on the mission in Yorkshire for twenty-eight years, enjoying a reputation as a zealous pastor, devoted to the poor. An account written by the long-suffering Lady Babthorpe, quoted by Challoner, relates that Thomas always travelled on foot in all weathers. He 'became so well-known to the heretics that he could not travel safely by day ... frequently passing whole nights without sleep'. Many times, wet and weary, he had to sleep in some outhouse because the householder could not safely admit him. One winter he fell and broke his leg which was badly set by a surgeon, which left him permanently lame. Afterwards he was obliged to travel on horseback. He was captured in 1616 at the house of Mr Vavasour at Willitoft in the East Riding and sent with his host and his entire family under guard to York. At his trial he would neither admit nor deny his priesthood, but he was condemned. On the scaffold he was offered his life if he would take the oath, which he refused. He was hanged, drawn and quartered at York 11 March 1616 at the age of seventy-one.

Blessed John Thules was the son of William Thules, the master of the local grammar school. He was born at Whalley, Lancashire, and baptised there on 28 December 1568. He was sent to Rheims in 1583, at the age of fifteen. From there he went to Rome in 1590 and was ordained at the Lateran 29 March 1592, by special dispensation, as he was still under the canonical age. His elder brother, Christopher, was also a priest, ordained at Rome in 1584. (Captured in Cheshire, Christopher suffered several terms of imprisonment, being committed to the Gatehouse August 1586, to Wisbech in 1590 and Framlingham in 1601. He was last heard of in 1622, a prisoner in the Clink.) A month after his ordination John was sent to England, predicting his likely martyrdom. About three months after his arrival he was apprehended in Northumberland, but managed to escape from custody. He worked on the mission all over England for twenty-two years, reported as being in Essex in 1605 and Lancashire in 1610. He was caught by William Stanley, 6th Earl of Derby, on 29 September 1615 at the house of Roger Wrenno at Chorley (see below) and the two of them were imprisoned at Lancaster. During a mass break-out from the jail John and Roger escaped. They walked all night, but discovered in the morning that they had gone in a circle and were re-captured only a mile from Lancaster. At their trial they denied breaking out of prison, stating that they had simply walked out when the opportunity arose. Roger explained that he had absconded 'so as not to die of hunger, as my brother had a little before. I had not eaten or drunk for two days.' This seems to imply that Wrenno's brother had died in prison. Offered their lives if they took the Oath of Allegiance they refused and were sentenced to death. During his ministry John had been less than charitable on occasions towards the Jesuits on the mission. He now deeply regretted this, and while awaiting execution arranged for a gold angel to be sent to every Jesuit priest he knew in the country. John and Roger were martyred together at Lancaster on 18 March 1616. En route to their execution attempts were made to forcibly drag them into a church. They succeeded in getting John inside, although his resistance left him with a head injury. Thules' severed head was displayed on Lancaster Castle and his quarters hung up in Preston, Warrington and Wigan.

Blessed Roger Wrenno was a weaver from Chorley, Lancashire. This is not the correct spelling of his surname, which some authors suggest might have been Warren. It was most likely Wrennal, and he may be identified with the Roger Wrennal, son of Robert Wrennal, baptised at Chorley in 1576. Roger was hanged for assisting Father Thules. When the attempt was made to force them into church, Roger successfully resisted, much to the anger of his guards. On the scaffold Wrenno was made to wait while they executed a group of criminals. When it came to his turn the rope broke and he was offered his life if he conformed but he re-climbed the ladder. After their executions, all the bodies, including John and Roger, were cut up in pieces and thrown into a heap so that it was impossible to identify which remains were those of the martyrs. The remains were left unburied for five days.

Blessed Thomas Tunstal was born at Whinfell, near Kendal, Westmorland. He went to Douai in October 1606, took the College oath in May 1607 and was ordained in 1609 returning to England the following year using the alias Richard Dyer. He spent four or five years in different prisons and around 1615 he joined the Benedictines. His final imprisonment was at Wisbech Castle, from which he escaped by letting himself down with a rope. He made his way into Norfolk and took shelter in a house near Kings Lynn. His hands were in a painfully bad way from rope burns which had become infected. He was recommended to seek the assistance of Lady Le Strange. This must have been Alice, wife of Sir Hamon Le Strange of the ancient family at Hunstanton. She kindly dressed his wounds and told her husband, who was a Member of Parliament and justice of the peace, all about the stranger and he quickly concluded that this must be the escaped priest whom he proceeded to have arrested, in spite of his wife's pleas. Thomas was committed to Norwich jail. Witnesses were brought at the next assizes to give evidence of his activities as a priest and he was condemned after refusing to take the oath. The next day, 13 July 1616, Thomas was hanged, drawn and quartered. He was allowed to hang until he was dead. His head was placed on St Bennet's gate and his four quarters hung from the city walls. A contemporary portrait of Thomas as a young man with abundant black hair and a moustache has survived.

Blessed William Southerne was born at Ketton, near Darlington, Co. Durham, in 1579. The son of William Southerne and Catherine Willey, he was baptised at St Andrew's church, Aycliffe, on 19 April. He was educated at the Jesuit academy at Vilna, Lithuania, then part of Poland, for six years before ill-health forced him to return home. He went to Douai before being sent to Valladolid in December 1598. There is some dispute as to the place of his ordination. Some sources claim he was ordained in Spain in 1604, but a report in 1615, from a man who had met Southerne, then living in rooms over a shop in Newcastle, states that the priest himself told him he had been ordained at Vilna. By 1605 William was back in England where he worked mainly in Northumberland and North Yorkshire. The precise date of his capture is not known but he was betrayed by William Johnson, another Durham-born priest, who had apostatised. A report states that Southerne was arrested at an inn by one Dales, a convicted murderer and a pursuivant in the service of Edmund, Baron Sheffield, President of the Council of the North, to whom William was sent. William was tried and condemned in 1618 which, for the government, was a diplomatically awkward moment because King James was deep in negotiations for a Spanish marriage for his son. Why Southerne had not been banished along with the seventy-four other priests in captivity at the time is a mystery. He was martyred at Newcastle-upon-Tyne 30 April 1618.

The Jacobean Martyrs, 1603-25

Apparently King James was furious when he heard the news of the execution, which he claimed was carried out without his knowledge. Whether that was true or not Lord Sheffield, whose commitment to pursuing Catholics was suspect because he had a recusant wife and many recusant relatives, was held to bear the responsibility and he was sacked.

In addition to these twelve martyrs other priests suffered and/or died in prison. George Fairburn, who came from Nottinghamshire and had been ordained in 1608, died of ill treatment in Newgate in 1615. The Benedictine, Father Robert Edmonds, was one of those who died in the Gatehouse in 1615. Also Chiswick-born Father John Maxey, who was ordained in Spain and served as a military chaplain in Flanders before returning to England in 1616. He was betrayed by his own father who urged that his son be harshly treated. After John's death in close confinement in the Bridewell in April 1617 his father instructed that he be buried in the prison rubbish dump. William York, born Kempsford, Gloucestershire 1581 was ordained at Seville in 1604, returned to England in 1605, and was in the New Prison in 1618. Kent-born John Windsor, a nephew of Sir William Windsor, was converted in Flanders by Father Thomas Sherwood. He returned to England where his uncle was in prison. When he was released John returned with him to France and studied at Saint-Omer. He was ordained at the English College, Rome April 1616 and came home in 1618. In 1621 he was in the New Prison. George Palmes from Yorkshire was ordained 1607 and joined the Jesuits in 1612. He was imprisoned at York in February 1621 and died on 13 August.

5 Blessed John Sandys was born in Lancashire and educated at Oriel College, Oxford. He became schoolmaster to the children of Sir William Winter in Gloucestershire. In 1583 he went to Rheims and was ordained there 31 March 1584. In October he returned to England and made his way to Gloucestershire to visit his old friends. No doubt through his connection with the Winter's he was entertained by the Dean of Lydney. The Dean had enemies, and hoping to get him into trouble, shortly afterwards they reported to the authorities that he had given hospitality to a priest. The Dean responded that he had believed John was simply 'an honest gentleman in Sir William's house' and had no idea he was a priest. John was arrested and tried under Sir Roger Manwood and condemned. He was martyred at Gloucester 11 August 1586.

The Jacobean Martyrs, 1603-25

6 Richard Norris was one of two priest brothers born at Milverton, Somerset. Richard was educated at Oxford and went to Rheims in 1578. He was ordained at Laon in 1579 and returned to England in August of that year when he became tutor to the children of Mr Owen in London. It is known that Richard said Mass at the homes of various Catholics in and around Holborn. He was closely associated with George Gilbert, the organiser of the band of young men who cared for priests on their arrival. As already related Gilbert went into exile in Rome. It may have been through Gilbert that Richard came into close contact with Edmund Campion. Norris was arrested in December 1581 and sent to the Marshalsea. He was tried and condemned on 5 February 1584 with thirteen other priests, including George Haydock and his four companions. Only these five of the group were executed. Norris was kept in prison until banished in January 1585. By May he was back in England but soon returned to the Continent where he died in 1590.

His younger brother, Silvester, arrived at Rheims in May 1585. At the age of fifteen he received the clerical tonsure. In August 1590 he was sent to Rome where he was a disruptive student, rebelling against the Jesuit discipline. He was ordained in the English College chapel by Bishop Owen Lewis in January 1595. He returned home in 1597 and, despite his earlier behaviour, had nothing but praise for the great kindness he received from the Jesuits in England. Following the Gunpowder Plot 'discovery', in December 1605 he was captured in Northamptonshire and sent to the Bridewell. He was one of the large group of priests banished in 1606. He headed for Rome and joined the Society of Jesus. He returned to England and died in Hampshire in March 1630.

7 Blessed Edward Oldcorne and Blessed Ralph Ashley. Edward was born in St Sampson's parish, York in 1561, the son of John Oldcorne, a prosperous bricklayer. Members of the Oldcorne family had suffered and died in prisons for their faith. Edward's father was not a Catholic, or at least he does not appear in the recusant returns; but his mother, Elizabeth, described in 1598 as 'old and lame', regularly does so and was imprisoned several times. She died soon afterwards in a York prison. Edward was educated at St Peter's School, York, where one of his contemporaries was Guy Fawkes. He intended becoming a doctor but in August 1581 he went to Douai, moved to Rome in February 1582 and was ordained at the Lateran 23 August 1587. In August 1588 he joined the Society of Jesus at the same time as John Gerard. He returned to England with Gerard and worked in the Midlands, mainly in Worcestershire, until the discovery of the Gunpowder Plot. Edward was

The Jacobean Martyrs, 1603-25

affectionate and self-effacing with an endearing innocence. He was also ascetic and wore a hair shirt. Father John Gerard relates the following story about Edward. He had developed a lesion in his mouth which became cancerous, for which he could find no remedy. He resolved upon a pilgrimage to St Winifred's Well, hoping to obtain some relief. While on his way to Holywell he stayed at a Catholic house and was told by the priest of the resident family that they had a stone that had been removed from the well. This was produced, and Father Oldcorne put the stone in his mouth, recommending himself to the prayers of St Winifred. Within a very short time the lesion had healed and Edward proceeded on his journey, bathing in the holy well and giving thanks for his healing. This must have been the occasion of the group pilgrimage that took place in 1605.

Ralph Ashley, sometimes called Raphael, was a Jesuit brother who had been a baker and servant at Valladolid. While on his return journey home to England Ralph had been captured by Dutch Calvinists and ill-treated. He met up with Father Oswald Tesimond in Brussels and early in 1598 they made the adventurous journey together to England - vividly described in Tesimond's autobiographical memoir. Ralph proved indispensable, as he spoke Flemish, and Father Tesimond accounted it 'a singular incident of Divine Providence' to have him as his companion. Travelling via Antwerp and then Middleburg, hoping to find a ship, they were hampered by the freezing weather and the blocks of ice that floated down the River Scheldt. They also had to be careful of the English garrison at Flushing, but found a Dutch ship willing to take them. It put to sea but had to return to port because of the foul weather. After a few days delay they eventually set sail. The weather was so awful the voyage took four days. They disembarked on the Thames, a mile or two downriver from the City of London, on 9 March. Ralph became the faithful companion of Father Oldcorne. The two were captured together at Hindlip Hall and were executed for alleged complicity in the Plot at Red Hill, Worcester on 7 April 1607. The day before the execution Father John Floyd SJ was arrested while trying to get into the prison to visit them. Edward died invoking the name of St Winifred. A number of relics of Oldcorne survive, including a rather gruesome one: his eye, which flew out of its socket when his head was struck off.

8 Father Oswald Tesimond was born in Yorkshire in 1563. He was educated at the free 'William and Mary' school in York where one of his fellow pupils was Guy Fawkes. At the age of seventeen in 1580 he entered the English College, Rome. On 13 April 1584 he joined the

The Jacobean Martyrs, 1603-25

Society of Jesus. After his novitiate he was sent to Sicily to complete his theological studies and afterwards he taught philosophy at Messina and Palermo. He was not sent to the English mission until November 1597 when he set out from Valladolid. He travelled to Bilbao, and found a ship ready to immediately depart for Calais. On board he found two other priests: John Ruffet and Roger Filcock q.v. (Ruffet, who came from Norfolk, had first returned to England in 1593 suffering from a serious illness that caused paralysis. In spite of this he was arrested on arrival, loaded with irons and was twice tortured on the rack. After his release he had gone back to Valladolid and been ordained. He was a prisoner in the Clink in 1602. Filcock was martyred with St Anne Line.) With nothing to eat or drink, Oswald endured a most uncomfortable voyage in a cramped space, lying on a heap of chestnuts, scarcely able to breathe as he was constantly choked by smoke. He landed at Gravesend 9 March 1598 and finally reached London, four months after setting out from Spain. He sought out Father Henry Garnet and was directed to a house called Morecrofts, near Uxbridge. He walked there from London and found Father Garnet in conference with other priests of the Society, and was given a warm welcome. After spending three days at the house they received a warning that a raid was imminent. Father Tesimond was amazed at the serenity shown by Father Garnet, who ordered anything of a Catholic nature to be hidden away and then counselled Tesimond and the other priests to take some refreshments and depart in the night, with the intention of meeting up again at Brentford. Tesimond and his companions walked until daybreak when, so tired they were hardly able to lift a foot, they were reunited with Father Garnet. They took a boat into London and at last found refuge at Father Garnet's house in Spitalfields. Living in the house was the aged mother of Father Robert Persons. Father Garnet looked after her for several years, often at great inconvenience, when he had to make hasty changes to his residence to avoid capture. Eight years later Father Tesimond found himself embroiled in the Gunpowder Plot. The proclamation for his arrest - still to be read in the Public Record Office - gives the following description of him: 'Of a reasonable stature, black hair, a brown beard cut close on the cheeks and left broad on the chin, somewhat long-visaged, lean in the face but of a good red complexion, his nose somewhat long and sharp at the end, his hands slender and long fingers, his body slender, his legs of a good proportion, his feet somewhat long and slender. His apparel of cloth, hose and jerkin much after the Italian fashion, the jerkin buttoned on the breast, his cloak buttoned down before with ribands hanging down on his breast, his hat narrow-brimmed with a

The Jacobean Martyrs, 1603-25

small band and a broad full crown, as now the fashion is.'

Oswald managed to evade capture and escaped the country in a small boat laden with dead pigs. He landed at Calais and made his way to Saint-Omer. He returned to Italy where he taught in Rome and again in Sicily. From there he was sent to teach at Valladolid and after postings at Florence and Naples he died in 1635, aged seventy-two.

There is another curious document in the State Papers relating to Father Tesimond. It illustrates the incredible gullibility of those making accusations against him. In 1610, Sir Edwin Rich wrote to King James from Naples, informing him that Father Tesimond had arrived and was plotting to send the King a poisoned, embroidered satin doublet!

9 John Cecil was born at Worcester in 1558 and educated at Oxford. He was ordained at the English College, Rome, in 1584. Cecil had at one time been a member of William Allen's household and had been sent by him to help in the foundation of the English College at Valladolid. By 1588, while in Spain, Cecil was already corresponding with Francis Walsingham. In 1591, trusted with delivering letters from Father Robert Persons SJ, then the Rector of the English College, Rome, Cecil betrayed him and several priests mentioned in the correspondence to Sir Robert Cecil. Back in France his superiors began to be suspicious about him, but amazingly he continued to enjoy their confidence and the friendship of prominent Catholics while continuing to supply the English government with information about them. Cecil had a colourful career in Spain, Italy, England and Scotland where he stayed with leading aristocrats. In 1594 he set out for Rome and was 'arrested' at sea by Sir Francis Drake. From his correspondence with Sir Robert Cecil it is clear that this was a pre-arranged subterfuge in an attempt to allay suspicions about his dealings with the English government. John was immediately set free. He carried on in similar vein until 1603 when he returned to England at the accession of King James. By now the government had decided it had no further use for him and he was imprisoned for a year before being banished. In spite of his wickedness and duplicity Cecil never seems to have formally apostatised. He died in Paris in 1626.

10 Dom Augustine Bradshaw (1576-1618), whose real name was John White, was born near Worcester. His parents were recusants. Father Edward Oldcorne, chaplain at nearby Hindlip Hall, introduced John to Father Garnet who arranged for him to go to Saint-Omer. In 1596 he moved to Valladolid. While suffering from a life-threatening illness in 1598 he made a vow to become a Benedictine if he recovered. John was

the first of the Valladolid seminarians to join the monastery of San Benito at Valladolid in April 1599. He was sent to Santiago de Compostela as a novice and took the name of Augustine. He was professed in 1600 and completed his education at Salamanca University. He returned to England with John Roberts in December 1602. In spring 1604 Bradshaw returned to Spain to attend the general chapter and ask his Spanish superiors about the establishment of an English monastery at Douai. In 1605 Thomas Arundell, Lord Arundell of Wardour, assumed command of an English regiment in the service of the Spanish Netherlands and took Bradshaw with him as chaplain general. The Jesuits, who resented a Benedictine being their superior, did all they could to get him dismissed. The plan for the Douai monastery having temporarily foundered due to Jesuit opposition, in 1606 Bradshaw was offered the old church of St Lawrence at Dieulouard, Lorraine. He frequently returned to England to supervise his Benedictine brothers working on the mission. He also spent much time in France where he was given the task of reforming a number of monastic houses. He died at the Cluniac Priory at Longueville, near Rouen. Contemporary accounts relate that Bradshaw was a warm-hearted, open-minded man with a winning personality, but he was also impetuous and not always prudent in his judgements. Without the assistance of John Roberts it is unlikely he would have succeeded as well as he did.

11 Francis Barnaby was born at Barnby, near Cawthorne, Yorkshire, in 1573. He was educated at Oxford and one of the Inns of Court. He went to Rheims in 1591 and was sent to Rome in 1593. He was ordained at Santa Maria in Aquiro, Rome, 30 November 1598. By June 1599 he was a prisoner in the Marshalsea but this was just a ruse to enable him to inform on his fellow Catholics. In 1601 he was sent to Framlingham Castle where he sided with the anti-Jesuit minority. He and Thomas Bluet q.v. were apparently banished in 1601 but, in fact, they were given safe-conducts to travel to Rome to press their case against the Jesuits. Barnaby got no further than Douai and after a somewhat turbulent short stay at the College he returned to England. In April 1602 he was purportedly a prisoner in the Clink. In truth he had liberty to come and go as he pleased, not only in England but overseas, treating the jail as no more than a place of lodging while supplying information to Bishop Bancroft of London. He had the nerve to sign the Protestation of Allegiance to Elizabeth in 1603. After many comings and goings, all for the purposes of spying, he was living in the Clink again by 1 November 1603. It was at this time that he supplied the government

The Jacobean Martyrs, 1603-25

with information about the Bye-Plot, leading to the apprehension and execution of Fathers William Watson and William Clark. In 1604 Barnaby was granted a pardon by the Archbishop of Canterbury, presumably because he had apostatised. He turned up in Ireland where he took the Oath of Allegiance in 1612. In 1621 he was living at his home at Barnby and supplying the Archbishops of York and Canterbury with information. The man was clearly an unprincipled scoundrel.

12 Blessed William (Maurus) Scott came from Chigwell, Essex. He was educated at Cambridge and became a Catholic. He went to Spain in 1604 and joined the Benedictines at San Facundo Abbey, Sahagun, taking the name of Maurus. He returned to England and worked for a year before being arrested and banished. This was repeated a number of times until 1612 when, thanks to the fanatical fury of Archbishop Abbot, he was finally apprehended. He was examined by Dr King, Bishop of London, who asked him, 'Are you a priest?' To which Maurus responded, 'My Lord, let me ask you, are *you* a priest?' 'No', was the Bishop's reply. 'No priest, no bishop', Maurus countered. He was condemned and hanged, drawn and quartered at Tyburn in the company of the Northamptonshire priest, Blessed Richard Newport q.v.

13 Dom Sigebert Buckley (1517-1610) is the link between the medieval monastic world and today's English Benedictines. He had been clothed as a monk in 1558 by Abbot Feckenham of Westminster. On 21 November 1607 two monks, Robert (or Walter) Sadler and Edward Mayhew, sought out Buckley in his cell in the Gatehouse prison where they were professed by him and Dom Thomas Preston, their superior. Roland Preston was ordained priest at Rome in 1590. He joined the Benedictines at Monte Cassino in 1592 taking the religious name of Thomas. He returned to England in 1603 and was arrested and imprisoned in the Gatehouse. He was later moved to the Clink where he remained for many years until released on a royal warrant in 1636. He died in London in April 1640. Sadler was ordained at Rheims in 1592 and the following year returned to England. He became a Benedictine as Dom Vincent. He died in London in 1621. Mayhew was born into a Catholic family near Salisbury in 1569. With his brother, Henry, he entered the English College at Rheims in 1583. He moved to Rome and was ordained by Bishop Owen Lewis in 1594, leaving for the English mission in 1595. Having served twelve years he joined the Benedictines. Dom Sigebert aggregated Sadler and Mayhew to Westminster and the English Congregation. In 1609 this was ratified by

the general chapter of the Congregation and confirmed by Pope Paul V Borghese (1605-21). Dom Sigebert, by now blind, spent his last years in Hampshire, dying in 1610 at the age of ninety-three, and was secretly buried. By 1612 there were seven of these monks, and in 1615 they occupied as their monastery the abandoned church of St Lawrence at Dieulouard in Lorraine. Mayhew was prior of St Lawrence's from 1613 to 1620. From 1623, until his death on 14 September 1625, he was chaplain to the priory of English Benedictine nuns at Cambrai and was buried there in the church of St Vedast. The priory had been founded in 1623 by nine young women, headed by Helen More, (in religion Sister Gertrude) daughter of Cresacre More and Elizabeth Gage, and the great-great-grandaughter of St Thomas More. Cresacre, of Barnburgh Hall, South Yorkshire, and a biographer of his martyred great-grandfather, had provided the original endowment for the convent. Catherine Gascoigne, daughter of Sir John Gascoigne and Anne Ingleby of Barnbow Hall, Barwick-in-Elmet, Yorkshire, was elected head of the community and served as abbess until 1676. The nuns were trained in the spiritual life by Dom Augustine Baker. The priory became the abbey of Our Lady of Consolation in 1641. In 1794, during the French Revolution, the nuns were expelled and eventually settled at Stanbrook Abbey, near Malvern, Worcestershire. Since 2009 a new Stanbrook Abbey has been located at Wass, North Yorkshire. Also as a result of the French Revolution, St Lawrence's, Dieulouard is now represented by Ampleforth Abbey in North Yorkshire.

Henry Mayhew, Edwards's brother, was ordained at Valladolid in 1592. He served at Seville until 1600 when he was sent to England. In 1611 he was arrested in Wiltshire and imprisoned at Newgate, where he remained until banished in 1613. He died at Douai in 1616.

14 Blessed Thomas Somers, whose alias on the mission was Wilson, was born at Skelsmergh, Westmorland. For some years he was a schoolmaster at a private Catholic school in the house of the Earl of Westmorland. Some of his pupils continued their education at Douai. In February 1605 he followed them and was ordained at Arras on 25 March. On 30 June 1606 he returned to England in the company of Father Matthew Flathers and was based in London. He may have lodged in Chancery Lane with his cousin, Mrs Cosins. In July 1610 he was apprehended by Lewis Owen, the informer, and was banished in the company of twenty other priests. They landed at Boulogne and Thomas made his way to Douai. He stayed for a time in Paris before returning to England on 29 October, but was soon recaptured and committed to Newgate until his martyrdom.

15 Doña Luisa de Carvajal y Mendoza (1568-1614) was born in Extremadura. She came from a noble Spanish family. She was left an orphan at a young age and was raised by her maternal uncle, the Count of Almazan, Viceroy of Navarre. He carried his religious asceticism to the point of fanaticism and encouraged his niece to some shockingly inhuman mortifications, such as being whipped and humiliated by her servants. Luisa felt especially drawn to England and, much moved by the martyrdom of Henry Walpole, she decided to learn English. She used part of her share of the family fortune to fund the Jesuit College at Louvain. This was transferred to Watten near Saint-Omer in 1612. Accompanied by William Davies, a Welsh priest ordained at Valladolid in 1603 and a nephew of the martyr of the same name, who had also baptised him, she went to England in 1605. She carried on a charitable ministry winning converts partly by giving help to poor women and taking care of their children. These activities led to her arrest in 1608. The intervention of Don Pedro de Zuñiga, the Spanish Ambassador, soon obtained her release. Following the martyrdom of Maurus Scott and Richard Newport, she organised the retrieval of their bodies at night and had them taken to her house. Father Michael Walpole, the future Jesuit Superior, used Doña Luisa's house at Spitalfields as his headquarters and acted as her confessor. After his banishment in 1610 Father Michael had returned to England in 1613 in the suite of the new Spanish ambassador, Don Diego Sarmiento de Acuña, future Count of Gondomar. Shortly afterwards Doña Luisa's house was violently raided. The house was virtually a secret convent and it may have been in the hope of capturing Father Walpole that the pursuivants were sent by Archbishop Abbot of Canterbury. Father Michael pretended to be a Spanish servant and evaded capture. Although she was arrested again, Doña Luisa was released through Spanish influence. The Spanish government was beginning to fear Doña Luisa was becoming a source of friction between their country and England and ordered her to return to Spain. Before she could do so, assisted by Father Michael, she died at the Spanish ambassador's residence in London on 2 January 1614; her 46th birthday. Father Michael collected all Doña Luisa's papers and accompanied her body to Spain in 1615. He died at Seville in 1620. In her will Doña Luisa left 14,000 ducats for the English mission.

451

Chapter Six

Charles I and the Civil War Martyrs, 1625-49

Adversity is not without comforts and hopes.

Essays, Francis Bacon, 1561-1626

The twenty-five-year-old Charles I, with his elevated and unshakeable belief in the divine right of kings, succeeded to the throne in March 1625. With his humane and cultured outlook and a Catholic wife, hopes were once more raised of toleration under the new monarch. In the final years of his father's reign the deposed Archpriest, George Blackwell, had been succeeded by George Birket, who died in April 1614, and in February 1615 William Harrison was appointed the third and last archpriest. He continued to petition Rome for a bishop until his death in May 1621. Harrison's pleas finally came to fruition two years later when, in 1623, seventy-year-old William Bishop 1 was appointed by Pope Gregory XV Ludovisi (1621-1623), to serve in England as Vicar Apostolic; the first Catholic bishop since the deposition of the hierarchy by Elizabeth. He landed at Dover about midnight on 31 July and despite his age, with a companion for guide, he walked through the stormy night the thirteen miles to the home of Sir William Roper, where he rested before continuing his journey into London the following day. (Sir William was a great-grandson of Sir Thomas More, his grandmother being Margaret Roper neé More.) In London he was given shelter by the widowed Lady Mary Dormer. At the time Prince Charles was in Spain, hoping to win the hand of the Infanta, the daughter of Philip IV, so there was a breathing space of toleration while the delicate negotiations were taking place. This, no doubt, influenced Rome in acceding to the demand of the clergy for a bishop in England. The negotiations failed, because the unsurprisingly high price demanded by Spain and Pope Gregory XV for granting the necessary dispensation for the marriage was a guarantee of some improvement in the situation of English Catholics. Given the attitude of Parliament, King James would never have been able to give such a pledge even if he had been minded to do so.

The Lord Chancellor, John Williams, Bishop of Lincoln, wrote to the Duke of Buckingham, then in Spain with Prince Charles, about William Bishop's arrival.

Dr Bishop, the new Bishop of Chalcedon, is come to London privately and I am much troubled thereabouts, not knowing what to advise H.M ... the only counsel were to let the judges proceed with them presently, hang him out of the way and the King to blame my lord of Cantuar or myself for it ... It is a most insolent part and an offence, as I take it, against our common law for an Englishman to take such a consecration without the King's consent, and especially to use any episcopal jurisdiction in this Kingdom without the royal assent ...

Bishop spent the summer travelling around administering confirmation. He set up a Chapter of twenty-four canons headed by a dean and divided the country into archdeaconries. The Chapter was to be a source of much division and controversy for years to come. William had planned a visitation of the whole of England but he died on 13 April 1624 while staying in Essex with Sir Basil Brooke whose son-in-law was Thomas More, a great-great-grandson of Sir Thomas. His successor, Richard Smith 2 was ordained bishop at Paris in January 1625 and arrived in England one month after Charles's accession. Opposition, both from the government - which issued warrants for his arrest in 1628 and 1629 - and from within his own flock, led to his retirement to France in August 1631. He never relinquished his authority until his death. His lasting legacy was his 'Chalcedon' catalogue of the English martyrs. The forerunner of all later works, it was based upon prison and court records that disappeared long ago. England had to wait thirty years before it received another bishop under Charles's younger son, James II.

The early years of Charles's reign were a time of relative peace for Catholics, and the numbers of priests steadily increased. Many in the Established Church began to regret the executions. Charles certainly found the idea of executing people for their religion abhorrent, but he had to tread cautiously. Although he had made promises at the time of his marriage to Henrietta Maria of France to repeal the most oppressive penal laws, Parliament had forced him to break his word. But Charles tried to circumvent the continued persecution of Catholics by Parliament and did his best in his own dithering way to reprieve priests. At the time when his most able and loyal minister, Thomas Wentworth, Earl of Strafford, was judicially murdered by attainder of Parliament in 1641, Charles, desperate to save Strafford, sought the advice of the Anglican bishops about defying Parliament and granting a reprieve. The Bishops advised him that he had two consciences, a public one and a private one. Thus, 'his public conscience as a King might not only dispense with, but oblige him to do, that which was against his conscience as a man.' And these were the prelates who accused the Jesuits of casuistry! (Charles gave way to Parliament and acquiesced in Strafford's execution; an action that haunted him with guilt for the rest of his life.) One wonders if similar advice was the self-justification he also adopted when yielding to other acts that were against his conscience, as in the case of signing the death warrants of condemned priests. With critical hindsight, it is easy to judge Charles, but what would we have done in his position?

The King often reprieved priests at the request of the Queen, whom he came to love deeply. She was a great benefactor of Douai College as well as being the god-daughter of Pope Urban VIII. Henrietta Maria had her own public chapel at Court served by several chaplains. The first English priest to be so appointed was George Leyburn in 1631. This was in the same month that Bishop Richard Smith left England for France. (Leyburn's appointment did little to protect him as a warrant was issued for his arrest in 1633 and he seems to have gone into hiding for several years.) Such open practice of Catholicism outraged the Protestants, who saw it as thinly disguised proselytising. There were a significant number of conversions by prominent figures of the reign, although Charles made known his disapproval and one, Walter Montagu, [3] was ordered by the King to absent himself from Court. At Somerset House in 1632 Henrietta Maria had built a splendid chapel staffed by a small community of resident French Capuchin Franciscans. They maintained a full round of daily services from 6 a.m. to Compline. The Catholics of the capital flocked to the chapel; the one place where they knew they would be able to worship in security. On the occasions when the morally chaste, music and art-loving Charles visited his wife at Somerset House, he would inspect the chapel and one of the Capuchin fathers recorded that he observed the King watching from a window the constant coming and going of the crowds. Once Charles joined the Queen and the company of Capuchins in their simple supper. It infuriated the Puritans. Their fanaticism blinded them to the fact that this was nothing more than a reflection of the King's innate courtesy towards the priests, whose cultivated conversation he appreciated. Such socialising may have been unwise and indiscreet but because Charles did not share the popular prejudices of many of his subjects, fatally he did not understand them or make allowances for them. Catholics were also able to readily frequent the chapels at the foreign embassies in London, which they did in large numbers. Attempts were even made to re-establish religious life by the Yorkshirewoman Mary Ward. [4]

Papal agents were received at Court, ostensibly as envoys to the Queen. The first of them was the Benedictine, Father Leander who compiled a report claiming that there were in England at that time 500 secular priests, about 250 Jesuits and 10 Benedictines. Leander was replaced by an Oratorian, the Italian Father Gregorio Panzani. He was

Charles I and the Civil War Martyrs, 1625-49

sent in 1632 by Cardinal Antonio Barberini, nephew of Pope Urban VIII, with a commission to investigate at first-hand the state of English Catholicism. He recognised that a bishop was necessary and played a part in reconciling the differences between the regulars and the secular clergy. He often had discussions about reunion of the Church of England with the Catholic Church with Secretary of State Sir Francis Windebank, and was received secretly by the King. He also had communications with the High Church Bishop of Chichester, Richard Montagu, about the possibility of reunion with Rome. Panzani was recalled to Rome in 1634 and became a bishop. He wrote an account of his time in England. He was followed from 1636 to 1639 by Douai-educated Father George Con, a Canon of St John Lateran and, like the Queen's confessor, the Oratorian, Robert Philip, a charming Scotsman whose company Charles particularly enjoyed. He was succeeded by the youthful priest, Carlo Rossetti, who used the pseudonym Count Rossetti. He was close to Queen Henrietta Maria but given the conflict in England at the time his mission was particularly difficult. He used what influence he had at Court to try and get priests exiled rather than executed. In 1641 Rossetti was summoned to the House of Commons but he fled England before the order from Parliament for his expulsion could be implemented. He later became a bishop and cardinal. The Pope sent gifts to the King to add to his already impressive art collection, but it did not stop Charles from using his influence to get Rome to quash all attempts to inaugurate proceedings for the canonization of Father Henry Garnet as a martyr.

Charles, a sincerely religious King, was far from being Catholic; indeed, he achieved the nearest thing to canonization in the Church of England for his faithfulness to the Church of which he was Supreme Governor. There are Anglican churches dedicated to King Charles the Martyr. The first monarch to be raised as a member of the Established Church, it was perhaps this certitude about his own Church that enabled him to be more tolerant of Catholicism. So sure was he of his position that, probably on the advice of Archbishop Laud, he determined to bring the Scottish Presbyterian Church into line with the Church of England. The rabid Scots Calvinists looked upon Anglicanism as little better than popery. When his Scottish subjects rejected all attempts to impose the Church of England Prayer Book on them the King took up arms in 1639 and marched towards Scotland, with the aim of imposing the Anglican liturgy. He demanded that his Catholic subjects heavily contribute to the cost of the expedition with men and money. His forces were defeated and Charles was forced to make concessions to the Scots. As we know with hindsight, this ill-conceived venture was the start of his undoing.

In his liturgical tastes, Charles was what today would be described as High Church. He personally accepted many of the Catholic Church's doctrines and reverenced the Virgin Mary and the saints. In York he had reconstructed part of the shrine of St William at the Minster. Like many Anglicans then and in later times, he called himself a Catholic, but that did not mean embracing the papacy; although he regretted the break with Rome and wished that more time could be spent in working towards reunion than in acrimonious controversy. The problem was that Charles was surrounded by those who shared his religious views, but they were in a minority.

It was all grist to the mill for his Puritan opponents who, in their ignorance, viewed the King's position as but one remove from papistry. He was supported (or was it the other way around?) by his Archbishop of Canterbury, William Laud (1573-1645), who also eventually paid for his convictions with his life. Laud, who used all his authority to try and enforce his doctrinal and liturgical ideas, seems to have genuinely sought better relations with Rome. If the Civil War had not erupted, how different could the history of the Catholic Church in England have been? The question will remain one of those tantalising 'might have beens' of history.

By 1628 Parliament demanded that the King rigorously enforce the penal laws and an act came into force (3 Car.1, iii); the only new piece of penal legislation of the reign, forbidding anyone to send their children abroad for a Catholic education. This was the only year in which Catholics were put to death. These were the Jesuit Edmund Arrowsmith and Richard Herst, a layman. After their condemnations, the executions were deliberately carried out with all speed to ensure that the royal reprieve would arrive too late. During the years of the King's personal rule without a Parliament from 1629 to 1640 there was an extended period of toleration. The penal laws remained in force, but although priests were condemned to death by the courts, thanks to Charles and his wife they were not executed. All that being said we must not paint too rosy a picture. Catholics were made to pay - literally - for their comparative toleration, and were frequently reminded that the favour they were enjoying was merely toleration, not approval. There was no change in policy, and Catholics remained subject to iniquitous fines for their recusancy. The Assize Judges were ruthless in insisting upon the enforcement of the Statutes. In 1635 a group of poor Catholics were prisoners in York Castle, deeply in arrears, as they were unable to pay their accumulated recusancy fines. They were summoned before Mr Justice Crawley and offered the Oath of Allegiance. When they all refused it they were subjected to the penalties of *praemunire* as punishment.

Charles or his ministers hit upon the idea of selling licences allowing the practice of their religion to those Catholics wealthy enough to be able afford them. An instance of this is the licence granted to the ancient Chichester family at Arlington Court, North Devon who maintained a domestic chapel. The licence for this - flying in the face of all penal legislation - was issued under the Great Seal, dated 14 March 1628, granting to John Chichester and Anne his wife, exemption from the pains and penalties of continuing as recusants, in exchange for an annual payment of a specified sum to the Crown. The fact was that recusant revenue had become an integral and indispensable part of government income, much as alcohol and petrol duty are today. Charles had inherited enormous debts from his profligate father, so the Catholics were squeezed even harder. The King was no doubt most gratified to find that his efficient finance minister had exacted a fivefold increase.

In the political sphere the Calvinists were in the ascendant and despite the King's efforts many priests died in prison. The Long Parliament, which met in November 1640, was dominated by Puritan fanatics hell-bent not only on punishing Catholics but also ridding the Church of England of its bishops and imposing Calvinism. Persecution was renewed and a proclamation was issued banishing all priests from the realm under pain of death. Charles continued to try and protect priests and the plight of Father John Goodman in 1641 became a test case in the struggle between the King and Parliament.

Goodman, a Welshman from Ruthin, was born in 1592. He was first cousin to Godfrey Goodman, the Catholic-minded Bishop of Gloucester. John was educated at Cambridge and became an Anglican minister, serving as curate at St Nicholas Olave, London. Dissatisfied with his religious position, he went to Paris and was there received into the Catholic Church by Father Richard Ireland. (Ireland was born in Westminster, London and educated at Westminster School. He was headmaster of the school from 1598 to 1610 when he fled to France, converted and was ordained priest in Paris in 1612.) John went to Douai in 1621 and then sought admission into the Society of Jesus at Watten, but did not remain and was ordained about 1631 in France before returning to England. He was a prisoner in Newgate by 1632 from where he was discharged in 1635. In 1637 he served a spell in the Gatehouse and was released only to be taken back into custody later that year. His final arrest was on 17 January 1640. He had to wait until August for his trial, but was found not guilty. However, a priest informer came forward to offer evidence against him and in January 1641 he was condemned to death at the Old Bailey. A few days later his reprieve by Charles at the Queen's request caused ferocious protests. Parliament petitioned the King for the execution to be carried out, sending unedifying delegations to meet Charles in order to vilify Catholics in general and demand Goodman's death. There was a bitter battle between the two parties and rather than be a cause of strife Father Goodman volunteered to submit to execution. He wrote to the King,

The humble petition of John Goodman condemned humbly showeth, that whereas your majesty's petitioner hath been informed of a great discontent in many of your majesty's subjects, at the gracious mercy your majesty was freely pleased to show unto your petitioner, by suspending the execution of the sentence of death pronounced against your petitioner, for being a Roman priest; these are humbly to beseech your majesty, rather to remit your petitioner to their mercy, than to let him live the subject of so great discontent in your people against your majesty: for it hath pleased God to give me the grace to desire with the prophet, that if this storm be raised for my sake, I may be cast into the sea, that others may avoid the tempest. This is, most sacred sovereign, the petition of him that should esteem his blood well shed, to cement the breach between your majesty and your subjects upon this occasion.

The priest's courageous offer impressed the House of Lords and caused a split between the Lords and Commons - of which Charles took advantage. He would not give way, even when the City of London refused him a desperately needed loan of £60,000 to enable him to pay his army. Father Goodman remained a prisoner in Newgate, where he died four years later in 1645.

Soon the King was embroiled in another trial of strength with his Parliament involving priests. Father Cuthbert Clopton alias Green, was born in 1607. His parents were both converts. His father came from Whorlton, Co. Durham and had married his cousin, Anne Clopton. She was the daughter of William Clopton of Clopton House, Stratford-upon-Avon. The house which Shakespeare purchased and re-named New Place had also been built by the Clopton family in an earlier generation. Cuthbert was ordained at Rome in 1636 and returned to England in 1638 as a chaplain and interpreter serving Giovanni Giustiniani, Venetian Ambassador in London 1638 to 1642.

On Saturday, 3 July 1641, while walking down Aldersgate Street, in the City of London, Father Clopton was accosted by Richard Carpenter, an apostate priest who had once been a fellow student at the English College, Rome. Saluting him with, 'Friend, I am glad to see you', he violently grabbed hold of Cuthbert, calling out loudly that he was a Romish priest. Carpenter, who was a nephew of Father Richard Blount, the Jesuit Provincial, then hauled Cuthbert before Sir James Campbell, the local Justice of the Peace. Campbell asked Carpenter for the warrant authorising Clopton's apprehension. Carpenter replied that his warrant was the command of Parliament that gave him power to apprehend anyone he believed to be a priest. Campbell then asked Cuthbert who he was and received the reply that he was a gentleman of the Venetian Ambassador's whom he served in the capacity of an interpreter. Asked by the Justice if he was a priest Cuthbert answered, that was for Carpenter[*] to prove; whereupon Clopton was committed firstly to the Counter and then to Newgate.

On Wednesday, 21 July Cuthbert was indicted at the Justice Hall of the Old Bailey before Sir Edmund Wright, Lord Mayor of London, Sir Edward Bromfield, Sir Thomas Gardiner, the Recorder of the City of London and Alderman Henry Bratt. Clopton was given permission to stand up in Court, accused persons usually being required to kneel.

On Friday, 23 July he and Father William Ward were tried at the Old Bailey before the Recorder of London, for their priesthood, which they did not admit, insisting that it was the Court's job to prove it; furthermore as the servant of a foreign ambassador, Clopton claimed diplomatic immunity. The apostate Carpenter, and the pursuivant James Wadsworth, who had once been a student at Saint-Omer, gave false testimony against Cuthbert and evidence was supplied against Father Ward by Wadsworth's colleague, Thomas Mayo, both of whom we shall meet again. During the court proceedings a personal letter from the King was delivered to the Recorder asking that Cuthbert be returned to the Ambassador. The letter was ignored and the jury found both priests guilty. At 5 p.m. later that afternoon they were summoned back to court and condemned to death under the Elizabethan Statute 27.

Ambassador Giustiniani appealed to the King, demanding an apology for the gross infringement of diplomatic privilege. Robert Rich, 1st Earl of Warwick (a title he bought for £10,000) the grandson of Richard Rich, was sent with a royal carriage to escort the Ambassador to Court to receive the King's apology. On the Sunday Charles issued Letters Patent, granting a free pardon to Clopton, instructing that he should be

---

[*] Carpenter was educated at Eton, Oxford and Cambridge and was converted by Peter Wilford OSB. He attempted to join both the Benedictines and Franciscans before going to Rome where he was ordained in 1635. He was very miffed when he apostatised and preached his recantation sermon at St Paul's because rather than praising him Archbishop Laud admonished him for speaking ungratefully against the Church of Rome. Laud angrily told him it was better for him to have stayed a Catholic than do what he had done. Carpenter was not pleased to be sent as vicar of a poor, obscure parish in Sussex. He later married and by 1654 was asking to be reconciled.

released.

The King's wishes continued to be ignored for several days and as Charles was about to leave for Scotland the desperate Ambassador had a personal interview with him, at which he expressed his anger that his instructions were being thwarted. Only after the King had exerted all his authority with both Houses of Parliament was Father Clopton finally released - on condition that he was sent abroad. He died in Rome in 1644 and was buried at the English College.

The seventy-six-year-old William Ward, whose real name was Webster, was not as fortunate as Clopton. Born c.1565, probably at Thrimby, Westmorland, it appears that he was raised as a Catholic, but little else is known of his early life. He entered the college at Douai in 1604 so was clearly a 'late vocation.' He was ordained at Rheims and sent to the English mission in October 1608. He actually landed in Scotland and was soon captured and spent the next three years in prison. When released he made his way to London, but was arrested and committed to Newgate before being banished in August 1613. He returned, but before long was in jail again. He was released from the Clink in 1632 but was back in the prison by 1637. Of his thirty-three years on the mission he spent twenty of them in various prisons.

Father Cuthbert Clopton wrote an account of William, and there is also a long memoir of him written by a priest contemporary who recalls that some held him to be passionate, as he could be fiery and fervent when speaking, but this was only because he cared so much about the salvation of those entrusted to his care. He spent a great deal of time hearing confessions, exhorting his penitents to greater virtue and the love of God. One of his favourite sayings was that, 'It was not easy to be saints in heaven, if we were not first saints here, and by perfect charity united to Almighty God.' He suffered greatly from a fistula, never being free from pain. He was generous to the poor but his own diet was very plain and simple and his clothing 'homely', although he had means to provide himself with better had he wished. When the times became more perilous for priests, in 1641 one of William's nephews came to London to try and persuade his uncle to move into seclusion in the country for a time, but he declined believing that his place was with his penitents.

He was finally arrested at midnight on Thursday, 15 July, in the house at Pye Corner near Smithfield of his nephew, John Wollan, by the apostate priest hunter Thomas Mayo, acting on a general warrant from the Speaker of the House of Commons. William was taken straight to Newgate. He was tried at the Old Bailey with Father Clopton on 23 July. Three witnesses, including Mayo, gave evidence against him. Mayo claimed to have attended Ward's Mass and had received absolution from him. William insisted that Mayo's evidence was false; that he had never heard his confession. Another witness was William Carpenter who had been ordained in Rome in 1630 but apostatised in 1637. Together with Father Clopton Ward was condemned. Father Clopton spent a long time with William in private on the Sunday before he died. He tells us that the two priests shed tears, not from sorrow or fear, but from William's thankfulness that his Saviour had thought him worthy to shed his blood for His sake. By 5 a.m. the following morning, Monday, 26 July 1641, Clopton was again with William, who he found very cheerful, especially pleased that he was to die on the feast of St Anne, to whom he had always had a particular devotion. He gave twenty shillings to Cuthbert to give to Mr Johnson, the Keeper of Newgate, for 'his kind usage towards him' and also left money to be distributed amongst the poor Catholics in the prison. Clopton then helped William to prepare himself, putting on him a clean cap, band and cuffs. At 8 a.m. he was led through the common jail by Keeper Meares and tied to the hurdle to be drawn from the prison by four horses. As he passed through Holborn he did his best to give his blessing to the occupants of the houses with which he was familiar. At the scaffold he gave the hangman and the man who had driven the horses some money before emptying his pockets of his remaining possessions and throwing them into the crowd. With the words, 'Jesu, receive my soul', he was hanged until he was dead and they stripped him while he was still hanging before dragging him by the heels to be dismembered. William Ward was the first priest to be executed for thirteen years; the first of many victims of the Long Parliament.

The numerical strength of Catholics at this time is difficult to quantify, but what figures are available suggests that in the counties of Lancashire and Durham and in South Wales Catholics could have made up approximately twenty per cent of the population. In Northumberland and Yorkshire the proportion was slightly less, whereas the great majority of the inhabitants of London were Protestant.

When the King left London at the outbreak of the first Civil War, nothing could save the priests who were apprehended, and in a six-year period from 1641 to 1646 at least twenty-two priests and laymen were executed by Parliament, and nine priests died in prison. Just how limited the King's powers had become is illustrated by the case of two priests from the North Riding of Yorkshire; eighty-one-year-old Blessed John Lockwood and thirty-seven-year-old Blessed Edmund Catterick or Catherick. Lockwood was born in 1561 at Sowerby, the eldest son of Christopher Lockwood and his wife Clare Lascelles,

Charles I and the Civil War Martyrs, 1625-49

daughter of Sir Robert Lascelles. John used Lascelles as his alias on the mission. He studied at the English College, Rome, and was ordained at the Lateran in 1597 at the late age of thirty-six, returning to England in 1598. He was to spend the next forty-four years on the mission. He was imprisoned at least twice, once at Newgate in 1610, when he was sentenced to death, but reprieved and banished. His final arrest was by a pursuivant named Langdale. It took place at Wood End, near Thirsk, at the house of a widow, Mrs Bridget Catenby, which had been his home for several years. Given his advanced age he was treated with great cruelty and indignity when escorted to York. He was unable to sit astride a horse so they laid him across the beast with John suffering sickness and fainting. When Langdale delivered his prisoner to the jail John gave him five shillings for 'giving him a great deal of trouble' in conveying him there.

Catterick, born 1605, was the son of Anthony Catterick of Carlton, Stanwick, near Richmond, Yorkshire and Joyce Pennington of Muncaster, Cumberland. He went to Douai in 1624, was ordained in 1630 and returned to England in 1634. His older brother, George, was also a priest active on the mission in Yorkshire. In 1642 he was apprehended on the road near Thornton Watlass by Justice Dodsworth, who may have been a relative by marriage, and committed to York Castle. The two priests were tried together and condemned but reprieved by the King who, prevailed upon by Parliament, gave way and signed their death warrants. Their martyrdom took place at York on 13 April 1642 while the King was in residence in the city and despite his protests at the barbarity. Father Catterick was appointed the first to die but Lockwood, noticing that he was showing signs of fear, stepped forward and asked that as the senior of the two he should be the first to die. Then turning to his companion he encouraged him saying, 'My dear brother in Jesus Christ and fellow sufferer, take courage, we have almost run our race, shall we faint and be tired when in sight of the prize?' John found it difficult to climb the ladder and asked the sheriff's patience declaring that it was hard work for a man of his age, 'however I will do my best; for who would not take thus much pains to get to heaven at the journey's end.'

Two men helped him up and he gave them a shilling each. Pausing at the top of the ladder to regain his breath, he called down to Edmund and asked how he was doing, and was pleased to hear that the younger priest was in good heart. With the prayer, 'Jesus my Redeemer, receive my soul', he was flung off the ladder. Edmund spoke little other than to pray for his persecutors and for the King. Pulling his cap over his eyes he exclaimed, 'Lord, my soul hath trusted in thee; let me never be

Charles I and the Civil War Martyrs, 1625-49

confounded.' The executioner behaved like a madman, tearing and slashing at the priests' bodies and flinging their entrails into the crowd. Edmund's head was placed on Micklegate Bar and, to show contempt for the King's authority, Lockwood's head was impaled on the north gate at Bootham Bar, close to Charles's residence, The Manor, so that he could not avoid seeing it. The priests' mangled quarters were rescued by Mary Poyntz. She was one of the original intimate companions of Mary Ward and eventually became superior of her order. She took the relics to her convent at Augsburg. Here they remained beneath an altar until the late 19th century when they were obtained by the monks of Downside Abbey, Somerset.

Not surprisingly, during the Civil War the Catholics staunchly supported the King, such as the immensely rich, Henry Somerset, 5th Earl, and later 1st Marquess, of Worcester. He and his son and heir, Edward, the remarkable inventor, contributed huge sums to the Royalist cause. (His second son, Thomas Somerset, was ordained priest in Rome and joined the Oratorians.) Whether or not Charles was deserving of such whole-hearted support is debatable. It was probably a case of 'better the devil you know', but for certain the Puritan alternative was too ghastly for Catholics to contemplate. Their numbers should not be exaggerated, but without the Catholic gentry the King would not have had officers of calibre experienced in warfare on the Continent, or been able to raise enough troops to form an effective army. It included priests who served as army chaplains, some of whom were killed or maimed in the conflicts. One such was the West Yorkshireman, Father Francis Pavier. His parents, Richard Pavier and Jane Oglethorpe, lived at Spofforth, where Francis was born in 1602. He was ordained at Lisbon in 1633 and came back permanently to England in 1636. Francis was killed while attending the wounded at the Battle of Marston Moor 2 July 1644. Catholics flocked to the royal standard, especially in Yorkshire and the rest of the North, where the King enjoyed strong support. Bishop Challoner gives an impressively long list of Catholics who lost their lives fighting for the King; a list headed by Robert Dormer, Earl of Caernarvon, Henry Constable, 1st Viscount Dunbar and Thomas, 2nd Baron Arundell of Wardour.

The recruitment policy backfired on the King, who was accused by his opponents of raising a papist army against the God-fearing Protestants. The memories of the Irish rebellion were still fresh. It started in October 1641 as an attempted coup d'état by the Catholic gentry, but rapidly degenerated into an uprising marked by appalling atrocities against the English and Scottish Protestant settlers; men, women and children. Thousands were slaughtered. Sad to recall, there

Charles I and the Civil War Martyrs, 1625-49

were instances of the Catholic clergy giving encouragement to the brutal excesses, although there were numerous examples of priests who risked their own lives to shelter endangered Protestants. No doubt the stories of cruelty gained much in the repetitious telling, but the fact remains that in the popular mind the blame was attributed to the Catholic Church, and many English Protestants were only too willing to believe that Catholics were forever plotting to massacre them.

The Catholics got a taste of things to come in 1645 when Parliament ordered that two-thirds of all the property of papists was to be seized just because they were papists. It was a license to plunder, and no one was spared the depredations, from the aristocracy to the humblest labourer.

In 1648 Parliament approved *Articles of Christian Religion* in which Catholic doctrine, especially the Mass, was ridiculed and condemned and the Pope was described as Anti-Christ. It was an additional sharp thorn in the crown they already had to bear when the Catholics found themselves on the losing side at the end of the Civil War.

The monarchy, having been first reduced to a cipher, was not brought down by a high-minded group of heroic patriots. We must forget all romanticised notions of a Parliament comprised of disinterested 'democrats'. Whilst the Puritan movement undeniably counted amongst its number many who were actuated by the highest motives, the House of Commons was mostly composed of squires and rich landed gentry, such as the skilful Parliamentary leader, John Pym, whose principal aim was promoting their own economic self-interest. The Commons was not anxious about the relief of the poor; an area in which the King was deeply involved. They were not concerned about the defence of the country; their small-minded, narrow self-interest dictated that they opposed the King when he tried to extend from the coastal areas the responsibility for paying the Ship Money tax in order to raise £180,000 per annum to fund the navy and build the ships that were to lay the foundations for England's future maritime greatness. (Not many years passed before the nation, under the Commonwealth, had to pay £800,000 in taxes for an army that was keeping it in subjection.)

Even after the army coup d'état against Parliament and the arrest of the King, Charles could still have regained his throne, albeit with much diminished powers, if, as a prisoner, he had agreed to the demands of the Puritans. Their price included even greater penalties being imposed on Catholics in England and Scotland; not least the compulsory education of their children by approved Protestants, as a means of quickly consigning their religion to extinction. Catholics who had

Charles I and the Civil War Martyrs, 1625-49

supported the King were to be exempt from any pardons. They also demanded the abolition of the Anglican Church and the establishment of a Presbyterian system. Charles professed that, 'I am constant for the doctrine and discipline of the Church of England, as it was established by Queen Elizabeth and my father; and resolve (by the grace of God) to live and die in the maintenance of it'. The King's honourable refusal to comply may have been either courageous or foolhardy. The Church he was defending was in a poor condition. It had become very unpopular with large sections of the population, not least because few of its ministers enjoyed any respect, either as men or as spiritual representatives. After the King's demise, and both monarchy and Church had been overthrown, the people realised, too late, that the victors, who hitherto had been full of platitudes about toleration, had no intention whatsoever of tolerating the opinions of any who differed from them. The assertion of the King at his trial in Westminster Hall that he stood for the rights and liberties of his subjects far more than any of his opponents, soon proved to be true.

After enormous pressure exerted on the 'judges' by Oliver Cromwell, to persuade them to sign the death warrant, Charles was executed, or more accurately, judicially murdered, in Whitehall on 30 January 1649. He met his death with magnificent courage and dignity, declaring that 'I go from a corruptible to an incorruptible Crown.' As Parliament had already abolished the Anglican *Book of Common Prayer*, no prayers were permitted to be said at his burial at Windsor. With his passing the Catholics were once more plunged into despair.

Edmund Arrowsmith

My loss may shine yet goodlier than your gain, when time and God give judgement.
       Marino Faliero, Algernon Swinburne, 1837-1909

Much of what we know about Edmund is taken from an anonymous account published in 1630 entitled *A true and exact relation of the death of two Catholics who suffered for their religion at the Summer Assizes held at Lancaster the year 1628*. The account was updated by an Irish-born Jesuit, Father Cornelius Murphy, and published in 1737. Edmund, the son of Robert and Margery Arrowsmith, was born at Haydock, in the parish of Winwick, near St Helens, Lancashire, in 1585. His father, born 1559, was a yeoman farmer. He married Margery

Gerard in 1584. Born in 1563, the daughter of Nicholas Gerard, she came from the same family as Father John Gerard of Bryn, just north of Haydock. Given her birth and family connections she was considered to have married 'beneath her'. The Arrowsmith's were also a well-known Catholic family. Edmund's grandfather died in prison for his faith. Robert and Margery's first child, was baptised Brian. Being recusants who sheltered priests, his parents suffered a great deal of persecution because of their religion. Once, while still a small child, Brian was left shivering in his nightshirt with his three younger siblings when the pursuivants took his parents and their servants off in the middle of the night to Lancaster jail. The children were taken in by kindly neighbours.

Robert Arrowsmith and his younger brother, Peter, after suffering several imprisonments, decided to go abroad, and served in the wars in Flanders. Peter died of wounds at Brussels and Robert went to visit his brother, Dr Edmund Arrowsmith, at Douai. The elder Edmund was born in 1563 and was ordained priest at Rheims in 1587. He did not enjoy good health and never returned to England, but taught at Douai and Rheims until his death in 1601. Robert went home to Lancashire and died shortly afterwards leaving Margery Arrowsmith a widow in poor financial circumstances.

Brian's education was first entrusted to an old priest with whom he lived for a time. It is believed that he attended the grammar school at Senely Green where his Protestant schoolmasters were fond of him. Obviously a pious child, Brian is said to have often recited the Jesus Psalter or Our Lady's Office on his journey to and from his lessons. At the age of twenty, Brian crossed the Channel and entered the English College, Douai, where he was Confirmed, taking the name Edmund, after his uncle; by which name he wished to be known. His studies were dogged by ill-health. He received all the minor orders in the church of St Nicholas, Douai on 14 June 1612 and was ordained at Arras on 9 December 1612. On 17 June 1613 he was sent by Dr Kellison, the Douai President, back to his native Lancashire. There, under the aliases of Bradshaw and Rigby, he became famous for his fearless and forthright mission. Reportedly small and unprepossessing in appearance, a contemporary - most probably Father John Southworth - recalled him as being, 'zealous, witty and fervent and so forward in disputing with heretics that I often wished him merrily to carry salt in his pocket to season his actions, lest too much zeal without discretion might bring him too soon into danger, considering the vehement and sudden storms of persecution that often assailed us'. Edmund was described as a man 'of great innocency in his life, of great sincerity in his nature, of great sweetness in his conversation and of great industry in his function. And he was ever of a cheerful countenance'.

In 1622 he was arrested and brought before Dr John Bridgeman, Bishop of Chester, who was at supper with some of his clergy. As it was Lent and the bishop and his guests were eating meat Edmund chided them for doing so. Edmund had a lively theological dispute with them, in which he was reported to have got the better of the argument. He was soon freed on the orders of King James. The King was anxious to promote a Spanish marriage for his son and needed to create a favourable impression, so he ordered all priests then in custody to be released. Because of the rapid increase in the number of priests, in 1623 Mutio Vitelleschi (1563-1645), the sixth Superior General of the Society of Jesus, erected England into a Province with Oxford-educated Father Richard Blount 5 as Provincial. He organised its members into Colleges covering different areas of the country. These eventually became the College of St Aloysius covering Lancashire, Cheshire and Westmorland; the College of St Ignatius for London; the College of The Immaculate Conception for Derbyshire; the College of St Chad for Staffordshire; the College of the Holy Apostles for Suffolk; the College of St Hugh for Lincolnshire and the College of St Francis Xavier for South Wales. In 1624 after making the Spiritual Exercises, Edmund joined the Society, becoming a member of the College of St Aloysius under its first Rector, Father John Worthington, the nephew of both Cardinal William Allen and of Dr Thomas Worthington, President of Douai. Edmund made a long retreat in Essex then went to London to undertake a short novitiate at the secret Jesuit house at Clerkenwell rented from John Talbot, 10th Earl of Shrewsbury. (Shrewsbury's mother was a Petre; his wife a daughter of Lord Arundell of Wardour.) Unfortunately the house was not secret enough for on 15 March 1628 it was raided and destroyed, but at least none of the priests or brothers present lost their lives. * The Attorney-General and future Lord Chief Justice, Sir Robert Heath, eventually released them on bail and was censured by Parliament for doing so, but he was acting on the direct instructions of King Charles, who had succeeded his father while Edmund was carrying on his ministry in Lancashire.

---

* Among the priests arrested at Clerkenwell was the future historian of the Elizabethan Jesuits in England, Henry More, great-grandson of Sir Thomas More. It was not long before Henry was back in jail where he seems to have remained until 1633. He then became chaplain to the Petre's at Ingatestone and Thorndon Hall, Essex. In 1635 he succeeded Richard Blount as Jesuit Provincial. His later years saw distinguished service in various academic capacities on the Continent. His history was published in 1660 and More died the following year, aged seventy-five.

Charles I and the Civil War Martyrs, 1625-49

In 1628 Edmund was in the neighbourhood of Brindle, when he had occasion to severely reprove a young Catholic man called Mr Holden. He was the son of the landlord of the Blue Anchor inn, Hoghton. Edmund often used the old, half-timbered inn as a secret refuge. Mr Holden had married his Protestant first cousin before a Protestant minister and the couple were now living at the inn. Edmund was in the process of obtaining a dispensation for them to be validly married by the Church and suggested that they separate until the marriage ceremony. Resentful of Edmund's reprimand, Holden betrayed him to a Justice of the Peace, informing him that Edmund was likely to be at the Blue Anchor.

The JP, Captain Rawsthorne, unwilling to cause problems for the landlord, sent a message to warn him of the imminent search, urging him to get the priest to leave quickly. This charitable conduct may not have been as unusual as it first appears if the contents of a letter from Richard Bancroft, Bishop of London, to Secretary Robert Cecil, now in the Public Record Office, are taken as evidence. Bancroft wrote that, 'In Lancashire, the most part being recusants, they stand in no fear, and have beaten many pursuivants and made them swear never to meddle with recusants again, and one they made to eat his own warrant! It is said also that in Lancashire, if a pursuivant came to the Justices and showed them his warrant they hindered him till they had sent to warn the recusant that a search would be made, and that if he have anything in his house he must convey it away.' Alerted by Holden, the innkeeper, Edmund packed up hastily and left the house on horseback. He made his dramatic escape through the lanes and fields of Brindle, but the Captain's young son and one of his servants caught up with him. Edmund's horse refused to jump the Moss Ditch, so he dismounted and ran along the course of the ditch hoping to find a narrower place, but was overtaken and apprehended. He was escorted to the Boar's Head inn in Hoghton Lane. What follows is taken from Edmund's own account of his arrest given at his trial.

As I was upon the road that very man ... rushed out upon me with a drawn sword. He was meanly dressed and on horseback. I made what haste I could from him, but being weak and sickly I was forced by him at last to the Moss where I dismounted and fled with all the speed I was able, which was not very great seeing I was loaded with heavy clothes, books and other things. At length he came up to me at the Moss Ditch and struck at me, though I had nothing to defend myself with but a little walking stick and a sword which I did not draw. With a blow he cut the stick close to my hand and did me some little hurt. I then asked him if his design was to take my purse and my life. He answered that perhaps it was; upon which I fled from him but was soon overtaken. Then up came this youth ... and others to assist him. They used me with much indignity and took me to an alehouse, and searched me to the skin, offering indignities which modesty forbids me to relate and which I resisted as far as I was able. That done they fell to drinking and spent nine shillings of my money in an hour; they told me that the Justice of the Peace, by whose warrant I was apprehended, was there in person, but that I would not believe. Upon this occasion I began to find fault with this man's wicked and rude behaviour, who seemed to be the ringleader and I besought him for Jesus' sake to give over his disordered life, drinking, dissolute talk and whatever might offend Almighty God.

Edmund was imprisoned in Lancaster Castle, where he continued to expound the Gospel to his fellow prisoners. Indicted under his alias of Rigby for being a priest and a Jesuit on 26 August, he was sent for trial at the assizes before the rabidly anti-Catholic former Attorney-General, Sir Henry Yelverton who requested Sir James Whitlock to assist him in hearing the case. The trial coincided with Parliament's order for the stricter application of the penal laws. Wasting no time Yelverton immediately demanded of Edmund, 'Are you a priest?' It was no part of Edmund's role to act as his own prosecution; it was up to the Court to prove his guilt as charged, so he answered equivocally, 'I would to God I were worthy'.

After trying a number of times to lead Edmund into an incriminating admission, Yelverton then changed tack by asking if he was not a priest, to which Edmund made no answer. Incensed, Yelverton launched into an attack on the prisoner. 'You may easily see he is a priest. I warrant you, he would not for all England deny his Order.' At this point a clergyman called Leigh, who was sitting as a Justice of the Peace, joined in the attack, accusing Edmund of seducing the people to popery. Edmund requested a public debate in which he would be allowed to defend his faith. This was refused, and Edmund responded that he was prepared to defend his religion not only with words but with his blood.

'You shall seal it with your blood', retorted Yelverton, 'I will not leave this town before you see your bowels burned before your face'. He repeated this and similar threats several times. 'And you, my Lord, must die', said Edmund.

He was ordered to answer directly how he justified going overseas to be ordained in defiance of the law. 'If any man can lawfully accuse me, I stand ready here to answer him,' replied Arrowsmith, knowing full well that they did not have sufficient evidence against him.

Apart from the accusation of Holden, the only witnesses they could produce were the boy and the servant who had apprehended him. They swore that Edmund had tried to convert them. It was at this point that Edmund asked leave to give his account of his arrest as quoted above, which he concluded thus: 'Upon my word and upon my life this, or to this effect, is all I said to him. Let him look on me and gainsay it if he can. As for that youth I deny not to have told him that I hoped when he came to riper years, he would look better into himself and become a true Catholic, for that and that alone, would be the means to save his soul: to which he made no answer at all. And I hope, my Lords, that neither they, nor any other can prove ill against me'.

This produced further invective from Yelverton, who told the jury that they should show no favour to Edmund. This made Arrowsmith smile, at which he was reproved for being a saucy fellow who had no better manners than to laugh at those who sat there in judgement for the King. On his knees Edmund begged them not to have such an opinion of him and prayed for the King and his judges, asking God in His mercy to confound heresy.

'Gentlemen of the jury', Yelverton said, 'look you how he wishes God to confound us all and root out heresy by which he means our religion.' He then proceeded to harangue the jury to find the prisoner guilty.

The Court then adjourned for dinner, which was a welcome respite to Edmund who was suffering from severe toothache. Despite the lack of any real evidence it did not take the jury long to find Edmund guilty of being a priest. Yelverton, not content with merely pronouncing the dreadful sentence, added 'Know shortly thou shalt die aloft between heaven and earth, as unworthy of either; and may thy soul go to hell with thy followers. I would that all priests in England might undergo the same sentence.' Edmund's response was to drop to his knees, make the sign of the Cross, and say simply, *'Deo gratias'* which he repeated in English, 'Thanks be to God.'

The jailer was ordered by Yelverton to treat the condemned man harshly. Edmund spent two days without food, loaded with heavy chains in a dark hole in which he could neither stand upright nor lie down but only sit crouching. The jailer provided him with a little pillow to put behind his back. No one was allowed to communicate with him except the Protestant minister, Leigh, who pestered him. The pending execution became a matter of public controversy. Even preparing the sheriff's warrant for the execution proved difficult as Sir James Whitlock, who had been prevailed upon to sit with Judge Yelverton, refused to sign the warrant. Eventually a vaguely worded warrant was drawn up without the judges' signatures. The townspeople of Lancaster were sure that the King would reprieve Edmund. At first no one could be found willing to carry out the execution, not even the prisoners in the jail. Then a butcher agreed that his assistant could be the executioner for a payment of £5, but the man fled. The gruesome task finally fell to an army deserter under sentence of death who was offered his liberty, a payment of forty shillings and the prisoner's belongings.

On Thursday, 28 August 1628 Edmund was told he was to die that midday. 'I beseech my Redeemer to make me worthy of it,' he exclaimed.

A large crowd had assembled as Edmund was led out to die. As he crossed the castle yard he raised his hand. This was a pre-arranged signal to a fellow priest and prisoner, John Southworth, who from his cell window above gave him absolution. As he reached the castle gates, a Catholic gentleman kissed and embraced him, until he was pulled away by force. Fastened to the hurdle with his head towards the horse's tail 'for greater ignominy', Edmund was dragged through the streets to the gallows. When he arrived at the scaffold he found Mr Leigh, the vicar cum-JP, who pointed out to him the boiling cauldron. 'Look you what is provided for your death,' was his callous greeting. 'Will you conform and lay hold of the King's mercy?' Patiently, Edmund answered, 'Good sir, tempt me no more. The mercy I look for is in heaven through the death and passion of my Saviour, Jesus Christ; and I humbly beg Him to make me worthy of this death.'

Among those present to witness the priest's death was John Southworth's father and it is comforting to think that he may have been able to make contact with his son imprisoned in the castle. Edmund knelt and prayed, all the while plagued by the Protestant ministers, whose interruptions he tried to ignore. Edmund prayed, 'I freely and willingly offer to Thee, sweetest Jesus, this my death in satisfaction for my sins and I wish that this little blood of mine may be a sacrifice for them ... I die for the love of Thee; for our holy Faith; for the authority of Thy Vicar on earth, the successor of St Peter, true head of the Catholic Church which Thou hast founded. In my death I only desire Thee, who are true life. Give me, good Jesus, constancy to the last moment.' The sheriff told him to make haste and so he rose with the words, 'God's holy will be done,' kissing the ladder as he climbed up resolutely. He prayed for the King and freely forgave all his persecutors. He asked the Catholics to pray for him but Parson Leigh falsely called out that none were present and offered to pray for him. Edmund replied, 'I neither desire your prayers, nor will I pray with you.' Standing on the ladder he addressed the crowd.

Bear witness ... that I die a constant Roman Catholic; and for Jesus Christ His sake, let not my death be a hindrance to your well doing and going forward in the Catholic religion, but rather may it encourage you thereto. For Jesus' sake have a care of your souls, than which nothing is more precious; and become members of the true Church, as you tender your salvation; for hereafter that alone will do you good ... nothing grieves me so much as this England, which I pray God soon to convert.

He then drew his cap over his eyes in readiness, but the persistent Mr Leigh made one more attempt to shake him, urging him to take the Oath of Allegiance and his life would be spared. 'You may live,' he cried, 'if you conform to the Protestant religion!' Wearily Edmund replied, 'Tempt me no more. I am a dying man. I will do it on no condition,' at which some of the ministers called out, 'Away with him!'

Covering his eyes again he was heard to say *'Bone Jesus,'* as he was thrown off the ladder. He was permitted to hang until he was dead before the rest of the sentence was carried out. His head and four quarters were displayed on Lancaster Castle. Judge Yelverton watched the execution from a window before sitting down to his dinner. With his venison they also brought in one of Edmund's quarters for him to see and he made a sick joke, comparing it unfavourably with his meat. The next day they executed Blessed Richard Herst or Hurst, 6 a young layman from near Preston on a trumped up charge of murder.

Edmund's right hand was rescued and given to his mother. It remained in safe keeping until 1822 when it was presented to the newly established St Oswald's parish at Ashton-in-Makerfield, close to Haydock where Edmund was born. The church also possesses a crucifix and small statue of the Blessed Virgin that belonged to the martyr. In 1970 the name of St Edmund Arrowsmith was added to the dedication of the church. Today the hand rests under a glass dome encased within a white marble tabernacle in the Lady Chapel of the church. The 'Holy Hand' has been an object of continuous veneration and there are detailed records of many well-attested miraculous cures (i.e. medically inexplicable) that have been attributed to Edmund's intercession through his relic, many of them involving non-Catholics.

Ambrose Barlow

Christ's law he taught, but first he followed it himself

The Parson's Tale, The Canterbury Tales, Geoffrey Chaucer, c.1340-1400

We are fortunate in possessing a good deal of contemporary biographical information about Ambrose. Bishop Challoner used manuscripts from St Gregory's Monastery, Douai, as his source, including one written by Ambrose's brother in 1642. Another manuscript entitled *The Apostolical Life of Ambrose Barlow* was written by an anonymous friend in the form of a letter to the martyr's brother. Ambrose was born at Barlow Hall, Chorlton-cum-Hardy, near Manchester, in November 1585. His pedigree was long and impressive; the fourth son of Alexander Barlow and Mary Brereton, daughter of Sir Urian Brereton of Handforth Hall, Cheshire, by his second wife, Alice Trafford, daughter of Sir Edmund Trafford. Alexander and Mary had fourteen children: eight boys and six girls.

The Barlows were a very ancient family who took their name from the place of their abode. Their history probably stretched back to Saxon times and they were recorded as living at Barlow as far back as the early thirteenth century, when the original hall was built near the River Mersey by Roger de Barlow in the reign of Edward I. They rose to prominence over the years and were related to every gentry family of note in Lancashire and Cheshire. Ambrose's great-aunt, Margaret Barlow, was the wife of the powerful Edward Stanley, 3rd Earl of Derby. The Barlow and Trafford families, along with the Premonstratensian Cockersand Abbey, were the owners of Chorlton. The Hall in which our martyr was born had been rebuilt c.1574 by Alexander Barlow senior. In the reign of Edward VI he was Member of Parliament for Wigan and in Queen Mary's reign he strongly supported the Catholic restoration in Manchester. But, as a Catholic, did not sit again after Elizabeth's accession. In 1559, when Laurence Vaux, q.v. the last Catholic Warden of the Collegiate Church, Manchester was forced into exile he consigned the deeds of the church to Alexander Barlow for safekeeping. In 1583, as part of a great round-up of Lancashire Catholic gentry, the pursuivants raided Barlow Hall in search of priests. None were found but Alexander was arrested and along with fifty others sent to Salford jail, where he died in 1584.

His son, Alexander Barlow junior, was knighted in the coronation honours of James I in 1603. In spite of the honour, Sir Alexander suffered grievously for his faith, being made to pay extortionate fines for the recusancy of himself, his wife and many children. He eventually fell foul of the law, enabling the King to refuse the monthly fines and take instead two-thirds of his estate. In 1609 the 'benefit' of his estate was bestowed on two of the King's favourites. When Sir Alexander died in April 1620 he asked to be buried with his father and ancestors in Didsbury Parish Church, but was instead buried at night, probably without any service, in the Collegiate Church of St Mary, St Denys and St George: since 1847 Manchester Cathedral. As we have already noted, the persecution extended to the dead, and it was not unusual for a recusant to be so treated.

In order to comply with the law, Alexander and Mary presented their son for baptism in the fourteenth-century St James's Parish Church, Didsbury, on 30 November 1585. He was given the name Edward. The entry in the baptismal register is still to be seen. It is certain that as staunch Catholics they would first have had him privately baptised by a priest. The Barlow's were closely related to the ancient Legh family; Elizabeth Legh was Edward's paternal grandmother. Where Edward attended school is unknown, but at twelve years of age he was sent to Adlington Hall, Cheshire as page to his relative, Sir Urian Legh. Although it was customary for sons of the gentry to serve their apprenticeship in the homes of a nobleman, it appears an odd choice in Edward's case because Sir Urian was a Protestant who had taken part in the Siege of Cádiz under the command of Robert Devereaux, Earl of Essex, in 1596. It seems that in this environment the young Edward conformed. The *Life* informs us that he was reclaimed through the influence of the widowed Lady Margaret Davenport of Bramhall, a neighbour of the Barlow family. Lady Davenport was a conspicuous recusant 'greatly infected with popery.'

Edward's elder brother, William, the third son of Alexander and Mary, had been educated at Douai and had joined St Gregory's Monastery, where he was ordained in 1608 taking the saint's name Rudesind, after the 10th century Spanish bishop and abbot. He became famous as a scholar and canonist and served as prior of St Gregory's from 1614 to 1621, when he became President General of the English Benedictine Congregation until 1629. He died in 1656 aged seventy-two. A younger brother, Robert, was also to enter St Gregory's where he was professed in 1630, dying in England a few years later.

At the age of twenty-three Edward also left for Douai. He studied under the care of the Benedictines at Anchin College. He made good progress and was sent by the President of Douai College, Dr Worthington, to the English College, Valladolid, where he arrived on 20 September 1610. After two years he returned to Douai, partly for reasons of ill health, but also it seems because he wanted to follow his brother and join the Benedictines. However, instead of remaining at Douai he was sent to the English Benedictine house near St Malo for his novitiate. He took the name of Ambrose, by which we shall henceforth call him. He did not stay long at St Malo but returned to St Gregory's, Douai, maybe because his brother, Dom Rudesind, had by then become Prior. On 5 January 1615 he made his solemn vows as a monk. Dom Ambrose was ordained priest in 1617 and shortly afterwards returned to work in England under the aliases of Brereton and Radcliffe.

His first call was at Barlow Hall to visit his family and no doubt he often went back to see his parents while they were alive. Evidently the ill health he suffered was the onset of consumption, because shortly after returning home he consulted a doctor about it. The doctor's advice was that he should drink new milk in the morning and eat a roasted apple at night. The advice must have been effective because Ambrose spent the next twenty-four years as a missionary in a relatively small geographical area, working around Manchester and south Lancashire. His life was orderly, dividing his time between spending one week touring the area and three weeks at home at his base. This was usually Morleys Hall, Astley, in the parish of Leigh. About seven miles from Manchester, the hall was the home of the Tyldesleys, a notoriously recusant family. Sir Thomas Tyldesley later became a Major General in the Royalist army. Ambrose's other regular base was at Wardley Hall, Worsley, the seat of the Downes family, who were his cousins. Ambrose's annual allowance was £8, which was paid from a pension left by Elizabeth Tyldesley for this purpose. He gave back £6 of the allowance for his board and lodging, even though he was away from his base for long periods.

He travelled a great deal, always on foot with a long countryman's staff on his back and often said Mass in several different places on the same day. In the circumstances in which he and other priests ministered this was not an unusual practice. No matter how busy he was, he never neglected his own prayer and meditation. He always had a servant to tend him on his journeys. They were all volunteers who were expected to pay for their own food and for that reason they mostly served for only short periods. Ambrose would present each of them with enough cloth to make a suit. One man who served him on and off for many years was Christopher Bate. Ambrose was noted for his humility, kindness, good humour, wit and patience. He could be strict with his penitents, reproving those Catholics who failed to give a good example; but never as strict as he was with himself. He criticised those among the Catholic gentry who were fearful of being seen to attend Mass, saying he did not like those who were simply 'peeping at God.' He would deflect slanders and insults - and he had to suffer plenty of them - with a joke. He had a hearty laugh and was described in the *Life* as 'so witty and cheerful in his conversation that of all men I ever knew he seemed most to represent the spirit of Thomas More.' He never allowed anything to rob him of his cheerfulness.

The poor, towards whom he showed great love, were always his first concern and his house was a refuge for them. Unlike other people, who could be condescending, he never stood on ceremony with the poor but gave a priestly example in the simple and frugal manner of his life. He never wore a sword and his outmoded grey clothes attracted attention for their plainness:

> ... the fashion thereof for the oldness might be the same that was in use when he first did leave or return into England; a long wasted jerkin and doublet, his breeches tied above the knees. The best hat that I ever saw him wear I would not have given him two groats for; the band about his neck of the country folks fashion, as poor as one is ordinary worn by any ... as I remember no cuffs at all. Instead of pantofles a pair of scurvy old slip-shoes which he continually wore indoors.

The *Life* tells us that Ambrose was careless of his beard, which he never bothered to trim or shave but let it grow as nature intended. He had naturally short curly hair, chestnut in colour. The writer of the *Life* was clearly something of an amateur artist and he painted a picture of Christ crowned with thorns for the altar. Ambrose asked him to teach him how to paint and he turned out to be an apt pupil.

Ambrose never drank wine and when asked why he abstained he replied, 'Wine and women make the wise apostatise.' Although personally austere and abstemious he was a good host. At Christmas, Easter and Pentecost he held 'open house' for all. At Christmas there would be boiled beef and pottage, goose and mince pies.

Ambrose would serve his guests and when everyone had eaten enough he would make a meal out of the leftovers; then, if anything remained, he would divide it amongst the poorest to take home with them. It was also his custom to give each man a gift of a grey coat and he encouraged the wealthier members of his flock to similar acts of charity. The writer of the *Apostolical Life* gives a vivid description of how Ambrose celebrated Mass. The foulest weather did not deter the Catholics, young and old, from coming to him, either day or night.

> Being come they hasted to the chapel, where the men having laid their hats upon a round table ... they passed by a fair coal fire to the altar; which upon the eve was ready dressed with clean linen and a venerable old vestment laid thereon, which came out but upon great days, with all other things poor and clean. The old picture before the altar was the arraignment of our Blessed Saviour. Against that time he used to prepare great wax candles, which he did help make himself ... how much I was edified in that place ...who seemed to represent the good Catholics in the primitive Church. They so truly united in charity, rejoiced to meet one another ... they spent the night modestly and devoutly, sometimes in prayer before the altar, otherwhiles singing devout songs by the fireside in another room ... that their singing might not disturb those that would be praying in the chapel. On great Holidays and most Sundays ... he used to preach ... in every place that he lodged at in his circuit.

Charles I and the Civil War Martyrs, 1625-49

He had a singular talent therein and could perform it with great facility without penning it. His style in preaching ... was the likest unto Scripture phrase of any that I ever heard; brief, plain and pithy. Oft I have called to mind how, upon the first Good Friday, I heard him to preach so movingly he did mention to us the passion of Our Saviour, and the words of St Paul which I had not taken notice of before, he made me ever to remember and highly to reverence.

Ambrose suffered his fair share of persecution, having evaded many narrow escapes from capture. He was imprisoned four times. Challoner states that while a prisoner in Lancaster Castle in 1628 Ambrose managed to gain access to Edmund Arrowsmith and administer the last rites to him. He was unexpectedly released before Arrowsmith's execution and was unaware that the Jesuit was already dead when, on 28 August, the very night of Edmund's execution, his fellow priest seemed to appear to him by his bedside and warned him that he too would one day be called to similarly suffer. It did not deter Ambrose, who continued travelling as before, passing openly through Leigh, where he was said to be 'as well known as their Parson'.

In March 1641 King Charles had reprieved seven priests under sentence of death. Parliament asked the King to rescind the reprieves and Charles replied to the request in a letter from York in which he said that if Parliament thought 'the execution of these persons so very necessary' he would defer to its judgement but made it clear that the responsibility for their deaths would rest with Parliament. The Commons seems to have baulked at taking the blame and the priests were left in prison. But Charles was forced by Parliament to issue a proclamation banishing all priests from the country within one month. Those who disobeyed would pay the penalty for treason. Ambrose was urged by his friends to go into hiding but he refused, saying, 'Let them fear that have anything to lose which they are unwilling to part with'.

His continual ill health was giving cause for concern but he would not consult a doctor. The *Life* tells us that 'he was to himself Dr Diet, Dr Quiet and the only Dr Merriman that I ever knew'. Early in 1641 he suffered a stroke, which caused a certain amount of paralysis down one side, and he was greatly concerned that if anything happened to him his flock would be deprived of the Sacraments.

The period fixed under the royal proclamation for Ambrose's banishment had expired and on Easter Sunday, 25 April 1641, Mr Gatley, the Vicar of Leigh, apparently having nothing more edifying to do on such a holy day, came with an armed gang to Morleys Hall to arrest him. The reverend gentleman had proposed to his congregation that instead of holding their Easter service they should proceed en masse to the Hall and catch the papists and their priest in their idolatrous worship.

So without any legal authority, armed with clubs and swords, gathering support as they went, about four hundred of them marched on the Hall. When they arrived they could be heard crying out 'Where is Barlow?' and shouting threats. Ambrose was still preaching after Mass and he ordered that the doors be opened to them and calmly surrendered. The congregation were allowed to leave after their names had been taken. The mob searched the house but found nothing of interest to them. Ambrose was taken to a Justice of the Peace at Winwick, who ordered him to be sent under armed guard to Lancaster, accompanied by the insults and jeers of the mob. He was put on a horse but because of the weakening effects of the stroke he had to be supported to prevent him from falling off. Some of the local Catholics would have tried to rescue him, but Ambrose told them to go home peaceably and not interfere: 'To die for this cause was more desirable than life'.

He was imprisoned at Lancaster Castle, during which time his friends tried to get him removed to London or sent into exile; but Ambrose was content to let matters take their course: he had to die sometime, he said, so what better cause could there be? In prison he found solace in reading *Consolations of Philosophy* by the Christian Roman statesman Severinus Boethius (480-524), written during his own imprisonment. King Alfred the Great had translated the *Consolations* into Anglo-Saxon and it was a work that had a profound influence on the medieval world. Boethius discourses on the transitoriness of all earthly greatness. Tradition has it that Boethius died a martyr and the relevance to his own situation would have been keenly appreciated by Ambrose. He was, however, deprived of the book when it was confiscated by his jailer.

After four months in prison he was brought to trial on 7 September before Sir Robert Heath, former Solicitor-General and Attorney-General, and future Lord Chief Justice. Heath was a reasonable and fair-minded man who had shown sympathy for religious prisoners, but he had received direct instructions from Parliament to ensure that the extreme penalty of the law was imposed on any priest caught in Lancashire in order to cow the papists, who were numerous in the county.

When the indictment was read, Ambrose immediately acknowledged that he was a priest and that he had carried on his priestly ministry for over twenty years. The judge asked why he had not obeyed the proclamation and left the country. He excused himself on two counts. Firstly, the proclamation specified Jesuits and seminary priests, whereas he was neither of these; he was a Benedictine monk. Secondly, he said that his poor health and his recent stroke had made it impossible for him to undertake such a long journey within the time allowed, as was known to those who had captured him. This elicited some sympathy in the Court so the judge tried a different approach. He asked the prisoner his opinion of the justice of the law that sanctioned priests being put to death.

Ambrose replied that the law was unjust and barbarous. 'For what law can be more unjust than this by which priests are condemned to suffer as traitors merely because they are Roman, that is true priests? For there are no other true priests but the Roman; and if these be destroyed, what must become of the divine law, when none remain to preach God's word and administer His Sacraments?'

Heath then asked Ambrose what was his opinion of those who made such laws and of those who were charged with putting them into execution. Sensible of the pitfalls inherent in the question, Ambrose said that he prayed God would forgive all involved.

The judge accepted the priest's illness in mitigation and informed him that he would set him free if he promised not to seduce the people any more.

'It will be easy to pledge my word to this since I am no seducer but a reducer of the people to the true and ancient religion. I have laboured to disabuse the minds of those who have fallen into error and I am resolved to continue until death to render this good office to these strayed souls'.

Heath could not help admiring Ambrose's honesty and courage. 'You speak boldly,' he said, 'to a man who is master of your life and who can either acquit or condemn you as he shall judge proper'. Ambrose answered that he could not deny the judge's powers adding, 'You have power given to you over me through a wicked policy, but be aware, although I appear before you in quality of a criminal, being as I am a minister of Jesus Christ and a priest of the New Law, in spiritual matters I am judge and I declare to you that if you continue to condemn the innocent and remain in the darkness of heresy it will be to my salvation and your damnation'. To this Heath responded that he had the advantage, since Barlow's sentence would be carried out first. Then he directed the jury to find the prisoner guilty.

The next day Ambrose was taken back to court to be sentenced to death, to which he responded with great serenity, 'Thanks be to God.' He then prayed that God would pardon all those who had been accessory to his death.

Heath seems to have genuinely regretted the priest's death but recognised that once Ambrose had openly confessed his priesthood there was nothing he could do to save him from the penalty of the law, especially in the face of demands from Parliament. Nonetheless, he acceded to Ambrose's request that he be given a cell to himself in order to prepare for his execution. Unknown to Ambrose, his fellow religious, meeting in General Chapter, had elected him to one of the English Benedictine titular offices as Prior of Coventry.

On Friday, 10 September 1641, carrying a wooden cross that he had made, Ambrose was placed on the hurdle and taken to his place of execution. Arrived at the gallows, he walked around it three times while reciting the *Miserere*. The Protestant ministers were all for entering into a dispute with him, but he told them that this was neither the time nor the place, for he had 'something else to do at present than to hearken to their fooleries'. He suffered with great fortitude as the dreadful sentence was carried out. His head was impaled on the tower of the Collegiate Church, Manchester. When the news of his martyrdom reached his brother monks at Douai, a celebratory *Te Deum* was ordered and Masses of thanksgiving were offered.

Many relics of the martyr survived. His left hand, once kept at Knaresborough, Yorkshire, is preserved by the Benedictine nuns of Stanbrook Abbey, now at Wass, North Yorkshire. His skull was obtained by Francis Downes of Wardley Hall, where it was kept for many years. The Downes family died out and the Hall passed into other hands. The whereabouts of the skull was forgotten. In 1745, during the time of the Jacobite Rising, when 'Bonnie Prince Charlie' reached Manchester, a detachment of rebel soldiers came to Wardley Hall and the tenant farmer, Mathew Morton, had to supply them with carts and horses. He was already finding it difficult to make ends meet and the loss of his property only made matters much worse. Morton resolved to abandon farming and try weaving instead. To accommodate the looms he decided to demolish a ruinous part of the old hall. In the process a box was discovered. Morton broke off the lid and found that it contained a skull, still with a full set of teeth and an amount of chestnut hair. The skull was subsequently enshrined in a niche of the hall staircase. Wardley Hall, where the skull has appropriately remained, has been the residence of the Bishops of Salford since 1930. To clear up all doubts, in the twentieth century scientific tests were carried out at St Bartholomew's Hospital, London, by pathologists and the anatomist, Professor Cave. As a result the skull relic was authenticated. In the 1960s the jawbone was removed and presented to the modest parish church of St Ambrose at Chorlton-cum-Hardy, that being the parish in which Ambrose's birthplace was located. Today there is a blue plaque outside Manchester Cathedral commemorating Edward Barlow.

What of the Barlow family? They were loyal to King Charles and supported him in the Civil War. Sir Alexander, the martyr's brother, was listed in 1641 as 'living in very reduced circumstances.' He died in 1642 and was succeeded by his son, a fourth Alexander, who died without issue in 1654. He was followed by his half-brother, Thomas, and he in turn by his son Anthony. The family remained faithful to the Church, and Anthony appears in the lists of recusants under George I. Anthony's son, Thomas, died of jail fever in Lancaster Castle in 1729. The last male heir of the family, Thomas, inherited Barlow and when he died in 1773 without issue, over seven hundred years of family history came to an end. Barlow Hall was ravaged by fire in 1879. One bay dated 1574, with its oriel window, survived. The hall is now the clubhouse of Chorlton-cum-Hardy golf club!

Alban Roe

Stone walls do not a prison make.

To Althea, Richard Lovelace, 1618-58

Bartholomew Roe was born at Bury St Edmunds, Suffolk, in 1580 or 1583. He was educated at Cambridge University and apparently, being of a naturally pugnacious disposition, he grew up an aggressive Protestant. The turning point in his life came while he was still at Cambridge when he went to visit friends at St Albans who told him about a recusant called David who was in prison there. Bartholomew resolved to visit him in order to persuade him of the error of his papist beliefs. It did not work out as he had intended. The prisoner was so sincere and resolute in his beliefs and argued his case so convincingly that Bartholomew returned to the university 'uneasy in mind' about his religion. As a result he embarked upon a course of reading and he also consulted Catholic priests.

In 1607 he became a Catholic and went to Douai, arriving on 13 November, and asked Dr Thomas Worthington, who had been President of Douai since 1599, to admit him to the English College as a 'convictor' - that is a student who financially supported himself. (Dr Worthington features in a long report from a spy sent to Lord Burleigh in 1601. It would be laughable were it not so chilling in its hate-filled venom. The writer, while aiming principally to condemn the Jesuits, manages to rope in all and sundry into his ungrammatical, splenetic invective. He 'knows not how to compare this cursed crew to anything better than the bawling three-headed dog of hell, whereof I will make the first head at Douai and in Flanders, the second, middle and chief head at Rome, the third and worst in Spain, the heart of the hell-hound Cerberus I reckon to lie in England and the other parts and members dispersed all over, and in this form I will anatomize this odious and ugly beast ... of all of which the most dangerous and pernicious are Doctor Worthington, President of the College of Douai.' In 1616 Worthington returned to the English mission, working mainly in Staffordshire, and he died at Biddulph Hall in 1627 aged 78.)

Regulations had recently come into force limiting the number of new scholars, so for a few months Bartholomew lived in lodgings while attending Douai University. He matriculated on 21 February 1608 and was then admitted to the college. In January 1611 he was expelled for insubordination and insolence so his pugnacity was clearly still a problem. The Vice-President and Procurator issued a report which stated that

Bartholomew Roe is most unsuited to the aims of this college on account of his contempt for the discipline imposed by his superiors, his leading some of the young men living in the college astray, and the great danger of his misleading more ... for among other things the said Bartholomew Roe, after a penance had been given to some students by their superior, publicly, before many others, took to task those who had performed the penance given them, saying, 'If it were my concern, I should not have done the penance'. On another occasion he incited two young men not to submit to the punishment ordered by a superior, with these and similar expressions: 'Are you willing to submit to so ignominious a punishment?'

Bartholomew's dismissal was conditional, 'for a time, until he became more suited to the college', although the college superiors nonetheless considered him a suitable candidate for ordination. Not prepared to take all this lying down he demanded a testimonial as to his character, which was refused. He was popular with his fellow students and twenty of them provided a testimonial to his good life and conduct. It may well be that the college authorities over-reacted to Bartholomew's 'sharp and ready wit, and a tongue well hung' which often led him into rash and indiscreet behaviour.

Bartholomew had been considering becoming a Benedictine and this too was unlikely to endear him to his Douai superiors. He may have been familiar with the recently established Benedictine monastery at Douai but, perhaps discretion being the better part of valour, he sought admission late 1612 or early 1613 to the order not at Douai but at another English Benedictine monastery: St Lawrence at Dieulouard near Nancy in Lorraine, which had been founded in 1606 by Dom Augustine Bradshaw in a disused collegiate church. The zealous and strictly observant Dieulouard community was still struggling to establish itself. In 1614 Bartholomew was professed under the name of Alban. In 1615 he was ordained priest and was sent to Paris to help in the foundation of the third community of the re-established English Benedictine Congregation. This was the monastery of St Edmund, King and Martyr. After the French Revolution this monastery moved to Douai and in the hostile, anticlerical political climate in France at the start of the twentieth century it moved to England where it has remained as Douai Abbey, Woolhampton, near Reading.

In the judgement of his superiors Alban was considered 'thoroughly qualified by a long practice of all religious virtues for the apostolic functions' and from Paris he was sent to England. He worked zealously in London for three years, gaining a reputation as a preacher, before being arrested and sent to the New Prison, Maiden Lane, in 1618. Here he remained, enduring great hardship, for five years until at the request of Count Gondomar, the Spanish Ambassador, he was included in King James' general amnesty of 1623 and sent into permanent exile. He made his way to the Benedictines at St Gregory's, Douai, but after only four months he was back in England to resume his work. In 1627 he was arrested by a professional priest hunter called Francis Newton.

This despicable man had once been an attorney-at-law but had been expelled from the legal profession for dishonesty. He and three equally disreputable cronies, James Wadsworth, Robert Luke and Thomas Mayo, formed a priest-catching co-operative purely for profit. They later boasted to have been responsible for the apprehension of thirty-seven priests, several of whom died in prison, as well as the execution of thirteen of them. Newton had Roe imprisoned at St Albans in the very cell - still to be seen - in the abbey gatehouse where he had first been led to the Catholic Faith.

Conditions at the prison were terrible and after two months, through the influence of friends, Alban was transferred to the Fleet Prison in London where he was to spend the next fifteen years. The Fleet, built beside the eastern bank of the now underground river of the same name, was just outside the city walls. It was one of the most ancient prisons consisting of several long buildings with four upper storeys, ranged around courtyards. The post of Keeper had been hereditary for hundreds of years. Principally for debtors, the Fleet was a notoriously corrupt institution. Like all prisons of the time it was run as a profit-making enterprise with the Keeper receiving the prisoners' payments.

The fees - which were extortionate - covered everything, such as putting on irons and taking them off and food and lodging; the larger the amount the prisoners paid to the Keeper, the better the accommodation they were allocated. There were even fees for visitors. If inmates were willing and able to pay enough they were allowed out of the prison on parole, provided they gave their word to return before nightfall.

Alban was to take full advantage of this laxity, especially in the later years. In spite of suffering from the pain of kidney stones - for which he endured more than one operation - he was the life and soul of the prison. His conviviality, gaiety and holiness endeared him to everyone and soon won the hearts of his jailers, who were invited to join him in games of cards while he told them amusing stories. There was a deeper purpose underlying all this socialising. As a result he was able to carry on an effective ministry, and not only amongst the prisoners. He was allowed to receive visitors, as well as being frequently allowed out on parole to minister to the Catholics of the city, returning to the prison at night. While ever he was permitted to follow this regime, what need was there for him to try and escape? Presumably through his influence, his brother James converted and joined the Benedictines and his sister became a nun. While in prison Alban translated Latin works into English, including St John Fisher's treatise on prayer.

The Long Parliament put an end to such tolerance. In 1641 Alban was moved to Newgate, and on 19 January 1642 he was brought to trial at the Old Bailey charged under Elizabeth 27 with being a priest and a seducer of the people. The main witness against him was an apostate Catholic. Alban, unhappy that the jury in their ignorance should be guilty of his death, at first declined to enter a plea. He was told that the penalty for this was the *peine forte et dure*: crushing to death. Alban responded that 'My Saviour has suffered far more for me than all that, and I am willing to suffer the worse torments for his sake'. The judge sent him back to prison telling him to think hard about it. Alban consulted some fellow priests and the next day, back in court, he agreed to a trial, pleading 'not guilty'. Accused of seducing people he said that if they meant by seduction winning souls for God then he confessed he had seduced a fair number. He was quickly pronounced guilty and received his barbarous sentence with serenity and a cheerful countenance. Making a low bow to the judge he thanked him, saying, 'How little this is in comparison to the bitter death which Christ suffered for me.' Pugnacious to the last Alban denounced the unjust law making it a capital offence to be a priest and he offered to dispute his faith in open court against all comers.

Charles I and the Civil War Martyrs, 1625-49

He spent the remaining two days asking his friends to pray that he might be worthy of martyrdom. Many Catholics came to visit him to offer comfort but found that the roles were reversed as Alban told them, 'Accept persecution with joy as coming from God. It is usually a mark of His favour, for at least it serves to increase our glory if we endure it with patient resignation.' On the morning of Friday, 21 January 1642, Alban and a fellow priest known as Richard Reynolds, said Mass at Newgate. At its conclusion Alban spoke to those present. 'When you see our heads up on London Bridge, take it that they are there to preach to you, to proclaim that faith for which we are about to die.'

There is some discrepancy or confusion about Alban's companion. Known to posterity as Blessed Richard or Thomas Reynolds, his real name was Thomas Green, his maternal family being called Reynolds; hence his alias. Some sources claim he was born c.1560 and ordained in 1592, that he had worked on the English Mission for fifty years and was aged eighty at the time of his death. The documentary evidence shows that he was born at Oxford in 1579 and was ordained at Seville in 1602, afterwards returning to England, from where he was banished in 1606. He soon resumed his work on the mission and was imprisoned again in 1628 and condemned to death. He was reprieved by the King at the request of Henrietta Maria. Imprisoned in Newgate in 1632, he was released two years later. He was in the Gatehouse in April 1635 but discharged a few days later, only to be rearrested. He spent the next seven years in prison waiting for the death sentence to be carried out. Said by a contemporary to be a 'remarkably mild and courteous' man, he was now very infirm and rather corpulent. Father Reynolds confided to Alban that he was fearful of his execution. Alban strengthened him with powerfully comforting words.

At 9 a.m. the priests were summoned and Alban walked out of the prison greeting the sheriff and his officers. Father Reynolds was already on the hurdle and Alban warmly embraced him and then, taking him by the hand, jokingly felt his pulse, asking him how he was. 'In very good heart,' replied Reynolds, 'blessed be God for it and glad I am to have for my comrade in death a man of your courage.' Making the sign of the Cross Alban said to the carter, 'Come on, let us be going'.

The road to Tyburn was lined with Catholics who ran forward to kiss the hands of the two priests and beg their blessing as they were drawn on the same hurdle. The day was wet and the road was deep in mud, so that their hands, faces and clothes were spattered with dirt. Alban declared that, 'they esteemed it more to be drawn up Holborn on a sledge for this cause, than if they were riding in the best coach the King had'. Seeing a Catholic man he knew he called out his name saying, 'My friend, do not be surprised at seeing me here; do you not know that am going to a great feast? Give my greetings to your master and tell him that you have seen me in a coach without wheels, and that I hope to be going to a place where I will pray God for him'. It was about 11a.m. when they arrived at Tyburn. On the scaffold the two priests gave each other absolution and Alban helped Father Reynolds up into the cart, from where, having asked the sheriff's permission, Thomas spoke to the crowd for almost half an hour. He forgave his enemies and prayed that the sheriff would merit the 'grace to be a glorious saint in heaven', at which that official was much moved. He addressed the executioner, 'Pray do your duty neatly, I have been a neat man all my life.' Alban had been speaking words of comfort to three felons who were also to be hanged, and he now turned to the people with a cheery greeting that was typical of his ebullient temperament, 'Well, here's a jolly company! I know you come to see me die: my fellow here has in great measure spoke what I would have said. However, I shall repeat the words I used at the bar. I say then, here again, for a man to be put to death for being a priest, this being the most sacred and highest order in the world, is an unjust and tyrannical law. I say that the law of the 27th of Queen Elizabeth, which condemns a man to death for being a priest, is a wicked, unjust and tyrannical law, a law not to be found in the whole universe, England excepted.' When the sheriff told him he could not vilify the law in that manner Alban desisted.

He presented his skull cap to a Captain Godfrey in the crowd; an act which got the captain into trouble with Parliament. He gave away all the money he still had to the executioner, asking him to drink to his health, but cautioning him not to get too drunk. He asked God to pardon his many sins and expressed the hope that his death would be satisfaction for them. He forgave his persecutors and asked the sheriff if his life would be spared if he conformed. The sheriff swore that if he abjured his Catholicism even at this late stage he would be freed.

'See then,' said Alban, 'what the crime is for which I am to die, and whether my religion be my only treason ... I wish I had a thousand lives then I would sacrifice them all for so worthy a cause.' A Protestant minister present was much affected by Alban's demeanour and went to speak to him. Alban told him, 'I will remember you', to which the minister replied, 'I pray you will'. Noticing one of the warders from the Fleet prison Alban jocularly said, 'You often told me that I should be hanged, and truly my unworthiness was such, I could not believe it; but I see you are a prophet.'

The two priests said the *Miserere* psalm in alternate verses. The executioner offered to cover their faces. Alban told him that he had

Charles I and the Civil War Martyrs, 1625-49

disposed of his handkerchief; but it did not matter because, 'I dare look death in the face, nor am I ashamed to be seen by those standing by.' Both of them called out the name of Jesus as they were simultaneously turned off the ladders. They were allowed to hang until they were dead, but the crowd made clear its displeasure at their deaths. In *Acts of the English Martyrs* by J H Pollen SJ, we read that on this occasion, as on so many others,

The Catholics piously vied with each other in taking away relics of the martyrs. Many dipped their handkerchiefs in the dismembered bodies; others carefully collected the bloodstained straw from the ground. About noon the quartered remains were returned to Newgate in baskets ready for boiling. For a few days the jailers made not a little profit from allowing Catholics into the prison to view the remains and take relics in return for a cash payment, before the heads and quarters were placed on poles over the city gates.

Count Egmont, later Duke of Gueldres, who was the Spanish Ambassador in London 1640 to 1645, collected a huge number of relics of the martyrs. He was present at the deaths of eleven priests, including Roe and Reynolds, and among his relics was a piece of the executioner's apron soaked in their blood. It is now preserved at Downside Abbey. The monks of St Lawrence, Dieulouard, were driven out during the French Revolution. In 1802 they found a home in North Yorkshire in a house donated by Lady Anne Fairfax. It was to become Ampleforth Abbey and College.

Henry Morse

All the bright company of Heaven hold him in their high comradeship.

Into Battle, Julian Grenfell, 1888-1915

Henry was born in 1595 at the house of his mother, Margaret Collinson, in the village of Brome, Suffolk, just south of Diss, close to the border with Norfolk. He was the seventh of the nine sons, out of fourteen children, of Robert Morse who came from Tivetsall St Mary, Norfolk, a short distance from Brome. In spite of his actual place of birth Henry always described himself as a Norfolk man. Robert was a man of some wealth, owning land and property, granaries and cattle. In his will he left a legacy to all his surviving children. Henry's share was £300 plus an annuity of £27 and the 'silver bell salt with cover' that had belonged to his maternal grandmother. He may have attended Norwich Grammar

Charles I and the Civil War Martyrs, 1625-49

School as a boy, but in May 1612 he entered Corpus Christi College, Cambridge. For whatever reason, whether religious or not, he did not remain long at Cambridge, leaving to study law at Barnard's Inn, one of the Inns of Court in London. While a student he attended the trial of St. John Almond. He later joined the Gray's Inn chambers of Richard Ross, who was his cousin by marriage. He appears to have conformed to the extent that he attended church occasionally. We know a great deal about his life from two contemporary biographies, the first written by his friend Father Ambrose Corby, the second by the great Jesuit historiographer, Father Philippe Alegambe, who had been one of Henry's professors in Rome. We are also fortunate that parts of the detailed journal which Morse kept in prison have survived. It is an invaluable record, especially for the last months of his life.

What made Henry decide to become a Catholic is unclear. All he tells us is that while at Gray's Inn he began to have religious scruples. The Inns of Court were full of Catholics or fellow travellers and he may have begun to have doubts from contacts he must have made among them. Henry's father, Robert, appears to have been a secret Catholic. He was certainly reported for recusancy to the Bishop of Norwich in 1583 for 'attending a secret Mass in the parlour of Stuston parsonage', situated between Brome and Diss. This suggests that the parson was one of those who had conformed while carrying on secretly ministering to Catholics. Robert was also accused of sheltering the priest Montford Scott q.v. Perhaps he was reconciled to the Church before he died, and this had a deciding influence on Henry. One of his older brothers, William, who was also a lawyer, had converted and gone to Douai in 1611. William is known to have been in London in the autumn of 1613 and it is surely not too fanciful to imagine that it was he who helped convert Henry. William was ordained at Arras in 1617 and returned to work in England in 1618 where he became a Jesuit. He died in Hampshire in 1649. Furthermore, another brother, Robert, had married Margaret, a daughter of Sir Henry Bedingfeld, described as 'the most obstinate papist' in the county. The Bedingfeld family were perhaps the most famous Catholic family in Norfolk, their home was (and is) the beautiful, moated Oxburgh Hall, in which the priest hole believed to have been constructed by Nicholas Owen can still be seen. It is inconceivable that Robert, yet another lawyer, had not converted when he married into the Bedingfeld family.

Whatever the deciding factor, in 1614 Henry obtained a licence allowing him to go abroad. He sailed from Gravesend to Dunkirk and arrived at Douai on 5 June, where he was formally received into the Catholic Church. Having decided to become a priest he returned to

Charles I and the Civil War Martyrs, 1625-49

England to obtain the inheritance left him by his father in order to pay for the cost of his priestly education. Unfortunately he was arrested on disembarkation. In spite of being in possession of a travel licence, when he refused to take the oath he was sent to London and put in the New Prison, Southwark, where he remained for the next four years, along with a great many other Catholics. Among his fellow prisoners were two Jesuits. The first, Father John Falkner, years later was chaplain to the Arundell family at Wardour Castle when it surrendered to the parliamentary forces in 1643 after a gallant defence by Lady Blanche Arundell. The second, Father Francis Wallis, Morse was to meet again in 1633 at Liège, where Wallis was then serving as rector.

The Spanish marriage proposed for Prince Charles was causing enormous anger around the country. Morse benefited from the amnesty to placate Spain granted by King James in June 1618, when he was included amongst the one hundred imprisoned priests sent into exile. He arrived back at Douai in early August where he was greeted by his brother, William, who was about to return to England. In December it was decided to send Henry to study at the English College, Rome, where that remarkable and holy priest Father Thomas Fitzherbert SJ [7] was Rector. Morse later acknowledged his debt of gratitude to Fitzherbert, who exercised great influence over him as well as being his good friend. He also formed lasting friendships with fellow students who later worked with him on the English Mission and were to share his imprisonments. While in Rome, Henry used the alias Cuthbert Claxton, a name he retained and by which he was known in England.

Although reported as being quick-tempered Henry was a very conscientious student who was always willing to help with the domestic chores of the college. He enjoyed acting as a tour guide to the English visitors to the Eternal City. He was ordained deacon in July 1620 and afterwards made a short visit to England. The precise date of his priestly ordination is not recorded but it was probably in May 1624. The following month he left for England. Before doing so he had asked permission to enter the Society of Jesus, and the Jesuit Superior General, Mutio Vitelleschi, had written to the Order's English Provincial, Richard Blount, advising him to receive Henry if he persisted in his desire. Henry wrote an account of his journey to Father Fitzherbert in Rome. Travelling via Brussels with two companions, they ran out of money because of the high cost of meals and Henry, having lent his companions money, had to borrow from the Jesuits at Liège. He eventually reached Saint-Omer and was provided by the college with all he needed to complete his journey home. Arrived in London he reported to Father Richard Blount, the Jesuit Provincial, at his secret lodgings.

Henry was listed amongst the twenty-four novices studying at the newly-established Jesuit novitiate at Edmonton, north of London, although few of them probably actually lived there. Henry cannot have been there for very long because he was sent to Northumberland to undertake his first year's training under Father Richard Holtby. Henry took up residence at St Anthony's, the home of Mrs Dorothy Lawson at Byker, on the north bank of the River Tyne, three miles from Newcastle. Mrs Lawson was the second daughter of Sir Henry Constable and his wife Margaret Dormer, of Burton Constable Hall, Holderness, East Yorkshire. Her equally resolutely recusant sister, Catherine, was the wife of Sir Thomas Fairfax of Gilling, 1st Viscount Fairfax. In 1596 Dorothy married Roger Lawson, a barrister of the Inner Temple, the son of Sir Ralph Lawson, but at thirty-six she had been left a widow. The Lawson's had been Lords of the Manor of Byker for generations. Dorothy lived at Hebburn but some months before Henry arrived she took up residence at St Anthony's. The house, described by Mrs Lawson's biographer as 'commodious for pleasure, and pleasant for all commodities; the rich and renowned river Tyne ebbing and flowing in such proportionable distance from the house that neither the water was inconvenient to it nor did it want the convenience of the water.' St Anthony's was one of the great Catholic centres of the North. Dorothy had her own chapel and library and there were plenty of hiding places. In addition to the local Catholics, foreign seamen engaged in transporting coal from Newcastle were welcomed at St Anthony's, named after the Franciscan saint of Padua.

The house was the chief residence of the septuagenarian Father Richard Holtby, [8] once tutor at Oxford to Alexander Briant. Holtby, who had succeeded Henry Garnet as Superior of the Jesuits, had spent most of his priestly life in the North. He was a skilled carpenter and the hiding places at St Anthony's were his work. He also made and embroidered the liturgical vestments. In this congenial environment Henry acted as chaplain, celebrating Mass daily and looking after the spiritual needs of the Catholics in the area. Soon the plague had broken out in Newcastle and Morse had his first taste of caring for its victims among the coal miners. King Charles had been forced to bow to the will of Parliament and priests had to be more cautious with so many pursuivants actively engaged in seeking them out.

Henry's arrest on Wednesday, 12 April 1626 was the result of an unlucky set of circumstances. He had been working in and around Durham and spent the previous night at an inn at Chester-le-Street before collecting a boy from Jarrow named John Berry, who was being sent to Douai to complete his education. Henry and the boy waited by the Tyne until the *Sea Horse*, a collier on its way to Calais, came into view. By previous arrangement, they hailed the captain, William Carew, and asked to be taken on board, where they changed into seamen's clothes. Somehow the customs officers at Newcastle had got wind of their plans and just below Tynemouth Castle the boat was ordered to drop anchor; it was then boarded and Henry and the boy were taken prisoner. At first Henry tried to pretend he was a foreigner who did not understand English, but when that did not work he tried to bluff his way out of the situation. When searched he was found to have rosary beads. In the end he had to admit that he was a Catholic and refused the oath when it was offered. But he would not admit to being a priest and nothing could be proved against him. The following morning Morse was twice examined by the mayor of Newcastle, William Liddel and the aldermen. When asked to take the Oath of Allegiance Henry refused.

While he was in custody another ship had been boarded and its passengers arrested. Among them was Father John Robinson SJ, posing as a Dutch merchant under the alias Zachary Vanderstyn. Catholic books were found in his possession and he was arrested. Robinson, who came from a recusant family - his parents had been imprisoned in York Castle - had been a student in Rome with Morse and the following day he was sent to join him in the ancient Newgate jail at Newcastle. Richard Neile, Bishop of Durham, suspecting that the area was a hotbed of smuggling Catholic books and conveying papists to and from the Continent, ordered raids to be made on all the known Catholic houses in the district.

Morse and Father Robinson were visited in jail by the steadfast Mrs Lawson, who provided them not only with a few comforts but also the necessary materials to enable them to say Mass. Soon they were removed to the appalling York Castle jail which was full of Catholics, men and women, kept in disgusting conditions in unventilated cells which often flooded; no wonder the death rate at the prison was so high. The two priests set about doing what they could to relieve their fellow sufferers, begging alms to provide sustenance and in the process converted a good number of the criminal inmates, which roused the ire of the Protestants of York. One case in particular achieved notoriety. A husband and wife were condemned to death for robbery. They were chained in a dungeon to await execution and Henry managed to gain access to speak to them. They greeted him with obscene oaths but by gentleness and patience he quieted them. He spent the night talking to them about the Catholic faith and by dawn they indicated their wish for absolution, which he gave them. A few hours later the couple appeared on the gallows and the crowd was eagerly anticipating their hanging. Imagine the furore when, instead of the cursing and shouting that had been expected, they declared themselves to be Catholics and died peaceably.

It was in his dark prison cell that Henry served out his novitiate. Under the guidance of Father Robinson he managed to make a retreat, complete the Spiritual Exercises and take his first vows.

Three years passed and then in March 1630 Henry was released and banished in perpetuity. At the same time Father Robinson was put on trial and sentenced to death. He was reprieved on the gallows at the last minute and left to spend a further eleven years carrying out his apostolate in the prison. When eventually released Father Robinson continued his work in Yorkshire where he died in old age. Morse made his way to the English Jesuit novitiate at Watten, where Father Henry Bedingfeld was Rector. In the autumn he was given employment as chaplain to the British mercenary soldiers fighting in the Spanish army in the Low Countries. He worked so hard, travelling about unceasingly ministering to the troops that he 'had strained himself to the limit of his endurance' and fell seriously ill. For a time he was not expected to live. Thanks to the extraordinary care of the Jesuit Fathers he recovered, but was not considered fit to return to arduous duties in the field so he was given an administrative post looking after all the temporal needs at Watten as well as serving nearby churches. He gave special attention to looking after the sick in the community. In 1633 Henry was moved to the Jesuit College at Liège where he undertook similar duties. By now he had recovered his health and Father Richard Blount asked for his return to England. Blount had recently arranged for some of his priests to travel to America to serve the Catholic immigrants in Maryland. Among them was Father Andrew White [9] who was smuggled on board the departing ship at the Isle of Wight. Father Andrew was destined to become the founding father of the English-speaking Catholic Church in the American colonies. Morse was appointed White's replacement in the London district.

The district was organised into a 'college'. Its minister was Father Philip Fisher (real name Thomas Copley) [10] but he departed for Maryland in 1637. Morse's closest companion was probably Norfolk-born Father Edward Lusher. Henry laboured in and around the poorest areas of Holborn and Bloomsbury, visiting the Catholics crowded together in the squalid slums of the parish of St Giles-in-the-Fields. In the autumn of 1635 London was again hit by an outbreak of the plague, and this time it was virulent and widespread. By the following spring the capital was in the throes of a major epidemic. The usual precautions were ordered, including sealing infected persons together with their families in their homes.

Henry will always be remembered for his heroic work in London during the plague, where he devoted himself to the sick with enormous courage. As Catholics were legally 'non-persons' they were not entitled to any assistance from the parish relief funds and depended entirely upon their co-religionists for help. In the absence of a bishop, the Chapter of secular priests governed the Church in England. Sadly, they and the Jesuits were often at loggerheads, usually as a result of mischief-making amongst some in the Chapter. In the dire situation, in April 1636 the Jesuits and seculars met to organise charitable relief. They agreed to co-operate in relieving sick Catholics. Father Matthew Wilson, the London Superior of the Jesuits, appointed Henry as their representative and the seculars nominated Father John Southworth. The two priests were to be responsible for the relief of Catholics in the panic-stricken city, whose civic leaders had all fled and where lawlessness reigned.

To prepare himself for the work Henry undertook a few days quiet retreat at Cheam, Surrey. The conditions in which the two priests laboured were indescribably foul, horrific and dangerous. The stench alone would have been unbearable and Henry found this a special trial. A contemporary writer, who said that 'death was everywhere', left a description of the symptoms of those suffering from the plague.

The pain of the swelling was in particular very violent, and to some intolerable; the physicians and surgeons may be said to have tortured many poor creatures even to death. The swellings in some grew hard, and they applied violent drawing-plasters or poultices to break them, and if these did not do they cut and scarified them in a terrible manner. In some those swellings were made hard partly by the force of the distemper, and partly by their being too violently drawn, and were so hard that no instrument could cut them, and then they burnt them with caustic, so that many died raving mad with the torment, and some in the very operation. In these distresses, some, for want of help to hold them down in their beds, or look to them, laid hands upon themselves. Some broke out into the streets, perhaps naked, and would run directly down to the river ... and plunge themselves into the water.

The screams and cries of those locked into their homes with dead plague victims were constant. Red crosses and often the words, 'Lord have mercy on us', were painted on the doors. At night, accompanied by the ringing of a bell and the cry of, 'Bring out your dead', the cart would come round to take away the bodies.

Henry had a list of 400 infected families, both Catholic and Protestant. Carrying a white rod and with 'a distinctive mark on his outer garment' to signify that he visited plague-infected houses, day and night Henry attended to the spiritual and physical needs of the Catholics, including laying out the putrid and disfigured corpses for burial at night in the specially dug communal pits where, uncofinned, they were tipped. It was work that Henry understandably found particularly repellent but, forcing himself to overcome his aversion, he courageously struggled on. Father Southworth was perhaps not always the easiest of persons to get on with. One gets the impression that in common with many 'northerners' John bluntly said what he thought. In the early days of their collaboration he found occasion to complain to the Chapter of Henry's 'unworthy timidity.' Although he heard confessions and gave Holy Communion to the dying plague-stricken, Henry did not always administer the Sacrament of Anointing, or Extreme Unction. Given his sensitivity it was probably true that he found it just too repulsive to touch their putrid foreheads, lips, nose and ears as well as fearing the contagion. Henry took the rebuke in good part, asked forgiveness for his lack of courage and made sure that in future he did not omit the anointing to the dying. At his later trial, many witnesses gave testimony to his administering the Sacraments to the Catholic sick and dying plague victims, as well as to the many converts he made through his equal kindness to poor Protestant families.

As conditions worsened, anxiety increased about the lack of money to continue providing relief. On 6 October 1636 Henry and Father Southworth issued a joint public appeal *To the Catholickes of England*, begging them for funds. In the appeal tribute was paid to the generosity of Protestants who were 'so ready to assist their distressed brethren' with alms. The response from the Catholics nationwide was generous, from the Queen downwards, and undoubtedly saved the lives of many who would otherwise have perished for lack of sustenance. When Father Southworth was arrested, Henry had to continue his work alone, assisted by two brave Catholic doctors: Thomas Turner and Dr More. The medical profession was, uniquely, the only one from which Catholics were not barred although both Turner and More had qualified at Padua, then the best medical school in Europe. For the second time Henry felt ill and it was realised he had contracted the plague. With the help of Dr Turner, who lanced his sores, and the fervent prayers of all his fellow Jesuits almost miraculously he recovered. After taking only a week's rest, despite his weakness, he forced himself to resume his work even if it meant that he had to drag himself from his bed to assist the dying.

In November 1636 Henry was arrested on the evidence of a nurse attendant, Mrs Frances Hall. She alleged that he had received a dying

Charles I and the Civil War Martyrs, 1625-49

Protestant couple named Seares, parishioners of St-Giles-in-the-Fields, into the Church. Knowing they were near to death the couple sent a message to a Catholic neighbour to send for Morse. He hurried to them and heard their confession and received them into the Church. Immediately after their bodies had been removed for burial Mrs Hall reported Morse to William Haywood, the rector of St Giles, who had remained at his post. He informed the local justice of the peace who sent a constable to apprehend the priest. The constable waylaid Henry the following day on his way to give Holy Communion to a dying Catholic. He was taken to the constable's house where, anxious about the safety of the Blessed Sacrament he carried around his neck, he consumed the Sacrament and hid the pyx. When Henry offered the constable some money he was allowed to go. He was later summoned for interrogation by the justice. The questions he was asked led Henry to believe that the justice was not really interested; indeed, he seemed annoyed that the priest had been apprehended. The justice told Morse that he was well aware the Catholics of London were most generous to their sick and, praising the work Henry was doing, he let him go. Morse returned to the constable's house and retrieved his pyx. When, shortly afterwards, the constable fell victim to the plague he was so impressed by Henry that he sent for him to receive him into the Church.

However Henry's fame was such that there were those determined to see him imprisoned; but in spite of being harassed he managed to evade being arrested, sometimes by bribing his would-be captors. Francis Newton, the disgraced lawyer who was responsible for the arrest of Alban Roe, together with his cronies - one of them an apostate priest - was intent on pursuing Henry. Morse himself described Newton as 'a man of infamous life and behaviour, being for many dishonest practices ... expulsed from the profession of an attorney-at-law ... and has been convicted of many abuses and corruptions'.

Newton's chance came on Monday, 27 February 1637 when, with fellow villain, John Cook, he accosted Henry in a street in Holborn as he was returning from visiting a sick woman. Henry demanded to see their warrant at which 'they jeered at me in reply and threatened to handcuff me, and this went on until we reached a tavern in Fetter Lane. Here at last they produced the warrant giving them authority. It had been issued as far back as 1632. I declared it was worthless and outdated.' The two pursuivants then took Henry in a boat up river to Westminster, 'all the way there Newton was pouring out a stream of curses, saying blasphemously that he wanted to see whether the saints I honoured would come to my aid.' Henry was taken to an inn in Broad Sanctuary where, he wrote, 'they immediately searched me to the skin' and took from him some religious medals. As Morse had been in close contact with plague victims and had suffered from the sickness himself - 'the sores on my body were scarcely healed' - it was illegal for an inn to admit him, but he was locked up for the night. The next day, 28 February, Newton and Cook attempted to extort money from Henry. He was given nothing to eat and Morse became increasingly anxious as to what would happen to the sick if he was detained for much longer. Cook then conducted Henry to the Sun tavern at Westminster and proceeded to negotiate his release for a payment of £5. It was now night and Henry did not have that amount of money with him so, in spite of the late hour, Cook escorted him to Holborn to try and obtain a loan from Catholic friends. He visited an apothecary named Hodson who agreed to provide the £5. On the excuse of going upstairs to fetch the money Hodson informed two Catholic gentlemen in the house what was happening. As a result the men charged downstairs, swords at the ready, and Cook fled from them as fast as he could run and Morse escaped from his clutches. Hoping to avoid further trouble from the Newton gang if he paid them the ransom demanded, two days later Henry returned to the Sun tavern. Here he was detained in solitary confinement during which he had to 'endure many insults and much ill-treatment because I insisted on having nothing to do with all the people who came and went, but passed those holy days of Lent in fasting and prayer.' Attempts were being made to interest the Queen in Morse's situation so to forestall her intervention on 2 March Newton approached Sir John Coke, the King's Secretary. Henry tells the story: 'He was a man who had a lifelong hostility to Catholics. Newton set his business before him and returned not merely with a commendation for the work he had done, but with a promise of a large reward and with a warrant also to examine my moral character and conduct. Moreover, he was not on any account to set me free, even at the Queen's bidding, unless he was first shown a written order for my release.'

Newton was determined to see Henry hanged and set about putting together a case for his prosecution. On 5 March Henry was brought before the Privy Council, accused of reconciling many people to the Church. By an unfortunate coincidence William Haywood, the rector of St Giles, chose that day to make his complaint about Morse, petitioning the Council 'for the glory of God' to take action against the great increase of Catholics in the parish. For the next three weeks Henry continued to be held at the Sun tavern in Newton's custody. On 26 March a warrant headed by Archbishop Laud's signature was issued by the Council for Henry's removal to Newgate and the transfer was carried out two days later. Because of the plague executions had been

Charles I and the Civil War Martyrs, 1625-49

postponed and the jail was grossly overcrowded. Henry was accommodated in a room up three flights of stairs, close by the prison chapel. His already fragile health deteriorated but he tried to keep up his Lenten devotions, as well as carrying on a ministry amongst the prisoners.

After four weeks in Newgate, on 22 April he was taken to the Old Bailey to stand trial. The proceedings lasted all day. Father Matthew Wilson, the Jesuit Provincial, was present in court and the same night he wrote a detailed account to the General of the Society of Jesus, Father Vitelleschi. Father Wilson also advised him that he was arranging for Henry to immediately take his final vows as a Jesuit. Although the trial followed the familiar pattern, Morse defended himself well. Newton was on hand to testify that Henry was a Jesuit priest. Morse protested that no one should believe the evidence of such a 'notorious rogue.' The presiding judge remarked, 'He may be a rogue. Still it is possible for you to be hanged on his testimony.' Many accusations were levelled against him of converting Protestants. It was clear that at least some of the evidence for this was fabricated, as several brave Catholics testified that they had always been of that religion and were not converts, such as the eighty-year-old widow, Cecily Crowe. She 'took her oath' that she, her daughters, and her son, who also gave evidence, had always been Roman Catholics and had it not been for Morse and the help he gave her she would have died either of starvation or sickness being shut up in her home. Margaret Allen, a poor woman of St Giles parish declared that she had sent for Morse when the family was struck down with the plague. 'He many times gave alms to me, my husband and my two little children, who all died of the plague, the parish not giving us anything, we being very poor and seven person in number shut up.' Another parishioner, Elizabeth Godwin, testified that being a poor labouring woman 'and being shut up for seven weeks, buried three of my little children.' Morse was the only one who relieved her with alms from Her Majesty. Yet another Catholic labourer, Edward Freshwater, had a similar story to tell. When Morse tried to visit the family he was refused permission to enter by the constables and had to hand money in through the window. Freshwater was shut up with his family for eight weeks. The only time the door was unfastened from outside was to collect the bodies of his children.

Morse insisted that whatever he had done he had not, 'in any interpretation done with the intent of alienating the King's subjects from their allegiance.' Thanks to the honest intervention of one of the judges, Sir William Jones, the jury was directed to ignore the first charge of 'perverting his Majesty's subjects' as there was 'not a scrap of real evidence' with which to convict Henry. Jones instructed the jury only to consider the second charge; that of being a priest. This resulted in Henry being found not guilty of persuading to popery, but guilty of being a priest. Morse thanked the presiding judge who remarked, 'Look, he actually thanks me because he has been found guilty,' to which Henry responded, 'My Lord, I thank you deeply from the bottom of my heart.' He was returned to Newgate to await sentence and on 23 April, the Tuesday of Easter week, he made his solemn profession as a Jesuit before Father Edward Lusher.* Henry wrote of his gratitude for this 'unexpected blessing' and prayed that 'while I live I may never cease to act in a manner worthy of this high honour, which I acknowledge I have done nothing to deserve from His divine hand ... may I bear always in my heart the testimony of my gratitude.'

Henry was unaware that after his trial Father George Con, papal representative to the Queen, had sought out the King and informed him of all the facts concerning the Jesuit's ministry to the sick. The King promised he would find a solution. When Henry was called back to the Old Bailey on 26 April, instead of being sentenced he was ordered back to prison, the King having given instructions for sentence to be deferred and that the prisoner be treated with respect.

After a further month in Newgate Henry wrote a personal letter to the King informing him of the circumstances of his arrest and trial and of the true character of Newton, on whose evidence he had been convicted. Henry begged the King who 'out of clemency and justice had preserved him from the sentence of death' to set him free 'from death in this prison' especially in view of his state of health. Henry's doctors, Turner and More, also sent a report to the King confirming how desperately ill he was. After three months in Newgate, Henry was released by the King on bail of 10,000 florins. Henry remained in London for about a year, but as his health was still giving cause for concern he was sent to minister to the Catholics of Devon and Cornwall. The choice of district may also have been influenced by the fact that this was where his brother William worked based in Exeter.

By early summer 1640 Morse was back in London. It was a time of great political and military tension. At the instigation of the tenacious

---

* Father Lusher was arrested in 1645 and condemned. He claimed immunity as a servant of the Spanish Ambassador who lodged a complaint, and in exchange for a promise that Lusher would be sent overseas within ten days, the House of Lords agreed that Lusher should be released. The Commons then voted on a resolution for his reprieve, which passed by a majority of five. An order was issued for the priest's banishment. Lusher was to emulate Morse. Aged 76, he died in London in 1665, a victim of the Great Plague, having contracted the disease while caring for the sick.

Charles I and the Civil War Martyrs, 1625-49

Newton on 17 June Henry was apprehended with Father John Goodman, whose story has been told earlier in this chapter. The arrest was made by John Gray, one of Newton's men, and Father Thomas Longueville, who had been a fellow student of Henry's in Rome. Thomas Longueville had a chequered career. Born at Stony Stratford, Buckinghamshire in 1598 he was ordained in 1622. For a time he had been in Newfoundland with Lord Baltimore. He was extremely anti-Jesuit, against whom he alleged several personal grievances, and it was presumably this hostility that led him to participate in Morse's arrest. The following day Henry was brought to Lambeth before William Laud, the beleaguered Archbishop of Canterbury, and members of the Court of High Commission. Morse 'pleaded the freedom granted to me under the King's own hand and the security of a thousand pounds that had been given in my name. and because I had committed no offence against the King I expected the Lord Archbishop and his court to grant me the favour which the King himself had been graciously pleased to bestow. Canterbury, however, answered that he had no intention of being compelled to act thus. At this I protested that I had been released by his Majesty, whose protection I now enjoyed. But his Lordship of Canterbury retorted that that was a point for the cognisance of another court, but one that carried no weight in his. And with this he ordered me to be taken back to Newgate.' Laud probably had no choice but to act as he did given that feelings were running so high against him in the capital and he had been threatened with violence from the mob. To release a Jesuit priest would have only added fuel to the fire.

On 3 July Morse and Goodman were released on the order of Secretary Windebank, clearly acting on behalf of the King who was now fully apprised of the vile activities of Newton and his gang. A royal proclamation ordered all priests to leave the country by April 1641, so Henry voluntarily left England. This was not only for the sake of his health, but also because his exile was considered prudent arising from the cause célèbre of Father Goodman's condemnation and reprieve by the King.

In 1641 Morse became chaplain to the English regiment in Flanders under the command of the Catholic Colonel Sir Henry Gage, the son of Sir John and Lady Margaret Gage neé Copley. His fellow chaplain was another future Jesuit martyr, the Northamptonshire priest Father Peter Wright. Morse and Wright worked tirelessly looking after the welfare of the soldiers and this bore fruit in the many conversions they achieved. Henry also gave retreats at the convents of the English Carmelites and Benedictine nuns in Flanders, and at Ghent he met two of the daughters of Mrs Dorothy Lawson whom he had known as children. Civil War having begun in England, Gage, accompanied by Father Wright, had returned home to fight for the King. Morse was also anxious to return home and while at Ghent in 1643, to his great joy, filled with premonitions of his probable martyrdom, his request was granted. It seems certain that Henry returned home on one of the ships escorting Queen Henrietta Maria from Scheveningen, Holland, where she had been seeking financial support for the King. The royal party disembarked at Bridlington. Because he was so well known in London it was thought prudent to keep Henry in the North of England and he was assigned by Father Christopher Simpson, Father Holtby's successor, to work in Cumberland. This formed part of the Jesuit 'College of St John' which also embraced Durham, Northumberland and Westmorland. Here Henry's colleagues included Fathers Ralph Corby, Thomas Rochester and Thomas Gascoigne. Morse ministered in Cumberland for about eighteen months. Given the terrain and the distances to be travelled, it cannot have been easy missionary territory.

Late one night while he was answering a sick call he accidentally ran into a troop of parliamentary soldiers and was immediately arrested and taken to the house of a local magistrate. The magistrate's wife happened to be a Catholic. She found the opportunity to speak to him in private and obtained confirmation of what she had guessed: that he was a priest. Regardless of the risk to herself, she secretly conducted Morse through the woods to safety, but the whole area was full of troops. He remained at liberty for six weeks, during which time the parliamentary troops gained control of Northumberland and Durham. When recaptured Henry was sent to Durham and lodged in filthy conditions before being transferred to Newcastle prison. On 19 November, together with Royalist supporters from the town, he was put aboard a coal boat bound for London. As the collier sailed down the Tyne Henry must have seen the sad sight of St Anthony's, which had been razed to the ground by the Scots in the fighting. He complained of being brutally ill-used by the crew on the voyage, during which appalling weather was experienced, before Yarmouth, on the Norfolk coast, was reached. Here the boat docked in order to make repairs. The town was the home of George, one of Henry's elder brothers. He was a wealthy man with shipping interests. When he heard of his brother's arrival he sent a message to his eldest brother, Robert, in Norwich. Robert, a distinguished lawyer, hastened to Yarmouth. He supplied Henry with ample funds, which he later distributed to the poor. Robert also tried every means at his disposal to obtain Henry's release. When this failed he gave money to the sailors on a promise that they would treat his brother better as the boat continued its journey to London. It made no difference as Henry records that he continued to be 'barbarously used'.

Finally reaching London, Morse was ordered to be imprisoned at Newgate. Hearing that the priest had arrived the Spanish Ambassador, Count Egmont requested that Henry be allowed to visit him. So en route to the jail Henry, who had never met Egmont before, was permitted to call on him where he received a warm welcome. Henry said Mass at which the ambassador served. That night Henry was locked up in Newgate where he joined many other priests among them William Henderson, who had worked in Henry's old area of St Giles; James Brown, John Hammond, Edmund Canam, Edward Tresham, Andrew Waferer alias Friar, Peter Wilford OSB, the Bridgettine, John Abbot and the Franciscan, Walter Coleman.

His brother, Robert, had preceded him to London trying everything he could think of to secure his release. Henry wondered if it was appropriate that 'so much endeavour' be made on his behalf 'and such extraordinary pains taken. Should I not entrust all things to the holy Providence of God and to the ordinary course of events? For my part I desire to be dissolved and to be with Christ. But if I am necessary to my people, I do not refuse to labour.' Robert offered huge sums of money on bond to the mayor and other officials if they would agree to his brother's banishment. It was all in vain. Parliament was in the ascendant and without the King the Catholics in London no longer had any protection. They were at the mercy of the pursuivants and many priests were arrested and imprisoned. Henry was brought to the magistrates' court on 1 January 1645 and was remanded to Newgate. At the earlier trial of Archbishop Laud one of the charges made against him by Francis Newton was that he had failed to bring Morse to justice. Viciously persecuted by the fanatic Puritan pamphleteer, William Prynne, who tampered with witnesses at the Archbishop's trial, Laud was attainted of treason by Parliament and executed on 10 January. The Anglican services were abolished and many churches were sealed up. On 17 January Morse was again brought to court: Wadsworth and Mayo were on hand to gloat. His appearance was brief. There was no trial. On the strength of his conviction nine years earlier, he was sentenced to death.

During the few days left to him before his execution Henry was in great demand from a constant stream of visitors. Father Ambrose Corby recorded that it was an amazing sight to see hundreds of people, Catholics and non-Catholics, from morning until night, wanting to see him and ask for his prayers and his blessing. They had to pay a fee to the jailers to be allowed in. One of his visitors was fellow Jesuit, Father Thomas Harvey, a cousin of the Marquess of Bristol. The priest's sister was known to Morse as she was the first Englishwoman to join the reformed Carmelites of St Teresa and had become prioress at Antwerp, where Henry had been chaplain. Harvey was well known to Newgate prisoners to whom he acted as a sort of unofficial chaplain. He took special care of those awaiting execution and was recorded as receiving many condemned prisoner converts into the Church. Francis Newton was on the look-out for him and obtained a warrant for his arrest, which cruelly stated that if Harvey was caught and condemned he was to be flogged at the cart's tail all the way from Newgate to Tyburn. Newton seized his opportunity and Father Harvey, along with twenty other visitors, was apprehended. They remained in custody until after Henry's execution when, all except Father Harvey, they were released on payment of a fine of £20. Harvey had to endure imprisonment until released through the influence of the Spanish ambassador who had a direct interest in that the priest had been born at Mechlin in the Spanish Netherlands during his parents' exile there.

Also among Henry's visitors were the ambassadors of the European powers or their representatives who came to see this hero of the Faith. One of them, the secretary to the Imperial Ambassador, came twice. 'Never in my life', he recorded, 'have I seen greater resolution in any man, nor a calmer expression on anyone's face; he was so happy and modest and was so affable to all.' On his last day Henry fasted; nor did he get any sleep, as he continued to receive visitors until the early hours of the morning. During the course of his last night a Catholic prisoner drew a portrait of Henry which was accounted a remarkable likeness. The portrait has survived.

At 4 a.m. on the morning of 1 February 1645, Henry recited the Litany of the Saints for the conversion of England and then offered a votive Mass of the Holy Trinity in Newgate, surrounded by many friends. Afterwards he had a brief rest before visiting all the condemned prisoners and speaking a few words of comfort to each. Everyone was astonished at his calm and smiling countenance. Among the prisoners was Father Christopher, a Franciscan from the north of Ireland. Arrested in Ulster he had been shipped to Newgate. Henry made a special point of embracing him. Later Father Christopher was to record, 'There was nothing belonging to this world in his expression: his face was so lit up with joy that if I had been a heathen, the experience of sweetness I then had would have won me to the faith he professed. And it was not a brief or fleeting experience; it has stayed with me to my old age.' At 9 a.m. Sheriff Gibbs came to conduct Henry to his execution. Henry fell to his knees and loudly thanked God in such a way that everyone was visibly moved. In a friendly gesture, taking Henry by the hand, the sheriff led him through the prison gate into the street. Gibbs personally laid straw on the hurdle and helped Henry to lie down. He was then tied on by ropes and dragged through the muddy streets to Tyburn, escorted by fifty mounted guards. When the procession reached the church of St Giles-in-the-Fields someone offered Henry a drink and he paused to pray for the souls of all those among the poor plague victims he had tended. Just before Tyburn was reached a magnificently decorated coach overtook the procession and the sheriff called a halt. From the coach alighted Melchior, Marquis de Sabran, the French resident. Kneeling down in the mud he begged Henry's blessing. Beneath the gallows Henry was made to wait half an hour for the arrival of a cartload of common criminals who were also to die. During the delay the Marquis de Sabran walked through the mud to the hurdle and took Henry by the hand asking him for his prayers for the peace of Christendom and to remember France. Henry then presented his handkerchief to the ambassador, that being all he had left to give. It was a memorable occasion. Not only the Marquis, but the ambassadors of all the European Catholic powers were present in their coaches, along with their diplomatic suites, to witness the priest's execution. As Henry rose from the hurdle he saw Count Egmont in his coach and, speaking to him in Latin, bade him farewell saying, 'Most illustrious Sir, I shall remember my promise, and when I come before God I shall not be unmindful of the kindness your Lordship has shown me.' Egmont then congratulated Henry on being allowed a martyrs death.

Henry was helped to climb the ladder and the rope was placed around his neck. He asked permission to address the crowd. 'I am come hither to die for my religion', he began. 'For that religion which was founded by Christ, established by the Apostles, and propagated through all the ages since to the present day by a visible hierarchy; a religion that rests on the testimony of the Scriptures, supported by the authority of the Fathers and Councils, outside which there is no salvation.' (See Appendix 5) The crowd began to murmur and Sheriff Gibbs begged Henry not to say anything that would upset them but to declare if he knew of any treason against the King or Parliament. 'I have a secret to declare,' said Morse, 'that highly concerns his Majesty and Parliament to know.' That caught the silent attention of the crowd. 'Gentlemen, take notice, the kingdom of England will never be truly blessed until it returns to the Catholic and apostolic faith ... This is the secret, Sir, if you will have it; this is the treason I have to disclose.'

Henry then spoke about his life and work during the plague. One of the Protestant ministers present took exception to this. 'You ought not to glory in your own works', he remonstrated. 'I will glory in nothing save my infirmities', Morse responded, 'All glory I ascribe to God, who was pleased to make use of so weak an instrument, and this day is pleased to call me to seal my faith with my blood, a favour I have begged these thirty years.' To which the minister replied, 'Well, you have now got your wish.' Henry concluded, 'And therefore I give the greatest praise I can to Almighty God. I pray that my death may be some kind of atonement for the sins of this kingdom; and if I had as many lives as there are sands on the seashore, I should willingly lay them all down for this end, and to testify to the truth of the Catholic faith.'

Henry was then told by the sheriff to say his final prayers. With his hands joined he prayed out loud, 'God eternal Father, Son and Holy Ghost, most humbly I ask pardon for all my offences, for I confess myself a great sinner. I repent from the bottom of my heart. As I pardon all those who have injured me, and especially those who now stain their hands with my blood, so I ask pardon of all whom I have in any way offended'. He ended by praying for 'England, his dearly-beloved country.' He asked that a nightcap be pulled over his eyes and a member of Count Egmont's staff came forward with one which he handed to the hangman with some money, requesting that it be returned to him after the priest's execution. Striking his breast three times Henry committed his soul into God's hands. He was left to hang until he was dead before the butchery began. He was stripped naked while still hanging. Count Egmont and the Marquis de Sabran came close to see the body being quartered. When this was completed the servants of the ambassadors dipped their master's handkerchiefs in Henry's blood. 'My Lords,' said Sheriff Gibbs, 'I regret that you should have witnessed such a shameful spectacle.' Henry's four quarters were displayed on the city gates and his head on London Bridge.

From Yorkshire, Father John Robinson, who had been Henry's fellow prisoner so many years before, wrote to Vincenzo Carafa, Jesuit Superior General, 'What likelihood is there now that I shall follow Father Henry Morse ... May he now be pleased to accept the prayers of his fellow soldier.'

The great historian of the period, Dame C V Wedgwood OM, in *The King's War 1641-47*, wrote of Henry Morse, '... and there ended a life of patient devotion and self-sacrifice by a death of exalted fortitude'.

Charles I and the Civil War Martyrs, 1625-49

Notes to Chapter Six

1 William Bishop was born at Brailes, Warwickshire, in 1553. His family had remained loyal to the Old Faith and many of their monuments, including members of the family who were priests through to the nineteenth century, may be seen in the magnificent parish church at Brailes, among them that of William's father who lived to the age of ninety-two. William was educated at Oxford and when he returned home he relinquished his interest in the family estate in favour of his brother and went to Rheims. After completion of his studies at Rome he was ordained in 1581, setting out for England at the end of the year. Claiming to be a merchant he was arrested on arrival at Rye, Sussex, early in 1582 and after interrogation was sent to the Marshalsea. Condemned to death in 1583 on the spurious charge of plotting to kill the Queen, he remained in prison until banished in January 1585. He went to Paris and became Doctor of Divinity at the Sorbonne. He was back in England in 1591 and in 1598 travelled to Rome to present the grievances of the English clergy about the Archpriest Blackwell. Rome clearly did not take kindly to their complaints and William was arrested and held prisoner in the English College. In 1599 he was put 'on trial' and forbidden to return to England. He went to Paris but was back in England by 1603 where he was one of the thirteen signatories of a Protestation of Allegiance to Elizabeth. It had little effect because he was arrested again, but released. In 1605 he was recorded as working in Herefordshire and by 1610 was in Oxfordshire. In 1611 he was once more a prisoner in the Gatehouse. When he was released he went to Paris and became a member of Arras College. In spite of his past record, in Paris on 4 June 1623 he was consecrated titular Bishop of Chalcedon and set off for England; the first bishop for over forty years.

2 Richard Smith (1567-1655) was the son of John and Alice Smith of Welton, Lincolnshire. He was educated at Trinity College, Oxford. He went first to Rheims and then, in 1586, to Rome, where he was ordained in May 1592. From there he went to Valladolid and taught philosophy for several years. In 1598 he was sent to Seville, and despite his desire to return to England was engaged in teaching for four years, followed by a period at Douai. In 1610 he at last returned home, but stayed for only two years before leaving for Paris as Superior of Arras College, which, with the financial assistance of Abbot Philip de Caverel of Arras, he had helped to establish as a place for higher studies by the clergy. While at the college he produced many works of apologetics and controversy. When William Bishop died, Smith was appointed his

successor. He was consecrated at Paris 12 January 1625 and returned to England in April. The Anglican bishops were incensed at his daring to exercise his episcopal functions and warrants were issued for his arrest. In the teeth of opposition from among the ranks of the Catholic clergy as well as the Protestants, he retired to France in August 1631 and was financially supported by Armand, Cardinal Richelieu. Deprived of that support when the Cardinal died in 1642, he took refuge with the Augustinian nuns in Paris and died there 18 March 1655.

3 Walter Montagu was the second son of Henry Montagu, 1st Earl of Manchester. Born in London he was educated at Cambridge. He was engaged on the Continent in diplomacy and acted as a secret service agent for the English government in France. In 1635 he became a Catholic and was found a position in Queen Henrietta Maria's household on his return to England but was asked to leave by the King. When the First Civil War broke out Montagu helped raise funds for the King from the Catholics, which earned him the enmity of Parliament and he left for France. Here he joined the Benedictines and through the influence of the Queen Regent of France was appointed Abbot of Nanteuil. In 1643 he came to England with important letters. He was arrested and sent to the Tower, where he remained until 1647, and was then banished by order of Parliament in 1649. He was appointed chaplain to the exiled Queen Henrietta Maria and lived at the Palais Royal, Paris, between visits to his abbey. He returned to England with the Queen in 1663 following the Restoration and resided at Somerset House. He returned with her to France in 1665. He helped officiate at the Queen's funeral in 1669 when she died at the convent of Chaillot. He was deprived of his abbacy in 1670 and became abbot of St Martin's, Pontoise. After his colourful career he died in Paris in 1677.

4 Mary Ward was born at Mulwith with Newby near Ripon in 1585. Her parents fell into the vagrant Catholic category being constantly on the move as far afield as Northumberland in order to avoid conviction. For several years she lived with her Babthorpe relatives at Osgodby where she received a fine education, learning Latin, French and German. Father Richard Holtby SJ acceded to her desire to enter the Poor Clares at Saint-Omer. She later established a convent for English Poor Clares at Gravelines. In 1609 she realised that she was not called to such a vocation and returned to London where she visited Catholic prisoners. A woman of vision, in 1609, with a number of companions she established a religious congregation at Saint-Omer teaching English girls seeking an education away from the persecution. She went on to

Charles I and the Civil War Martyrs, 1625-49

establish other religious houses in Germany, Austria and Italy. In 1618, on a return visit to London, Mary was arrested and condemned to death without trial, but friends raised money to obtain her release. Her congregation was modelled upon the Jesuits, with whose order she hoped to amalgamate. Defying the prejudices of the time she courageously organised the first communities of active, unenclosed women in the history of the Church. This brought her into conflict with Rome and in 1631 her order of 'Jesuitesses' was suppressed, though the severity of this was mitigated somewhat after Mary had an audience with Pope Urban VIII. She returned to London in 1639 and, hoping to open a Catholic school, had a meeting with Queen Henrietta Maria. Because of the Civil War, by 1642 she and her sisters moved to Heworth near York. It was here, after a lifetime of unceasing activity, that Mary died in January 1645, surrounded by her faithful companions. She was buried in the cemetery by the church at Osbaldwick, near Heworth. Mary's ideas about the role of women were centuries in advance of her time and came in for much criticism. Known as the English Ladies or later the Institute of the Blessed Virgin Mary, today Mary's foundation is called the Congregation of Jesus and still flourishes at the famous Bar Convent at York.

5 Richard Blount was born 5 October 1563 into a well-to-do family at Blount Hall, Leicestershire. Educated at Balliol College, Oxford, in 1583 he entered the English College, first at Rheims and then at Rome, where he was ordained in 1589. He returned to England via Spain in 1591, posing as a returning prisoner of war sailor. Lord Howard of Effingham himself examined Richard but found nothing suspicious about him. In 1596 he joined the Society of Jesus and spent about eight years sheltered by the Darell family at their ancestral home, Scotney Castle, near Lamberhurst, Kent. The castle was raided in 1597, when Thomas Darell had been sent to London as a prisoner; his wife confined to the house of a Justice of the Peace, and his servants sent to jail. Mr Darell had commissioned the construction of several priest holes and armed with provisions, for about a week Father Blount had remained hidden in a secret compartment under a staircase. He escaped detection. About a year later, at Christmas-time 1598, one of the Protestant servants informed the Justices, and they raided the house again in the middle of the night. Richard, with nothing on but his breeches, and accompanied by his serving man, managed to get into a hiding place within the thick stone walls. Mr Darell was absent from home, but his wife and children were locked up in a room over the gatehouse while the searchers took possession of the house, which they searched for ten

days. The rain fell heavily and the searchers, wet and weary, made a fire in the hall to warm and dry themselves; and there they sat, drinking. Father Blount, who had resolved to die in hiding rather than give himself up, seizing the opportunity of the stormy night, asked his man to go out and investigate. When apprised of the situation, Richard came out of hiding. Barefoot, the two men climbed over two walls about ten feet high, and clambered to a broken tower about sixteen feet above the moat, which at that point was eighty feet wide and far too deep to be able to wade across. Taking his courage in his hands Blount leaped from the tower into the icy moat. He intended that his man would jump down after him, hoping to carry him over the moat, but he realised that he was too weak to be able to do this, fearing they might both drown in the attempt, so he swam across to the other side, directing his man to another place where the water was shallower and he could wade through it. After losing their way, the two of them finally made it to the house of a nearby Catholic husbandman, who loaned them some clothes and shoes. They then walked fourteen miles across rough country and found shelter at the house of a Catholic gentleman. Here Richard remained for three weeks to recuperate, his legs and feet being injured and inflamed. He was then conveyed to London to the care of a doctor.

Richard moved into secret lodgings with a lady in London; and here he spent the remainder of his life. His residence was so secret that we do not have a clue where it might have been located. A great many of the letters he both sent and received have survived, which throw light upon the situation of Catholics under Elizabeth and James. He narrowly escaped capture when he was on his way to meet Father Robert Southwell at the Bellamy's house at Harrow. For fifteen years Richard managed to keep out of sight of the servants in the house, apparently living as a recluse and only going out at night and returning home at daybreak. Even among the wealthy circles in which he moved he was legendary for his rich apparel. One description of him was in 'a gold-laced suit. A cloak lined through with velvet ... rings on his fingers, a watch in his pocket ... a stiletto at his side.' Yet at home he dressed very simply, often in threadbare clothes. His greatest grief was that his brothers remained Protestants. One of his converts was Thomas Sackville, Earl of Dorset, Lord High Treasurer under James I. Anne of Denmark, James's consort, was believed to be a secret Catholic. She had given scandal when she had refused to receive communion at her coronation. Early in 1605, while pregnant, by some means she made contact with Father Blount and asked to receive the Sacraments of the Catholic Church from him. She also undertook not to attend Anglican services. As the Queen was persuaded to attend the Church of England, her Catholicism cannot have been very deep-rooted, although Richard reprimanded her for doing so. Blount also had direct contact with King James. Following upon the crazy conspiracy involving Father William Watson, which Richard and Henry Garnet had helped frustrate, Richard was sent a letter from Rome, advising of an alleged plot to assassinate the King. He rode all the way to Salisbury to deliver the letter personally to James. The King reacted kindly to Father Blount; as a result he was granted a royal pardon for having been ordained priest. In 1617 Richard became Superior of the Jesuit Mission and when England was made into a Province, Blount became the first Provincial. He died in London on Whit Sunday, 13 May 1638, having been Superior for twenty-one years. By a special privilege his funeral, conducted by the Capuchin friars, took place late at night in Queen Henrietta Maria's chapel at Somerset House. It was attended by all the Jesuits of the London district. Richard was afterwards buried in the cemetery attached to the chapel. Normally reserved for the Catholic members of the Queen's household, it was the only Catholic cemetery in London.

6 Blessed Richard Herst was born near Preston. He was a yeoman farmer but also a well-known recusant. John Bridgeman, Bishop of Chester sent pursuivants to arrest him, and in doing so a scuffle ensued with Herst's farm servants. In the course of the fracas one of the three pursuivants, called Dewhurst, fell and broke his leg. Unfortunately the leg turned gangrenous and Dewhurst died. Before he did so he made a statement confirming that it was the result of an accident, absolving Herst and his servants from blame. In spite of that Herst was accused of murder and brought to trial. Hearing of Dewhurst's statement, the jury was unwilling to convict him, but Judge Yelverton told them that the authorities were determined to make an example of Herst, and therefore they must deliver a guilty verdict against such an obstinate recusant. The real reason for his condemnation was apparent when his wife was asked to urge her husband to take the oath. She responded that she loved Richard but had rather see him face death than wrong his conscience. Herst was offered his freedom, even on the scaffold, if he took the oath. The sheriff came for him about one in the afternoon. As he was led out of prison carrying a picture of Christ crucified, he looked up to see Edmund Arrowsmith's head impaled at the top of the castle saying, 'You have sent that blessed martyr to prepare the way for us.' The executioner was fumbling over fastening the rope and Richard said to him, 'Tom, I think I must come and help you.' He was martyred at Lancaster 29 August 1628. He left behind six young children and a heavily pregnant wife. Three beautiful letters that he wrote to his

spiritual father before his death, one on the morning of his execution, are extant. The last one reads:

> Now I take my last leave. I am now dying, and I am as willing to die as ever I was to live, I thank my Lord and Saviour, who I trust will never fail me. I have comfort in Christ Jesus and his blessed Mother, my good angel and all the blessed saints. And I am much comforted in the valiant and triumphant martyr that is gone before me and I do much to trust in his good prayers. How I have been used, you will hear, and likewise what I had offered to myself if I would have taken the oath. I hope my friends will truly understand ... I would I had as many lives to offer as I have committed sins ... I pray you remember my poor children, and encourage my friends about my debts, and let it appear that my greatest worldly care is to satisfy them, as far as my means will extend. Once again adieu. I desire to be dissolved and be with Christ Jesus. I trust we shall meet again in heaven to our eternal comfort; now I take my last leave, this execution day, about eight of the clock and commit you to Christ Jesus.

7 Father Thomas Fitzherbert (1552-1640) came from the famous recusant family of that name. He was the eldest son of William and Elizabeth Fitzherbert of Swynnerton, Staffordshire, and a grandson of judge Sir Anthony Fitzherbert. He was educated at Oxford where, in 1572, he served a year in prison for recusancy. In 1580 he married Dorothy East and they had a son, Edward, but two years later, wanting freedom to practise his religion, he retired to France. He then moved to Spain, where for many years he served Philip II on various diplomatic missions. After his wife's death in 1588 he went to the English College, Rome, and on 15 August 1602 he was ordained. He published a book against the ideas of Machiavelli. In 1613 he joined the Society of Jesus. He became superior of the English Jesuit mission, living at Brussels from 1616 to 1618, and then Rector of the English College, Rome, from 1618 to 1639. This distinguished and eminent priest died in Rome 17 August 1640, aged eighty-eight and was buried in the English College chapel.

8 Richard Holtby was born in the hamlet of Fryton, near Hovingham, North Yorkshire, in 1553. He was educated at Oxford and Hart Hall, Cambridge. He did not take a degree but arrived at Douai on 3 August 1577, and just eight months later, on Holy Saturday, 29 March 1578, he was ordained. His eleven fellow ordinands included Alexander Briant, Joshua Pulleyn, John Hart and John Bennet. Richard returned to England in February the following year and commenced his mission in the northern counties. Early in 1581 he played host to Edmund Campion for several quiet days, during which time the Jesuit made the finishing touches to his book *Ten Reasons*. No doubt influenced by his famous guest, Richard decided to become a Jesuit. In 1582 he rode to London to find Father Jasper Heywood, the Jesuit Superior, but failing

to locate him he sold his horse and used the proceeds to fund a ship's passage to France. He made his way to Paris and there, under the guidance of Father Thomas Darbyshire, he made the Spiritual Exercises of St Ignatius. He joined the novitiate for the English Province of the Society at Verdun in 1583 and concluded his studies at Pont-à-Mousson. He was then made Superior of the Scots College there in 1587. Sadly, ten of his students died of the plague and he buried them with his own hands in the outlying fields. Richard survived and returned to England in 1590, landing on the Yorkshire coast with Father John Curry. He became superior of the Jesuit 'College of St Michael' which covered the whole of Yorkshire. Although very active on the English mission, he was never once apprehended. This was not due to shortage of information about him that was supplied to the government by spies and apostates and he had several narrow escapes. In one spy's report he is described as, 'a little man with a reddish beard.' In 1594, while staying with the Trollope family in Co. Durham, Richard and the eldest son of his host travelled a considerable distance for the baptism of a child. As they approached the house on their return they saw that the place was surrounded and a search was taking place. They were spotted and had to run for their lives. They remained hidden in a wood for two days and nights, sleeping the first night in a tree and the second in a cave. Richard seems to have been a jack-of-all-trades: mason, gardener, carpenter and embroiderer. He constructed several hiding-places in various locations. Father John Gerard described him as 'father of all the Churches' from Yorkshire to the Scottish border. Following the martyrdom of Father Henry Garnet in 1606, Richard was chosen to succeed him and he may have taken up residence in London at this time. He showed great prudence as leader of the forty-two Jesuits under his care on the mission. He was Superior for three years. Richard wrote a long account of the persecution in the North. The venerable priest died in County Durham in May 1640 at the age of eighty-seven.

9 Father Andrew White was born in London in 1579. He studied at Douai and in Spain and was ordained in 1605 and returned to England in that perilous Gunpowder Plot year. In 1606 he was captured and banished and shortly afterwards joined the Society of Jesus. Back in England Andrew began advising George Calvert, 1st Baron Baltimore about the possibilities of colonisation in America. Calvert was the same age as Andrew having been born at Kiplin, near Catterick, North Yorkshire in 1579. The Calvert's were a strongly recusant family. His father suffered relentless harassment for his religion. Removed from parental care George was sent to a Protestant school and while at

Charles I and the Civil War Martyrs, 1625-49

Oxford he conformed. He married a Protestant and their children were baptised as Protestants. Calvert entered the royal service, faithfully serving King James, and he held many important posts in England and Ireland, culminating in his appointment as one of the two principal Secretaries of State in 1619. In 1625 he was given his peerage, taking the title Baltimore after his estate in Ireland. Then to the surprise of many Calvert resigned all his offices except his membership of the Privy Council and publicly declared his return to Catholicism. Godfrey Goodman, Bishop of Gloucester alleged that Calvert had always been a secret Catholic; which is probably true. Calvert's interest in the New World was not just for commercial reasons. He saw it as a possible refuge for persecuted English Catholics. His first settlement was in Newfoundland but it did not prove successful so in 1632 he obtained a royal charter to found a colony further south in what was to become the state of Maryland. Calvert died within weeks of the granting of the charter but he is nonetheless regarded as the founder of Maryland. He left the settlement to his son, Cecil, so named in honour of Robert Cecil. He in turn was succeeded by his own son, Leonard, the first colonial governor of Maryland. In November 1633 Andrew White accompanied the first colonists to Maryland as the superior of the Jesuit mission. He was joined by a fellow Jesuit from the English Mission, Father John Altham vere Grosvenor. On 25 March 1634 he celebrated the first Mass in English-speaking America and laboured for the next ten years converting many native Indians as well as colonists. He wrote a famous account of the early history of Maryland and compiled a grammar, dictionary and catechism in the local Algonquin language. The English Puritan, Richard Ingle, was a tobacco trader to the Americas, although he was in reality little better than a pirate. He was at odds with the Catholic leaders in Maryland and when Leonard Calvert seized his ship Ingle managed to escape. In 1645 he returned and attacked the colony in the name of Parliament, imprisoning its Catholic royalist leaders and looting all their property. He took over the government of the colony and arrested Fathers Andrew White and Philip Fisher, sending them back to England in chains where they were committed to Newgate. Here they remained until January 1648. Andrew, by now 69 years of age, begged to be allowed to return to Maryland but this was refused and he died in 1656.

10 Philip Fisher, whose real name was Thomas Copley, was the eldest son of William Copley and the grandson of Sir Thomas Copley of Gatton, whose history has already been related. Philip/Thomas was born during his parents' exile in Madrid in 1596. He arrived in

Charles I and the Civil War Martyrs, 1625-49

Maryland in 1637 and being a man of great ability he took over the care of the Jesuit mission. In 1645 he was arrested with Father White and sent back to England. When he was released from prison in 1648 he boldly returned to Maryland where he found a Catholic community that had flourished in his long absence. It cannot have been an easy assignment given the unspeakably atrocious tortures and horrific martyrdoms of his fellow Jesuits at the hands of the Iroquois, Huron and Mohawk Indians that were taking place at this time. *
Philip/Thomas was recorded as 'the most distinguished man among the fourteen Jesuits who had worked in Maryland.' He then attempted to join the mission in Virginia. He wrote to Vincenzo Carafa, the Jesuit Superior General in Rome:

A road has lately been opened through the forest to Virginia; this will make it but a two days' journey, and both places can now be united in one mission. After Easter I shall wait upon the Governor of Virginia upon business of great importance.

Philip/Thomas died in Maryland in 1652.

---

* These were the heroic proto-martyrs of North America. René Gupil was born 1608 near Angers, France. He was a surgeon before joining the Society of Jesus. He served the mission to the Huron Indians until captured by the Iroquois in 1642 and taken to Ossernenon, on the Mohawk River, New York where he was killed. Isaac Jogues was born 1607 at Orléans. He worked among the Mohawks and had already suffered tortures and mutilation from their enemies, the Iroquois, whose slave he became for a time. He escaped and returned to France but resumed his work in Canada. In 1646, while on a peace mission to the Iroquois at Ossernenon he was attacked and killed with tomahawks by a Mohawk clan. Jean de Lalande was also martyred in the same year. Noel Chabanel was martyred by the Hurons in 1649. Jean de Brèbeuf was born in Normandy in 1593. He worked tirelessly amongst the Hurons with whom he lived, learning their language, along with his Jesuit companion, Gabriel Lalemant. In 1649 they were captured in a raid by the Iroquois. Their deaths were unbelievably horrific, among the most abominable in the annals of Christian martyrdom. They were appallingly tortured, mutilated, burnt and their remains eaten. These martyrs were all canonized in 1930.

Chapter Seven

Puritan Parliament and the Commonwealth

Oppression stretches his rod over our land.

Samson, William Blake, 1757-1827

The French Ambassador in London under the Protectorate, Antoine de Bordeaux-Neufville, was of the opinion that, generally speaking, Catholics fared better under Cromwell than they had done for decades. Many historians have tended to follow that opinion. Insofar as only two of them paid the ultimate price on the scaffold that is true, but it is all a matter of relativity. Initially, Parliament was supposedly in control, but real power lay with the military dictatorship of Oliver Cromwell and the army. During the Civil War the Puritan soldiery had often behaved barbarously; gratuitously vandalising and robbing churches. Before the execution of the King a more austere Puritan regime had been introduced. The celebration of Christmas had already been abolished and in the Articles of Christian Religion passed by Parliament in 1648 the Catholic Faith was specifically attacked. The Mass was described as abominable and the Real Presence in the Eucharist condemned as superstitious gross idolatry. A new catch-all oath was introduced: the Oath of Abjuration. It stated:

 I do abjure and renounce the supremacy and authority of the Pope over the Catholic Church in general, and over myself in particular. And I hold it as of faith that there is no transubstantiation in the Supper of our Lord, or in the elements of bread and wine, after their consecration by any person whomsoever. And of the same faith I hold that there is no purgatory; that the Consecrated Host, crucifixes or images ought to be honoured with *cultus,* and that no *cultus* is due to them. I also believe that no salvation can be obtained by works; and I abjure all doctrine in confirmation of the aforesaid points, and I renounce them without any equivocation, mental reservation or secret evasion whatever, taking my words now uttered according to the common and usual acceptation of the same.

 It is blindingly obvious that no true Catholic could possibly take such an oath. Cromwell said he wished to 'meddle not with any man's conscience'. This is an honourable statement of an ideal and he may have sincerely meant what he said, but in practice it was a very different story of intolerance, and one not confined to just religious matters.

 England under the Commonwealth and Protectorate must have been a pretty joyless place. Draconian laws seeking to enforce strict morality were enacted. Sex outside marriage was punishable by three months in prison - later increased to six months - for both parties. For those guilty of adultery the punishment was death. Women who had an illegitimate child were treated as criminals. Heavy fines were imposed for swearing and drunkenness. The traditional amusements of the populace were ruthlessly suppressed. The pleasure gardens were closed; Morris dancing was banned as a heinous sin; the maypoles were pulled down and the theatres closed. When surreptitious performances of plays were given, often in taverns, the premises were raided by the troops and the actors were arrested and sent to prison. All the wrongs, of which the Puritans had accused King Charles, were practiced on an unwilling people with tyrannical infringements of individual liberty. Martial law obtained, and there were flagrant violations of *habeas corpus*. For example, William Prynne, who was a thorn in Cromwell's side, was imprisoned without trial for three years. Hoist with his own petard one has scant sympathy for the man. William M Lamont, referring to Prynne's pamphlet, *The Sword of Christian Magistracy,* writes that it is 'one of the most blood-curdling pleas for total repressive action from the civil authority in the English language.' (vide *Puritanism and Historical Controversy,* 1996). Virulently anti-Semitic, Prynne opposed Cromwell's plan to lift the ban on the legal residence of Jews in England. The majority of the country was dis-enfranchised to ensure that the deeply unpopular minority regime was kept in power, until Cromwell found Parliament too obstructive and unceremoniously dispensed with it. Like all dictators, Cromwell's power base was the army or more specifically, the highly-paid and strictly disciplined, Ironsides, and it is not too fanciful to compare their tactics with Hitler's Blackshirts.

In 1650 the law requiring attendance at the Anglican Church was repealed. The Established Church was no longer recognised; its deprived clergy were forced to worship secretly. (Some may be so unchristian as to here invoke the colloquial idiom 'a taste of their own medicine', but we shall refrain from such uncharitable thoughts.) Anything of beauty that still remained in the churches was vandalised; even the ancient tombs were mutilated and desecrated. The antiquarian and biographer, John Aubrey, wrote about the destruction he found at Oxford University where all the stained glass windows depicting saints and religious symbols had been smashed. Old St Paul's Cathedral in London was used as a thoroughfare for porters and carriers. Even dunghills accumulated in the building. Booksellers and tobacconists had stalls. There was a glazier's workshop and the chapels were used for storage. The vaults were occupied by a carpenter and used partly as a wine cellar. Little wonder that Cromwell had no compunction about using the place as stabling for the army's horses.

By the Act that made Cromwell Lord Protector in 1653, religious liberty was granted with the exception of 'popery'. Cromwell - no doubt genuinely - believed that he was an instrument of divine retribution. Vide the Irish situation, which although it is not strictly within the ambit of this book illustrates religious policy. Nowhere was Cromwell's messianic delusion more vividly illustrated than in Ireland, where Catholics were denied all mercy, being cruelly massacred, including women and children. The 'lucky' ones were transported as slaves to the sugar plantations of the West Indies. Bishops and priests were executed. In 1653 Catholicism was banned in Ireland. Statute 27 of Elizabeth, making it a treasonable offence simply to be a priest, was extended to Ireland. Priests were banished or sent to camps specially set up in the Arran Islands. Cromwell's treatment of the Irish will forever be a stain upon his memory.

Under the Commonwealth and the Protectorate of Cromwell - an autocratic and dictatorial monarchy in all but name - the Catholics were made to suffer severely for their support for the King. Cromwell was not averse to profiting personally from their misfortune. For example, he was the chief beneficiary of the confiscation of the estates of the imprisoned Edward Somerset of Raglan, 2nd Marquess of Worcester. At the time of King Charles's trial (of which the pre-determined outcome was never in doubt) Cromwell conveniently managed to transfer responsibility from himself onto God. He declared that, '... since the Providence of God has cast this upon us, I cannot but submit to Providence'. As Arthur S Turberville wrote in *Commonwealth and Restoration* (1936),

Cromwell was a very complex character. Constantly probing his own heart, he was incapable of self-analysis. In expression he was ever forcible, but seldom lucid. But his actions were definite enough. After a long and wandering exposition of the Scriptures, Oliver would break into fierce personal denunciations, and then clinch his argument with one peremptory sentence and the appearance of a file of soldiers.

A man of contradictions, alongside his belief in his messianic mission Cromwell was also a pragmatist. At least he harboured no delusions about his own political position. On his return from Ireland, a flattering courtier, referring to the cheering crowd that greeted the Protector, said to him, 'Your Highness may see by this that you have the voice of the people as well as God'. Cromwell answered him, 'As to God, we will not talk about Him here; but as for the people, they should be just as noisy if they were going to see me hanged'. Somewhat surprisingly, he had friendly relations with a number of Catholics, and the Protector briefly toyed with the idea of entering into discussions with Rome about toleration for private Catholic worship. However, Catholics continued to be denied all freedom of worship and the penal laws were vigorously applied against them. Shockingly, there are cases of Catholic children being flogged for refusing to attend Puritan religious instruction. To give one instance from 1654: at a village near Alnwick, Northumberland, there was a nine-year-old boy who was the only Catholic in his class. When the Protestant ministers visited the school to instruct the children the boy asked leave to go home. He was told he had to listen to the instruction and his request was refused so he slipped out and ran home. When he returned to school the next day he was severely flogged by the master.

At a time of extremely high taxation, the taxes for Catholics were doubled. This policy of the Commonwealth and Protectorate almost succeeded in taxing Catholics out of existence. Those who had actively supported the King had their properties compulsorily sold up by Parliament. The first of these sequestration ordinances came into force in 1643. Committees of sequestrators were appointed for all counties in England and Wales, empowering them to seize two-thirds of the estates of all Catholics, the proceeds to be used for the prosecution of the war. A great many Catholic families fell foul of this and succeeding legislation, some of them, unable to cope any longer with the heavy financial burden, finally lapsed into Protestantism. In Yorkshire Sir Walter Vavasour had to find a staggering lump sum of £20,000; and Sir Thomas Gascoigne not less than £3,000 to discharge their sequestration. Families such as the Cholmley's of Brandsby had to endure their property being sold; and the estate of Thomas Tankard of Brampton was sold up leaving him with just a small cottage in Wensleydale. Robert Knightly owned a large property in Essex, which was demolished in order to use the materials to help repair the fort at Tilbury.

These examples could be multiplied many times. The ordinances permitted one fifth of the value of the seized estate of a recusant to be used to support his wife and children on condition that the children must be raised as Protestants or swingeing deductions were made from the fifth. The level of rigour in the execution of these ordinances varied. The Sayer family of Worsall, North Riding, were harshly treated. When John Sayer's property was sold up his widow and children were denied even the fifth.

On the other hand there is the example of Captain Edward Saltmarsh, son of a Puritan family, who, after serving in the

Parliamentary army, married the widowed Gerardine Meynell, a Catholic, daughter of William Ireland of Nostell Priory, and settled at Kilvington Castle, North Yorkshire. He used his position to help his wife and her relations to evade the sequestration of their property. He later became a Catholic himself and had two sons, Gerard and Peter - who was baptised by none other than Blessed Nicholas Postgate - who both became priests and served on the English mission. (Gerard was ordained at Rome in 1676. Around 1700 he became tutor to Thomas Howard, 8th Duke of Norfolk and accompanied him for four years on his foreign travels. After serving as chaplain to the duke's mother at Worksop he became chaplain to the duke himself until 1709 when he was dismissed because the duke's new sixteen-year-old wife, Maria Shireburn of Stonyhurst, wanted her own Jesuit chaplain. By 1723 he was living in Holborn, London where he was chaplain once more to the dowager duchess Mary. He died in 1732. Peter was ordained in 1686 and served as chaplain to the Blue Nuns at Paris from 1691-95 and the Benedictine nuns at Pontoise until 1697. He returned to England and in 1706 was appointed archdeacon of Sussex. He died in London 1724.)

There are countless appeals recorded from Catholics begging for relief from the crippling fines imposed on them or the forfeiture of their entire estates. Notwithstanding the draconian Parliamentary ordinances many priests continued their ministry; Catholics flocked to the chapels of the foreign embassies to hear Mass and the number of reported conversions greatly increased. In 1655, six Masses were being said every day in the chapel of the Venetian Ambassador to cope with the numbers of English worshippers. It became such a problem that the Government passed a law forbidding English Catholics to frequent the chapels of foreign embassies.

During the period of the Civil War, when the Puritans were in the ascendant, in addition to the five martyrs (Roe, Reynolds vere Green, Lockwood, Catterick and Morse) we have already described, twelve other priests were martyred in the years 1642 to 1646. 1 To demonstrate the rabid, anti-Catholic fanaticism fostered by Parliament, it is salutary to describe in some detail the case of one of them, Blessed Hugh Green, who was martyred with unspeakable barbarity and obscenity in 1642.

Hugh, the son of a Protestant London goldsmith, was born c.1585. He was educated at Peterhouse, Cambridge, graduating BA in 1605 and MA in 1609. He converted and arrived at Douai in July 1610, was ordained 14 June 1612 and sent to the English mission later that year. Working under the alias Ferdinand Brooks or Brown, he laboured for many years, his main place of residence being Chideock, Dorset, the home of Lady Arundell. When the proclamation was issued in 1642

Puritan Parliament and the Commonwealth

banishing all priests, in March Hugh set out for Lyme Regis intending to take ship believing he still had a couple of days grace before the decree took effect. As he was boarding a ship for France he was accosted by a customs official and Hugh admitted that he was a Catholic priest leaving England in accordance with the proclamation. He was told that he was several days too late, the closing date enabling him to take advantage of the decree having already passed. In spite of Hugh protesting his good intentions to comply, he was arrested and imprisoned in Dorchester jail. Five months later he was tried and condemned. On Friday 19 August 1642 the fifty-seven-year-old priest was taken to a hill outside Dorchester for execution. A long, detailed and harrowing account of his martyrdom was written by Mrs Elizabeth Willoughby and a friend who were close eye-witnesses.

Mrs Willoughby was clearly a woman of extraordinary courage who accompanied the hurdle taking Father Green to his execution. Here he was made to wait until three poor women were hanged. Mrs Willoughby relates that in the crowd on horseback was a 'reverend father of the Society of Jesus' who, in spite of the great danger in which he had placed himself, gave Hugh absolution. She continues:

Now is our martyr brought to the foot of the ladder by the sheriff, where falling upon his knees, he remained in devout prayer for almost half an hour: then he took his crucifix and Agnus Dei from his neck and gave them this devout gentlewoman, my assistant in this relation; his beads he gave to another and last of all he gave to me most unworthy his book of litanies and also from the gallows he threw down to me his band, spectacles and priest's girdle.

Hugh spoke at some length in defence of the Catholic Church and protested his innocence of any crime, other than his priesthood. The many ministers present called upon the sheriff to shut him up and get on with the execution. Hugh expressed his forgiveness from his heart for all those who had a hand in his death and asked forgiveness of any whom he may have offended. Mrs Willoughby's account continues:

Then he called to me and desired me to commend him heartily to all his friends. I told him I would, and that some of them were gone before him, and with joy expected him. Then on my knees I humbly begged his benediction; so did five others and he cheerfully gave us his blessing making the sign of the holy Cross over our heads ... pulling his cap over his face, his hands joined before his breast, in silent prayer he expected his happy passage.

At last the ladder was turned with the help of the hangman who sat astride the gallows and Hugh was seen

to cross himself three times with his right hand as he hanged; but instantly the hangman was commanded to cut him down with a knife which the constable held up to him, stuck in a long stick, although I did my utmost to have hindered him. Now the fall which he had from the gallows, not his hanging, did a little astonish him ... The man that was to quarter him was a timorous unskilful man, by trade a barber named Barefoot ... he was so long dismembering him that he came to his perfect senses and sat upright and took Barefoot by the hand ... but the people pulled him down by the rope which was still about his neck: then did this butcher cut his belly on both sides and turned the flap upon his breast, which the holy man feeling, put his left hand upon his bowels, and looking on his bloody hand laid it down by his side; and lifting up his right hand he crossed himself saying three times Jesu, Jesu, Jesu, mercy! The which, although unworthy, I am a witness of, for my hand was on his forehead ... the Catholics were pushed away by the unruly multitude, except myself, who never left him until his head was severed from his body. While he was thus calling upon Jesus, the butcher did pull out his liver instead of his heart, and tumbling his guts out every way to see if his heart were not among them; then with his knife he raked in the body of the blessed martyr, who even then called upon Jesus ... and his forehead sweat; then it was cold and presently again it burned; his eyes, nose and mouth run over with blood and water. His patience was admirable, and when his tongue could no longer pronounce that life-giving name Jesus, his lips moved and his groans gave signs of those lamentable torments which for more than half an hour he suffered. Methought my heart was pulled out of my body to see him in such cruel pains, lifting up his eyes to heaven and not yet dead; then I could no longer hold but cried out upon them that did so torment him: upon which a devout gentlewoman understanding he did yet live went to the sheriff and on her knees besought him to see justice done and to put him out of his pain, who at her request, commanded to cut off his head; then with a knife they did cut his throat and with a cleaver chopped off his head ... Then was his heart found and put upon a spear and showed to the people and so thrown into the fire ... Then did this gentlewoman and myself go to the sheriff and beg his body, the which he gave to us. Now did the devil roar and his instruments, the blinded Dorcestrians, did fret and chafe and told the sheriff he could not dispose of his quarters to papists ... And truly I believe if we had tried to carry them away they would have thrown us into the fire for our number was small and they many thousands. Their fury did so rage against us that we were forced to withdraw ourselves ... so great was their malice to Catholics ... from ten o'clock in the morning till four in the afternoon the ungodly multitude stayed on the hill and sported themselves at football with his head, and put sticks in his eyes, nose, ears and mouth and then they buried it near to the body.

To give him due credit, Cromwell was genuinely reluctant to execute priests. As a result only one priest, Peter Wright, 2 was martyred under the Commonwealth and one, John Southworth, under Cromwell's Protectorship, which no doubt had a bearing upon the judgement of historians. However, this gives a false impression because there was no let-up in the persecution and dozens of priests were sentenced to death and reprieved only to be left to die in harsh prison conditions. 3

John Southworth

The path of duty ... the way to glory.

On the death of the Duke of Wellington, Alfred, Lord Tennyson, 1809-92

John Southworth (pronounced 'Sutherth') was related to the famous Catholic family of that name whose seat since the early fourteenth century was Samlesbury Hall near Preston. Sir John Southworth, born c.1526, had been prominent during Queen Elizabeth's reign. He was knighted in 1547 and by 1562 was High Sheriff of Lancashire. A staunch adherent of the Old Faith, along with most of the Lancashire gentry, he suffered the penalties for being a recusant. Rather surprisingly, in 1568 William Downham, Bishop of Chester, reported him to William Cecil for not attending church and for speaking out against the Book of Common Prayer. Sir John must have been too outspoken in his opposition to ignore as Downham was believed to let his responsibilities towards crushing recusancy go by default for fear of offending the gentry. In 1581 Edmund Campion had been his guest at Samlesbury, and for this offence in 1582 Sir John had been imprisoned in Salford jail and the New Fleet prison, Manchester. In 1584 he was transferred to London. He died at Samlesbury in November 1595.

Bishop Challoner tells us that John Southworth was 'a younger son of the ancient family of Samlesbury', from which we may infer he meant a junior branch; but neither the precise year of John's birth nor his birthplace is known for certain, though it may have been Samlesbury Hall. The saintly Bishop suggests 1592 as the year of John's birth, but if John's age was indeed seventy, as claimed by some at the time of his death, the martyr must have been born c.1584. It is most probable that Challoner is correct and John was sixty-two years old at the time of his death.

John entered the English College, Douai, on 14 July 1613 to begin his priestly studies. His health gave cause for concern and he went home to Lancashire for nearly a year before returning to Douai on 25 March 1617. He used the alias Lee, which was most likely his mother's maiden name. On 31 March 1618 he received the sub-diaconate at Valenciennes with George Machell. He was ordained deacon on Palm

Sunday, 8 April and priest on 14 April, Holy Saturday, by Francis Van de Burch, Archbishop of Cambrai, offering his first Mass the next day, Easter Sunday. After a further year of study, in April 1619 he left Douai to try his vocation as a Benedictine. Which monastery he entered is not recorded, but clearly this did not suit him and on 13 December of that year he received his *viaticum* (money for the journey) from Dr Kellison, President of Douai. In the company of Edmund Broughton, a Douai student, he crossed from Calais to Dover in disguise and made his way to London where arrangements had been made for his safe, temporary residence with another priest. He worked in the London area for the next five years.

In 1624, not in the best of health, he was banished and arrived at Douai on 24 March. He remained in Flanders for about a year, spending some months at Douai College. On 29 July 1625 he was assigned as confessor to the Benedictine nuns of the Assumption of Our Lady at Brussels. The convent had been founded in 1598 by Lady Mary Percy, daughter of Blessed Thomas Percy, executed in 1569 after the Northern Rising.

By 1626 John was back in Lancashire. The following year he was arrested and imprisoned in Lancaster Castle at the same time as Edmund Arrowsmith and Ambrose Barlow. In September 1628 he was tried and condemned to death, but he was reprieved by the King and ordered to be detained in Wisbech Castle. The move never took place and he remained a prisoner at Lancaster for three years where, looking down from his cell window, he was able to give Edmund Arrowsmith absolution as he was led out to his execution.

On 24 March 1630 orders came for John to be banished by royal warrant, along with fifteen other priests, and he was moved from Lancaster to the Clink prison in Southwark in readiness. On 11 April he was named as one of the priests to be delivered into the custody of the French Ambassador, Charles de l'Aubespine, Marquis de Châteauneuf. When the group of priests arrived at Douai in May John was not one of their number. It is doubtful if he ever left the country as he was recorded as still being in the Clink in 1632, where his prison conditions were much ameliorated as a result of the interest shown in him by Queen Henrietta Maria. This led to complaints to the Privy Council from the pursuivant John Gray, that in common with other priest prisoners, John Southworth 'condemned' enjoyed too much liberty, being allowed to go abroad out of the prison. John's name also appears as a signatory to a number of appeals and petitions between 1630 and 1636. Among them were letters in July 1632 to Bishop Richard Smith and Pope Urban VIII respectively, urging the speedy return to England of the self-exiled Bishop.

For the next twenty-five years John carried on his ministry in London, usually from secret lodgings in and around Westminster, which was in those times an area of some of the most appallingly, filthy slums in the capital. When the plague broke out in 1636 we have already seen how he worked with Henry Morse, heroically tending the sick. As earlier related, Catholics did not receive any financial help from the parish, unless of course they conformed, and no doubt many died rather than apostatise. Many testified that the parish gave them nothing because they were recusants and had it not been for the Queen's alms given by the two priests they would have starved to death. When Morse succumbed to the plague it was John's turn to struggle on alone until Henry recovered. Robert White, the curate of St Margaret's, Westminster, lodged a complaint about Southworth with Archbishop Laud, describing Southworth as a 'dangerous seducer'. His petition to the Archbishop stated that, 'This man, under the pretence of distributing alms sent from the Friars at Somerset House and other Papists doth take occasion to go into divers plague-stricken houses in Westminster' and used his charitable work to proselytise and 'pervert' people to the Church of Rome. White implored Laud to take steps to speedily apprehend Morse and Southworth.

On 6 October 1636 John issued a joint appeal with Henry Morse *To the Catholickes of England*. It began:

> We underwritten being appointed to serve the infected Catholicks of the City and Suburbs of London, with our spiritual assistance, having seen with our eyes the extreme necessity which many of the poorer sort are fallen into, by reason of the present sickness, do thinke ourselves obliged even in conscience, to make the same knowne unto you, by a publicke letter, to the end that those, whom God hath blest with sufficient ability and meanes, taking so weighty a matter into their serious consideration, may, through the help of his holy grace, resolve with themselves forthwith, to do what in them lieth, and what in such an exigent Christian charity and duty bindeth everyone unto, for the necessary support and relief of so great a multitude.
>
> We do protest unto you seriously, even upon our soles and consciences, that the greatness of this calamitie exceedeth all belief, in so much as we should never have imagined in the least part, of that which really is, had not our owne eyes, and daily experience attested the same unto us, and we may truly averre, that this so great a desolation amongst our poor brethren, joined with the small means and power we have, to relieve them, is a far more grievous affliction unto us than all the labours and dangers, which we undergo daily for their spiritual aid and comfort.

The appeal goes on to describe in detail the appalling conditions of the sick, many of whom found 'their languishing paine' worse than death itself. It expresses the hope that the example of the Protestants in the City may be an example to the Catholics to imitate their generosity and charity. The appeal resulted in a considerable sum being raised for the relief of the suffering Catholics. But the pursuivants were relentless in their pursuit of John and Father Morse. Sir Dudley Carleton, Clerk of the Privy Council, was prevailed upon to issue a warrant for John's arrest and imprisonment in the Gatehouse. From there he addressed a 'humble petition' to King Charles via the Queen, protesting that his care was for the poor and sick, whom he had 'laboured only to preserve from perishing' and he begged the Queen 'to move his Majesty' not to keep him in jail for the sake of those who depended upon his help. The appeal was successful. He was set free after only a few days by the Secretary of State, Sir Francis Windebank.

In 1637 John and Father Goodman were apprehended by Francis Newton, the priest catcher, and, like Morse, were held by him at the Sun tavern at Westminster whose landlord was a man named Spencer. Newton hoped to make even greater money out of such detentions if the priests or their friends could be persuaded to buy their freedom. The situation must have come to the attention of Sir Francis Windebank, because on 28 November 1637 he ordered the two priests to be removed from the tavern to the Gatehouse, swiftly followed by orders for their release. John was at liberty for about three years until he was arrested again at some unknown date, appeared before the High Commissioners, and was sent to the Clink Prison. On 24 June 1640 a decree addressed to the keeper of the Clink from the Commissioners of Causes Ecclesiastic stated, 'John Southworth, a Popish recusant, has been convented before us for matters of ecclesiastical cognizance, and has refused to give sufficient bond for his appearance to answer the matters objected against him. We having understood that he was formerly committed by a warrant from the Council to the Clink, and is still a prisoner there, have therefore thought fit by virtue of our commission to remand him back to the said prison until order be given for his enlargement.' (*Domestic Papers, Charles I, Vol.28*) On 16 July 1640, from his house in Drury Lane, Secretary Windebank issued a warrant for John's release 'forthwith', but before the year end he was back in the Gatehouse as is clear from a State Paper dated 2 December which refers to him as 'a condemned man now out of the Clink and in the Gatehouse'. The Long Parliament, now conscious of its ascendancy, was furious at Windebank's continued protection of priests, albeit with the King's authority, and he was denounced. He was indicted of releasing twenty-seven priests, including John Southworth. With the

Puritan Parliament and the Commonwealth

King's permission in 1642 Windebank fled from London overnight and escaped to France in an open boat, where he died a Catholic in Paris in 1646. (His sister, Mildred, married Robert Read of Linkenholt, Hampshire. Her son Thomas became principal of Magdalen College, Oxford until he converted to Catholicism in 1646. He went to Douai and was ordained priest in 1648.)

For the next fourteen years John was continuously harassed in his work, being regularly imprisoned and released, usually through the intervention of the Queen. In 1653 the Chapter appointed John, along with Father Andrew Knightly, 4 as a Collector for London and Middlesex, with the task of raising money for the maintenance of the clergy.

With the execution of the King Southworth lost his protector and the renewed persecution under the Commonwealth rendered his position even more vulnerable. Following information from a pursuivant called Jefferies, on the night of Monday, 19 June 1654 John was taken from his bed and arrested by Colonel Charles Worsley. This is described in a letter from Lorenzo Paulucci, Venetian Secretary in London to the Venetian Ambassador in France and corroborated by the Jail Delivery Rolls showing his committal to Newgate for trial on Wednesday, 21 June. Beneath the entry in the Newgate Register, in the hand of a prison clerk, are added the words 'to be hanged, drawn and quartered'. On Saturday, 24 June John was brought to trial at the Old Bailey. The magistrate begged him to plead 'Not guilty' to the charge, but John felt this was dishonest and a denial of his priesthood, so he readily confessed to being a priest. Despite all the pleadings and delaying tactics employed by the magistrate and his promise that John's life would be spared, he could not prevail upon John to plead not guilty to the charge and he was pronounced guilty. On Monday, 26 June he was again called to Court when Serjeant William Steel, the Recorder of London, had no alternative but to pronounce the death sentence which he did in a voice choking with emotion and tears running down his face. Falling upon his knees John said, 'Lord God, I humbly thank thee, who hath made me worthy to suffer for Thy sake.' Then standing up he said to the Recorder, 'I thank you for what you have done, and for your civilities to me, and I pray God to give you His holy grace, that you and all this nation be converted to the true Roman Catholic and Apostolic Faith, and remain in heaven for ever with Jesus Christ in glory.'

The foreign ambassadors in London all made strong representations to Cromwell to grant Southworth a reprieve. It appears that the Lord Protector, 'averse from such cruelty', was personally inclined to accede to their request. Following representations from the Portuguese

Ambassador, João de Sá, Count of Peneguião, Cromwell promised that he would secure a reprieve for 'God forbid that my hand should be consenting to the death of any for religion.' But the next day the Protector sent his apologies to the ambassador for being unable to honour his promise, having been overruled by the Council which advised him that the law, which he had sworn to uphold, should be allowed to take its course. 'It was not that Cromwell approved of sanguinary punishments in matters of religion, but that he had no objection to purchase the goodwill of the godly by shedding the blood of a priest'. (John Lingard, *History of England.*))

On 28 June John was dragged to Tyburn to face death with a group of felons. A detailed eyewitness account of the execution was preserved by Bishop Challoner. Despite it being a stormy day with heavy rain, thunder and lightening, the crowd was huge, numbering several thousand. Over two hundred coaches containing important personages, ambassadors and their retinues attended. John, weak and looking much older than his 62 years, insisted on wearing his cassock and his four-cornered cap on the scaffold. Around his neck was a silver cross hung from a ribbon. He was made to wait until eight men and a woman had been executed. He read out a speech that he had prepared.

Good people, I was born in Lancashire. This is the third time I have been apprehended, and now being to die, I would gladly witness and profess openly my faith, for which I suffer. And though my time be short, yet what I shall be deficient in words, I hope I shall supply with my blood, which I will most willingly spend to the last drop for my faith. Neither my intent in coming into England, nor practice in England, was to act any thing against the secular government. Hither I was sent by my lawful superiors to teach Christ's faith, not to meddle with any temporal affairs. Christ sent his apostles; his apostles their successors; and their successors me. I did what I was commanded by them, who had power to command me, being ever taught that I ought to obey them in matters ecclesiastical, and my temporal governors in business only temporal. This, and only this, according to my poor abilities, I laboured to perform. I had a commission to do it from him, to whom our Saviour, in his predecessor, St Peter, gave power to send others to propagate his faith. This is that for which I die, O holy cause! and not for any treason against the laws. My faith and obedience to my superiors is all the treason charged against me: nay, I die for Christ's law, which no human law by whomsoever made, ought to withstand or contradict. This law of Christ commanded me to obey these superiors and this Church, saying whoever hears them hears himself ... I was brought up in the truly ancient Roman catholic apostolic religion, which taught me that the sum of the only true Christian profession is to die. This lesson I have heretofore in my lifetime desired to learn; this lesson I come here to put in practice by dying, being taught it by our blessed Saviour, both by precept and example. Himself said, He that will be my disciple, let him take up his cross and follow me ... To follow his holy doctrine and imitate his holy death, I willingly suffer at present; this gallows 'looking up' I look on as his cross which I gladly take to follow my dear Saviour. My faith is my crime, the performance of my duty, the occasion of my condemnation. I confess I am a great sinner; against God I have offended, but am innocent of any sin against man; I mean the commonwealth and government. How justly then I die, let them look to who have condemned me. It is sufficient for me that it is God's will: I plead not for myself but for you poor persecuted Catholics whom I leave behind me. Heretofore liberty of conscience was pretended as a cause of war, and it was held a reasonable proposition that all the natives should enjoy it who should be found to behave themselves as obedient and true subjects. This being so, why should their conscientious acting and governing themselves according to the faith received from their ancestors, involve them more than all the rest in that universal guilt? ... It has pleased God to take the sword out of the king's hand and put it in the Protector's. Let him remember that he is to administer justice indifferently and without exception of persons. For there is no exception of persons with God, whom we ought to resemble. If any Catholics work against the present government, let them suffer; but why should all the rest who are guiltless (unless conscience be their guilt) be made partakers in the promiscuous punishment with the greatest malefactors? I therefore desire the Lord Protector would grant them a liberty of conscience equal with their fellow subjects and that he may so govern as may be for the honour of God and the good of the people.

Here John was interrupted, and urged to make haste, so he requested all the Catholics present to pray for him and with him. Raising his eyes and hands to heaven in silent prayer he then closed his eyes and submitted quietly to execution. He was cut down while alive and the butchery was carried out but he made no sound.

After the execution, Don Alonso de Cárdenas, the Spanish Ambassador, bought the mangled remains from the hangman for forty shillings. According to Challoner it was at the behest of the Howard family that the head and quarters were sewn together by James Clark, a surgeon, and the body, expensively embalmed with rich spices, was smuggled to Douai. It was the object of great local veneration and at least one inexplicable cure took place of a college student close to death. Later the body was encased in a lead coffin and placed under the altar of St Augustine of Canterbury in the college church. There the body remained until the outbreak of the French Revolution, when Douai College was suppressed. For greater security, on 4 May 1793 Father Thomas Stout buried the college treasures deep in the basement for safety. John Southworth's coffin was removed from the college church 'with as much respect as circumstances would admit' and buried below the kiln furnaces. Close by was buried silver church plate, relics of Sir Thomas More, St Thomas Becket and the cardinal's biretta of St Charles Borromeo. By 1863 the premises were being used as a cavalry barracks and after a search some of the college silverware was found, but not John's relics.

In 1927 the former college buildings were sold to Douai Town Council, which decided to demolish them to make way for a new road. While excavations were taking place on 15 July, under what had been the kiln area, the workmen found a lead coffin about 5'8" in length, moulded to the shape of a human body. The leaden shell had been made in two halves, the upper part fitting onto the lower, rather like a lid on a tin box. When it was opened a body wrapped in discoloured linen was found within. It was quite well preserved, especially the head, which was inclined towards the right shoulder. When unwrapped, the face had a coppery tint; the mouth was slightly open and there were still traces of a beard and moustache, but the eye sockets were empty; the ears had been removed and the hands severed at the wrists. The following day, a workman digging in the same plot, discovered a much deteriorated wooden box covered in pieces of lead. In it was found the degraded Borromeo biretta and some rough, brown hairy material. Unfortunately it was not realised that this was a remnant of the hair shirt of St Thomas Becket and was thrown away.

Steps were taken to identify the body. By means of X-rays and other tests, it was established that the body had been quartered, embalmed and sewn together and could be identified beyond doubt as John Southworth. Permission was obtained from the French and British Foreign Offices to transfer the body to England. In December 1927 the body was brought back to St Edmund's College, Ware, Hertfordshire, where it was enshrined in a casket in the chapel. After John had been beatified it was decided to move his relics to Westminster Cathedral.

Clothed in a 'Roman-style' red chasuble, a black four-cornered cap on his head, his face covered by a silver mask, John's body was placed in a glass reliquary. On 1 May 1930 the relics were solemnly placed in the chapel of St George and the English Martyrs in Westminster Cathedral, where they appropriately still rest at the heart of the London district where the martyr spent so many years of his priestly life.

The Southworth family, exhausted by iniquitous fines and persecution, gradually had to dispose of their estates. The Lower Hall at Samlesbury had been sold in 1620 to the Catholic Walmsley family. In 1679, at the height of the 'Popish Plot' furore, the Southworth family had at last been obliged to sell old Samlesbury Hall after 300 years of ownership.

Puritan Parliament and the Commonwealth

Notes to Chapter Seven

1 In addition to Blessed Hugh Green, whose story has been related in detail, the other eleven priests were as follows:

Venerable Edward Morgan, a Welshman from Flintshire, was born in 1584. He was converted by Father John Bennet SJ in 1601 and in 1604 travelled to Douai. He joined the English College, Rome, in 1606. He then had a spell with the Jesuits at Saint-Omer, but left after beginning to exhibit mental health problems, which delayed his ordination: this took place at Salamanca in 1618. By May 1628 he was a prisoner at Flint for refusing the Oath of Allegiance. In 1632 he was condemned to have his ears nailed to the pillory and transferred to the Fleet, London, where he remained a prisoner for ten years until the Puritan Parliament decided to execute him. He was condemned to death at the Old Bailey on 23 April 1642, together with John Francis Quashet, a Scottish Friar Minim. Quashet was not executed but later died in Newgate. Edward was martyred at Tyburn on 26 April. While he awaited execution he was wearied by the large number of visitors who wanted to see him, not only many Protestants, whose respect he gained by the patient way he answered their queries, but also Catholics, who made their confessions to him. He was greatly embarrassed by the way in which his visitors, wishing to keep a memento of him, cut off his buttons, and in the end he was forced to yield up to them his cloak, which they cut up among them while providing him with a new one to wear to Tyburn. He found means to say Mass, which moved him profoundly, as well as finding solace in the visit of a Jesuit priest. He told the priest of the great hardship he had endured during the last two years of his imprisonment, during which he had incurred a debt of £22 in order to procure basic necessities for himself. He begged that the priest would find means of paying the debt and this was achieved by the contributions of Catholics. At 8 a.m. on the day of his execution he was placed on the hurdle, but his head was too low and the rope around his neck was so tight that he could scarcely breathe. By the time they reached Holborn this was noticed and he was made more comfortable. While this was being done a bystander offered him a glass of wine, which he accepted gratefully. The crowd around the gallows, including coaches and horsemen, was so great that it was only with great difficulty that the sheriff's men could force their way through with the hurdle. As Edward climbed up into the cart there were shouts of 'Silence' so his last words could be heard. He took as his text the Gospel of St John, 'The good shepherd lays down his life for his sheep.' His lucid and memorable speech,

Puritan Parliament and the Commonwealth

offering his life for the good of his country and reconciliation between King and Parliament, made a great impression on his hearers. As the rope was fixed round his neck he said he was now to be sent to heaven on a string, at which one of the ministers present chided him for joking. 'Indeed', Morgan replied, 'it is no joking matter to me, but very serious, but why should anyone be offended at my going to heaven cheerfully? For God loves a cheerful giver.' He was allowed to hang until dead before he was cut down. Why Edward Morgan has not been included among those beatified by the Church is a mystery, and it does not reflect well if the underlying reason was his bout of mental illness, which he had clearly overcome.

Blessed Thomas Bullaker was a doctor's son, born at Midhurst, near Chichester, Sussex, c.1602. His was a Catholic family that suffered for recusancy. At the age of eighteen he went to the Jesuit College at Saint-Omer, then to Valladolid, Spain. In 1622, he joined the Franciscan Recollects at Abrojo, taking the name of John Baptist. He completed his studies at Segovia and was ordained priest about 1627. He spent some time in Segovia and Ávila. As his order was engaged in sending missioners to the West Indies Thomas volunteered, but was refused and told that his work was to be on the English mission. In 1630 he took ship from Bordeaux and landed at Plymouth, but on his arrival the ship's master alerted the mayor and Thomas was arrested. He was transferred to the county jail at Exeter and was tried at the Lenten Assizes, but the trial was halted for lack of evidence and Thomas was released on bail. He moved to London where he made a particular apostolate serving sick prisoners. On Sunday, 11 September 1642, as he was saying Mass at the home of Mrs Margaret Powell, in St Sepulchre's parish, he was apprehended by the pursuivant Wadsworth, one of Francis Newton's gang, and taken before the sheriff of London. Thomas wrote a long and detailed account of his arrest and trial. He was committed to the New Prison and on the following Tuesday was taken to Westminster to be examined by a committee of Parliament. Wadsworth appeared and laid before the committee the vestments that he had taken from Thomas. He was then sent to Newgate to await trial with Mrs Powell. Both were sentenced to death but Mrs Powell was reprieved. On 12 October Thomas was drawn to Tyburn, where he tried to speak about the Real Presence of Christ in the Eucharist, but was ordered to desist. He was cut down while still alive to face dismemberment. His head was set up on London Bridge.

Blessed Henry Heath was born to Protestant parents at Peterborough in

1599 and was baptised on 16 December at St John's church. He was educated at Corpus Christi College, Cambridge, where, as a result of his reading of the Fathers of the Church, he decided to become a Catholic. He went to London, and through contacts was introduced to Father George Muscot, who received him into the Church and sent him to Douai with a letter of recommendation.* While at Douai Henry decided he wished to join the English Franciscans at St Bonaventure's and took the name of Brother Paul of St Magdalen. After his ordination he spent the next nineteen years at his convent where he had a distinguished career, being elected Guardian three times, as well as being professor of divinity at the university. During this time his father crossed to Douai, was received into the Church and became a lay brother at the convent. Henry desperately wanted to work on the English mission and badgered his superiors to be allowed to do so. They finally agreed in 1643 and he lost no time in setting out for England. He took ship from Dunkirk where he met a German gentleman who paid for his passage. He arrived at Dover with nothing but what he stood up in and walked all the way to London. He called at the Star Inn near London Bridge, but when it was discovered that he did not have any money, he was thrown out. He wandered the streets until at nightfall weariness caused him to shelter in the doorway of a house. When the householder came home and found him he sent for the constable and Henry was taken before the Lord Mayor who, when Heath admitted he was a priest, had him committed to Newgate. His trial was a formality, and being convicted under 27 Elizabeth, he was sentenced to death. While he waited for his execution he received a great many visitors so that he could scarcely get a moment's rest. On 17 April 1643 he was taken to Tyburn. His last prayer was 'Jesus, have mercy on this country! Jesus, convert England! England turn thyself to the Lord your God!' He was allowed to hang until dead.

Blessed Arthur Bell was born 13 January 1591 into a wealthy family at Temple Broughton, Hanbury, Worcestershire and baptised at Feckenham. His father died when he was eight-years old and Dorothy,

---

* Muscot, whose real name was Fisher, was born at Earls Barton, Northamptonshire. He led a perilously eventful life on the mission being arrested and imprisoned several times. In 1629 he was sentenced to death which was commuted to life imprisonment through the intervention of Queen Henrietta Maria. This did not stop him from conducting an effective apostolate and making many converts, even among the felons in the jail. In January 1641, while still a prisoner, he was appointed President of Douai College. The Queen again intervened and he was allowed to leave the country to take up his post. He died at Douai in 1645.

his mother, arranged for Arthur to be educated privately by her wealthy brother, Francis Daniel, at Acton, Suffolk. At the age of twenty-four he went to Saint-Omer and was then sent to Valladolid. He was ordained at Salamanca 14 April 1618 and on 8 August he joined the Franciscans at Segovia. Father John Gennings, then in process of restoring the English Franciscan province, sent for Arthur to join the new convent at Douai. In 1632 he was sent to Scotland as provincial with the aim of restoring the Franciscan order. In this he was unsuccessful. He worked for a time at Gravelines and Brussels before being elected Guardian at St Bonaventure's for two years. In September 1634 he was sent back to England where he worked for nine years, until arrested by parliamentary soldiers at Stevenage on 6 November 1643. Stripped half naked, he was taken to London on horseback where he was examined by a parliamentary committee and sent to Newgate. While there a letter from his superior was delivered to him recalling him to Douai as he had once again been elected Guardian by his brethren. Arthur replied saying that if he was set at liberty he would obey with alacrity. He was tried on 7 December, when Wadsworth and Mayo appeared as witnesses against him, and Serjeant Green, the Recorder, pronounced sentence. A short while before the trial seized documents had come into Parliament's possession sent by the Archbishop of Cambrai at the behest of Pope Urban VIII. In the papers certain priests were nominated to make enquiries into the executions of priests, take depositions from witnesses upon oath and send accounts of them to Rome. One of the priests nominated was Arthur Bell. It cannot have been pure coincidence that Parliament published this information on the day of Bell's trial. On 11 December he was taken to Tyburn for execution. When he was stripped he was found to be wearing his habit underneath his clothes. The guards did their utmost to try and prevent any relics being taken, but this did not deter people from dipping their handkerchiefs in his blood. The serene and confident way in which he met his death so impressed his executioner that he became a Catholic.

Blessed Thomas Holland, the son of Ann and Richard Holland, a gentleman, was born in 1600 at Sutton, near Prescot, Lancashire. At a young age he was sent to Saint-Omer and from there went to Valladolid. When Charles, Prince of Wales, arrived in Madrid in his abortive attempt to woo the Infanta Maria, the college at Valladolid decided it was only courteous that the English seminarians should present their compliments to him. Thomas Holland was chosen to give a Latin oration before the Prince assuring him of the loyalty of the seminarists. In 1624 he joined the Society of Jesus and served his novitiate at Watten, Flanders. He was ordained at Liège and served his order in various capacities at Ghent and Saint-Omer, making his final vows in 1634. His health was not good and it was decided to send him back to England in 1635 where he had to spend months in close confinement in London as the pursuivants were so active. Most of his ministry, under the aliases of Hammond and Saunderson, seems to have been exercised at night in disguise, at which he was particularly adept. In October 1642 he was apprehended and committed to the New Prison for two months before being transferred to Newgate. He was tried at the Old Bailey on 7 December and although no substantial evidence was produced against him he was condemned, much to the disgust of the Lord Mayor, Sir Isaac Pennington. As he awaited his execution he was visited by a great many people, including French, Spanish and Dutch with whom he could converse fluently in their own languages. On the day of his execution he was able to say Mass before being drawn to Tyburn. The ministers present urged the hangman to cut the rope before he was dead, but this was ignored. He was martyred on Monday, 12 December 1642 before a huge crowd, which included Count Egmont and all the members of his suite.

Blessed John Duckett, born in 1614, was a North Yorkshireman from Underwinder, Sedbergh. His parents were church papists, but John was reconciled in 1631 by Father Andrew North. He went to Douai in 1633 and was ordained at Cambrai in 1639. He was a man of prayer and would often spend whole nights in contemplation. After ordination he was at Arras College in Paris for three years. Before he returned to England he spent two months preparing himself with the English Carthusians at Nieuport, where his kinsman, John Duckett, the son of James Duckett the martyr, was prior. About Christmas 1643 John arrived in Co. Durham. On 2 July the following year, in the company of two laymen, he was on his way to baptise two children, when he was waylaid by parliamentary soldiers near Wolsingham and was carried off to prison at Sunderland. John gives his own account of his examination, 'They committed me to prison, making no doubt of my being a priest by reason of my holy oils and such like things they found about me ... I would not answer directly that I was no priest, they threatened to put fired matches between my fingers till I would confess what I was. But when their threats would not prevail, they sent me to jail again, and put irons on me ... In the meantime they were examining the two that were taken with me; who, when I heard they would be shipped and sent away, seeing it was because I would not confess what I was ... I confessed myself to be a priest to free them.' John was sent to London in the company of Father Ralph Corby, where they were both examined by a parliamentary committee and sent to Newgate. They were tried on 4 September before the Recorder, Mr Glyn, and convicted of being priests. The night before his execution he wrote a farewell letter to Richard Smith, Bishop of Chalcedon: 'I fear not death; I shall receive it joyfully, for that Christ is my life and death is my gain. Never since my receiving of Holy Orders did I so much fear death as I did life, and now when it approaches can I faint?' John was always a humble and cheerful man and at 10am when the time came for him to go to Tyburn, wearing his cassock, he climbed onto the hurdle himself saying to those who stood about crying, 'Why do you weep for me who am glad of heart this happy day?' On the way, raising his head from the hurdle, he gave his blessing to all that called for it but said very little on the gallows, preferring to remain in silent prayer. He was executed on 7 September 1644 with Ralph Corby and five felons found guilty of coining. It coincided with the news of the defeat of the parliamentary forces in Cornwall under the Earl of Essex. Dame C V Wedgwood in *The King's War 1641-1647*, comments that the execution of the priests was intended to divert 'the attention of the people from the tidings of disaster.' Since 1899 a tall, Celtic style commemorative 'Duckett's Cross' has marked the spot at Redgate Banks, near Wolsingham, where John was arrested.

Blessed Ralph Corby, whose real name was Corbington, was born 25 March 1598 at Maynooth, near Dublin. He came from a deeply religious family from Co. Durham. His parents, Gerard and Isabella, had moved to Ireland hoping to find greater freedom to practise their faith. When Ralph was five years old the family returned to England and lived partly in Lancashire and partly in Durham, moving about to avoid the persecution. The family then went to Flanders, and at the age of fifteen Ralph entered the Jesuit College at Saint-Omer, along with his brothers. After six years he was sent to Segovia and Valladolid where he was ordained priest. He returned to Flanders and in 1625 commenced his novitiate in the Society of Jesus at Watten. After further study at Ghent, in 1632 he was sent to the English mission where he worked in Co. Durham, mainly among the poorer Catholics, travelling around the scattered villages on foot, which seems to have seriously affected his health. On 8 July 1644, while preparing to say Mass at a country house not far from Newcastle, he was apprehended by parliamentary soldiers, who scarcely gave him time to remove his vestments before rushing him off to Sunderland where a committee of sequestrators was in session. He obeyed their instruction to sign a confession that he was a priest and together with Father John Duckett he was put on board a ship bound for London. On arrival they were examined before a parliamentary committee at Westminster and were taken through the streets under the guard of a company of drum-beating soldiers to Newgate, where they were kept close prisoners until their trial at the Old Bailey. After condemnation Ralph and John were kept in terrible conditions among the common felons and loaded with irons until the Keeper of Newgate intervened and transferred them to better lodgings. A great many visitors came to see them, including the European envoys in London. The French resident, the Marquis de Sabran,[*] made his confession to Ralph, who gave him a gift of rosary beads, which were sent to Anne of Austria, the Queen Mother of France. The Duchess of Guise spent a whole night in their company praying, and she also made her confession to Ralph. Afterwards she bought the chalice which he used at his last Mass. Ralph told everyone that they had no cause to weep for him, rather if they loved him they ought to rejoice and congratulate him that he was going to meet so great a happiness. He wore his religious habit to his execution and on the scaffold declared that he embraced death with open arms, rendering his life to the Saviour who died for us all. The sheriff would not allow the two priests to be cut down until he was sure they were dead. After the butchery he ordered that everything should be burned, so that the 'papist dogs' would have nothing to keep as relics. Ralph's family all became religious. His father and a brother were lay-brothers in the Society of Jesus; two other brothers were Jesuit priests; his mother and two sisters were Benedictine nuns.

Blessed Philip Powel was born on 2 February 1594 at Trallong, Brecknockshire, Wales. He was educated at Abergavenny Grammar School before being sent to London, at the age of sixteen, to read law at the Middle Temple under the tuition of David Baker, who later became a Benedictine monk under the name of Augustine. He went to Flanders in 1614 to join the English Benedictines at St Gregory's, Douai, and was ordained in 1618. On 7 March 1622 he set out to return to England. For the first few months he lived with his old tutor, Mr Baker, who sent

---

[*] The son of the Marquis, Louis de Sabran (1652-1732), was born in Paris. He was educated at Saint-Omer. He married an English lady and after her death became a priest in 1679, joining the Society of Jesus in 1688. He worked in England in the reign of James II, to whom he was a court chaplain, where he engaged in vigorous theological debates with Anglican spokesmen. When William of Orange invaded in 1688 it was to Louis de Sabran that James entrusted the responsibility of getting the infant Prince of Wales safely out of the country.

him to a family called Risden in Devon. Philip served the mission in Devon, Cornwall and Somerset for over twenty years, acting for part of the time as chaplain to the Poyntz family at Leighland, North Somerset.

At the outbreak of the Civil War he moved to Yarcombe, South Devon and then to Parkham, North Devon. He served as a chaplain in the royalist army under General Goring in Cornwall. When the area was overrun by parliamentary troops and Gorings' forces were disbanded, on 22 February 1646 he took a small boat bound for Wales, but the vessel was boarded by Captain Crowder, some of whose men identified Philip as a priest. He was committed prisoner below deck where he was stripped of all except his shirt. On 11 May he was sent to London to St Catherine's jail, Southwark, before being moved to the King' Bench, where before two judges he gave an account of his whole life. On 29 May he was committed to the common jail where he contracted pleurisy. It was not until 9 June that he was well enough to be carried to the King's Bench bar in Westminster Hall to answer the charges. He was called again on the 12th and 16th June, where he ably argued his defence, claiming that as he was taken at sea and not, strictly speaking, in England, the Elizabethan statute did not apply. After his condemnation the judge asked if he would like to choose on which day to die. Philip replied that with so much to answer for it was not an easy matter to be provided well to die. 'Consider, my lord, what time your lordship would allot to yourself and appoint that to me', and so left it to the judge's discretion rather than name the day of his own execution. On 3 August 1646 he was taken to Tyburn. When the sheriff prevented him from continuing his speech to the crowd he pulled his cap over his eyes and waited silently. He was made to stand for about fifteen minutes because the carter could not bring himself to drive the cart away, and another man had to do the job. He hung until he was dead, but his head and quarters were not put on public display as usual: they were buried in the churchyard at Moorfields.

Blessed Edward Bamber, the son of Richard and Jennet, was born c.1597 at a manor house called The Moor, Great Carleton, Poulton-le-Fylde, near Blackpool. Little is known of his early life other than that he studied at Saint-Omer and Seville, although Challoner is mistaken in stating that he was also at Valladolid. He was ordained at Cádiz 6 July 1626 and shortly afterwards joined a ship at Sanlúcar de Barrameda bound for Le Havre. It seems Edward intended to return to Saint-Omer, but the ship ran into bad weather and was forced to shelter at Plymouth, where he was apprehended and searched. As he had on him a certificate confirming his ordination, the authorities were furnished with proof of who he was. On 4 December 1626 he was sent to London where he was imprisoned for three months. On 13 March 1627 Edward renounced his faith and was granted a pardon and released. How genuine was his apostasy may be judged from the fact that he made his way to his native Lancashire, and worked on the mission there for about thirteen years. He was first captured near Standish and may have been chaplain to Ralph Standish at Standish Hall, the moated manor house near Wigan. While being escorted to Lancaster he was lodged at the Old Green Man inn, Claughton-on-Brock from which he contrived to escape as his guards were drunk. He managed to find shelter with Mr Singleton of Broughton Tower. He was finally caught in 1643 and imprisoned in Lancaster Castle for three years, being brought to trial in 1646, when two false Catholics gave witness against him. On 7 August 1646 he was drawn to the place of execution with two priest companions: John Woodcock and Thomas Whitaker. With them was a felon named Croft and on the scaffold Bamber urged him to repent, confess his sins and be absolved and join the Catholic Church, following the example of the penitent thief in the Gospel. The ministers present were outraged, but in spite of their threats Edward stood his ground. Croft publicly confessed his crimes and asked forgiveness for them and in front of everyone Edward absolved him, to the intense mortification of the ministers. Taking a handful of coins he threw them to the crowd saying that God loved a cheerful giver. He then turned to Father Whitaker, who was terrified of what was to come, and spoke words of encouragement and comfort to him, at which the sheriff ordered him to be turned off the ladder immediately. He was cut down before he was dead to suffer a most savage butchery. Someone wrote an ode about his death which says,

> Few words he spoke, they stopped his mouth,
> And choked him with a cord;
> And lest he should be dead too soon,
> No mercy they afford.
>
> But quick and live they cut him down,
> And butcher him full soon;
> Behead and tear and dismember straight,
> And laugh when it was done.

Blessed John Woodcock was born at Clayton-Le-Woods, near Preston, Lancashire, in 1603. His father was Protestant, his mother Catholic, and it was she who sent her son to the Jesuits at Saint-Omer. He then studied at the English College, Rome, where he decided he wished to join the Franciscans. He applied first to the Capuchins, but was rejected, so he turned to the English Franciscans at St Bonaventure's, Douai, and was accepted, being clothed by Father Henry Heath. He made his profession one year later to Father Arthur Bell, taking the name of Father Martin of St Felix. He was ordained in 1634 and afterwards acted as chaplain at Arras to Mr Sheldon, an English exile, until in 1640 he was sent to England. Because of ill-health he asked to be recalled in 1642 and returned to Douai. In 1644 he requested to return to the English mission, landing at Newcastle-upon-Tyne. He made his way into Lancashire to see his parents, but his father, frightened for his son's safety, urged him to go away. The local garrison had been alerted to John's arrival and he was disturbed while saying Mass at the home of the Burgess family and arrested by soldiers at Bamber Bridge. Next day he was committed to Lancaster Castle, where he spent the next two years without trial. While standing on the ladder John tried to address the crowd, but was quickly silenced by the sheriff and flung off. Like Father Bamber he was butchered alive.

Blessed Thomas Whitaker, the son of Thomas, master of the free school at Burnley, Lancashire, and his wife Helen Starkey, was born 1611 and baptised at St Peter's church 26 September. Through the generosity of the recusant Townley family, in 1622 he was sent to continue his studies at Saint-Omer, and in 1634 went to Valladolid, where he was ordained in March 1638. The following month he returned to England using the alias Starkey. He worked in Lancashire around the Fylde area; Goosnargh, Kirkham and St Michael's-on-Wyre. Early in the Civil War he was arrested while travelling to Lancaster, but in the middle of the night managed to escape by letting himself down from an upstairs window. Luckily for him next morning he ran into a Catholic, who took him in. He was again arrested by a gang of pursuivants armed with swords and clubs at the house of Mr Midgeall at Goosnargh and committed to Lancaster Castle on 7 August 1643. En route he managed to escape but was quickly recaptured. He spent six weeks in solitary confinement in the Castle before being allowed access to the common jail. His imprisonment without trial lasted nearly three years until he was condemned and sent for execution with Fathers Bamber and Woodcock. On the scaffold he could not hide his fear, having to watch as his two companions were butchered before him. His younger brother, Humphrey Whitaker, was also a priest, ordained at Rome in 1638. He spent most of his life teaching at Douai and Lisbon and was president of the latter college from 1651 until his death in 1653.

Puritan Parliament and the Commonwealth

2 Blessed Peter Wright was born into a recusant family at Slipton, Northamptonshire, in 1603. His father died when he was young, leaving a large family of children, so Peter was obliged to find work as a clerk in a lawyer's office at Thrapston. Here he lived for several years and conformed to the Established Church; at least outwardly. He was reconciled and crossed to the Netherlands and eventually made his way to the Jesuit College at Liège. In 1629 it was intended that he should be sent from Ghent to Rome but Peter asked that he be admitted to the Society of Jesus. He served his novitiate at Watten, followed by years of study at Liège, where he was ordained, probably in 1636. He became a military chaplain, serving the English regiment of Colonel Henry Gage in the Spanish Netherlands. Here he met Henry Morse. Gage greatly esteemed Peter and kept him by his side for seven years. In 1643 King Charles summoned Colonel Gage home to serve him in the Civil War. He was made Governor of Oxford and given a knighthood. Peter returned to England with Gage and ministered to the soldiers. He was with Gage in September and November 1644 when Gage tried to relieve the siege of Basing House, near Basingstoke, Hampshire. The magnificent house, held for the King, was the home of the Catholic John Paulet, 5th Marquess of Winchester. In the parliamentary assault, led by Oliver Cromwell himself, six priests were killed. On 11 January 1645 Colonel Gage was killed near Abingdon, Peter administering the last sacraments to him. Peter then became chaplain to the Marquess of Winchester, *based at his house in Holborn, London. While he was preparing to say Mass on 2 February 1651 the priest hunters broke in and were detained on the stairs by the Marquess, long enough for Peter to climb out of a window and onto the leads. It did not take long for the pursuivants to work out what had happened when they saw the altar prepared and the open window. They climbed up onto the leads and arrested him. He was committed to Newgate where he had several other priests for company, including Father Thomas Dade, superior of the Dominicans, and shared a bed in a cell with Father Charles Cheney. He was tried at the Old Bailey on 14 May before Lord Chief Justice Sir Henry Rolle, William Steel, the Recorder and the Lord Mayor, Thomas Andrews. Evidence was given against him by the priest catchers Mayo and Wadsworth and the apostate former Dominican priest, Thomas

---

* Paulet and his wife were imprisoned in the Tower and offered an allowance with the proviso that their children were to be brought up as Protestants. In 1649 it was decided not to try him for high treason but he was kept in prison. His estates were declared forfeit and in 1656 he was again in prison for debt. He did not recover his lands until the Restoration in 1660. In 1669 he married, as his third wife, Isabella Howard, daughter of Blessed William Howard, Viscount Stafford.

Puritan Parliament and the Commonwealth

Gage, brother of Colonel Henry. (Gage married and was appointed rector of Deal in 1651. He supported the parliamentarians, became chaplain to a general and accompanied him on an expedition to the West Indies and died in Jamaica in 1656.) Peter was found guilty and condemned. Every effort was made to obtain a reprieve, but as it was the Whitsun recess Parliament was not in session. From morning until night a great number of Catholics came to the prison to see Peter who made a general confession of his life to Father Cheney, after which he declared that he had never known so much joy in his soul. On Whit Monday, 19 May, he and Father Cheney celebrated Mass, after which came the knocking at the gates to summon him to his execution to which he responded, 'I come, sweet Jesus, I come.' His progress on the hurdle appeared more of a triumphant procession as people crowded around to ask his blessing. As the hurdle passed his house the Marquess of Winchester and all his family were waiting on the balcony and they bowed their heads low when Peter raised himself up and gave them his final blessing. It was a hot, sunny day and the crowd at Tyburn was huge. An eye witness estimated the numbers up to 20,000 with two hundred coaches and five hundred horsemen. Thirteen felons were appointed to die at the same time and as these were being hanged Peter, his eyes closed, his hands clasped before him, occupied his time in prayer for almost an hour. Offered his life if he renounced his Faith he courteously refused. He also declined to have his face covered. With the rope around his neck he kept his final speech brief, saying he did not want to detain his audience. He declared, 'This is a short passage to eternity' and thanked God that He had granted him such a death of which he was so unworthy. He was allowed to hang until dead before the mutilation began. His remains were taken for burial by friends, who were permitted to carry away his head, which was taken to the Jesuits at Liège. A piece of the rope with which he was hanged is now enshrined at St Paul's Catholic Church, Thrapston.

3 ... *harsh prison conditions*. To give the lie to the erroneous perception of leniency towards Catholics in the period there follows just a representative selection of priests who suffered during the rule of Parliament and under the Commonwealth.

1642: *Edward Wilkes*, alias Thomson, seminary priest, born at Knaresborough. Arrested at Malton he was set in the stocks on market day, when he was identified and sent to York Castle. He was tried and convicted but died before his execution. *Boniface Kemp* OSB who had been professed at Montserrat, Spain, and *Ildephonse Hesketh* OSB both served as chaplains to the Royalist army at the battle of Marston Moor. They were wounded and apprehended by parliamentary soldiers and greatly ill-used. Both died in prison in Yorkshire. *Lawrence Mabbs* OSB died Newgate.

1645: Venerable *Brian Cansfield* SJ was born at Tatham, Lancashire, in 1582. In 1604 he joined the Society of Jesus in Flanders. He returned to England in 1618 and worked on the mission in Lancashire, Lincolnshire and Yorkshire under the alias of Barton. In 1645 the wife of a Yorkshire judge was reconciled to the Catholic Church and her furious husband ordered the priest hunters to search for the priest responsible. Father Cansfield was arrested while saying Mass. He was violently struck and abused before being imprisoned in York Castle in a damp, filthy cell. He was starved and beaten before it was discovered that they had got the wrong priest and he was released. Aged sixty-three he was a physically broken man and he died a few days later. The Welshman, Venerable *John Goodman*, whose story has been told, died in Newgate aged fifty-three. *Walter Coleman*, a Franciscan whose name in religion was Father Christopher of St Clare, died in Newgate.

1646: *Richard Bradley* SJ came from Lancashire. He joined the Jesuits at the age of eighteen. After ordination he served as a missioner among the English soldiers in Belgium. After his return to England he was captured by parliamentary soldiers. Aged forty-one he died of jail fever on 30 January, a close prisoner at Manchester awaiting trial. *John Felton* SJ died after seven months in prison at Lincoln. *Peter Wilford* OSB was ordained at Valladolid in 1607. In 1608 he joined the Benedictines, taking the name Boniface. He was sentenced to death in May 1642 and died in Newgate 12 March aged sixty-two.

1647: *Thomas Blount* came from Shropshire and was educated at Saint-Omer, Valladolid and Lisbon where he was ordained in June 1641. He joined the English mission in 1642. Arrested and condemned to death he died in Shrewsbury jail, aged thirty-one.

1648: *Thomas Foster* SJ was born 1590 at Earswick, Yorkshire, and ordained by St Robert Bellarmine in 1614. He died in Lincoln jail on 31 March; *Andrew Waferer* OSB, was born in Huntingdonshire. He was converted by Father Robert Hawkesworth and shortly afterwards imprisoned. He was ordained at Valladolid in 1603. Captured by the pursuivant Wadsworth in 1641 he was condemned to death but reprieved by the King and died in Newgate, aged seventy-two.

Puritan Parliament and the Commonwealth

Edmund Cannon, born 1578 in Essex, was a student at Seville where he was ordained in 1602. By 1610 he was working in Oxfordshire and was in the Clink in March 1622. He was released on bond in 1626 having taken the Oath of Allegiance. He was back in the Clink in 1632 and then moved to Newgate. Condemned to death in 1641 his execution was fixed for 13 December but he was reprieved at the request of the French ambassador and left in prison.

1650: *John Abbot* alias Rivers, nephew of George Abbot, Archbishop of Canterbury. Converted at Saint-Omer by Father John Floyd he was ordained 1612 and became a Bridgettine in 1623. Several times imprisoned he was condemned to death April 1641 and died in Newgate aged sixty-two; Yorkshireman *John Jackson*, ordained 1598, had been archdeacon of Wiltshire. Condemned to death in December 1641 sick and prematurely aged he was reprieved by the King and died in Newgate aged seventy-seven. *Robert Cox* OSB, sentenced to death but not executed, died in the Clink, Southwark.

1651: *John Smith* SJ, of Nidderdale, Yorkshire died in York Castle 21 December.

1652: *John Worthington* SJ, who had been arrested when a boy, was Rector of the College of St Aloysius. He was arrested in Lancaster in 1643 and paraded through the streets in a mock religious procession, after his vestments had been publicly burned. He remained a prisoner for ten years. He died on 25 January. *George Gage* was the second son of Sir John and Lady Margaret. Ordained in 1626 he returned to England and was immediately arrested at Dover on information from the spy James Wadsworth and sent to the Clink. In 1629 he was released through the influence of Queen Henrietta Maria who took him into her service for a time as her 'cupbearer'. He worked on the mission in Sussex and was grief stricken when he learned that his apostate brother, Thomas, had betrayed Father Peter Wright. In 1649 he became archdeacon of London and suffered several imprisonments. He died in Newgate 28 July.

1660: *George Anne* SJ, born 1595, came from the recusant family at Frickley, near Wakefield. He was ordained at Santo Spirito in Sassia, Rome by Peter Lombard, the long-exiled Archbishop of Armagh, on 25 March 1620. (Santo Spirito was originally the church of the Anglo-Saxon pilgrim's hospice in Rome, established by King Ine of Wessex (688-726). George came to England in 1621 and joined the Jesuits in

Puritan Parliament and the Commonwealth

1623. Aged sixty-three, on 24 June he died in York Castle, as had his recusant grandfather, Richard Anne, in 1600. Peter Lombard was born in Waterford c.1555 but was sent to Westminster School and then to Oxford, where one of his professors, the historian William Camden, thought highly of his talents and believed he had turned him into an Anglican. That turned out to be false optimism as Peter went to Louvain, graduated Doctor of Divinity and was ordained. In 1594 he became provost of Cambrai cathedral. Called to Rome, he so impressed Clement VIII that in 1601 he was appointed Archbishop of Armagh, even though there was no hope of him ever going to Ireland to claim his see because of the swingeing penal laws. James I harboured a bitter personal dislike for Lombard who spent the rest of his life in Rome serving the papacy in various capacities, including Pontifical Commissions. He died in 1625.

Other priests imprisoned/condemned included:

John Hackshott, the son of the martyr Thomas Hackshott, was born in London some months before his father's execution. He entered Douai in 1616 and was ordained and sent to England in 1625. He was captured in December 1632 and jailed for five years in both the Gatehouse and New Prison. Released in 1637 he became chaplain to a family in Lincolnshire. He was re-arrested and condemned to death at Newgate 8 December 1641. He was reprieved but still a prisoner in July 1648. He died in 1663.

Edmund Cole alias William Marsh was an Anglican minister who was converted by Father John Percy SJ. He went to Valladolid and was ordained in 1624. He worked on the mission in Berkshire and Hampshire. Indicted as a priest in 1642 he was condemned, but banished.

John Whitbread alias Wilmot and Peter Turner was born in London 1595. He was imprisoned in 1619 and banished in 1621. Ordained in 1625 he was arrested by Francis Newton in 1637. Condemned at Newgate 10 April 1641 he was reprieved but was still in prison in July 1648.

Charles Cheney, who shared a cell and bed in Newgate with Peter Wright, was born in Hampshire in 1604. At the age of eight he was sent abroad to be educated by the Jesuits. He entered Douai in 1618 but was asked to leave to leave in 1622 for lack of application to his studies.

However he persisted in his vocation and was admitted to the English College, Rome in 1633. He was ordained at Rome in February 1636. Arrested and condemned in 1651 for saying Mass his release was begged by the Spanish ambassador. If he was released it cannot have been for very long because in 1652 he was back in Newgate.

George Machell of Whinfell, Kendal, Westmorland, was born 1587. He entered Douai in 1607 and later that year was sent to the English College, Rome. He was a troublesome student and was sent back to Douai in 1612. Expelled from Douai he was re-admitted in 1614 and again expelled in 1616. However he returned and was ordained at Cambrai in April 1618. He worked in London from 1632 onwards under the alias Baker. It was claimed he frequented taverns far too often! He was arrested for saying Mass at Holborn in February 1651. Committed to Newgate he was condemned to death and left in Newgate.

Yorkshireman *Basil Norton*, born 1595, was a relative of Sir John Conyers of Norton Conyers. He entered Douai May 1613 but returned to England in 1615 due to health problems. In January 1616 he was imprisoned at Newgate for refusing the oath. Banished in July 1618 he returned to Douai and was ordained at Cambrai in September 1621. By April 1642 he was again in Newgate, where he remained for nineteen years until released in 1661. He died the following year and was buried at St Giles-in-the-Fields.

Richard Worthington, son of Thomas Worthington and Mary Allen, a niece of Cardinal Allen, was born in 1606 at Louvain where his parents were in exile. He entered the English College, Rome in 1623 and was ordained at Naples in 1631. In April that year he came to London where he was a chaplain to the Venetian ambassador. On 15 August 1643, the feast of the Assumption, he was living at the Spanish ambassador's house and used his coach to visit Lady Tresham, who was ill, in order to give her the sacraments. On his return the coach was stopped in the street and Worthington was pulled out and arrested. He was condemned to death but the ambassador secured his release. In 1652 Richard became chaplain at St Monica's, Louvain where he remained until his death in 1657.

4 Father Andrew Knightly was the son of Edward Knightly of Offchurch, Warwickshire, and the grandson of Sir Valentine Knightly of Fawsley, Northamptonshire. Andrew was Edward's twelfth child.

Puritan Parliament and the Commonwealth

The Knightly's were a famous Puritan family but the numerous Offchurch branch remained staunchly recusant until 1688. Andrew's sisters, Elizabeth and Dorothy, were nuns on the Continent. When Andrew was ordained is unknown and the first reference to him on the mission occurs in 1632 when he was working in his native county. At some point he must have moved to London when, along with John Southworth, he was appointed Collector for London and Middlesex. The following year he was appointed archdeacon of Middlesex and Vicar General to Bishop Richard Smith. In all the unseemly dissension among the secular clergy Knightly supported Smith but when the Bishop left for France and died in Paris in 1655 Andrew wielded the most senior authority writing to Rome to complain of the hopelessness of his position. Said to be a great age he died in 1660. His public will states that he was a gentleman of St-Giles-in-the-Fields, where he requested to be buried. Reflecting his family's status he left considerable property and land in Warwickshire and Leicestershire to his nephews and godsons. In his private will he left money to his nun sister in Lisbon, to Douai College and to various religious orders in England, as well as to Father Basil Norton, then a prisoner in Newgate.

Chapter Eight

Charles II and the 'Popish Plot', 1660-1685

Truth sits upon the lips of dying men.

The Scholar Gypsy, Matthew Arnold, 1822-88

When the ineffectual Richard Cromwell - who briefly succeeded his father as Lord Protector - abdicated, the exiled King was invited to return home. Charles II entered London to a triumphant and tumultuous welcome on 29 May 1660; his 30th birthday. The restoration of Charles to his throne aroused fresh optimism amongst the Catholics, hopeful that their loyalty to the Stuarts would at last secure some toleration. Charles was conscious of owing a debt of gratitude to his Catholic subjects for their service to his father in the Civil War. Furthermore in 1651, as Prince of Wales, he had attempted to claim his throne. After his defeat at the Battle of Worcester it was largely Catholics who gave him refuge. Charles Giffard escorted the prince to his family home, White Ladies Priory, so called because it had been a nunnery until 1535. At the time it was occupied by a family of tenants; the Penderell's. The Giffard's then moved the fugitive to their nearby Boscobel House, on the Shropshire/Staffordshire border, where Charles hid in the famous oak tree and in the priest's secret chamber in the attic. (One of the Giffard sons, Peter, was studying for the priesthood at Lisbon where he was ordained in 1653. He served in England until his death in 1689.) Charles was next moved to Moseley Old Hall, a rather remote late Elizabethan house with a secret chapel. The home of Thomas Whitgreave, it was his chaplain, the Benedictine priest, Father John Huddleston, a former chaplain in the Royalist army, who saved Charles's life by hiding him in the priest hole beneath a trapdoor when the parliamentary soldiers came to search the house. It was an act of bravery the King never forgot and significantly it was also the time from which Charles's interior conversion to Catholicism can probably be dated. Huddleston, who represented all that was best about English Catholicism, later recalled that Charles declared that when he was in possession of his crown 'both you and all of your persuasion shall have as much liberty as any of my subjects.' During the first months of his return the King relaxed the persecution and priests were released from prison. On 25 October 1660 Charles issued a declaration of toleration for tender consciences, while waiting for Parliament to settle religious

546

Charles II and the 'Popish Plot', 1660-1685

policy. The King stated that no one should be disquieted or called in question for differences of opinion in religious matters, as long as they did not disturb the peace. That instrument of persecution, the Council of the North, which had been abolished in 1641, was not restored. At the insistence of Parliament, in 1663 Charles had to issue a directive ordering the enforcement of the penal laws. Until then most Catholics were allowed to live in peace and many priests were allowed to work discreetly. Charles, although brought up amongst Catholics, was a pragmatist when it came to matters of religion or indeed any other matters. Having spent his youth in exile he was determined, as he declared, never to go on his travels again, so that all his policies were designed to ensure his continued tenure of the throne. Charles had many personal affinities with the Church, having a Catholic mother, a beloved Catholic sister and dependence upon the Catholic Louis XIV for financial support. He had a Catholic wife, the Portuguese princess, Catherine of Braganza. His illegitimate daughter, Charlotte Fitz-Charles, became a nun at Dunkirk. Her mother, Catharine Pegge, had a priest brother, William, who was ordained and sent to England in 1666. Another illegitimate daughter, Lady Mary Tudor, married the Catholic 2nd Earl of Derwentwater, Edward Radclyffe. Charles's brother James, Duke of York, and his first wife, Anne Hyde, both converted. James married, as his second wife, an Italian Catholic princess, Mary Beatrice d'Este of Modena. Charles's Scottish/French Stuart cousins were Catholics and one, Ludovic, 10th Seigneur d'Aubigny, son of the 3rd Duke of Lennox, was a priest, ordained by Bishop Richard Smith in Paris in 1652. He became almoner to Queen Catherine of Braganza in 1661 but died on his way to Rome to be made a cardinal in 1665.

During Charles's reign the Chapter was able to set up a more formal organisational structure of archdeaconries covering England and Wales. No slander was too foul or allegation too far fetched to level at the Catholics, who in turn had been accused of being responsible for the Great Plague of 1665, in which as many as 80,000 may have died, and the Great Fire which destroyed much of the City of London the following year. Despite his public religious ambivalence and scepticism, Charles made an effort to protect the Catholics from molestation by the Puritan bigots. His room for manoeuvre was, however, limited because the Civil War had so weakened the authority of the Crown. He tried to honour his nuptial contract to ensure that his consort, Queen Catherine, was allowed free practise of her religion. Father Philip Thomas Howard OP, 1 great-grandson of Saint Philip Howard, had a position of influence at Court. He was grand almoner to the Queen and lived at St James's Palace in receipt of a salary. During

Charles II and the 'Popish Plot', 1660-1685

Queen Henrietta Maria's exile the Puritans had imprisoned and then banished her Capuchin priests and desecrated their chapel. On her return to England in 1663 she reinstated the Capuchins.

As has already been noted with the career of the remarkable Mary Ward, throughout the reigns of Charles I and II there was no shortage of vocations to the priesthood and religious life, especially from the gentry families. There was a steady flow of English candidates to religious houses on the Continent. Many gentry families over several generations had established close associations with particular religious orders. Post-Reformation this was reinforced because of the problems of educating their children at home. Yorkshire families were prominent in producing an extraordinary number of vocations - priests, monks and nuns - such as the Gascoigne's and Ingleby's who favoured the Benedictines. The records are very scanty and imprecise but in the seventeenth century from the West Riding of Yorkshire alone came at least thirty-three Benedictines and thirty-five Jesuits, plus Carthusians, Franciscans and Dominicans.

In 1670 Parliament complained to the King about the 'growth of popery'. Much to the resentment of the Protestants, Charles brought prominent Catholics into his government. As he once remarked in conversation with Edward Hyde, Earl of Clarendon, 'For my part ... I had rather trust a Papist rebel than a Presbyterian one'. While Parliament was prorogued in 1672, Charles issued a Declaration of Indulgence allowing toleration to Catholics; but when Parliament reconvened he was forced to withdraw it. Parliament retaliated by passing the Test Act, (25 Car. II, ii) which disbarred anyone from holding any public office who did not take an oath insulting the Catholic Church and specifically denying the Real Presence of Christ in the Eucharist. Five years later a new Act 'for the more effectual preserving the King's person and government, by disabling Papists from sitting in either House of Parliament' came into force, requiring every member of either House to take an oath making a blasphemous declaration against Catholicism, thus all Catholics were effectively excluded from Parliament. Although aimed ostensibly at all Catholics, the Act was a further swipe at James, Duke of York, who was banished to Scotland.

In spite of the King's efforts active persecution never abated and priests continued to die in prison. Thomas Vaughan of Courtfield was born in 1606. Educated at Douai he was ordained in 1627 by his uncle, William Gifford OSB, Archbishop of Rheims, a former student of the English College, Rome. He returned to England in 1628 and worked on the mission in Wales, joining the Society of Jesus in 1632. He died in Cardiff jail in 1675. In the same year Father William Pugh, whose

Charles II and the 'Popish Plot', 1660-1685

alias was Captain Pugh, was arrested for saying Mass in a chapel at Llanthony, Monmouthsire.

The final six of the Forty Martyrs were all victims of the fierce persecution of 1678-81 that amounted to nothing less than a pogrom against Catholics. The infamous so-called 'Popish Plot' was invented and fomented by a miserable, unscrupulous reprobate named Titus Oates, in collusion with the deranged clergyman Dr Israel Tonge and later, his disreputable crony, the Chepstow-born William Bedloe. At this distance in time it is impossible for us to conceive how such an incorrigible scoundrel as Titus Oates could have provoked the country into such a frenzied, anti-Catholic hysteria. Titus was born at Oakham, Rutland, in 1649. Jane Lane (the pen name of Elaine Kidner Dakers) commenced her 1949 biography of him with, 'The England of sixteen hundred and forty-nine suffered two national tragedies: the execution of King Charles the First, and the birth of Titus Oates.' He seems to have been a chip off the proverbial old block. His father, Samuel, a former chaplain in Cromwell's army, was a self-appointed Anabaptist preacher. A weak and vacillating character, he followed whatever course best suited his material advantage. He was a sensualist who liked to baptise his female converts in the nude at night and, to quote Jane Lane, cloaked 'his animal instincts with a convenient religious cant.' The physically unprepossessing Oates, with his enormous jutting jaw, tiny sunken eyes, slobbering mouth and wailing voice was a backward child, detested by his parents and disliked by his schoolfellows and he developed a massive inferiority complex. He had been a failure at everything he attempted. He was expelled from the Merchant Taylors' School for theft and expelled from Cambridge, where his tutor pronounced him a 'great dunce'. Notwithstanding his lack of academic attainment, he became an Anglican vicar at Bobbing in Kent in 1673 but was soon dismissed for theft, drunkenness, blasphemy and sodomy. For false allegations of sodomy against a young schoolmaster - who had probably spurned his advances - he was ordered to pay £1,000 in damages and was bound over for perjury. Unable to pay he was imprisoned first at Hastings then at Dover but managed to escape. In 1675 he began service as a naval chaplain before being ousted for sodomy. Unemployed, he moved to London where he frequented some insalubrious haunts that may well have been the 'gay clubs' of their day.

Titus ingratiated himself with the Jesuits, who charitably supplied him with funds and found him a job as chaplain to the Protestant's in the household of the Earl Marshal of England, Henry Howard, Earl of Norwich. (Howard, great-grandson of St Philip Howard, became 6th

Charles II and the 'Popish Plot', 1660-1685

Duke of Norfolk in December 1677. As a Catholic he was debarred from sitting in the House of Lords when he refused to subscribe to the 1673 Test Act. Rather than conform he chose exile and went to live in Bruges in a house attached to a Franciscan convent. He returned to England three years later and died in 1684.) In less than three months Oates was dismissed by Howard. And then, unbelievably, on 3 March 1677 Titus was received into the Catholic Church by a somewhat disreputable priest named William Berry, who was generally regarded by his colleagues as unhinged. Unemployed again Oates was on his uppers. Accepting the new convert's sincerity at face value the elderly Jesuit Provincial, Father Richard Strange, assisted him to enter the English College, Valladolid, where he arrived in June 1677. This seems extraordinary given that Titus was so deficient in Latin, the language in which studies were mostly conducted. The Jesuits, and Strange in particular, have come in for criticism for not thoroughly investigating Oates's background but he was such a plausible villain. Certainly the Jesuits were to pay a heavy price for their lack of judgement, but they were in good company where Titus was concerned. When the new student's ignorance of Latin was discovered he was promptly dismissed from Valladolid, his superiors paying for his passage home on a ship from Santander. When he left Oates stole part of the College register. This, no doubt, later proved to be an invaluable source of information for him when it came to identifying and accusing priests. It was during his stay in Spain that he first encountered William Bedloe.

Returned to London and feigning penitence with many hysterical tears, Oates once more wormed his way into the Catholic community and was given a second chance by Father Strange who recommended him to the college at Saint-Omer where it was hoped he might improve his education. Oates arrived on 10 December 1677 and the college was greatly shocked by his grotesque appearance and his lewd conversation with the boys who were his fellow students. Needless to say when his sexual proclivities were discerned he was very soon ejected during a visit by the new Provincial, Thomas Whitbread, who had succeeded Strange in January 1678. Provided by the Jesuits with clothes and money Titus returned to England in June 1678 full of malice and venomous hatred for Catholics and Jesuits in particular. Oates later claimed he had only joined the Jesuits in order to spy on them. Back in London he attempted to blackmail the Jesuits but when he was given short shrift he swore vengeance. He teamed up with Israel Tonge, an acquaintance he had known through his father. Tonge was another former Anglican vicar, a university graduate who had held various livings before turning fanatic Puritan under the Commonwealth. At the

Charles II and the 'Popish Plot', 1660-1685

Restoration he reverted to the Established Church and was lucky enough - for an ex-Puritan - to obtain the living of St Mary Staining in the City of London. His luck ran out when the church was burned to the ground in the Great Fire of 1666. Whether or not this was the direct trigger, he clearly became mentally unbalanced, exhibiting all the symptoms of a mammoth persecution complex. Having returned from a spell in Tangier as an army chaplain he appears to have spent most of his time writing turgid, wildly incoherent, anti-Catholic, particularly anti-Jesuit, pamphlets. His contemporaries all believed he was a madman. Titus informed Tonge that while at the Jesuit college he had learned about a meeting of members of the Society planned for London. This was nothing more than one of their regular meetings or 'Consults' but it served as the germ of the idea that led to the concoction of the 'Plot'. At a later stage Oates and Tonge caused severe embarrassment to their Whig paymasters when, at a banquet given in Oates' honour by the City of London, the two of them got into a heated argument as to which of them was the originator of the conspiracy.

A thoroughgoing rogue who inhabited the criminal underworld, William Bedloe had been involved in various nefarious schemes, which had led to his imprisonment. It was to save his skin from his latest dubious escapade that Bedloe offered to turn 'Kings evidence' and reveal what he knew of the 'Plot'. Taking his cue from Titus Oates, as the days went by he enlarged and embroidered his original allegations until they reached preposterous proportions. He claimed that forty thousand men were to be ready in London, who were to be joined by forty thousand more from Spain and ten thousand from Flanders, after the murder of the King. Bedloe alleged that there were to be Catholic uprisings all over Wales and that a Jesuit priest, Father Charles Pritchard, was going to murder the Duke of Buckingham. The mind boggles that these ludicrous ravings could have been given any credence other than in the prevailing climate of mass hysteria in which 'the native good sense and humanity of the English character' was temporarily extinguished. (John Lingard, *History of England*).

There was a large measure of personal spite and revenge against Catholics not only in Oates's accusations but also in the fabrications of other so-called witnesses. Prominent among them was Stephen Dugdale. A Catholic convert he was steward to Walter, 3rd Lord Aston of Forfar at Tixall Hall, Staffordshire, where he cheated the estate workers of their wages. In September 1678 Dugdale was dismissed by Lord Aston for embezzlement. With the outbreak of the 'Plot' Dugdale jumped on the bandwagon perjuring himself by giving false testimony. Deeply saddening though it is to recall, there were also a number of

Charles II and the 'Popish Plot', 1660-1685

other Catholics who were terrorised into providing false information, for example Miles Prance, a London silversmith in Covent Garden. Born in Cambridgeshire in 1646, the son of Simon Prance and Anne Shepherd, his two brothers, Thomas and Charles, were priests and two of his sisters were nuns. Prance was known to Queen Catherine and to the Jesuits for whom he had done work. There were also priests who at the outbreak of the 'Plot' apostatised, such as London-born John Portman who gave evidence against Sir Miles Stapleton and Viscount Stafford, and Exeter-born John Travers SJ, who despicably took advantage of the prevailing climate and turned on his former colleagues, supplying false evidence against them. Even worse was Father John Sergeant. Born in Lincolnshire in 1623 and converted by George Gage he was ordained at Lisbon in 1649. He hated the Jesuits and proved something of a maverick priest given to publishing pamphlets. When the 'Plot' broke out he had retired to Amsterdam returning in October 1679 when, before the King and Council, he gave shamefully false evidence trying to besmirch the memory of Father John Gavan SJ. As Gavan had been martyred four months previously Sergeant's lies could not do him any more harm, but in any case nobody, least of all the King, believed Sergeant. Nonetheless, Sergeant was granted a royal pardon and was paid a weekly subsidy until the end of the reign, but he was shunned by his fellow Catholics. (In old age Sergeant continued issuing vitriolic and libellous publications abusing his fellow priests. He died in 1707 and was buried in St Pancras churchyard.)

The nub of the 'Plot' was the assassination of the King and his replacement by his Catholic convert brother James, Duke of York, who would then bring in a foreign Catholic army to massacre the Protestants and force the nation back to Catholicism. The whole affair would have been farcical were it not for the appalling consequences. The last persecution in which Catholics were actually put to death for their faith, it is one of the most shameful episodes in the whole of British history. The eighteenth-century statesman, Charles James Fox, called it 'an indelible disgrace upon the English nation'.

Oates and Tongue prepared a dossier of forty-three paragraphs setting out their fictional plot. Not content with simply alleging that the King was to be murdered there were several strands to the 'Plot': Charles was to be killed in triplicate by being shot with a silver bullet and stabbed as well as poisoned by the Queen's physician! After that the Catholics would burn down the main towns and cities and all Protestants were to be massacred. In August Tongue had a meeting with his friend Christopher Kirkby, a bankrupt merchant who had

Charles II and the 'Popish Plot', 1660-1685

wheedled an appointment as a tax-gathering clerk to the Lord Treasurer, the anti-Catholic Thomas Osborne, Earl of Danby. Kirkby, who shared Tonge's delusions, was known by sight to the King and he agreed to present the dossier to Charles when he was taking his morning walk in St James's Park. Kirkby duly presented the dossier to the King who then spoke to him alone in the palace. Kirkby told Charles that the Benedictine, Thomas Pickering and the Jesuit brother, John Grove, planned to shoot him and if this did not succeed then he was to be poisoned by Sir George Wakeman, the Catholic physician to Queen Catherine. (Wakeman's brother, Edward, was a priest. Their mother, Mary, was a daughter of Richard Cotton of Warblington.) The King told Kirkby to bring Israel Tonge to the palace that evening. Confronted by the mad and incoherent Tonge, who would not name Oates as the source of his information, Charles was sceptical about the whole story but, erring on the side of caution, he thought it prudent to have it investigated, so he handed the affair over to Lord Treasurer Danby and went off to Windsor. In September 1678 Oates and Tonge sought out a Justice of the Peace, Sir Edmund Berry Godfrey, and presented to him their spurious allegations of Catholic plots. Godfrey was a courageous and conscientious official who had remained in London carrying out his duties throughout the Great Plague. The mysterious death of Sir Edmund, whose body was found on Primrose Hill in October, was the catalyst the plotters needed to lend some semblance of credence to their allegations when 'the Catholics' were accused of his murder, although they had nothing to gain by Godfrey's death. It was not unusual for magistrates to be assaulted, so it is likely that Godfrey, who often went about with a bodyguard for protection, was attacked by a criminal seeking revenge. He may have recognised his assailant who then had to kill him. (Sir Edmund was a somewhat melancholy man, who was in a state of depression, and some modern historians have argued that he committed suicide.)

The rabidly anti-Catholic Anthony Ashley Cooper, Earl of Shaftesbury, and leader of the Whig opposition to the King eagerly seized upon Oates as a heaven-sent opportunity and shamelessly exploited the 'Plot' for his own political aims. Shaftesbury's 'vaulting ambition' was matched by his ruthlessness in attaining his ends and Oates's sensational allegations were just what he needed to persuade the country that their liberties were being threatened by the papists. Charles called Shaftesbury 'the greatest rogue in England'. His methods in manipulating public opinion were reminiscent of those employed by John Pym and his cronies against Charles I: playing upon the prejudices and passions of the mob and employing groups of men to

Charles II and the 'Popish Plot', 1660-1685

intimidate members of the Commons to demonstrate in his favour whenever someone opposed him. Not content with fanning the flames of fanaticism, Shaftesbury actively connived with Oates and his cohorts to tailor their false information to the advantage of the exclusionist cause - that is excluding the Duke of York from the succession to the throne and supplanting him with the Protestant James Scott, Duke of Monmouth, King Charles' eldest illegitimate son. Shaftesbury tried to persuade Charles to legitimise Monmouth, but fond as he was of his handsome son, the King would not entertain the idea. Shaftesbury was not acting from altruistic motives; he saw the weak, vain, unintelligent Monmouth as a puppet king, while he became the real ruler of the country. John Dryden (1631-1700), the dramatist and poet laureate, in his great poem, *Absalom and Achitophel*, satirising the 'Popish Plot', had nothing but invective for Shaftesbury, the Achitophel of the poem: 'In friendship false, implacable in hate, resolved to ruin or to rule the state'.

> Achitophel, grown weary to possess
> A lawful fame, and lazy happiness,
> Disdained the golden fruit to gather free
> And lent the crowd his arm to shake the tree.
> Now, manifest of crimes, contrived long since,
> He stood at bold defiance with his prince:
> The wish'd occasion of the Plot he takes;
> Some circumstances finds, but more he makes
> By buzzing emissaries, fills the ears
> Of listening crowds, with jealousies and fears
> Of arbitrary counsels brought to light,
> And proves the King himself a Jebusite.

Shaftesbury did not stop at supplying false evidence when it suited his purpose. He also resorted to imprisonment and brutal treatment to compel so-called witnesses to provide lying testimony. After Oates testified before the Privy Council, in gratitude for his disclosures, he was awarded a monthly salary of £40 and allocated an apartment in the Palace of Whitehall. Carried away on a tide of his own notoriety and influence, and enjoying his new-found celebrity status, Titus Oates's allegations mushroomed alarmingly in number and scope. He was bold enough to raid the Jesuit residence which was attached to the Spanish embassy. The ambassador, Count Egmont, prevented the soldiers from taking away Venerable Edward Mico SJ, his chaplain who was ill in bed with a fever. The priest was brutally treated by the raiders and placed under house arrest. He died shortly afterwards.

Charles II and the 'Popish Plot', 1660-1685

King Charles, under no illusions as to the true purpose of the allegations, never believed in the existence of any Catholic plot. Finding it all too preposterous to be taken seriously, he made the mistake of treating the whole affair too light-heartedly. When the full import of the 'Plot' was realised, the King's efforts to mitigate its terrible consequences proved ineffectual. On 20 November 1678, under pressure from Parliament, he was forced to issue a proclamation for the arrest of priests. The real plot, as Charles knew very well, was the Whig conspiracy against his brother. Deploring the incredible credulity of his subjects Charles personally exposed Oates as a 'most lying scoundrel' when he questioned him before the Council and advised that he should be ignored. It was of no avail, as people who had been whipped up into an anti-Catholic frenzy were prepared to believe anything, however ludicrous. In spite of being thoroughly ashamed of himself for so doing, for reasons of political expediency, Charles capitulated to the advice of George Savile, Earl of Halifax, that the 'Plot' must be treated as if it were true, 'whether it were so or not'. Even the non-Catholic Samuel Pepys was dragged into Oates's farrago of nonsense. (It is salutary to note that intelligent, cultured men like Pepys and John Evelyn reveal in their diaries a readiness to believe that there might be some truth in the most fantastic rumours about papists.) Pepys, the Secretary to the Admiralty, was targeted by Shaftesbury and accused of being a secret papist because he maintained his loyalty towards his former employer, the Duke of York. Pepys' clerk, Samuel Atkins, was taken into custody at Newgate and every ploy was used to frighten him into accusing his master, which he would not do. Lord Shaftesbury fabricated charges that Pepys had leaked naval intelligence. The stratagem did not work. Despite being held in the Tower Pepys steadfastly refused to say anything incriminating against his friend the Duke of York, although the spurious charges against him were not dropped until June 1680.

Oates, who clearly made up his stories as he went along, frequently contradicted himself and had to wriggle and squirm his way out of his predicament. His so-called evidence being demonstrably false and his documentation forged, Oates was praised as the saviour of the nation, and his wicked perjury was only revealed when it was too late.

Blessed Edward Coleman, a married man, had been secretary to Mary of Modena, Duchess of York since 1673. He was born at Brent Eleigh, Suffolk, and educated at Cambridge. He was the Catholic convert son of an Anglican minister. Coleman was an active proselytiser for his faith and an over-zealous meddler in religious and political affairs. Some of his contacts in France, whose close alliance with England he favoured, were extremely indiscreet to say the least;

Charles II and the 'Popish Plot', 1660-1685

not to mention the payments he had received from the French government for his services. Lord Treasurer Danby thought Coleman exercised a dangerous influence on James, Duke of York. Coleman, who was a friend of the magistrate, had been warned by Sir Edmund Berry Godfrey that he had been accused by Oates of planning to kill the King in exchange for which he would be given the post of Secretary of State under the new reign. It was all pure fantasy, of course, but the death of Berry Godfrey enabled Oates to make use of it to lend some semblance of credibility to his allegations. Coleman had corresponded with Father François de la Chaise, confessor to Louis XIV of France, about finding lawful means of bettering the condition of Catholics in England. On the evidence of this correspondence, combined with the lies of Oates, a warrant for Coleman's arrest was issued to William Bedloe. Edward voluntarily gave himself up to the Secretary of State, Sir Joseph Williamson, and the same day was brought before the Council. Oates was present at the meeting but failed to even recognise Coleman. Edward was tried for treason on 27 October before Lord Chief Justice Sir William Scroggs and Mr Justices Wild and Jeffreys. Oates embroidered his 'evidence' to such a ludicrous extent that even the prosecution were uncomfortable and under cross-examination Oates got himself hopelessly tangled up in his own lies. He became evasive and tried to make excuses. It was palpably obvious that it was physically impossible in the timescale for Oates to have been in the places at which he claimed to have witnessed the many incidents he invented. Coleman was nonetheless found guilty and, protesting his innocence of involvement in any 'Plot' he was executed at Tyburn on 3 December 1678. This was followed on 24 January 1679 by the executions of the Jesuit, William Ireland [2] and his servant John Grove. [3]

The conspirators were bold enough to try and draw the King's Catholic consort, Queen Catherine, into the 'Plot'. Oates and Bedloe claimed to have overheard her planning with her priests to poison her husband. No rational person lent any credence to these allegations but Charles ordered Oates to be taken to the Queen's residence, Somerset House, to identify the rooms he had described in which he alleged the conversation had taken place. Titus was unable to recognise any of the rooms and the accusations were quickly quashed. He next tried attacking those attached to the Queen's court. Her physician since 1670, Sir George Wakeman, was accused of plotting to poison the King. In 1678 one of the Queen's chaplains, Father Thomas Tilden, commonly called Dr Godden, was accused of hiding the body of Sir Edmund Berry Godfrey for three days at Somerset House. Born at Dartford, Kent in 1622 he was converted by Father George Gage and

Charles II and the 'Popish Plot', 1660-1685

went to Lisbon in 1643 and was ordained in 1649. He became president of the Lisbon College in 1654. He was engaged to teach English to Catherine of Braganza prior to her marriage to Charles II and accompanied her to London in 1662. Another of those accused of Berry Godfrey's murder was Father John Bradsheet who had been ordained at Ávila in 1658 and was based in Staffordshire. His sister was a servant of Tilden's so this was, no doubt, thought by Oates and Bedloe too good a connection to pass up. A proclamation was issued for Bradsheet's arrest but he was never apprehended. Tilden escaped to France in January 1679. (Tilden remained in exile in France until the accession of James II when he returned to his duties at Somerset House. He died in November 1688 and was buried in the cemetery attached to Somerset House chapel.)

His servant, Lawrence Hill, was not so lucky; nor was his fellow employee at Somerset House, Robert Green, an elderly married Irish Catholic whose job was to arrange the cushions in the Queen's chapel. As a craftsman who was familiar with Somerset House Miles Prance had been one of the many accused by Bedloe of complicity in the murder of Sir Edmund Berry Godfrey. Placed in irons and threatened with torture, Prance in turn falsely accused Hill and Green, and a Protestant servant named Henry Berry, of involvement in the death of Godfrey. Prance, brought before the King, confessed that his evidence was false, 'upon his salvation' and repeated this confession before the Council. Returned to Newgate he was persuaded to recant and Green, Hill and Berry were tried on 5 February with Prance as chief prosecution witness. Father Bradsheet's sister appeared as a defence witness but her evidence was dismissed when it was revealed that her brother was a priest. Tilden's niece, Mary, also bravely gave evidence for the defence at the trial. She provided an alibi for Hill that he had not left the house that night, which led Scroggs to outrageously suggest that she must have been in bed with Hill all night in order to be sure. Mrs Hill was in court and called out that Prance 'knows all these things to be as false as God's true, and you will see it declared hereafter, when it is too late'. These two humble Catholics were found guilty and martyred at Tyburn on 21 February 1679. Addressing the crowd Hill said, 'I am now come to the fatal place of execution, and in a little time must appear before the tribunal of God Almighty, who knoweth all things; and I hope it will be happy for me, because I am innocently put to death. I take God, men and angels to witness, I am innocent of the death of Justice Godfrey; and believe it will be well for me because I die innocently; and hope through the merits of my blessed Saviour to be saved.' Then Green spoke, 'I desire all your prayers and as for Sir

Charles II and the 'Popish Plot', 1660-1685

Edmund Berry Godfrey ... I never saw him to my knowledge in my life.' Green and Hill were buried at St Giles-in-the-Fields. (Hill had a son, John, who was educated at Lisbon at the expense of Queen Catherine. He was ordained priest and returned to England in 1703.)

Another of the Queen's chaplains was Father John Huddleston [4] He was the one priest whom the conspirators dare not touch. As the saviour of the King's life after the Battle of Worcester, he was specifically exempted by royal proclamation from all harassment.

Aside from the King, there seem to have been few contemporary personages of any cool commonsense inclined to view the proceedings dispassionately. The diarist and author John Evelyn - certainly no Catholic sympathiser - was one. He wrote of Oates as a 'vain, insolent man. Such a man's testimony should not be taken against the life of a dog'. Today it is hard for us to imagine the extent of the incredible paranoia, bigotry and hate engendered by the 'Plot'. Yet we know from more recent history how easily the public can be whipped-up into a violent rent-a-mob. Shaftesbury's propaganda had done its work and twenty-one Catholic peers were excluded from the House of Lords, although he failed to get the ban extended to the Duke of York. Scores of priests made their escape to the Continent, including the future bishop and Vicar Apostolic of the Eastern District, Bonaventure Giffard. The less fortunate ones included Richard Fincham, who was arrested but allowed to go abroad; John Parsons, arrested in Hertfordshire in January 1679 and imprisoned in the Gatehouse, and Henry Rootes, named by Oates as Henrique, the name he was called at Seville where he was ordained. In the witch-hunt hundreds of innocent lay people suffered imprisonment in the countrywide round-up of known Catholics. There were over 2,000 in London prisons alone. Many of them died in prison, the victims of the insanitary conditions and disease.

A typical case is that of Sir Henry Tichborne of the ancient Hampshire family which had given two martyrs to the Church: Venerable Nicholas Tichborne 1601 and Venerable Thomas Tichborne 1602. On 21 November 1678, having been accused by William Bedloe, Sir Henry was arrested on a warrant from Lord Chief Justice Sir William Scroggs, and committed to Winchester prison for high treason. In December he was removed to the Tower where he was kept in close confinement for eighteen months. Throughout that time he was never examined or questioned or formally charged. Eventually he was released on a writ of *habeas corpus* and told to return home. It is a story that could be multiplied many times.

In the febrile atmosphere gripping the country in February 1679

Charles II and the 'Popish Plot', 1660-1685

Parliament decreed that all recusants had to be summoned by special warrants to take the Oath of Allegiance. The upheaval provoked a mass exodus abroad of Catholic peers and gentry; among them Robert Brudenell, 2nd Earl of Cardigan, Thomas Howard, 3rd Earl of Berkshire, Francis Browne, 3rd Viscount Montague and Lord and Lady Fairfax of Gilling. In Leicestershire, Lady Smith and her three children were thrown into jail for their refusal until released by order of the House of Lords. Less prominent or poorer recusants did not have such privileges and were rounded up and sent to jail for their refusal. Some of them were committed indefinitely and remained in prisons for several years. This is borne out by the order issued in January 1685 for the release of 730 named recusants who had refused to take the oath. 228 of these were in Durham and 239 in Hereford, most of them women. Large numbers of priests were apprehended, mostly betrayed by opportunistic apostates and informers. Among those affected were a group of Mary Ward's nuns taken at Ripon and York, together with their Jesuit chaplain. The scanty records of Yorkshire alone show the great numbers of Catholics who were summoned, most of whom refused the oath and were imprisoned in York Castle, where several of them had died by 1680. The oath was tendered a second time before an Assize Judge. As the penalty for refusal was *praemunire* it is unsurprising that many gave in and, with mental reservations, took the oath, such as the forty reported to have done so at Winchester. The anti-Catholic bandwagon gathered momentum in April 1679 when, apparently not satisfied that the existing recusancy laws were sufficient, an anti-popery bill was introduced in the House of Commons. The Lords debated a bill to remove all papists from London, especially expelling all Catholic traders and merchants from the City. They abandoned the proposal when warned that this would wreak havoc with the City trade. They then considered measures for the compulsory exile of the Catholic gentry to destroy their influence. By December 1679 the King, presumably in an effort to take some of the heat out of the situation, set up a Committee for Suppressing Popery. The Committee began its work by ordering that all the priests in custody should be brought to trial.

No one indicted could remotely expect to receive even a faint semblance of a fair trial; the proceedings were a travesty. Sir William Scroggs (1623-83), who presided at most of the earlier trials discriminated against, scurrilously abused and vilified the accused Catholics. Those Catholics brave enough to give evidence for the defence found themselves insulted and their veracity impugned. Scroggs enunciated two absolutely incredible principles as the basis for the proceedings at the trials: 1. Although it was true that the witnesses against the accused had committed serious misdemeanours, none of these should be admitted in court as in any way impairing the value of their testimony, especially as they had received royal pardons for their crimes: 2. No Catholic witness for the defence was to be believed, as it should be presumed that they had received dispensations to lie under oath. So even though the priests on trial defended themselves ably and through cross-examination clearly demonstrated that their accusers were manifestly guilty of blatant perjury, it was of no avail.

On 13 June 1679 the trial opened at the Old Bailey of five Jesuits: Thomas Whitbread, [5] William Harcourt, [6] John Fenwick, [7] John Gavan [8] and Antony Turner. [9] Its importance may be gauged from the fact that it was heard not only by Scroggs and the judges of the King's Bench, but also by George Jeffrey's, Recorder of London and Francis North, Chief Justice of Common Pleas, with the Attorney-General and Solicitor-General. The accused priests had arranged for a large group of boys from Saint-Omer to be brought over to London to give evidence to rebut the claim of Oates that he had been at the Jesuit 'Consult' in London in April 1678 when, in fact, he had been at the college. Five of the boys were arrested but released after interrogation. Oates took the stand and when asked to explain why he had not recognised Father Gavan when he had appeared before the Privy Council and why he could not be more specific about other parts of his testimony he blustered and faltered. Scroggs told him, 'I perceive your memory is not good.' Oates then faced an uncomfortable barrage of questions from Father Gavan, who seemed to be the dominant personality among the accused priests. Oates response was to complain to the bench that he was being abused and one of the judges reproved Gavan. Whitbread and Fenwick then challenged details in Oates's account and although he was unable to provide an explanation the judges chose to ignore it. Stephen Dugdale then gave 'evidence'. He was not of the low-life category of Oates and Bedloe which meant that when he denounced innocent victims it made his apparently plausible 'evidence' seem more credible. Lying through his teeth he turned in an accomplished performance which, in spite of his having failed earlier to recognise Harcourt, earned him the praise of Scroggs. He was followed for good measure by Prance and Bedloe. Then came the fourteen defence witnesses from Saint-Omer to swear that Oates had been at the college during the first six months of 1678. Their testimony was derided and impugned by the judges who told the jury that they had clearly been instructed what to say and given permission to lie. The court became very noisy and boisterous and proceedings were held up as a result.

Charles II and the 'Popish Plot', 1660-1685

Scroggs commenced his summing-up for the jury with the incredible statement that as the evidence had been long and confused it 'is almost impossible for anyone to remember it; neither would I if I could'. He finished with a ranting diatribe against Catholics in general. The jury took just fifteen minutes to find the priests guilty. The five were martyred together on 20 June before a huge crowd of spectators who stood in silence for over an hour while they made their final speeches.

The tide began to turn with the delayed trial for treason of the Queen's physician Sir George Wakeman and three Benedictine monks; William Wall alias Marsh, William (Augustine) Rumley and James (Maurus) Corker, which opened on 18 July 1679. Dom Maurus had been arraigned with the five Jesuits, but, managed to obtain a postponement of his trial, thereby saving his life. The wicked triumvirate of Oates, Bedloe and Dugdale were witnesses for the prosecution. When Dugdale deposed that after the King's murder all Protestants were to be killed the prosecuting counsel incredulously asked, '*All* Protestants?' to which Dugdale replied in the affirmative destroying his credibility with the court. Oates had earlier failed to even recognise Wakeman when he appeared before the Council in September 1678. Wakeman asked Oates to explain why he had not recognised him, to which Oates responded with monumental insolence, 'I am not bound to answer that question.' Scroggs told Oates that he must answer the question, but as he did not have an answer Wakeman was able to demolish his lying testimony.

Oates and Bedloe got themselves thoroughly confused with their contradictory testimony and Scroggs questioned the veracity of their evidence, with the result that Wakeman and the monks were acquitted. Bedloe had the nerve to challenge Scroggs, claiming that he had not summed up the evidence correctly. One wonders at what stage Scroggs began to examine his conscience over his judgment in the cases of the fifteen innocent men he had already sent for execution.

In addition to Edward Coleman, John Grove, Lawrence Hill and Robert Green two other laymen were put to death; Richard Langhorne [10] and William Howard, Viscount Stafford, the grandson of Philip Howard. [11] Over thirty priests, most of them Jesuits, were condemned to death. The Benedictine brother, Thomas Pickering, and fifteen priests were executed, [12] including the six who are numbered among the Forty Martyrs. With the addition of Archbishop Oliver Plunket, [13] twenty-three innocent Catholics were barbarously executed for a wicked fiction. The tragedy was described by Jane Lane in her biography of Titus Oates as 'a series of judicial murders without parallel in the story of these nations'. To quote Professor J P Kenyon in

Charles II and the 'Popish Plot', 1660-1685

The Popish Plot (1972), 'If there really had been a Popish Plot it was against human nature to suppose that one of these men would not have cracked, or if not one of these, then one of the scores of Catholic priests and laymen now in prison, often barely surviving under loathsome conditions and with little prospect of release'. In fact, although they had all been offered a pardon for their confessions, not one of the victims of the 'Plot' ever made the least acknowledgment of any guilt in thought, word or deed because they had no guilt to admit.

Shaftesbury openly revealed his hand when, taking advantage of the national hysteria, he brought forward an Exclusion Bill in May 1679 to remove the Duke of York from the succession. The King was stung into action and in July dissolved Parliament. But Shaftesbury and his disreputable cohorts kept the pot boiling for as long as they could. In January 1680 seven priests were put on trial purely for their priesthood with Oates on hand to testify against them. They were three Dominicans, David Kemish or Kemys q.v. and Lionel Anderson, plus Scotsman Andrew Lumsden; William Russell, a distinguished Franciscan who was Rector of Mount Grace Priory, Yorkshire; two seculars, Charles Parry and Henry Starkey q.v. and the Benedictines James (Maurus) Corker q.v. and William Marshal, who had been acquitted with George Wakeman. All except Lumsden were condemned to death under Elizabethan statute 27, but none of them were executed. Russell remained a prisoner until 1684 when he was banished. Parry and Marshal remained in prison until the end of the reign. In February 1680 the Jesuit Anthony Hunter and the Benedictine Jerome Hesketh were tried at the Old Bailey. There was no witness against Hesketh and he was released, but Hunter was condemned on the strength of Oates's testimony and he died in Newgate in 1684. Evidence of the attitude towards priests at the time may be gleaned from the story of Father John Francis Dickenson. In October 1680 an Irish Protestant woman named Martha Cook accused him of trying to convert her. At the time she was in Newgate where she had been committed for the crime of coin clipping. This was a very serious offence regarded as treason and carried the death penalty. (In 1690 Thomas Rogers was hanged, drawn and quartered and his wife Anne burnt alive for this crime.) Father Dickenson was arrested and convicted. The real reason for betraying him soon became apparent: Cook claimed the £100 reward for exposing the priest and was released.

In 1681 the conspirators finally overreached themselves in seeking to impeach the Duke of York as a recusant and on the strength of the change in public mood the King decided that countermeasures had to be taken. He ordered Shaftesbury's arrest for high treason and Oates to be

Charles II and the 'Popish Plot', 1660-1685

thrown out of his apartment at Whitehall. Charles then dissolved Parliament and issued a declaration to be read in all the churches setting out his reasons for the dissolution. So came to an end what, to quote Jane Lane again, was 'the bloodiest hoax in history'.

In the face of the baying Protestant extremists in Parliament, the powers of the King to stop the bloodshed had proved to be limited. It became politically expedient for him to allow the executions of condemned priests whom he believed to be innocent, and while he managed to reprieve many others they remained in prison where sixteen died from ill-usage. [14] The story was told by Queen Catherine herself that she kept in her chamber portraits of the five Jesuit martyrs who perished in June 1679. Whenever Charles visited her he would kiss their hands and beg their forgiveness as it troubled his conscience so much to be reminded of their innocence. Those priests who had managed to survive the holocaust were released on the accession of James II.

When Charles II suddenly collapsed on 2 February 1685 and it soon became clear that he was dying, Thomas Ken, Bishop of Bath and Wells, exhorted him to receive the Anglican sacrament. As the King had been Catholic in his religious beliefs for a great many years he declined to do so. At the height of the 'Plot' in 1679 Charles had taken from Sir William Waller, Justice of the Peace for Westminster, a crucifix said to contain a fragment of the True Cross, which he had confiscated from a priest (The fanatically anti-Catholic Waller was personally responsible for the arrest of most of the priests since 1678. All the Catholic books and vestments he had confiscated he publicly burned.) The King secretly wore the crucifix for the rest of his life and left it to his brother. On his deathbed, the cynical Charles finally honoured the promise he had made fifteen years previously to his adored sister. Queen Catherine begged the Duke and Duchess of York to get a priest to her husband who she knew to be a Catholic at heart. The night before he died Charles was asked by his brother if he wished to see a priest. The King whispered back, 'Yes, with all my heart!' The old Benedictine, Father John Huddleston, who had saved the King's life thirty-four years before, was smuggled into the bedchamber and he formally received Charles into the Catholic Church, giving him absolution and Holy Communion and anointing him. The King once sardonically declared that he was one of those bigots who regarded malice as a far greater sin than a few sexual peccadilloes; and he told Bishop Burnet, 'I cannot believe almighty God would damn a man for all eternity for taking a little irregular pleasure out of the way'. There is no reason to believe that Charles' deathbed conversion was not

Charles II and the 'Popish Plot', 1660-1685

perfectly sincere.

And what became of the conspirators? King Charles was content to bide his time and allow Shaftesbury enough rope with which to eventually hang himself. As Charles had astutely foreseen, when it became apparent that, in order to satisfy his own ambitions, Shaftesbury was prepared to install the bastard Duke of Monmouth on the throne, there was a strongly adverse public reaction. In 1681 the Earl fled in disguise to Holland, where he died in 1683. Most of the others were later found guilty and punished for their perjury. Israel Tonge is said to have died of starvation. William Bedloe died blaspheming and cursing those who had suborned him to accuse so many innocent men. Stephen Dugdale continued his career of giving false evidence against former colleagues. He contracted syphilis which he claimed was the result of a Catholic having poisoned him! He became an alcoholic and died in March 1683 raving in his *delirium tremens* about the spectres he could see. Miles Prance voluntarily retracted everything he had said and pleaded guilty to perjury. He was sentenced to be whipped and pilloried. King James II pardoned Prance for his perjury.

The arch-villain Titus Oates met his nemesis in the person of Lord Chief Justice Sir George Jeffreys, the selfsame judge who had condemned innocent priests on the strength of his testimony. Oates was first indicted in January 1685 and his trial fixed for 8 February. The postponement of the trial was not attributable to the King's death on 6 February, but because no barrister could be found willing to defend Titus. When finally tried in May 1685 Oates attempted to call many eminent personages as witnesses in his defence. Few of them responded and those that did became parties to his condemnation. Theophilus Hastings, 7th Earl of Huntingdon, who had shown animus towards Catholics and some sympathy for the Duke of Monmouth, was asked by Jeffreys how the Lords had reacted to Oates's allegations in 1678. Huntingdon replied, 'Mr Oates's discovery found a good reception in the House of Lords, but it was grounded upon the opinion that what he said was true and that he was an honest man ... But since that time, it being apparent that there were so many great contradictions, falsities and perjuries in his evidence, upon which so much innocent blood had been shed, I believe a great many persons who were concerned in the trials of those unfortunate men are heartily afflicted and sorry for their share in it, and I do believe that most of the House of Peers have altered their opinion as to this man's credit and look upon his evidence, as I do, to be very false.' On the first day of the trial twenty-one prosecution witnesses gave evidence that contradicted Oates's perjuries. On the second day forty were called, many of them respectable Protestant servants, who confirmed every single movement for every day of Father William Ireland's whereabouts in Staffordshire in 1678, thereby vindicating his alibi. Oates's only response to this was that Ireland's testimony had not been believed at his trial. He even had the audacity to charge Jeffreys with hypocrisy for his part in the 'Plot' trials. Sir George was astonished at Oates's monumental effrontery, declaring, 'Is it not a prodigious thing to have such actions as these today defended in a court of justice, with that impudence and unconcernedness as though he would challenge even God Almighty to punish his wickedness.' Solemnly proclaiming that 'the justice of the nation lies under a very great reproach' Jeffreys told the jury that his blood curdled 'to see a fellow continue so impudent as to brazen it out as he has done'. He described Oates as a 'shame to mankind' and a 'monstrous villain' who had 'pawned his immortal soul' and he lamented the 'wickedness of an age which had caressed and rewarded' such men as Oates and the 'infamous' Bedloe who had caused the deaths of so many innocent persons. Found guilty of perjury Oates was sentenced to be paraded round all the Courts in Westminster Hall wearing a paper hat proclaiming his crime. He was fined a thousand marks, whipped through the streets, put in the pillory - where he was pelted by the mob that he had once shamelessly manipulated - and imprisoned for life. Judge Jeffreys, passing sentence, remarked, 'When a person shall be convicted of such a foul and malicious perjury as the defendant is, I think it impossible for the courts, as the law stands, to put punishment upon him in any way proportionable to the offence that has drawn after it so many horrid and dreadful consequences.' Many, including members of the judiciary, thought that the sentence was lenient in view of the heinous nature of the crime. Sir Francis Wythens, who participated in Oates' trial declared, 'I do not know how I can say but that the law is defective that such a one is not to be hanged.'

When William, Prince of Orange came to power in December 1688 he knew he had to keep his Protestant promoters sweet, so he ordered Oates's release from the Kings Bench prison and awarded him a pension. Titus, who went to Court to kiss the King's hand, rented a 'handsomely furnished' house in Axe Yard, Westminster. In 1693 he married a wealthy draper's daughter who was half his age. The event was lampooned with lewd ribaldry by the pamphleteers and coffee-houses. The unfortunate girl had £2,000 which Oates managed to dissipate in six months. Titus next became a Baptist preacher at Wapping until he was thrown out in 1701 for being a hypocrite and defrauding that non-conformist organisation of the proceeds of a rich

old lady's will. He died in complete obscurity in July 1705 and was buried in an unknown grave. If it were not such an anachronism, an apposite epitaph for Oates might have been an extract from Rudyard Kipling's *Epitaphs of the War:*
>I lied to please the mob. Now all my lies are proved untrue
>and I must face the men I slew.

†

John Plessington

Voice of truth amid the storm of lies ...voice of love amid the roar of hate.

Henry E G Rope, 1880-1978

John was born c.1637 at Dimples Hall, Garstang, Lancashire. He was the son of Robert Plessington or Pleasington and Alice Rawstone. Royalist Catholics, the family had suffered much because of their beliefs. John was educated by the Jesuits at their secret school at Scarisbrick Hall near Ormskirk. (The original 13th century moated manor was replaced in 1595 and by 1607 it was a substantial house with its own Catholic chapel. An Edward Scarisbrick married Margaret Barlow, daughter of Alexander Barlow and aunt of St Ambrose Barlow. Because of their Catholic faith the family played little part in local affairs. Many sons of the Scarisbrick family became Jesuits, each of them using the alias Neville. 15 The Jesuits continued their occupation of the Hall throughout the 18th century. Scarisbrick Hall was rebuilt by the famous Catholic convert architect Pugin and is one of the finest Victorian-Gothic buildings in existence. It is still a private school.) John went abroad to study for the priesthood, firstly at Saint-Omer, from where he moved to the English College of St Alban, Valladolid, in 1660. Here he was ordained deacon under the name of John Scarisbrick. He was ordained priest at Segovia on 25 March 1662 and in April 1663 he was sent to England.

He ministered until 1669 in Lancashire and at Holywell, North Wales, where St Winifred's Well had remained a place of pilgrimage throughout the penal times. Using the alias William Scarisbrick, he then worked for the next sixteen years in Cheshire, using Puddington Hall near Burton, on the Wirral, as his base. The Hall was the ancestral home of the Massey family. The head of the family, Edward Massey, with his wife Alice Braithwaite sheltered John. When Edward died in

Charles II and the 'Popish Plot', 1660-1685

September 1671 leaving John £5 in his will, Plessington remained with his son and heir, William. In 1679 when the Oates 'Plot' was at its height, Plessington was betrayed by a Catholic and arrested by a man named Thomas Dutton, who was paid for his trouble. John was imprisoned for two months in Chester Castle. He was never accused of being implicated in the 'Plot' but was charged under the old Elizabethan statute solely with being a priest. He was tried in May 1679, when three witnesses testified that they had seen him exercise his priestly functions, and he was condemned to death. The judges who sentenced him, Sir Job Charlton and George Johnson, wrote to inform Parliament, asking if John should be reprieved. Parliament ordered the execution to be carried out.

John was kept in prison until 19 July 1679 when he was taken from Chester Castle to be hanged, drawn and quartered on Gallows Hill - now known as Barrel Well Hill - at Great Boughton, Aldford, beside the River Dee near Chester. The remarkable speech that he made from the scaffold was afterwards printed and circulated.

Dear Countrymen, I am here to be executed, neither for theft, murder nor anything else against the law of God, not any fact of doctrine inconsistent with monarchy or civil government. I suppose several now present, heard my trial at the last assizes, and can testify that nothing was laid to my charge except my priesthood; and I am sure you will find that priesthood is neither against the law of God, nor monarchy, nor civil government ... But I know it will be said, that a priest ordained by authority derived from the See of Rome, is by the law of the nation, to die as a traitor; but if that be so what must become of all the clergymen of the Church of England? for the first Protestant bishops had their ordination from those of the Church of Rome, or not at all; as appears by their own writers; so that ordination comes derivatively from those now living. As in the primitive times, Christians were esteemed traitors and suffered as such by national laws, so are the priests of the Roman Church here esteemed, and suffer as such. But as Christianity then was not against the law of God, monarchy or civil policy, so now there is not any point of the Roman Catholic Faith (of which Faith I am) that is inconsistent therewith, as is evident by induction in each several point. That the Pope has power to depose or give license to murder princes, is no point of our belief. And I protest in the sight of God and the court of Heaven, that I am absolutely innocent of the plot so much discoursed of, and abhor such bloody and damnable designs; and though it be nine weeks since I was sentenced to die, there is not anything of that laid to my charge, so that I may well take comfort in St. Peter's words, I Peter. Let none of you suffer as a murderer, or as a thief, or as an evil-doer, or as a busybody in other men's matters; yet if any man suffer as a Christian let him not be ashamed or sorry. I have deserved a worse death, for though I have been a true and faithful subject of my King, I have been a grievous sinner against God.

Charles II and the 'Popish Plot', 1660-1685

Thieves and robbers that rob on highways, would have served a greater perfection than I have done, had they received so many favours and graces from Him as I have. But as there was never a sinner who truly repented and heartily called to Jesus for mercy, to whom He did not show mercy; so I hope by the merits of His passion, He will have mercy on me, who am heartily sorry that I ever offended Him. Bear witness good hearers, that I profess, that I undoubtedly and firmly believe all the articles of the Roman Catholic Faith, and for the truth of any of them, (by the assistance of God), I am willing to die; and I had rather die than doubt any point of faith taught by our holy mother the Roman Catholic Church. In what condition Margaret Plat, one of the chiefest witnesses against me, was before and after she was with me, let her nearest relatives declare. George Massey, another witness, swore falsely, when he swore I gave him the Sacrament and said Mass at the time and place he mentioned; and I verily think he never spoke to me, or I to him, or saw each other but at the assizes week. The third witness, Robert Wood, was suddenly killed, but of the dead why should I speak. These were all the witnesses against me, unless those that only declared what they heard from others. I heartily and freely forgive all that have been, or are in any way instrumental to my death, and heartily desire that those that are living, may heartily repent. God bless the King and the royal family, and grant His Majesty a prosperous reign here and a crown of glory hereafter. God grant peace to the subjects and that they live and die in true faith, hope and charity. That which remains, is that I recommend myself to the mercy of Jesus, by whose merits I hope for mercy. Jesus, be to me a Jesus.

His quartered remains were wickedly returned to the Massey family at Puddington Hall; they were instructed to hang them from the four corners of their house, but the local people would not allow this and for a time they lay on an oak table in the entrance hall. Afterwards the remains were buried in the nearby churchyard of St Nicholas's at Burton, the location of the grave being handed down from generation to generation. In 1837 Father Ralph Platt of Puddington asked to be buried in the same grave. Attempts have been made - the last in 1962 – to locate and exhume John's relics, but have proved unsuccessful.

A rose-coloured chasuble believed to have belonged to John is kept at St Winefride's parish church, Little Neston, and at St Francis's church, Chester there is a piece of linen stained with his blood. At St Winifred's parish church, Holywell John is depicted in a stained glass window. Today a memorial plaque in Burton churchyard commemorates John Plessington and since 1980 his name has been recorded on a memorial plinth at the Gallows Hill site. Also on the plinth is commemorated George Marsh, who was burned there for heresy in 1555. The contrast between the two men thus remembered could not be greater. Marsh was a pugnacious and obstreperous

Protestant, who was actually treated with great consideration. Every effort was made to reconcile him, but he seems to have been hell-bent on provoking his own death.

✝

Philip Evans

Bring me my harp ... I would play one more tune before I die. Last night an angel called ... play, and come through the gates of death.

Dafydd Y Gareg Wen: David of the White Rock

Philip, the son of William Evans and Winifred Morgan, was born at Monmouth, Wales, in 1645 and was educated at Saint-Omer. On 7 September 1665, at the age of twenty he joined the Society of Jesus and served his novitiate at Watten. Philip was highly thought of by his superiors, who praised him for his frankness, modesty and cheerfulness, qualities that remained with him all his life and won him universal affection. In 1675 he was ordained priest at Liège and sent back to work in South Wales. He laboured zealously without molestation until November 1678. As everywhere else, the situation of the Church in South Wales at this time was fraught with difficulties and missionary conditions were hard, but the number of priests was maintained and the Franciscans were active in the area. Using the alias 'Captain Evans' Philip frequented the home of Thomas Gunter at Abergavenny where it was said '100's go to Mass when not 40 go to church.' He also regularly visited Charles Prodger at Wern-ddu, Llantilio Crosseny and Christopher Turberville, as well as making visits to Powis Castle.

Following the scare of the 'Plot' John Arnold, of Llanvihangel Crucorney near Abergavenny, the psychopathically fanatic anti-Catholic Member of Parliament for Monmouth, Justice of the Peace and tireless hunter of priests, offered a reward of £200 for Philip's capture. Arnold was a close crony of William Bedloe. The youngest of the Jesuits on the mission, Philip was advised to flee but would not hear of deserting his post. Betrayed by Edward Turberville, his host's apostate younger brother, who was a despicable informer, on 4 December 1678 Philip was caught at Sker House, Porthcawl, the home of his friend Christopher Turberville, and taken prisoner to Cardiff Castle. Refusing to take the oath when proffered, he was put in an underground cell. Here he spent five months while the authorities scoured the countryside trying to find evidence against him. They finally found a poor old woman and her daughter and a deformed dwarf named Mayne Trott, who had once been at the Spanish Court but was now an apostate in the service of John Arnold. They were suborned to testify at the Spring Assizes that Philip was a priest. Trott's evidence was intended to implicate Philip in the 'Plot' but it was unsupported, so the court had to rely upon the evidence of the two women that they had seen him celebrating Mass and had received Communion from him.

The trial took place on Thursday and Friday, 8 and 9 May at the Shire Hall, Cardiff. The judge, Mr Justice Owen Wynne, was a kindly man. He indicated to Philip that if he would deny the evidence he would go free. Philip, knowing it would be perjury to deny the truth of the evidence, remained silent. The judge told the jury that if they believed the evidence of the two women they must find Evans guilty under the Elizabethan Statute 27, which they quickly did. After receiving his sentence with head bowed, Philip thanked the judge and jury.

The execution was delayed for eleven weeks during which Philip was treated reasonably and allowed a great deal of liberty out of his cell. He wrote a short letter to his superior, Father David Lewis, who being in prison himself was most grateful and derived comfort from the message. We learn in these weeks of Philip's skill at games and music. It was during a game of tennis that the news was brought to him by the under-sheriff that he was to die the following day: Philip remarked, 'What haste is there?' and calmly finished the game. He spent his last hours playing the Welsh harp and talking cheerfully to the many people who came to say goodbye. His sister, Catherine, (Barbara in religion) was a Blue Nun at Paris and, in a letter that has survived, Philip wrote to her the day before his execution informing her of his situation. He asked for her prayers and promised to pray for her, telling her to be joyful, rather than mourn for him.

About 9 a.m. on 22 July 1679 the under-sheriff, Charles Evans, came to the cell where Philip and Father John Lloyd were held. A blacksmith was sent for to remove their irons, but Philip's were so well riveted on that the smith took an hour to get them off, causing him considerable pain in the process, although Philip urged him on regardless. The two priests asked if they could walk to the place of execution, but this was refused and they were both put into a cart, their arms pinioned. When they arrived at Gallows Field they prayed for a while and then asked who was to die first: Mr Evans was the reply. Philip, bowing to the crowd, addressed them in Welsh and English.

I need not tell you why we are brought here to suffer; our sentence of condemnation is sufficient witness that it was not for any plot, or any other crime, but for being priests; consequently I die for religion and conscience's sake. I shall not speak much of the goodness of my cause because I think it will be needless; but it is so good that I would not give the happiness of dying for it, for all the crowns of the world. Sure, if a man ever speaks the truth, it must be at the hour of death, therefore I hope nobody will doubt of what I say. If I have or had any enemies in the world, which I do not know that ever I had in my life, I do heartily forgive them for anything done or said against me; and if I have offended anybody, I am heartily sorry for it and ask them forgiveness. I pray God bless and prosper the King. Beg the prayers of all, and in particular the Catholics here present.

He then knelt down and prayed with some friends around him, and taking his leave of them went up the ladder, pausing to say the following:

Sure this is the best pulpit a man can have to preach in, therefore I cannot forebear to tell you again that I die for God and religion's sake, and I think myself so happy that if I had never so many lives, I would willingly give them all up for such a cause. If I could live it would be but for a little time though I am but young. I think myself happy that I can purchase with a short pain an everlasting life. I do forgive all those that have any hand in my death, accusation or condemnation. I give thanks to those that have been kind to me, and to you Mr Sheriff. Adieu, Mr Lloyd, though for a little time, for we shall shortly meet again. Pray for me and I shall return it when it pleases God that I shall enjoy the beatific vision. If any of you that see me willingly die for my religion have any good thought upon it, I shall think myself happy.

As he climbed to the top of the ladder he stopped and said in a clear voice, 'Into your hands, O Lord, I commend my spirit,' and giving a sign to the executioner, he was turned off, but the ladder being too short it turned around with him so that Richard Jones, one of the sheriff's bailiffs, grabbed hold of his legs and twisted them round after his body so that he would hang straight from the rope.

John Lloyd

All at rest thou liest and the fierce breath of tempests can no more disturb thy ease.

TheTimber, Henry Vaughan, 1622-1695

John, the son of Walter Lloyd, was born into a Catholic family at Brecon, South Wales in 1630. He was probably a nephew of his namesake, a Jesuit priest who studied at the English College in Valladolid. John's brother, William, was a priest and his sister, Mother

Charles II and the 'Popish Plot', 1660-1685

Margaret Bruno, like Philip Evan's sister, was in the convent of the Blue Nuns in Paris where she died in 1674. John studied humanities at Ghent before entering the Royal English College of St Alban, Valladolid, in 1649 where he took the missionary oath on 16 October. He was very popular because of his lovable innocence and humility. Having completed his theology and philosophy studies he was ordained priest on 7 June 1653 and the following year returned to South Wales, where he laboured for the next twenty-four years. He visited the home of Howel Carne at Colwinston and was known to frequent and say Mass at Trivor, the large farmhouse home of Walter James and his family in the parish of St Maughans, north of Monmouth. The house had several secret hiding places and the room used as the chapel can still be seen today.

On 20 November 1678 John was apprehended at the home of John Turberville at Pen-llyn near Cowbridge, Glamorgan, and sent to join Philip Evans in Cardiff Castle. (The Turberville family at Pen-llyn had been sheltering priests for nearly a century. The first Welsh student to take the missionary oath in 1579, Father Morgan Clynnog, nephew of Dr Maurice Clynnog, first rector of the English College, Rome, had lived with Jenkin Turberville between 1596 and 1602.) John was tried with Philip, being convicted on similar evidence and condemned. The two priests enjoyed each other's company while awaiting execution and were taken to the gallows together. When it was known that Philip was to die first, the two priests embraced one another, and John gave Philip absolution. He then had to stand by and watch his comrade suffer.

When it came to his own turn he kissed the gallows and gave a short speech, which was later printed. Saying that he had never been a good speaker all his life he declared, 'My fellow sufferer has declared the cause of our death, therefore I need not repeat it ... I shall only say that I die for the Catholic and Apostolic faith, according to these words in the Creed, I believe in the holy, Catholic Church; and with those three virtues, faith, hope and charity. I forgive all those that have offended me; and if I have offended anybody I am heartily sorry for it and ask their forgiveness. I beg the prayers of all and in particular of the Catholics here present, desiring them to bear their crosses patiently and to remember that passage of Holy Scripture, 'Happy are they that suffer persecution for justice, for theirs is the kingdom of heaven'. He then climbed the ladder and thanked all who had been kind to him, in particular Mr Carne, the sheriff. Striking his breast three times, he said 'Lord have mercy upon me a sinner,' and as he was saying 'Into Thy hands, Lord, I commend my spirit,' he was turned off the ladder.

John's priest brother, William, was arrested in November 1678 and imprisoned in Brecon jail. In April 1679 he too was found guilty of being a priest and was sentenced to death. He suffered such harsh treatment in prison that, aged sixty-five, he died six days before his scheduled execution.

John Wall

Now there is waiting for me the prize of victory awarded for a righteous life.
St Paul, *Second Letter to Timothy*

John, the son of William and Dorothy Wall, was born into a wealthy recusant family in 1620. He was the eldest of several sons. It is possible that his birthplace was Chingle Hall, an old moated house near Kirkham, Lancashire. John's family originated from Aldeby in Norfolk. William Wall had a considerable estate in Norfolk but being Catholic he decided to move to Lancashire for the easier practise of his religion in an area where Catholics were numerous. He was connected with the Wall family at Chingle and this may also have influenced his decision. John was baptised by Edmund Arrowsmith. He was sent to Douai at an early age, and on 5 November 1641 entered the English College, Rome, under the name of John Marsh. He had hoped to be a convictor, but as his father was unable to pay the fees he was maintained at the Pope's expense. He was ordained in the chapel of The Apostles Peter and Paul in the Vatican on 3 December 1645. His brother, William, who was four years his junior, also studied at Douai and arrived at the English College, Rome, just two days before John's ordination.

After completing his studies, on 12 May 1648 John left for England, paying a visit to the Holy House shrine at Loreto en route. He returned to Douai in 1650 and on 1 January 1651 he joined the Franciscans at St Bonaventure's Convent, which had been founded by John Gennings, brother of St Edmund Gennings. Now a very old man, John was still living at the convent. The new novice was given the name Joachim of St Anne, in honour of the parents of the Virgin Mary. Two years later he was appointed Father Vicar and later novice master at St Bonaventure's, where he remained until 1656, the year in which, accompanied by a small group of friars led by Father Leo Randolph, he returned to England. They first made their way to Father Leo's home, the early 16th century timber framed manor house at Wood Bevington, Salford Priors, Warwickshire. (The manor, a listed building, still exists.) Here it was decided that John would concentrate his activities in the counties of Warwickshire and Worcestershire.

We have considerable information about his apostolate from an account written by an anonymous priest friend. John laboured on the mission for twenty-three years under the name of Francis Johnson, eventually settling his headquarters for his final years at Harvington Hall near Kidderminster. This was the home of the widowed Lady Mary Yate, the daughter and heiress of Humphrey Pakington, Lord of Chaddesley Corbett and Harvington who died in 1631. Mary's mother, Abigail Sacheverell, came from Morley, Derbyshire. Her family had remained faithful and had been constantly in trouble with the authorities for their recusancy since Elizabethan times. Mary Pakington married Sir John Yate from yet another steadfast Catholic family. After her husband's death Abigail lived at Harvington Hall until her death in 1657. The following year Sir John died and his widow, Mary, moved into Harvington Hall and became a great benefactor to the poor. (There is a fascinating connection between the Pakington's and one of the earliest Henrician martyrs, Blessed John Haile. Not long before he was arrested in 1535 there is a record of his having sold land in Worcestershire to John Pakington. The land was confiscated by the Crown before the sale was complete and Pakington asked Thomas Cromwell to use his influence to ensure that the land was transferred to him.) Harvington Hall had several hiding holes in which priests could be concealed. They can still be seen today and are considered some of the best surviving examples of the work of Nicholas Owen. Lady Mary continued to shelter priests for the remainder of her long life. Prominent among them was Worcester-born Sylvester Jenks, for whose education at Douai she had paid. After his ordination he was based at Harvington Hall from 1686. In August 1687 James II was in Worcester and attended Mass at the recently erected Catholic chapel. Jenks gave the sermon and as a result he was appointed a royal preacher and moved to London at Christmas 1687 on a salary of £60 per annum.

There is the heartening story told of how John Wall, shortly before his capture, was visiting Kings Norton and would have been apprehended had it not been for the goodness of a Protestant named Thomas Millward who bravely hid him in his house. In gratitude John told Millward that if he was ever required to die for his faith he would offer his life's blood for the Protestant's soul.

In October 1678 when the tumult of the 'Plot' burst out, John happened to be visiting London as a guest of the Queen's Capuchins at Somerset House. Most of the information we have comes from John's own written account. While in the capital he called on the French Jesuit, Claude de la Colombière. Claude had been confessor at the

Charles II and the 'Popish Plot', 1660-1685

Visitation convent at Paray-le-Monial to the visionary of the Sacred Heart, Saint Margaret Mary Alacoque. On the recommendation of King Louis XIV, in 1676 he had been sent to London as preacher to the Duchess of York, Mary of Modena. He lived frugally at St James's Palace and, being subject to Father Thomas Whitbread, the English Jesuit Provincial in London, he knew all the fathers of the Society of Jesus who were soon to be martyred. John sought out Claude at St James's Palace, announcing himself as a poor Friar Minor come to seek the strength and counsel of the Sacred Heart of Jesus. John spent the day in conversation with Claude, stayed to supper and was persuaded to remain overnight, Claude giving up his bed to his guest while he slept on the floor. The following morning, the feast of All Saints, John said Mass in Claude's oratory. 'Because all Catholics are obliged to obey the King's commands in all things that are not against our religion', John obeyed the order arising from the 'Plot' frenzy that required all Catholics to leave London. In the middle of the night on 24 November Claude was dragged from his bed at St James's Palace and arrested. He was sent to the Kings Bench Prison, where he was very ill. It was feared that he would be executed but the French Ambassador, Jean-Paul de Barillon, Marquis de Branges, intervened on the direct orders of Louis XIV and Claude de la Colombière was sentenced to banishment, which took place in January 1679. Claude died in 1682 and was canonized in 1992.

John returned to Worcestershire but not to Harvington. Why he did not go back to Harvington is unknown. Maybe he did not want to cause Lady Mary additional problems. He took up residence just two miles away at the home of the Finch family, Rushock Court, near Bromsgrove. In December he was arrested there by the sheriff's deputy who had come during the night to apprehend a defaulting debtor. John tells the story.

The officers coming to the house in the morning and not finding the like person, they broke down all the doors and amongst the rest my chamber door, before I was out of my bed, and by mistake arrested one instead of the other, and although the deputy's men coming into my chamber and looking round about did think they were mistaken and that I was not the man, yet some other soldiers coming into my chamber, one of them said he knew me therefore he would have me before the Justices and bade his companions secure me, and would not let me out of his sight till they had carried me before the Justice and that without either constable or warrant ... when I came before the Justice of peace I told him the accident that had brought me before him ... if I had taken the oaths I had been presently freed; but I told him ... that it was against the faith and religion I professed and against my conscience, and I would never offend against either, not even if I suffered for it.

Charles II and the 'Popish Plot', 1660-1685

The name of the JP was Mr Townsend of Elmley Lovett. When John refused to take either the Oath of Supremacy or the Oath of Allegiance the justice's compassionate wife tried to persuade him to save himself from further trouble, but John responded that he would not be moved by any fear of danger to go against his conscience. Mr Townsend then accompanied John to the magistrate at nearby Westwood Park, Hampton Lovett, Sir John Pakington, who happened to be a cousin of Lady Mary Yate. He was questioned at length by Sir John who once more proffered him the oaths to read out loud. John told him,

I am ready to swear as follows, that ever all my life I have been, and now am, and ever will be to my last breath as faithful a subject to the King as any subject whatsoever; and as faithful as if I had taken the oaths now offered by them to me 100 times over. But as for these oaths offered to me I could not take them, whatever I suffered.

John was then taken under guard to prison in Worcester Castle where he spent a cold winter with inadequate food. Here he remained for five months. At the January Quarter Sessions 1679, he was brought before Mr Justice Street at the Guildhall under the name of Johnson. Asked if he was a Jesuit he responded,

It would be easy for me to say no, but by saying it I may prejudice others who hereafter may be asked the same question. If they did not answer no, it might be taken as an argument against them. Therefore, gentlemen, I desire that whatever proofs may be brought against me may now be produced and thereupon I will answer for myself. But I beseech you, gentlemen, not to urge me to answer aye or no to any question before some witness has appeared or argument been adduced against me. For neither the law of God nor of man obliges anyone to be witness against himself, even though he were guilty, any more than to be his own executioner. If there be witnesses who can prove what they swear against me, then my life is at the King's mercy. But in the meantime I remain guiltless, even if I decline to answer your questions, yes or no; because the fact of my saying no would be no sufficient testimony to acquit and free me.

Having retired for consultation the justices committed John for trial at the Lent Assizes, where they told him they had no doubt that there would be 'evidence enough to send him to the gallows.' Much of John's suffering is known to us from his own account written while in jail.

Imprisonment in our times especially when none can send to his friends, nor friends come to him, is the best means to teach us how to put our confidence in God alone in all things ... As for my part, God give me His grace, and all faithful Christians their prayers, and I am happy enough. As for others, I pray God that the evil examples of those who swear against their consciences may not be guides for the rest to follow, nor their deeds a rule to their actions. We all ought to follow the narrow way, though there may be

Charles II and the 'Popish Plot', 1660-1685

difficulties in it. It is an easy thing to run the blind way of liberty, but God deliver us from all broad, sweet ways ... Our Saviour promises a hundredfold and life everlasting for everything that we forsake for His sake. Who well considers this will be content to leave both friends, fortune and freedom by imprisonment for their faith, till such time as it shall please God and the King to release them. And in the meantime they will have this comfort, that they are giving testimony that they fear God and honour the King. They fear God because they choose rather to suffer persecutions than to swear against their consciences; they honour the King because they are willing to suffer the penalties that he commands, and yet remain faithful subjects to him.

On Tuesday, 15 April he appeared before Mr Justice Littleton and Mr Justice Atkyns and pleaded not guilty. From the account of the protracted proceedings he defended himself under examination with great skill and dexterity. We know what was said in detail because John himself wrote a lengthy account of the trial. Four witnesses were called. Three of them had to be subpoenaed and stated that they knew nothing of which to accuse John. Under examination all that could be got from them was that they had seen John pray and read passages from the Bible. The second witness admitted to being a Catholic so Atkyns told him to go away as he was likely to be too prejudiced in John's favour. The fourth witness was an apostate named Rogers, who had a personal grudge against him. When John heard 'how insignificant and absurd' some of the accusations were he 'inconsiderately smiled.' This caused offence to the judge and John begged his pardon. John said that though his life might seem to be a matter of very small account to the judge, yet it was all he had. 'It was as great a gift of God to him as theirs to them, and therefore God had laid on him a great obligation to defend it. Therefore', he continued, 'being thus brought before your Lordship, in a case where my life and credit are at stake, I humbly beseech your lordship to deal by me accordingly, as I presume from your prudence and worthiness, you will not refuse to do.'

Before the jury was sent out John asked leave to address them.

Suppose that all proofs which the witnesses have brought against me were alleged against the jury, or some of them, so that if the arguments were judged by them conclusive, some of the jury would lose part of their estates and credit, or be in danger of their lives; which of those on whom this peril were likely to fall would judge such arguments as were alleged against me sufficient to condemn them to the loss of their estates, or credit, or to endanger their lives? Deal with me therefore as if it were your own case.'

John was found guilty - not of any connection with the 'Plot' but simply for being a priest under the Elizabethan statute. John made a final plea. He argued that he was a priest before the King returned to England 'and whatever I did before His Majesty's coming cannot make me now guilty, because his Majesty, before his return, put out several proclamations that none should ever be troubled for their religion or conscience sake, and since his return he has done the same, not only by proclamation, but not long since, in the declaration that everyone should freely practise his own religion, of whatever persuasion.' But the judge countered, 'However that may be, if you are a priest now in England, you are guilty.' After hearing his sentence John bowed courteously to the judge and responded, 'Thanks be to God. God save the king and I beseech God to bless your lordship and all this honourable bench'. Later he wrote:

I was not, thank God, troubled with disturbing thoughts either against the judge or the jury, nor any of the witnesses, for I was then of the same mind as by God's grace I ever shall be and I esteemed the judge and jury the best friends that ever I had in my life. I was so present with myself, whilst the judge pronounced sentence of death, that at the same time I offered myself and the world to God.

Littleton, the presiding judge, who told John he had spoken well, indicated that he did not intend John should die without knowing the King's wishes. Before being conducted back to prison, John tells us he was approached by a number of Protestant gentlemen who had been present in court. In a conversation lasting about half an hour, they expressed their regret and sorrow for his plight; but John assured them that they should not grieve for him for he was quite joyful, being ready to die tomorrow if required.

By order of the Privy Council in May John was sent on horseback to London for interrogation by Oates, Bedloe and Dugdale. He was put in Newgate where his brother William was already a prisoner, accused of aiding and abetting Sir George Wakeman to poison the King. To their sorrow the brothers were denied the opportunity to meet. John was 'very strictly examined' several times during the month he was detained in London, but Bedloe publicly pronounced him innocent of any plotting. After a spell in Newgate, the Council ordered him to be sent back to Worcester, whither he returned on 18 July to await execution. In a letter to a friend who had sent him some money he gave a detailed account of his London interrogations. John was offered his life on more than one occasion if he would renounce his religion. 'I could not buy my own life at so dear a rate'. He added, prophetically, 'This is the last persecution that will be in England; therefore I hope God will give us all His holy grace to make the best use of it'.

Lord Chief Justice Sir William Scroggs and Mr Justice Atkyns arrived at Worcester in August for the Summer Assizes. They sent for John to be brought to their lodgings and told him bluntly that he would

Charles II and the 'Popish Plot', 1660-1685

die in a few days for being a Roman priest unless he would secure his reprieve by taking the oath and conforming. John thanked the judges for their trouble but refused their offer. He was returned to prison and kept in close confinement. On 18 August he was informed that he was to die on the 22nd. What comfort it must have been for him to be allowed a visit from a fellow Franciscan, Father William Leveson. At the time Leveson's brother, Francis, yet another Franciscan priest, whose religious name was Ignatius of St Clara, was also a prisoner in Worcester jail. (Venerable Francis Leveson died in the jail 11 February 1680, aged thirty-four, after fourteen months in terrible conditions as a close prisoner, the authorities having failed in that time to find any witnesses prepared to swear against him.)

William Leveson was permitted to see John on the 20th, and in a letter written on 25 August to his fellow Franciscans, he described his visit. 'I found him a cheerful sufferer of his present imprisonment and ravished, as it were, with joy with the future hope of dying for so good a cause. I found, contrary to both his and my expectation, the favour of being with him alone'. To his great surprise Father Leveson was allowed to visit John again on the 21st. He writes, '... the day before his execution I enjoyed the privilege for the space of four or five hours together; during which time I heard his confession and communicated him, to his great joy and satisfaction'. John must have been extraordinarily composed, judging from the letter he wrote to the provincial of the English Franciscans.

This is the last act of my duty which I shall ever be able to offer to your Paternity in this world. I shall have long been in the other world before this letter comes into your hands. But this will make clear that, according to my bounden duty, I begged the blessing of you my Father, before I suffered; and also pardon for all my negligences and faults ... from the first moment it was my happy lot to be admitted into the ranks of this seraphic order and to be numbered among your brethren. One day of my life remains to me after writing this. The times were so evil that they removed from me all possibility of writing to you, nor did they allow me or anyone else on my behalf, to give an account to your Paternity of my condition ...For the space of nine months I have been imprisoned as a child in the womb. And now that the nine months have elapsed, I hope that my Mother the Church will bring me forth to God, and that I shall enjoy light perpetual.

On Friday, 22 August 1679, John was taken to be executed with two common criminals at Redhill, which was about a mile from the castle, overlooking Worcester. The sheriff asked him if he found it repugnant to die with two felons whereupon John remarked upon the appositeness of being executed with two thieves, just as Christ had been. There was a huge crowd but Father William Leveson managed to stand close to the

Charles II and the 'Popish Plot', 1660-1685

scaffold and again gave John absolution before he died. Leveson informs us that while the criminals were hanged, John kissed the ladder, kissed the rope, kissed the hangman's hand and gave him ten shillings.

While in prison John had written a long and beautiful speech, a copy of which he had given to Father Leveson and was later printed. The sheriff allowed John the time to read the speech in full. In it he discoursed on the three virtues of faith, hope and charity.

By faith we are all to believe whatever God has revealed to us in this world, and by hope all are to expect what He has promised in the world to come. And when God bestows such faith and hope it is in order to bring all to true charity and love of Him; for who can fail to love that Infinite Goodness in which he believes and hopes? ... St Paul declares, "There is but one lord, one faith, one baptism, even as you are called, in one hope of your calling." This being most true, let every rational Christian, in his most retired thoughts, consider how this unity of faith and this hope of our calling, can stand with a multitude of sects and opinions, opposed to one another, with which this nation abounds ... I come to the third virtue - that of charity. It is true that this body of mine in this shipwreck is full of sin, but when the shipwreck is over, I shall come to inherit that Rock that shall never fail. Now welcome shipwreck, that makes the body suffer, but brings the soul to a haven of joy! Many talk much of charity, but few understand and still fewer practise it. This is the greatest virtue. "Though you speak with the tongues of angels and have not charity, it availeth nothing. Charity suffers all things, hopes all things, bears all things". It has pleased our Saviour to declare that no man has greater charity than that he lays down his life for his friend. I therefore do willingly undergo this death I am to suffer now to testify that I love my friend and neighbour as myself; whilst I undergo this death for myself and them, seeing that it is for the profession of my faith I die, that they, whilst they live, may more happily serve God in the same belief. And I testify I love God above all, because I forsake the world and myself in death, rather than offend Him by doing anything against my conscience ... O Blessed Trinity, give me eternal life. Let my body die to the world for love of Thee, that my soul may live forever and live in Thee, my God.

He asked God to bless the King and give him a long and happy reign, to bless the nation and Parliament. 'I will offer my life in satisfaction for my sins and for the Catholic cause. I beseech God to bless all my benefactors and all my friends ... and all those that suffer under this persecution; and to turn our captivity into joy; that they that sow in tears may reap in joy'.

Having placed the rope around John's neck, the hangman asked him to give a sign when he wished to be turned off, but John declined to give any sign simply saying, 'do it when you will', and closed his eyes. The ladder was quickly removed and John was left hanging, presumably dead. His body was disembowelled and quartered and his

Charles II and the 'Popish Plot', 1660-1685

head cut off. Many in the crowd are said to have wept and some called out that this was no way to destroy popery: 'It is enough to make us all papists!'

Father Leveson obtained the head, which he gave to Father Leo Randolph who later conveyed it to St Bonaventure's at Douai where it remained until at least 1743. The relic was acquired by the Poor Clare nuns of Aire who, in the French Revolution, brought it with them to England. They later returned to France and joined a convent at Gravelines. In 1836 some of the community came back to Scorton, near Darlington, England, but, so the story goes, afraid of what the English Customs officers would think of their bringing the head into the country, it was buried in the cloister garden at Gravelines. In spite of later searches being made to recover the relic it was not found. John's quartered body was buried in the churchyard of St Oswald's, Foregate Street, Worcester. The actual site of the grave was probably lost when part of the churchyard was destroyed for road widening. There is now a memorial inscription in the churchyard and it remains a place of pilgrimage for Worcestershire Catholics. In 1879 a memorial cross was erected to commemorate John in the churchyard at Harvington. It reads: In memory of Father John Wall OSF, in religion Father Joachim of St.Anne, who obeying God rather than man, for twelve years ministered the sacraments to the faithful in this and other parts of Worcestershire in daily peril of death.

Since 1923 Harvington Hall, as a result of a generous benefaction, has belonged to the Catholic Archdiocese of Birmingham, which has carried out extensive conservation and restoration.

John's brother, William, was ordained at the Lateran in 1649 and sent to England in 1650. He was soon back at Douai where he taught for about two years. In 1668 he joined the Benedictines at Lambspring, taking the name Dom Cuthbert. He joined the English mission under the alias Marsh. Arrested during the 'Plot' he was tried with Sir George Wakeman at the Old Bailey on 18 July 1679. William boldly told the court that all Europe was astonished at the proceedings in England, where the blood of so many innocent persons was spilled upon the oaths of a band of profligate wretches that were not fit to breathe. Lord Chief Justice Scroggs was not best pleased by this and launched into a vicious attack upon the Catholic Church. Notwithstanding Scroggs' hostility, and despite Oates giving lying testimony against him, William was acquitted, but remained in prison. He was again brought to trial the following January accused of being a priest and condemned to death. He was reprieved by the King, although still confined to prison; but, contrary to some authorities who assert that he died there, he survived

Charles II and the 'Popish Plot', 1660-1685

until freed on the accession of James II and served as one of the King's chaplains at St James's Palace. He died at the Abbey of Lambspring, in October 1704. As a postscript it may be added that five years after John Wall's martyrdom, his Protestant shelterer, Thomas Millward, was received into the Catholic Church by Father Leo Randolph.

John Kemble

In qua fide puer natus fui in eadem senex morior
I will die as an old man in the same faith in which I was born

St Jerome (c.341-420)

John was born in 1599 into a Catholic family at Rhyd y Car farm in the parish of St Weonards, Herefordshire. His father, John Kemble, came from an old Wiltshire family. Why some of the Kemble's moved to Monmouthshire is unclear, but it has been surmised that it was to enable them to practise their religion in greater safety in a rural area where Catholics remained numerically strong. In King James's time, John Kemble senior was well-known to the authorities, being reported as a dangerous recusant who harboured priests. John's mother, Anne Morgan, came from a prominent family at Skenfrith. Her grandfather, John Morgan, was the local steward of the Duchy of Lancaster and the last governor of Skenfrith Castle. The handsome altar-tomb of he and his wife may still be seen in Skenfrith's sturdy 13th century parish church dedicated to St Bridget, as well as the seventeenth-century Morgan family box pew. So John's ancestry was a mixture of Welsh and English. John was probably the youngest child and while a small boy, his family moved into the Herefordshire parish of Llangarron. Bishops Robert Bennett of Hereford and Fraser Godwin of Llandaff were determined to enforce the penal laws. At Christmas 1604 John Kemble and his wife were listed among the 'principal and most dangerous recusants of the diocese of Hereford.' In 1605 the High Sheriff of Herefordshire reported that John Kemble was sheltering 'one Stampe, a Jesuit'. This was Thomas Stamp who was a seminary priest, not a Jesuit. He came from Derbyshire and was already a priest when he arrived at Douai. For several years he was chaplain to Sir George Peckham at his houses in London and Denham. By September 1586 he was a prisoner in the Gatehouse. In January 1588 he was sent to Wisbech. He was released in May 1594 and an informer reported that

Charles II and the 'Popish Plot', 1660-1685

he was hiding at John, Baron Lumley's house in Greenwich. He may have gone to Herefordshire to try and get himself out of harm's way.

Although there is no written record of his arrival we know that at a young age, following in the footsteps of his elder brother, Walter, John was smuggled to Douai to be educated; a perilous undertaking for all concerned. Walter eventually became a Benedictine priest at Douai.

At the age of eighteen, using the alias Holland, John entered the seminary at Douai, then under the presidency of Harrowden-born Dr Matthew Kellison. He was ordained deacon on 22 February 1625 and the following day was ordained priest by Herman Ottemberg, Bishop of Arras. He said his first Mass on 2 March, the feast of St Chad. On 4 June of that year he was sent home to begin his apostolate in his native area of Hereford and the Welsh border country. John is unique among the martyrs for his extraordinarily long ministry of fifty-four years. The centre of his ministry was Pembridge Castle at Welsh Newton, the home firstly of his uncle, George Kemble, and then of his nephew, Captain Richard Kemble. The chapel, reached by a stone staircase, was hidden in the top storey of the keep at the south-west corner. Today what remains of Pembridge is a farmhouse. In the adjoining parish of Llanrothal the Jesuits were given the Cwm or Combe estate by Edward Somerset of Raglan, 2nd Marquess of Worcester. It consisted of adjoining farmhouses managed by a Catholic farmer named Peter Pullen.

Here they had established a community, the 'College of St Francis Xavier' whose priests served nearly forty places in South Wales and Herefordshire. With their help John founded mission centres around the Monnow Valley which delineates the border between England and Wales. The Monnow Valley had remained a stronghold of Catholicism, owing much to the patronage of Catholic peers. The Carmelites were also active on the Herefordshire borders and ran a secret school. Under King Charles I Monmouthshire topped the list of twenty-nine counties for the number of convictions of recusants. In some places there were hardly any Protestants to be found. Even today the valley remains a secluded, inaccessible area of narrow lanes, its medieval churches, such as those at Skenfrith, having strong defensive towers; a reminder that this was Marcher country. There were many Catholic families in Herefordshire and Monmouthshire who sheltered John and at whose houses he and other priests said Mass. These centres would have included the home of Sebastian Needham at Hilston House, St Maughans; the wealthy Milbourn's at Wonastow Court; the Mynors family at their fortified medieval manor, Treago Castle, and the Jones family in Wonastow parish whose house, Treowen, was well supplied

Charles II and the 'Popish Plot', 1660-1685

with hiding places. During the Civil War Pembridge Castle was held for the King and was forced to surrender to the parliamentary forces after a siege in 1646. It was severely damaged but John continued to make it his headquarters. In 1649 John visited London on clergy business while back home many of the castle lands were seized as forfeit for the recusancy of the family. His nephew, Captain Richard Kemble, distinguished himself at the Battle of Worcester in 1651. When Prince Charles's horse was killed Kemble gave him his own mount on which to escape. In February 1670 when Parliament presented an address to King Charles II about the 'Growth of Popery', the Cym and the Jesuits operating from there were explicitly cited as an example of popish activities. Parliament recommended that they 'should be punished for their insolencies.'

When the 'Plot' spread out its vicious tentacles from London into the countryside, few places were more vulnerable than the Welsh borders because there was such a concentration of Catholics. Priests were imprisoned in Monmouth, Cardiff, Brecon, Denbigh, Chester and many other towns. In the winter of 1678 priests in fear of their lives went into hiding or fled the country. Many hunted priests perished of hypothermia, hunger and exhaustion as they moved about the open country and mountains in wintertime trying to elude their captors. Father James Richardson SJ was chaplain to the Vaughan Family at Courtfield, Welsh Bicknor, then in Monmouthshire. (Over the centuries the Vaughan's gave many sons and daughters in the service of the Church, the most famous being Cardinal Herbert Vaughan, Archbishop of Westminster (1832-1903). Five of his brothers became priests, three of them bishops, and his five sisters became nuns.) Father Richardson had to hide in a forest for a fortnight in the depths of winter. At night Mrs Vaughan went bravely into the forest to take him food. When the pursuivants came looking for him he had to climb a tall tree where he remained hidden for days. Catholic houses and property, including Courtfield, were ransacked and trashed by the authorities in the hope of finding a priest. The Cwm was raided and John was urged by his friends to flee. 'I'm too old now', was his answer. He said he had but a few years to live and would remain at his post. After all it 'will be an advantage to suffer for my religion'.

In spite of his wife and children being Catholics, Captain John Scudamore of Kentchurch Court led the searchers to Pembridge Castle in November 1678. John calmly surrendered to his arrest and was dragged off through the snow to the county jail in Hereford. While John was in prison, the governor made a pen and ink portrait of him which has been preserved. He remained in prison over three months until sent

Charles II and the 'Popish Plot', 1660-1685

for trial in March 1679, when he was condemned at the assizes to be hanged, drawn and quartered for being a seminary priest.

On 23 April he and Father David Lewis were sent to face examination in London for complicity in the 'Plot'. Too frail to ride properly, John was strapped to a horse, his face to the animal's tail 'like a bundle of merchandise', as one eyewitness described it, and taken on the painful journey to Newgate to join Father Roger Hanslepp, a priest born in 1642 at Up Hatherley, Gloucestershire. Ordained in 1675 he had been tried and condemned at Gloucester on 21 April 1678 and ordered to be sent to Newgate. On 23 May Oates, Bedloe and Dugdale were instructed by the House of Lords to interrogate the priests. Kemble was promised his life and liberty if he 'confessed' but Oates failed to implicate John in the imaginary 'Plot, or obtain any information from him. On 28 May the Privy Council ordered him to be sent back to Hereford, this time walking most of the way. He was returned to prison, sick and exhausted and in great pain, as witnessed by a fellow prisoner, Father Charles Carne,[14] who was in Hereford jail at the same time awaiting his fate. On 9 June he wrote a letter on Kemble's behalf to a Mrs Elizabeth Sheldon in London. She clearly had been a benefactor to John during his time in the capital.

> I hope you will pardon these, though from an unknown hand, it is to acquaint you that Mr Kemble is arrived to Hereford, but weary and sickly. God reward you and all the other benefactors for your very great charity to him and his companions. I am desired by him that good friends take care there be a stop put to execution; it is reported here (how true I know not) that the day is appointed for that dismal fact ... I hope good friends (if possible) will prevent the tragedy. I am a prisoner in the same place on the same account, though not yet condemned. Next assizes I am to receive my doom. Mr Kemble, though being incapable of expressing himself, your petitioner desired me to do so on his behalf; he gives his humble service to yourself and to all pious benefactors.

There is a most interesting relic in the form of a letter between an unknown lady and Kemble. (Could this possibly have been the same Mrs Sheldon?) The lady wrote to him in prison to tell him that she and her mother had endeavoured to persuade the keeper to let them in to see him, but without success; so she asked him for his prayers and blessings. On 13 June John wrote a short reply in the margins of the letter and returned it to her, enclosing a lock of his hair as a keepsake. The letter, albeit very damaged, and the hair have survived. John's last letter, it reads:

> This poor old condemned man whom you so charitably visited in Newgate, to whom you delivered four pounds in the night before our removal, came

safely to Hereford on the Saturday following. But I have been so bruised in body that I have not been able to sit so long as to write to you according to your commands; be pleased therefore to excuse my want, not of dutiful respect to you and your worthy companions to whom I shall ever acknowledge myself unspeakably obliged, but to my miserable condition. You shall have of me as long as I live a true and faithful beadsman, but your full requiter must be the Almighty rewarder of all your good works. What I left in your hands I beseech you let be sent with what convenience may be. I am sorry I am able to do no more and had not been able to do so much had not you and your friends' extraordinary charity assisted me. I pray you expect no compliments from him that never knew how to make use of them and pardon this my shortness and bad writing which I perform in great pain.

On 11 July the Privy Council ordered the death sentence to be carried out on all priests found guilty. John appeared before Lord Chief Justice William Scroggs and Sir Robert Atkyns at Hereford Town Hall on 4 August. While awaiting execution he was allowed visitors, among them the children of Captain Scudamore, the man who had arrested him. With the children he shared the sweets sent in by friends. When asked why he treated them with such kindness, he replied that their father had been the best friend he had ever had.

On 22 August Humphrey Digges, the under-sheriff of Hereford, came to tell John that he was to die that day. He asked for time to pray and smoke a last pipe. The under-sheriff admired the old man and he and the prison governor joined John in smoking a pipe and drinking a cup of wine. The incident was the origin of the Herefordshire custom of referring to a parting pipe as a 'Kemble pipe'. John was drawn on a hurdle to Wigmarsh Common (now known as Widemarsh) north of the city to the gallows, where a huge crowd had assembled. As it was customary John spoke to the people while standing in the cart. His last words were taken down and printed.

It will be expected that I should say something, but as I am an old man it won't be much, and not having any concern in the plot, neither indeed believing there was any: Oates and Bedloe not being able to charge me with anything when I was brought up to London, though they were both with me, makes it evident that I die only for professing the old Roman Catholic religion, which was the religion that first made this kingdom Christian and whosoever intends to be saved must die in the religion. I had almost forgot to have said something, which I shall declare now: that is I desire God to forgive all those that have been anyways accessory to the bringing of me to this place. It is my prayer now, and shall be unto Almighty God not to punish them for so doing; and if I have offended any man in thought, word or deed, I am heartily sorry for it and beg his pardon as I pardon those that have anyways offended me.

Charles II and the 'Popish Plot', 1660-1685

The hangman was greatly upset. John shook him by the hand and tried to encourage him saying, 'My friend, Anthony, be not be afraid, do thy office well. I forgive thee with all my heart; you are doing me a greater kindness than discourtesy'.

He then pulled his cap over his eyes and prayed for a while in silence on his knees, after which he announced that he was ready and they might carry out their duty whenever they pleased. Three times he repeated 'Into Thy hands, O Lord, I commend my spirit,' before the cart was pulled away. The hangman was clumsy and the knot of the rope had not been correctly placed so John hung for half an hour, slowly and painfully strangulating, the blood bursting from his mouth, nose and ears. No one had the heart to cut him down and so he was left to die. Such was the respect in which he was held that he was spared the disembowelling and quartering, but his head was cut off. John Kemble was eighty years of age. Even his persecutors declared that they had never seen anyone die so like a gentleman and so like a Christian.

His body was begged by his nephew, Richard Kemble, and buried beside the churchyard cross at Welsh Newton, Monmouth, under a plain slab that reads:

JK Dyed the 22 of August Anno Do 1679.

The village, three and a half miles north of Monmouth, is situated on the A466, the main road between Hereford and Monmouth. The small Norman church of St Mary still retains its twelfth-century carved stone rood screen. John's grave immediately became and continues to this day a much-loved place of pilgrimage and many miraculous cures have been attributed to the martyr's intercession at his resting place. One of the first was the cure from throat cancer of Scudamore's own daughter. In 1805 the great Brecon-born actress, Mrs Sarah Siddons, née Kemble, with her brother Charles, who belonged to the famous Kemble family acting dynasty, toured the Wye Valley and visited the grave of their martyred relative. She sent a yearly donation to have it kept in decent order.

The martyr's left hand being under his head was accidentally severed at his execution. It was retrieved by a woman in the crowd who wrapped it in her apron. It now rests above the altar of the Lady Chapel in St Francis Xavier's Catholic Church, Hereford, in a most beautiful silver-gilt, enamelled reliquary. The hand lies in a crystal cylinder supported by the figures of saints and angels. Its base is set with the precious stones which the book of Revelation says adorn the foundation stones of the Holy City of God, the New Jerusalem. The inscription reads: *The hand of the Rev. John Kemble, a priest of Hereford, who out of hatred of the Catholic faith and the Christian priesthood, was hanged at Widemarsh, outside the gate of Hereford, 22 August 1679.*

The reliquary was donated by a grateful father, Robert Monteith of Carstairs, Scotland, whose son recovered from a life-threatening illness after being touched by the hand. In 1995 an inexplicable cure was attributed to the hand's healing powers. Father Christopher Jenkins suffered a massive stroke and lapsed into a deep coma; his life was despaired of. After the hand had been applied to his forehead he quickly made a full recovery. The Catholic Church at Monmouth possesses other relics of the martyr; among them his missal dated 1623, with marginal comments in his handwriting, a silver chalice, the oak benches that served as his altar and his portable altar stone.

David Lewis

My soul, there is a country far beyond the stars ... There, above noise and danger, sweet peace sits crown'd with smiles.

Peace, Henry Vaughan, 1622-1695

David Henry Lewis was born at Abergavenny in 1616. His father was Morgan Lewis, who had conformed, presumably for material advantage. His mother was Margaret Pritchard, who remained Catholic. The Pritchard family produced several priests. She was also a niece of the saintly Dom Augustine Baker OSB, lawyer, monk and mystical writer, who died of the plague in London in 1641. David, the eldest of nine children, strangely seems to have been the only one who was raised as a Protestant. He was educated at the Royal Grammar School, Abergavenny, of which his father was head. Another former pupil was Blessed Philip Powel OSB, who was martyred at Tyburn in 1646. Just like his two Benedictine predecessors, when he left school at sixteen David was sent to study law at the Middle Temple in London. After three years in London he travelled to Paris and joined the household of Comte Savage as tutor to his young son. While in Paris he was received into the Catholic Church by Father William Talbot, procurator of the Jesuit mission. He returned home to spend two years with his family at Abergavenny and had the joy of seeing his father reconciled to the

Charles II and the 'Popish Plot', 1660-1685

Church before his death.

Both his parents having died, David sought the advice of Father Charles Browne, Superior of the Jesuit mission in Wales, about his future. On 3 November 1638 he entered the English College, Rome, under the alias of Charles Baker. One of his fellow students was John Wall. After four years in Rome he was ordained priest at San Lorenzo in Damaso 20 July 1642. Later that year, on the feast of the first Christian martyr, St Stephen, he preached a short sermon before Pope Urban VIII. On 19 April 1645, following the example of his maternal uncle, Father John Pritchard, he joined the Society of Jesus and served his novitiate at Sant'Andrea, Rome. Immediately after he was professed in 1646 he was sent to the mission in Wales, but was quickly recalled to Rome to become spiritual director at the English College. This proved to be a short posting because there was a greater need for David's talents in his homeland, and in 1648 he returned to Monmouthshire to work in South Wales and Herefordshire for the next thirty years. This was not an easy task in the aftermath of the Civil War, when many priests were in great danger from the parliamentarian authorities, and several of David's colleagues were imprisoned during the years of the Commonwealth.

His apostolate was carried out in the Jesuit missionary district known as the College of St Francis Xavier, with its headquarters at the Cwm, isolated converted farmhouses near Llanrothal. (The Cwm, though changed, still stands today.) The Cwm was not a college in any conventional sense of the name; it was an administrative centre and a place of rest and refuge for the priests serving on the mission. There were around twenty-five priests on the mission when David joined them and they had to subsist on a communally shared meagre annual income. Some priests were attached as chaplains to the houses of prominent Catholic landowners from where they could minister to the Catholics in the surrounding area. For example, Father William Morgan SJ was fortunate to be chaplain to William Herbert, Earl of Powis, at magnificent Powis Castle, near Welshpool. Most however led a peripatetic existence serving the area allotted to them. This was how David laboured, traversing the often mountainous country, mostly on foot. To avoid the persecutors he often took long, circuitous routes at night in order to visit and serve the poorest of his flock, for whom he evinced a special love and devotion. It earned for him the name *Tad y Tlodion*: the Father of the Poor. From 1666 to 1671 David was Superior of the South Wales district. He again held that post from 1674 until his death.

John Arnold, of Llanvihangel Court, in 1670 had reported to the

Charles II and the 'Popish Plot', 1660-1685

House of Lords that at the Cwm were six Jesuit priests and 'at Llantarnam, an eminent papist's house in Monmouthshire, there is a room fitted up chapel wise for saying Mass where Father David Lewis, a popish priest, has said Mass for many years past.' The local authorities may have sympathised with the Catholics because little action was taken. In 1678 Arnold presented to the Commons a report giving details provided by informers about Catholic activities in Monmouthshire and Herefordshire. It repeated the information that David Lewis publicly said Mass in the chapel at the home of the Morgan family at Llantarnam, near Cwmbran, as well as other houses around Abergavenny, such as that of the attorney Thomas Gunter, who had also been host to Philip Evans. The Gunter's, who were relatives of David Lewis, suffered greatly for their faith. They owned a large mansion in Cross Street, Abergavenny and had a chapel in the attic.

Llantarnam, founded 1179, was originally a Cistercian abbey which was suppressed in 1538. In 1559 the abbey was granted by Elizabeth I to the Earl of Pembroke, from whom the Morgan family bought the property in 1561. The Morgan's were staunch recusants and their wealth enabled them to eventually buy exemption from paying further swingeing fines for non-attendance at church. In their mansion, built from the abbey materials, they had a Catholic chapel. Lady Frances Morgan was an aunt of David Lewis's and he lived at Llantarnam Abbey for several years before moving into a cottage next to the blacksmiths workshop when his presence threatened to endanger the family. Lady Frances died in 1676 and Llantarnam passed to her son, Sir Edward, a Justice of the Peace, who nevertheless remained a Catholic. His chapel was attended by the Catholics from the surrounding area. The abbey was rebuilt by Wyatt in Elizabethan style in 1835 and little remains of the medieval buildings. Used by the RAF during the Second World War, in 1946 the abbey was acquired by the Sisters of St Joseph of Annecy who are still in residence. Aptly their order was established in 1650; contemporaneous with David Lewis. How completely David would have identified with the *Maxims of Love* composed for the sisters by their founder, the Jesuit Jean-Pierre Médaille, (1610-69) who wrote, 'Have for God a love that is generous, embracing all that love is capable of, and all that a heart can love in God and for God ... a love unable to be uprooted by any created power.'

When the full fury of the 'Plot' burst upon Monmouthshire the hunt was on for every priest. In December 1678 a joint committee of the Lords and Commons ordered Herbert Croft, Bishop of Hereford since 1661, to root out the Jesuits at the Cwm, which was raided and ransacked. (Croft, son of Sir Herbert Croft of Croft Castle, Herefordshire, like his father before him, had been a convert to Catholicism. But unlike his father, who died living with the English Benedictines at Douai in 1622, he had reverted to the Church of England and wrote anti-Catholic pamphlets.) Croft sent a report of the raid to the House of Lords.

In the parish of Llanrothal there were two houses called the Upper and Lower Combe, with a walled court before each of them, having lands belonging to them worth about three score pounds per annum ... One of these houses is a fair genteel house wherein there are six lodging chambers, each one a convenient study to it ... besides several other lodging rooms. The other house is also a good country house, with several chambers and studies to some of them ... these houses are seated at the bottom of a thick woody and rocky hill, with several hollow places in the rocks wherein men may conceal themselves and there is a private passage from one of the houses into this wood. In one of these houses there was a study found, the door whereof, very hardly to be discovered, being placed behind a bed and plastered over like the wall adjoining, in which was found a great store of divinity books and others in folio and quarto, and many other lesser books, several horse loads ... many whereof are written by the principal learned Jesuits.

The priests had managed to get away in time but a great deal of valuable material and vestments were seized, as well as the many books. These were carted of to Hereford where they still remain in the famous cathedral library. One of those books is inscribed with the name of Thomas Gunter.

David went into hiding at Llantarnam, but his whereabouts were betrayed and early in the morning of Sunday, 17 November 1678 he was arrested by a troop of dragoons while preparing for Mass. He was taken to the home of the magistrate Charles Price at Llanfoist, just west of Abergavenny. Price was a cousin by marriage of William Bedloe. Here John Arnold and another magistrate, Thomas Lewis, awaited David's arrival. All the details of his arrest, imprisonment and trial are known from the *Narrative* written by Lewis and published after his death. On that Sunday afternoon, escorted by twelve armed men, he was carried in a triumphal procession through Abergavenny to the Golden Lion inn; here William Jones, the Recorder, held a makeshift court in an upstairs room. A former servant of the priest gave evidence that he had seen him say Mass many times, so he was committed for trial. Afterwards he was escorted to Arnold's house at Llanvihangel Crucorney, where he arrived about midnight and was kept overnight under guard. The following morning he was conducted on horseback under armed guard to Monmouth prison, where he was kept in close

Charles II and the 'Popish Plot', 1660-1685

confinement. A friend paid the fourteen shillings cost of providing the prisoner with a bed, candles and a fire. David tells us that he was locked up by night and barred up by day so strictly that he was never allowed to leave his room, but friends managed to smuggle information to him. During Christmas week 1678 he received a visit from two magistrates who told him that Charles Price, a servant of the Marquess of Worcester at Raglan Castle, had been accused by William Bedloe of being involved in the 'Plot'. David was questioned under oath as to what he knew about the matter. David replied, 'Upon oath, and under my hand I give it, that to my knowledge I never saw Bedloe, I never spoke to him, I never had any correspondence with him directly or indirectly, I further depose that I never heard, I know nothing of the Plot, till common fame had spread it over the country.'

It must have been heartbreaking for him to hear about the arrests of other priests and the destruction of his life's work in the mission. A few instances may be recalled of the fate of David's priestly friends and colleagues. Father Ignatius Price SJ was born in 1610 in Monmouthshire. Under the alias of Walter Price he served the Jesuit mission for thirty-five years, based at the Cwm. At the age of sixty-nine he fled his pursuers for two months, usually at night in the snow, with only the bare minimum of clothes to keep him warm. He rarely found any shelter because the Catholics were too afraid to offer him hospitality so he had to sleep outdoors wherever he could. He succumbed to a violent fever and died. Not content with hounding the man to his death, the magistrate, Charles Price of Llanfoist, who was a relative, ordered his grave to be opened, ripped apart his shroud and removed the silver cross around the priest's neck. Father Thomas Neville, aged eighty-four, was caught and killed by pursuivants at Raglan in the winter of 1679. Father Charles Pritchard SJ, another Monmouthshire priest, was born in 1637 and joined the Jesuits in 1663. He had been named as one of the murderers of Sir Edmund Berry Godfrey and the would-be murderer of the Duke of Buckingham in the malevolent accusations of William Bedloe. (The fact that Father Pritchard had never left South Wales in the sixteen years of his apostolate shows how random the allegations were.) A reward of eighty crowns was offered for his capture, which he managed to evade for nearly eighteen months, hiding by day and emerging only at night to serve the needs of local Catholics. His health collapsed under the weight of strain and anxiety he endured. One night he suffered a bad fall, which hastened his end, and on 14 March 1680 he was buried secretly in the garden of a house where he had found shelter. The old Carmelite priest who ran their school, Father Nicholas Rider, was

Charles II and the 'Popish Plot', 1660-1685

arrested but bailed by some local Protestants. Taken to London, he was again arrested and bailed but sought sanctuary in the Spanish Embassy, where he died. Father George Loop, a Herefordshire Carmelite, escaped from Captain Scudamore disguised as a farmer's wife. He successfully made his way through various villages all the way to Worcester. Father Thomas Andrews, who lived near Llantilio, hid in the woods before being taken in by a Catholic widow called Jane Harris. When the pursuivants raided her house Father Andrews had escaped. Mrs Harris was arrested and for a time was held in the same jail as David Lewis. Father Andrews, worn out by his hardships, died of exposure and was buried in the floor of a barn.

Not only the clergy but also the laity in South Wales had to bear the brunt of the persecution. The penal laws were rigorously enforced against them for the first time in years. Their homes were raided and property confiscated. Many were thrown into prison for refusing to take the Test Oath, and reduced to penury by the iniquitous bail requirements to secure their release.

On 13 January 1679, a bitterly cold day with heavy snow, David was transferred to the new county jail at Usk. En route a stop was made at an inn at Raglan and whilst there a messenger arrived at the door asking to speak with David urgently. The message was that Father Ignatius Price lay dying in a barn about half a mile away and wanted to see him. All David could do was to send back a message 'for his soul's happy passage out of this turbulent world to an eternity of rest.'

The jail at Usk, situated in Bridge Street, had once been a friary belonging to the Grey Friars. There David encountered many lay friends who had refused to take the Test Oath. On 28 March David was brought to trial at the Lenten Assizes before Sir Robert Atkyns. Having had legal training, he was able to conduct a worthy defence, challenging some of the jurors selected. Arnold then challenged several more and the sheriff, despairing of ever nominating a jury, suggested sarcastically that Arnold should just call whom he pleased. At this Judge Atkyns told the sheriff 'not to be saucy.' After some difficulty, a jury was finally sworn which was to the satisfaction of John Arnold - but not of Lewis, who feared that they were all ignorant men. The prosecution witnesses, one of whom was Mayne Trott who had testified against Philip Evans, testified to having seen David say Mass and carry out other priestly functions. One witness, Dorothy James, made a slanderous statement about David and then laughed loudly when her evidence was concluded. Atkyns rebuked her: 'When the gentleman is for his life, it is no jesting matter.' David disputed the evidence, including evidence of his identity; he questioned the worthless

593

Charles II and the 'Popish Plot', 1660-1685

character of some of the witnesses, a number of whom, like Dorothy James, were motivated by malice, which, by calling witnesses, he was able to expose, and vigorously refuted aspersions cast upon his good name.

However proficient his defence, the outcome of the trial was never in doubt: he was found guilty of being a priest under 27 Eliz. I, c.2. Sir Robert Atkyns declared, 'It is enough that you have exercised the functions of a priest in copes and vestments used in your Church, and that you have read Mass and taken confessions. He that uses to read Mass commits treason.' When the death sentence was pronounced David bowed to the judge. Together with John Kemble, he was sent to London for questioning in Newgate by Oates and Bedloe. Lord Shaftesbury told David that if he provided evidence about the 'Plot' and renounced his Catholicism his life would not only be spared but he would be well rewarded. Neither being able to implicate them in the 'Plot', nor persuade them to apostatise, Lewis, Kemble, John Wall and Roger Hanslepp were ordered on 28 May to be taken back to their respective prisons, and David was returned to Usk. Father Hanslepp was returned to Gloucester for execution, but for reasons unexplained this was not carried out and he was still alive in 1685.

David spent three months awaiting his execution during which time, thanks to the connivance of the jailer, Catholics were allowed access to him and he was able to administer the Sacraments to them. In prison David composed his final speech, a manuscript copy of which, written on jail paper, in beautiful handwriting has survived. High Sheriff James Herbert of Coldbrook kept finding excuses to delay the execution in the hope that a reprieve might be granted by the King. On 11 July the Privy Council issued orders that all condemned priests should be executed forthwith, but still the High Sheriff prevaricated. John Arnold, angry at the delay, asked Lord Shaftesbury to order the sheriff to carry out the execution.

Poor Sheriff Herbert, who was fined for neglect of duty, had to face further headaches on the day fixed for the execution, which took place at Usk on 27 August 1679 at a place known as the Coniger, before a great crowd. The workmen refused to erect the gallows, so the sheriff had to bring a convict from the jail; this man, on a promise of securing his freedom, set up a makeshift effort of two poles with a crossbeam. However, they were not high enough to allow sufficient drop for a body, so a trench had to be dug beneath to create more space. The convict had to beat a hasty retreat when the crowd threw stones at him. The official hangman refused to carry out the execution and fled the town. A blacksmith was induced to perform the task when offered a

Charles II and the 'Popish Plot', 1660-1685

handsome sum as a bribe.

Standing on a stool below the gallows, David delivered his eloquent speech in Welsh which was afterwards published. He defended himself again from any imputations on his character then explained what was the true cause of his untimely death. 'Why thus sledged to this country Tyburn? Why this so untimely death of mine? It was for no plot.' He avowed himself a loyal subject of the King, for whom he prayed daily, and abhorred all plots, of which he knew nothing. He alluded to his interrogation at Newgate, in which he had been offered his life, proving that he died for reasons of conscience and his religion. He declared,

Here is a numerous assembly; may the great Saviour of the world save every soul of you all. I believe you are here met not only to see a fellow native die, but also to hear a fellow native speak. My religion is Roman Catholic; in it I have lived above forty years; in it I now die and so fixedly die, that if all the good things in this world were offered to me to renounce it, all should not remove me one hair's breadth from my Roman Catholic faith ... A Roman Catholic priest I am; a Roman Catholic priest of that religious order called the Society of Jesus I am; and I bless God who first called me. I was condemned for saying Mass, hearing confessions and administering the sacraments. As for saying Mass, it was the old and still is the accustomed and laudable liturgy of the holy Church; and all the other acts are acts of religion tending to the worship of God and therefore dying for this I die for religion.

David forgave with all his heart those who had any part in bringing about his death. He named his 'capital persecutor' John Arnold, 'who hath been so long thirsting after my blood.' He declared that he bore neither him nor anyone else ill will but only love, and for whom he asked God to give the grace of true repentance. He said, 'Forgive and you shall be forgiven; I profess myself a child of the gospel and the gospel I obey.' Turning to his fellow Catholics he urged them, 'Fear God, honour your King; be firm in your faith ... bear your sufferings patiently and forgive your enemies.' He made a humble act of contrition and then uttering the words, 'Sweet Jesus, receive my soul,' the stool was pulled away.

A Protestant gentleman took the hand of Father Lewis and prevented the executioner from cutting him down before he was dead. He was disembowelled, but the crowd, many dipping cloths in his blood, protested that his body should not be quartered. He was, therefore, spared this indignity and all his remains were taken in a large procession and buried in the churchyard of old St Mary's Priory, Usk. There they still rest on the north side of the pathway close to the west porch of the church.

Charles II and the 'Popish Plot', 1660-1685

Some years ago this author helped meet the cost of a new grave slab to replace the sunken and broken older one. The new grave stone, headed *Ad majorem Dei gloriam* - the motto of the Society of Jesus - is inscribed with details of David's life, death and canonization. Monmouthshire honours its martyr priest. There are plaques at various sites associated with David Lewis. At Usk the site of execution is marked with a blue plaque in Welsh and English, mounted on a rock. In the Catholic church of St Francis Xavier and St David Lewis - which is located opposite the place of his execution - there is a shrine containing a piece of the rope with which he was hanged and a piece of linen stained with his blood. Many other relics have survived, including a travelling chalice belonging to David at the Catholic church in Abergavenny and bloodstained cloth kept by the Sisters of St Joseph at Llantarnam Abbey.

David's grave continues to be a place of pilgrimage. To those who may ask why pilgrimages should still be made to the places associated with the martyrs, the answer is eloquently supplied by the American poet, playwright and Nobel laureate, T S Eliot, who in his verse drama *Murder in the Cathedral* wrote:

Wherever a martyr has given his blood for Christ there is holy ground and the sanctity shall not depart from it.

St John Chrysostom, memorably echoing Tertullian of Carthage's (Quintus Septimius Florens Tertullianus) c.160-c.225 immortal phrase, 'The blood of martyrs is the seed of Christians', wrote, 'The blood of martyrs is to the churches as water is to a garden'. And he applauds pilgrimages to honour the saints because they are examples to encourage those who come after them to walk the same path.

Charles II and the 'Popish Plot', 1660-1685

Notes to Chapter Eight

1 Philip Thomas Howard was the son of Henry, Earl of Arundel, grandson of the martyred Philip Howard. His brother was Henry, 6th Duke of Norfolk. His mother was Elizabeth Stuart, daughter of Esmé, 3rd Duke of Lennox, so he was related to the Royal Family. At the age of sixteen he joined the Dominicans in Italy. Professed in 1646, he took the name of Thomas in religion and was ordained in 1652. Devoted to the cause of the conversion of England, he founded a college for the education of English Catholic boys. Because he occupied a prominent position at Court he faced much hostility and opposition from the Puritan faction and returned to the Continent. In 1672 he was nominated by the Pope as Vicar Apostolic of England, but because of opposition from the Chapter of secular clergy, who wanted a diocesan structure restored, the nomination was withdrawn. In 1675 he was made a Cardinal and took up permanent residence in Rome where he tried to promote the interests of English Catholics, and in 1679 was named Cardinal Protector of England and Scotland. He rebuilt the English College at Rome. Through his influence, the number of Vicars Apostolic was increased to four at the accession of James II in 1685. He tried to exert influence, albeit from a distance, on the new King to be more cautious about pushing forward his policy of toleration in the face of Protestant opposition. He took part in three papal conclaves. He died in 1691, much mourned, and was buried at Santa Maria sopra Minerva, his titular church in Rome.

2 Blessed William Ireland - real name Iremonger - came from a Yorkshire family; the eldest son of William Iremonger of Crofton Hall and Barbara Eure of Washingborough, Lincolnshire. He was born in Lincolnshire in 1636. He was educated at Saint-Omer and entered the Society of Jesus at Watten in 1655 aged only nineteen. He was professed in 1673 and after ordination became chaplain to a convent of Poor Clares. He returned to England in 1677 and was appointed Procurator of the English Province. He was arrested by Titus Oates on the night of 28 September 1678. Oates swore that on 1 September Ireland had been in London at a Jesuit meeting plotting to kill the King. Thanks partly to the efforts of his sister, Anne, witnesses were able to testify that Ireland was in Staffordshire at the time of the alleged meeting, providing a solid alibi to discredit Oates's claim. They included William Harrison, coachman to Sir John and Lady Southcote. However, Scroggs told the jury to ignore the defence witness testimony. He proposed to the jury that even if the precise dates and

times alleged by Oates were wrong, that did not mean the substance of his accusation was not true, and therefore the inaccuracies did not invalidate his testimony! A woman named Sarah Pain then claimed to have seen Ireland in Fetter Lane, London on 20 August. On the strength of the lying 'evidence' of Stephen Dugdale, after a very short recess the jury returned a guilty verdict and Ireland was condemned. Scroggs thanked the jury for being 'good Protestants' sarcastically adding, 'much good may their thirty thousand masses do them!' On his return to Newgate William wrote a journal recording where he had been every day from 3 August to 14 September while he was absent from London. He was able to cite the exact dates on which he had stayed with many prominent persons such as Lord Aston, Sir John Southcote (who was married to Lord Aston's daughter, Elizabeth) and several gentry families in Hertfordshire and Staffordshire, being seen by many people every day of the period. On 1 September he had been at the house of Mr Gerard at Hilderston, Staffordshire. After two reprieves by the King, on Friday, 24 January 1679 William and John Grove were dragged to Tyburn, pelted and abused all the way by the mob. At the gallows William addressed the crowd, 'We are come hither, as on the last theatre of the world, and do therefore conceive we are obliged to speak.' He expressed his forgiveness for anyone who had a hand in his death and then tried to explain his itinerary in Staffordshire at the time he was alleged to have been plotting in London, but the sheriff told him to be quiet as nobody would believe him. Hanged, drawn and quartered his remains were buried at St Giles-in-the-Fields.

3 Blessed John Grove was the servant to Father William Ireland SJ. He lived at Wild House, which was part of the Spanish Embassy occupied by Jesuits. He was imprisoned at Newgate and Oates swore that Grove was to receive £1,500 for his part in the assassination of the King. He was hanged, drawn and quartered with William Ireland at Tyburn. On the scaffold he protested his innocence and asked God to forgive those who were the cause of his death. He was buried at St Giles-in-the-Fields.

4 Father John Huddleston OSB was born in 1608 at Leyland, Lancashire, one of the sixteen children of Joseph and Helen Huddleston; a recusant family. John studied at Saint-Omer and the English College, Rome, where he was ordained in 1637, returning to England in 1639. He served as a chaplain to the Royalist army in the Civil War. He seems to have spent most of his ministry in Staffordshire, but at what date he joined the Benedictines is unknown.

Charles II and the 'Popish Plot', 1660-1685

It was Father Huddleston who hid the future Charles II at Moseley after the Battle of Worcester, thus saving his life. John's uncle, Richard, born at Leyland in 1583, was also a priest who as a boy had been taught by Blessed Thomas Somers. Richard Huddleston had written *A short and plain way to the faith and church*, which Charles had enjoyed reading while in hiding at Moseley. At his restoration Charles appointed John a chaplain to his mother, Queen Henrietta Maria, at Somerset House. After the Queen Mother's death he became attached to the chapel of Queen Catherine. He was the one priest who was safe from prosecution during the 'Plot' furore. He remained safe after James II had fled in 1688 and continued in the service of Queen Catherine. He published his uncle Richard's book, along with his own account of his role in rescuing Charles II and the King's deathbed conversion. John was quite senile when he died at Somerset House at the age of ninety in September 1698 and was buried at St Mary-le-Strand.

5 Blessed Thomas Whitbread, alias Harcourt, was born in Essex c.1618. Educated at Saint-Omer, he joined the Jesuits on 7 September 1635 and was ordained in 1645. He served on the mission from 1647 onwards, mostly in the eastern counties where he was at various times superior of the Lincolnshire and Suffolk districts. At the time of the 'Plot' he was the Jesuit Provincial and it was he who had dismissed Oates from Saint-Omer. Despite suffering serious illness, he was brutally treated after his arrest by the vengeful Oates in London before dawn on Michaelmas Day, 29 September 1678. Awaiting his recovery he could not be moved to Newgate until three months later. Along with William Ireland and John Fenwick he was indicted at the Old Bailey on 17 December, but for lack of evidence against them Thomas and Father Fenwick were sent back to Newgate. He was tried with four fellow Jesuits at the Old Bailey on 13 June 1679 when Stephen Dugdale once again obliged by swearing that the five Jesuits plotted to kill the King. Sir John and Lady Southcote, their son Edward and their daughter - who had not been called at Ireland's trial - appeared as witnesses. Under cross-examination from Lord Chief Justice Scroggs their testimony confirmed that Father William Ireland had indeed been with them at Tixall, Staffordshire, and elsewhere from 5 August to 9 September, corroborating coachman Harrison's earlier testimony. It was too late to help Ireland, who had been executed six months earlier, but it served to discredit Oates. However, Lord Chief Justice Scroggs dismissed the evidence on the grounds that as the earlier jury had found Ireland guilty they must have believed Oates! King Charles was so disgusted at the conduct of the trial of Whitbread and his companions that for forty-

Charles II and the 'Popish Plot', 1660-1685

eight hours he refused to sign the death warrants. Affirming his innocence Whitbread was hanged, drawn and quartered at Tyburn on 20 June 1679 and his remains were buried with his fellow martyrs somewhere near the north wall of St Giles-in-the-Fields church, which was on the road to Tyburn. When Oates was tried for perjury and found guilty in 1685, Sir Edward Southcote and his uncle, Lord Aston, newly released from the Tower, were subpoenaed to give evidence against him. They repeated their testimony about Ireland's whereabouts in 1678 and were then believed.

6 Blessed William Harcourt, whose real name was Barrow, was born c.1610 at Kirkham, Lancashire. Educated at Saint-Omer, he joined the Jesuits at Watten in 1632, was ordained in 1644, and returned to England in 1645 working in the London district for thirty-five years. He served as financial manager for the English province from 1671 to 1677 and was elected Superior in 1678. He urged his fellow Jesuits to leave the country but believed it was his responsibility to remain in London, constantly changing his address and adopting disguises in an attempt to avoid capture. A servant in a house where he was temporarily lodging betrayed him and he was arrested on 7 May 1679. He was hanged, drawn and quartered at Tyburn with Whitbread and his companions.

7 Blessed John Fenwick, whose real name was Caldwell, was born at Durham in 1628. His parents disowned him when he converted to Catholicism. In 1654 he went to Saint-Omer and became a member of the Society of Jesus at Watten on 28 September 1656. He was ordained in 1664 and was appointed procurator of the college at Saint-Omer. In 1674 he was sent to the English Mission. Along with William Ireland and John Grove he was arrested by Oates and a party of soldiers on the night of 28 September 1678. Had he not been executed, it would have been necessary to amputate his leg as it had gone gangrenous from the heavy irons cutting into it while in prison. Offered a pardon on the gallows John declared that he could not acknowledge any guilt for a non-existent plot nor would he lie to save his life. He was hanged, drawn and quartered at Tyburn with Whitbread.

8 Blessed John Gavan was born in London in 1640. Educated at Saint-Omer, he became a Jesuit in 1660, was ordained at Rome in 1670 and returned to England in 1671. He served on the mission mainly in Staffordshire, being based for several years at Wolverhampton, the town that was the headquarters of the Jesuit College of St Chad. His labours must have been rewarded because by the time of King James II

Charles II and the 'Popish Plot', 1660-1685

Wolverhampton had an unusually large number of Catholics with their own chapel. Gavan had a reputation as a scholarly priest and an eloquent preacher. He came to London hoping to find means of escaping to the Continent but was apprehended on 23 January 1679. He was hanged, drawn and quartered at Tyburn with Whitbread. After his condemnation, Lord Shaftesbury visited Father Gavan with a promise of pardon if he would confess to the conspiracy. 'I would not murder my soul to save my body', was his response. Like his companions John made a speech on the scaffold, a speech which bears out his reputation for fluency. 'Dearly beloved countrymen, I am come to the last scene of mortality, to the hour of my death; an hour which is the horizon between time and eternity; an hour which must make me a star to shine forever in heaven above or a firebrand to burn everlastingly among the damned souls in hell below.' Protesting his innocence he said that if this was not the truth then, 'I wish with all my soul that God may exclude me from his heavenly glory and condemn me to the lowest place of hell fire.'

9 Blessed Antony Turner, the son of a Protestant minister, was born in 1628 near Melton Mowbray, Leicestershire,. He went to Cambridge and, after he, his brother Edward, and his mother had converted he went to the English College, Rome. In 1653 he went to Flanders, entered the novitiate of the Society of Jesus and was ordained 1659. His brother, Edward, followed him into the Society and died in prison in 1681. Returning to England in 1661, Antony served the mission mainly in Worcestershire. When the 'Plot' was at its height he was told by his superiors to leave the country. So in January 1679 he travelled to London seeking funds to enable him to make his escape to the Continent. His quest having failed, he decided to give himself up and was imprisoned at Newgate. He was hanged, drawn and quartered at Tyburn with Whitbread. In his final speech Father Turner said, 'I am bound in conscience to do myself that justice as to declare upon my innocence from the horrid crime of treason with which I am falsely accused. I am as free from the treason I am accused of as a child that is just born. I die a Roman Catholic and humbly beg the prayers of such for my happy passage into a better life.' When the 'Plot's' final victim, St Oliver Plunket, Archbishop of Armagh, after a sham farce of a trial was executed at Tyburn on 1 July 1681, he asked to be buried at St Giles-in-the-Fields with the Jesuits. Another Irish victim of the 'Plot' was Peter Creagh, Bishop of Cork, and great-nephew of Archbishop Richard Creagh q.v. He spent two years in prison falsely accused by Oates but was acquitted in 1682.

Charles II and the 'Popish Plot', 1660-1685

10 Blessed Richard Langhorne was a married, Bedford-born, barrister of the Inner Temple, which he entered in May 1647 and was called to the bar in November 1654. He lived in Shire Lane, Holborn, with his wife, Elizabeth, who was a Protestant. Langhorne was eminent in his profession, acting as legal adviser to the London Jesuits, handling their property transactions. It was, no doubt, this eminence that made him a target for Oates with whom he had had previous dealings. In 1677 Langhorne's youngest son, Charles, was a student at Valladolid. A newly arrived fellow student was Titus Oates. After five months he was expelled for 'serious moral lapses'. As Oates was returning to England, Charles - somewhat naïvely - asked him to deliver a letter to his father. This was duly delivered and the unsuspecting Richard, learning that Oates was next going to Saint-Omer, asked him to take a letter for him to the Jesuits at the college, thanking them for their care and education of his sons.

Arrested on 7 October 1678, without any legal proceedings, Richard was kept in virtual solitary confinement in Newgate for eight months. On 14 June 1679 he was tried at the Old Bailey, where Oates cited the letters he had delivered two years previously, falsely alleging that they contained treasonable correspondence. Richard acknowledged receipt of his son's letter from Spain but denied that it contained anything but family matters. Oates and Bedloe swore that Richard had taken part in consultations for killing the King. Stephen Dugdale also gave evidence against him. Richard was able to bring witnesses to discredit the evidence, but he was found guilty and condemned. He was reprieved for a time in the hope that incriminating information might be extracted from him, but Richard stoutly maintained his innocence and the falseness of all that was sworn against him. On 14 July 1679 he was taken to Tyburn, where he handed to the sheriff a long speech which he had written, asking that it should be published. He was allowed to read parts of the speech from the scaffold. He said, 'I take it to be clear that my religion is the sole cause which moved my accusers to charge me with the crime, for which upon their evidence I am adjudged to die, and that my being of that religion which I here profess, was the only ground which could give them any hope to be believed, or which could move my jury to believe the evidence of such men.' He related how he had been offered a pardon and other inducements and preferments if he had agreed to renounce his religion, 'but blessed be my God, who by his grace hath preserved me from yielding to those temptations and strengthened me rather to choose this death, than to stain my soul with sin, and to charge others, against truth, with crimes of which I do not know that any person is guilty.' He forgave Oates and Bedloe and

Charles II and the 'Popish Plot', 1660-1685

prayed that they would be moved to true repentance. He begged that God would bless the nation and not lay the guilt of his blood on the country. He kissed the rope as it was placed over his head, asking the hangman if it was correctly positioned. This was confirmed, and the hangman asked his forgiveness which he freely gave him. As he stood in prayer someone called out to him, 'The Lord have mercy on your soul,' to which Richard replied, 'The Lord in heaven reward your charity.' Then crossing himself he said, 'Blessed Jesus, into thy hands I recommend my soul; now at this instant take me into paradise. I desire to be with my Jesus. I am ready and you need stay no longer for me.' The cart was pulled away and he was hanged, drawn and quartered. His remains were buried at St Giles-in-the-Fields.

Two of Richard's sons, Charles and Francis, became priests. Charles was ordained in 1683 and came to England the following year. He was in London in 1686 but then appears to have returned to the Continent. In 1709 he was made a chaplain to the *de jure* James III at Saint-Germain-en-Laye, and he died there in 1723. Francis, who also studied at Saint-Omer and Valladolid, was ordained at Madrid in 1682. He was with his brother in London in 1686 and by 1704 was at Saint-Germain, where he died in 1709.

11 **Blessed William Howard, Viscount Stafford**, was born in the Strand, London, on 30 November 1612, the youngest of the three sons of Thomas, Earl of Arundel, only son of the martyred Philip Howard. At the coronation of Charles I in 1626 he was made a Knight of the Bath. In 1637 he married Mary, Baroness Stafford, and he was allowed to take the title himself in 1640, when he was created a viscount. They had eight children: three sons and five daughters. William naturally supported the King but in 1642 went into exile. When Charles II regained his throne William was restored to all his honours. As a Catholic he was excluded from the House of Lords under the legislation of 1673. He lived the life of a country gentleman, enjoying the company of his family, but was also somewhat litigious in asserting his rights. In 1675 he conducted his Dominican nephew, Philip, to Rome when he was made a Cardinal. On 25 October 1678, for no apparent reason other than he was an easy target, Stafford was included in the list of five impeached Catholic peers accused by Titus Oates of involvement in the 'Plot'. King Charles immediately dismissed the allegations, but Lord Shaftesbury had the peers arrested. Howard was sent to the Tower along with William Herbert, 1st Earl of Powis, John, 1st Baron Belasyse, Henry, 3rd Baron Arundell of Wardour and William, 4th Baron Petre. They were soon joined by Walter, 3rd Lord Aston who

Charles II and the 'Popish Plot', 1660-1685

had been accused by Stephen Dugdale, his former steward, who he had dismissed from his service for fraudulent practices. Charles's scepticism is easy to understand given the proven loyalty of the peers to his family. Lord Belasyse had played a conspicuous part in the Civil War, fighting at Edgehill and Naseby for his father, Charles I, and was wounded several times. Under Charles II he held a number of official posts but had to resign them all when he refused to take the oath under the Test Act. Lord Henry Arundell too had fought on the royalist side in the Civil War and after the Restoration was appointed Master of the Horse to the Queen Mother, Henrietta Maria.

William Howard was kept prisoner for a year before being suddenly taken for trial for treason at Westminster Hall in November 1680. Evidence was given against him by the apostate Edward Turberville and by Stephen Dugdale who claimed that Lord Stafford had offered him £500 to kill the King. Another witness was John Portman, a London-born priest who had apostatised at the outbreak of the 'Plot'. He had already given evidence against Sir Miles Stapleton in Yorkshire. (See Blessed Thomas Thwing.) No written evidence was produced at the trial and it appears no serious attempt was made to investigate the perjured testimony, but the cowardice of the Lords in the face of the popular frenzy ensured that William was found guilty. On Wednesday, 29 December 1680 he was beheaded on Tower Hill. He was full of confidence in the mercy of God, knowing he died for nothing more than his faith. He died with a quiet dignity and heroism, certain that one day the truth would be known and 'all the world will then see and know what injury has been done to me'. His last letter to his wife and the speech he made on the scaffold all confirm William's character as a 'generous, devout, charitable man' as stated in the 'Memoir' of him written by Dom James (Maurus) Corker OSB, his confessor.

Howard was the only one of the five Catholic peers to be tried and executed; the remaining four were never brought to trial. Lord Aston was released in the summer of 1680. He died in 1714. Baron Petre died in the Tower in January 1684. Lord Belasyse was released in February 1684 and was appointed First Lord Commissioner of the Treasury by James II. He died in 1689. The Earl of Powis was also freed in 1684 and in May 1685 he, Arundell and Belasyse petitioned the House of Lords which annulled all the charges against them. On 4 June the attainder against Viscount Stafford was posthumously reversed. William Herbert was created Marquess of Powis by James II, to whom he was steadfastly loyal. It was he who conveyed Queen Mary and the infant Prince of Wales to their French exile in 1688. Sacrificing his

Charles II and the 'Popish Plot', 1660-1685

huge fortune and estates he chose exile with his King and died at the Jacobite court at Saint-Germain in 1696. Lord Arundell was released from the Tower in February 1684. Under James II he held the office of Lord Privy Seal. He retired from public life when William of Orange gained the throne and died in 1694. William Howard was the last Englishman to be martyred for his Catholic faith.

Dom Maurus, the son of a vicar of Bradford, had been one of three Benedictines arrested for the 'Plot' but the postponement of his trial certainly saved his life. He was tried with Sir George Wakeman in July 1679 and acquitted. He was sentenced to death for his priesthood on 17 January 1680 and remained in Newgate until 1685, when he was released by James II. While still in prison he was confessor to Archbishop Oliver Plunket and accompanied him to Tyburn for his execution. Dom Maurus was elected President of the Anglo-Benedictine Congregation at Paris in 1689 and Abbot of Lambspring in 1693. He resigned and returned to England in 1696. He died at Paddington, London on 22 December 1715.

12 The remaining three priests and the Benedictine brother executed were as follows:

Blessed Thomas Pickering was born in Westmorland c.1621. He was a Benedictine lay brother professed at St Gregory's, Douai, in 1660 and returned to London in 1665. As one of a small group of Benedictines who were attached to the Queen's chapel at Somerset House, he acted as steward to the community and was known to the King and Queen. In 1675 when Charles was forced by Parliament to order the Benedictines to leave England, Pickering was allowed to remain, presumably because he was not a priest. In 1678 he was alleged to have skulked around St James's Park with concealed pistols waiting to kill the King. The accusations made against him by Oates and Bedloe - including that 30,000 Masses would be said for the success of his evil enterprise - were patently ludicrous, as both the King and Queen said so, but he was found guilty. After reprieves from the King his execution was delayed for several months; but Parliament demanded his death and he was hanged, drawn and quartered at Tyburn on 9 May 1679 and buried at St Giles-in-the-Fields.

Blessed Nicholas Postgate was born either 1598 or 1599 into a Catholic family at Kirkdale House, near Egton Bridge, North Yorkshire. His mother was Margery and his father James Postgate, a farmer of Deane Hall. In 1604 they were indicted as recusants, accused of being married

Charles II and the 'Popish Plot', 1660-1685

by a Catholic priest and of having their children secretly baptised. While a teenager Nicholas was part of the travelling company of 'Egton Interlude Players' who performed shows, which often contained satirical comments on the contemporary political and religious situation, much to the annoyance of the authorities. Escorted by Father Francis Greene, at the age of twenty-one, Nicholas arrived at Douai 4 July 1621. He was ordained at Arras 20 March 1628 and sent to England 29 June 1630. He was attached to Lady Jane Hungate, widow of Sir William, at Saxton in Elmet until her death in 1642 and possibly also to the Gascoigne's at nearby Barnbow. Then he moved to the East Riding with Mary, Dowager Viscountess Dunbar, widow of Henry Constable 1st Viscount, until her death in 1659. But it is clear that he was an active missionary over a wide area of Yorkshire during these periods. He worked selflessly on the mission for almost fifty years, tramping the North York moors over great distances in all weathers, his base being a cottage at Ugthorpe. Nicholas himself wrote, 'I have always worked to help poor Catholics. I live as a poor man amongst the poor. I often repeat to myself those words "Why look for rest when you were put into the world to labour?" I am working right to the limits of my strength.' In 1665 he did, in fact, ask Douai for another priest to assist him. A letter of his survives in which he gives an indication of the progress of his ministry, citing the number of children he had baptised (595), couples he had married (226), burials he had conducted (719) and the number of converts he made (2,400). A well-known figure in North Yorkshire, in 1679 he was arrested at the home of Matthew Lyth at Littlebeck, near Sleights, Whitby, by John Reeves, who received a reward of £20. When asked if he was a popish priest, he replied, 'Prove it'. Despite being interrogated by Sir William Cayley at Brompton, near Northallerton, he could not be brought to divulge any information. However, he had on his person communion wafers and devotional books and was committed to York Castle to await trial at the Assizes. He was condemned to death, not for any complicity in the 'Plot', but simply for being a priest. He said that it was but 'a short cut to heaven'. That the victims of the 'Plot' were almost randomly selected is demonstrated by the fact that another priest, who came from and worked in the same area as Postgate, escaped execution. Andrew Jowsey, born at Ugthorpe c.1646, was arrested at Egton, put on trial but acquitted on 9 December 1678. On the scaffold Nicholas asked the sheriff, 'Pray tell the King that I never offended him in any manner of way,' and he asked forgiveness of all as he forgave those who had wronged him and brought him to such a death. Aged over eighty he was hanged, drawn and quartered at York 7 August 1679. In an

Charles II and the 'Popish Plot', 1660-1685

extraordinary gesture, Catholics were allowed to take away his remains in a cart for burial; sadly where that took place is unknown. His clothes and few possessions were sold to Catholics at extortionate prices. One of the martyr's hands is now preserved at Ampleforth Abbey, North Yorkshire. Few priests have been as much loved by their flock; a love that has endured to this day in the memory of the people of North Yorkshire. That Nicholas Postgate had to wait until 1987 to be beatified beggars belief.

Blessed Charles Meehan was born in Ireland c.1640. He became a Franciscan and completed his formation with the English friars at Douai. He was probably ordained in 1672. He lived for a time with the Franciscans at Louvain, in Germany and Rome. He set out to return to Ireland in June 1678. Fatefully for him, his ship ran aground on the North Wales coast and when he came ashore he was arrested at Denbigh. From his possessions it was determined that he was a priest and given the rampant anti-Catholic hysteria of the time he was condemned for his priesthood. He was hanged, drawn and quartered at Ruthin on 12 August 1679. On the scaffold he declared, 'Since God has been pleased to give me the grace of martyrdom, blessed be his Holy Name.'

Blessed Thomas Thwing was born in 1635 at Heworth, near York, the son of George Thwing of Heworth Hall and Kilton Castle and Anne, daughter of Sir John Gascoigne of Barnbow Hall, Barwick-in-Elmet. The Thwings were a great recusant family who had suffered for generations for adherence to their Faith. Many of them had been imprisoned and numerous members of the family lived vagrant lives to avoid conviction. It was at the house of William Thwing at Heworth that his sister, Ann, had been caught on 2 February 1593 sheltering Blessed Anthony Page of Harrow. [16] William was in York at the time, but when the searchers came to the house Father Page, who was hidden in a cavity under the haystack, was soon discovered. William was arrested, despite declaring his ignorance of the priest's presence. When he was put on trial, Ann, to protect her brother, protested he was unaware of Father Page in the house. As a result William was surprisingly acquitted. Ann was imprisoned in York, and was still there three years later, without ever having been brought to trial.

The Thwing family had already given a martyr to the Church; Thomas's uncle, Blessed Edward Thwing, executed at Lancaster in 1600. Thomas was educated at Saint-Omer and Douai. After ordination he returned to England in 1665 and acted as chaplain at Carlton

Charles II and the 'Popish Plot', 1660-1685

Towers, East Yorkshire, to the Stapleton family, who were his cousins. He established a school located at Quosque Hall, the Stapleton's Dower House. In collaboration with his maternal uncle, the deeply pious Sir Thomas Gascoigne, he was responsible for inviting Mary Ward's Institute of the Blessed Virgin to settle at Dolebank, Ripon in 1677 and later at the Bar, York, in a house donated by Sir Thomas. Three of Thomas Thwing's sisters were members of the community, which he served as chaplain. Sir Thomas Gascoigne had three brothers; Francis, the youngest, was a priest; John became abbot of Benedictine Lambspring, Germany and Michael was also a monk at the monastery. Two of Sir Thomas Gascoigne's employees - Robert Bolron and Lawrence Mowbray - had been dismissed for dishonesty and they sought revenge by latching onto the 'Plot'. Perhaps casting themselves in the roles of the Oates and Bedloe of Yorkshire they accused Sir Thomas, his daughter, Lady Anne Tempest, and their Catholic friends of being involved in a conspiracy to murder the King. On the night of 7 July 1679 Thwing was arrested with Sir Thomas at Barnbow Hall and imprisoned in York Castle. In November Sir Thomas, who was eighty-five years old, very lame and deaf, along with his daughter and Sir Miles Stapleton, was taken to London and arraigned for treason in January 1680. (Since 1676 Father John Lodge, whose alias was Bates, had been chaplain at Carlton Towers to Sir Miles Stapleton, who had helped pay for his education at Douai. Lodge was also arrested and imprisoned. How long he was in jail is not clear but he did not return to Carlton Towers until 1693 so it is likely he was a prisoner for all those years. Father Lodge was still active in Yorkshire in 1731.) Bolron and Mowbray provided the most bloodcurdling evidence against the accused. At the trial in January 1680 under Sir William Dolben and Sir Francis Pemberton, Protestant witnesses came forward to testify on behalf of Sir Thomas and against Bolron and Mowbray, revealing their true characters. As a result Sir Thomas was found not guilty. Lady Tempest and Sir Miles were sent back to York for trial with Thomas Thwing who had spent nearly a year in prison before being brought before the assizes on 17 March 1680. Many of the gentry summoned to the trial as jurors did not appear, indicating their reluctance to stand in judgement of the accused. The prosecuting attorney commented, 'I perceive the best gentlemen stay at home.' The jury was subject to so many challenges that the proceedings had to be abandoned until the next assizes in July. The 'evidence' produced against the prisoners was no more than a list of names of those Catholics willing to subscribe to defraying the cost of establishing the Institute of the Blessed Virgin in York. It was presented by the prosecution as a list of persons willing to

Charles II and the 'Popish Plot', 1660-1685

kill the King. The remainder of the prosecution case rested on the lies of Bolron. Nineteen Protestant witnesses came forward for the defence, including prominent pillars of society such as Sir Thomas Yarborough. Presiding at the trial were two Justice's of the King's Bench, Sir William Dolben - whose brother became Archbishop of York – and Sir Edward Atkyns, younger brother of Judge Sir Robert Atkyns. Dolben summed up impartially, pointing out the inconsistencies in the evidence. He conceded that the prosecution had failed and Lady Tempest and Sir Miles were acquitted. When he died in 1705 Sir Miles left Carlton Towers to his nephew Nicholas Errington of Northumberland. (How was he related to Blessed George Errington?) Sir Thomas Gascoigne died in 1686 at the age of ninety-three in retirement at the Benedictine monastery at Lambspring. Judged even by the normal standards of the day, Thomas Thwing's trial, again under Atkyns and Dolben, was a monumental farce, but he was condemned. Upon receiving the verdict, Thwing simply said, 'I am innocent'. The King ordered a stay of execution, but under pressure from the House of Commons, which passed a special remonstrance, this was withdrawn and the King signed the death warrant on 13 October. Thomas was hanged, drawn and quartered at York on 23 October 1680. His dismembered remains were buried in the churchyard of St Mary Castlegate, York. Thomas was the last of the long line of seminary priests to suffer martyrdom.

[13] St Oliver Plunket was born 1629 in County Meath into a wealthy family of Norman descent. In 1647 he entered the Irish College, Rome and was ordained in 1654. Because of the intense persecution in Ireland, where Catholicism had been outlawed, it was impossible for Oliver to return to his native country for many years. He served in Rome as a theology professor until appointed Archbishop of Armagh and Primate of All Ireland in July 1669. He arrived in Ireland in March 1670 and set about trying to reorganise the ravaged Church. Over the next four years he confirmed 480,000 Catholics. He founded an integrated Jesuit-run college in Drogheda for both Catholics and Protestants. When the Test Act came into force in 1673 Plunket had to go into hiding and his college was razed to the ground. With the advent of the 'Popish Plot' Archbishop Peter Talbot of Dublin was arrested and Plunket again went into hiding. He refused to abandon his flock and was imprisoned in Dublin Castle in 1679 when falsely accused by Arthur Capel, Earl of Essex of plotting a French invasion. Capel, who had been Lord Lieutenant of Ireland, hoped to resume that office by discrediting his successor, the Duke of Ormonde. Lord Shaftesbury,

knowing that no Irish jury would ever convict Plunket, had him removed to Newgate, London. At the first trial the grand jury found no case to answer but he was not released. His second trial, at Westminster Hall, has been described as a travesty of justice and a disgrace to the country, when he was denied the opportunity to call defence witnesses from Ireland. Gilbert Burnet attended the trial and was in no doubt as to Plunket's innocence, who he praised as a wise and sober man who wanted only to live peaceably and look after his flock. Sir Francis Pemberton presided and when passing sentence declared that Oliver's treason was his "setting up of your false religion." For the crime of 'promoting the Roman faith' Oliver was found guilty of high treason to which he responded *Deo Gratias*. Barillon, the French Ambassador, pleaded personally with King Charles for mercy but the King, while frankly acknowledging that he knew Plunket was innocent, felt that he could not take such a bold step at that time. Capel himself made a similar plea to Charles who rounded on him angrily declaring, "His blood be on your head; you could have saved him but would not, I would save him but dare not." Plunket was hanged, drawn and quartered at Tyburn on 1 July 1681; the last Catholic martyr to be put to death in England. His mutilated body was buried at St Giles-in-the-Fields but was exhumed in 1683 and taken to Lambspring Abbey, Germany. His head was taken to Rome and in 1921 it was enshrined in St Peter's Church, Drogheda, where it remains. Most of his body rests at Downside Abbey. Oliver was canonized in 1975.

14 The list of all those who suffered in the 'Plot' is too great to detail, but a small selection of those not already mentioned will serve to convey the extent of the endurance of the many who died in prison and/or from ill-treatment.

Venerable Thomas Bedingfeld SJ, real name Downes, chaplain to the Duke of York, died in the Gatehouse on 21 December 1678 while awaiting trial.

Venerable Francis Nevill SJ died in prison at Stafford in 1678.

Robert Pugh was born c.1610 in Caernarvonshire. Ordained in 1633 he joined the Society of Jesus but was dismissed from the order in 1645 for joining the Royalist army without permission. He worked on the mission in Wales and London. Arrested in December 1678 he was imprisoned in Newgate. While awaiting trial he died there of the harsh treatment to which he was subjected 22 January 1679.

Charles II and the 'Popish Plot', 1660-1685

Thomas Jenison SJ came from a wealthy family and renounced his inheritance in favour of his younger brother, Robert, who apostatised and gave evidence against him. After spending nearly a year in prison he died in jail in London 27 September 1679.

Placid Aldhelm, a Benedictine, was a convert minister. A chaplain to Queen Catherine, he died in Newgate in 1680.

Richard Birkett died in prison under sentence of death at Lancaster 1680.

Richard Lacy SJ (real name Prince) died in Newgate 11 March 1680.

John Morgan was born in London in 1627 and was ordained in 1654. Arrested and condemned in April 1679 he was reprieved by the King and died in Newgate 21 March 1680.

David Kemish or Kemys, Dominican, an old man at his trial in 1679. He had been confessor to Dowager Lady Arundell when arrested. He was too weak to stand and too deaf to hear. He died in Newgate a few days later. Tried with Kemish was the Benedictine, *Henry Starkey*. Born in Cheshire in 1612 he was ordained at Lisbon April 1638. He had served in the Royalist army in the Civil War and had a leg blown off by a cannonball. Because of his disability, he was refused entry to Douai but accepted by the Benedictines in 1649, taking the name Hugh. He returned to England in 1661 and was arrested in January 1679 and condemned to death but remained in Newgate until 1683. After release he lived in France, where he died in 1688.

William Atkins SJ died in prison at Stafford under sentence of death 17 March 1680 aged eighty. The bedridden Father Atkins was so feeble that he had to be carried into the courtroom and so deaf that he could not follow the proceedings at his trial in August 1679. When the verdict was delivered it had to be shouted into his ear and he thanked the judge.

Thomas Wilkinson SJ was born in Lancashire. He studied at Valladolid and was ordained at Segovia with John Plessington in 1662. Arrested in 1679 he was imprisoned at Morpeth, Northumberland, where he was poisoned by a doctor on 12 January 1681.

Edward Turner SJ died in the Gatehouse 19 March 1681.

Charles II and the 'Popish Plot', 1660-1685

William Allison was imprisoned in York Castle October 1679 and died a prisoner under sentence of death in 1681.

Benedict Constable, a Benedictine, died in prison at Durham 11 December 1683.

John Bully, born 1627 at Chideock, Dorset. He fought for the Royalists in the Civil War and was ordained at the Lateran, Rome, in 1654. He was arrested and imprisoned at Winchester in December 1678. He was tried at the Old Bailey in April 1681 when Miles Prance gave evidence against him. Condemned to death, he was not executed but kept in Newgate. In November 1681 he was transported to the Scilly Isles, where he died in 1687.

Andrew Bromwich was born at Oscott House, Handsworth, near Birmingham. He was condemned with William Atkins at Stafford in spite of taking the Test Oath. He remained in prison for nearly ten years. He died at Oscott House in 1702 and was buried in the Bromwich vault at Handsworth church. (The property at Oscott became the first seminary of that name until the new college was opened in 1844. It then became known as Old Oscott and was leased by Cardinal Nicholas Wiseman to John Henry Newman who re-named it Maryvale.)

William Bennet SJ (real name Bentney) was born in 1609 in Cheshire. He joined the Jesuits and served on the mission from 1640. He was arrested and imprisoned in Leicester jail. He was tried at Derby in March 1682 and condemned to death, but remanded back to Leicester. It seems likely that he was released on the accession of James II in 1685, but was re-arrested in 1688 and sent back to Leicester prison, where, kept in filthy conditions, he died on 30 or 31 October 1692, aged eighty-four.

[14] Father Charles Carne, born 1639, was the fifth son of William Carne, and his Catholic wife, Jane, of Nash Court, Glamorgan, Wales. Raised as Protestants, Charles and an elder brother converted and went to Douai in 1653. After his ordination Charles returned to England and became chaplain to the Monington family of Sarnesfield, Herefordshire. He was arrested during the 'Plot' furore and reportedly took the oath; it did not save him being imprisoned at Hereford. Charles expected that he would soon follow Kemble, but when tried at the assizes in August 1679 he was acquitted because of discrepancies in the evidence submitted. He continued his ministry and died at

Charles II and the 'Popish Plot', 1660-1685

Sarnesfield in 1712.

15 Scarisbrick alias Neville Jesuit priests included: Edward 1639-1708; he was one of Titus Oates' intended victims but survived to become a chaplain to James II. He died in Lancashire. Edward 1663-1735; he served in Derbyshire and at Bushey Hall, Watford. Edward 1698-1778; he was superior of the Derbyshire mission.

16 Blessed Anthony Page came from the well-known recusant family at Harrow-on-the-Hill.* He was educated at Christ Church, Oxford where he matriculated 23 November 1581. He entered the English College, Rheims, 30 September 1584, was ordained deacon at Laon in 1590 and priest at Rheims on 21 September 1591. In January 1592 he returned to England. He seems to have worked in Yorkshire and was reported as being at a house on the coast. His apostolate did not last very long because he was arrested early in 1593, during the massive general search of Yorkshire and Durham that took place, when hundreds of suspect houses were raided. Anthony Champney, who was his contemporary at Rheims, described Father Page as a wonderfully modest man with a winning personality and he seems to have been liked by his jailers, although every effort was made to get him to conform. While awaiting execution he wrote a number of letters that have survived to his family and friends, which were sent to Father Richard Holtby for re-direction. Anthony Page was martyred at York on 20 April 1593.

---

* As a footnote of history the Manor of Uxendon, Harrow passed from the Bellamy family to the Page family in the early 17th century. The Pages' were still at Uxendon in the late 18th century. There are Bellamy and Page graves and memorials at St Mary's parish church, Harrow-on-the-Hill. Sir Richard Page of Uxendon (1603-1653) was knighted in 1645 for his services to King Charles I at the battles of Edgehill and Newbury.

Epilogue

They shall fight against you, but they shall not prevail against you, for I am with you, says the Lord.

Jeremiah 1:19

There were great hopes when James II acceded to the throne: the first Catholic monarch for 127 years. In spite of his Catholicism he was genuinely welcomed, enjoying the support of the majority of the people who remembered him as a successful Lord High Admiral. However, James was very different from his brother in temperament. Charles was a consummate master of dissimulation, or put more bluntly, a capacity for telling lies when it suited political expediency. Hard working and conscientious, honest and forthright to the point of tactlessness, James did not share this aptitude with his brother. As a result he completely misread the mood of the times, believing that his welcome as King gave him a mandate to relieve and favour his fellow Catholics while at the same time continuing to protect the position of the Anglican Establishment. It did not. His imprudent determination to follow a policy of liberation for all, Protestant non-conformists as well as Catholics, brought down upon him the wrath of his enemies. Emboldened by the defeat of the rebellion against him in the summer of 1685 led by his bastard nephew, the Duke of Monmouth, James began to openly favour Catholics, appointing many to positions of authority. Catholics became university fellows, Lord-Lieutenants, JP's and judges, aldermen and mayors. What relief, albeit short-lived, Catholics must have felt when the oppression was lifted and the Benedictines, Jesuits and Franciscans established houses.

At Rome on 9 September 1685 Dr John Leyburn, nephew of Father George Leyburn, was consecrated Vicar Apostolic for the whole of England and Wales. Leyburn was born near Kendal, Westmorland in 1620. He was educated at Douai and returned to England and for about twelve years he was chaplain to Francis Browne, 3rd Viscount Montague and tutor to his son and heir. In 1670 he succeeded his uncle as President of Douai College. He resigned in 1676 and went to Rome where he became secretary to Cardinal Philip Howard. He arrived in London as Vicar Apostolic in October 1685 and was given lodgings at St James's Palace. He was said to go about 'in a long cassock and cloak, with a golden cross hanging to a black ribbon about his neck; and goes in a chair or sedan.' James attended Mass in public at Court in great splendour. The new royal chapel at Whitehall, which opened at Christmas 1686, was magnificently fitted out with white marble,

Epilogue

exquisite artworks and carvings by the incomparable Grinling Gibbons, as well as thrones for the King and Queen opposite the altar. John Evelyn, the diarist, went to hear the Italian music, appreciated the magnificence, but bewailed that he 'should ever have lived to see such things in the King of England's palace.' (In 1687 Christopher Wren was commissioned to enlarge the chapel which, sadly, was looted and destroyed in 1688.) The Jesuits were able to open churches as well as establishing free schools in London, Wolverhampton, Lincoln, Durham, Wales and elsewhere. Their substantial Savoy College on the bank of the River Thames was open to all, regardless of religion, and attracted hundreds of boys.

Contrary to the caricature of him painted by his Whig opponents, James was not the bigot presented in Protestant propaganda, which had a vested interest in maintaining the falsehood. He had genuine friendships with dissenters, including the Quaker William Penn, one of the future Founding Fathers of America. Hundreds of Quakers were released from imprisonment on James's accession. Penn probably influenced the drafting of the first Declaration of Indulgence for the Liberty of Conscience, which James issued on 4 April 1687. Penn retained his affection and friendship for James long after he had lost his throne. Indeed, Penn became a Jacobite, meeting up with fellow-sympathisers supporting the exiled Stuarts. The Declaration, the first real step towards establishing religious freedom, suspended all penal laws for failure to conform to the Church of England for Catholics, non-Anglican Protestant dissenters and Jews. It permitted everyone to worship wherever they saw fit and removed the requirement of taking religious oaths, such as the Test Act, before being employed in government or military offices. It is difficult to put a number on exactly how many people the Declaration was likely to benefit. It has been estimated that the Catholics accounted for about one-seventh of the population, and to these has to be added the various Protestant Dissenters. This attempt by James to secure toleration was interpreted by his enemies as a thinly disguised means of returning England to the obedience of Rome. It brought about the King's downfall. Perhaps if James had adopted a more cautious, longer term approach things might have been different. Cardinal Howard, Queen Mary and even the Pope, Blessed Innocent XI Odescalchi (1676-89) counselled moderation. On the other hand it probably would not have made any difference, as the anti-Catholic bigots were so implacable in their opposition. Even under James the Catholics were not free from prosecution under the penal laws. The Baptists and Quakers supported the King but, incredible though it may seem, there were actually groups of Dissenters, e.g. the

Epilogue

Presbyterians, whose hatred of Catholicism was so great that they were prepared to oppose James's Declaration, and thereby deny themselves of the benefits, if it meant sharing those benefits with the Catholics. It may have been that James was in a hurry for perfectly understandable reasons. His brother, Charles, had died at the age of fifty-three. He was fifty-one when he came to the throne; by the standards of his time that was old. Perhaps if he had been gifted with foresight to know that he had another sixteen years to live, he might have adopted a more *festina lente* approach.

Bishop John Leyburn faced an impossible task trying single-handedly to oversee the Church in England and Wales. In 1687, on a pastoral tour of Northern England, he had confirmed 21,000 people. He was a moderating influence, trying to curb the King's zeal for the Catholic cause, particularly with regard to his high-handed actions in installing Catholic fellows at Magdalen College, Oxford.

In January 1688 Pope Innocent XI agreed to divide the Church administration into four vicariates under the episcopal care of Vicars Apostolic. John Leyburn headed the London District. James Smith, President of Douai, was named for the Northern District. Smith, who was born at Winchester in 1645, was appointed President of Douai College in 1682. On 13 May 1688 he was consecrated by Archbishop Fernando d'Adda, the papal nuncio, in the royal chapel at Somerset House. Afterwards he made his way north to York where he was received in August by the Catholic clergy who sang a welcome *Te Deum*. On one of his pastoral visitations in Yorkshire he had his crozier vindictively confiscated by Thomas Osborne, Earl of Danby. Michael Ellis OSB, whose baptismal name was Philip, was a son of the Anglican rector of Waddesdon, Buckinghamshire. Ellis was allotted the Western District, also embracing Wales. While still a pupil at Westminster School he converted and in 1670, at the age of eighteen, became a Benedictine at St Gregory's, Douai. He returned to England in 1685 and became a court preacher to James II. He was consecrated by Archbishop d'Adda in May 1688. Bonaventure Giffard was appointed to the Midland District. Born at Wolverhampton he was sent to Douai with his brother, Andrew, to be educated. He became a Doctor of Divinity at the Sorbonne. Giffard was consecrated on 22 April 1688 in the royal chapel at Whitehall by Archbishop d'Adda in the presence of the King and Queen. The new bishops, who were granted a salary of £1,000 per annum, supplanted the contentious Chapter which had governed the English mission for many years.

When James tactlessly tried to reinforce his Declaration of Indulgence on 27 April 1688, Archbishop William Sancroft of

Epilogue

Canterbury, Thomas Ken of Bath and Wells and five other bishops opposed the King's wishes by refusing to read the Edict of Toleration, as instructed. James, determined to have his way, foolishly ordered their arrest and imprisonment. The 'Seven Bishops' were put on trial in June and they were acquitted. Public indignation was aroused on behalf of the Bishops, and as a result of the King's actions, the Anglican episcopate actually became suddenly popular, for probably the first (and only) time in the nation's history. (It is salutary to note that in 1689, when required to take the oath of allegiance to William and Mary, under the Protestant Succession Act of that year, five of these same bishops, including Sancroft and Ken, refused. Having taken an oath to James and his heirs they honourably refused to recognise his daughter, Mary, and her bisexual husband, William of Orange, as legitimate sovereigns, believing that James Francis Edward, the Prince of Wales, was the *de jure* King James III in succession to his father. The Bishops were deprived, and their example was followed by hundreds of Anglican clergy who were known as Non-Jurors. Many became poverty stricken and dependent upon charity having lost their livelihoods and sometimes had to endure persecution from the new government. As the Non-Juror bishops consecrated successors their schism from the Church of England continued for many years. Indeed, it lingered on until 1788 when, on the death of James II's grandson, Prince Charles Edward Stuart, 'Bonnie Prince Charlie', most of the Non-Jurors felt able to give their allegiance to George III.)

In today's more tolerant climate, James's religious policy of establishing a level playing field between the different religious communities strikes us as nothing more than long overdue common justice; but it was attempted far too insensitively and it proved to be his undoing. This was especially true of his attempt to repeal the Elizabethan statute 27. When it became clear that Parliament was unlikely to agree James committed the blunder of planning to 'pack' Parliament to get the measure through.

After miscarriages and the deaths of four children in infancy, the last straw for many English Protestants was the birth of a healthy Catholic son and heir to James and Mary in 1688. So the King's opponents entered into a conspiracy to dethrone him in favour of his dour Dutch Protestant nephew and son-in-law, William of Orange, and his long-suffering wife, Mary. Some of the conspirators may have been acting from genuine convictions, but most of them were seeking to preserve their own economic self-interest. Given the passage of time that had elapsed since the suppression of the religious houses and Rome's oft repeated acceptance of the *status quo*, it seems incredible that pending

Epilogue

James II's accession there were those who still feared their Church acquisitions would somehow be re-possessed. James had never given any indication that this was intended nonetheless prominent Parliamentarians expressed their anxieties that they might lose their property. John Hampden, supporting the Exclusion Bill, said, 'Can it be imagined we shall not pay severely for having shed so much blood of these martyrs as they call them and for having so long enjoyed their Holy Church land?' Gilbert Burnet fuelled these fears with propaganda claiming that under a Catholic king there was a threat to their property. When the Church's policy on the issue was re-stated Burnet's response was that popish guarantees should not be trusted. After the overthrow of the King it was left to Sir Edward Warcup to express the general relief felt when he wrote 'Now we may hope to call our Church lands our own again.' William of Orange landed at Torbay on 5 November to begin his bid for the throne. James had enjoyed recognition as a conspicuously brave man all his life but when the so-called 'Glorious Revolution' was launched his nerve inexplicably failed him. Perhaps it was the indefensible betrayal of the traitorous John Churchill, future Duke of Marlborough, or his abandonment by his own Protestant daughters, Mary and Anne, playing the roles of Goneril and Regan, that tipped the balance, but by the end of the year James had fled to France. Many followed the King's example; many of those who did not had arrest warrants issued or were arrested. Catholic chapels were attacked and destroyed. The Yorkshireman, Father Paul Stephenson, who had been appointed by James II a Public Preacher at the Catholic chapel in York in 1685, was arrested and imprisoned in the Kidcote and the castle. Father Ralph Clayton, who came from Shrewsbury, only returned to England in March 1688 as chaplain to Bishop Bonaventure Giffard. Ralph was arrested in Kent and imprisoned in Newgate. The layman, Henry Hills, was a London printer to Charles II and James II and had been master of the Stationer's Company in 1684. When he became a Catholic he suffered so much abuse he followed James into exile in 1688. The Jesuits from Savoy College left London but were arrested at Canterbury and imprisoned. Charles Palmer SJ, rector of the college was captured at Faversham and imprisoned at Newgate where he died in 1690 aged seventy-four.

Three of the Vicars Apostolic were arrested. John Leyburn and Bonaventure Giffard were detained at Faversham, Kent en route for Dover, intending to join King James. Leyburn was sent to the Tower and Giffard to Newgate and they remained prisoners until July 1690. Leyburn was outlawed in 1701 but he died peacefully in London in June 1702. In 1703 Giffard was appointed to succeed Leyburn in the

Epilogue

London District and from 1708 to 1713 he also had to govern the Western vicariate, assisted by his priest brother as his vicar-general. For years afterwards Giffard lived a hunted life, hounded from pillar to post, constantly having to move lodgings; frequently being hauled before the courts on the evidence of paid informers. Giffard died in 1734, aged ninety-two, having been Vicar Apostolic for forty-six years, and was buried in St Pancras churchyard alongside his brother, Andrew. (In 1909 the brothers' remains were removed to St Edmund's College, Ware.) Giffard was succeeded in the London District by his coadjutor, Benjamin Petre. Michael Ellis was sent to Newgate and when released went into exile, firstly at Saint-Germain and then Rome. His repeated requests to be allowed to return to England were refused. In 1708 he was appointed Bishop of Segni in Italy. He died in 1726. Bishop James Smith escaped and went into hiding in the north. He was never captured but carried out his religious duties in great secrecy. He sought refuge at the home of Francis Tunstall at Wycliffe, on the Yorkshire/Durham border. Here he remained until his death in May 1711.

With the departure of King James, the Catholic community was plunged into despair. James's Declaration of Indulgence became void under the deeply unpopular William of Orange. The new reign saw a recasting of the machinery of repression against Catholics. Superficially the new regime might have fostered a façade of toleration but in practice the persecution continued. In 1699 the recusancy laws were simplified with an Act 'for further preventing the growth of Popery' (11 & 12 Gul.III, 4) which actually increased the penalties on priests and Catholic schoolteachers. The confinement to a radius of five miles from home was reinforced and all recusants who neglected to take the new oath within six months of reaching the age of eighteen were rendered incapable for life of inheriting any property or of buying or selling land. It often came down to a matter of recusants being offered a new Oath of Allegiance to William and Mary, phrased in such a way that no faithful Catholic could take it, thereby ensuring not only a speedy conviction, but also social exclusion, and with it all hope of preferment. A reward of £100 was offered for the capture of a priest and Hurst Castle on the Solent was earmarked as a special place of imprisonment for Catholic clergy. A similar reward was available for the conviction of a Catholic sending children abroad to be educated. Any Catholic running a school could be imprisoned for life. Catholics continued to be subject to double taxation. Other petty restrictions were imposed such as a law against Catholics being allowed to own a horse worth more than £5.

In 1700 - twelve years after James II had attempted it - toleration

Epilogue

was extended to non-Anglican Protestants, but not to Catholics. Parliament passed a new law bypassing priesthood as such but making the saying of Mass a crime punishable by life imprisonment. The same Act forbade Catholics to own or inherit land, and Catholic heirs to property found themselves dispossessed. Under the solidly Anglican Queen Anne, nothing changed. Despite generally giving their political allegiance to the Stuarts, many Catholics refused to take the Oath of Allegiance to Anne because of its wording, although recusants were not unduly molested in her reign. Nonetheless there are many instances of priests being arrested; for example, the Yorkshireman, John Danby, who was imprisoned at York in 1708. There was only one new Act (12 Anne,2,c.14) which extended the existing laws against Catholics sending their children to be educated abroad. Anne, who declared her abhorrence of Catholicism, cynically and hypocritically approved the clause in the Treaty of Utrecht 1713, which guaranteed 'free exercise of their religion' to the Catholics of Gibraltar when Spain ceded the Rock to Britain: a freedom denied to her British subjects.

The early eighteenth century has generally been regarded as the nadir of the Catholic Church in Britain, when the numbers of priests declined and those remaining continued to be constantly harassed and imprisoned, some dying in jail under George II as late as the 1730's. The records show that in the seven years up to 1738 eighty-one priests had died, and in the same period only forty-eight new priests had been ordained. Repression of Catholics continued throughout the eighteenth century, albeit in methods that subtly differed from the crude persecution of the two previous centuries. The Anglican establishment was virulently anti-Catholic and regarded all papists as dangerous and incapable of responsible citizenship. The Archbishops of Canterbury were fond of lecturing the Catholic gentry on the obscurity in which they ought to live. The government of George I increased the fines on Catholics, particularly those caught teaching. It also increased the rewards paid to informers.

The failure of the two Jacobite rebellions dashed any lingering hopes of a Catholic Stuart restoration. In the aftermath of the 1715 rebellion there was a burst of renewed persecution. A number of priests were arrested, such as forty-six-year-old, Northumberland-born James Gardiner, and London-born John Verhuyck alias Liddell. William Caton from Upper Rawcliffe, Lancashire, who worked near his home around St Michael's-on-Wyre, was convicted at Lancaster in January 1716, as was William Winckley. Father Winckley lived with his brother, Edward, at Banister Hall, near Blackburn and because of their recusancy the estate was forfeited. William Quartermain or Wilmot,

Epilogue

(depending upon which was his true name and which his alias) was a Yorkshire priest ordained at Valladolid in 1676. He had been identified by Titus Oates as Wilmot alias Quartermain during the 'Plot'. He became secretary to Vicar Apostolic John Leyburn in 1685. He was arrested in 1716 at the Cross Keys inn, Holywell. The inn, run by Thomas Parry, regularly accommodated secular priests and had a chapel. Quatermain was betrayed by apostate priest Richard Hitchmough who stated that the inn actually belonged to the clergy and was rented from them by Parry. A priest of scandalous life in 1718 Hitchmough returned to Holywell, which had remained a recusant centre, and destroyed and plundered the Catholic chapels. Hitchmough was responsible for the arrest of several priests. They included Welshman Peter Wynne, a resident priest at Holywell, and seventy-three-year-old Peter Gooden, who ran a little private school near Lancaster and had already been apprehended in the Oates 'Plot'. The mission in and around Preston, Lancashire - where there had been support for the Jacobite rebels - was specially targeted. Catholic places of worship were destroyed, including the chapel at the ancient Ladyewell shrine at Fernyhalgh whose priest, the notable spiritual writer Christopher Tootell or Tuttell - who had served there since 1699 - had to go into hiding suffering many privations. On one occasion he hid for nine hours under a pile of hay in a remote barn. In 1723 he returned and rebuilt the chapel. He died there in 1727. (Ladyewell today is still a thriving pilgrimage centre. Its church, St Mary's, was built in 1795.)

Two statutes were passed by Parliament which ipso facto made all Catholics traitors and confirmed that two-thirds of the property of all convicted recusants belonged to the State.

In 1722 an Act 'for granting an aid to his Majesty by levying a tax upon Papists' (9 Geo. I, 18) came into force, imposing a special extra tax on Catholics, over and above the Land Tax, on which Catholics already paid double. The measure raised £100,000. One by product of this measure was that the survey conducted by the government into the value of Catholics' property, in order to levy the tax, gives us an indication of the number and geographical distribution of Catholics at the time. Yorkshire tops the list by far, followed by Lancashire and Staffordshire. The double Land Tax remained in force into the nineteenth century.

The 1745 rebellion failed to attract the support of the Catholics of the North of England, but large numbers of them were nonetheless summoned to take the Oath of Allegiance, and some of the prominent gentry were arrested, without any evidence of wrongdoing. Catholic

Epilogue

Mass centres - literally houses or cottages which were used for worship - were attacked by mobs, sacked and their contents publicly destroyed. Among those arrested in Yorkshire at the behest of paid informers were seven priests. One, the Dominican, John Green, apprehended near Morley, was fined and imprisoned for several months. The remaining six met with similar treatment. All confessed to being priests and remained in York Castle until 1747, when they were released on condition that they left the country.

In Queen Anne's reign there were said to be 20,000 Catholics in London and, despite an obvious increase in numbers, this figure was still being given in 1746 in the returns of the London Vicariate. The wealthier Catholics tended to live in Soho and frequented the various embassy chapels, such as the Sardinian chapel in Lincoln's Inn Fields, or Mass 'houses' in Westminster or the City. Where ever they attended Mass it remained a dangerous undertaking. Doorkeepers would be employed to check in worshippers and then would lock the door, signalling that it was deemed safe for Mass to begin.

Sporadic outbursts of active persecution continued such as that which took place in 1767, when several priests were prosecuted. Father James Webb had been appointed by Bishop Challoner priest in charge of the chapel of St Mary and St Michael in Virginia Street, close to the Thames in East London. Its congregation consisted for the most part of poorer labourers and dock workers. The chapel was entered from King's Head Alley, which enabled escape to be made through the warren of adjoining courts. Father Webb was arrested and spent seventeen months in Newgate before being brought to trial at Westminster on 25 June 1768 before William Murray, Lord Mansfield, the Lord Chief Justice. Mansfield was determined that the prosecution should fail. He castigated the informer who had obtained the £100 reward, rubbished the evidence and instructed the jury to acquit Webb; which they did. Father John Baptist Maloney, convicted of saying Mass at Croydon, was condemned to life imprisonment but banished after serving a few years of his sentence and ended his days in America. Although the old law carrying the death penalty was never again exercised incredibly it remained on the Statute Book until 1843.

150 years of persecution had taken its toll: worn down by the penalties inflicted upon them, many families finally conformed. Externally it appeared that the Church was dwindling into insignificance, but modern scholarship has tended to redress the balance of this depressing picture. Internally the Church remained spiritually vigorous, developing its own very English devotional traditions, and although growth was very patchy, in some of the larger

Epilogue

towns it actually showed a small numerical increase. Just how many Catholics there were is impossible to guess, but one estimate suggests that by the late eighteenth century there were between 50,000 and 60,000, about half of whom were in London. The Church was kept afloat largely by the remaining faithful Catholic gentry, many of whom, despite their impoverishment, managed to survive, often going into business or trade; and by the unassuming efforts of the Venerable Richard Challoner, by the time of whose death in 1781 at the age of ninety there was a glimmer of hope on the horizon.

In the teeth of much vocal opposition the first Catholic Relief Act was passed in 1778. A modest reform it repealed the legislation prescribing life imprisonment for priests and Catholic teachers and enabled Catholics to own land, but they were still not allowed to hold office or be free from double taxation. The reform provoked the notorious Gordon Riots in London in 1780 organised by the Protestant Association led by the deranged Lord George Gordon. His mob destroyed many Catholic places of worship, including the Virginia Street chapel and the Sardinian chapel. Even Lord Mansfield's house was attacked. From his secret lodgings the Vicar Apostolic, Bishop Challoner, could hear the baying mob that was searching for him. He escaped to Finchley where he hid until the riots were over. The aged bishop never recovered from the shock of the riots. Shortly afterwards he was seized with paralysis and died two days later. If anything the mayhem and wanton destruction only served to strengthen the resolve of those committed to Catholic relief. An Act of 1782 permitted Catholic schools. A new Relief Act followed in 1791 in which, momentously, priests were legally allowed to exercise their ministry and licensed Catholic chapels were permitted. It also entitled Catholics holding land over a stipulated value to vote. Catholics were at last enabled to serve on juries and to gain access to professions, such as the law, from which they had been excluded.

Religious refugees from revolutionary France greatly increased the numbers of priests; so many, in fact, there was a surplus and in certain locations, e.g. Barwick-in-Elmet, in the West Riding, camps were established to accommodate them. Then there were the immigrants from Ireland who swelled the numbers of Catholics, further increased by a growing influx of converts. In 1829 the Duke of Wellington's government passed the Catholic Emancipation Act. This removed many of the remaining restrictions on Catholics in the United Kingdom. Emancipation had been long in coming, but throughout all the desolate years of waiting Catholics knew from the teaching of the Church that Resurrection was only achieved by following the suffering *Via Crucis*

Epilogue

of Calvary. They took consolation from the assurances of Christ: 'Blessed are you when they shall revile you and persecute you and speak all that is evil against you, untruly, for my sake. Rejoice and be glad, for your reward is very great in heaven.' They may also have been heartened to read the comments about their Church from the influential historian Lord Macaulay as expressed in his 1840 *Essay on Leopold Von Ranke's History of the Popes during the Sixteenth and Seventeenth Centuries*. Macaulay was certainly no Catholic sympathiser, far from it; indeed, he was prone to the prejudices of his time and in the same essay bemoaned the fact that a 'more enlightened' world was not more favourable to Protestantism and unfavourable to Catholicism. Nonetheless he gave this appraisal:

> There is not, and there never was on this earth, a work of human policy so well deserving of examination as the Roman Catholic Church. The history of that Church joins together the two great ages of human civilisation. No other institution is left standing which carries the mind back to the times when the smoke of sacrifice rose from the Pantheon, and when camelopards and tigers bounded in the Flavian amphitheatre. The proudest royal houses are but of yesterday, when compared with the line of Supreme Pontiffs. That line we trace back in unbroken series, from the Pope who crowned Napoleon in the nineteenth century to the Pope who crowned Pepin in the eighth; and far beyond the time of Pepin the august dynasty extends ... The Papacy remains, not in decay, not a mere antique, but full of life and youthful vigour. The Catholic Church is still sending forth to the farthest ends of the world missionaries as zealous as those who landed in Kent with Augustine, and still confronting hostile kings with the same spirit with which she confronted Attila. The number of her children is greater than in any former age ... Her spiritual ascendancy extends over vast countries ... Nor do we seen any sign which indicates that the term of her long dominion is approaching. She saw the commencement of all the governments and of all the ecclesiastical establishments that now exist in the world; and we feel no assurance that she is not destined to see the end of them all. She was great and respected before the Saxon had set foot in Britain ... when Grecian eloquence still flourished at Antioch, when idols were still worshipped in the temple at Mecca. And she may still exist in undiminished vigour when some traveller from New Zealand shall, in the midst of a vast solitude, take his stand on a broken arch of London Bridge to sketch the ruins of St. Paul's.

In 1850, with the prior knowledge of the British Government, Blessed Pope Pius IX Mastai-Ferreti (1846-1878) restored the Catholic hierarchy. This was accompanied by 'No popery' demonstrations and accusations of papal aggression from the press, which triggered physical attacks on priests and convents. The Pope had sensitively ensured that none of the new bishops would use the titles of the ancient

Epilogue

sees now held by the Anglican Church. Nevertheless Parliament retaliated by passing the Ecclesiastical Titles Act in 1851. This made it a criminal offence for anyone outside the Church of England to use an episcopal title of any city or town in the United Kingdom. This meant that any Catholic bishop using a territorial title e.g. Westminster, was doing so illegally. (The Act was a dead letter. It was never legally enforced and was repealed in 1871.) While Edward Stanley, 14th Earl of Derby, was briefly Prime Minister in 1852 he engineered a royal proclamation banning Catholic processions and the wearing of religious dress in public by Catholics. This sparked a new wave of bigotry fostered by Orangemen in the Manchester and Liverpool areas. With the connivance of local police constables, who actively took part, churches were attacked and vandalised, the Sacred Hosts being scattered in the streets. Catholic schools and the homes of Catholics were ransacked and burned and the mindless violence led to loss of life. The *Manchester Guardian*, accusing Derby of loosing bigotry on the streets in order to shamefully court popularity, described the 'irretrievable disgrace' of the Protestant 'bullies and ruffians' who indulged in 'the most cruel and cowardly murder ... not in self-defence, but in brutal and licentious phrenzy.'

In this climate Bills were introduced in the House of Commons attacking convents, which were to be subject to compulsory regular inspections, and seeking to impose 12 months imprisonment with hard labour for any nuns who refused to co-operate. There were even calls for convents to be abolished. Such was the hate-filled hostility towards women religious that when the Sisters of Mercy volunteered to work in the horror of the hospitals of the Crimea they were vilified, and Florence Nightingale came in for vitriolic criticism from press and politicians for working with them. In fact, the sisters, who formed the hard core of the nursing staff at all six hospitals 1855-56, were the unsung heroines of the Crimean War.

In modern times the site of the Tyburn gallows has been marked by a memorial stone in the traffic island at the junction of Edgware Road and Bayswater Road, a few yards beyond Marble Arch. Some 300 yards further up the road is Tyburn Convent, a haven of tranquillity amidst the traffic noise of London, where the nuns maintain unceasing prayer before the Blessed Sacrament, night and day. Founded in 1903 by the Benedictine Adorers of the Sacred Heart of Jesus the convent is a shrine to the martyrs of whom they possess many relics. Although it was unknown to the nuns at the time of their foundation it was the fulfilment of a prophesy made in 1585 by a Marian priest, Father Gregory Gunne, who before he was banished predicted that one day a

Epilogue

convent would stand at Tyburn.

Today, in a world of ungodly scepticism, the Catholics of England and Wales enjoy the blessing of being able to openly practise their Faith. How little in these days of freedom can we even begin to imagine what the grinding tyranny of two centuries of persecution meant to the faithful few.

The Forty Martyrs came from every walk of life from the highest nobility to the lowest of the poor. Regardless of their station, their faith clearly meant everything to them, to the extent of ultimately giving their lives for it. Through all their vicissitudes they lived their faith wholeheartedly, often full of humour. The martyrs - to borrow from the Rule of St Benedict - were 'Men who have no other purpose in life but God. Is there any other purpose for anyone?' We can find solace in the reflections of Cardinal William Allen on the martyrs; that we should have joy in the Lord 'because the victory won by Christ's confessors predominates over earthly sorrow for the grievousness of their suffering.'

May the sacrifices they and our Catholic forebears made never be forgotten.

Appendix 1

The Ikon of the Forty Martyrs of England and Wales

The ikon was painted, or more correctly 'written'- to use the traditional, designation - because an ikon is meant to be 'read', by Anna Dimascio who came into the Roman Catholic Church from our sister Orthodox Church. The English word ikon is derived from the Greek *eikon*, meaning an image. It is the same word used in the Bible in Genesis: *'God created man in His image'* and again in St Paul's letter to the Colossians: *'Jesus is the image of the invisible God.'* So in Christian tradition an ikon is a holy image representing Christ, the Mother of God, the saints or the mysteries of the Faith. Ikons, the most ancient form of Christian art, date back to apostolic times.

I had been researching the project of an ikon for many years ever since attending the canonization of the Forty Martyrs in Rome in October 1970. Anna and I collaborated to translate the fruits of that research into iconography. Great care was taken to remain faithful to historical authenticity wherever possible e.g. costume. At the same time we had to ensure that this was not achieved at the expense of the ikon failing to maintain the integrity of true ikonographic traditions. One source of reference was the, albeit stylised, contemporary portraits and engravings of some of the martyrs, particularly those of the Stuart period, but not with the aim of reproducing an exact likeness.

Many hours were spent in composing harmonious groupings of the forty saints so that the historical and spiritual affinities amongst them were manifest. For example, the six Welsh martyrs are grouped together as are the three women; likewise those who shed their blood together or knew each other personally. The ikon, measuring 18 x 24 inches, took one year to complete and was solemnly blessed with the prescribed ritual of incense and holy water, by Bishop Alan Clark of East Anglia in his domestic chapel at Norwich in January 1992. It was now a holy object for prayer and the veneration of the saints whose images were depicted.

Although copyright, I have given reproductions of the ikon to many churches, abbeys and schools - both Catholic and Anglican - throughout England and Wales. Although no reproduction can hope to do justice to the vibrant richness of the original, the ikon has been featured in newspapers, magazines and diocesan year books. A tribute, I hope, to the extraordinarily gifted Anna Dimascio, who sadly died of cancer at a tragically young age.

Appendix 2

Prayer to the Forty Martyrs of England and Wales

O God, almighty and everlasting, you fashioned the forty holy martyrs of England and Wales after the likeness of your Son, who is glorified through His death for the world's salvation: listen now to their prayers, and grant us the strength that their love and faith imparts, so that we may come to the fullness of life. Through Jesus Christ our Lord. Amen

Appendix 3

Beatification and Canonization

The Catholic Church teaches that there is a close personal, spiritual union between Heaven and earth; that all those who have died and whose souls have attained the Beatific Vision (i.e. enjoying the immediate knowledge of God, "face to face") are able, through prayerful intercession, to help those on earth. The doctrine, expressed in the Creed as the Communion of Saints, is intimately bound up with the doctrine of the Church as the Mystical Body of Christ, present on earth and in Heaven.

All who attain Heaven are saints and it is perfectly permissible for anyone to ask privately for the intercession of someone they believe to be a saint. Public veneration is a different matter, requiring the official sanction of the Church after the appropriate procedures laid down in Canon Law. The process is usually initiated by the bishop of the diocese in which the candidate lived and/or died. In cases of martyrdom the process is primarily concerned with proving the fact of martyrdom. The rules laid down by Pope Benedict XIV Lambertini (1740-58) require proof not only that the person actually suffered death but that the death was accepted with resignation; that it was inflicted out of hatred for the Faith or its practice. Furthermore, the mindset of both victim and persecutor is also examined because the victim must not have borne any rancour towards their persecutor but rather shown love and forgiveness. After exhaustive enquiries and examination of all available evidence that meet the criteria the person can be declared Blessed. Canonization - when the person is declared a Saint - is an even more stringent process in which the Church usually requires evidence of two miracles.

Appendix 4

The Seal of Confession

Although it caused him anguish Henry Garnet knew he was on sure ground in adopting the course he took. From time immemorial the Catholic Church has held to the absolute confidentiality of confession. The Fourth Lateran Council of 1215 summed up that teaching:

Let the priest absolutely beware that he does not by word or sign or by any manner whatever in any way betray the sinner: but if he should happen to need wiser counsel let him cautiously seek the same without any mention of person. For whoever shall dare to reveal a sin disclosed to him in the tribunal of penance we decree that he shall be not only deposed from the priestly office but that he shall be sent into the confinement of a monastery to do perpetual penance.

Current Canon Law (983) states, 'The sacramental seal is inviolable; therefore it is absolutely forbidden for a confessor to betray in any way a penitent in words or in any manner *and for any reason.*' [Author's italics] A priest who breaks the confessional seal is subject to automatic excommunication. There may be cases where things said in confession may be revealed but always and only with the penitent's express permission and without revealing the penitent's identity.

Before the Reformation in England the issue was clear; the state accepted the Canon Law of the Church, but since the Reformation the legal position has been a rather "grey area." Some countries respect the confessional seal in varying degrees but in the United Kingdom there is no legislation on the subject of disclosure of information obtained in religious confession. It appears that a priest has no legal right to insist on the privilege of absolute confessional confidentiality. The fundamental principle under the rules of evidence requires that any witness shall provide the whole truth as it is known to him and this applies to everyone. In the 19th and 20th centuries there were a number of cases involving both Catholic priests and Anglican clergy in which differing interpretations were reached by the Courts depending upon the circumstances of the particular trial. Some judges accepted the plea of confidentiality and did not press the matter; others insisted that the priest witness was compelled to reveal what he had heard. Priests were certainly committed for contempt of court for refusing to disclose information gained in confession.

In his treatise *The Principles of the Law of Evidence,* William Mawdesley Best (1809-69) expresses the opinion that the priest privilege should not only be granted, but that there are grounds for believing that the right to the privilege is an existing one.

In 1873 judge Sir Robert Phillimore in his *The Ecclesiastical Law of the Church of England,* wrote: It seems to me at least not improbable that, when this question is again raised in an English court of justice, that court will decide it in favour of the inviolability of the confession, and expound the law so as to make it in harmony with that of almost every other Christian state.

Appendix 5

Extra Ecclesiam Nulla Salus – outside the church there is no salvation

As will already have been noted, similar remarks were made by several other martyrs. They have to be understood in their proper theological context. The teaching of the Catholic Church on the matter is quite straightforward. Father Edward Hawarden (1662-1735) a prolific and learned writer - and an ecumenist before his time - clearly explained it in his work of 1728, *Catholics not uncharitable in saying that none are saved outside the Catholic Communion*. As there is only one baptism and one Church - the Catholic Church - baptism makes the recipient of the Sacrament a member of the Catholic Church as all profess in the Creed: *unam, sanctam, catholicam et apostolicam Ecclesiam*. Only by formal apostasy is membership of that Church lost.

In his encyclical of August 1863, *Quanto conficiamur moerore (On promotion of false doctrines)* that arch-conservative, Blessed Pope Pius IX, clearly enunciated that not everyone outside the Church would be damned, without compromising the fundamental principle that outside the Church there is no salvation; a precept which is so evidently in accordance with both Christ's explicit teaching in the Gospels and St Paul's letter to the Ephesians. 'There are', Pius writes, 'those who are struggling with invincible ignorance about our most holy religion. Sincerely observing the natural law and its precepts inscribed by God on all hearts ... they live honest lives and are able to attain eternal life by the efficacious virtue of divine light and grace. Because God knows, searches and understands the minds, hearts, thoughts and nature of all, his supreme goodness and mercy will by no means permit anyone at all who is not guilty of deliberate sin to suffer eternal punishment ... God forbid that the children of the Catholic Church should even in any way be unfriendly to those who are not all united to us by the same bonds of faith and love. On the contrary, let them be eager always to attend to their needs with all the kind services of Christian charity ... and strive to guide them back to Catholic truth and to their most loving Mother who is ever holding out her maternal arms to receive them lovingly back into her fold. Thus, firmly founded in faith, hope and charity and fruitful in every good work, they will gain eternal salvation.' Or put most simply, those in invincible ignorance of the true faith will not be held guilty of this by God.

The Second Vatican Council reiterated this teaching most forcefully.

In *Nostra aetate,* its Declaration on the Relation of the Church to Non-Christian Religions proclaimed by Pope Paul VI in October 1965, we read that the Church, 'regards with sincere reverence those ways of conduct and of life, those precepts and teachings which, though differing in many aspects from the ones she holds and sets forth, nonetheless often reflect a ray of that Truth which enlightens all men.' The Council did not suggest that non-Catholic religions are equal to the Church, but it recognised that those religions may possess a reflection of the truth. That is summed up in *Lumen Gentium,* the Council's Dogmatic Constitution on the Church promulgated in November 1964. 'The sole Church of Christ which in the creed we profess to be one, holy, catholic and apostolic ... subsists in the Catholic Church ... Nevertheless, many elements of sanctification and of truth are found outside its visible confines.'

Finally, *The Catechism of the Catholic Church*, promulgated by Pope John Paul II in 1997 states, 'How are we to understand this affirmation, often repeated by the Church Fathers? ... This affirmation is not aimed at those, who through no fault of their own, do not know Christ and His Church. Those who ... nevertheless seek God with a sincere heart, and, moved by grace, try in their actions to do His will as they know it through the dictates of their conscience - those too may achieve eternal salvation ... The Catholic Church recognises in other religions that search, among shadows and images, for the God who is unknown yet near since he gives life and breath and all things and wants all men to be saved. Thus, the Church considers all goodness and truth found in these religions as a preparation for the Gospel and given by him who enlightens all men that they may at length have life.'

List of Sources

Abrami, J, O.Carm., *St Margaret Clitherow,* Carmelite Press, 1980
Ackroyd, P, *The Life of Thomas More,* Chatto & Windus, 1998
Acts of the Privy Council of England: New Series, Dasent, J R, [ed.] 32 vols., HMSO, 1890-1918
Allen, Cardinal William, *A Brief History of the Glorious Martyrdom of the Twelve Reverend Priests: Father Edmund Campion and his Companions,* 1582, edited by J H Pollen SJ, Burns & Oates, 1908
------, *Letters and Memorials of Cardinal William Allen,* edited by Fathers of the London Oratory. *(Records of the English Catholics under the Penal Laws II)* David Nutt, 1882
Anglo, S, *Images of Tudor Kingship,* Seaby, 1992
Anon, *Jesuits in Conflict: Historic Facts Illustrative of the labours and sufferings of the English Mission and the Province of the Society of Jesus in the Times of Queen Elizabeth and her Successors. First Series.* Burns & Oates, 1873
Anstruther G, OP, *The Seminary Priests*
------, *vol.1 Elizabethan,* St Edmunds College, Ware, 1968
------, *vol.2 The Early Stuarts,* Mayhew-McCrimmon, 1975
------, *vol.3 1660-1715,* Mayhew-McCrimmon, 1976
------, *A Hundred Homeless Years,* Blackfriars, 1958
------, *Vaux of Harrowden,* R H Johns, Newport, 1953
Ashley, M, *The English Civil War,* Sutton, Stroud, 1990
------, *Charles II,* Weidenfeld & Nicholson, 1971
------, *James II,* J M Dent, 1977
------, *Charles I and Oliver Cromwell,* Methuen, London, 1987
Atteridge, A H, *The Elizabethan Persecution,* Harding & More, 1928
Aveling, Dom J C H, OSB, *The Catholic Recusants of the West Riding of Yorkshire 1558-1790.* Proceedings of the Leeds Philosophical & Literary Society, 1963
------, *Northern Catholics: the Catholic Recusants of the North Riding of Yorkshire,* London, 1966
------, *The Handle and the Axe: Catholic Recusants from Reformation to Emancipation,* Blond & Briggs, 1976
------, *Catholic Recusancy in the City of York 1558-179,* Catholic Record Society, 1970
------, *Post Reformation Catholicism in East Yorkshire, 1558-1790* East Yorkshire local History Series No.11, 1960
Baskerville, G, *English Monks and the Suppression of the Monasteries,* London, 1937
Bassett, B SJ, *The English Jesuits,* Burns & Oates, 1967
Baumer, F, le van, *The Early Tudor Theory of Kingship,* New Haven, 1940
Bellamy, J, *The Tudor Law of Treason: an Introduction,* Routledge & Kegan Paul, London, 1979

List of Sources

Belloc, H, *James II,* Philadelphia, J.B.Lippincott Co., 1928
------, *How the Reformation Happened,* New York, R.M.McBride, 1928
Bernard, G W, *The king's reformation: Henry VIII and the making of the English Church,* Yale UP, 2005
------, *The Tudor Nobility,* Manchester UP, 1992
Berrington, J, *The Memoirs of Gregorio Panzani: Birmingham, 1793,* Gregg, 1970
Betts, J R, *Blessed Peter Wright SJ,* Northampton, The Becket Press, 1997
Bingham, C, *James VI of Scotland,* Weidenfeld & Nicholson, 1979
------, *James I of England,* Weidenfeld & Nicholson, 1981
Birt, H N, *The Elizabethan Religious Settlement,* Bell, 1907
Black, J B, *The Reign of Elizabeth, 1558-1603,* 2nd ed. Oxford Clarendon Press, 1959
Booty, J E, *John Jewel as Apologist for the Church of England,* SPCK, 1963
Bossy, J, *The English Catholic Community 1570-1850,* Darton, Longman Todd, 1975
------, *Under the Molehill: An Elizabethan Spy Story,* Yale UP, 2002
Boyan, P A & Lamb, G R, *Francis Tregian: Cornish Recusant,* Sheed & Ward, 1955
Bridgett, T E, CSSR, and Knox, T F, *Queen Elizabeth and the Catholic Hierarchy,* Burns & Oates, 1889
Brooks, F W, *York and the Council of the North,* St Anthony's Press, 1954
Browning, A, *The Age of Elizabeth,* London, T.Nelson, 1935
Bruce, M L, *Anne Boleyn,* Harper Collins, 1972
------, *The Making of Henry VIII,* London, 1977
Bryant, Sir A, *Charles II,* London, 1935 [rev.ed.] Cassell & Co., 1955
Budiansky, S, *Her Majesty's Spymaster: Elizabeth I, Sir Francis Walsingham and the Birth of Modern Espionage,* Viking, 2005
Burnet, G, *History of the Reformation of the Church of England,* ed. Pocock, Oxford, 1865
Burns, G, *Gibbets and Gallows:The Story of Edmund Arrowsmith* Burns & Oates, 1944
Burton, E H, *The Life and Times of Bishop Challoner (1691-1781)* 2 vols., Longmans, Green & Co, 1909
Burton, E H, and Pollen, J H, SJ, *Lives of the English Martyrs. 2nd series the Venerable Martyrs 1583-88,* London, 1914
Bush, M, *The Pilgrimage of Grace: A Study of the Rebel Armies 1536* Manchester University Press, 1996
------, and D Bownes, *The Defeat of the Pilgrimage of Grace,* Hull, 1999
Butler, A, *The Lives of the Saints,* 4 vols., 1756-59, edited and revised by H J Thurston SJ and D Attwater, Burns Oates, 1986 ed.
Calendar of State Papers, Domestic Series, of the Reigns of Edward VI, Mary, Elizabeth, James I, 1547-1625, preserved at the Public Record Office, edited by R Lemon, 11 vols., Longman Green,1856-1865

List of Sources

Calendar of State Papers, Domestic Series, of the reign of Charles I, 1625-1649 preserved at the Public Record Office, 23 vols., Nendeln, Liechtenstein, Kraus Reprint, 1967

Calendar of State Papers, Domestic Series, of the reign of Charles II, preserved at the Public Record Office, ed. M A Everett Green, Vaduz, Kraus Reprint, 1965

Camden, W, *Annales of Queen Elizabeth*, ed. W T MacCaffrey, University of Chicago Press, 1970

Camm, Dom B, OSB, *Forgotten Shrines*, Macdonald & Evans, 1910

------, *Courtier, Monk and Martyr: Blessed Sebastian Newdigate*, Art and Book Company, London, 1901

------, *A Benedictine Martyr in England: Dom John Roberts*, Bliss & Sands, 1897

------, [ed.] *Lives of the Martyrs declared Blessed by Pope Leo XIII in 1886 & 1895*, 2 vols., London, 1904-05

------, *Tyburn and the English Martyrs*, 3rd edition. Burns, Oates & Washbourne, 1924

Campion, E, SJ, *Ten Reasons Proposed to his Adversaries for Disputation in the Name of Faith,* transl. by J Rickely, SJ, Manresa Press, 1914

Caraman, P, SJ, *A Study in Friendship: Robert Southwell & Henry Garnet*, India, 1991

------, *The Western Rising 1549,* West Country Books, 1991

------, *Henry Garnet 1555-1606 and the Gunpowder Plot*, Longmans, Green & Co., 1964

------, *Henry Morse: Priest of the Plague*, Longmans, Green & Co., 1957

------, [ed.] *The Other Face: Catholic Life under Elizabeth I ,* Longmans, Green & Co.,1960

------, [ed.] *The Years of Siege: Catholic life from James I to Cromwell* Longmans, Green & Co., 1966

------, [ed.] *William Weston: the Autobiography of an Elizabethan* Longmans, Green & Co., 1955

Carlton, C, *Charles I: The Personal Monarch,* Routledge, Kegan Paul, 1983

Carr, D, *The Reformation in England: To the Accession of Elizabeth I* St Martin's Press, New York, 1968

Catholic Encyclopaedia, Robert Appleton Co., New York, 1913

Catholic Record Society, *Documents Relating to the English Martyrs*

Catholic Record Society: x-xi *The Douai College Diaries 1598-1654,* edited by Burton & T L Williams, 1911

------, xxx, *Registers of the English College, Valladolid 1589-1862,* edited by E Henson, 1930

------, xlvii-xlviii, *History of the English Persecution of Catholics and the Presbyterian Plot,* by Warner, J, edited by T A Birrell, 2 vols. 1953 & 1955

------, Vol.21, *Ven.Philip Howard, Earl of Arundel,* ed. J H Pollen SJ and W MacMahon SJ, 1919

List of Sources

Cavendish, G, *The Life and Death of Cardinal Wolsey*, ed.Sylvester, E.E.T.S., 1959
Chadwick, H, *St Omers to Stonyhurst: A History of Two Centuries*, Burns & Oates, 1962
Chadwick, O, *The Reformation*, Pelican History Series, 1964
Challoner, Bishop, *Memoirs of Missionary Priests Secular as well as Regular and of Catholics of both sexes that have suffered death in England on religious accounts 1577-1681*, issued 1741 new edition revised and corrected by J H Pollen, Burns, Oates & Washbourne, 1924
Chambers, M C E, *The Life of Mary Ward, 1585-1645*, 2 vols., ed. H J Coleridge SJ, Burns & Oates, 1882
Chambers, R W, *Thomas More*, Jonathan Cape, 1935
Chapman, H W, *Lady Jane Grey*, Jonathan Cape, 1962
Chauncy, Dom M, *The History of the Sufferings of Eighteen Carthusians in England*, translated from Latin, Burns, Oates & Washbourne, 1890
Chronicle of the Greyfriars of London, ed. J G Nichols, Camden Society Old Series, vol.53, London, 1852
Clark, F L, *William Warham, Archbishop of Canterbury*, Oxford, 1993
Clark, J S, [ed.], *The Life of James II, collected out of Memoirs Writ of His own Hand*, 2 vols., London, 1816
Clayton, J, *The Historic Basis of Anglicanism: A Short Survey of the Foundations of the Anglican Communion*, Sands, 1925
Cobbet, W, *Complete Collection of State Trials*, vols. III and VII, London, R Bagshaw, 1809-1828
------, *A History of the Protestant Reformation in England and Ireland*, Burns, Oates & Washbourne, 1929
Collins, T, *Martyr in Scotland: The Life and Times of John Ogilvie*, Burns Oates, 1955
Connelly, R, *The Eighty-Five Martyrs*, McCrimmons, 1987
------, *No Greater Love: Martyrs of the Middlesbrough Diocese*, McCrimmons, 1987
------, *Women of the Catholic Resistance 1540-1680*, Pentland Press, 1999
Constant, G, *The Reformation in England. I The English Schism: Henry VIII*, transl. by E Scantlebury, London, 1934
Cornwall, J, *The Revolt of the Peasantry 1549*, Boston, Routledge and Kegan Paul, 1977
Courson R. de, *The Condition of English Catholics under Charles II*, Translated by Mrs F.Raymond-Barker, CTS, London, 1899
Cox, J C, Rev., *Three Centuries of Derbyshire Annals*, Bemrose and Sons, London, 1890
Crabites, P, *Clement VII and Henry VIII*, Routledge, 1936
Cross, C, *The Puritan Earl, The Life of Henry Hastings, Third Earl of Huntingdon, 1536-1595*, St Martin's Press, New York, 1965
Davey, F, *Blessed Cuthbert Mayne*, Longmans, 1960
Davies, M, *St John Fisher*, The Neumann Press, 1998

List of Sources

De Silva, A [ed.[*The Last Letters of Thomas More,* Wm.B.Erdmans Publishing, Michigan, 2000
Devlin, C, SJ, *The Life of Robert Southwell, Poet & Martyr,* Sidgwick and Jackson, 1967
Dickens, A G, *The English Reformation,* Batsford, 1989
------, *Thomas Cromwell and the English Reformation,* English Universities Press, 1959
Dictionary of National Biography, new ed., eds. H G Matthews and B Harrison, Oxford University Press, 2004
Dixon, Watson R, *History of the Church of England from the abolition of the Roman jurisdiction 1529-1570,* 6 vols. Smith Elders & Co, G.Rutledge & Sons; Oxford Clarendon Press, 1895-1902
Dodd, C [vere H Tootell], *History of England 1500-1688,* Wolverhampton 1742/London 1839-40, with Notes, Additions and a Continuation by Rev. M A Tierney, 5 vols., reprinted 1971
Dodds, M H & R, *The Pilgrimage of Grace 1536-37 and the Exeter Conspiracy 1538,* 2 vols., Cambridge, 1915
Doernberg, E, *Henry VIII and Luther,* Stanford University Press, 1961
Duffy, E, *The Stripping of the Altars,* Yale University Press, 1992
------, [ed.] *Challoner and His Church. A Catholic bishop in Georgian England,* Darton, Longman and Todd, 1981
------, *Fires of Faith,* Yale University Press, 2009
------, *Voices of Morebath: Reformation and Rebellion in an English Village,* Yale UP, 2001
Dugmore, C W, *The Mass and the English Reformers,* Macmillan, 1958
Dures, A, *English Catholicism 1558-1642: community and change,* London, 1983
Edwards F, SJ, *The Jesuits in England from 1580 to Present Day,* Burns & Oates, 1985
------, *Guy Fawkes: The Real Story of the Gunpowder Plot?* London, Hart-Davis, 1969
------, *Robert Persons: The Biography of an Elizabethan Jesuit, 1546*-1610, Institute of Jesuit Sources, 1995
------, [ed. & transl.] *The Elizabethan Jesuits*: *Historia Missionis Anglicanae Societas Jesu, 1660* of Henry More, Phillimore, 1981
------, *The Marvellous Chance; Thomas Howard, Fourth Duke of Norfolk and the Ridolphi Plot,* Hart-Davis, 1968
------, *Plots and Plotters in the Reign of Elizabeth I,* Four Courts, 2002
------, [ed.] *The Gunpowder Plot: The Narrative of Oswald Tesimond, alias Greenway,* Folio Society, 1973
Ellis, T P, *The Catholic Martyrs of Wales,* 1932
Elton, G R, *Reform and Reformation 1509-1558,* Harvard University Press, 1977
------, [ed.] *The Reformation 1520-1559,* Cambridge University Press, 1990

List of Sources

------, *The Tudor Constitution: Documents and Commentary*, 2nd ed. Cambridge University Press, 1982
Emmison, F G, *Tudor Secretary: Sir William Petre at Court and Home*, Harvard University Press, 1961
Encyclopaedia Britannica
English Historical Documents Williams, C H, [ed] *1485-1558,* Eyre & Spottiswoode, London, 1967
Erickson, C, *Bloody Mary*, John Dent, 1978
Evelyn, J, *The Diary*, Bray, W, 2 vols., London, 1901
Faludy, G, *Erasmus of Rotterdam*, Eyre & Spottiswoode, 1970
Farmer, D H, [ed.], *Oxford Dictionary of Saints,* 5th ed., 2003
Fea, A, *Secret Chambers and Hiding Places,* 3rd revised ed., London, 1908
Fincham, K, [ed.] *The Early Stuart Church 1603-1642,* Macmillan, 1993
Fletcher, A and D MacCulloch, *Tudor Rebellions*, London, 1997
Foley, H SJ, *Records of the English Province of the Society of Jesus,* 8 vols., Manresa Press, 1877-1884
Foss, E, *Biographical Dictionary of the Judges of England 1066-1870* Longman, Brown, Green & Longmans, London, 9 vols., 1848-1870
Foxe, J, *The Book of Martyrs,* ed. Pratt, 8 vols., London, 1874
Fraser, A, *Mary, Queen of Scots*, Weidenfeld & Nicholson, 1969
------, *The Gunpowder Plot: Terror and Faith in 1605*, Weidenfeld & Nicholson, 1996
------, *King Charles II*, Weidenfeld & Nicholson, 1979
------, *Cromwell Our Chief of Men*, Weidenfeld & Nicholson, 1973
Frere, W H, *The Marian Reaction*, SPCK, London, 1896
Froude, J A, *History of England from the Fall of Wolsey to the Defeat of the Spanish Armada,* 1856-70, vols. vii-xii, Everyman's Library
------, *The Divorce of Catherine of Aragon*, London, 1891
Fullerton, G, *The Life of Luisa de Carvajal,* Burns & Oates, 1873
Gamache, Father Cyprien de OFM Cap, *Memoirs of the Mission in England of the Capuchin Friars of the Province of Paris from the year 1630 to 1669, as Translated in the Court and Times of Charles I,* London, 1848
Gardiner, S R, *What the Gunpowder Plot was,* Longmans, Green & Co.1897
------, *History of England, 1603-1607,* London, 1883
Gasquet, Cardinal F A, *A History of the Venerable English College, Rome*, London, Longmans, Green & Co., 1920
------, *Henry VIII and the English Monasteries,* G Bell, London, 1910
------, *The Last Abbot of Glastonbury*, George Bell & Sons, 1908
------, *The Greater Abbeys of England*, Chatto & Windus, 1922
------, *English Monastic Life*, Methuen, 1924
Gee, H, *The Elizabethan Clergy and the Settlement of Religion 1558-1564*, Oxford Clarendon Press, 1898
Gennings, J, *The Life of Edmund Gennings*, Burns & Oates, London, 1887
Gerard, J, SJ, *The Autobiography of an Elizabethan*, transl. and ed. by P Caraman, SJ, Longmans, Green & Co., 1951

List of Sources

------, *A Narrative of the Gunpowder Plot,* Morris J, SJ, [ed.], in *The Condition of English Catholics.* 2nd ed., Longmans, Green & Co., 1872

Gillow, J, *A Literary and Biographical History or Bibliographical Dictionary of English Catholics,* 5 vols., Burns Oates, 1885-1902 ed.

------, *The Haydock Papers: A Glimpse into English Catholic Life under the Shade of Persecution,* Burns & Oates, 1888

Graves, Law, T, [ed.] *A Historical Sketch of the Conflicts between Jesuits and Seculars in the Reign of Queen Elizabeth,* David Nutt, 1889

Haigh, C, [ed.] *The English Reformation Revised,* Cambridge University Press, 1987

------, *The Last Days of the Lancashire Monasteries and the Pilgrimage of Grace,* Chetham Society, Manchester, 1969

Haile, M, *The Life of Reginald Pole,* New York, Longmans, Green & Co., 1910

------, *An Elizabethan Cardinal: William Allen,* Isaac Pitman & Sons, 1914

Hamilton, D B, *Anthony Munday and the Catholics, 1560-1633,* Ashgate, 2005

Handover, P M, *The Second Cecil 1563-1604,* Eyre & Spottiswoode, 1959

Hardy, W J, *Documents Illustrative of English Church History,* Macmillan & Co, 1914

Harper-Bell, C, *The Pre-Reformation Church in England 1400-1530,* Longman, 1996

Harting, J H, *Catholic London Missions,* Sands & Company, London, 1903

Haswell, J, *James II,* Hamish Hamilton, 1972

Havran, M, *The Catholics in Caroline England,* Stanford UP, 1962

Hayward, F M, *Padley Chapel and Padley Martyrs,* Derby, Bemrose & Sons, 1903

Hay, M V, *The Jesuits and the Popish Plot,* Sands & Company, 1934

Hayley, K H D, *The First Earl of Shaftesbury,* Oxford, 1968

Haynes, A, *The Elizabethan Secret Services,* Sutton Publishing, 1992

------, *Walsingham, Elizabeth's Spymaster,* Sutton Publishing, 2004

------, *The Gunpowder Plot,* Sutton Publishing, 1994

Hemphill, B, Dom, OSB, *The Early Vicars-Apostolic of England 1685-1750,* London, Burns & Oates, 1954

Hendricks, L, O.Cist, *The Carthusian Martyrs,* London, 1931

------, *The London Charterhouse; its Monks and Martyrs,* Kegan Paul, Trench, 1889

Hicks, L, SJ *An Elizabethan Problem,* Burns & Oates, London, 1964

Hilliard Atteridge, A, *The Elizabethan Persecution,* Harding & Moore Ltd, London, 1928

Hirst, J H, *The Blockhouses of Kingston-upon-Hull and who went there,* Browns & Sons, 1913

Hodgetts, M, *Secret Hiding Places,* Dublin, Veritas, 1989

Hope, W H Saint-John, *The History of the London Charterhouse from its Foundation until the Suppression of the Monastery,* W H Allen, London, 1925

Hopkirk, M, *Queen over the Water,* John Murray, 1953

List of Sources

Howell, T B, *Howell's State Trials*, ed. D S Thomas, London, Routledge, Kegan Paul, 1972 edition
Hughes, P, *Rome and the Counter-Reformation in England*, Burns Oates, 1942
------, *The Reformation in England*, revised ed., New York, Macmillan, 1963
Hutchinson, R, *The Last Days of Henry VIII*, London, 2005
------, *Elizabeth's Spymaster*, London, 2006
------, *Thomas Cromwell*, London, 2007
Hyland, K, Rev.St.George, *A Century of Persecution*, Kegan, Paul, Trench Trubner, London, 1920
Janelle, P, *Robert Southwell the Writer*, Sheed & Ward, 1935
Jardine, D, *A Narrative of the Gunpowder Plot*, John Murray, 1857
------, [ed.] *Criminal Trials II: The Gunpowder Plot*, London, 1835
Jessop, A, *One Generation of a Norfolk House*, Burns & Oates, 1879
------, *Letters of Father Henry Walpole, SJ.*, Norwich, 1873
Jones, J R, *The Revolution of 1688*, New York, Norton, 1972
Jordan, W K, *Edward VI: The Young King*, Harvard University Press, 1968
------, *Edward VI: the Threshold of Power*, London, Allen & Unwin, 1970
Kelly, C, *Blessed Thomas Belson*, Smythe, Gerrards Cross, 1987
Kelly, J N D, *The Oxford Dictionary of Popes*, Oxford UP, 1986
Kenyon, J P, *The Popish Plot*, William Heinemann, 1972
------, *Stuart England*, 2nd ed., Penguin, 1985
Ker, C, *The life of the Venerable Philip Howard, Earl of Arundel*, Longmans, 1926
Kirk, J, *Biographies of English Catholics*. ed. By J H & E H Pollen, London, Burton, 1909
Knowles, D, OSB, *Bare Ruined Choirs*, Cambridge, 1976
------, *The Religious Orders in England*, vol. 3, *The Tudor Age* Cambridge University Press, 1948-59
------, *The Monastic Order in England*, Cambridge University Press, 1940, 1976 ed.
Knox, T F, *Records of the English Catholics under the Penal Laws 1st & 2nd Douai Diaries*, London, 1878
------, *Letters and Memorials of Cardinal Allen*, London, 1882
Lane, J, *Titus Oates*, Andrew Dakers, 1949
Law, T Graves, *A Calendar of the English Martyrs of the 16th & 17th Centuries*, London, 1896
Lee, F G, *The Church under Queen Elizabeth: An Historical Sketch*, Revised Ed. W H Allen, 1892
Letters and Papers, Foreign and Domestic, of the reign of Henry VIII, 1509-1547, eds. J S Brewer, J Gairdner and R H Brodie, 21 vols., London, 1862-1910
Lingard, J, *The History of England from the First Invasion of the Romans to the Accession of William and Mary 1688*, 10 vols., James Duffy, Dublin, 1874
Lloyd, C, *Formularies of Faith put forth by authority during the reign of Henry VIII*, Oxford, 1856

List of Sources

Loades, D, *The Reign of Mary Tudor 1553-58*, 2nd ed., Longman Group, 1991
------, *The Cecils,* Bloomsbury, 2009
London Encyclopaedia, edited by B Weinreb & C Hibbert, 1983
Longley, K M, *Saint Margaret Clitherow,* Anthony Clarke, 1986
  [being a revised and updated edition of the book published 1966 under the pen- name Mary Claridge]
Lunn, D, *The Catholic Elizabethans,* Downside, 1998
MacCulloch, D, *Thomas Cranmer: A Life,* Yale University Press, 1997
------, *Tudor Church Militant: Edward VI and the Protestant Reformation,* Penguin, 1999
------, *The Reign of Henry VIII: Politics, Policy and Piety,* Basingstoke, 1995
Mackie, J D, *The Early Tudors,* Oxford University Press, 1952
Magee, B, *The English Recusants,* Burns, Oates & Washbourne, 1938
Marks, A, *Who Killed Sir Edmund Berry Godfrey?* Burns & Oates, 1905
------, *Tyburn Tree: Its History and Annals,* Brown Langham, 1908
Marius, R, *Thomas More,* Alfred Knopf, New York, 1984
Marshall, A, *The Strange Death of Sir Edmund Berry Godfrey,* Sutton Publishing, 1999
Mathew, D J, *Catholics in England,* Longmans Green, 1936
------, *Catholicism in England: the Portrait of a Minority 1535-1935,* 2nd ed., Eyre & Spottiswoode, London, 1948
------, *James I,* Eyre & Spottiswoode, London, 1967
Mattingley, G, *Catherine of Aragon,* Little, Brown and Company, 1941
------, *The Defeat of the Spanish Armada,* Jonathan Cape, 1959
McGrath, P, *Papists and Puritans under Elizabeth,* Blandford Press,1969
Merriman, R, *Life and Letters of Thomas Cromwell,* 2 vols, Oxford, 1902
Meyer, A O, *England and the Catholic Church under Queen Elizabeth,* 1915 transl. from the German by J R McKee, Routledge, Kegan, Paul, 1967
Miller, J, *Popery and Politics in England 1660-88,* Cambridge University Press, 1973
Monro, M, *Blessed Margaret Clitherow,* New York, Longmans, Green, 1947
Moorhouse, Geoffrey, *The Pilgrimage of Grace,* Weidenfeld & Nicholson, 2002
More, Thomas, *St Thomas More: Selected Letters,* ed. E F Rogers, Yale, New Haven and London, 1961
Morris, J A, *Richard Topcliffe: 'a most humbell pursuivant of Her Majestie',* The Military College of South Carolina, 1964
Morris, J H, SJ, [ed.] *Troubles of Our Catholic Forefathers as related by themselves* 1st, 2nd and 3rd series, including a transcript of *A True Report of the Life and Martyrdom Mrs Margaret Clitherow,* by Father John Mush, Burns & Oates, London, 1872-77
------, *The Catholics of York under Elizabeth,* London, 1891
------, *The Condition of Catholics under James I,* 1871
Muller, J A, *Stephen Gardiner and the Tudor Reaction,* London, 1926, 1970 ed., New Octagon

List of Sources

Neale, J E, *Queen Elizabeth*, Jonathan Cape, 1934
------, *Elizabeth and her Parliaments, 1559-81,* London, 1953
Neame, A, *The Holy Maid of Kent*, London, Hodder & Stoughton, 1971
Newton, D, *Catholic London*, Hale, 1950
Nicholls, M, *Investigating the Gunpowder Plot*, Manchester University Press, 1991
Norman, E.R, *Roman Catholicism in England from the Elizabethan Settlement to the Second Vatican Council*, Oxford University Press, 1986
Oman, C, *Henrietta Maria*, Hodder & Stoughton, 1936
------, *Mary of Modena*, London, Hodder & Stoughton, 1962
Palmer, W, *Life of Mrs Dorothy Lawson of St Anthony*, Charles Dolman, 1855
Paul, J E, *Catherine of Aragon and Her Friends*, Burns & Oates, 1966
Peacock, E, [ed] *A list of the Roman Catholics in the County of York in 1604. Transcribed from the original manuscript in the Bodleian Library and edited with genealogical notes.* Savill & Edwards, London, 1872
Phillips, G E, *The Extinction of the Ancient Hierarchy*, Sands & Co., 1905
Pollard, A F, *Wolsey*, London, 1929
Pollen, J H, SJ, *The English Catholics in the Reign of Elizabeth 1558-1580* Longmans, Green & Co., 1920
------, *Acts of the English Martyrs*, London, Burns & Oates, 1891
------, *Father Henry Garnet and the Gunpowder Plot*, London, 1888
------, *Queen Mary and the Babington Plot*, Edinburgh, 1922
Pollock, J, *The Popish Plot: A Study in the History of the Reign of Charles II,* London, Duckworth, 1903
Porter, L, *Mary Tudor*, Portrait, 2007
Prescott, H F, *Mary Tudor*, revised ed. New York, Macmillan Company, 1953
Prynne, William, *The Popish Royal Favourite*, London 1643
Pritchard, A, *Catholic Loyalism in Elizabethan England*, University of North Carolina, 1979
Purdie, A B, *The Life of Blessed John Southworth,* Burns Oates & Washbourne, London, 1930
Questier, M C, *Catholicism and Community in Early Modern England c1550-1640* Cambridge University Press, 2006
Read, C, *Secretary Cecil and Queen Elizabeth*, New York, Knopf, 1955
------, *Mr Secretary Walsingham and the Policy of Queen Elizabeth,* Oxford U P, 1925
Reid, R R, *The King's Council in the North*, Rowman and Littlefield, 1975
Reynolds, E E, *The Roman Catholic Church in England and Wales*, Anthony Clarke, 1973
------, *St John Fisher*, Anthony Clarke, 1955
------, *The Field is Won: St Thomas More*, Burns & Oates, 1968
------, *The Trial of St Thomas More,* Burns & Oates, 1964
------, *Thomas More and Erasmus*, Burns & Oates, 1965
Rex, R, *Henry VIII and the English Reformation*, Basingstoke, 1993
Rhodes, W E, [ed,] *The Apostolical Life of Ambrose Barlow*, Chetham Society, 1909

List of Sources

Richards, D, *Britain under the Tudors and Stuarts*, Longmans, Green & Co., 1951
Richardson, W C, *History of the Court of Augmentations, 1536-1554*, Oxford University Press, 1961
Ridley, J, *The Life and Times of Mary Tudor*, Weidenfeld & Nicholson, 1973
------, *Thomas Cranmer,* Oxford, 1962
Roper, W, *The Life of Sir Thomas More, knight,* ed. Hitchcock, E.E.T.S., 1935
Rose Troup, F, *The Western Rebellion*, Smith & Elder, 1913
Routh, E M G, *Sir Thomas More and his Friends*, Oxford, 1934
Rouse, A L, *Tudor Cornwall*, Macmillan, 1969
------, *The England of Elizabeth*, Macmillan, 1973
------, *The Tower of London*, Cardinal, 1972
Sacred Congregation for the Causes of Saints, *Cause of the Canonization of the Blessed Martyrs John Houghton, etc.: Official Presentation of Documents,* Vatican Polyglot Press, Rome, 1968
Salmon, T, [ed], *A Compleat Collection of State Trials for High Treason,* 4 vols, London, 1719
Salome, M, *Mary Ward: A Foundress of the 17th Century,* Burns & Oates, 1901
Sander, N, *The Rise and Growth of the Anglican Schism 1585,* with a continuation by Edward Rishton, transl. by D Lewis, London, 1877
Savine, A, *English Monasteries on the Eve of the Dissolution in P.Vinogradoff [ed] Oxford Studies in Social and Legal History*,Vol. 1. Oxford, 1909
Scarisbrick J J, *The Reformation and the English People*, Blackwell, Oxford,1984
------, *The Jesuits and the Catholic Reformation*, The Historical Association,1989
------, *Henry VIII*, Eyre Methuen,1968
Simpson, R, *Edmund Campion*, London, 1896, revised and edited by Peter Joseph, Gracewing, 2010
------, *The Penal Laws: Instances of the Sufferings of Catholics,* Burns, Oates & Washbourne, 1930
Singer, S W, *The Life of Sir Thomas More by his son-in-law William Roper*, London, 1822
Smith, L B, *Henry VIII: The Mask of Royalty*, Panther, London, 1973
------, *Treason in Tudor England: Politics and Paranoia*, London, 1986
------, *The Elizabethan Epic*, Panther, 1966
Smith, A G, *The Babington Plot,* Macmillan, 1936
Smyth, C H, *Cranmer and the Reformation under Edward VI*, Cambridge 1926
S.N.D, *William Howard, Viscount Stafford 1612-1680*, Sands & Co.,1929
Southern, A C, [ed.] *An Elizabethan Recusant House, comprising the Life of Lady Magdalen Viscountess Montague,* Sands, 1954
Southwell, R, *An Epistle of Comfort*, edited by M Waugh, Burns & Oates, 1956
------, *An Humble Supplication to Her Majestie,* edited by R C Bold, Cambridge University Press, 1953

List of Sources

Spink, H H, *The Gunpowder Plot and Lord Mounteagle's Letter*, 1902
Squiers, G, *Secret Hiding Places*, London, 1933
Stanton, R, *A Menology of England and Wales*, London, 1892
Starkey, D, *Six Wives: The Queens of Henry VIII*, Harper Perennial, London 2003
------, *The Reign of Henry VIII: Personalities and Politics*, London, 2002
Steer, F W, *The Life of Philip Howard*, edited from the 1630 anonymous *Life Howard* Phillimore,1971
Stonor, R J, *Stonor*, 2nd ed., Newport, R H Johns, 1952
Stow, J, *The Annals of England collected out of the most Authentic Authors, Records and other Monuments of Antiquity*, London, 1605
Strype, J, *Annals of the Reformation*, Clarendon Press, Oxford, 1824
Sturge, C, *Cuthbert Tunstall*, London, Longmans, Green, 1938
Tanner, J R, *Tudor Historical Documents 1485-1603,* Cambridge, 1940
Thaddeus, Father, The *Franciscans in England 1600-1850*, Art & Book Company, 1898
Thomson, J A F, *The Early Tudor Church and Society*, Longmans, London, 1993
Thompson, E M, *The Carthusian Order in England*, SPCK, 1930
Todd, J M:, *Reformation,* London, Darton, Longman & Todd, 1971
Trappes-Lomax, M, *Bishop Challoner*, Longmans, Green & Co., 1936
Trevor-Roper, H R, *Archbishop Laud,* Macmillan & Co., London, 1962
Trimble, W R, *The Catholic Laity in Elizabethan England 1558-1603*, Harvard University Press, 1964
Trudgian, R F, *Francis Tregian*, Alpha Press, 1998
Turner, F C, *James II,* Eyre & Spottiswoode, 1948
Waugh, E, *Edmund Campion*, Oxford University Press, 1980
Wedgwood, C V, *The King's Peace 1637-41*, Collins Fontana, 1972
------, *The King's War 1641-47*, Collins Fontana, 1973
------, *Oliver Cromwell*, Duckworth, 1973
Whatmore, L E, *The Carthusians under King Henry VIII*, University of Salzburg, 1983
Whelan, H, *Snow on the Hedges*: A Life of Cuthbert Mayne, Fowler Wright , 1984
White, F O, *Lives of the Elizabethan Bishops of the Anglican Church*, Skeffington, 1898
Wilkie, W H, *The Cardinal Protectors of England: Rome and the Tudors before the Reformation,* Cambridge UP, 1974
Williams, M E, *The Venerable English College, Rome*, Dublin, Cahill, 1979
------, *St Alban's College, Valladolid: Four Centuries of English Presence in Spain,* 1986
Williams, N, *Elizabeth I,* Weidenfeld & Nicholson, 1967
------, *Thomas Howard, Fourth Duke of Norfolk*, Barrie & Rockliff, London, 1964
Williamson, H Ross, *The Gunpowder Plot,* London, 1951

List of Sources

Willis, B, *A History of the Mitred Abbeys,* vols. 1 & 2, Bowyer 1718-1719
Willis-Bund, J W, *A selection of cases from the State Trials,* Cambridge University Press, 1879-82
------, *Vol. 1 and Vol. 2 part1: Trials for Treason*
------, *Vol. 2 part 2: The Popish Plot*
Wilson, D, *In the Lion's Court: Power, Ambition and Sudden Death in the Reign of Henry VIII,* London 2002
Woodward, G W O, *The Dissolution of the Monasteries,* Blandford Press, 1966
Wriothesley, C, A *Chronicle of England during the reigns of the Tudors from 1485 to 1559,* ed. W D Hamilton, Camden Society, 2 vols., 1875-77
Wright, T, *Three Chapters of Letters relating to the Suppression of the Monasteries, edited from originals in the British Museum,* Camden Society/J B Nichols & Son, London, 1843
Yeo, M, *Claude de la Colombière,* Burns, Oates & Washbourne, 1940
Yepez, D, *Historia Particular de la Persecucion de Inglaterra, 1599*
Youings, J, *The Dissolution of the Monasteries,* Allen & Unwin, 1971

PAMPHLETS, BOOKLETS AND JOURNALS

Arrowsmith, E, *A True Account of the Life and Death,* 1630, Vice-Postulation
Benson, G, *An account of the city and county of York from the Reformation to the year 1925* Yorkshire Archaeological Society Vol. 3, 1925
Bliss, W, *Notes on the Religious belief of Anne of Denmark,* English Historical Review, Vol.4, 1889
Bushell, D, *The Bellamies of Uxendon,* Harrow Octocentenary Tracts, Cambridge, 1914
Camm, Dom B, OSB, *The Life of Blessed [St] John Wall,* 1932, reprinted 1972
Canning, J H, 'The Titus Oates Plot in South Wales and the Marches', in *St Peter's Magazine* 1923-24
Caraman, P, SJ, *St Philip Howard,* CTS, 1985
Crean, P J, *Life of the Venerable William Davies,* CTS, 1958
De Rosa, P, *Blessed Alexander Briant,* Vice-Postulation
Dickens, A G, *The First Stages of Romanist Recusancy in Yorkshire, 1560-1590,* Yorkshire Archaeological Journal, Vol. 35, 1943
------, *The Extent and Character of Recusancy in Yorkshire, 1604,* Yorkshire Archaeological Journal, Vol.37, 1945
Edwards, G, *St Ambrose Barlow,* CTS, 1984
The Eighty-Five Blessed Martyrs, Martyrs Office
Elvins, M T, *The Sussex Martyrs,* CTS, 1983
Fee, W, *Martyrs of Northumberland and Durham,* CTS, 1979
Fitzherbert, M, *St Philip Howard,* revised M T Elvins, CTS, 1975
Foley, B C, *Blessed John* Paine, Vice-Postulation, 1961
------, *The Eighty-Five Blessed Martyrs,* CTS, 1987
Forster, A, *Blessed Eustace White,* Vice-Postulation

List of Sources

Goulder, L, *Church Life in Medieval England and Wales. The Parishes*, Guild of Our Lady of Ransom, 1988 ed.
------, *Church Life in Medieval England and Wales. The Monasteries.* Guild of Our Lady of Ransom, 1990 ed.
------, *Westminster,* Guild of Our Lady of Ransom, 1967 ed.
------, *London, The Tower and Environs*, Guild of Our Lady of Ransom, 1989 ed.
Hallett, Rt.Rev.Mgr, *St Thomas More*, CTS, 1957
Humphreys, J, *The Habingtons of Hindlip and the Gunpowder Plot,* Transactions of the Birmingham and Midlands Institute, Vol. 31, 1905
Harting, E M, *The Diary of a Recusant*, The Month, Vol. CXVIII, 1911
Hodgetts, M, *Harvington Hall*, Archdiocese of Birmingham, 1991
Johnston, F R, *St Richard Reynolds*, Syon Abbey, 1961
Knox, T F, *The Last Survivor of the English Hierarchy, Thomas Goldwell, Bishop of St Asaph*, The Month, Jan-Feb, 1876
Leatherbarrow, J S, *The Lancashire Elizabethan Recusants,* Chetham Society, New Series, Vol. 110, Manchester, 1947
MacCulloch, D, *'The Myth of the English Reformation'*, Journal of British Studies, 1991
McGoldrick, T A, *St Margaret Clitherow*, CTS, 1971
Morris, J, SJ, *The English Martyrs*, CTS, 1961
Nassan, M, *St Robert Southwell*, CTS
O'Dwyer, M, *Blessed Anne Line*, Vice-Postulation
Oxburgh Hall Guide, National Trust, 1990
Petre Lord J, *Ingatestone Hall Guide,* Leighprint
Rice, F, *St John Boste*, Darlington Carmel, 1993
Smith, R L, *St John Fisher*, CTS 1960
Stark, A, *Thomas More*, Guild of Our Lady of Ransom, 1978
Stonor, Dom J, OSB, *Six Welsh Martyrs*, Vice-Postulation
Tigar, C, SJ, *Henry Walpole*, Vice-Postulation, 1970
------, *Forty Martyrs of England and Wales,* Stella Maris, 1961
Tyburn Convent, *They died at Tyburn 1535-1680*, 1961
Walsh, J, SJ, [compiler] *The Forty Martyrs of England and Wales*, CTS, 1997 ed.
Waugh, M, *Blessed Ralph Sherwin*, CTS, 1962
------, *Blessed John Plessington*, CTS, 1961
------, *Blessed Nicholas Owen: Jesuit Brother and maker of hiding holes*, 1959
Whatmore, L E, *Blessed Margaret Ward*, 1961
Whitfield, J L, *Blessed John Southworth*, CTS, 1959

ARTICLES

Barry, P, 'The Penal Laws', in *L'Osservatore Romano,* English ed. 30/11/1987
Molinari, P, SJ, 'Canonization of Forty English and Welsh Martyrs', in *L'Osservatore Romano*, English ed. 29/10/1970

Index of Persons

A

Abercrombie, Robert SJ 388, 390
Abbot, George 83, 395, 421 423, 428, 431, 449, 451, 542
Abbot, Henry (lay martyr) 378, 379
Abbot, John 501, 542
Abel, Thomas D.D. (priest martyr) 59, 72
Adams, John (priest martyr) 118
d'Adda, Fernando 616
Agazzari, Alfonso SJ 211, 212
Alacoque, Margaret Mary St 575
Alban, St 47
Aldhelm, Placid OSB 611
Aldobrandini, Pietro 389
Alegambe, Phillipe SJ 488
Alfield, Thomas (priest martyr) 206, 345, 353
Alexander VI 28
Allen, Catherine 69, 170
Allen, Helen 170
Allen, John 30
Allen, John 169
Allen, Margaret 497
Allen, Mary 140, 544
Allen, William (Cardinal) 69, 121, 125, 140, 144, 145, 146, 147, 158, 169, 185, 189, 191, 193, 201, 213, 226, 258, 313, 314, 315, 316, 345, 346, 353, 360, 367, 378, 447, 467, 545, 626
Allison, William 612
ALMOND, ST JOHN 425-431, 440, 488
Almond, John O.Cist. 106, 426
Altham, John vere Grosvenor 512
Amias, John (priest martyr) 364
Anderson, Sir Edmund 114, 130
Anderson, Lionel OP 562
Anderton, Robert (priest martyr) 114,
Andleby, William (priest martyr) 208, 378
Andrews, Thomas 341
Andrews, Thomas 539
Andrews, Thomas 593
Anne, Queen 419, 618, 620, 622
Anne of Cleves 60, 61, 64
Anne of Denmark 390, 508
Anne, George SJ 541
Anne, Richard 523
Aquaviva, Claudio SJ 286, 298, 301, 302

Arden, Edward 113
Arden, Mary 113
Arnold, John 569, 570, 589, 591, 593, 594, 595
Array, Martin 208, 209, 290
ARROWSMITH, ST EDMUND 455, 465-472, 477, 509, 522, 573
Arrowsmith, Edmund 384, 466
Arrowsmith, Peter 465
Arrowsmith, Robert 465, 466
Arundell, Lady Anne 176
Arundell, Blanche, Lady 489
Arundell, Catherine 179
Arundell, Dorothy 177
Arundell, Henry (Lord Wardour) 603, 604
Arundell, Sir John 176, 179, 180, 184, 261
Arundell, Thomas (Lord Wardour) 448, 463, 467
Ashby, Thomas (lay martyr) 59
Ashe, Margaret 422
Ashley, Ralph SJ (martyr) 403, 406, 407, 408, 443, 444, 445
Ashton, Margaret 126-128
Ashton, Roger (lay martyr) 130
Aske, Robert 38-41, 49
Askwith, Robert 253
Asleby, George OCist. 42
Aston, Walter, (Lord Forfar) 551, 598, 600, 604
Atkins, Samuel 555
Atkins, William SJ 611, 612
Atkinson, Anthony 277, 279
Atkinson, James 412, 413
Atkinson, Matthew OSF xxi
Atkinson, Thomas (priest martyr) 383, 440
Atkinson, William 383
l'Aubespine, Charles de, Marquis de Châteauneuf 522
d'Aubigny, Ludovic 547
Atkyns, Sir Edward 578, 609
Atkyns, Sir Robert 577, 578, 586, 593, 594, 609
Aubrey, John 515
Audley, Thomas (Lord Audley) 17, 22, 32, 58, 64, 67, 310
Augustine of Canterbury, St 145, 291, 421, 424, 527, 624
Augustine of Hippo St xviii, 16, 18

647

Index of Persons

Ayling, William 37
Aylmer, John 104, 120, 163, 175, 221, 259, 339, 359, 371

B

Babington Anthony, 117, 118, 158, 293, 379
Babington, Francis 105
Babthorpe, Lady Grace 139, 440
Babthorpe, Leonard 139
Babthorpe, Sir Ralph 139
Bailey, Laurence (lay martyr) 393
Bailey, Thomas 105
Baker, Augustine OSB 450, 535, 588
Baines, Richard 148
Baldwin, John 258
Baldwin, William SJ 412, 413, 414
Bale, John 51, 102
Bales, Christopher (priest martyr) 291
Balland, Nicholas 53
Ballard, John 117, 118, 157, 315, 403
Bamber, Edward (priest martyr) 536, 537, 538
Bancroft, Richard 158, 384, 396, 418, 419, 448, 468
Bandersby, William 106
Barillon, Jean-Paul, Marquis de Branges 575, 610
Barkworth, Mark OSB (priest martyr) 336, 337, 384, 385, 386, 413
Barley, Dorothy 222
Barlow, Alexander 473, 566
Barlow, Sir Alexander 473
Barlow, Anne 438
Barlow, Anthony 481
BARLOW, ST AMBROSE 472-481, 521, 566
Barlow, Lewis 146, 170, 171
Barlow, Margaret 473
Barlow, Margaret 566
Barlow, Robert 474
Barlow, Thomas 481
Barlow, William (Rudesind) OSB 474
Barlow, William 155
Barnaby, Francis 417, 446, 449
Barnes, John 245
Barnes, Ralph OCist 42
Barnes, Richard 245
Barnes, Robert 325, 412
Baronius, Cardinal Cesare 427
Barton, Elizabeth 3, 15, 60, 61, 62, 72

Barwise, Robert 261, 324
Barwys, John 375
Bate, Christopher 475
Bateson, Leonard 143
Batmanson, John 10
Battie, Anthony (lay martyr) 143, 168
Bayne, Ralph 154
Beaufort, Margaret 63, 64
Beaumont, Sir Francis 281, 282, 306, 307, 378
Beaumont, Francis 281
Beaumont, Jane 162
Beche, John vere Marshall OSB (abbot martyr) 55, 56, 57, 58, 59
Beckham, Margery 299
Becket, Thomas St xix, 9, 46, 327, 412, 528
Bedingfeld, Sir Henry 488
Bedingfeld, Henry SJ 492
Bedingfeld, Thomas SJ vere Downes 610
Bedloe, William 550, 551, 556, 557, 558, 560, 561, 564, 565, 569, 578, 585, 586, 591, 592, 602, 605, 608
Bedyll, Thomas 11, 12, 14, 20, 21, 23, 24, 25, 43
Beesley, George (priest martyr) 336, 371, 372
Beesley, Richard 336
Belchiam, Thomas OSF (priest martyr) 71
Belasyse, Lord John 603, 604
Bell, Arthur OSF (priest martyr) 531, 532, 538
Bell, James (priest martyr) 106
Bell, Thomas 149, 426
Bellamy, Anne 294, 295, 325
Bellamy family 202, 293, 294, 295, 297, 370, 371, 374, 379, 381, 508
Bellarmine, Robert St 136, 174, 372, 420, 541
Belson, Augustine 365
Belson, Thomas (lay martyr) 365, 366, 371
Benedict XIV 628
Bennet, John SJ 173, 233, 510, 529
Bennett, William SJ vere Bentney 612
Bennett, Robert 351, 437, 582
Bennett, William 317, 318
Berden, Nicholas 152, 153, 369, 370, 379
Bere, Richard 56, 69

648

Index of Persons

Bere, Richard O.Cart. (martyr) 69
Berkeley, Gilbert 355
Bernard, St 411
Berry, John 490
Beza, Theodore 211, 228
Bickerdike, Robert (lay martyr) 276, 277
Bickley, Ralph SJ 152, 210, 211
Bigod, Sir Stephen 41
Bird, James (lay martyr) 129, 130
Bird, Robert 25
Bird, William 25
Birket, Catherine 373
Birket, George 115, 373, 383, 452
Birket, Richard 611
Bishop, William 344, 435, 452, 505
Blackburne, Lancelot 144
Blackall, Christopher 327
Blackwall, Nicholas 325
Blackwell, George 172, 261, 347, 394, 427, 452, 505
Blake, Alexander (lay martyr) 175, 291, 292
Blethyn, William 107
Blonham, Laurence OCist 42
Blount, Charles (5th Lord Mountjoy) 62
Blount, Charles (8th Lord Mountjoy) 298
Blount, Sir Michael 295, 320
Blount, Richard SJ 293, 458, 467, 489, 492, 507, 508, 509
Blount, Thomas 541
Blount, William (4th Lord Mountjoy) 62
Bluet, Thomas 417, 448
Blundell, William 392, 393, 396
Bocher, Joan 79
Boderie, Antoine Le Fèvre de la 419
Bocking, Edward OSB 61
Bodey, John (lay martyr) 129
Body, William 75
Boethius, Severinus 4778
Bold, Richard 287
Boleyn, Alice 71
Boleyn, Anne 1, 2, 3, 4, 11, 17, 27, 53, 63, 66, 64, 65, 71, 72, 73, 91, 155, 309, 319
Boleyn, George (Viscount Rochford) 17
Boleyn, Mary 2, 319
Boleyn, Thomas (Earl of Wiltshire) 17
Bolron, Robert 608, 609
Bonner, Edmund 7, 84, 85, 89, 90, 154, 286
Bonnewe, Florence 54
Bordeaux-Neufville, Antoine de 514
Borgia, St Francis 189
Borromeo, Charles St 210, 375, 528
Bosgrave, James SJ 202, 213, 345
Bosgrave, Thomas (lay martyr) 152, 176, 177
BOSTE, ST JOHN 255, 274-285, 306, 372
Boste, Nicholas 274
Bourchier, Thomas OSF 44
Bourne, Cardinal Francis OP xx
Bourne, Gilbert 154, 355
Bowes, Marmaduke (lay martyr) 245
Bowes, Richard 106
Bowker, Alexander 149
Boxall, John 96, 155
Bradbridge, William 180, 181
Bradley, Richard 541
Bradshaw, Augustine OSB vere John White 417, 419, 448, 450, 483, 588
Bradsheet, John 557
Braithwaite, Alice 566
Bramston, Thomas 360, 361, 362
Brandon, Charles (Duke of Suffolk) 38
Brandon, Lady Frances 88
Branton, Stephen 348
Bratt, Henry 459
Bray, William 315
Braybrooke, James 344
Brébeuf, Jean de St 513
Brereblock, John 208
Breres, Mary 328
Brereton, Mary 473
Brereton, Sir Urian 473
Bretton family 132-134
Bretton, John (lay martyr) 127-129
BRIANT, ST ALEXANDER xiii, 205, 215-220, 225, 229, 490, 510
Bridgeman, John 467, 509
Bridget of Sweden, St 17, 177
Briggs, Thomas 105
Brigosa, John 148
Brindholme, Edmund (priest martyr) 59
Brinkley, Stephen 195, 339
Bristow, Richard 201, 202, 338

649

Index of Persons

Bromfield, Sir Edward 459
Bromley, Sir Edward 403
Bromley, Sir George 233, 234
Bromley, Sir Henry 404, 405, 406, 407
Bromley, Sir Thomas 199
Bromwich, Andrew 612
Brookby, Anthony OSF (priest martyr) 70
Brooke, Sir Basil 453
Brooksby, Eleanor née Vaux 137, 142, 166, 281, 288, 402, 403
Broughton, Edmund 522
Broughton, Mark OSB 420
Brown, Dorothy 138, 139
Brown, James 501
Browne, Anthony OSF 44
Browne, Anthony (1st Viscount Montague) 121, 266, 275
Browne, Anthony-Maria (2nd Viscount Montague) 207, 374, 392, 439
Browne, Charles SJ 589
Browne, Francis (3rd Viscount Montague) 559, 614
Browne, Magdalen (Viscountess Montague) 115, 121
Browne, Mary 207, 266
Browne, William (lay martyr) 393
Browne, Sir William 222
Brudenell, Robert (Earl of Cardigan) 559
Bruno, St 8
Brushford, John 175
Buckley, Sigebert OSB 419, 449, 450
Bulkeley, Katherine 398
Bull, Simon 227, 263, 341
Bullaker, Thomas OSF (priest martyr) 530
Bullock, Dr George 231
Bullock, Peter 168, 169
Bulmer, Sir John 41
Bully, John 591, 612
Burch, Francis Van den 522
Burden, Edward (priest martyr) 137, 260, 363
Burnet, Gilbert 17, 55, 77, 84, 93, 563, 618
Burrows, Frances 69, 288
Buxton, Christopher (priest martyr) 161, 259, 360
Byrd, William 185, 207, 221, 287, 288, 301, 337, 402

C

Cabrini, Francis Xavier St 411
Cadwallador, Roger (priest martyr) 437
Calverley, Edmund 359, 362
Calvert, George (Lord Baltimore) 511, 512
Calvert, Leonard 512
Calvert, Millicent 241
Calvert, William 241
Camden, William 102, 157, 201
Campbell, Sir James 459
CAMPION, ST EDMUND xv, 107, 118, 142, 152, 178, 186-206, 210, 211, 214, 219, 220, 222, 225, 228, 229, 242, 250, 266, 278, 293, 300, 301, 312, 337, 338, 339, 340, 341, 342, 343, 344, 346, 354, 370, 379, 387, 400, 416, 444, 509, 521
Campion, Edward vere Edwards priest martyr) 259, 359
Canam, Edmund 501
Cansfield, Brian SJ 541
Cantilupe, Sir Nicholas de 9
Capel, Arthur (Earl of Essex) 609, 610
Capes, John 429
Carafa, Vincenzo 504, 513
Cárdenas, Alonso de 527
Carew, John 280
Carew, Sir Peter 77
Carew, William 491
Carey, Catherine 2, 319
Carey, Sir George (2nd Lord Hunsdon) 114, 180, 185
Carey, Henry (1st Lord Hunsdon) 2, 110, 317, 319
Carey, John (lay martyr) 152, 176, 177
Carey, Sir William 2
Carleton, Sir Dudley 524
Carne, Charles 585, 612
Carpenter, Richard 458, 459
Carpenter, William 461
Carter, William (lay martyr) 141, 163
Carvajal, Luisa de 422, 451
Catenby, Bridget 462
Catesby, Robert 393, 402, 409
Catherine of Sweden, St 15
Catherine of Aragon 1, 2, 3, 4, 6, 15, 26, 38, 43, 50, 56, 62, 63, 65, 70, 71, 72, 73

650

Index of Persons

Catherine of Braganza 547, 552, 553, 556, 557, 558, 563, 599, 611
Catterick, Anthony 462
Catterick, Edmund (priest martyr) 461, 462, 518
Caton, William 620
Catton, Thomas 49
Cavell, Edith xviii
Caverel, Philip de 420, 505
Cawarden, Sir Thomas 50
Cawood, John 163
Cayley, Sir William 606
Cecil, John 416, 417, 447
Cecil, Sir Robert (Earl of Salisbury) 122, 158, 171, 260, 295, 351, 357, 377, 385, 392, 393, 394, 402, 405, 410, 416, 447, 468, 512
Cecil, Thomas (2nd Lord Burghley) 137, 166, 171, 390
Cecil, William (1st Lord Burghley) xiii, 91, 93, 96, 100, 103, 107, 108, 111, 112, 117, 119, 126, 133, 142, 154, 156, 157, 161, 176, 187, 188, 189, 196, 200, 218, 223, 224, 230, 278, 279, 285, 295, 311, 315, 317, 318, 338, 348, 356, 377, 390, 521
Chaderton, William 369
Chaise, François de la 554
Challoner, Richard xx, xxv, 120, 160, 162, 164, 165, 168, 218, 228, 277, 328, 334, 355, 369, 426, 440, 463, 472, 477, 521, 527, 536, 622, 623
Champney, Anthony 322, 325, 333, 363, 611
Chaplain, William 174
Chapuys, Eustace 19, 49
Charles I 345, 372, 397, 429, 452-465, 470, 477, 481, 489, 514, 524, 532, 539, 548, 553, 603, 604, 613
Charles II 546-564, 584, 599, 603, 604, 610, 618
Charles V 2, 60
Charlton, Sir Job 567
Chartres, Richard 4, 5, 26
Chauncy, Maurice 8, 10, 11, 12, 13, 15, 21, 23, 24, 25, 82
Chedsey, William 103
Cheney, Charles 539, 540, 543
Cheney, Richard 187
Chichester, John 457

Churchill, John (Duke of Marlborough) 420, 618
Clapton, Mrs Grace 284, 285
Clapton, William 277, 278, 435
Clark, Alan 627
Clark, James 527
Clark, Thomas 148, 149
Clark, William 260, 417, 449
Claxton, James (priest martyr) 257, 358, 359
Clayton, Francis 149
Clayton, James 258
Clayton, Ralph 618
Clement VII 2, 3, 31
Clement VIII xxv, 323, 390, 417, 427, 543
Clement, John 69
Clement, Margaret 24, 69
Clement, Mother Margaret 69, 170, 253
Clibburn, Gerard 275
Cole, Edmund 543
Clifford, Henry (Earl of Cumberland) 17
Clifford, Lord John 39
Clifford, Rosamund 398
Clench/Clinch, John 246, 248, 249, 250, 277, 326, 373
Clinch, John 262
Clitherow, Anne 69, 244, 250, 253
Clitherow, Henry 244, 253
Clitherow, John 238, 240, 241, 244, 245, 246, 249, 251, 253
Clitherow, John 238, 244
CLITHEROW, ST MARGARET xii, xiii, 166, 236-254, 325, 347, 435
Clitherow, Richard 238
Clitherow, Thomas 253
Clitherow, William 238
Clitherow, William 253, 254
Clopton, Anne 458
Clopton, Cuthbert 458-461
Clopton, William 458
Clynnog, Maurice 208, 209, 210, 572
Clynnog, Morgan 208, 572
Cobham, Sir Henry 301
Cockerel, James (prior martyr) 42
Coke, Sir Edward 135, 296, 299, 421, 430
Coke, Sir John 496
Cole, Henry 103

651

Index of Persons

Coleman, Edward (lay martyr) xxiv, 555, 556, 561
Coleman, Walter OSF 501, 541
Colet, John 29, 66
Colleton, John 196, 198, 202, 204, 344, 355
Collins, John 30
Collinson, Margaret 487
Colombière, Claude de la St 574, 575
Colt, Jane 66
Comberford, Henry 240, 249
Con, George 455, 498
Coniers, Samuel 354
Constable, Benedict OSB 612
Constable, Henry (1st Viscount Dunbar) 463, 606
Constable, Sir Henry 149, 489
Constable, John 364
Constable, Lady Margaret née Dormer 149, 490
Constable, Mary (Viscountess Dunbar) 606
Constable, Robert 41
Cook, John 494
Cook, Lawrence 25
Cook, Martha 562
Cooper, Anthony Ashley (Earl of Shaftesbury) 553, 554, 555, 558, 562, 564, 594, 600, 609
Cooper, John 141
Cooper, John 190
Cooper, Richard 429
Cooper, Thomas 114, 131
Copley, Bridget 285, 386
Copley, John 412
Copley, Sir Thomas 99, 100, 285, 336, 512
Copley, William 100, 512
Corby, Ambrose 488, 501
Corby, Ralph (priest martyr) 500, 534, 535
Corker, James (Maurus) OSB 561, 562, 604
Cornelius, John (priest martyr) 152, 176, 177
Cornforth, Thomas SJ 429
Cottam, Thomas (priest martyr) 118, 202, 204, 213, 230, 340, 343
Cotton, George 266, 267, 386
Cotton, John 286, 386
Cotton, Richard 386, 553

Courdres, Martin de OSA 59
Courtenay, Henry (Marquess of Exeter) 17, 58, 65
Coverdale, Miles 78, 79, 155
Covert, Thomas OSF (priest martyr) 70
Cox, Richard 90
Cox, Robert OSB 542
Cranmer, Thomas 3, 18, 32, 38, 52, 60, 65, 68, 71, 74, 75, 78, 79, 80, 85, 87, 88, 89, 90, 97, 137, 155, 156, 346
Creagh, Peter 601
Creagh, Richard 188, 601
Cresswell, Joseph SJ 302, 347
Croft, George 30
Croft, Herbert 590
Croft, Sir Herbert 590
Cromwell, Oliver 51, 465, 514, 515, 516, 520, 525, 526, 538, 546
Cromwell, vere Williams, Richard 51
Cromwell, Richard, 546
Cromwell, Thomas 4, 5, 6, 12, 13, 14, 16, 17, 18, 21, 22, 24, 25, 27, 31, 32, 33, 34, 35, 36, 37, 38, 39, 41, 42, 43, 44, 45, 47, 50, 51, 52, 53, 54, 55, 56, 60, 61, 62, 64, 65, 69, 70, 71, 72, 73, 89, 93, 207, 574
Crockett, Ralph (priest martyr) 259, 360, 362
Crow, Alexander (priest martyr) 162, 163
Crowe, Cecily 497
Crowther, Thomas 175
Curry, John 152, 208, 511
Curteys, Richard 104

D

Dacre, Elizabeth 310
Dacre, Sir Leonard 109
Dacre, Thomas (Lord of Gilsland) 310
Dacre, William (Lord of Gilsland) 115
Dade, Thomas OP 539
Dalby, Robert (priest martyr) 364, 365
Danby, John 620
Daniel, Francis 531
Darbyshire, Thomas SJ 96, 174, 286, 511
Darne, Christian 422
Darrell, Anthony 133
Darrell, Thomas 507
Davenport, Lady Margaret 474

Index of Persons

Darcy, Sir Arthur 41
Darcy, Dorothy 171
Darcy, Lord George 171
Darcy, Lord Thomas of Chiche 58
Darcy, Lord Thomas of Templehurst 41
Dauntsey, William 69, 70
Davies, Richard 370
Davies, William (priest martyr) 151, 172, 173
Davies, William 397, 398
Davies, William 451
Davies, William, 435
Davy, John O.Cart. (deacon martyr) 69
Dawson, Thomas 390
Dean, William (priest martyr) 257, 259, 344, 345, 353
Dee, John 92
Dering, John OSB 61
Devereux, Robert (Earl of Essex) 266, 336, 380, 474
Dibdale, Robert (priest martyr) 118, 262
Dickenson, Francis (priest martyr) 292, 375
Dickenson, John Francis 562
Dickenson, Roger (priest martyr) 131
Digges, Humphrey 586
Dimock, Robert 190
Dingley, Sir Thomas (lay martyr) 58
Dix, William 315
Doe, John 198
Dolben, Sir William 608, 609
Donne, Henry 194
Dormer, Lady Mary 452
Dormer, Robert (Earl of Caernarvon) 463
Douglas, George (priest martyr) xxiii, 120, 160
Dowdall, James (lay martyr) 143
Downes, Francis 480
Downham, William 231, 521
Drake, Sir Francis 180, 431, 436, 447
Draycott, Anthony 103
Drury, Robert (priest martyr) 435
Dryland, Christopher SJ 152, 153, 265, 370, 377
du Bellay, Jean 7
Duckett, James (lay martyr) 143,168 533
Duckett, John (priest martyr) 533, 534

Dudley, John (Duke of Northumberland) 75, 80, 83, 88, 154, 276
Dudley, Margaret 310
Dudley, Robert (Earl of Leicester) 88, 107,133, 187, 188, 196, 199, 208, 224, 287, 363
Dugdale, Stephen 551, 560, 561, 578, 598, 599, 602, 604
Dugdale, Sir William 52
Duke, Edmund (priest martyr) 282, 372
Dutton, Thomas 567

E

Eastgate, John OCist 42
Eastgate, Richard OCist 42
Ecclesfield, Francis 277, 278
Edes, Richard 413
Edmonds, Robert OSB 443
Edward the Confessor St 46, 81
Edward I 473
Edward III 9
Edward IV 35, 64, 73, 89
Edward VI 46, 48, 51, 60, 69, 75-80, 85, 87, 88, 92, 94, 95, 103, 107, 121, 155, 222, 231, 255, 276, 398, 426
Edwards, David 232, 233, 235
Edwards, Francis 362
Egerton, Thomas 203, 341
Egmont, Count (Duke of Gueldres) 487, 501, 503, 504, 503.533, 554
Ely, Humphrey 279, 340, 341
Eliot, George 196, 197, 198, 202, 204, 205, 223, 224, 225, 226
Ellis, Michael OSB 616, 619
Elizabeth I xiii, 2, 4, 5, 43, 46, 48, 83, 86, 90, 91, 92, 94, 95, 96, 97, 98, 100, 103, 104, 105, 107, 108, 109, 110,111, 112, 113, 114, 116, 117, 119, 120, 121, 123, 131, 133, 134, 135, 141, 142, 143, 149, 153, 154, 155, 156, 157, 161, 162, 164, 169, 170, 177, 178, 180, 183, 184, 185, 186, 187, 188, 189,199, 201, 203, 204, 205, 206, 207, 208, 212, 213, 214, 216, 217, 221, 224, 225, 226, 230, 231, 234, 235, 240, 248, 251, 256, 257, 260, 263, 270 276, 277, 278, 279, 281, 283, 284, 285, 286, 292, 294, 295, 296, 273, 298, 301, 304, 305, 306, 307, 308, 309,310, 311, 312, 313, 314, 315, 316,

653

Index of Persons

318, 319, 322, 324, 325, 326, 327, 339, 340, 343, 344, 345, 352, 353, 354, 355, 357, 358, 361, 363, 375, 376, 379, 380, 382, 387, 389, 390, 401, 402, 403, 411, 426, 437, 452, 465, 473, 521, 590
Emerson, Ralph SJ 141, 142, 190, 196, 210, 339, 379
Epson, Thomas OSB 25
Erasmus, Desiderius 29, 52, 62, 64, 67, 68
Errington, George (lay martyr) 254, 277, 281, 351, 373, 379, 609
Ralph (3rd Baron Eure) 130, 245, 246
Evans, Charles 570
EVANS, ST PHILIP 569-571, 572, 590, 593
Evans, William 569
Evelyn, John 555, 558, 615
Evingham, Richard 179
Ewens, Matthew 306
Exmew, William O.Cart. (priest martyr) 26, 56, 63
Eynon, John OSB (priest martyr) 57

F

Fairfax, Lady Anne 487
Fairfax, Sir Thomas 249
Fairfax, Sir Thomas (Viscount Fairfax) 490
Falkner, John 489
Faringdon, Hugh vere Cook OSB (abbot martyr) 55, 56, 57, 58
Farnese, Alexander, (Duke of Parma) 301
Fawcet, Roland 251
Fawkes, Guy xiv, 393, 394, 402, 444, 445
Feckenham, John OSB 81, 87, 89, 90, 96, 361 449
Felton, John (lay martyr) xxiv, 112, 156
Felton, John SJ 541
Felton, Thomas (martyr) 257, 358
Fenn, James (priest martyr) 355
Fenn, John 355
Fenn, Robert 355
Fenwick, John vere Caldwell SJ (priest martyr) 560, 599, 600
Feron, Robert 63
Ferrers, Henry 63
Ferrers, Katherine 63

Fetherston, Richard (priest martyr) 59, 73
Fieldsend, William 106
Fettiplace, Bessels 197
Filby, George 340
Filby, John 340, 366
Filby, William (priest martyr) 198, 199, 202, 229, 230, 340, 362, 364
Filcock, Roger SJ (priest martyr) 336, 337, 384, 386, 446
Filcock, Simon 384
Fincham, Richard 558
Fisher, John (Cardinal/martyr) xix, xx, xxi, 2, 4, 7, 15, 22, 27, 31, 41, 57, 60, 64, 65, 123, 484
Fisher, Philip vere Copley SJ 100, 492, 512, 513
Fitzalan, Henry (Earl of Arundel) 310
Fitzalan, Mary 310
Fitz-Charles, Charlotte 547
Fitzherbert, Sir Anthony 17, 123, 124, 510
Fitzherbert family 123-125
Fitzherbert, Sir Thomas 124, 273
Fitzherbert, Thomas SJ 125, 190, 195, 489, 510
Fleet, John 406
Fleetwood, William 257, 270
Fletcher, John 426
Flower vere Floyd, Richard (lay martyr) 259
Floyd, Henry SJ 383
Floyd, John SJ 445, 542
Floyd, Owen 259
Ford, Thomas (priest martyr) 179, 196, 201, 202, 338, 342, 344
Fordam, Christopher 248
Forest, John OSF (priest martyr) 44, 70
Forster, Sir Humphrey 198
Fortescue, Adrian (lay martyr) 58, 71, 72, 212
Fortescue, Isabel 328
Foster, Isabella 136
Foster, Seth 136
Foster, Thomas SJ 541
Foster, Thomas 136
Foster, William 136
Fox, Charles James 552
Foxe, John 79, 83, 84, 85, 86, 310, 311, 3456

654

Index of Persons

Frank, John 325, 401
Freeman, William (priest martyr) 369
Freshwater, Edward 497
Fulthering, John (lay martyr) 393
Fulthrop, Edward (lay martyr) 379
Fulwood, Richard SJ 109, 401

G

Gage, Elizabeth 450
Gage, Francis 336
Gage, George 542, 552, 556
Gage, Sir Henry 336, 499, 500, 539, 540
Gage, John 336
Gage, Sir John 336, 499, 542
Gage, Lady Margaret 297, 335, 336, 499, 542
Gage, Thomas 336, 540
Gage, William SJ 336
Gardener, John 363
Gardiner, Bernard 324
Gardiner, German (lay martyr) 59, 74,
Gardiner, James 392
Gardiner, James 620
Gardiner, Stephen 74
Gardiner, Sir Thomas 459
Garlick, Nicholas (priest martyr) xxii, 124, 126, 128, 157, 161, 172, 360
Garnet, Brian 408
Garnet, Eleanor 69
Garnet, Henry SJ (priest martyr) xiii, 69, 107, 125, 129, 130, 152, 161, 164, 165, 166, 169, 174, 176, 260, 263, 273, 281, 286, 287, 288, 290, 296, 297, 298, 299, 305, 306, 308, 319, 321, 324, 327, 331, 334, 337, 376, 377, 379, 384, 389, 399, 400, 401, 402, 403, 404, 405, 406, 407, 408, 409, 410, 411, 412, 413, 433, 434, 445, 446, 447, 455, 490, 509, 511, 629
Garnet, Margaret 69, 324
Garnet, Richard 412
GARNET, ST THOMAS xvi, 385, 407, 412-415, 419, 420
Gascoigne, Catherine 450
Gascoigne, Francis 608
Gascoigne, John 608
Gascoigne, Sir John 450, 607
Gascoigne, Michael, OSB 608
Gascoigne, Thomas 500
Gascoigne, Sir Thomas 517, 608, 609,

Gates, John 129
Gaudy/Gawdy, Justice Francis 226, 330, 331
Gavan, John SJ (priest martyr) 552, 560, 600, 601
Geldard, Janet 239, 242
Geldard, Lancelot 239, 240
Geldard, Percival 240
Gellebrand, Nicholas 153
GENNINGS, ST EDMUND 152, 261-264, 268, 269, 270, 274, 377, 387, 573
Gennings, John OSF 262, 264, 532, 573
Geoffrey, Martin 76
George I 481
George II 620
George III 617
Gerard, John SJ xiii, 101, 109, 119, 124, 151, 152, 158, 166, 173, 174, 260, 273, 289, 302, 305, 306, 308, 317, 321, 323, 324, 325, 326, 328, 331, 332, 333, 335, 336, 339, 352, 382, 393, 399, 400, 401, 404, 405, 407, 408, 410, 414, 415, 435, 443, 444, 445, 466, 511
Gerard, Marjery 465, 466
Gerard, Miles (priest martyr) 292, 375, 376
Gerard, Sir Thomas 173, 317, 318, 352
Gervase, George OSB (priest martyr) 436
Gibson, John 135
Gibson, William (lay martyr) 254, 352, 379
Gibson, William 42
Gibson, William 252
Giffard, Charles 546
Giffard, Bonaventure OSB 558, 616, 618, 619
Giffard, Peter 546
Giffin, Maurice 322
Gifford, Gilbert 117, 158
Gifford, William OSB 548
Gilbert, George xix
Gilbert of Sempringham, St 222
Giustiniani, Giovanni 458, 459
Glanville, Sir John 164
Godfrey, Sir Edmund Berry 553, 556, 557, 558, 592
Godfrey, Cardinal William xx
Godsalf, George 223, 227

655

Index of Persons

Godwin, Elizabeth 497
Godwin, Fraser 582
Gold, Henry 61
Goldwell, Thomas 154, 211, 347, 354, 356, 362
Gondomar, Diego de Sarmiento 399, 429, 431, 439, 440, 451, 483
Good, John 174
Gooden, Peter 621
Goodman, Godfrey 457, 512
Goodman, John 457, 458, 499, 524, 541
Gordon, Lord George 623
Gorkum, Martyrs of 164
Goter, John xxv
Gratley, Edward 313, 314, 315, 316, 365, 367
Graves, Hugh 240
Gray, John 499, 522
Grayson, Thomas 236, 237
Greaves, Francis 429
Green, Hugh (priest martyr) 518, 529
Green, John 363
Green, John OP 622
Green, Robert (lay martyr) 557, 561
Green, Thomas O.Cart. (priest martyr) 69
Greene, Francis 606
Greenwood, William O.Cart. (martyr) 69
Gregory the Great St 18, 47, 145, 264, 291, 421, 424
Gregory XIII xix, xx, 27, 113, 125, 146, 177, 191, 210, 346, 375
Gregory XIV 170
Gregory XV 452
Gregory, Arthur 306
Grene, Christopher SJ xix, 279
Grenville, George 183
Grenville, Sir Richard 180, 181, 182, 183, 184
Gray, Lady Catherine 277
Grey, Henry (Marquess of Dorset) 88
Grey, Lady Jane 46, 80, 88, 90
Grey, William (Lord Grey de Wilton) 76, 78
Griffith, John (priest martyr) 58
Grimston, Ralph (lay martyr) xiv, 193
Grindal, Edmund 97, 103, 104, 142, 426
Grissold, Clement 434
Grissold, Robert (lay martyr) 392, 434
Grove, John (lay martyr) 553, 556, 561, 598, 600
Gunne, Gregory 625
Gunston, Sir David (lay martyr) 59, 74, 327
Gunter, Thomas 569, 590, 591
Gunter, William (priest martyr) 257, 357
Gupil, René St 513
Guzman de Silva, Don Diego 377
Gwent, Richard 24
Gwyn, Catherine 231, 234
GWYN, ST RICHARD 231-236
Gwynneth, John 107
Gylham, William 31

H

Habington family 402, 403, 404, 406
Hackshott, John 543
Hackshott, Thomas (lay martyr) 383, 543
Haile, John (priest martyr) 17, 63, 574
Hales, Sir Christopher 27
Hall, Elizabeth 137
Hall, Frances 493
Hambley, John (priest martyr) 118, 120, 160, 258
Hammerton, Sir Stephen 41
Hammond, John 501
Hampden, John 618
Hampden, Sir John 63
Hansby, Agnes 162
Hanse, Everard (priest martyr) 199, 364
Hanslepp, Roger 583, 592
Hanson, John 96
Harcourt, William vere Barlow SJ (priest martyr) 560, 600
Hardesty, Robert (lay martyr) 368
Hardesty, William 193, 280, 282
Hargrave, Richard 141
Harman, Julian 196, 198
Harrington, Sir John 3890
Harrington, William (priest martyr) 194
Harris, Jane 593
Harris, John 59
Harris, Thomas 182
Harrison, James (priest martyr) 143, 168

656

Index of Persons

Harrison, John 175
Harrison, Matthew (Matthias) 143
Harrison, Richard (abbot martyr) 42
Harrison, William 452
Harrison, William 597
Harold II 37
Hart, John SJ 202, 213, 340, 342, 510
Hart, William (priest martyr) 150, 175, 244, 249, 349, 350
Hartley, William (priest martyr) 195, 259, 337, 343
Harvey, Thomas SJ 501
Harwood, John OCist. 54
Hastings, Henry (Earl of Huntingdon) xiii, 104, 125, 132, 138, 139,143, 162, 163, 243, 276, 277, 278, 279, 280, 281, 283, 284, 285, 303, 307, 309, 348, 374, 378
Hastings, Theophilus (7th Earl of Huntingdon) 564
Hatton, Sir Christopher 199, 317
Hawarden, Edward 631
Hawkesworth, Robert 165, 541
Hawksworth, William 193
Haydock, Ewan 353
Haydock, George (priest martyr) xxii, 353, 354, 356, 444
Haydock, Richard 353
Haydock, William OCist. 42
Haywood, William 495, 496
Heath, Dorothy 369
Heath, Henry OSF (priest martyr) 530, 531, 538
Heath, Nicholas 31
Heath, Nicholas 84, 95, 154, 310
Heath, Sir Robert 467, 478, 479
Heath, Thomas 168
Hebburn, Anthony 435
Henderson, William 501
Heigham, William 333
Hemsworth, Stephen 106
Henley, Walter 47
Henrietta Maria, Queen 372, 453, 454, 455, 458, 485, 494, 496, 497, 498, 500, 506, 522, 523, 524, 542, 548, 599, 604
Henry II 8, 398
Henry V xxv, 10, 15
Henry VII 51, 61, 70
Henry VIII 1, 2, 3, 4, 5, 6, 7, 8, 11, 12, 13, 15, 16, 17, 18, 20, 21, 22, 23, 25, 26, 28, 30, 31, 33, 34, 35, 36, 37, 38, 39, 40, 41, 42, 43, 44, 45, 46, 47, 48, 50, 52, 53, 54, 55, 56, 57, 58, 59, 60, 61, 62, 63, 64, 65, 66, 67, 68, 70, 71, 72, 73, 74, 79, 80, 87, 88, 89, 93, 94, 97, 105, 107, 143, 155, 188, 221, 229, 255, 285, 309, 398, 426
Herbert, James 594
Herbert, William (Earl of Powis) 589, 603, 604
Heron, Giles (lay martyr) 25, 69, 70
Heron, Sir John 25
Herst, Richard (lay martyr) 456, 472, 509
Hesketh, Ildephonse OSB 540
Hesketh, Jerome OSB 562
Hewett, John (priest martyr) 259, 363
Heywood, Jasper 313, 344, 510
Heywood, John 74
Heywood, Oliver 107
Hide, Leonard 345, 346
Hildesley, William 198
Hill, Lawrence (lay martyr) 557, 558, 561,
Hill, Richard (priest martyr) 282, 373
Hill, Thomas 392
Hills, Henry 618
Hilton, Andrew 274, 275, 362
Hillyard, William 307, 378
Hitchmough, Richard 621
Hobbes, Robert OCist. 42
Hodge, John 182
Hodgkins, John 155
Hodgson, Edmund 163
Hodgson, John 163
Hodgson, Robert 163
Hodgson, Sidney (lay martyr) 270
Hogg, John (priest martyr) 282, 373
Holcroft, Thomas 55
Holford, Thomas (priest martyr) 257, 267, 324, 370
Holgate, Robert 79
Holiday, Richard (priest martyr) 282, 373
Holland, Hugh 30
Holland, Richard 532
Holland, Thomas SJ (priest martyr) 532, 533
Holmes, Robert 264, 265
Holtby, Richard SJ 126, 136, 152, 193, 215, 277, 303, 304, 308, 378, 490, 500, 506, 510,, 511, 613

657

Index of Persons

Hooper, John 90
Hopton, Cecily 218
Hopton, Sir Owen 218, 224, 316, 317
Hore, Richard 182
Horne, William O.Cart.(martyr) 25, 69
Horner, Nicholas (lay martyr) 291, 292
Horner, William 259
Horsey, Ralph 176
Hotham, Sir John 133
Hothersall, George 325, 326
HOUGHTON, ST JOHN 10-25, 56,
Houghton, Richard 195
Houghton, Sir Richard 166
Houghton, Simon 422, 423
Howard, née Dacre, Anne (Countess of Arundel) 290, 295, 310, 311, 312, 315, 316, 321, 337
Howard, Catherine Queen 45, 60, 62, 309
Howard, Charles (Lord Effingham/Earl of Nottingham) 256, 319, 410, 412, 507
Howard, Elizabeth 313, 321
Howard, Lord Henry 312, 313
Howard, Henry (Earl of Surrey) 285, 309
Howard, Henry (6th Duke of Norfolk) 549, 550, 597
Howard, Isabella 539
HOWARD, ST PHILIP xxiv, 152, 158, 170, 285, 296, 309-322, 367, 381, 439, 549, 561, 597
Howard, Philip Thomas (Cardinal) 322, 547, 597, 614, 615
Howard, Thomas (2nd Duke of Norfolk) 10, 42, 319
Howard, Thomas (3rd Duke of Norfolk) 5, 17, 23, 40, 44, 67, 68, 112
Howard, Thomas (4th Duke of Norfolk) 170, 308
Howard, Thomas (8th Duke of Norfolk) 518
Howard, Thomas (Earl of Arundel) 438, 439, 603
Howard, Thomas (Earl of Berkshire) 559
Howard, Lord William 312, 313, 315, 411
Howard, William (Viscount Stafford, lay martyr) xxv, 332, 539, 321, 561, 603, 604

Huddleston, John OSB 546, 563, 598, 599
Huddlestone, Sir Edmund 328
Huddlestone, Jane 324
Hughes, John 234
Hume, Cardinal Basil OSB 321
Humphrey, Laurence (lay martyr) 131, 132
Humphreys, James 182
Hungate, Lady Jane 606
Hunt, Eleanor 137
Hunt, Gilbert 167
Hunt, Thomas vere Benstead (priest martyr) 143, 163, 164
Hunt, Thurstan (priest martyr) 143, 166, 167
Hunter, Anthony SJ 562
Hussey, Lord John 41
Hutton, John 243, 244
Hutton, Mary 243
Hutton, Matthew 134, 136, 281, 285, 349, 390, 426
Hutton, Peter 243
Hutton, Richard 106
Hutton, William 240, 243, 350
Hyde, Anne (Duchess of York) 547
Hyde, Edward (Earl of Clarendon) 548

I

Ile, Hugh 144
Ingham, Richard 127-128
Ingle, Richard 512
Ingleby, Anne 450
Ingleby, Francis (priest martyr) xiii, 244, 245, 246, 276, 351, 366
Ingleby, Sir William 132, 137, 351
Ingram, John (priest martyr) 279-284
Ingworth, Richard 26, 32
Innocent XI 615, 616
Ireland, John (priest martyr) 59, 74
Ireland, Richard 457
Ireland, William vere Iremonger SJ (priest martyr) 556, 565, 597, 598, 599, 600

J

Jackson, John 542
Jackson, Richard 324
James I xii, 83, 95, 100, 120, 125, 145, 185, 253, 260, 266, 325, 340, 372, 388, 395, 397, 409, 410, 413, 415, 418, 423,

Index of Persons

428, 429, 431, 442, 443, 447, 452, 467, 473, 483, 489, 508, 512, 582
James II 452, 535, 545, 548, 552, 554, 555, 556, 557, 558, 562, 563, 564, 574, 582, 595, 597, 600, 603, 604, 605, 608, 610, 612, 613, 614, 616, 617, 618, 619
James, Edward (priest martyr) 259, 359, 360, 361
James, Dorothy 593
James, Roger OSB (priest martyr) 57
James, Walter 572
Jebb, Robert 130
Jeffreys, Sir George 556, 564, 565
Jeffreys, Sir John 182, 183
Jenison, Thomas SJ 611
Jenkins, Christopher 588
Jenkins, David 196, 197, 198
Jenkinson, Henry OCist 42
Jenks, Roland 216
Jenks, Sylvester 574
Jerome, St 16, 18, 425
Jewel, John 90, 101, 104
Jogues, Isaac St 512
John of Beverley, St xxv
John of Bridlington, St xix, xxv
John Chrysostom, St xxi, 82, 425, 596
John Paul II xxiii, 632
Johnson, George 567
Johnson, Robert (priest martyr) 201, 202, 213, 341, 344
Johnson, Thomas O.Cart. (martyr) 69
Johnson, William 442
Jones, Edward (priest martyr) 292, 376
JONES, ST JOHN 322-327, 412
Jones, Nicholas 294, 295, 325
Jones, Sir William 497
Jordan, Agnes 45, 46
Jowsey, Andrew 606
Julius II 28
Julius III 81

K
Kellison, Matthew 466, 522, 583
Kelloway, Francis 315
Kemble, Charles 587
Kemble, George 583
Kemble, John 580
KEMBLE, ST JOHN 582-588, 594, 612
Kemble, Richard 583, 587
Kemble, Walter OSB 583

Kemish, David OP 562, 611
Kemp, Boniface OSB 540
Kemp, David 258
Kempe, John 182
Ken, Thomas 563, 617
Kendall, Thomas 271
Kennet, Samuel 342
Kilbeck, William 371
Killingale, Anne 138, 139
Killingale, Henry 138, 139
Kingsmill, Catherine 196, 198
Kingsmill, George 331, 434
Kingsmill, Morpheta 46
KIRBY, ST LUKE 201, 202, 210, 213, 228-230, 343
Kirkby, Christopher 552
Kirkham, Richard 393
Kirkman, Richard (priest martyr) 244, 347, 348
Kitchin, Anthony 95
Knaresborough, John xix
Knight, William (lay martyr) 254, 352, 379
Knightly, Andrew 525, 544, 545
Knightly, Edward 544
Knightly, Robert 517
Knightly, Sir Valentine 544
Knollys, Sir Francis 215, 366
Knowles, Simon xiii, 141
Knox, John 154
Knyveton, William 215

L
Lacey, Brian (lay martyr) 270
Lacey, William (priest martyr) 150, 244, 347, 348
Lacy, Richard SJ vere Prince 611
Laithwait, Thomas SJ 392, 433
Lalande, Jean de St 513
Lambton, Joseph (priest martyr) 284, 373, 374
Lampley, William (lay martyr) 259
Langhorne, Charles 602, 603
Langhorne, Francis 603
Langhorne, Richard (lay martyr) 561, 602, 603
Langley, Anne 162
Langley, Richard (lay martyr) 136, 162, 163, 346
Larke, John (priest martyr) 59, 74
Lascelles, Agnes 136

Index of Persons

Lascelles, Clare 461
Lascelles, Sir Robert 462
Latimer, Hugh 44, 52, 72, 79, 85, 87, 89, 102
Laud, William 455, 456, 459, 496, 499, 501, 523
Laund Anne 189
Lawrence, Peter 58
LAWRENCE, ST ROBERT 8-20
Lawson, Dorothy 490, 491, 499
Lawson, Sir Ralph 490
Lawson, Roger 490
Layton, Richard 32, 33, 35, 42, 56
Lee, Rowland 3, 11, 16, 20, 43, 47
Legh, Elizabeth 474
Legh, Thomas 32, 35, 47, 55
Legh, Sir Urian 474
Leigh, Gilbert 132
Leigh, Richard (priest martyr) 259, 358, 359
Leigh, Valentine 359
Lellis, de Camillus St 154
Leo X 1, 29, 43
Leo XIII xx
Lessius, Leonard SJ 286
Le Strange, Alice 442
Le Strange, Sir Hamon 442
Leveson, Francis OSF 579
Leveson, William OSF 579, 580, 581
Lewin, Christopher 373
LEWIS, ST DAVID 570, 585, 588-596
Lewis, Morgan 588
Lewis, Owen 144, 209, 375, 449
Lewis, Thomas 591
Leyburn, George 454, 614
Leyburn, John 616, 618, 621
Liddel, William 491
Lillie, John SJ xiii, 334, 335, 401
Linacre, Thomas 29, 66
LINE, ST ANNE xiii, 152, 332-337, 382, 435, 446
Line, Roger 333
Lion, John (lay martyr) 143
Lister, Jane 169
Lister, Thomas SJ 266, 404
Litchfield, Clement 89
Littleton, Humphrey 406, 409
LLOYD, ST JOHN 571, 572-573
Lloyd, Walter 572
Lloyd, William 573, 574

Lockwood, Christopher 462
Lockwood, John (priest martyr) 462, 463, 464, 519
Lodge, John 609
Lomax, James 174
Lombard, Peter 543, 544
London, John 32,
London, John 399
London, Roger OSB 58
Longueville, Thomas 500
Loop, George 594
Louis VII 46
Louis XIV 548, 557, 576
Lowe, Joan 196, 198
Lowe, John (priest martyr) 118, 119
Loyola, Ignatius St 221, 250
Ludlam, Robert (priest martyr) xxii, 124, 160, 161
Luke, Robert 484
Lumsden, Andrew OP 563
Lusher, Edward SJ 493, 499
Luther, Martin 1, 5, 72, 194
Lyth, Matthew 607

M

Mabbs, Lawrence OSB 542
Machell, George 522, 545
Machiavelli, Niccoló 5, 511
Mackerell, Matthew 41, 42
Major, Anthony 279, 280
Mallet, Dorothy 167
Mallet, James 6
Maloney, John Baptist 623
Man, Henry 20
Manners, Sir Oliver 174, 332
Manners, Roger (Earl of Rutland) 332
Manny, Sir Walter de 9
Manwood, Sir Roger 182, 184, 259, 444
Marillac, Charles de 1, 46
Markland, Alexander 378
Marsden, William (priest martyr) 114,
Marsh, George 569
Marsh, John 258
Marshall, Thomas 105
Martin, Gregory 145, 164, 170, 178, 184, 188, 201, 310, 311, 338
Martin, Richard (lay martyr) 259
Mary I xvi, 2, 3, 15, 30, 46, 48, 53, 62, 68, 69, 70, 73, 74, 77, 78, 80-87, 90, 91, 96, 97, 98, 99, 103, 105, 106,

Index of Persons

107, 124, 155, 156, 175, 187, 196, 208, 221, 222, 223, 231, 236, 286, 310, 322, 399, 427, 474
Mary II 618, 619, 620
Mary of Modena 556, 565, 576, 605, 616, 618
Mary Stuart (Queen of Scots) 109, 112, 116, 117, 119, 120, 124, 157, 158, 173, 221, 250, 276, 298, 306, 310, 389
Maskew, Bridget 254
Maskew, Thomas 254
Mason, John (lay martyr) 263, 270
Massey, Edward 567
Masters, Richard 42
Masters, Richard 61
Matthew, Tobie 278, 285, 338, 372, 373, 374
Matthew, Sir Tobie 372
Maxey, John 444
Maxfield, Thomas (priest martyr) 431, 439, 440
Maxfield, William 352
Maxfield, William 439
May, Henry 237, 242, 244, 245, 247, 250
Mayhew, Edward OSB 449, 450
Mayhew, Henry 449, 450
Mayler, Henry 429
MAYNE, ST CUTHBERT 178-186, 212, 221, 296, 346, 431
Mayne, William 178
Mayo, Thomas 458, 459, 460, 482, 500, 531, 538
Médaille, Jean-Pierre 590
Medeley, William 122
Meehan, Charles OSF (priest martyr) 607
Mendoza, Bernardino de 227
Mercurian, Everard SJ 189, 190, 191, 209
Meredith, Jonas 315, 380
Metham, Thomas 146, 171
Metham, Sir Thomas 171
Meynell, Gerardine 518
Mico, Edward SJ 554
Middlemore, Humphrey O.Cart. (priest martyr) 11, 22, 63
Middleton, Alice 66
Middleton, Anthony (priest martyr) 292, 376
Middleton, Jane 236
Middleton, Robert (priest martyr) 143, 166, 167, 171
Middleton, Thomas 236
Mileham, Nicholas 42
Miles, Francis 420
Miller, Ralph 194
Milner, Ralph (lay martyr) 131
Millward, Thomas 574, 582
Molinari, Paolo xxii
Mompesson, Henry 412
Mompesson, Sir John 264
Mompesson, Lawrence 148
Montford, Thomas 392
Monteith, Robert 588
Moore, William 58
Moore, William 223
Mordaunt, Lord Henry 438
More, Cecily 69
More, Cresacre 450
More, Elizabeth 69
More, Helen 450
More, Henry SJ 207, 467
More, Hugh (lay martyr) 257, 358
More, Sir John 66
More, Thomas 453
More, Sir Thomas (lay martyr) xix, xx, xxi, 1, 2, 4, 9, 15, 19, 22, 24, 25, 27, 29, 41, 53, 57, 60, 62, 64, 65, 66, 69, 70, 74, 105, 115, 123, 141, 186, 207, 285, 411, 416, 450, 452, 453, 475, 528,
More, Sir William 115, 266
Moreland, William 271
Morgan, Anne 582
Morgan, Edward (priest martyr) 529, 530
Morgan, Sir Edward 590
Morgan, Lady Frances 590
Morgan, Henry 154
Morgan, John 582
Morgan, John 611
Morgan, Polydore 268, 269
Morgan, William SJ 589
Morgan, Winifred 569
Morone, Cardinal Giovanni 209
Morris, George 107
Morris, James 436, 437
Morris, John SJ xx
Morris, Robert 233, 234
Morse, George 500
MORSE, ST HENRY xv, 487-504, 523, 539

661

Index of Persons

Morse, Robert 487
Morse, Robert 488, 500
Morse, William SJ 488, 498
Morton, Sir George 176
Morton, John (Cardinal) 66
Morton, Matthew 479
Morton, Robert (priest martyr) 257, 357
Mowbray, Lawrence 608
Mowbray, Thomas de 11
Mudd, James 253
Mudd, Maud 238
Mudd, Michael 241
Mudd, Thomas O.Cist 106, 426
Munday, Anthony 202, 204, 220, 230, 338, 386, 387
Murphy, Cornelius SJ 465
Murray, William (Lord Mansfield) 622, 623
Muscot, George vere Fisher 531
Mush, John xii, xiii, 138, 149, 162, 238, 240, 241, 242, 244, 247, 251, 252, 253, 262, 346, 347, 380, 436
Mush, William 262, 436

N
Napper, George (priest martyr) 437, 438
Neale, John 208
Needham, Sebastian 583
Neile, Richard 491
Nelson, John (priest martyr) 171, 186, 211
Nelson, Martin 146, 171
Nelson, Thomas 171
Neri, Philip St 210
Nevill, Francis SJ 610
Neville, Charles (6th Earl of Westmorland) 109, 277, 285
Neville, Lady Margaret 277, 278, 284, 285
Neville, Thomas 592
Newdigate, Sebastian O.Cart. (priest martyr) 21, 22, 63
Newman, Cardinal John Henry xviii, 92, 612
Newman, William 335
Newport, Richard (priest martyr) 437, 438, 449, 451
Newton, Francis 483, 495, 496, 497, 498, 499, 502, 524, 530, 543

Nichols, George (priest martyr) 365 366
Nichols, John 229, 230
Nightingale, Florence 625
Norris, Richard 399, 444
North, Andrew 533
North, Sir Edward 25
North, Francis 560
Northburgh, Michael 9
Norton, Basil 544, 545
Norton, Benjamin 129, 139
Norton, John (lay martyr) 143, 165
Norton, Margaret 165
Norton, Thomas 357
Norton, Thomas 216, 217, 346
Nowak, Edward xxiii
Nutter, John (priest martyr) 354
Nutter, Robert (priest martyr) 167, 344, 354, 356

O
Oates, Titus 549-567, 578, 580, 585, 586, 594, 597, 598, 599, 600, 601, 603, 605, 608, 613, 621
Ogilvie, St John 432
Oglethorpe, Jane 463
Oglethorpe, Owen 91, 154
Oldcorne, Alice 243
Oldcorne, Edward SJ (priest martyr) 266, 291, 401, 403, 404, 405, 406, 407, 408, 444, 445, 447
Oldcorne, John 444
Osbaldeston, Edward (priest martyr) 149
Osbaldeston, Thomas 149
Osborn, Edward 206
Osborne, Thomas (Earl of Danby) 553, 556, 616
Ostcliff, George 106, 202
Ottemberg, Herman 583
Owen, George 398
Owen, John 362
Owen, Lewis 418, 421, 450
OWEN, ST NICHOLAS 270, 289, 325, 398-408, 488, 574

P
Page, Anthony (priest martyr) 382, 383, 607, 613
Page, Francis SJ (priest martyr) 169, 335, 336, 382, 383

662

Index of Persons

Paget, Thomas (Baron Beaudesert) 190
Paine, Jerome 227
PAINE, ST JOHN 179, 220-228
Pakington, Humphrey 574
Pakington, John 574
Pakington, Sir John 576
Palaser, Thomas (priest martyr) 143, 164, 165
Palmer, Charles SJ 618
Palmer, Katherine 46
Palmes, George 96
Palmes, George SJ 443
Panzani, Gregorio 396, 454, 455
Parker, Matthew 90, 96, 155
Parker, William (Lord Monteagle) 393, 394, 403, 404
Parkyn, Robert 107
Parlour, Hugh 165, 383
Parr, Katherine, Queen 50, 54
Parr, Sir Thomas 50
Parry, Charles 562
Parry, William 122
Parsons, John 558
Paschal, John 210, 211, 212, 214, 437,
Paslew, John OCist. (abbot martyr) 42
Pate, Richard 154
Pattenson, William (priest martyr) 148
Paulucci, Lorenzo 525
Pavier, Francis 463
Pavier, Richard 463
Paul III 65
Paul V 450
Paul VI x, xx, xxi, 632
Paulet, Sir Amias 119
Paulet, John (Marquess of Winchester) 539
Paul of St William 59
Peacock, John 42
Peckham, Sir Edmund 119
Peckham, Sir George 582
Pegge, Catharine 547
Pegge, William 545
Pemberton, Sir Francis 608, 610
Penn, William 615
Pennington, Sir Isaac 533
Pennington, Joyce 462
Pepys, Samuel 555
Percy, John SJ 543
Percy, Lady Mary 522

Percy, Thomas (Earl of Northumberland, lay martyr) xxiv, 109, 110, 426, 522
Percy, Thomas 419
Percy, Sir Thomas 41
Perkins, Francis 265
Perpetua, St 378
Persons, Robert SJ 84, 121, 125, 146, 150, 174, 189, 190, 192, 193, 195, 196, 199, 211, 212, 215, 216, 217, 228, 287, 293, 302, 338, 341, 343, 372, 379, 446
Peterson, William 59
Peto, William, OSF 43, 322
Petre, Lady Anne 196, 221, 222, 226
Petre, Benjamin xxv, 619
Petre, John (1st Baron Petre) 207
Petre, Richard 96
Petre, Robert (3rd Baron Petre) 207
Petre, Sir William 53, 54, 96, 201, 207 221
Petre, William (2nd Baron Petre) 207
Petre, William (4th Baron Petre) 603, 604
Petre, William (13th Baron Petre) 207
Pettingat, Samuel 147, 148
Phelippes, Thomas 152, 306, 315
Philip II 81, 111, 121, 144, 256, 303, 510
Philip, Robert OSB 455
Philips, John 182
Philpot, Clement (lay martyr) 59
Pibush, John (priest martyr) 143, 165,
Pickering, John OSD 42
Pickering, Thomas OSB (brother martyr) 553, 561, 605
Piers, John 254
Pierson, Walter O.Cart. (martyr) 69
Pike, William (lay martyr) 159
Pilcher, Thomas (priest martyr) 120, 158, 159
Pitts, Arthur 195, 209, 353
Pius IV 108
Pius V St 109, 110, 112, 113, 156, 188, 204, 293, 358, 411
Pius IX 624, 631
Pius XI xx
PLASDEN, ST POLYDORE 262, 267, 268-271, 274
PLESSINGTON, ST JOHN 566-569, 611
Plessington, Robert 566

663

Index of Persons

Plumtree, Thomas (priest martyr) xxiv, 112, 155, 156
Plunket, St Oliver (Archbishop martyr) 561, 601, 605, 609, 610
Pole, Edward 175
Pole, Sir Geoffrey 346
Pole, Henry, (Lord Montague) 64, 276
Pole, Margaret (Countess of Salisbury, lay martyr) 58, 59, 64, 73, 74, 276
Pole, Reginald (Cardinal) 81, 82, 84, 91, 170, 208, 276, 346,
Pollard, James SJ vere Sharpe 397
Pollard, Richard 56
Poole, David 124, 154
Popham, John 166, 169, 182, 203, 296, 316, 317, 327, 335, 341, 383, 384, 410
Pormort, Thomas (priest martyr) 291, 374, 375
Port, Elizabeth 173
Port, Sir John 173
Portman, John 552, 604
Postgate, Nicholas (priest martyr) xxii, xxiii, 518, 605, 606, 607
Pound, John 120
Pound, Thomas 120, 340, 341
Powel, Philip OSB (priest martyr) 535, 588
Powell, Edward D.D. (priest martyr) 59, 72
Powell, Margaret 530
Poyntz, Mary 463
Poyntz, Sir Nicholas 355
Prance, Miles 552, 557, 560, 564, 612
Preston, Thomas 133
Preston, Thomas OSB 449
Price, Charles 591
Price, Charles 592
Price, Ignatius/Walter SJ 592, 593
Pritchard, Charles SJ 551, 592
Pritchard, John 589
Pritchard, Margaret 588
Proctor, Sir Stephen 137, 168
Prodger, Charles 569
Prynne, William 501, 515
Pugh, Robert 172
Pugh, Robert 610
Pugh, William 548
Pullan, Michael OSB xiv
Pullan, Robert xiv
Pulleyn, James xiii
Pulleyn, Joshua SJ xiii, 123, 334, 510
Pulleyn, Maria xiv
Pulleyn, William xiii
Punte, John 42
Pym, John 464, 553

Q

Quartermain, William 620, 621
Quashet, John Francis 529

R

Radclyffe, Edward (Earl of Derwentwater) 547
Raleigh, Sir Walter 176, 180, 270, 271
Randolph, Leo OSF 573, 581, 582
Ravis, Thomas 414, 420
Rawlins, Alexander (priest martyr) 262, 265, 308, 309, 370, 376, 377, 378
Reding, Thomas O.Cart. (martyr) 69
Rawstone, Alice 566
Reeves, John 604
Reynold, William 140
REYNOLDS, ST RICHARD 14-20, 56, 61, 123
Reynolds, Richard (Thomas) vere Green (priest martyr) 485-487
Reynolds, Thomas 154
Reynolds, Walter 26
Rich, Sir Edwin 447
Rich, Hugh OSF 61
Richard, Sir Rich 13, 62, 66, 227, 459
Rich, Robert (Earl of Warwick) 227, 459
Richard III 73
Richardson, Lawrence (Johnson) (priest martyr) 208, 343
Richardson, William 59
Richardson, William (priest martyr) 143, 169
Richelieu, Cardinal Armand de 506
Rider, Nicholas 593
Ridley, Nicholas 79, 80, 85, 87
Ridolfi, Roberto di 111, 112
RIGBY, ST JOHN 327-332
Rigby, Nicholas 327
Rishton, Edward 202, 204, 208, 210, 340, 343, 344
ROBERTS, ST JOHN xiv, 244, 380, 416-425, 448
Robertson, Thomas 96
Robertson, Thomas 105
Robins, William 173

664

Index of Persons

Robinson, Christopher (priest martyr) 281, 372
Robinson, John (priest martyr) 259, 362
Robinson, John SJ 491, 504
Robsart, Amy 187
Roche, John (lay martyr) 255, 256, 257, 258
Rochester, John O.Cart (martyr) 23, 68
Rodes/Rhodes, Francis 246, 248, 250
ROE, ST ALBAN 481-487, 495, 518
Rogers, John 79
Rolle, Sir Henry 539
Rookwood, Ambrose 413, 414
Rookwood, Edward 162
Rookwood, Robert 162
Rootes, Henry 558
Roper, John, Lord Teynham 401
Roper, Margaret 19, 68, 452
Roper, Sir William 452
Roper, William 69, 74, 141, 186
Roscarrock, Nicholas 208, 212, 213
Ross, Richard 488
Rossetti, Carlo 455
Rouse, Anthony 261, 414, 415
Rowsham, Stephen (priest martyr) 120, 159, 362
Rudall, Thomas 106
Ruffet, John 446
Rugg, John OSB (monk martyr) 57
Rumley, William OSB 561
Russell, Lord John 57, 77, 78
Russell, William OSF 562
Ryprose, Elizabeth 54

S

Sá, João de, Count of Peneguião 526
Sabran, Louis de SJ 535
Sabran, Melchior Marquis de 503, 504, 535
Sacheverell, Abigail 574
Sackville, Elizabeth 46
Sackville, Margaret (Countess of Dorset) 312, 316, 319
Sackville, Robert (Earl of Dorset) 312
Sackville, Thomas (Earl of Dorset) 508
Sadler, Sir Ralph 109, 119
Sadler, Robert (Walter) 449
Salmon, Patrick (lay martyr) 152, 177
Salt, Robert O.Cart. (martyr) 69
Greenwood, William 69
Saltmarsh, Edward 517, 518
Saltmarsh, Gerard 518
Saltmarsh, Peter 518
Sancroft, William 616, 617
Sanders, Elizabeth 196
Sanderson, Henry 165
Sandys, Edwin 97, 104, 132, 133, 240, 242, 426
Sandys, John (priest martyr) 399, 443
Savile, George (Earl of Halifax) 555
Saville, Sir John 308
Sayer, Abraham 149
Sayer, John 517
Sayer, Richard 165
Scory, John 104, 155
Scott, Cuthbert 95, 154
Scott, James (Duke of Monmouth) 554, 564, 614
Scott, Montford (priest martyr) 270, 371, 488
Scott, William (Maurus) OSB 418, 422, 432, 438, 439, 449, 450
Scroggs, Sir William 556, 557, 558, 559, 560, 561, 578, 580, 586, 597, 598, 599
Scroope, Winifred 437
Scryven, Thomas O.Cart. (martyr) 69
Scudamore, John 324
Scudamore, Captain John 584, 586, 587, 593
Scudamore, Sir John 324, 370
Sedbar, Adam OCist. (abbot martyr) 42
Sedgwick, Thomas 105
Sergeant, John 552
Sergeant, Richard (priest martyr) 381
Seton, George (5th Lord Seton) 276
Sewell, Hugo 262
Seymour, Edward (Duke of Somerset) 46, 75, 77, 88, 154, 346
Seymour, Jane Queen 38, 54, 88
Seymour, Sir Thomas 54
Shakespeare, William 48, 113, 266, 290, 337, 458
Shaw, Henry 146, 172, 221
Sheffield, Lord Edmund 391, 442, 443
Sheldon, Elizabeth 585
Shelley, Edward (lay martyr) 259
Shelley, Elizabeth 46
Shelley, Frances 436

665

Index of Persons

Shelley, Richard 116, 317
Shelley, William 336
Shelley, Sir William 221
Sherlock, Anthony 406
Sherson, Martin 258
Shert, John (priest martyr) 202, 223, 344
SHERWIN, ST RALPH 152, 201, 202, 205, 206, 207-215, 220, 221, 225, 228, 343, 378, 437
Sherwood, Henry 261
Sherwood, John 261
Sherwood, Richard 152, 261
Sherwood, Richard 261
Sherwood, Thomas (lay martyr) 186
Sherwood, Thomas 443
Shirley, Sir Thomas 312
Siddons, Sarah 587
Sidney, Sir Philip 188
Simpson, Christopher 500
Simpson, Richard (priest martyr) 161
Singleton, Robert 59, 74
Singleton, William 387
Sixtus IV 28
Sixtus V 256
Skevington, Sir William 229
Slade, John (lay martyr) 129
Sledd, Charles 202, 203, 220, 229, 230, 338, 342, 353
Slyfield, Ralph 381
Slythurst, Thomas 103
Smith, Francis 144
Smith, James 393
Smith, James 616, 619
Smith, John SJ 541
Smith, Richard xix, xx, 115, 374, 454, 505, 522, 534, 545, 547
Snow, Peter (priest martyr) xiv, 193
Solzhenitsyn, Alexander xviii
Somers, Thomas (priest martyr) 420, 421, 423, 424, 436, 450, 599, 425
Somerset, Edward (Lord Herbert of Raglan/2nd Marquess of Worcester) 516, 583, 592
Somerset, Henry (1st Marquess of Worcester) 463
Somerset, Thomas 463
Somerville, John 113
Southcote, Sir Edward 600
Southcote, Sir John 597, 598
Southwell, Sir Richard 285
SOUTHWELL, ST ROBERT 169, 177, 259, 266, 285-299, 305, 306, 316, 319, 320, 357, 359, 375, 379, 386, 408, 508
Southworth, Christopher 356
Southworth, Sir John 133, 356
SOUTHWORTH, ST JOHN 466, 471, 493, 494, 519, 520, 521-528, 545
Stonnes, James 105
Speed, John (lay martyr) 285
Spenser, William (priest martyr) 368
Sprott, Thomas (priest martyr) 143, 163, 164
Stack, George 25
Stafford, Lady Mary 603
Stamford, Ralph 399
Stamp, Thomas 582
Standish, Ralph 537
Stanesby, John 435
Stanihurst, Sir James 188
Stanley, Edward (3rd Earl of Derby) 473
Stanley, Edward (14th Earl of Derby) 625
Stanley, Henry (4th Earl of Derby) 317
Stanley, William (6th Earl of Derby) 441
Stanley, Sir William 355
Stanney, Thomas SJ 131, 265, 288, 351
Stanney, William 264
Stapleton, Brian 246, 254
Stapleton, Sir Miles 552, 604, 608
Stapper, Harry 144
Starkey, Helen 538
Starkey, Henry OSB 562, 611
Starkey, Thomas 18
Steel, William 525, 539
Stern, Edmund 24
Stephenson, Paul 618
Stevens, Richard 155
Stevenson, Thomas 357
Stillingfleet, Cuthbert 134
Stokesley, John 4, 11, 15, 45
STONE, ST JOHN 26-28
Stonor, Dame Cecily 194, 195, 338
Stonor, John 195, 339
Storey, John (lay martyr) 90, 112, 156, 188, 387
Stourton, Lord Charles 185
Stourton, Lord Edward 394

Index of Persons

Stout, Thomas 527
Strange, Richard SJ 550
Strange, Thomas SJ 395
Stransham, Edward (priest martyr) 369
Stransham, George 122, 361, 362
Stuart, Prince Charles Edward 617
Stuart, Lady Elizabeth 597
Stuart, Esmé (Duke of Lennox) 597
Stuart, James Francis Edward (James III) 535, 603, 604, 617
Stuart, Ludovic 547
Stukeley, Sir Thomas 191
Sugar, John (priest martyr) 392, 434, 435
Sutton, Abraham 352
Sutton, Robert (priest martyr) 257, 259, 352, 439
Sutton, Robert (lay martyr) 361
Sutton, William SJ 174, 352
Swale, William OCist 42
Swallowell, George (lay martyr) 282, 283, 284
Swithun, St 47
Sykes, Edmund (priest martyr) 120, 141, 160, 364

T
Talbot, George (6th Earl of Shrewsbury) 124, 215
Talbot, John (10th Earl of Shrewsbury) 467
Talbot, John (lay martyr) 143, 165
Talbot, Peter 609
Talbot, William SJ 588
Tallis, Thomas 37
Tankard, Thomas 517
Tarugi, Cardinal Francesco 427
Taylor, Hugh (priest martyr) 245
Taylor, Richard 356
Taylor, Ursula 351
Taylor, Valentine 144
Tedder, William 258, 375
Tempest, Lady Anne 608, 609
Tesh, Anne 246, 254
Tesh, Edward 246
Tesimond, Oswald SJ 401, 403, 404, 409, 445, 446, 447
Thirkeld, Richard (priest martyr) 244, 350
Thirkell, Henry 291
Thirlby, Thomas 95, 154

Thirsk, William OCist. (martyr) 42
Thomson, William (priest martyr) 293, 333, 381
Thompson, James (priest martyr) 244, 348
Thorne, John OSB (priest martyr) 57
Thorpe, Robert (priest martyr) 129
Thules, Christopher 440
Thules, John (priest martyr) 440, 441
Thwing, Ann 607
Thwing, Edward (priest martyr) 167, 356, 357, 607
Thwing, Thomas (priest martyr) 604, 607, 608, 609
Thwing, William 607
Tichborne, Sir Henry 558
Tichborne, Nicholas (lay martyr) 383, 558
Tichborne, Thomas (priest martyr) 169, 383, 558
Tilden, Thomas 556, 557
Tilletson, Francis 122, 165
Tonge, Israel 549, 550, 551, 553, 564
Tootell, Christopher 621
Topcliffe, Richard 125, 140, 157, 161, 162, 163, 165, 206, 255, 259, 263, 268, 269, 270, 271, 272, 273, 274, 278, 281, 291, 294, 295, 296, 297, 303, 304, 305, 306, 324, 325, 333, 339, 343, 357, 365, 375, 376, 412
Towneley, John 122
Trafford, William 22, 25
Trafford, William OCist. (abbot martyr) 42
Travers, John (priest martyr 44
Travers, John SJ 552
Tresham, Edward 501
Tregian, Francis 120, 179, 180, 181, 182, 183, 184, 185, 206, 213
Tregian, Francis 185
Tregian, Thomas 179
Tregonwell, Sir John 53, 54
Tremayne, Richard 182
Trenchard, George 176
Tresham, Francis 394
Tresham, Sir Thomas 48, 144, 192, 193, 206, 361, 369, 379, 3934
Trewe, John 248
Trollope, John 126
Trott, Mayne 570, 593
Tuchiner, Anthony 322, 381

Index of Persons

Tudor, Lady Mary 547
Tunstall, Cuthbert 84, 144, 154
Tunstall, Francis 619
Turberville, Christopher 569
Turberville, Edward 569, 604
Turberville, James 154
Turberville, Jenkin 572
Turberville, John 572
Turner, Antony SJ (priest martyr) 560, 601
Turner, Edward SJ 601, 611
Turner, Dr Thomas 494, 498
Twist, Ann 121
Tyldesley, Elizabeth 475
Tyldesley, Sir Thomas 475
Tynbygh, William 9, 63
Tyrell, Anthony 117, 118, 119, 153, 157, 171, 181, 208, 222, 228, 229, 258, 259, 288, 315, 363, 365, 366, 379
Tyrwhit Robert 190
Tyrwhit, William 190
Tyrye, Michael 426

U

Urban VIII xix, 454, 455, 507, 522, 532, 589

V

Vallenger, Stephen 301
Vaughan, Dominic 371
Vaughan, Cardinal Herbert 584
Vaughan, Richard 435
Vaughan, Thomas 548
Vaux, Anne 137, 142, 166, 281, 288, 401, 402, 403, 406, 409
Vaux, Edward (4th Baron Vaux of Harrowden) 401, 402
Vaux, Elizabeth 401, 402, 429
Vaux, George 401
Vaux, Henry 313
Vaux, Laurence 175, 473
Vaux, William (3rd Baron Vaux of Harrowden) 69, 142, 192, 194, 206, 281, 288, 312, 313, 339, 380, 401
Vavasour, Dorothy 239, 240, 243
Vavasour, James 243
Vavasour, Dr Thomas 239, 240, 243, 346,
Vavasour, Sir Walter 517
Velasco, Don Alonso de 423
Venise, Roger 144
Verhuyck, John 620
Verstegan, Richard 206, 368
Vesey, John 77
Vitelleschi, Mutio SJ 467, 487, 497
Vivian, John 257
Vowell, Richard 42

W

Wade, Richard OCist 42
Wade, Sir William 414, 415, 433
Wadsworth, James 459, 483, 501, 530, 532, 539, 541, 542
Waferer, Andrew OSB 501, 541
Waire, John (friar priest martyr) 58
Wakeman, Sir George 553, 556, 561, 562, 578, 605
Wakeman, Roger 174
Waldegrave, Sir Edward 103
WALL, ST JOHN 573-582, 589, 594
Wall, William OSB 573, 581, 582
Waller, Sir William 563
Wallis, Francis SJ 489
Walpole, Christopher SJ 302
Walpole, Edward SJ 302, 324
WALPOLE, ST HENRY 299-308, 378, 422
Walpole, Michael SJ 302, 397, 422, 451
Walpole, Richard SJ 302
Walpole, Sir Robert 299
Walsingham, Sir Francis 111, 116, 117, 118, 119, 133, 147, 152, 153, 156, 157, 158, 162, 178, 196, 223, 224, 230, 258, 288, 293, 30`, 306, 313, 315, 317, 341, 346, 355, 365, 369, 370, 377, 447
Warcop, Agnes 137
Warcop, Anne 378, 379
Warcop, Thomas (lay martyr) 193, 378
Walworth, James O.Cart. (martyr) 22
WARD, ST MARGARET 254-259, 359
Ward, William vere Webster (priest martyr) 459, 460, 461
Warham, John 105
Warham, William 2, 3, 60, 61, 63
Warnford, Peter OSB 158
Waterson, Edward (priest martyr) 284, 373, 374
Waterton, Thomas 348
Watkinson, Robert (priest martyr) 169, 383, 384

668

Index of Persons

Watkinson, Thomas (lay martyr) 129
Watson, Christopher 190
Watson, Thomas 90, 154
Watson, William 254, 255, 256, 257, 260, 261, 417, 449, 509
Watts, William 193
Way, William (priest martyr) 359
Webb, James 622
Webley, Henry (lay martyr) 257, 353
Webley, Thomas (lay martyr) 345
WEBSTER, ST AUGUSTINE 8-20
Webster, Frances 239
Webster, Margaret 239
Webster, Richard 372
Weddell, Agnes 239, 242
Weddell, Anne 239, 242
Weddell, John 239, 240
Welbourne, Thomas (lay martyr) 393
Wells, Alice 137, 268
Wells, Gilbert 264
Wells, Henry 130, 264
WELLS, ST SWITHUN 130, 262, 263, 264-268, 269, 270, 274, 369, 370, 371, 377
Wells, Thomas 264
Welsh, Robert 78
Wentworth, Matthew 132
Wentworth, Thomas (Earl of Strafford) 453
West, Lady Mary 158
West, Nicholas 65
Weston, Edward 156, 384, 387
Weston, Sir Henry 99
Weston, William SJ 118, 287, 313, 325, 339, 370, 379, 408, 418
Weston, Sir William 48
Wharton, Christopher (priest martyr) 137
Wharton, Henry 137
Wharton, Lord Thomas 137
Wharton, William 262
Whitaker, Humphrey 538
Whitaker, Thomas (priest martyr) 537, 538
Whitbread, John 543
Whitbread, Thomas SJ (priest martyr) 550, 560, 575, 599, 600, 601
White, Andrew SJ 492, 511, 512
White, Dorothy 258, 370
WHITE, ST EUSTACE 270, 271-274

White, John 91, 154
White, Robert 523
White, Sir Thomas 187
Whitehead, Isabel 136
Whitgift, John 142, 150, 176, 311, 396, 413
Whiting, Richard OSB (abbot martyr) 55, 56, 57
Whitlock, Sir James 469
Whytford, Richard 15, 62
Widmerpool, Robert (lay martyr) 259, 360
Wigginton, Giles 248, 250
Wiggs, William 345, 346
Wilcox, Robert (priest martyr) 259, 359, 360
Wilford, Peter OSB 459, 501, 541
Wilson, Matthew 493, 497
Wilson, Sir Thomas 102
Wilkes, Edward 540
Wilkinson, Thomas SJ 611
Wilkinson, William 243
William III (of Orange) xxi, 535, 565, 605, 617, 618, 619
Williams, George 351
Williams, John 182
Williams, John 452
Williams, Richard (priest martyr) 375
Williamson, Sir Joseph 556
Williamson, Thomas 106
Williamson, Thomas 115
Willoughby, Elizabeth 519
Winckley, William 620
Windebank, Sir Francis 455, 499, 524, 525
Windsor, Martin xiii
Winifred, St 445, 566
Winter, Sir William 443
Wintour, John 408
Wintour, Robert 408
Wintour, Thomas 408
Wiseman, Edmund 198
Wiseman family 69, 290, 306, 323, 327, 333, 400, 402, 403
Wiseman, Jane 137, 323, 324, 325, 326, 328, 333
Wiseman, Cardinal Nicholas 612
Wollan, John 460
Thomas, Wolsey Cardinal 2, 7, 29, 31, 61, 66, 67
Wood, William, (prior martyr) 42

669

Index of Persons

Woodcock, John OSF (priest martyr) 537, 538
Woodfen, Nicholas (priest martyr) 265, 364, 369
Woodhouse, Thomas, (priest martyr) 189
Woodward, John 207, 208, 214
Worsley, Charles 525
Worthington, John 139, 140, 467, 542
Worthington, Richard 139, 140
Worthington, Richard 544
Worthington, Robert 139, 140
Worthington, Thomas 139, 149, 165, 344, 467, 474, 481, 482
Worthington, Thomas 139, 140
Wray, Sir Christopher 202, 203, 204, 214
Wren, Sir Christopher 615
Wrenno, Roger (lay martyr) 441
Wright, Sir Edmund 459
Wright, John 426
Wright, Peter SJ (priest martyr) 499, 520, 539, 542, 543
Wriothesley, Anne 120
Wriothesley, Charles 15, 32, 44, 58
Wriothesley, Henry (3rd Earl of Southampton) 265, 266
Wriothesley, Thomas (Earl of Southampton) 120, 265, 312
Wyatt, Sir Thomas 88, 89, 90
Wyatt, William 208
Wynne, Justice Owen 570
Wynne, Peter 621
Wythens, Sir Francis 565

Y

Yarborough, Sir Thomas 609
Yate, Edward 198
Yate, Francis 195, 196, 198
Yate, Jane 197, 198
Yate, Sir John 574
Yate Lady Mary 574, 576
Yaxley, Richard (priest martyr) 365, 366
Yelverton, Sir Henry 469, 460, 472, 509
Young, Richard xiii, 118, 257, 270, 306
Young, Thomas 97, 104
Younger, James 148

Z

Zouche, Elizabeth 54

www.ingramcontent.com/pod-product-compliance
Lightning Source LLC
Chambersburg PA
CBHW031321230426
43670CB00006B/205